BOOKS

By Harold Burris-Meyer and Edward C. Cole

SCENERY FOR THE THEATRE

THEATRES AND AUDITORIUMS

By Harold Burris-Meyer

ACOUSTICS FOR THE ARCHITECT
(*with Lewis S. Goodfriend*)

SOUND IN THE THEATRE
(*with Vincent Mallory*)

By Edward C. Cole

STAGE MANAGER'S MANUAL

Scenery for the Theatre

Scenery for the Theatre

The Organization, Processes, Materials, and Techniques
Used to Set the Stage

Revised Edition

Harold Burris-Meyer and Edward C. Cole

Contributing Authors—Nicholas L. Bryson, James F. Göhl,
Austin O. Huhn, Harvey Sweet, Douglas C. Taylor, Gene A. Wilson

Illustrated with photographs, drawings, tables, and graphs

Little, Brown and Company—Boston-Toronto

.

Published simultaneously in Canada
by Little, Brown & Company (Canada) Limited

PRINTED IN THE UNITED STATES OF AMERICA

To Anita Burris-Meyer and Alice Cole

Preface

Scenery contributes to the experience that is theatre in that it provides physical support to the actors, singers, and dancers. It establishes the environment for the performance-audience confrontation developed by the playwrights and by the directors, the composers, conductors, musicians, and choreographers. And it must accomplish these tasks within physical, organizational, and financial limitations. If this book is to be realistic and authoritative, it must then relate scenery to the conceptual thinking, designing, and planning which affect it and to the organizations by which the production is planned, produced, and operated. This the book undertakes to do. But it treats details of associated elements of theatre only to the extent to which scenery is affected by them.

It does not explore or expound the aesthetic theory and the practice of the designer. It avoids a detailed examination of stage lighting, but of necessity recognizes the demands which lighting exerts upon the theatre structure and the scenery. Nor does it delve deeply into sound and acoustics, though, as with lighting, it considers equipment that impinges upon stage space and scenery, as well as the sound effects which are frequently included in the assignments of technical staff and property men. Costume is considered as a factor only when costumed actors come on the stage and into physical relationship with the scenery. Theatre management is not of prime concern, but since the preparation and execution of the physical production must be organically integrated with the total process of theatrical production, it is necessary to look at its managerial aspects.

Though much of the material this book contains is as applicable today as it was thirty-two years ago, when it was first published, a number of considerations make a new, revised, and expanded edition mandatory.

A new generation of theatres is in the making. Scenery must be appropriate to, and accommodated in, lately restored theatres of the nineteenth century, early twentieth-century theatres with fixed prosceniums, and new theatres with extended, open, proscenium, thrust, and arena stages. Scenic requirements vary from nothing (bare stages) to realistic sets extending halfway around the audience.

New scenic materials and processes are available and uses of some materials have been extended: plastics, metals, and paints.

The craft of the scene technician and technical director in the American theatre now demands a degree of engineering competence hardly necessary a generation ago.

There is now a considerable literature dealing with the technical aspects of theatrical production. There are excellent texts for the beginner. Technical theatre magazines published in several countries help to keep the theatre in phase with scientific progress. Characteristics of materials are treated in great detail and are well presented in handbooks and catalogs. The bibliography lists publications which supplement the material presented here. The theatre craftsman must develop his own competence by carrying his skills beyond those in current use and applying creative imagination to the uses of materials and techniques suggested here or still under development.

The title page lists six contributing authors, experts in one or more of the scenic techniques introduced or vastly improved during the last generation.

James F. Göhl, designer and teacher, master of his craft, has written and illustrated the chapter on scene painting, the most comprehensive manual on the subject now in print. The scenery panels for the color plates were executed by him and by Thomas Ford, charge man in the Feller Scenery Studios.

Illustrations and text on the fabrication of many scenic elements in a variety of thermoplastics were supplied by Nicholas L. Bryson.

Harvey Sweet wrote the text and furnished the illustrations covering techniques of using rigid expanded polystyrene and polyurethane.

Douglas C. Taylor, technical director, contributed text and illustrations on metalworking in scene construction.

The bibliography lists works by Messrs. Bryson, Sweet, and Taylor which treat these subjects in greater detail than this volume does.

Gene A. Wilson has set forth the techniques of using glass-reinforced plastic — fiber glass — to produce scenery and properties.

Austin O. Huhn has supplied the description and illustrations of special-effects techniques used in television and cinema sound stages.

From his vast and unique collection of photographs of scenery under construction, taken in the Nolan Scenery Studios, Munro Gabler has provided seventy-five which effectively illustrate the best current techniques and methods.

Curtis J. Senie made new line drawings and revised drawings from the first edition, numbering over a hundred, which appear throughout the book.

Dorothy Wilken supervised the rendering of the graphs, which appear in the Appendix.

Our editors at Little, Brown — William S. Jarrett, A. L. Hart, Jr., William D. Phillips, and Jean Whitnack — and Moses F. Carr, Jr., Harriet Sears, and Susan Brendel of the design and production staff, styled the book and put it together. Georgina Johnston compiled the index. We thank them for their skillful assistance.

The exacting task of typing, often from crabbed copy, has been accomplished with signal skill, accuracy, and dispatch, by Eleanor Belanic, Margaret Beyer, Gail Mau, Linda Ruth Thompson, Linda Searles Thompson, and Dorothy Wolff.

We cite with gratitude the kindness and generosity of our professional associates and fellow showmen, and of all those who have supplied information and illustrative material, as tabulated in the back of the book.

Contents

Tables

Scenery for the Theatre

1.1 Proscenium and setting. Siena, 1560

1.2 Drawing for scenery, sixteenth century. Vicenzo Scamozzi, designer

The state of the theatre

1

Before beginning a study of the technical planning, manufacture, and use of scenery, it is necessary to survey the structural and operational aspects of the theatre that affect the form and structure of the scenery. This chapter and the two succeeding ones are accordingly devoted to a brief statement of those elements in the history of the theatre that affect present-day scenery, a résumé of the characteristics of theatres as they affect scenery, an outline and brief analysis of theatre organization, and a statement of the process by which a production is planned.

So closely allied and so interdependent are the arts and crafts which find their common expression in the theatre that it is as difficult to find anything essentially new in the technical phases of dramatic production as it is to find basic novelty in dramatic situations. Scenery, stage machinery, light, and effects perform much the same function today as they have since they were first used. There have been improvements and additions, but almost nothing has been discarded.

Painted scenery was used in the time of Sophocles. Many realistic props are called for in the scripts of the comedies of Aristophanes. The Romans used painted structural scenic units: in comedy, practical (functioning) windows and balconies on the façades of private houses; in tragedy, realistic and imposing columns on public buildings. Hills, trees, rocks, and caverns formed the background for Roman satyric drama. The Renaissance brought the painted drop and the wing and border setting. Since then no basically new scenic structures have been developed. The unframed drop, the framed wing, the flat, and the three-dimensional weight-bearing platform have all been for centuries essentially as they exist today. In the nineteenth century scenery started to undergo a transition, largely due to the influence of Adolphe Appia. Two-dimensional

scenery

painted scenery began to give place to three-dimensional scenery, which depended for dramatic significance on its design and the effective use of light. There is nothing essentially new or different in the modern skeleton sets required by central and thrust stages, or elaborate multilevel scenic structures often used on open and extended stages.

Flat and three-dimensional scenery, then, constitutes our tangible scenic medium. With it, it is possible to set the stage in conformity with the demands of any type of play — realistic, stylized, expressionistic, or abstract — or in conformity with any of the current isms.

machinery

Most scenery has been constructed so that moving it has not required its complete disassembly. Moreover, despite Aristotle's enunciation and Richelieu's enforcement of the principle of unity of place in drama, scenes have been and are changed within the play. The script of *Götz von Berlichingen* calls for fifty-two scene changes. Appropriate stage machinery has usually been forthcoming to meet the demand for scene changes.

Scenery can be moved vertically and horizontally, and the Greeks had machinery for facilitating movement in both planes. The *ekkyklema,* the wagon stage much as we know it now, carried set pieces into the acting area. The *mēchanē,* a crane and windlass, made possible Medea's exit in a chariot drawn by dragons. Used to deposit a god on the stage, it aided in the solution of many knotty dramaturgical problems. The *periaktos,* a revolving prism devised by the Greeks, reappeared in the Renaissance and is now used for wing masking in conjunction with revolving stages. The curtain, raised from a well, was used by the Romans. The gridiron appeared in the seventeenth century. The nineteenth century brought traps and devices for tilting, raising and lowering, and revolving the stage floor. All these have remained essentially the same, except that motive power for vertical operations became hydraulic in the nineteenth century, and in the twentieth, electric. Steel has replaced wood and hemp. Projected patterns have to some extent replaced paint. Wagons, treadmills, and motion pictures integrated with action on the

1.3 A Renaissance stage machine used in the Teatro Farnese at Parma, Italy, about 1600, for the appearance from above of a deity surrounded by attendants. Two frames, each consisting of five timbers swivel-pinned together and supporting seats for the attendants are hung on ropes which are either pulled or wound on drums to alter the configuration of the frames. Two configurations are shown. The seats are also swiveled to hang plumb, whatever the frame configuration may be. A single seat above the frames carries the deity and the ring above it carries more attendants

1.4 An effect created by the machine in Figure 1.3. The frames, carrying cupids and attendants with the throne of Venus and a halo of flowers and cupids above, have been lowered into the view of the audience. Clouds conceal the rough structure of the machine, and the ropes, presumably, are invisible or ignored

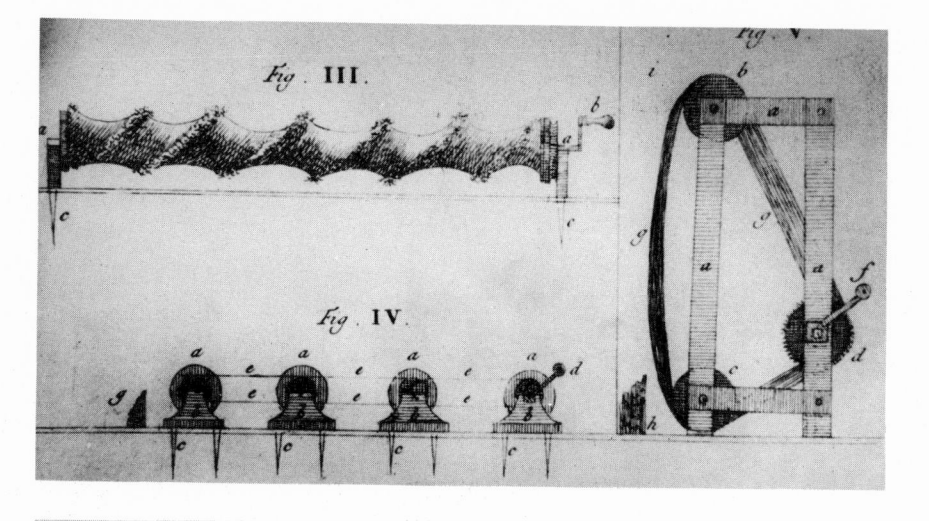

1.5 Machines to make waves (left) and a waterfall (right). Four cylinders, with spiral ridges adorned with fluffy white material, are arrayed on the stage floor, parallel to the proscenium with a ground row (*g* in "Fig. IV") concealing their lower halves. To simulate waves, they are belted together and driven by a crank. To simulate a waterfall, a fabric loop is passed around three rollers and is driven by a crank attached to one of the rollers. These were machines used in the Teatro Farnese in the early seventeenth century

1.6 Folding platforms and stairs, operated on ropes from drums above: a perspective sketch looking upstage. On the left, the platforms are in position for use; on the right, they have been flown, the lower stairs and the platform tops folding to afford more clear fly space. Teatro Farnese, early seventeenth century

stage have given scenery a dramatic significance impossible when it is moved only to change static settings. Although basic construction procedures have remained unchanged, detailed techniques have embraced developments in materials and tools and have both reacted to and influenced changes in dramaturgy and presentation.

Artificial light was first used in the theatre to provide visibility. Before the advent of electric lighting, light had been used only occasionally to create atmosphere and mood. These functions are now taken for granted. The requirements they establish as well as the additional demands of naturalness, design, and especially emphasis have led to the development of ever more efficient light sources and increasingly precise and flexible control. Stage lighting can, within certain limits, establish and

light

1.7 Setting for *Man of La Mancha*. Howard Bay, designer. The flown staircase over the thrust stage is reminiscent of a Renaissance effect

alter the appearance of scenery. It cannot replace scenery. It does complement scenery and can do some scenic jobs very well. Used in combination with other devices, light is increasingly important in producing effects.

Sound and light, alone or in combination, were first used principally for spectacle but are now part of almost every play. As effect apparatus has become susceptible of precise control, the effect has gained in dramatic importance. The audience will react to effects almost as intensely as to anything an actor can do — the rain in *Rain,* for instance, or the disembodied voice of the ghost in *Hamlet,* the tired tenement in *One Third of a Nation* or the brainstorm in *The Adding Machine.* Percussion and rumble devices of ancient and medieval origin are still useful. But electronic control of sound and the magnetic record have given sound the flexibility of light. Here, for the moment, technical development has outrun artistic competence.

The theatre always seeks and thrives on novelty, not only in achieving on the stage the realism and ubiquitousness which the cinema provides so easily, but in producing plays by Sophocles, Plautus, Shakespeare, Goldoni, Cibber, Sheridan, and Schiller in the manner of their first production, or in a modern manner, or in any other way which will render them dramatically effective. For novelty, the witches in *Macbeth* may be Haitian voodoo priests. Hamlet may use a pistol. A messenger may be replaced by a television receiver. Valkyrie may ride through the skies.

In the play of modern authorship all the technical features of modern civilization must appear and work convincingly on the stage, and that which is not yet, must be. The secret of eternal youth must be out. The post-Armageddon era must be the present. Assorted brands of metaphysics must be convincing for two hours. The earth must yield up its treasure and the sea its dead.

The structure of the theatre affects the demands made upon scenery and limits what can be accomplished with it. Most theatres have been built with a view to accommodating a single form of performance. But since the theatre usually lasts longer than the person who specifies its use, it imposes limitations on what the next user may do. Insofar as the scenery is affected, theatres are big (seating 2,500 or more), normal for legitimate production (seating 800 to 1,400), or little (seating under 400). Optimal seeing and hearing conditions limit audience size to about 800 on one floor or 1,200 in a theatre with one balcony. The size of the theatre directly affects scenery in three ways: the cost to build, mount, and operate; the size of the shops where scenery is built and painted; and the relative difficulty of transportation.

There are exceptions. In endowed or state-supported theatres, monuments to civic pride, there is often no intention to break even, and so far as scenery is concerned the sky is the limit. Experimental theatres found in some academic institutions are wont to mount productions whose scenic demands have no economic justification. Occasionally, a producer in the commercial theatre will shoot the works for whim or

effects

novelty

theatres

1.8 Boxes, forestage, proscenium, and setting in the restored Ford's Theatre, Washington, D.C.

reputation's sake, even going so far as to rebuild part of the theatre, as David Belasco did when he produced *Mima*.

The standard proscenium in the commercial theatre of early twentieth-century vintage, still standard in New York, has a stage so small that the scenery must often be constructed with extreme ingenuity to fit into it and work once it's there.

The stages of community or school theatres often limit scenery by especially galling technical deficiencies, which are compounded by shortage of funds. Common shortcomings are lack of flying equipment, insufficient stage depth, and inadequate lighting instruments and control. One new school theatre even has a ceiling of acoustical tile over the stage.

The arena stage is justified only on economic grounds, but some producers view the inherent limitations as a challenge and relish the task of minimizing the losses of dramatic effect by attempting to balance them with startling innovations. They then attempt to justify this theatre type on the basis of bold, imaginative production, never admitting that the boldness and imagination would accomplish more on a stage capable of accommodating scenery and oriented toward an audience at considerably less than 180°.

Thrust stages limit scenery in that nothing can be flown over the thrust section of the stage, and scene changes must therefore be done *a vista* on the floor. Because of the wide audience splay, sightlines severely limit the useful playing area and impose restrictions on the scenery.

Advantages are rarer than limitations. The theatre in which shops are integral, enabling scenery to be designed, built, subjected to trial setup,

TABLE 1.1. AVERAGE DIMENSIONS OF THE COMMERCIAL THEATRE

Proscenium Height	Proscenium Width	Stage Depth	Stage Width	Gridiron Height	Apron Width
28'1"	37'7"	31'1½"	70'	61'	2'2"

painted, rigged, lighted, and rehearsed all in the same building, can get better scenery for less money and operate it more economically than a theatre with any other kind of arrangement. The theatre in which it is possible to store the sets not in use, with minimum disassembling, has a distinct economic advantage, particularly for repertory. Furthermore, scene design is easy, scenery flexible, and construction simplest in a theatre with an adequate stage.

The theatre in the nightclub, supper club, hotel, or gambling house is yet another type and growing in number. Designed for spectacle, these theatres often impose tremendous scenic demands: the broken dam in the Stardust, Las Vegas, and the underwater ballet in the Lido, Paris.

Producing organizations are of many kinds, but the type of organization is not necessarily tied to any particular type of theatre. The commercial theatre is most often found in the standard proscenium theatre, as in New York. Average dimensions are given in Table 1.1, and the equipment is limited to gridiron, counterweight or rope system, traps, house switchboard, company switch, and a few permanent leads to box booms and balcony front lighting positions. The producer must bring in all other equipment required by the show. Commercial productions appear off Broadway in converted movie houses, converted stores, abandoned or active churches, and hotels.

The arts center, usually owned and operated by a nonprofit corporation, has a standard pattern: an opera house/concert hall (capacity: 2,500 plus) and a legitimate theatre (capacity: 800–1,200). These theatres offer considerable scope to the scene designer. They are well equipped and can often accommodate repertory. An example is shown in Figure 1.9.

Community theatre tends to grow. It starts in the abandoned firehouse and ends in the community arts center, complete with professional staff and resident company.

Some of the best theatres in America are to be found on university campuses. In educational institutions the theatre is a laboratory. In teaching theatre, a building that is wrong is just as bad as a book that is wrong. This realization has resulted in many very good plants, of which a number are occupied by professional companies. Permanently installed equipment is often sufficient for any kind of production: gridiron, several cycloramas, devices for moving the stage floor, complete electrical control and lighting equipment, sound and effect machines, and so on. In their best form these plants can offer great variety in the physical relationship between performance and audience by functioning as either extended, open, proscenium, or thrust stages.

Outdoor theatres require scenery that cannot be affected by rain or blown away by a strong wind. These requirements result in the use of

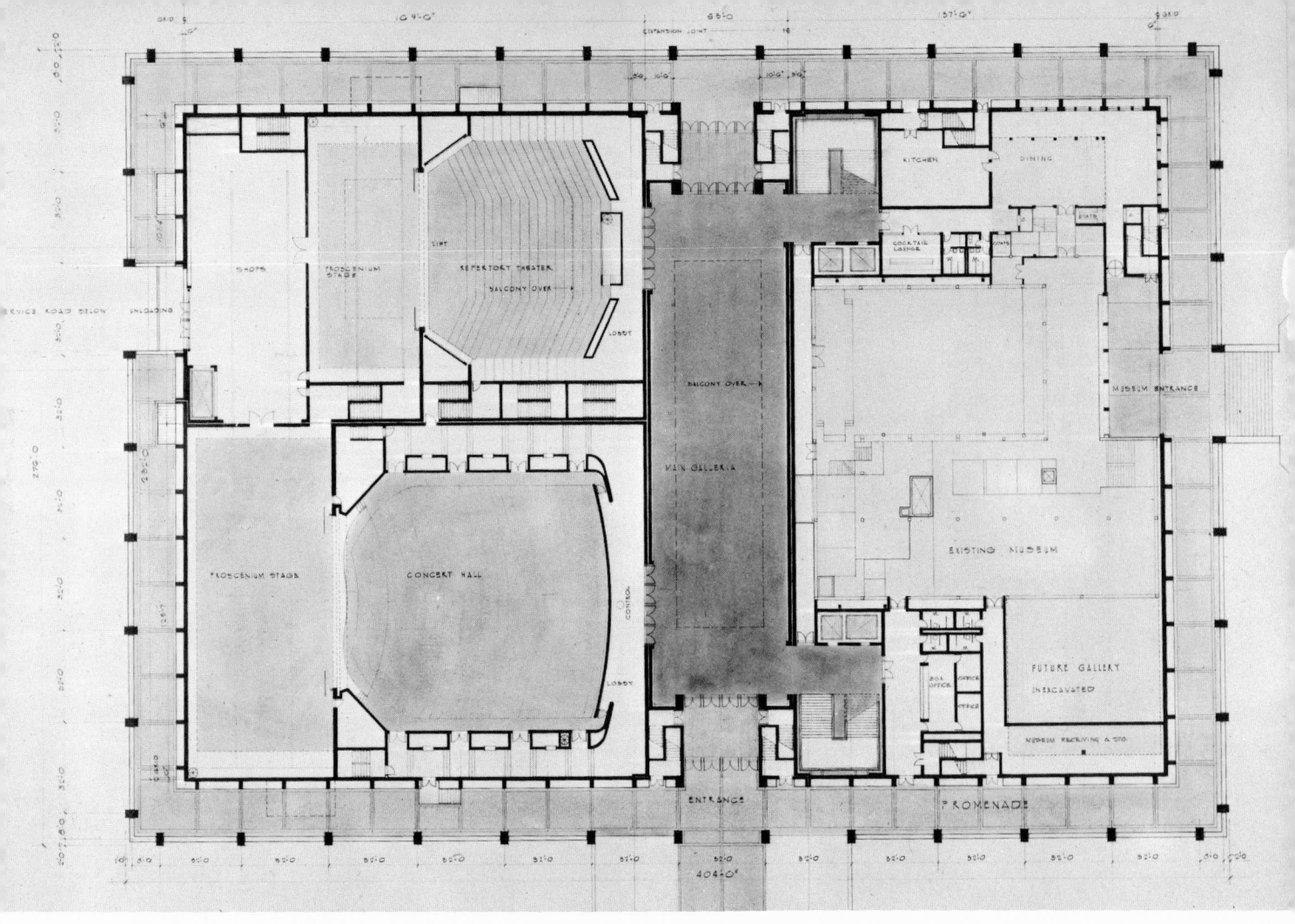

1.9 Atlanta Cultural Center, Atlanta, Georgia. Main floor plan.

physical dimensions

few movable units. The unit set which is built in place and stands all season is preferred.

The human dimension establishes the scale for the scenery. The size of the stage and the requirements for moving and handling scenery determine the dimensions of the scenic units and of the parts into which they may be divided. Average commercial stage dimensions have been tabulated (Table 1.1), but averages for other types are less meaningful. Opera houses often have proscenium stages, 80′ or more wide and a useful depth at least half of that, a high proscenium arch, and a grid-iron height of 100′ more or less. Many small community theatres have proscenium openings less than 30′ wide and so little fly space or back-stage scenery space that they are restricted to single, unit, or suggested sets.

If the scenery is to be moved, the means of transportation also affects its planning and construction. Loading doors on trailer vans and inside dimensions of cargo airplanes impose new limits on the size of scenic units — usually less than the 5′ 9″ maximum for one dimension which obtained for generations when intercity scenery transportation was provided by railroad baggage cars.

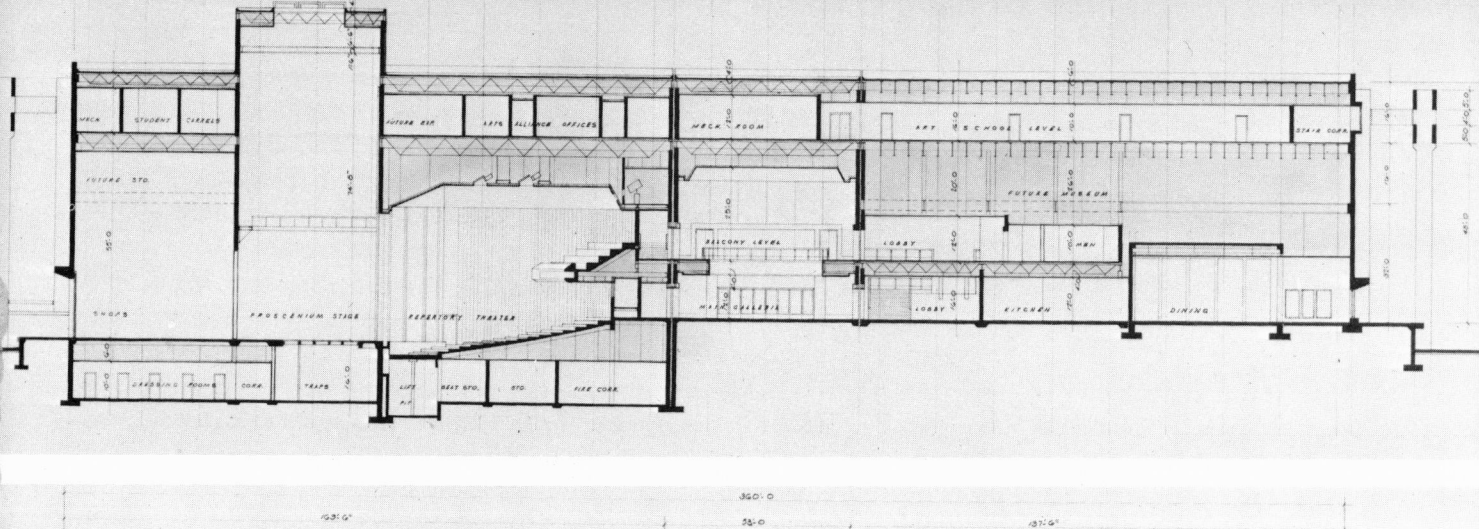

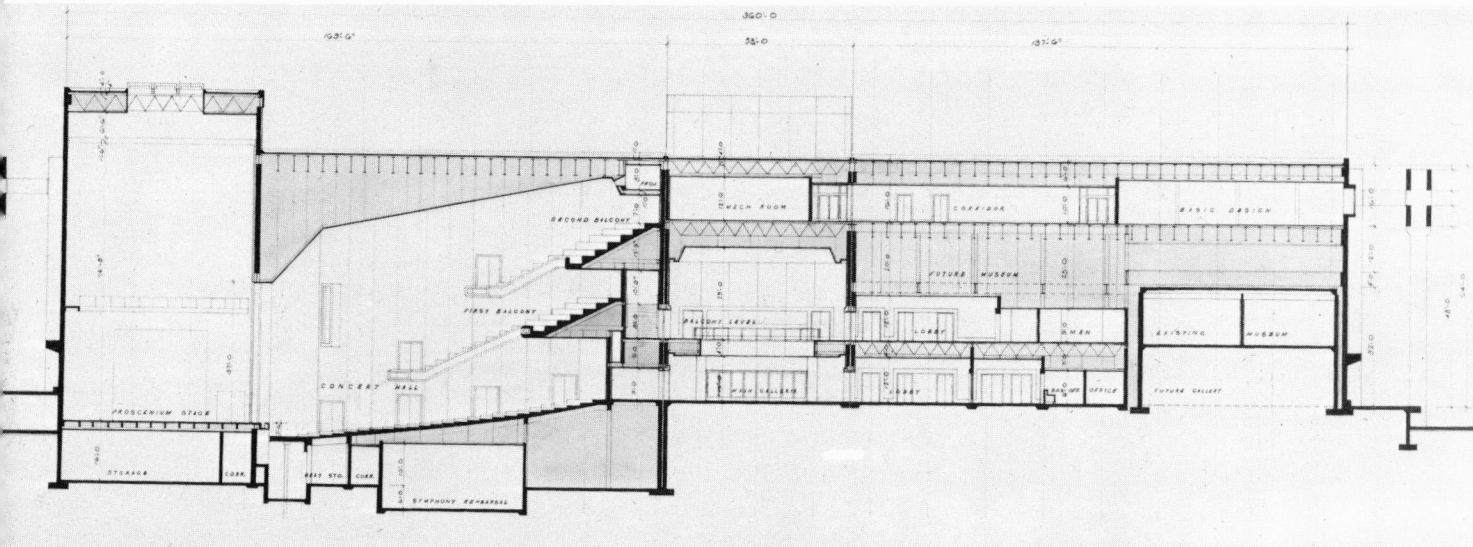

Sections through the Repertory Theatre (above) and the Concert Hall (below)

So scenery must be planned and built to conform to such an array of limitations that efforts to break out of them go on all the time. Experimental theatre is a term which implies trying new things with scenery as well as with all other theatre elements.

No criticism of theatre structure is particularly useful unless a criterion is set up. It is impossible to design the universal, ideal theatre plant because the theatre structure will always bear the mark of those who have conceived it. However, the guiding principle in theatre design, as in industrial design, must be *efficiency*, if the theatre is to be economically and artistically successful. Theatre efficiency is the accomplishment of all theatrical tasks in the least time (man-hours), under conditions of maximum comfort and safety for audience and staff, and subject only to the artistic demands of the play.

Efficiency backstage can be achieved only if there is plenty of stage floor area and adequate equipment. During the last half century, an increasingly large proportion of the sets used in theatres have required horizontal moving. Very few multiset productions can now be handled by flying alone. Therefore, requisites for stage efficiency are:

efficiency

• Stage floor area equal to that of the auditorium plus one-third, with clear space at either side of the stage equal to the proscenium width plus 5′; depth, twice the acting area. This arrangement provides adequate room for the most space-consuming method of scene shifting.

• Gridiron height at least three times proscenium height.

• Scene, paint, electrical, and property shops, and storage space in or adjacent to the stagehouse, with short, clear paths of movement to the stage. All shops capable of being acoustically isolated from the stage.

• Quick and easy access to dressing rooms.

• Complete working circulation to all parts of the theatre: lobby, projection and spotting booths and ceiling, orchestra pit, light and sound control room.

• Equipment to provide vertical and horizontal movement: flying systems, traps, elevators, wagons, revolving stage.

• Drop, tab, draw, and contour curtains, projection surfaces, and cycloramas.

• Microphone and loudspeaker outlets.

• Multiscene preset light-control console located where the operator can see the stage.

• Stage manager's panel, including machinery controls, intercommunication and cue-system panel, and rehearsal P.A. control.

developments and trends
dramaturgy

Since 1938 playwrights have been turning away from the classical three-act form and writing plays that are more loosely plotted. Perhaps this trend can be attributed to the influence of radio, motion picture, and television drama, in which there are few practical limitations on the number of possible locales, perhaps to an expression of rebellion against established forms or classical restrictions. Plays calling for the representation onstage of many locales, either simultaneously or in quick succession, have increased in number. The storytelling logic of this is apparent when one considers the absurdity of the single set in *Life with Father* — the Day family is forced to live its entire life in the breakfast room. This is not to say that the play in one realistic set and the play with scene changes only during intermissions are extinct. There are examples of them in any season. As a result, there are added to the traditional scene techniques two salient categories of scenery: sets for *a vista* scene changes in response to the demands of playwright, director, and audience for presentations unbroken by technical pauses; and elaborate and strong scenic structures in response to demands of playwrights that several contiguous locales be shown simultaneously — upstairs and downstairs, indoors and outdoors, and the like. Designers, directors, and technicians have all been forced to extremes of ingenuity to evolve methods of changing scenery within view of the audience and to achieve scenic structures capable both of supporting the loads and forces of action on raised levels and being dismantled for transportation.

structure of scenery

Structure has undergone elaboration, enrichment, and refinement. Scenery that shakes when a door is closed, stair railings that move when actors lean on them, and wrinkles in wall surfaces are no longer tolerated. Furthermore, the hopeful expectation of a long run, which attends most Broadway and off-Broadway openings, imposes the re-

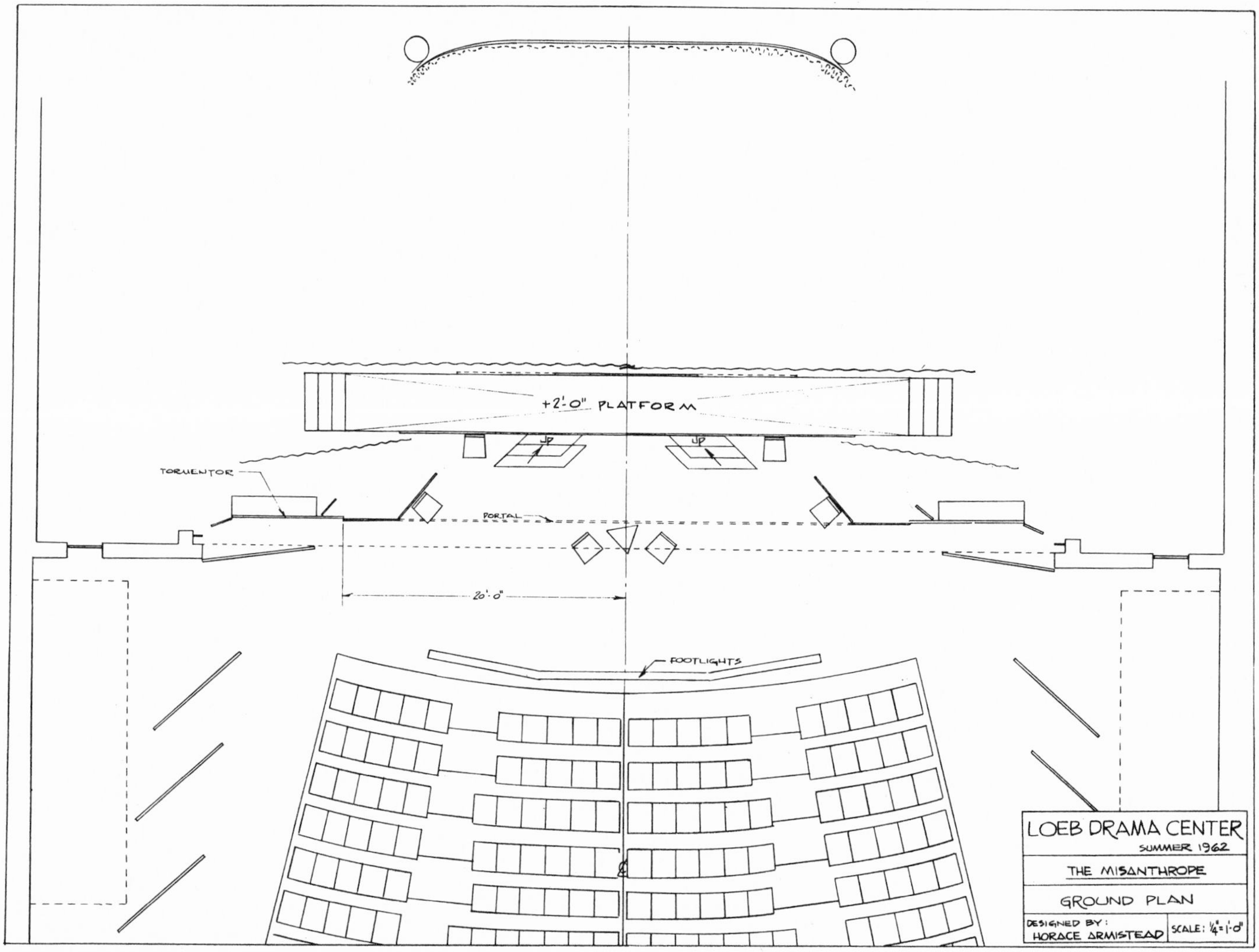

Within the plan drawing, the following labels appear:

+2'-0" PLATFORM

TORMENTOR

PORTAL

20'-0"

FOOTLIGHTS

LOEB DRAMA CENTER
SUMMER 1962
THE MISANTHROPE
GROUND PLAN
DESIGNED BY:
HORACE ARMISTEAD   SCALE: ¼"=1'-0"

1.10 The first of three arrangements of the flexible stage of the Loeb Drama Center, Harvard University. Here the floor plan and setting for *The Misanthrope* have the form and style of the Molière period. The pit elevator is at stage level, making possible entrances from left and right onto the forestage. Horace Armistead, designer

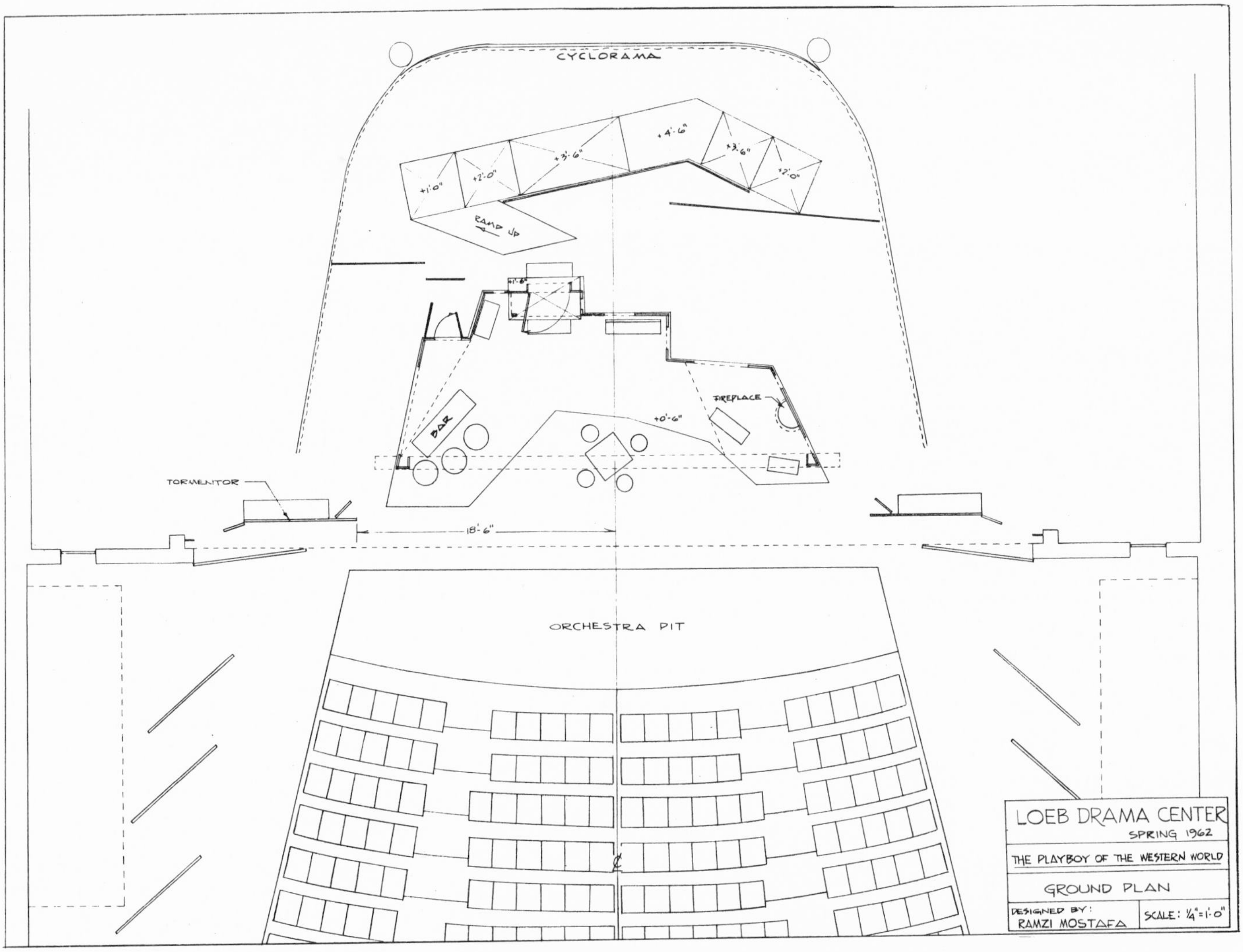
CYCLORAMA
+1'-0"
+2'-0"
+3'-6"
+4'-6"
+3'-6"
+2'-0"
RAMP UP
+1'-6"
FIREPLACE
+0'-6"
BAR
TORMENTOR
18'-6"
ORCHESTRA PIT
LOEB DRAMA CENTER
SPRING 1962
THE PLAYBOY OF THE WESTERN WORLD
GROUND PLAN
DESIGNED BY:
RAMZI MOSTAFA
SCALE: ¼"=1'-0"

1.11 The plan and setting for *The Playboy of the Western World* are in the conventional proscenium form with orchestra pit. Ramzi Mostafa, designer

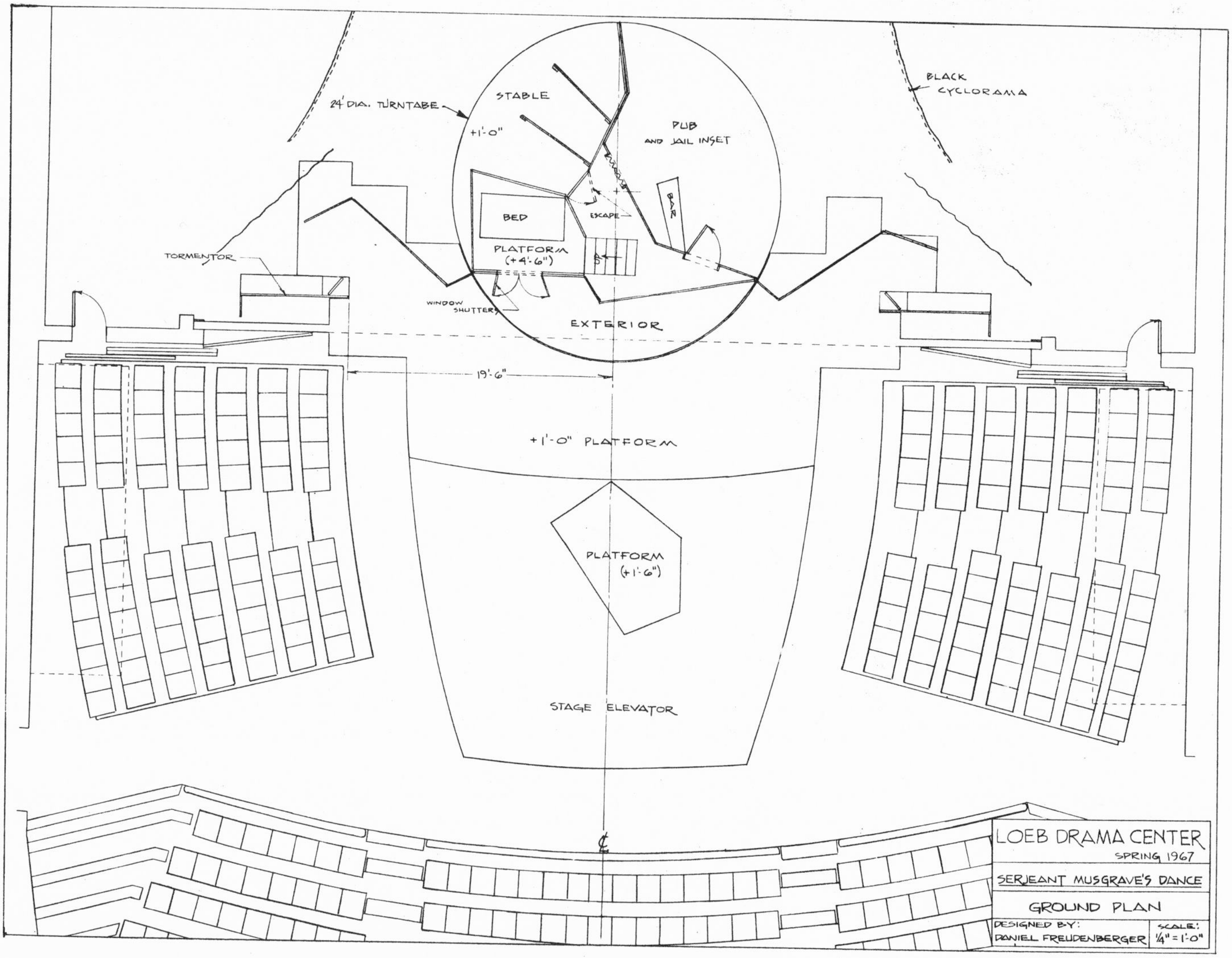

24' DIA. TURNTABE

STABLE
+1'-0"

BLACK
CYCLORAMA

PUB
and JAIL INSET

BAR

BED

ESCAPE

PLATFORM
(+4'-6")

TORMENTOR

WINDOW
SHUTTER

S

EXTERIOR

19'-6"

+1'-0" PLATFORM

PLATFORM
(+1'-6")

STAGE ELEVATOR

¢

LOEB DRAMA CENTER
SPRING 1967
SERJEANT MUSGRAVE'S DANCE
GROUND PLAN

DESIGNED BY:
DANIEL FREUDENBERGER

SCALE:
¼" = 1'-0"

1.12 For *Serjeant Musgrave's Dance,* the two front sections of seats have been raised and rolled to the sides. The pit elevator and the thrust stage elevator have been raised and a revolving disc installed for scene changes. Daniel Freudenberger, designer

15

1.13 Setting for *Twelfth Night* at the Hopkins Center, Dartmouth College. With both side stages opened and set with scenery, action may extend beyond the proscenium. The forestage elevators are lowered to produce a change in stage level

quirement of durability on all scenery built for New York production; the show that closes after one performance is nonetheless built to run for two years.

Aside from demands exerted by playwrights in their scene plots, designers and technicians have responded to technological developments in the world outside the theatre by using new materials and devices to achieve traditional effects in better ways and to create new effects. The creative urge has often been happily coupled with the competitive drive

1.14 A Doric colonnade and pediment related the *Agamemnon* of Aeschylus scenically and thematically to the *Homecoming* of Eugene O'Neill when both plays were presented in one program at the Yale School of Drama. Thaddeus Gesek, designer

for novelty to the ultimate benefit of the playwright, director, actor, and producer and to the edification of the theatregoer.

The revision of the building code of the city of New York received intensive study by qualified experts for a period of four years; it was examined in public hearings and enacted into law by the New York City Council on October 22, 1968. As the law governing the building of theatres in the first theatre city in the United States, it has already served, and will in the future serve, as the model and standard reference for authorities in other cities in revising their own laws and in granting variances from existing obsolete laws. Salient practical benefits of the new code are options in the arrangement of seats; freedom to locate theatres above, below, or at grade level; freedom to vary the line separating the performance and audience areas; and elimination of the fire curtain in favor of other protective devices which do not demand so rigid a location. New theatres for New York City, planned to take advantage of this code, are under construction as this edition of *Scenery for the Theatre* goes to press.

laws governing the construction of theatres

Directors, actors, and teachers of actors are increasing their demands for free creation and expression even to the presentation of improvisations, performances developed from scenarios, and unscripted and loosely constructed *happenings,* although the members of the Dramatists Guild in production contracts still claim and receive the author's jurisdiction over script changes. Composers, painters, and sculptors, perhaps impatient with the abstract character of music and the inertness of the plane surface and static forms, are now discovering living, moving, vocal actors as media for *their* creative expression, and research engineers are testing products of modern technology in the generation of emotional responses in audiences. As a result, designers and technicians receive demands for unusual (to put it mildly) scenery and properties but are simultaneously the beneficiaries of imaginative thinking by wearers of the key of Sigma Xi.

Thespis unfettered

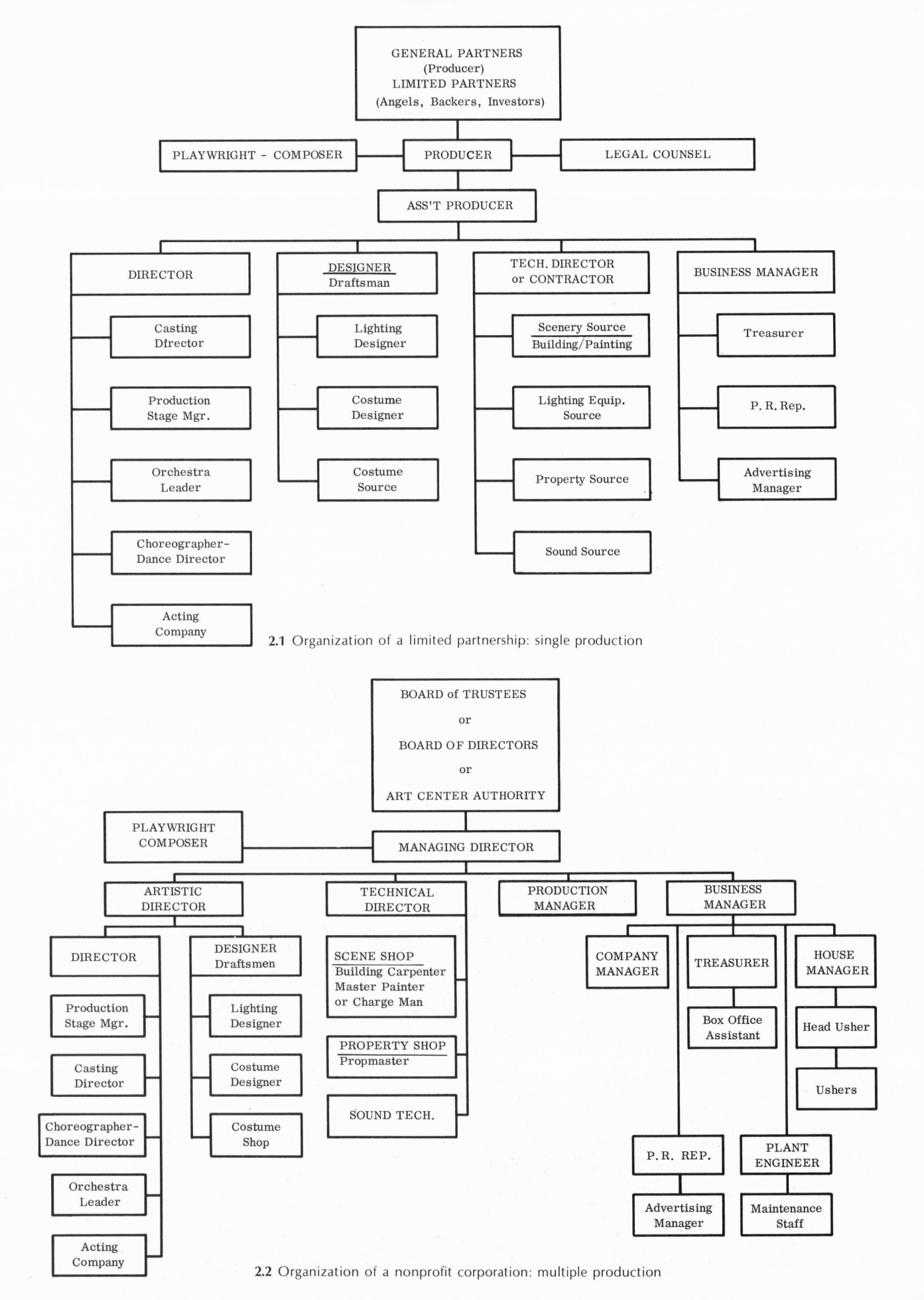

2.1 Organization of a limited partnership: single production

2.2 Organization of a nonprofit corporation: multiple production

Organization for production 2

The simplest statement of the steps in the production of a play is the following:

1. An organization is formed.
2. A play is selected.
3. A theatre is obtained.
4. The production is designed, planned, and cast.
5. The production is prepared by various departments, each performing a logical division of the work.
6. An audience is promoted.
7. The divisions of the production are assembled.
8. Technical and dress rehearsals are held.
9. The production is performed.
10. The production runs.
11. The production tours.
12. The production is terminated.
13. Receipts and expenditures are totaled, and a balance is struck.

This summarizes what happens to most plays that are produced. Each step in the sequence, save perhaps 10 and 11, must be taken. There are infinite variations possible in the organizations performing the tasks listed and to some extent in the order in which they are performed. Since this book is concerned with scenery, actors and playwrights will be mentioned only as their work relates to the physical production.

Insofar as the preparation and operation of scenery is concerned, there are two basic types of theatre organization: First, the organization which produces a single play and presents it in an owned or leased theatre, or troupes it into a succession of theatres on the road; most commercial productions are presented by organizations of this type. Second, the organization which produces and presents a series of plays in sequence (stock) or in alternation (repertory). This type of organization includes resident professional theatres, most community theatres, and almost all school theatres. The civic center sometimes has a resident repertory opera company.

The organization charts (Figures 2.1 and 2.2) list the essential personnel engaged in producing a play, indicate lines of authority, and give the responsibilities and duties of those concerned with the preparation and use of scenery.

the producer
single production

Commercial theatre. In the standard commercial theatre in the United States, the producer — an individual or corporation — initiates a limited partnership for each separate production. Shares in each production (units, pieces of the show) are sold to individual investors (limited partners); the producer is the general partner. The partnership may or may not own motion picture, TV, book, and record rights. It is dissolved when major sources of income are exhausted. Personnel are hired for the production run (or limited engagement) of the single play. Income is from box office receipts, concessions, and rights. The theatre, which is rented, costs thirty to forty percent of the box office gross. Legal counsel is important because of the large number of intricate contracts that are implicit in the system.

Eat, drink, and see the show. The show in the nightclub, supper club, or the gambling house is organized as a combination production, except that the house supplies the capital, and the admission charge is absorbed in the cover charge or the bar bill or the house percentage. It is often a variety show, headlining a number of different acts in succession throughout the season. Individual acts seldom require much in the way of scenery and carry only a few essential props. By contrast, some of the most elaborate spectacles requiring technical virtuosity are staged in nightclubs.

Amateur production. A social organization of one kind or another decides to produce a play or "put on a show" for any reason whatsoever. Lack of theatrical knowledge makes sound organization and professional guidance necessary. All work is voluntary — possibly under a paid director.

multiple production

Multiple-production organizations include resident companies which are tenants in municipal or civic-center theatres, community theatres, resident professional theatres, schools, festivals, and summer stock. The multiple-production organization is at best a corporation tailored to the particular needs of a functioning theatre, with a complete producing staff employed for the season or longer. Most multiple-production organizations are nonprofit. Their income is derived from gifts, public or private educational appropriations, or government and foundation subsidies, as well as from box office receipts, subscriptions, and concessions.

Resident company. A movement toward the decentralization of the professional theatre, begun in the fifties, resulted in the establishment of some thirty resident professional theatres in regional centers about the United States by the mid-sixties. Often referred to as resident repertory companies, they are similar to the old-time resident stock company, but with important variations: they depend heavily upon patrons and subscription for an assured income; they run one play for three to five weeks, providing a similar period for the preparation of the next play; they import actors who are specially suited to certain roles; and they undertake sundry theatrical services to the community, such as children's theatre, theatre in the schools, reduced admissions for students and senior citizens, and citizens' participation in the affairs and operation of the company. Unfortunately, many companies have elected to play in theatres which are too small to provide the financial support of a first-class operation with the ancillary activities and have to depend upon philanthropy to balance the books, a condition which impairs autonomy. Limited finances also affect the salaries which can be paid and tend to restrict the selection of actors and actresses.

School theatre. This type of theatre is a permanent organization with a transient personnel. Production departments are headed by faculty members or by students working under faculty supervision. The various positions of duty are rotated among the student workers. The demarcation of responsibility must be established very clearly because students do not have the same familiarity with the whole process or its parts as experienced workers do. To compensate for the students' lack of experience, procedures and methods must be expounded with particular thoroughness. The assistant in each position becomes the number one man in that position the following year, thus assuring continuity and enabling some accumulation of expertise. It follows that in a school the whole production process must be fairly rigid and less amenable to variations than in an organization of permanent or professional personnel, in which the initiative of expert individual members can be applied to the peculiar demands of the particular production.

Income is from the school operating budget, box office receipts, tuition, and student activity fees.

Summer theatre. Of whatever kind, the summer theatre takes advantage of the all-pervasive American vacation by extending into the winter in benign climates.

Summer stock revives popular classics and standard plays. It is an inexpensive tryout ground where author and producer may tinker with a new play and gauge audience reaction, "give it the poison-ivy test," before a lot of money is spent on a metropolitan production. It also serves as a training ground for young actors and technicians, and offers something approaching a vacation with pay to the established actor. The amazing thing about summer stock is that the audience bears up so well under a barrage of often inferior plays, hastily and meagerly produced in makeshift, poorly appointed theatres. The encouraging facts are that summer theatre tryouts have produced such outstanding productions as *Man of La Mancha.* Shakespeare festivals from coast to coast have made knowledge of the Bard part of American culture, and thousands of young aspirants have gained practical experience and derived inspiration and skill from contacts with hundreds of old pros.

the director

Whatever the type of organization, the director concerns himself with the design of scenery since it must agree with his interpretation of the play and satisfy all the requirements of the stage action. He is concerned with its construction and operation because it must have planned stability and appearance, and must shift with the requisite speed and silence.

the designer
single production

Commercial theatre. The designer, a free-lance specialist, designs sets and designs or selects properties. He may also design costumes; otherwise a costume designer is employed. His contract provides that he must furnish sketches, color schemes, models, and working drawings of all sets, be available for consultation and changes until the show opens, and usually light the show. Sometimes, a lighting designer is employed to do the lighting, or it may be done by an employee of the company which supplies the lighting equipment. The last third of the designer's fee is not paid until after the show opens. The designer is a member of the scenic artists' union. He is employed only by the production. Some designers develop semibinding associations with certain producers.

multiple production

Resident company. The designer may be resident or employed for a single production. His responsibilities are the same as in the combination production.

Community theatre. Scene designer–technician is a common combination. Costumes are rented or made, seldom bought.

Summer theatre. The designer, besides designing, often paints the scenery and may hunt set and trim props. Economy of money, space, and labor is his first consideration. A few excellent and prosperous summer theatres now have their scenery built and painted in professional shops.

School theatre. In general, design is by the director or by faculty members or students in the art or home economics departments. Professional schools have departments of stage design with faculty or student designers. In these departments, sketches, color layouts, working drawings, costume plates, and patterns are made. The costume department undertakes the manufacture as well as the design of costumes. Organization varies, but the aim is to follow the practice of permanent theatre organizations.

the technical director
single production

A technical director is employed only to articulate the technical elements of production, and then only for elaborate productions. When a technical director is not employed, a representative of the scenic construction company, the designer, and production stage manager work out a scheme for handling sets. The scene designer or lighting designer lights the show, and all unspecified jobs fall to the production stage manager. A scene technician employed by the scenic construction company plans and supervises the construction of the settings.

multiple production

Resident company. The technical director is in direct charge of all technical elements of production. He plans and supervises the construction and operation of all settings and may light the productions. He prepares and executes the scheme for scene changes and alternation of productions. He plans and supervises all changes in permanent technical equipment. He is the backstage efficiency engineer and may serve a number of theatres or work under a general technical director who supervises technical production for a group of theatres.

Community theatre. The technical director's job is similar to that of technical director for the resident company. When the theatre has no technical director, the duties are divided between director, designer, and stage manager. Technical organization of community theatres is generally loose.

School theatre. A technical director is found in professional schools, where he teaches technical production. In production his duties are the same as those listed for the resident company. The designer–technical director is usually the second full-time salaried member of a school theatre organization.

In the planning of either single or multiple productions the variety of components, the variations within components, the intricacies of human relationships, and complexities of techniques render a smooth course from inception to completion difficult. A production manager who is thoroughly knowledgeable in all the arts, crafts, and techniques, and skilled in estimating and planning, who comprehends the time and work requirements and is keenly aware of the obvious chances for error as well as the hidden pitfalls and unforeseen eventualities, can do much to make the production process *efficient* by eliminating wasted effort and time, by the maximum use of limited facilities, and by the planned elimination of overtime. He can make the work *effective* by coordinating the related components of production in time and space, and *pleasant* by obviating clashes between departments and persons which might be caused by lack of coordination, misunderstanding, or poor communication. In a producing organization, this person is severally called production stage manager, assistant producer, company manager, production coordinator. His appropriate title heads this paragraph.

His duties are entirely confined to planning the season or the production in consideration of all known, predicted, and apprehended factors in the situation, and supervising the fulfillment of the plans. He is responsible only to the producer and has executive authority and decision in engaging and assigning subordinate personnel, scheduling work, scheduling the use of the stage, and coordinating the efforts of various departments. He exercises this authority only after consultation with, and thorough understanding and careful consideration of, all persons and departments working on the production. He must prepare and utilize the following documents:
* Season schedules broken down into the several steps in the preparation of each production, the places where the work is done, and the days when it is done.
* Production schedule for each show from the date of selection of play to opening night and even to the strike of the show, detailed as to work, time, place, and functional units.
* List of available personnel.
* Table of the permanent organization.
* Table of organization for each production, showing personnel hired or assigned to each show and their duties.

the production manager

PROPOSED PREPRODUCTION RESPONSIBILITY CHART

Column groups: **TOP MANAGEMENT / BOARD**, **ADMINISTRATION**, **PRODUCTION STAFF**, **THEATRE STAFF**

Columns (left to right):
1. Board of Directors
2. Pres., Board of Directors
3. Publicity Committee
4. Program Committee
5. Finance Committee
6. Artistic Director
7. General Manager
8. Comptroller
9. Publicity Director
10. Assistant to Gen. Manager
11. Executive Assistant
12. Production Coordinator
13. Production Assistant
14. Technical Director
15. Director
16. Conductor
17. Choreographer
18. Scene + Prop Designer
19. Light Designer
20. Costume Designer
21. Stage Manager
22. Assistant Stage Manager
23. Assistant Stage Director
24. Assistant Conductor
25. Show Technician
26. Costume Coordinator
27. Sound Coordinator
28. Orchestra Manager
29. Resident Stage Manager
30. Qet Resident Stage Manager
31. Qep Resident Stage Carpenter
32. Qep Resident Stage Carpenter
33. Qep Resident Electrician
34. Front of House Manager
35. Maintenance

Task	1	2	3	4	5	6	7	8	9	10	11	12	13	14	15	16	17	18	26	28	29	31	32	33	34
ESTABLISH OVERALL AIMS	FD	FD																							
RECOMMEND PROGRAM				GS		DS	CN		CN																
APPROVE PROGRAM	FD	FD				NT	NT		NT																
RECOMMEND SCHEDULE OF PERFORMANCES						DS	GS																		
APPROVE " " "	FD	FD				DS	DS																		
SET OVERALL BUDGET	FD				DS		CN	CN																	
RECOMMEND BUDGET BREAKDOWN					GS	CN	DS	CN																	
APPROVE " "	FD	FD				NT	NT	NT																	
ESTABLISH PUBLICITY POLICY	FD	FD		GS		CN	CN		DS																
SET OVERALL PRODUCTION SCHEDULE						CN	GS					DS		CN											
APPROVE OVERALL PRODUCTION SCHEDULE						NT	FD					DS	NT	NT											
HIRE ADMINISTRATION STAFF						CN	FD	CN	CN	CN															
RECOMMEND PLAY, OPERA, OR CONCERT				GS		WD	CN			NT															
APPROVE " " "	FD	FD				WD	NT																		
RECOMMEND SCRIPT + OR SCORE VERSION				GS		WD	CN																		
APPROVE " " "	FD	FD				WD	NT																		
RECOMMEND DIRECTOR				GS		WD	CN																		
APPROVE "	FD	FD				WD	GS					NT													
RECOMMEND CONDUCTOR				GS		WD	CN								CN										
APPROVE "	FD	FD				WD	NT					NT			NT										
RECOMMEND CHOREOGRAPHER				GS		WD	CN								CN	CN									
APPROVE "	FD	FD				WD	GS					NT			NT	NT									
RECOMMEND CASTS OR PERFORMERS				GS		WD	CN								CN	CN	CN								
APPROVE " "	FD	FD				WD	NT					NT			NT	NT	NT								
RECOMMEND STAGE MANAGER						CN	GS					CN			CN										
APPROVE " "						NT	FD					NT			NT										
RECOMMEND ASSISTANT DIRECTOR						DS	CN								GS	CN									
APPROVE " "						FD	FD								NT	NT									
RECOMMEND ASSISTANT CONDUCTOR						DS	CN								CN	GS									
APPROVE " "						FD	FD								NT	NT									
RECOMMEND SCENE DESIGNER				GS		WD	CN	CN	CN						CN	CN	CN								
APPROVE " "	FD	FD				WD	DS	NT	NT						NT	NT	NT								
RECOMMEND LIGHT DESIGNER				GS		WD	CN	CN	CN						CN	CN	CN	CN							
APPROVE " "	FD	FD				WD	DS	NT	NT						NT	NT	NT	NT							
RECOMMEND COSTUME DESIGNER				GS		WD	WD	CN	CN						CN	CN	CN	CN							
APPROVE " "	FD	FD				WD	DS	NT	NT						NT	NT	NT	NT							
RECOMMEND SHOW TECHNICIAN						GS	DS	CN	CN					CN											
APPROVE " "						NT	FD	NT	NT					NT											
EMPLOY RUNNING CREWS							GS	DS	CN					CN					CN		WD				
EMPLOY ORCHESTRA							GS								CN					WD					
PUBLICITY + ADVERTISING			GS					CN	CN		DS														
BOX OFFICE								CN	GS	DS															
COMPLIMENTARIES	CN	CN						CN	GS	CN	DS														
PROGRAM PRODUCTION	CN	CN					GS	CN	DS			CN										DS			
HOUSE MANAGEMENT							GS	CN														DS			
USHERS + STAFF							CN	CN															DS		
PROGRAM SELLERS							CN	CN																DS	
MAINTENANCE							CN	CN																	DS

Legend:

- **WD** — WORK DONE BY
- **GS** — GENERAL SUPERVISION
- **DS** — DIRECT SUPERVISION OVER WORK DONE
- **CN** — PERSON TO BE CONSULTED
- **NT** — PERSON TO BE NOTIFIED
- **FD** — FINAL DECISION TO BE MADE BY

2.3 A chart on which are analyzed the organization and operation of a production. This chart discloses such faults as excessive concentration of responsibilities in certain individuals (director-designer, resident stage manager-stage carpenter) and generally inadequate communication. Following this study, its maker proposed changes, set forth in a series of charts, some of which are shown below (Figures 2.4 and 2.5) and in Chapter 14 (Figures 14.2 and 14.4)

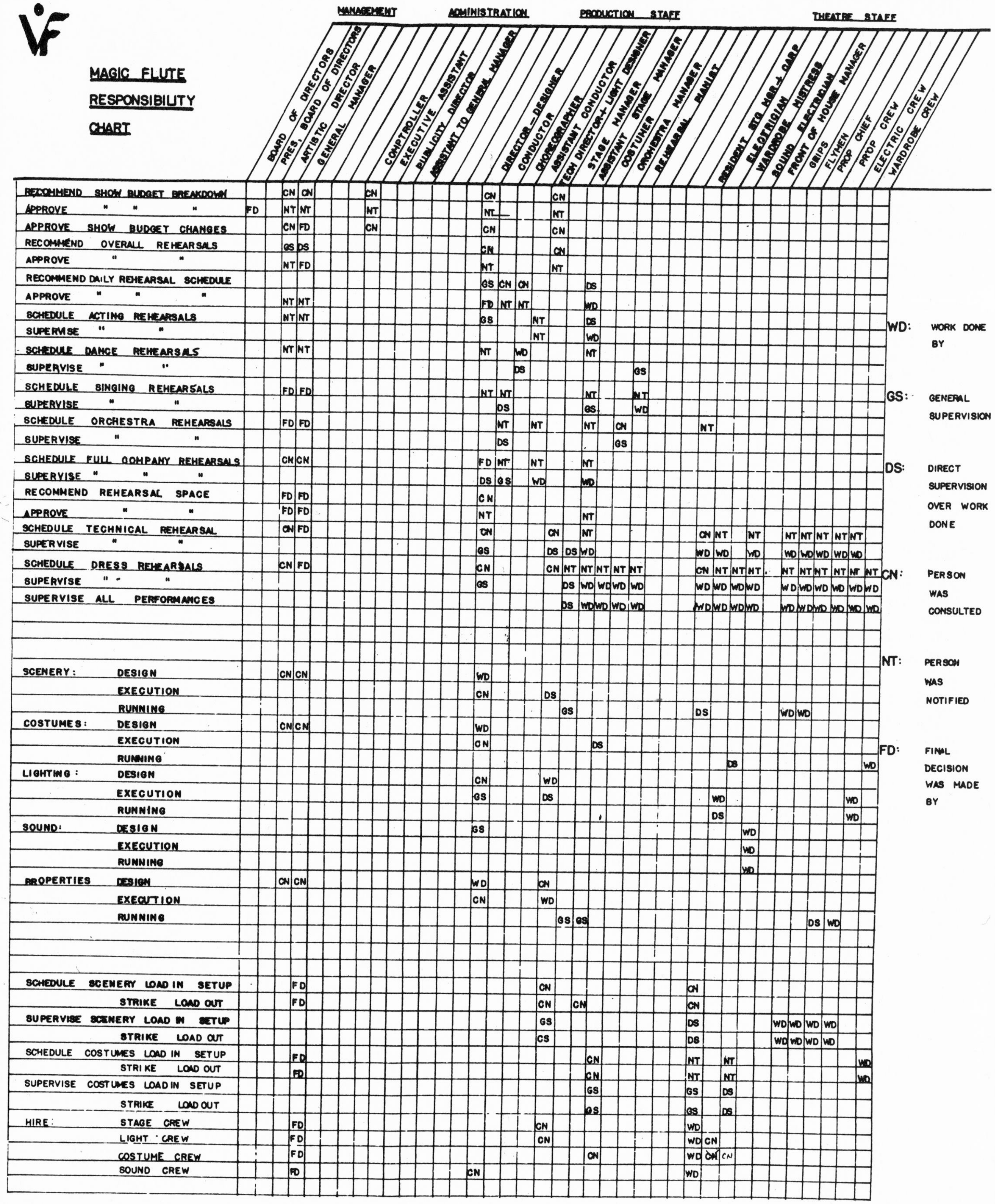

MAGIC FLUTE RESPONSIBILITY CHART

	MANAGEMENT				ADMINISTRATION				PRODUCTION STAFF										THEATRE STAFF										
	Board of Directors	Pres. Board of Directors	Artistic Director	General Manager	Comptroller	Executive Assistant	Publicity Director	Asst. to General Manager	Director-Designer	Conductor	Choreographer	Assistant + Light Designer	Tech Director + Light Designer	Stage Manager	Assistant Stage Manager	Costumer	Orchestra Manager	Rehearsal Pianist	President Stg Mgr + Carp	Electrician	Wardrobe Mistress	Sound Electrician	Front of House Manager	Grips	Flymen	Prop Chief	Prop Crew	Electric Crew	Wardrobe Crew
RECOMMEND SHOW BUDGET BREAKDOWN			CN	CN	CN				CN		CN																		
APPROVE " " "	FD		NT	NT	NT				NT		NT																		
APPROVE SHOW BUDGET CHANGES			CN	FD	CN				CN		CN																		
RECOMMEND OVERALL REHEARSALS			GS	DS					CN		CN																		
APPROVE " "			NT	FD					NT		NT																		
RECOMMEND DAILY REHEARSAL SCHEDULE									GS	CN	CN			DS															
APPROVE " " "			NT	NT					FD	NT	NT			WD															
SCHEDULE ACTING REHEARSALS			NT	NT					GS			NT		DS															
SUPERVISE " "												NT		WD															
SCHEDULE DANCE REHEARSALS			NT	NT					NT		WD			NT															
SUPERVISE " "										DS							GS												
SCHEDULE SINGING REHEARSALS			FD	FD					NT	NT				NT			NT												
SUPERVISE " "										DS				GS		WD													
SCHEDULE ORCHESTRA REHEARSALS			FD	FD						NT	NT			NT	CN			NT											
SUPERVISE " "										DS					GS														
SCHEDULE FULL COMPANY REHEARSALS			CN	CN					FD	NT	NT			NT															
SUPERVISE " " "									DS	GS	WD			WD															
RECOMMEND REHEARSAL SPACE			FD	FD					CN																				
APPROVE " "			FD	FD					NT					NT															
SCHEDULE TECHNICAL REHEARSAL			CN	FD					CN		CN		NT						CN	NT		NT		NT	NT	NT	NT	NT	
SUPERVISE "									GS			DS	DS	WD					WD	WD	WD			WD	WD	WD	WD	WD	
SCHEDULE DRESS REHEARSALS			CN	FD					CN		CN	NT	NT	NT	NT				CN	NT	NT	NT		NT	NT	NT	NT	NT	
SUPERVISE " "									GS			DS	WD	WD	WD	WD			WD	WD	WD	WD		WD	WD	WD	WD	WD	
SUPERVISE ALL PERFORMANCES												DS	WD	WD	WD	WD			WD	WD	WD	WD		WD	WD	WD	WD	WD	
SCENERY: DESIGN			CN	CN					WD																				
EXECUTION									CN				DS																
RUNNING											GS								DS							WD	WD		
COSTUMES: DESIGN			CN	CN					WD																				
EXECUTION									CN							DS													
RUNNING																					DS								WD
LIGHTING: DESIGN									CN			WD																	
EXECUTION									GS			DS								WD								WD	
RUNNING																				DS								WD	
SOUND: DESIGN									GS													WD							
EXECUTION																						WD							
RUNNING																						WD							
PROPERTIES: DESIGN			CN	CN					WD				CN																
EXECUTION									CN				WD																
RUNNING											GS	GS														DS	WD		
SCHEDULE SCENERY LOAD IN SETUP				FD							CN								CN										
STRIKE LOAD OUT				FD							CN	CN							CN										
SUPERVISE SCENERY LOAD IN SETUP											GS								DS					WD	WD	WD	WD		
STRIKE LOAD OUT											CS								DS					WD	WD	WD	WD		
SCHEDULE COSTUMES LOAD IN SETUP				FD												CN			NT	NT									WD
STRIKE LOAD OUT				FD												CN			NT	NT									WD
SUPERVISE COSTUMES LOAD IN SETUP																GS			GS	DS									
STRIKE LOAD OUT																GS			GS	DS									
HIRE: STAGE CREW				FD							CN								WD										
LIGHT CREW				FD							CN								WD	CN									
COSTUME CREW				FD												CN			WD	CN	CN								
SOUND CREW				FD				CN											WD										

Legend:

WD: WORK DONE BY

GS: GENERAL SUPERVISION

DS: DIRECT SUPERVISION OVER WORK DONE

CN: PERSON WAS CONSULTED

NT: PERSON WAS NOTIFIED

FD: FINAL DECISION WAS MADE BY

2.4 A proposed preproduction responsibility chart which is limited to the planning phase and shows changes, in both organization and operation, from Figure 2.3

COMMITTEES AND COMMUNIQUES

Legend:
- CP – CALL + PRESIDE AT MEETING
- MT – MUST ATTEND MEETING
- NT – MUST BE NOTIEDOF RESULT OF MEETING

2.5 A chart of committees and communiqués which clarifies procedures regarding attendance at meetings and the distribution of essential working information. In an operation as complex as theatrical production the coordination of personnel, space use, and time depends upon the prompt receipt of accurate and complete information

Sound, other than the actors' voices, is traditionally the business of the **musical director, conductor,** and orchestra for sound emanating from musical instruments or special percussion devices; the **property master,** for sounds emanating from standard nonelectronic sound machines; and the **sound technician,** for sound electronically produced, reproduced, and distributed. The sound technician designs and supervises the manufacture of special sound-producing and reproducing apparatus, electrical and mechanical; he maintains this apparatus and coordinates all work with sound. He installs and operates the public address system if electronic reinforcement is needed and the theatre does not have a system of its own. He obtains or makes, dubs, and edits the tape recordings used in the show, and operates the sound control system. He is concerned with scenery because loudspeaker units and microphones must often be flown, built into the scenery, or moved during shifts. In general, he is concerned with all acoustical problems of the production and responsible for their solution.

The musical director and conductor are concerned with scenery only when musicians or music sources are used onstage. In such cases, the position of offstage ensembles and movement of people during the scene shifts are sometimes critical.

Stage lighting has established itself as an art of tremendous importance. The effectiveness of the play, to say nothing of the scenery, often depends upon it. It has been, and is, practiced by designers, directors, technical directors, and representatives of the organizations which build and supply stage lights. In resident theatres, some community theatres, and the best professional schools, experts in stage lighting are staff or faculty members. In Europe, the technical director is the stage-lighting expert. In American and English commercial production, he is a freelance or is attached to a producing organization. His generally accepted title is lighting designer. The lighting designer may be involved with scenery at the planning stage if the lighting problems are intricate or if there is to be projection.

Scenery is built on contract by a scenic construction company and paid for before the show opens. It is sold, given away, or destroyed at end of run, or stored for road tour or revival.

Lighting equipment is rented from a manufacturer or supplier who repossesses it when the show closes. Rental-purchase on the basis of a weekly payment of 10 percent of the purchase price, once a regular practice, is now infrequent.

Trim props are often built in the scene shop. Set and hand props are purchased or borrowed from dealers. Props may be purchased in ten weekly installments from stage-property concerns, and will be repossessed if the show closes within ten weeks. Props are usually sold or otherwise disposed of at end of run or stored for road tour.

The actor furnishes his own modern costumes. Modern dresses, gowns, and the like are purchased wherever available. Period and special costumes are made on contract by a commercial costumer and disposed of at the end of the run.

sound

lighting

sources of scenery, lights, props, costumes
single production

Resident company. Scenery is built in the theatre's own shops, or shops which serve a number of theatres in the same center. Shops and scenic construction are within the economic and administrative unit of the theatre or a group of theatres. Sets are sometimes built on contract by a scenic construction company and kept as long as the play is in repertory.

Complete lighting and control equipment is part of the permanent equipment of the theatre. It is rigged, operated, and maintained by the staff electrician.

Properties are bought, as in commercial production, or made in the theatre's own shops.

In repertory, costumes are made or taken from stock. Otherwise they are rented or purchased from commercial costumers who have made them on contract, as in commercial production.

Community theatre. Scenery is usually built in the theatre or in improvised shops, or onstage if shops are lacking. It is kept for reuse or salvage.

Lighting equipment is purchased from a manufacturer as permanent theatre equipment.

Properties are borrowed, purchased, or built in the theatre and saved for other shows.

Costumes are borrowed, bought, rented from commercial costumers, or made by volunteers.

School theatre. Scenery is built by students on the premises, rebuilt from stock, or purchased from other productions. It is stored for reuse or salvage.

Lighting equipment is purchased from a manufacturer, from second-hand dealers, or from other productions. It may be designed and made by students and kept as permanent theatre equipment.

Properties are borrowed or rented, seldom purchased. In professional schools props are often built.

Costumes are borrowed, rented, or made by students and saved if owned. Professional schools have costume departments for designing and making costumes.

variations

Many and varied talents are often to be found in one person. Theatre organization is flexible enough to accommodate them. Not only may one person fill several roles in the producing organization, but he may appear, without change of title, in the operating organization (see Chapter 14).

In commercial theatre a large staff often works on business and planning between productions, and many of its members assume various functions in the producing organization when it starts work on a show. A man may be play reader, casting director, play doctor, and business agent during the summer, then act as director, stage manager, or company manager in production. A designer may prepare a script for production and promote financial backing, as well as perform all functions which are normally his. This sort of alternation or combination of functions occurs to some extent in almost all producing organizations.

The technical director may be the same person as the designer. The designer in the school or community theatre may be his own draftsman, may design costumes, may paint the scenery, and may prepare the lighting plot. The latter is usually part of his contractual responsibility in commercial production.

The casting director may be or become the stage manager. The stage manager may be and often is the assistant director. One scene designer who was a distinguished actor sometimes appeared in the plays he designed. A well-known officer in a producing company manages a number of productions (producer), sometimes designs the scenery (designer), paints it and supervises its installation in the theatre (technical director), and lights the production (designer, technical director). Playwrights, actors, directors, composers, and designers often invest in the productions in which they work.

The summer theatre usually produces its own scenery, often with apprentice labor, irrespective of the type of organization which operates the theatre: college, community, or commercial. The producing organization is also the operating organization: the carpenter builds the scenery, rigs it, shifts it, and scavenges it at the end of the run.

The greatest effectiveness in preparing a production is achieved when **the centralized shop** the organization is complete and permanent. In some European state theatre organizations, for example, the same shops supply scenery, properties, and costumes to a number of affiliated theatres. In single-play production in New York, scenic construction firms (studios) build and paint the scenery and properties, make the costumes, and supply lights and electronic sound control equipment; they have largely supplanted the individual firms which supplied only one of these services. Centralized shops for art centers serve several theatres, and in universities they serve both theatre and television studio.

In the case of the centralized commercial shop, the producer and the construction firm enter into a single contract whereby the whole physical production is delivered to the theatre ready to install and use.

Theatrical labor is unionized. In commercial and resident profession- **labor** al production and in civic centers, all employees belong to one or another of the nine principal theatre unions. There are nearly seven hundred locals, branches, and area offices. Responsibilities, working conditions, and pay rates are established by the unions and are made part of employment contracts. These regulations apply to persons involved in preparing a production as well as to those running it. To some extent they circumscribe the production process, but in many instances they help to guarantee a standard of performance.

In some resident professional, summer stock, and community theatres, unions supply department heads, and nonunion apprentices make up the crews and house personnel. Some schools and community theatres use only student, apprentice, and volunteer labor. The practice of charging apprentices tuition and using them as labor still flourishes in some summer theatres.

The European repertory theatre is equipped by virtue of purpose, **comment** organization, plant, and permanence of staff to give plays their best production. Resident and community theatres in the United States often aim at, and may someday succeed in, adopting those elements of the European repertory theatre which are essential to good and efficient production, but lack of funds, public apathy, unfamiliarity with repertory methods, and subservience to the star system have retarded development.

The flexibility of the commercial single-production organization is both a boon and a disadvantage. The advantages are adaptability to the demands of the individual production and the ability to make use of particular talents. Seldom does a person fit exclusively into the rigid pattern of scene designer, director, or technical director. One technician can design, another can do lighting, and so on, while a director may fancy his virtuosity in writing press releases.

The demands of productions differ. One requires little technical knowledge because it has a single simple set; another requires feats of engineering because of its complexity. One depends very little on lights for its dramatic values because it is domestic comedy in one set, and another depends upon the skill of a lighting designer for changes in locale, atmosphere, and mood, and for visual dramatic effects.

The producer must determine his personnel needs when planning the production and employ only such people as are required, rather than retain a whole staff of experts, several of whom may be unnecessary on certain productions. For example, a permanently employed costume designer might not earn his wages on modern-dress productions, so the producer hires a scene designer who can also exercise color and style control over the actresses' dresses and coiffures and the actors' ties, suits, hose, and shoes.

The disadvantage of a flexible combination of talents for the production of individual plays is potential misunderstanding. The normal consequence of multiple free-lancing is that each individual worker, from the producer down, develops his own technique, which differs from that of any other worker in his field. The producer may have an individual idea of his relation to the balance of the organization and of his prerogatives. The designer may have an individual idea of his responsibilities and executive authority.

In the chapters that follow, the production process is treated on the basis of a completely staffed, permanent, producing organization. When the work of an individual or department is discussed, it is assumed that there is such an individual or department in the producing organization.

the schedule   Producing organizations customarily announce the schedule for the coming season late in the preceding spring or early summer. This is necessary in resident, community, and university theatres in which season subscriptions are sold. In commercial theatre, though union contracts limit rehearsal time to four weeks for legitimate productions and six for musicals, production planning must often begin six months or more ahead of opening date because of the amount, diversity, and intricacy of technical elements of production, the availability of scene shop time, and the time required to engage personnel and negotiate contracts.

Planning the production

3

The basic scheme for a dramatic production may come from any one of a number of sources but it is most often found in the manuscript of a playwright, submitted to a producer, approved by the play reader, and found to the producer's liking. The playwright may have such clear ideas of every detail of the production that planning the production can be limited to carrying out the directions written into the script. The verbal descriptions of the settings may be so meticulous that they leave no feasible alternative approach to the scene designer. Stage business may be so precisely stated and so inherently right for the action that the director's task becomes one of supervising the actors' adherence to the stage directions. The plays by George Kelly and some by Eugene O'Neill are notable in this respect.

Scripts which include all details of production are rare. In revivals of plays of past generations, plans for the production have to be formulated since the acting scripts and prompt books are seldom available, and even if they are, a production in the exact historical manner may have little appeal for modern audiences. In the scripts of new plays, particularly by new authors, the playwright rarely contributes more than the idea, plot, and dialogue, and is eager to have experts in the allied fields of dramatic production contribute their wisdom and ability to the realization of his play upon a stage.

A dramatic production may be a figment of a producer's imagination. He may have no more than an initial idea for a production, which may or may not be based on an existing script, poem, or group of performers. He may submit the idea to the appropriate members of his staff, or, in combination production, he may assemble a group of writers, designers, composers, and so on, for the purpose of making that idea into a production.

Scene designers often cherish fond schemes for producing famous plays or great works of literature in dramatic form, which have been adapted to suit scenic schemes. Norman Bel Geddes's project for *The Divine Comedy* is well known; his *Lysistrata* project achieved production under his own aegis. Actors and actresses occasionally create the opportunities to act parts which they wish to play, by becoming impresarios in the necessary production ventures.

In point of time, a play is generally not included in the season's schedule until the planning is done. It can easily be seen that the planning may be complete, exhaustive, and may take many years, or it may be tentative or totally lacking. However, the sequence and the essential elements of planning are the same, no matter when it is done or by whom.

planning sequence

Usually the playwright furnishes the original idea for the production. He finds, probably through his play agent, a producer who is interested in doing his play. The producer has, or can raise, the necessary financial support for the project. The producer and the playwright discuss the general requirements of the production, and, particularly in combination production, the people who may be chosen to carry out the divisions of the work of production: director, actors, scene designer, technical director, costume designer, and so on. They agree, ultimately, on the principal people (often not until they have discovered that many of their first choices are either contracted to someone else, in Europe, or in Hollywood) and call them together.

At the first conference, the project is discussed, the author's views are heard, and the others offer their opinions pro and con, ask questions, and contribute ideas. Seldom is agreement immediate. Seldom does one meeting serve to elucidate everyone's ideas of the aims of the production. Sometimes the designer expresses no interest or has definite ideas which do not agree with those of the author or of the director. Sometimes the playwright and the director cannot develop a common interpretation of the script. Sometimes the director finds that the principal actors whom the author wants do not see the characters as he does. Sometimes failure to reach mutual understanding results in the termination of a project at its very inception.

The importance of mutual understanding at the start of a project cannot be stressed too strongly. Many chronicles of the theatre are based upon the failure of a group of people, embarked upon a theatrical venture, to reach a candid expression and interchange of views before the production was begun. For the sake of an appearance of harmony and accord, prominent and seemingly intelligent people will ignore what they know to be basic differences of opinion, and as work progresses, set about to achieve their own objectives by underground methods. This practice is not native to the theatre alone, but the failure of many theatrical ventures can be traced to it.

The nature of theatrical endeavor renders complete understanding of a projected enterprise difficult. The extreme specialization of each worker and the emphasis of each specialist upon his own particular field;

the very fact that each production is in many respects new and unprecedented; the differing opinions, schools of thought, theories, experiences, and preconceptions related to every step of the production process and every detail of theatrical performance — all militate against a clarity of understanding at the beginning of work on a production and continued agreement as the production progresses.

In order that this treatise shall not stop at this point, it will be assumed that the production staff — namely, the author, producer, director, scene and costume designers, and possibly the principal actors — have reached an agreement on the basic values to be presented in the production and that they part as friends, each to prepare the plans for his own phase of the production.

The director begins a detailed study of the script. The author, director, theatre poet, or play doctor rewrites scenes which proved to be weak when the play was read at the conference. The principal actors, if any are chosen at this time, begin work on characterizations. The producer, in combination production, procures a theatre and starts his publicity. The technical workers make plans and specifications. The ensuing period of planning is one of frequent meetings, interchange of ideas, gathering of specific data, and development of the whole broad scheme.

The scene designer inaugurates the planning of the scenic investiture of the production. He has complete responsibility to the producer for all the visual elements of the production except, or possibly including, the costumes. Briefly surveyed, his task is:

scene design

• To make himself familiar with the background material upon which the scene is to be based. To plan each setting with respect to all essential requirements (as stated in the script or prescribed by the director) and limitations (stage space and equipment, budget, etc.)

• To make complete and clear representations of each setting, in sketch rendered in color, ground plan, and model, from which all other workers on the production may ascertain when necessary the nature of the scenery.

• To make detailed drawings and specifications for the builders, stage carpenters, and flymen who are to construct and install the scenery on the stage.

• To evolve a workable scheme of handling the scenery in shifts of allowable time duration.

• To supervise the execution of all parts of the scenic scheme from beginning to end.

Because theatrical production is an art, or at the least partakes of the artistic spirit, and the scene designer is an artist, he is not in the least interested in designing scenery which copies, imitates, or even suggests the work of any other designer, except when his assignment calls for designing *in the style of* a certain painter or an ancient theatre designer, say, Galli Bibiena or Inigo Jones. He is rightly concerned that the scenery be his own original creation, in his own style and manner.

3.1 The sketch

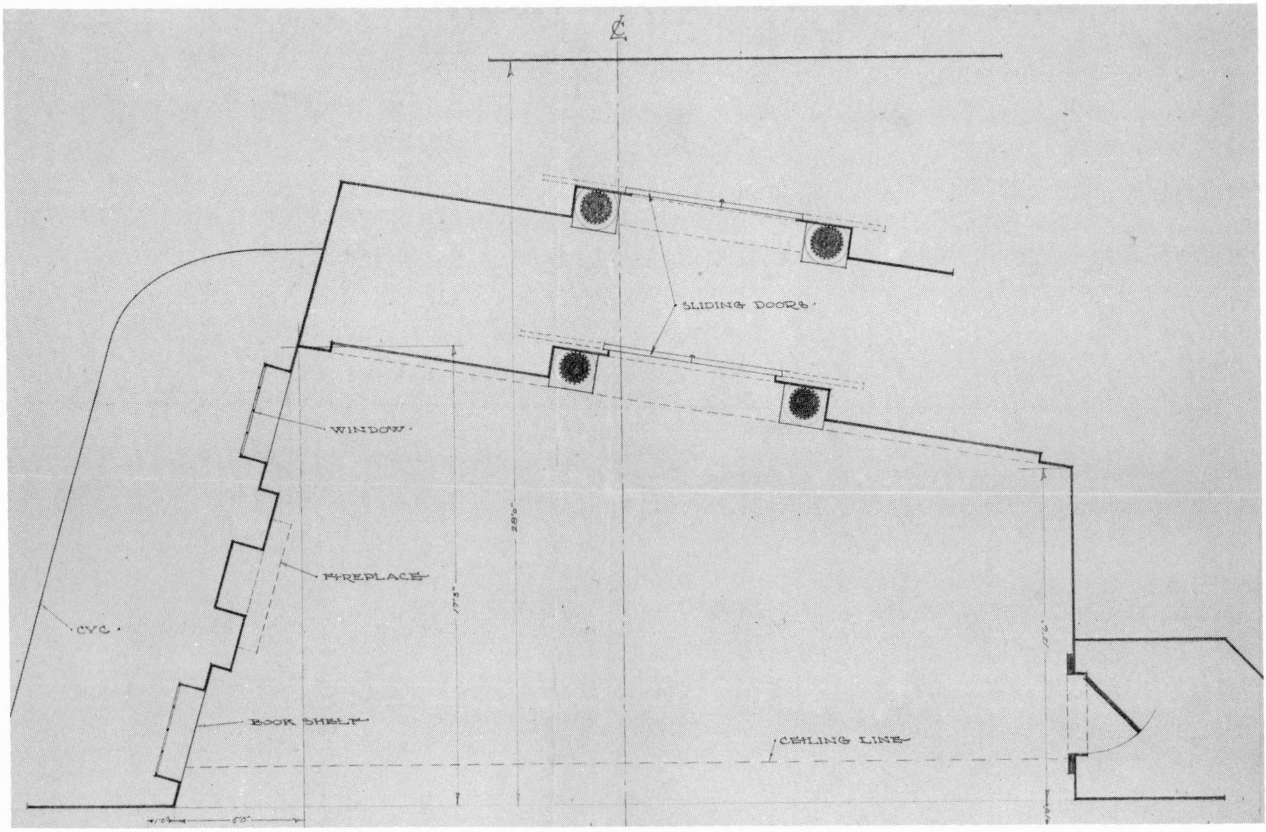

3.2 The ground plan

Sketch, ground plan, and model for *First Lady* by Katherine Dayton and George
S. Kaufman. Donald Oenslager, designer; Sam Harris, producer

The original elements in the planning done by the scene designer are represented in sketch, ground plan, and model (Figures 3.1, 3.2, and 3.3). Each sketch depicts the set as it is to appear under stage lights. It shows clearly the conformation of the set, the period of architecture, the colors, the nature and location of all furniture, draperies, pictures, and other decoration, the position of entrances and exits, and the scale of the scenery in relation to the actors who are to play in it. If there are a number of variations in the visual aspect of one set of scenery, the designer makes a separate sketch to show each one. The ground plan shows graphically the arrangement of the scene on the stage floor, the position of all items of scenery and furniture, the entrances and exits, the extensity and height of all levels, the position and size of all steps, open traps, and ramps. The model combines the pictorial nature of the sketch with the precise factual character of the ground plan. It shows in small scale the space relationships of all parts of the scenery and all the properties. It aids the producer and director in visualizing the total effect of the scenery on the stage. The model may be set behind a model proscenium and lighted to give an approximation of the final appearance of the scenery under lights. Using small-scale figures, the director may even use the model in planning the actors' movements.

sketch, ground plan, and model

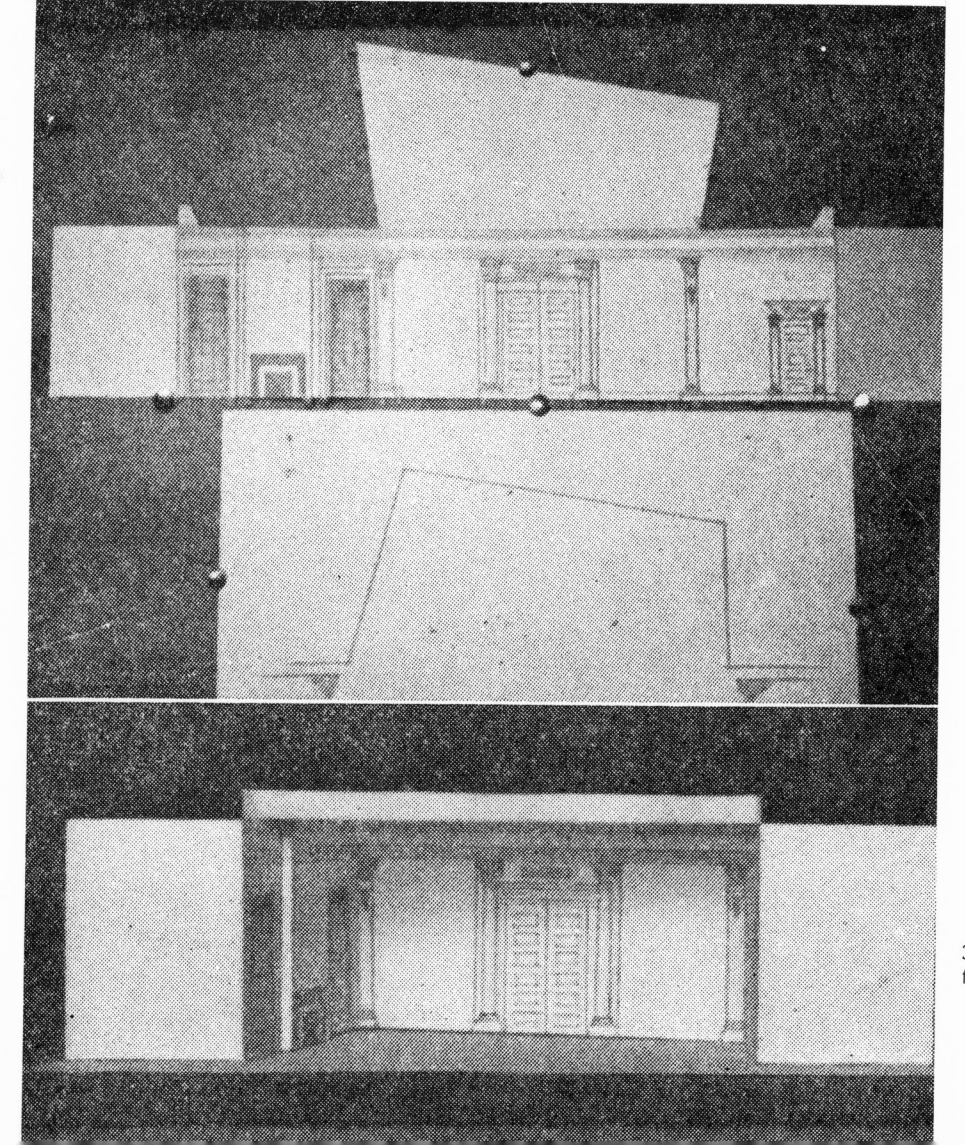

3.3 The model. Above: before folding. Below: folded and fastened

The model is all but indispensable when the scenic investiture is complex or of a novel character. Through its use, the designer can solve in advance the problem of rapid changes of scenery, and the capacity of the stagehouse (which, contrary to many designers' beliefs, is limited) can be made concretely perceptible.

Sketch, ground plan, and model define, to a considerable extent, the scope of the production. They must therefore be approved by the producer and all members of the production staff whose work they limit or influence. In most organizations, the author of the play, the producer, and the director each have the right to reject the scene designs. In combination production, the right is assured the author by contract, is inherent in the function of producer, and may or may not be granted the director. However, a director may, and often will, dissociate himself from a production if the designs for the scenic investiture fail to carry out his ideas of how the play should be interpreted. The scene designer, accordingly, must satisfy the three persons listed as well as he can without betraying his concept, and the process of satisfying all of them generally involves a number of revisions.

the director's requirements

The director is concerned with these elements of scenery:
- Style, as it relates to the style of the acting.
- Locale and atmosphere, as they relate to stage business.
- Mood, as it blends or clashes with the mood inherent in the script.
- Space relationships in the settings, as they dictate the positions of actors and the paths of movement.
- Scene shifts, as their time requirements interrupt or contribute to the tempo of the play.

style

The style of a setting is a function of the architectural detail, the lines, the forms, and colors, and the juxtaposition of parts in the design. It is shown as a prominent, integral characteristic of the whole design. If there has been a preliminary discussion of the production as described in the foregoing paragraphs, there should be very little difficulty in determining after a quick examination of the sketch whether or not the designer has created a style harmonious with the style of the other elements of the production.

Particular styles go in and out of favor. Since 1930 there has been a gradual swing away from realism toward the use of design elements (that is, form, area, color, brush strokes, texture) for more active dramatic expression: attempts to express the emotional tonality of the play in the design elements; attempts to make stage sets successful visual compositions (the sets are often more effective in the sketch, which can be viewed as an entity by a single observer, than in the realized stage set, which can only be seen and appreciated piecemeal by any single spectator); response to the stimuli of the various *isms* of the visual arts — cubism, abstractionism, dadaism, op, pop — with attempts to express the meaning of the play through visual symbols or to elicit an emotional reaction from the audience; concurrence with the cinematic requirements of loosely plotted plays which demand that many locales be placed onstage either simultaneously or in quick succession; and attempts to reduce the costs of making and handling scenery by eliminating unessential parts, making parts serve many purposes, and "letting the audience use its imagination," under proper stimulus, of course, from the play and the actors.

Locale is the geographic placing of the scene, either in a general or in a particular way. "Scotland" may be a sufficient indication of locale for the presentation of a Scotch play in Boston, but the "south shore of Cape Cod" is the degree to which locale might have to be particularized for the presentation of a Massachusetts play to the same audience. The designer's idea of locale is set forth in his architectural detail, his choice of properties, furniture, and interior decoration, his land contours and vegetation for exterior sets. The station of life of the characters in the play is indicated by these elements at the rise of the curtain, and there must be agreement between what the scenery says the characters are and what they, by the speeches and actions, show themselves to be, if the performance is to have convincing unity.

Atmosphere, which resembles and yet differs from locale, is the condition of the natural elements which surround the play. Thus, a gray sky which forebodes an approaching storm creates an atmosphere different from that created by a gray sky through which the sun is about to break. The designer depicts the atmosphere in his rendering of sky, his depiction of light through windows, his indication of natural effects, such as flowers and green fields, or by his total exclusion of natural effect from the scene.

As the style of the play may range between naturalism (the careful depiction of intimate details of daily living) to symbolism (plot, dialogue, character, in fact any production element with hidden or obvious second or third meanings) to abstractionism (some or all elements of the play lacking all or most resemblance to real phenomena), so the scenic investiture may run the same gamut. Locale, in the nonrealistic styles, need not be specific in time or place if this is not essential to the play. Natural representations are not obligatory as the genesis of visual and auditory effects.

The mood of a scene is that quality which emanates from it as a result of the concurrence of all its elements to produce an emotional reaction in the observer. The quality of mood is best delineated by such adjectives, as heavy, light, somber, ominous, gay, rollicking. It parallels in drama the composer's instructions to the player in music: allegro, vivace, lento, doloroso, con spirito. Among the qualities of scenery it most stubbornly defies analysis because it is a total effect rather than a single specific quality of the design. The discussion of mood frequently leads to altercations between artists in the theatre, probably because each may approach the mood of the play subjectively conditioned by acquired preconceptions. Since agreement on mood is essential, it is important that the designer make painstaking efforts to present clearly, and the director endeavor to understand precisely, the mood of the play as set forth in both the script and the sketches.

The foregoing aspects of the scenery upon which the director and the designer must agree are the most difficult of resolution because they

locale

atmosphere

influence of style on locale and atmosphere

mood

stage space

involve, to a considerable degree, intangible theory. In representing and discussing space relationships and scene shifting, the director and designer are dealing with physical and mathematical fact. The minimum space through which an actor can move, to cite an example, is an absolute quantity which can be determined by measurement. The number of people in the audience who will and will not see stage business performed in a certain space on the stage can likewise be accurately shown on scale drawings. The director can see in advance whether or not the movements which he has planned for the actors agree with the positions of the furniture as indicated by the designer. All the details of spacing in the settings are examined by the director and designer in conference over the sketches and ground plans.

shifts The director is concerned with the arrangement for shifting the scenery only insofar as the time required for the shifts affects the continuity in audience attention to the play. The director may specify to the designer the maximum time allowances for scene shifts, if they are important, and the designer may make those allowances a governing condition in the creation of his entire scenic scheme. The director and designer and technical director, in another instance, may devise together a progression of the scenery and action which is uninterrupted by changes, or the author may call for such a progression.

mock-up or rehearsal scenery A director may ask that practical, full-sized simulations of parts of the scenery be built and furnished for rehearsals. His reason may be to make certain that the sightlines of a small set are satisfactory or that sufficient space is available, or to supply structure upon which choreography may be developed. Such mock-ups are skeletal and workable. The producer must approve the expenditure.

designer vs. author and producer The author, as the originator of the project and the person most familiar with the background, characters, and action of the play, and the producer, as the sponsor of the project, are concerned with the broad aspects of the designer's scheme. The author wants truthful locale, atmosphere, and surroundings for his characters. The producer wants a production of artistic merit with some degree of novelty and attractiveness. Sometimes, the designer and director, or the designer and producer, have reached an understanding so complete — through working together continually — that a roughly drawn ground plan with a few words of explanation are sufficient basis for the acceptance by director or producer of the designer's entire scheme.

Some producers and directors wish to know much more about the scenery than others. Some believe themselves to be the sole intelligent judges of the fitness of wallpaper patterns, paint colors, decorative detail, and furniture. Others are content if they know that the entrances and other practical parts of the settings are designed in location and size satisfactory to the action. Unfortunately, in the heat of production, producers, directors, and authors sometimes change their minds about what they want scenically or otherwise, and fail to inform the scene designer. The director may find it convenient to make a nonpractical window practical, or to cut an entrance. A change may be authorized by the director and not by the producer. If the necessary corrections are not made before the set designs go to the shop, the scenery comes to the stage as originally designed, and in the ensuing fray it is up to the scene designer to prove that his designs are correct and approved. It is therefore a practice in some organizations for the designer to get a dated approval signature from author, director, and producer on every design and each revision as a measure of self-protection.

It is conceivable, though hardly probable, that designer and director may agree at the beginning on the extent to which the designer may plan the action of the play, and the director dictate the style and details of the décor. After the director and designer reach an initial understanding on the broad interpretation of the play, and a later one regarding the essential form of the settings, each thereafter proceeds on his own course of action without invading the other's sphere of jurisdiction, but maintains close liaison during the preparation of the production.

The planning of the production is, up to this point, kept oriented by the designer's sketches, ground plans, and models. They serve to get the various departments of production under way. From them the costume designer learns the colors and forms of the backgrounds, and he can proceed to make sketches, collect samples, and make color plates. The lighting designer gets the size and shape of the scenery, its position on-stage and in the flies, the areas of stage action to be lighted, and the openings through which light can be directed toward the stage. He can proceed to make a plan for the location of lighting instruments and can even suggest to the designer the desirability of facilitating certain positions by adjustments of the scenery. The sound technician begins to think practically about the location of microphones and loudspeakers, and to suggest to the designer the provision of mounting positions, spaces, and special openings or coverings in the scenery. The technical director establishes from the ground plans and models the workability of the scenery, learns what is necessary to build the scenery and to light the show, the necessary scenic provision for sound and effects, and makes a tentative cost estimate on the technical production. But sketches, ground plans, and models serve only to get the technical production started. As soon as his first renderings are approved by producer, playwright, and director, the designer must proceed with detailed planning and make his complete drawings.

The scene designer makes mechanical drawings to convenient scales to show the exact shape, size, and appearance of the scenery as he wishes it. They include the following drawings and specifications:

designer's drawings and specifications

To the scale ½″ = 1′ 0″:
• Ground plan of each set. The set is shown in relation to the permanent structure and equipment of the stage: proscenium, act curtain, tormentors, floor traps, and cyclorama, if there is one. The size and location of all architectural items, thicknesses and backings of all openings, and alternate portions of all movable parts are shown. Areas covered with special floor coverings, steps, inclines, and platforms are

shown, and amount of rise indicated. Widths and hanging positions of drops and borders are shown. Principal points in the set are located by dimensions with reference to a fixed line across the stage at the proscenium and a center line of the stage perpendicular to the proscenium. Each object is identified for recognition in other drawings.

• Front elevations of all flat scenery: wall areas, backings, drops, borders, wings, ground rows, and set pieces. All architectural detail is shown in position. The following particulars are either drawn or mentioned in notes on the drawings: hardware such as hinges, latches, knobs; radii and centers of all curves; special effects such as secret panels; practical parts, surface materials, and battens for applied properties and lighting fixtures. Size and location of all parts are stated in dimensions, and parts are labeled to correspond to the ground plans.

• Front elevations and requisite additional views of all three-dimensional scenery: stairs, ramps, platforms (see "Models" below). The front elevations are supplemented by cross sections to show thickness, moldings, change of shape, interrelation of surface planes, and parts not completely presented in the elevations.

To the scale 1″ = 1′ 0″ or 3″ = 1′ 0″ (the choice of scale depends upon the complexity of detail in the object to be drawn):

• All architectural parts: doors, windows, mantels, ceiling beams, columns, pilasters, cornices.

• All exterior objects such as trees, hedges, rock walls.

Actual size:

• All irregular ornamental parts such as ceiling coffers, panels, corbels, plaques, newel posts, and spindles, and all objects which are to be turned, carved, or molded. Elevations and indicative sections are drawn.

• Patterns of designs to be applied to surfaces of scenery or to draperies.

• Sections of all moldings which are to be specially cut or made up by assembling or altering stock moldings.

Specifications to accompany these drawings:

• Indication of all practical parts and the nature of their use in the action of the play.

• Statement of loads which scenery must support.

• Surface covering and finish wherever it is to be other than scenery cloth, sized.

• Floor-covering materials other than the regular stage floorcloth.

models

Scale models of parts of the scenery which are not easily represented in mechanical drawing are substituted for detail drawings. Such scenery as irregular rock formations, complex arrangements of levels, stone walls, misshapen trees, and other natural forms may be accurately modeled in wood, plaster of Paris, soap, Styrofoam, or sponge rubber.

drawings of properties

Similar mechanical drawings are made of all objects classed as properties which are to be fabricated: elevations of draperies with detailed specifications of the amount and kind of materials to be used, their

3.4 Painter's elevation of a portion of the *First Lady* set. It is sufficient to show all the colors required and to indicate the desired visual effects

3.5 The completed setting for *First Lady*

color, and the method of cutting and draping; three or more views of each object of furniture to appropriate scale; full-sized details of all parts to be carved, turned, or molded; complete specifications for the surfacing and finishing of each piece; full-sized patterns of designs to be applied to fabrics.

The designer's drawings are made on tracing paper. A sufficient number of black-on-white prints are made to supply all persons requiring them. Prints of the ground plan are given to the stage manager and the lighting designer. A full set of designer's drawings, along with sketches and the model, are submitted to the technical director, to be used in calculating costs and making the technical analysis.

painting specifications

The scene designer prepares complete instructions for the scene painters (see Figure 3.4). These consist of scale elevations of all surfaces of scenery to be painted, rendered in color exactly as they are to appear when finished, verbal description of the procedure to be followed, and patterns or stencils of all designs to be applied to the scenery.

technical planning
appraisal of the job

Before the designer's drawings are completed, the technical director has started to estimate the work to be done and the amount of time it will require. He must, in fact, bring three major factors into balance before he can be sure that the work will progress to a successful conclusion: the magnitude of the job, the available time, and the budget. These factors also concern the scene builder in commercial production, who must estimate his costs and bid for the job of building and perhaps painting the scenery for the show. If he estimates high, he may exceed the producer's budget and lose the job; if he estimates low, he may get the job, but lose money doing it.

The appraisal of the magnitude of the job is made by finding the answers to a series of questions: How many sets? What type of sets are they — interior or exterior, full-stage or part-stage, framed or unframed, simple or complex in structure, simple or complex in ornament, what percentage stock materials, what percentage special? What are the time allowances for scene changes? How much time will be required to build, paint, and rig each set? How much time will be required to rehearse shifts? To light? To set the sound? What are the properties? How much time will be required to build or procure them?

Both the magnitude of the job and the time available have a direct bearing on the cost of the production. Overtime work increases costs out of proportion to the value of time thus gained. Inversely, cost limitations also have a direct bearing on the magnitude of the job. The technical director appraises the scenery, as represented in the designer's sketches, drawings, and models, in terms of materials and man-hours of labor. If the estimates exceed the budget allotment for scenery, the producer and designer must agree to reduce the amount of the scenery and thus reduce man-hours, or consent to substitution of cheaper materials or to a reduction of the complexity of the scenery.

the available time

This is the time between the date when work can begin and the date of the first dress rehearsal. In this time the scenery must be built, painted, assembled, lighted, and rehearsed. The available time, which is often short, must be apportioned very carefully to avoid expensive overtime work and to prevent the early parts of the work from lagging, thereby causing undue pressure of work toward the end of the production period.

In the combination system, where scenery production contracts are let to independent concerns, the technical director simply reports the bids to the producer. The contracting concerns assume the responsibility for the costs of completing, on specified dates, their phases of the total job. The technical director acts to coordinate their separate functions, attending to delivery of built scenery from shop to paint studio and from studio to stage. The scene designer or an assistant scene designer generally performs the technical director's functions under such an organization.

Thus the technical director puts in order the general approach of all departments to the problem of producing the scenery. He compiles into a timetable (Figure 3.6) the sequence of events or deadlines which affect all departments and distributes copies among department heads for criticism and to avoid conflicts. Minor alterations are made if necessary, and the schedule is put into effect. The degree of detail which this schedule includes depends upon the complexity of the production and the urgency of each department's holding exactly to its finishing dates. If there is ample time, the technical director will distribute the extra days throughout the work period, and reserve one or two free days just before dress rehearsal as a safety factor.

The scene designer compiles for the lighting designer a statement of the lighting desired. This takes the form of numerous small sketches based on his original sketches of the settings; they illustrate changes in the lighting and may even include ground plans with suggested positions for lighting instruments. The designer pays particular attention to the direction, intensity, color, and general composition of the lighting, and leaves the technical procedure to the lighting designer.

In combination production, sketches, plans, models, designs, color sketches, and lists are the basis for bids by manufacturers of and dealers in scenery, lights, and properties. The production is prepared by the successful bidders, and the technical planning by the producing organization is next concerned with the assembly of the production on the stage. In repertory or similar organizations the production process is complete within the organization and proceeds as indicated above.

As they receive the requisite data from director, stage manager, designer, and technical director, the backstage department heads do their planning, often with the collaboration of and always subject to the approval of those to whom they are responsible.

Lighting is an integral part of the design of the scenery and, in professional practice, is the responsibility of the scene designer. Scene designers may assume and discharge this responsibility personally or they may assume it and delegate the work either to assistant designers or to lighting designers in their employ. Alternatively they may work with a lighting designer engaged by the producer. In New York, lighting designers are members of a special section of Local #829 of the United

interrelation of departments during planning

lighting

Production Time Table		"Cake Before Breakfast"				
Day	Date	Actors	Scenery	Properties	Lights	Sound
Mon.	Nov. 1	Scripts typed	Designs selected			
Tues.	2	Readings				Plot to Effect Man from Stage Mgr.
Wed.	3					
Thur.	4		Act I Drawings to Scene Technician	Plot to Prop. Master	Plot to Electrician	
Fri.	5			Act I Drawings to Prop. Master		
Sat.	6					
Sun.	7	Principals cast			Layout and schedule of instruments	
Mon.	8		Act II Drawings to scene technician		Estimate	
Tues.	9		Act I Built Transfer to paint shop	Act II Drawings to Prop. Master	Procure Equipment	
Wed.	10	Extras cast		Deadline Act I Trim.		
Thur.	11	Begin Rehearsals				
Fri.	12		Act III Drawings to Scene technician			
Sat.	13		Act I painted. Transfer to stage	Act III Drawings to Prop. Master		Stage Mgr. check effects
Sun.	14		Act II built Transfer to paintshop.	Deadline Act II Trim.		
Mon.	15					
Tues.	16					
Wed.	17					
Thur.	18		Act II Painted Transfer to stage	Deadline Act III Trim.		
Fri.	19					
Sat.	20		Act III Built Transfer to paint shop			
Sun.	21					
Mon.	22					Director hear sound effects
Tues.	23					
Wed.	24		Adjust stage equipt			
Thur.	25		• • •			
Fri.	26	Run through for technical departments		Deadline Handprops.	Mount and focus instruments	
Sat.	27		Act III painted Transfer to stage	Deadline Furniture	"	
Sun.	28		Rig Act I			
Mon.	29			Trim Act I	Light Act I	
Tues.	30	Handprops. at rehearsal	Rig Act II	Handprops. at rehearsal		
Wed.	Dec. 1	Rehearse with sound effects		Trim Act II	Light Act II	Sound with all subsequent rehearsal
Thur.	2		Rig Act III			
Fri.	3		Rehearse scene changes.	Trim Act III	Light Act III	
Sat.	4	Rehearse with scenery and lights	Rehease with actors		Rehearse with actors	"
Sun.	5	Dress Rehearsal	"	"	"	"
Mon.	6	" "	"	"	"	"
Tues.	7	" "	"	"	"	"
Wed.	8	Opening Performance	"	"	"	"

3.6 A production timetable

3.7 Lighting layout, ground plan, and section

No.	MAKE	USE	Act I	Act II	Act III	Lamp	Wattage	Pocket	Dimmer	Dimmer Watt
INSTRUMENT SCHEDULE "DECADE" by Marion Hazard Setting-J.Larsen Lighting-A.H.Ross										
SPOTLIGHTS										
1.	Century LeKolite	Area 1L	54	54	54	T-20	500	HL-1	5	500
2.	" "	" 2L	"	"	"	"	"	" 2	6	"
3.	" "	" 3L	"	"	"	"	"	" 3	7	"
4.	" "	" 1R	26	26	26	"	"	HR-1	8	"
5.	" "	" 2R	"	"	"	"	"	" 2	9	"
6.	" "	" 3R	"	"	"	"	"	" 3	10	"
7.	" Baby	" 4L	54-F	54-F	54-F	G-30	400	1B-1	17	"
8.	" "	" 5L	"	"	"	"	"	2B-1	18	"
9.	" "	" 6L	"	"	"	"	"	3B-1	19	"
10.	" "	" 7L	"	"	"	"	"	1B-2	20	"
11.	" "	" 4R	26-F	26-F	26-F	"	"	2B-2	21	"
12.	" "	" 5R	"	"	"	"	"	4B-1	22	"
13.	" "	" 6R	"	"	"	"	"	4B-2	23	"
14.	" "	" 7R	"	"	"	"	"	2B-3	24	"
SPECIAL SPOTS										
15.	Century Baby	Door Special	26	26	26	G-30	400	4B-3	52	1000
16.	" "	Arch "	62	62	62	"	"	2B-4	53	1000
17.	Pevear Box	Stair "				Fr.	"	5U-1	54	1000
FLOODS										
18.	Cyclorama	Hall Backing	26-F	26-F	26-F	PS-40	500	5U-2	46	1000
19.	"	" "	"	"	"	"	"	5U-3		
20.	"	Backing Door R	62-F	62-F	62-F	"	"	1PR-1	12	
21.	"	Exterior Backing	26	26	26	"	"	1U-3	G	4000
22.	"	" "	"	"	"	"	"	"	"	
23.	"	" "	"	"	"	"	"	"	"	
24.	"	" "	"	"	"	"	"	"	"	
25.	"	Daylite Diffuser	"	"	"	"	"	1U-4	35	1800
26.	"	" "	"	"	"	"	"	"	"	
27.	"	" "	"	"	"	"	"	"	"	
PROJECTORS										
28.	Century	Sun	54	54		G-40	500	1U-1	H	4000
29.	"	"	"	"		"	"	1U-2		
STRIPS										
30.	Kleigl Compart.	Foots L	Primaries R-G-B	A21-23	60-240 / 60-240 / 100-400	FL-1,2,3	33 / 45	550 / 250 / 1000		
31.	" "	" C	"	" " "	100 / 480	F-1,2,3	47	1000		
32.	" "	" "	"	" " "	60 480 / 100 800	"	48 / 49	1000 / 1000		
33.	" "	" R	"	" " "	60-240 / 60-240 / 100-400	FR-1,2,3	12 / 13 / 44	250 / 550 / 1000		
34.	Century Compart.	Borders	26,57,& Red Cell	PS-30	200-1600	A-3B-2	29	1800		
35.	" "	"	" " " "	"	" R-3B-4	30	"			
					" B-X-1	31	"			
SPECIALS										
36.	Floor Lamp	Above fireplace			Fr.	G-25	Z-40	2FL-2	4	250-6h

3.8 An instrument schedule. Outlets and control board setup

Scenic Artists. This book presumes a lighting designer in the producing organization, in conformity with any one of the three arrangements just mentioned.

The lighting designer has the scene designer's more or less complete list of lighting requirements. He receives from the stage manager a list of acting areas to be lighted, a plot of the lighting effects required by the action, and a cue sheet locating in the action of the play the occurrence of each effect. He integrates the designer's lighting requirements with those of the action, confers with designer, stage manager, and director in case of conflicting requirements, and compiles a lighting layout (Figure 3.7) composed of:

• Ground plan and vertical section of each set in position on stage, showing all lighting instruments in position, and the areas they light.

• An instrument schedule (Figures 3.8 and 3.9) for each set, giving

DIMMER	LOCATION	NO OF INST	TYPE	LAMP	COLOUR	USE	NOTES
1	1ST BEAM / 2ND BEAM	17,83 / 5	8" LEKO	2M/T-20	3,17,36,54	AA1 + AA7	REMOTE COLOUR CONTROL PLUG AS DESIRED
2	"	18,19 / 6	"	"	"	AA2 + AA8	"
3	"	21,22 / 7	"	"	"	AA3 + AA9	"
4	"	24,25 / 8	"	"	"	AA4 + AA10	"
5	"	27,28 / 9	"	"	"	AA5 + AA11	"
6	"	29,30 / 10	"	"	"	AA6 + AA12	"
7	BOOTH	1	12" D.C. ARC		9,7,17,36,38	ACCENT	FIVE COLOUR FRONT OPERATED
8	"	2	"		"	"	"
9	ELECT #4	7,9	16" B.P.	2M/GA8	AS DESIRED	SPECIAL	
10	1ST BEAM	20,21,26	12" FRESNEL	2M/GA8	54/54	CURTAIN WARMERS	
11	1ST BEAM / 2ND BEAM	32 / 11	8" LEKO	2M/T-20	3,17,36,64	AA1 + AA7	REMOTE COLOUR CONTROL PLUG AS DESIRED
12	"	34 / 12	"	"	"	AA2 + AA8	"
13	"	35 / 13	"	"	"	AA3 + AA9	"
14	"	36 / 14	"	"	"	AA4 + AA10	"
15	"	38 / 15	"	"	"	AA5 + AA11	"
16	"	40 / 16	"	"	"	AA6 + AA12	"
17	2ND BEAM	3	12" Incandescent Followspot	8M/T-32	3,1,17,36,38	ACCENT	
18	"	4	"	"	"	"	
19	ELECT #4	1,3,5	16" B.P.	2M/GA8	AS DESIRED	SPECIAL	
20	1ST BEAM	35,37,39	12" FRESNEL	2M/GA8	54/54	CURTAIN WARMERS	
21	ELECT #1	1,2	12" FRESNEL	2M/GA8	3,54	AA13	
22	"	4,5	"	"	"	AA14	
23	"	6,7	"	"	"	AA15	
24	"	9,10	"	"	"	AA16	
25	"	11,12	"	"	"	AA17	
26	"	14,15	"	"	"	AA18	
27	SL LAD #1	1,2,3,4,5,6,7,8	6" LEKO / 8" LEKO	1+2 500/T-12 3+4 750/T-24 5-8 1000/T-24	3,17	SIDE ACCENT	
28	SR LAD #1	"	"	"	"	"	
29	SL LAD #1	8,9,10,11,12,13,14	8" LEKO	1000/T-2A	"	"	
30	SR LAD #1	"	"	"	"	"	
31	ELECT #2	16,17	12" FRESNEL	2M/GA8	17,86	AA13	
32	"	19,20	"	"	"	AA14	
33	"	21,22	"	"	"	AA15	
34	"	24,25	"	"	"	AA16	
35	"	26,27	"	"	"	AA17	
36	"	29,30	"	"	"	AA18	
37	SL LAD #2	1,2,3,4,5,6,7,8	6" LEKO (1+2) / 8" LEKO (3-8)	1+2 500/T-12 3-6 750/T-24 7+9 1000/T-24	3,17	SIDE ACCENT	TO BE USED WHEN CYC OUT
38	SR LAD #2	"	"	"	"	"	"
39	SL LAD #2	9,10,11,12	8" LEKO	9+10 1000/T-24 11+12 2M/T-30	"	"	"
40	SR LAD #2	"	"	"	"	"	"
41	SL SIDE SLOTS / SR SIDE SLOTS / ELECT #2		6" LEKO / 8" LEKO / 16" B.P.	1000/T-12 1000/T-2A 1000/Q-40	3 AS DESIRED	ACCENT	PLUG AS DESIRED
42	SL SIDE SLOTS / SR SIDE SLOTS / ELECT #2		8" LEKO / 16" B.P.	750/T-24 1000/T-2A 1000/Q-40	AS DESIRED	"	"
43	SL SIDE SLOTS / SR SIDE SLOTS / ELECT #2		8" LEKO / 16" B.P.	750/T-24 1000/T-2A 1000/Q-40	AS DESIRED	"	"
44	SL SIDE SLOTS / SR SIDE SLOTS / ELECT #2		8" LEKO / 16" B.P.	1000/T-24 1000/T-2A 1000/Q-40	AS DESIRED	"	"
45	SL SIDE SLOTS / SR SIDE SLOTS / ELECT #2		8" LEKO / 16" B.P.	1000/T-24 1000/T-2A 1000/Q-40	AS DESIRED	"	"
46	SL SIDE SLOTS / SR SIDE SLOTS / ELECT #2		8" LEKO / 16" B.P.	1000/T-2A 1000/T-2A 1000/Q-40	AS DESIRED	ACCENT	PLUG AS DESIRED
47	SL LAD #3	1,2,3,4,5,6,7,8	6" LEKO / 8" LEKO	1+2 6" LEKO 3-6 750/T-24 7+8 1000/T-24	3,17	SIDE ACCENT	TO BE USED WHEN CYC OUT
48	SR LAD #3	"	"	"	"	"	"
49	SL LAD #3	9,10,11,12	"	9+10 1000/T-24 11+12 2M/T-30	"	"	"
50	SR LAD #3	"	"	"	"	"	"
51	FOOTLIGHTS	1-7	8X8 STRIP	150/R-40 FL	R	BLENDING	USE ROUNDELS
52	"	"	"	"	B	"	"
53	"	"	"	"	G	"	"
54	"	"	"	"	A	"	"
55	ELECT #1	1-8	"	150/R-40 FL	R	BLENDING + TONING	"
56	"	"	"	"	B	"	"
57	"	"	"	"	G	"	"
58	"	"	"	"	A	"	"
59	ELECT #3	1-8	"	150/R-40 FL	R	"	"
60	"	"	"	"	B	"	"
61	"	"	"	"	G	"	"
62	"	"	"	"	A	"	"
63	ELECT #5	1-8	"	150/R-40 FL	R	"	"
64	"	"	"	"	B	"	"
65	"	"	"	"	G	"	"
66	"	"	"	"	A	"	"
67	ELECT #6	1-8	"	150/R-40 FL	R	"	"
68	"	"	"	"	B	"	"
69	"	"	"	"	G	"	"
70	"	"	"	"	A	"	"
71	ELECT #8	1-32	CYC	150/R-40 FL	R	CYCLORAMA	1,2,11,12 DEAD HUNG USE ROUNDELS
72	"	"	"	"	B	"	"
73	"	"	"	"	G	"	"
74	"	"	"	"	A	"	"
75	ELECT #9	"	"	150/R-40 FL	R	"	"
76	"	"	"	"	B	"	"
77	"	"	"	"	G	"	"
78	"	"	"	"	A	"	"
79	FLOOR-US.	1-12	8X8 STRIP	150/R-40 FL	R	"	USE ROUNDELS
80	"	"	"	"	B	"	"
81	"	"	"	"	G	"	"
82	"	"	"	"	A	"	"
83	FLOOR-US	1-14	8X8 STRIP	150/5-40 FL	R	"	"
84	"	"	"	"	R	"	"
85	"	"	"	"	B	"	"
86	"	"	"	"	B	"	"
87	"	"	"	"	G	"	"
88	"	"	"	"	G	"	"
89	"	"	"	"	A	"	"
90	"	"	"	"	A	"	"

NOTE	CONTROL — 90, 6 KW. DIMMERS	TOTAL NUMBER OF INSTRUMENTS — 288	ALL COLOUR CINEMOID

3.9 Compare this instrument schedule with that in Figure 3.8. The increase in the number of instruments indicates the elaboration of stage lighting since 1938 and the number of instruments required to equip a stage for a rapidly changing festival repertory season

in detail the specifications of each instrument, circuits, loads, dimmers, switches, and all equipment and accessories required.

• Control board specifications and setup, and tentative cue sheet for each scene.

He estimates the cost of lighting the production and submits it to the producer.

Because the art of stage lighting is complex and full of electrical and optical technicalities, it is often difficult for the lighting designer to explain lighting methods and terminology, and for the scene designer and director to understand them. Nevertheless, as it is important for the scene designer and director to agree on major factors in the scenery, so is it important for the scene designer, director, and lighting designer to agree, before the work is begun, on the effects to be produced. It is advantageous for the scene designer and director to know the theory and practice of stage lighting.

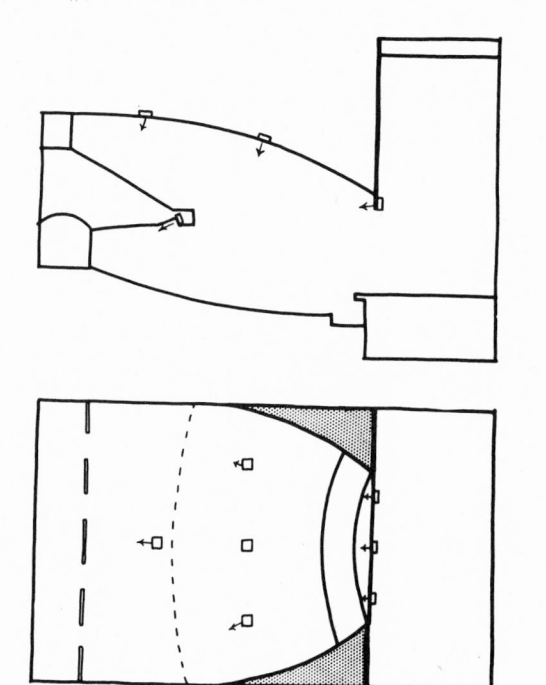

3.10 Permanent installation: loudspeakers in the ceiling and under the balcony for auditory perspective about the house; loudspeakers in the proscenium for stereophonic reinforcement

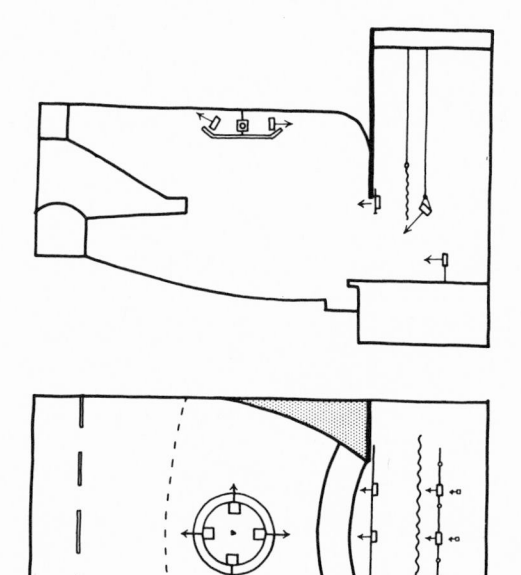

3.11 Temporary installation: four loudspeakers in the chandelier reflecting sound from the ceiling and walls, three in a false proscenium, and others, either hung behind a border or on stands behind a drop, for dubbing voices onto dancers or mimes.

sound

The sound technician receives from the author and the director a list of sound requirements. He arranges with the designer and the technical director for the location of his apparatus so that it will not be masked or interfered with by standing or moving scenery, props, and the like. He makes the necessary acoustical and electrical interference tests, designs and draws specifications for apparatus, and arranges for its procurement; in collaboration with the stage manager he works out sound plot, setup, and cue sheet (Figure 3.12).

#	Scene No.	Scene Description	Time	Warning	Cue	Sound	Source	Input No.	Input Control Setting	Input Channel Color
3a	1	Macbeth			{ Segue	Prokofiev	W E T T	2		G
4					{ Segue	Witches	Spotter D-1	3	16	3R
5				wierd sisters	-- charms wound up	witches				
6				inhabitants o the earth	- that you are so - speak	witches	Spotter D-1			
7				thane of Candor	- be king hereafter	witches				
8				seeds of time	neither beg nor fear	witches	Spotter 6-A2-9B Screen D-1			strike 3R
9a					Banquo and Macbeth- all hail	Thunder witches				
10				let us speak	till then, enough. Come.	Orch	Pit	4 5 6	16 16 16	4R 5W 6G
11					Segue	Voice	Booth	1	16	W
12						Orch.	Pit	4 5 6	16 16 16	4R 5W 6G
13	II	Tempest		Beginning of Overture	Opening of curtain	Ariel	Tent	1		1W
14				thats my noble master	go, hence with diligence	Orch.	Pit	4 5 6	16 16 16	4R 5R
15				Keep a good tongue	shall not suffer indignity	Whistle cut!	Spotter D2	3		3W
16				I am subject to	of the island	Ariel	Tent	1		W
17					thought is free	Tabor + Pipe	Spotter D2	3		3R
18										
19				forgive me my sins	I defy thee	Thunder	Thunder Screen	2		2W
20				Lead monster	I'll follow, Stephano	Orch. Thunder	Pit	2		2W
21				let it be tonight	tonight: no more	Ariel	Spotter D-2	3		3W
22					Segue you and your ways	Prospero	Booth	1		1W
23					Follow, I pray you	Orch.	Pit	4 5 6	16 16 16	4R 5W
24					End of Orchestra	Voice	Booth	1		1W
25	III	Dream		Voice Line	O.K. charlie	orch	Pit	4 5 6		4R 5W
26				Sing me now asleep	then to your offices	Fairies	Spotter D-3	3		R
27				Segue	end of music	Fairies	Spotter D-3	3		
28				your cue is past-it is never time	as true as truest horse	Bottom	Spotter D-4	3		
29				doth move me	I love thee	Bottom				
30				Segue	I have enough to serve mine own turn	Bottom				
31				weeps every little flower	enforced chastity	Bray				
32				thy sleek, smooth head	my gentle joy	Bottom				
33				to say what dream it was	me thought I was	Bray				
34				Segue	sing it at her death	Orch.	Pit	4 5 6		R W
35				Segue	End of overture	Voice	Booth	1		W
3 4		Tocatta					Western Elec. D-5	2		W
		Intermission								
40		Overture		Stage Mgr.	Stage Mgr.	Orch	Pit	4 5 6		4R 5W
41	V	Jones		Segue	End of orch.	Drum	Drum	2		W

(vertical note in Warning column, scene II/III: "Check Thunder Channel")

3.12 Setup and operating sheet for a demonstration of the theatrical use of electronically reproduced sound at Stevens Institute of Technology

48

Output No.	Output Channel Color	Output Control Setting	Speaker Plug	Panel Jack	Speaker Location	Operating Technique
1 2 3	G		1 2 3	L M N	Overhead Speakers	Background music Fade with Banquo & Macbeth
6 7 8	R	28 28 28	6 7 8	E F G	Stand Speakers	
						lift spotter
						set spotter on
						lift spotter
						put spotter on
1 2 3	R W G	16 16 16	1 2 3	A B C	Procen-R Expo Procen-L	1 ft. spotter, strike disc #1, at end of witches shift drum to input #2, booth mike to input #1, Backstage over head to proscenium
4 5 6	W		2 4 5 6	B H I J		Inputs 4,5,6 green to stereo setup.
1 2 3	R W G	16 16 16	1 2 3	A B C	Procen-R Expo Procen-L	
						shift output to pit
2,4,5,6,7	W		2 4 5 6 7	B H I J D		End of orchestra shift prosc. to backstage overhead
1 2 3	R W G		1 2 3	A B C		
2 4 5 6 7	W		2 4 5 6 7	B H I V D		Put spotter on
1 3			1 3	E - G		Lift spotter
2 4 5 6 7 8	3		2 4 5 6 7 8	B H I J M N		add speakers for Thunder
2 4 5	W		2 4 5	B H I		
						up on 8th bar & out
4 5	W		4 5	H I		
2 4 5 6 7 8	W		2 4 5 6 7 8	B H I J M N		Thunder on word cues
1 2 3	R W G		1 2 3	A B C		
2 4 5 6	W		2 4 5 6	B H I J		
1 2 3	R W G		1 2 3	A B C		Hook up & set stage witch speakers
6 7 8	R		6 7 8	L M N	OHSR OHSC OHSL	Fade up Fairies - spot to be sure to get first note
6 7 8	R		6 7 8	L M N		End Disc at end of music - strike disc & put on Ass disc
6 7 8	R		6 7 8	E F G	Stage Stand Speaker	Drop Spotter — Follow Bottom with Speakers
						Drop Spotter
						Lift Spotter
						Spot
						Spot - Run to end of cut
					Center Stand	Spot - strike disc
1 2 3	R W G		1 2 3	A B C		
4 5 6	W		2 4 5 6	B H I J	Exp. WH EH Bal.	
	W		1 2 3 4 / 5 6 7 8	A B C N / I J L N	PR Exp PL WH / EH Bal OHSR OHSL	
			Intermission shift	1 2 3 4 5 6 7 8 / A B C L N H I K		
2 3	R W G	16 16 16	1 2 3	A B C	Procenium Rt. Cen. Lt.	Start drum on last note orchestra - inaud.
6 7 8	W		8	K	Floor	

49

3.13 Costume designer's working sketch. Design by Frank Bevan for Aquilina in Thomas Otway's *Venice Preserved*, produced at the Yale School of Drama

The costume designer, when his designs have been approved, arranges for purchase or manufacture of costumes, sets fitting dates, and prepares, in complex productions, a costume operation chart. The property master lists, locates, and plans the procurement of properties, and prepares the lists and plans he will use in the assembly and running of the show.

While all paper planning is in progress, the technical director must work out a scheme by which all elements of production can be made and assembled without conflict, and must husband his stage space while plans are on paper, for he cannot stretch the stage after the show is built.

As can easily be seen, planning a production involves a progressively larger number of people, whose work is closely interrelated. To keep the planning oriented and the building up to schedule, and to prevent conflicts, some organizations have production meetings at frequent intervals, attended by all members of the organization involved in planning the production. Such meetings are particularly valuable when changes in script or set design are undertaken after production has started, since all plans can be altered at once, and all conflicts ironed out before any time or work is wasted. Between meetings or at times when pressure of work precludes meetings, the production manager assumes the functions of coordinator and expediter.

Department heads see the production in terms of their own departments, and are therefore often able to make valuable suggestions for improving or simplifying the production, as well as pointing out the limitations within which work assigned to their departments will have to be done. The earlier in the production process that such suggestions can be made and presumptive limitations pointed out, the better it is for the show. Woe to the department head who does not make director, producer, and author understand presumptive limitations at this first meeting. Silence is taken for acquiescence and a guarantee by the department head that the job can be accomplished.

In some organizations, with department heads long accustomed to working together, planning may seem to be perfunctory and yet may be both thorough and effective, even though it involves only occasional and casual conferences.

4 Planning the scenery

From this point onward, the study of scenery, which is, after all, the subject of this book, will be pursued by as straight a path as possible. Scenery starts on the drawing board, and the drawing-board phase of its development is the subject of this chapter. Some of the planning of the scenery is, to be sure, done during production planning, just as part of the production planning is done before the play is included in the season's schedule. Such scenic planning enables the departments of production whose work affects or is affected by scenery to get under way. It is far from complete, for the scene designer's drawings show only the external, visible aspects of the scenery. There still remains the determination of sightlines, of how the scenery will be disposed onstage, how it will fit together, how it is to be moved, what weight it must support, and how it is to be prepared within time and budget limitations. Until these questions are answered, the planning of the scenery cannot be completed.

sightlines   When each set is tested in position on the stage, and this is done on the model, on plans, and finally when the set is assembled, a major item in the test is the examination of the critical sightlines, to test the range of visibility of the audience. There are two requirements which govern the visibility from the auditorium to a set onstage:

• All important parts of the set and all acting areas must be visible to all spectators.

• No part of the stage outside the setting, none of the stage paraphernalia, no unfinished portion of the scenery, and no actors waiting offstage may be visible to any spectators.

The technical director checks the sightlines to see if these requirements are satisfied. Checking may indicate the necessity for pieces of scenery which are not specified and may also demonstrate the unworkability, from a director's point of view, of some portion of the scenery.

Checking the sightlines is, in the American professional theatre, the scene designer's responsibility. The contracting scene builder constructs only such scenery as the designer specifies, and if certain pieces fail to mask openings when they are set onstage, it is the scene designer's fault. Inasmuch as many functions are in this book assigned to the technical director which are commonly in America performed by the scene designer, it is well for the scene designer to assume that, if he is working in the American professional theatre, he must be, to a considerable extent at least, his own technical director.

Sightlines are lines of vision from points in the auditorium to points on the stage. In the auditorium only certain vantage points are critical and only the sightlines from those points to a limited number of points in any set on the stage are necessary to settle the whole problem of visibility and masking.

To satisfy the requirement of visibility, it is necessary to ascertain the limit of vision of the spectators in the seats farthest from the center on either side, of the spectator in the highest balcony seat past objects over the stage, and of the spectator in the lowest seat past objects on the floor. Sightlines drawn from these four extreme positions past each consecutive object which protrudes in the range of vision delineate the stage space (three dimensions) which can be seen by *all* spectators.

Thus in Figure 4.1, sightlines from A and B past the proscenium walls, past the jog in the stage right wall, and past the edges of the opening in the back wall show that only the shaded portion of the stage is visible to all spectators. The director must be informed of this limitation of the usable acting area so that he will place important stage business within the shaded area.

The sightlines just described cause considerable restriction of areas outside the main walls of the set. On the ground plan, these areas may appear to be usable for action, but when tested, they prove to be practically useless because of the limited number of spectators who see them. The area beyond the upstage center doorway in Figure 4.1 is an example of this: The sightline proves that only the bottom tread of the flight of steps can be seen by the whole audience.

Any piece of scenery or large property which protrudes laterally into the acting area masks a portion of the area upstage of it from view by some of the spectators. The jog in the stage right wall is an example.

Figure 4.2 shows in cross section a set which contains large platforms, a backdrop, and a masking border. The sightline from A past the footlights shows that a portion of the stage floor is invisible. Sightlines from A and B show that the floors of both platforms are invisible to the entire orchestra. A sightline from B past the bottom of the balcony and a sightline from C past the bottom of the teaser show the upward limits of vision for the whole audience. The sightline from C sets the height limit at which actors on platforms are visible from the balcony. The shaded portion indicates the zone of vertical stage space which is visible to the entire audience and hence most useful for objects, stage business, or action.

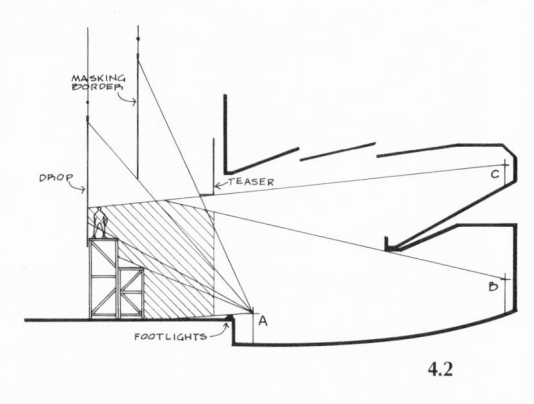

4.1

4.2

Scene designers, in locating important pieces of scenery, properties, and entrances, must subject them to this test of audience visibility. A scene designer is wise if in laying out ground plans he works with reference to a ground plan of the theatre on which are shown the extreme side seats of the auditorium and balcony and the natural sightlines — that is, those inherent in the structure of the theatre.

American commercial theatres, particularly those in New York City, are notoriously bad with respect to sightlines from side seats of both orchestra and balcony. Designers are forced to extremes of ingenuity to avoid the hackneyed slanting sidewalls and yet show important detail in the sides of their sets. This situation is often made still worse by the necessity of closing in the proscenium to gain backstage space. The horizontal sightlines from proscenium boxes are especially bad.

Figure 4.2 also illustrates the use of sightlines to determine the position and size of borders. Modern stagehouses are seldom high enough to accommodate drops or cycloramas which will mask the top of an open scene and still fly up out of sight when the scene is changed. The height of a backdrop or cyclorama is generally limited to one half the height of the gridiron, and a masking border is hung downstage of it, to conceal its top and the space above it. As the section drawing indicates, the closer to the proscenium the border is hung, the smaller it may be and the lower it must be hung to conceal the top of the drop. It is desirable to hang borders high despite the fact that high borders must be large, because:

• The higher they are hung, the fewer spectators see them, and they are rarely decorative.

• The higher they are hung, the less they intercept rays from lighting instruments mounted on the first light pipe or the first light bridge. The top limit of their hanging height is determined by the trim of scenery or lights which must be concealed and which are hung upstage of them.

To satisfy the requirement of complete masking, it is necessary to ascertain the range of *extreme* vision of the spectators in the corner seats nearest the stage, past objects on the *opposite* side of the set; of the spectator in the highest balcony seat past objects on the stage floor; and of the spectator in the seat lowest and nearest the stage past objects over the stage.

Figure 4.3 shows sightlines from A and B past the sides of the opening in the back wall to indicate the necessary width of the backing. The sightline from A past the downstage side of the opening in the sidewall shows the required width of that backing. Since the spectator at B cannot see through the sidewall opening at all, there is in this case at C another sightline which indicates that the backing must be set close to the scenery and also shows the spectators to the right of line C who cannot see action in the space outside the set at that entrance. Sightlines from A and B past opposite edges of the proscenium show that unless curtains fill the space between the tormentor and proscenium wall, the tormentor must be extended offstage (or downstage) to intercept the sightline.

Figure 4.4 shows an interior set which has a window in the back wall

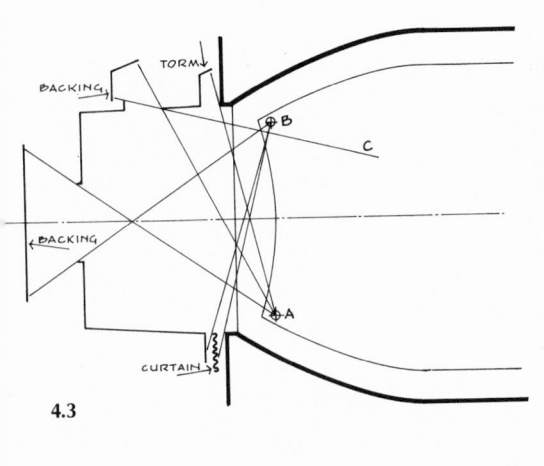

4.3

and an entrance in the sidewall. The sightline from A past the top of the window opening shows how high the backing must be. The sightline from B past the bottom of the window shows that a portion of the stage floor and the bottom of the backing would be visible if there were no ground row. The second sightline from B past the top edge of the ground row demonstrates that the ground row adequately conceals the bottom of the backing and the floor.

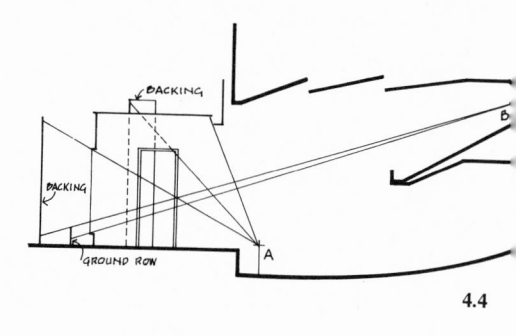

4.4

The sightline from A past the edge of the teaser indicates the necessary downstage extensity of the ceiling. The sightline from A through the upper downstage corner of the doorway in the sidewall indicates the necessary height of the backing at its highest point. In order to determine the height of the backing for any sidewall opening, it is necessary to use whatever sightline has the greatest angle to the horizontal and extends the farthest upstage before intersecting the backing.

In numerous instances, the solution of the problem of visibility and masking in a set is effected only by compromise. As shown in Figure 4.5, the height of the scenery, the height of the teaser, the placing of lights in the teaser, the downstage extension of the ceiling, the possibility of lighting from the ceiling slot, and the visibility of the spectators in the front row of the orchestra and the last row of the balcony are involved. If the designer wants a low set and low ceiling, the teaser must be lowered or the ceiling brought very close to the first border lights. If the teaser is lowered, the balcony spectator sees less of the back wall, does not see an actor on the platform, and the light beam from the auditorium ceiling is cut off. Hence all of the factors must be weighed in determining the final position of the teaser and height of the set and ceiling.

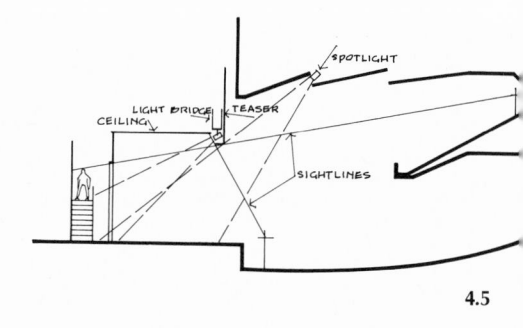

4.5

Sightlines, besides showing what zones of the stage are visible to all or any spectators, inversely indicate the parts of the stage which are totally invisible and consequently useful as positions for lights or as storage positions for scenery and properties. It goes almost without saying, but must be stated, that stage manager, stagehands, and actors waiting for entrances must keep out of the audience's sight. They do not always do this.

In the application of visibility tests to any set or group of sets, the technical director may use the scene designer's ground plan of the set and the section upon which the technical analysis of the rigging is made. It is essential, however, that he have the exact location of the critical spectator positions measured from the three coordinates: horizontally, the auditorium center line and the proscenium line; and vertically, the stage floor level. A technical director working entirely in one theatre, may well have plans and sections of the entire stage and auditorium duplicated in black-on-white prints for use in both technical and sightline analysis. Where alterations in plan are necessitated as a result of sightline tests, they are made on the authorization of the scene designer and to the specifications set by him.

In designing and specifying scenery to satisfy the tests for sightlines, the scene designer presumably knows the theatre into which the scenery is to go. If, because of the vagaries of booking, the theatre is changed while the show is in rehearsal, he must study the sightline problems of the second theatre and possibly order changes in the scenery. If the scenery is scheduled to go into several road theatres on a tryout tour or a post–New York road tour, there must be on-site tests of sightlines for audience visibility by the scene designer in a tryout theatre or by the stage manager in a road-tour theatre, and the best possible solutions achieved. A rule which obviates the second assistant stage manager's climbing the stairs to the second balcony is: If a seat can be seen from a point onstage then the point onstage can be seen from that seat.

These forms of theatre contain inherent sightline problems. One is in the province of the architect and is either solved when the building is built or remains forever unsolvable: the problem of actors *covering* (concealing) other actors for some spectators somewhere in the house at all times during the action.

As shown in Figures 4.6 through 4.8, no matter on what axis A and B may be aligned, there will be spectators in the relative positions of 1 and 2. The scene designer is concerned with this particular sightline problem only insofar as he may aggravate it by placing platforms in the acting area to intensify the covering phenomenon.

open stage and arena

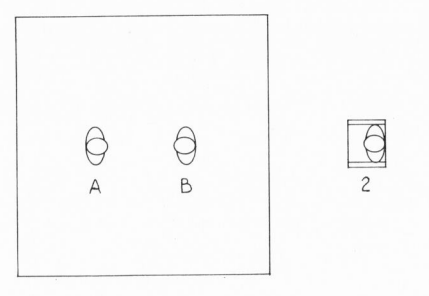

4.6 A covers B for Spectator 1; and B covers A for Spectator 2

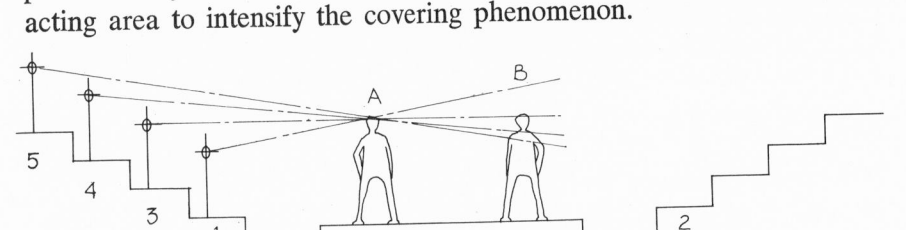

4.7 Only if successive rows of seats are raised adequately is the covering problem solved for Spectators 3, 4, and 5

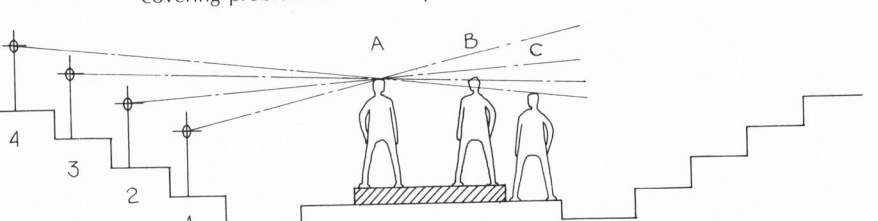

4.8 A covers B for Spectators 1, 2, and 3. A and B cover C for all spectators on the side shown

Of paramount importance to the scene designer is the sightline from the highest seat on one side of the house over the head of an actor standing at the far side of the acting area (Figure 4.9). This sightline shows the designer a zone, above the sightline, in which he may place opaque scenery, and a zone below the line within which the scenery must be either transparent or constructed of such thin members that the audience's view through or around them is not jeopardized.

4.9

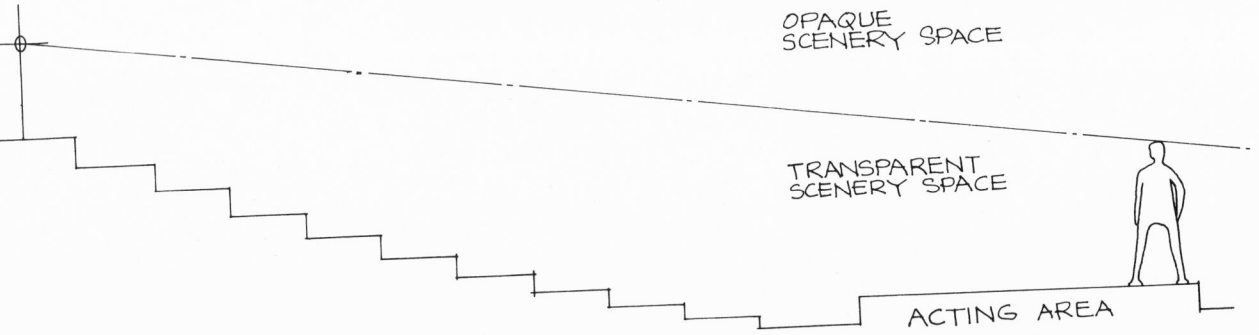

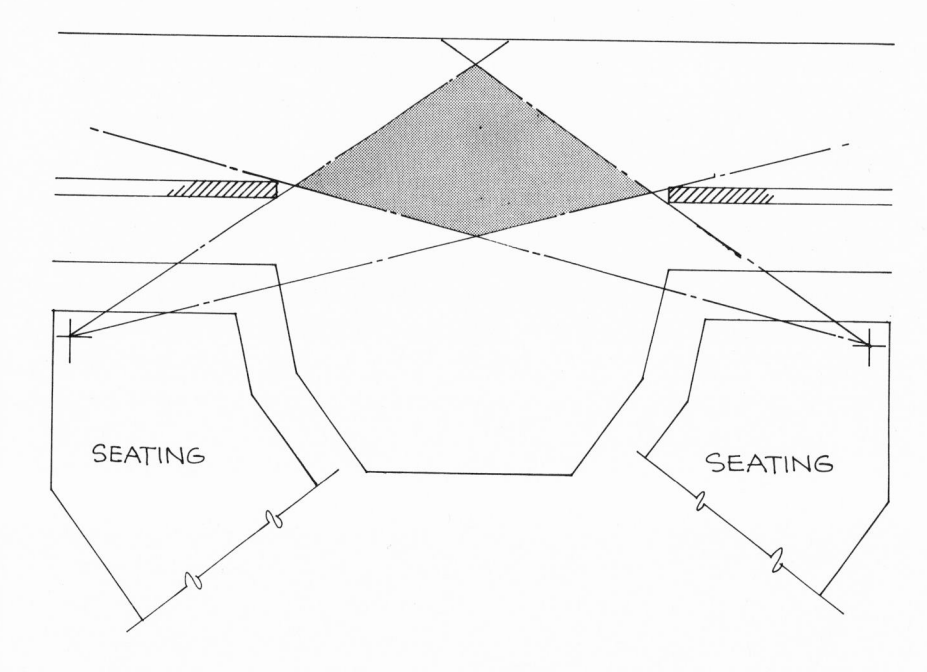

SEATING

SEATING

4.10

The extent to which the audience wraps around the thrust portion of an open stage determines the amount of the stage which can be seen by all spectators, as shown by the shaded area in Figure 4.10. As with any proscenium, the sightlines from the nearest seat past the proscenium on the opposite side determines the extent of the required masking.

For an extended stage the horizontal sightlines follow the directive for a proscenium stage. For the vertical sightlines, the plotter must use the steepest sightline from a balcony seat past the lowest part of the side-stage teaser to determine the high limit of visibility, and the flattest sightline from a balcony seat past the balcony rail to determine the low limit of visibility. The latter is important in determining where actors are visible from all balcony seats.

extended stage

When one set of scenery, properties, and miscellaneous apparatus must be replaced by another in the short space of from ten seconds to four minutes, the smallest item of apparatus to be moved and the least movement of it must be determined in advance. With space on stages, particularly American stages, as restricted as it is, each item of scenery and apparatus must, so to speak, earn its keep. To particularize a law of physics, scenery, props, and lighting equipment cannot occupy the same space at the same time.

tests for fit and
movement

On a floor plan and a section of the entire stagehouse, drawn to small scale (Figure 4.11), each set of scenery is tested for fit on the stage. Additions and alterations to stage equipment are drawn. Teaser trim, ceiling trim, drop and border trim are decided. The scenery is divided into units for handling in scene shifts, and the movement of each unit to and from storage is tested, if necessary, by the movement of models or paper templates on the plan. Flying positions are determined. Overhead storage space required by each piece is tested, and the movement of each, flown into the flies past other pieces, is checked.

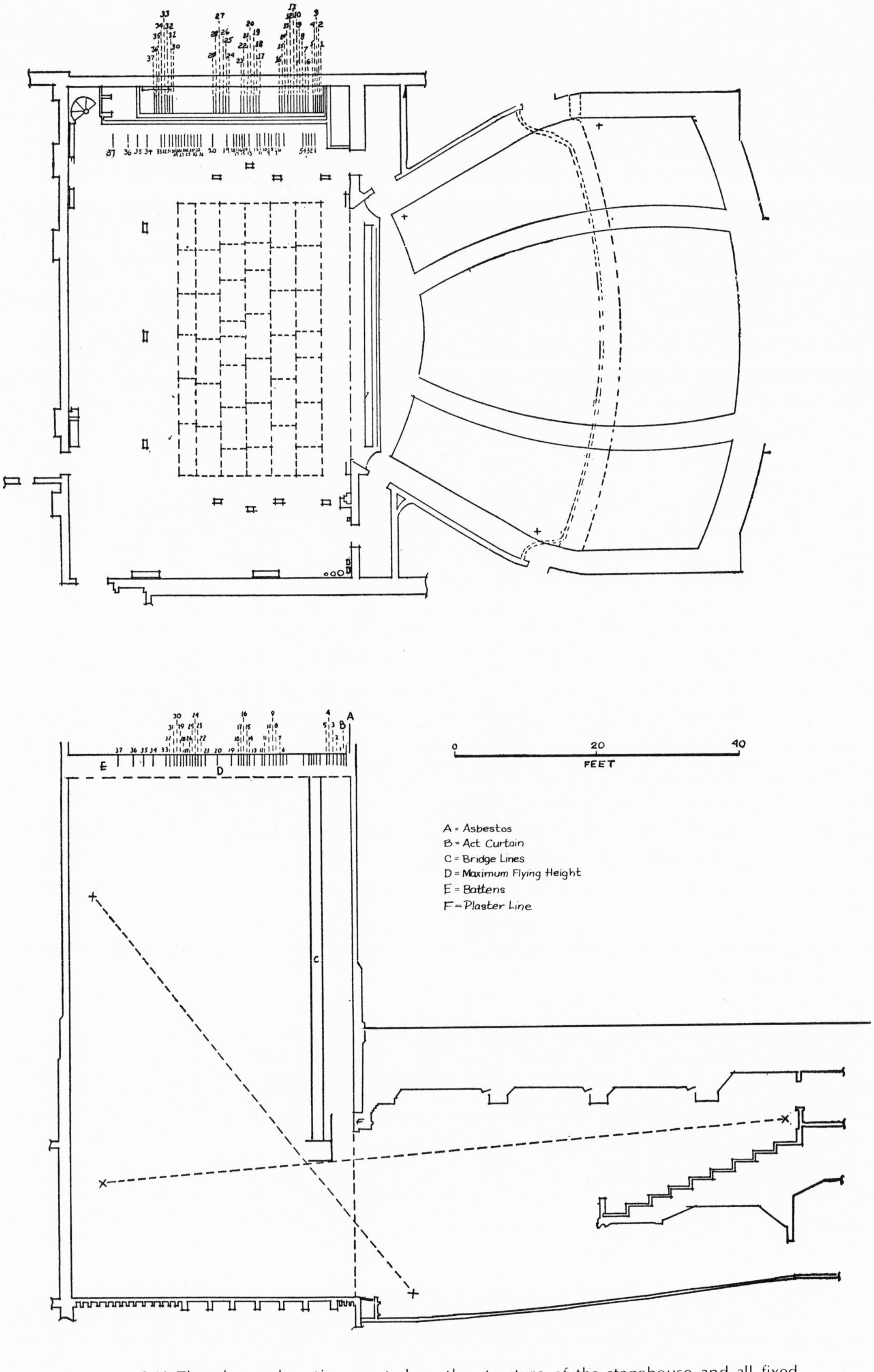

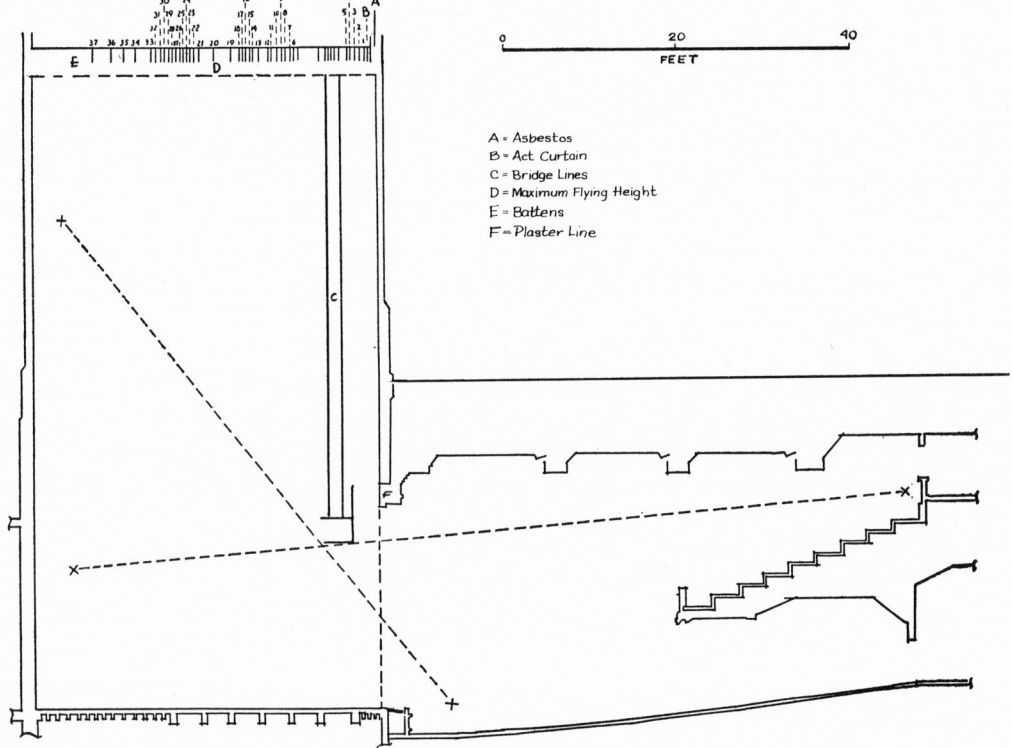

A = Asbestos
B = Act Curtain
C = Bridge Lines
D = Maximum Flying Height
E = Battens
F = Plaster Line

4.11 The plan and section must show the structure of the stagehouse and all fixed objects which might limit placement and movement of scenery, props, or lighting equipment. Models of settings and of the stage may be used in three-dimensional tests

On the plan and section, lighting equipment is located and the requisite space is provided according to the requirements of the lighting designer. Necessary adjustments and alterations in the scenery design and the rigging scheme are made. Movement and position of properties and sound apparatus are studied, and space allowances are made for the storage of properties and other paraphernalia.

The speed of the scene shifts is calculated on a basis of the number of major moves required for each shift. Sometimes the whole technical plan of a multiset production is conditioned by the necessity of making one of the scene changes in a few seconds.

The analysis of the scenery into units for handling involves the determination of the motive power for each unit, and the inclusion in the building requirements of all additional parts which make the moving possible, such as wagons, superimposed floor, tracks, grooves, caster pieces, lift jacks, tip jacks, trusses, and stiffeners.

strength Scenery must be strong. Scenery is constantly being handled, moved from theatre to theatre, transported from city to city. Some scenery must support not only its own weight and the weight of other attached pieces, but also the active weight (live load) of one or more actors. Scenery must sometimes withstand the impact of objects thrown against it. The loads and impacts which scenery must withstand determine the structural design and the materials to be used. The technical director determines his structure and materials by calculation, or by reference to the graphs in the Appendix and to engineering handbooks and tables.

portability Scenery is divided into units for handling onstage. It must usually be further subdivided into pieces. Pieces are the smallest parts into which it is necessary to divide scenery for purposes of construction and transportation. A back wall may be a unit for handling onstage; yet for construction and transportation it may be divided into numerous pieces — several flats, a door, a window, etc. As a part of the technical analysis, the sizes of openings through which the pieces must be moved is noted, for they limit the piece dimensions. Moreover, since the division of the set into units and pieces must never jeopardize its appearance, means must be contrived as a part of the process of division to make the joints invisible or, at the worst, inconspicuous.

dependability and economy Insofar as dependability and economy are functions of design, they must be considered in the technical analysis. Dependability of scenery — that is, the movement of each piece, the operation of each machine, the descent of each unit from the flies, the operation of sliding panels, traps, or other mechanical aids to the action which must occur with unchanging precision nightly, beginning with the first dress rehearsal — is assured only by *strong structure, clear paths of movement,* and *good maintenance.* The first two of these may be planned on the basis of the technical analysis. Economy is a function of material (the technical analysis establishes the limits of choice of material), the complexity of design, and the time required for construction.

orders for materials The technical director and the designer must be concerned about the availability of the materials from which the scenery is to be built — a

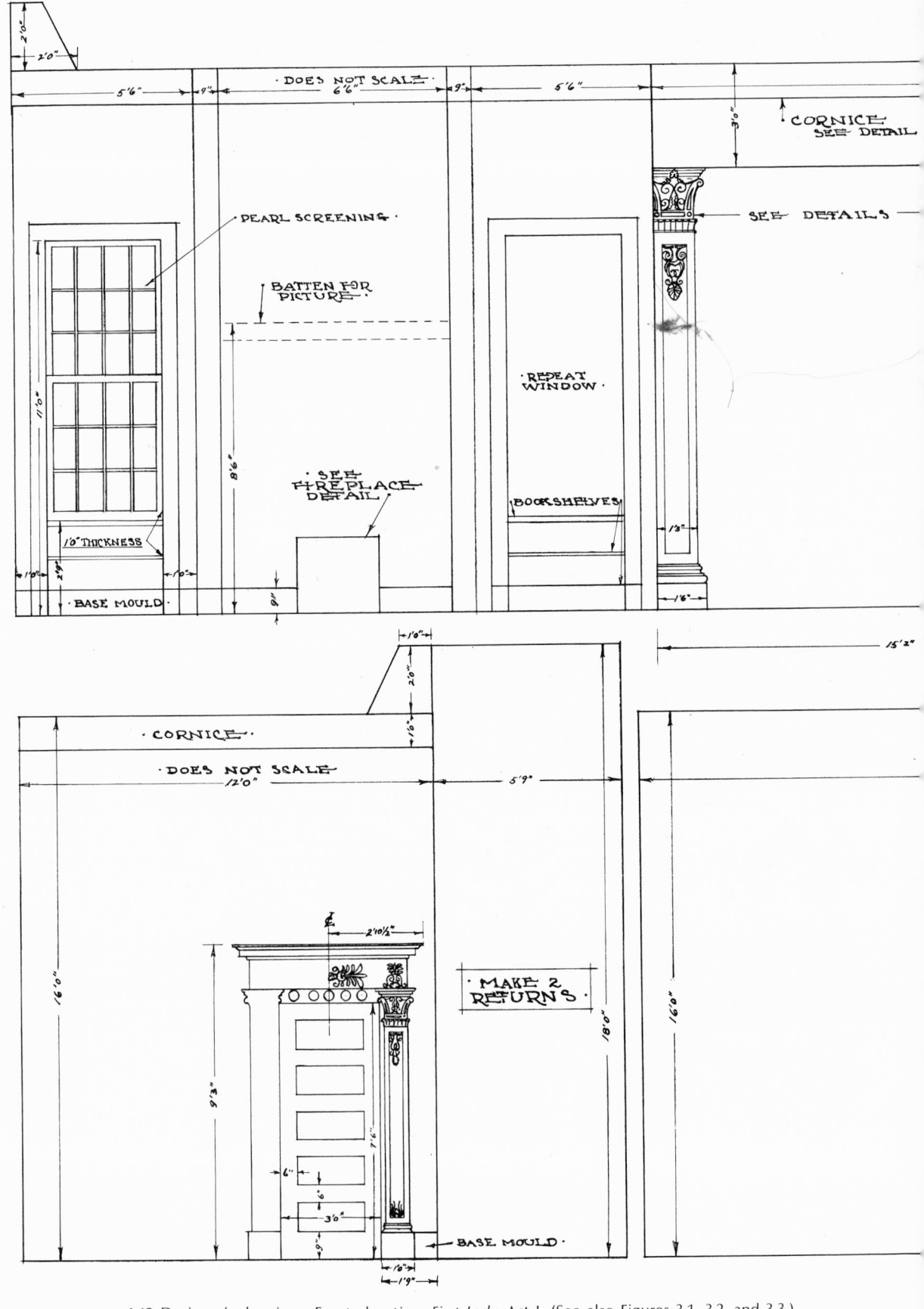

4.12 Designer's drawings. Front elevation, *First Lady*, Act I. (See also Figures 3.1, 3,2, and 3.3.)

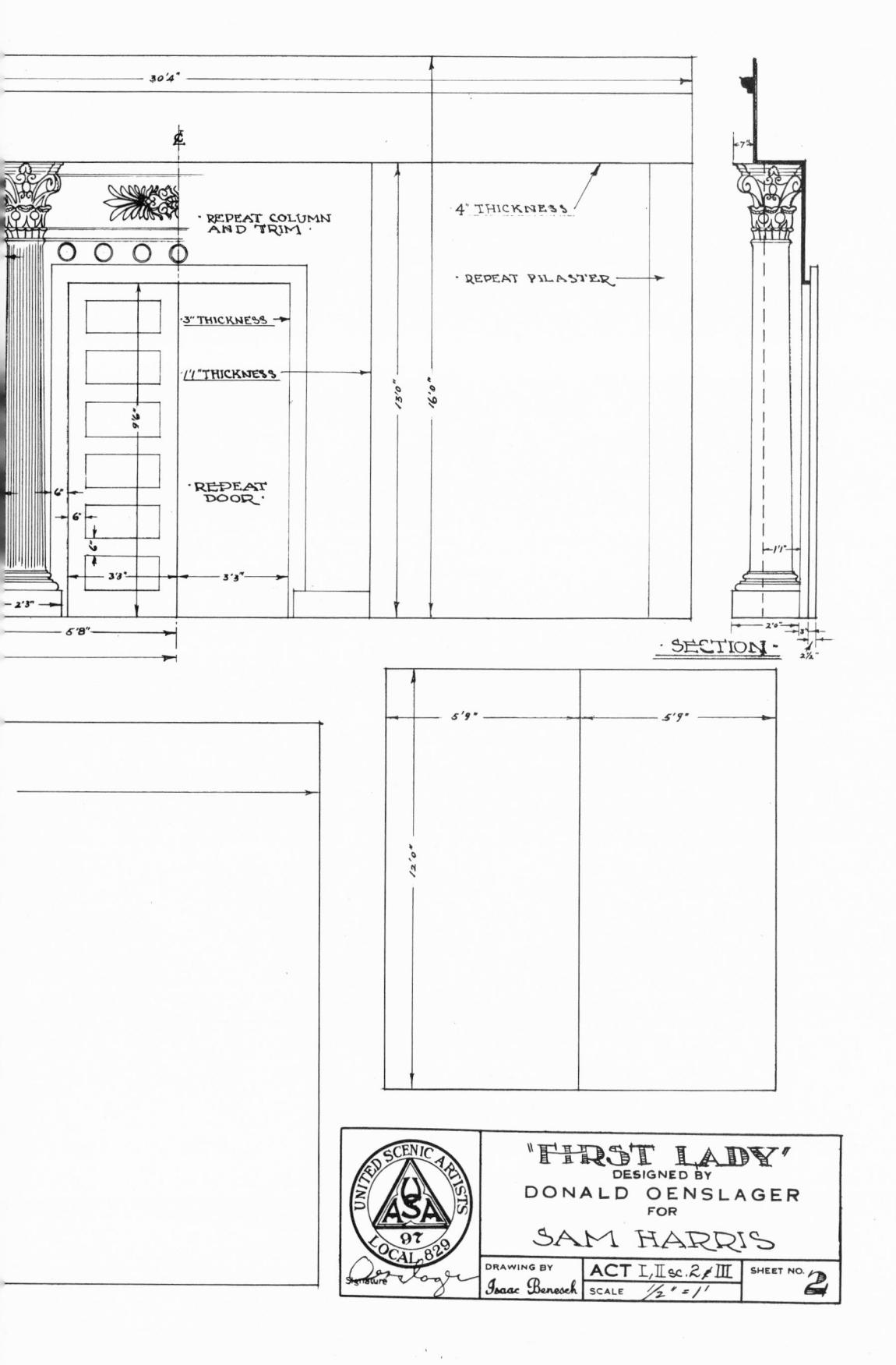

30'4"

· REPEAT COLUMN
AND TRIM ·

4" THICKNESS

· REPEAT PILASTER

·3" THICKNESS ·

·1'1" THICKNESS ·

13'0"

16'0"

·REPEAT
DOOR·

2'6"

6"

6"

6"

3'3"

3'3"

2'3"

5'8"

· SECTION ·

7'

1'1"

2'0"

3"

2½"

5'9"

5'9"

12'0"

"FIRST LADY"
DESIGNED BY
DONALD OENSLAGER
FOR
SAM HARRIS

| DRAWING BY | ACT I, II sc.2 & III | SHEET NO. |
| Isaac Benesch | SCALE ½" = 1' | 2 |

4.13 Working drawings. Rear elevations of flats, *First Lady*, Act I

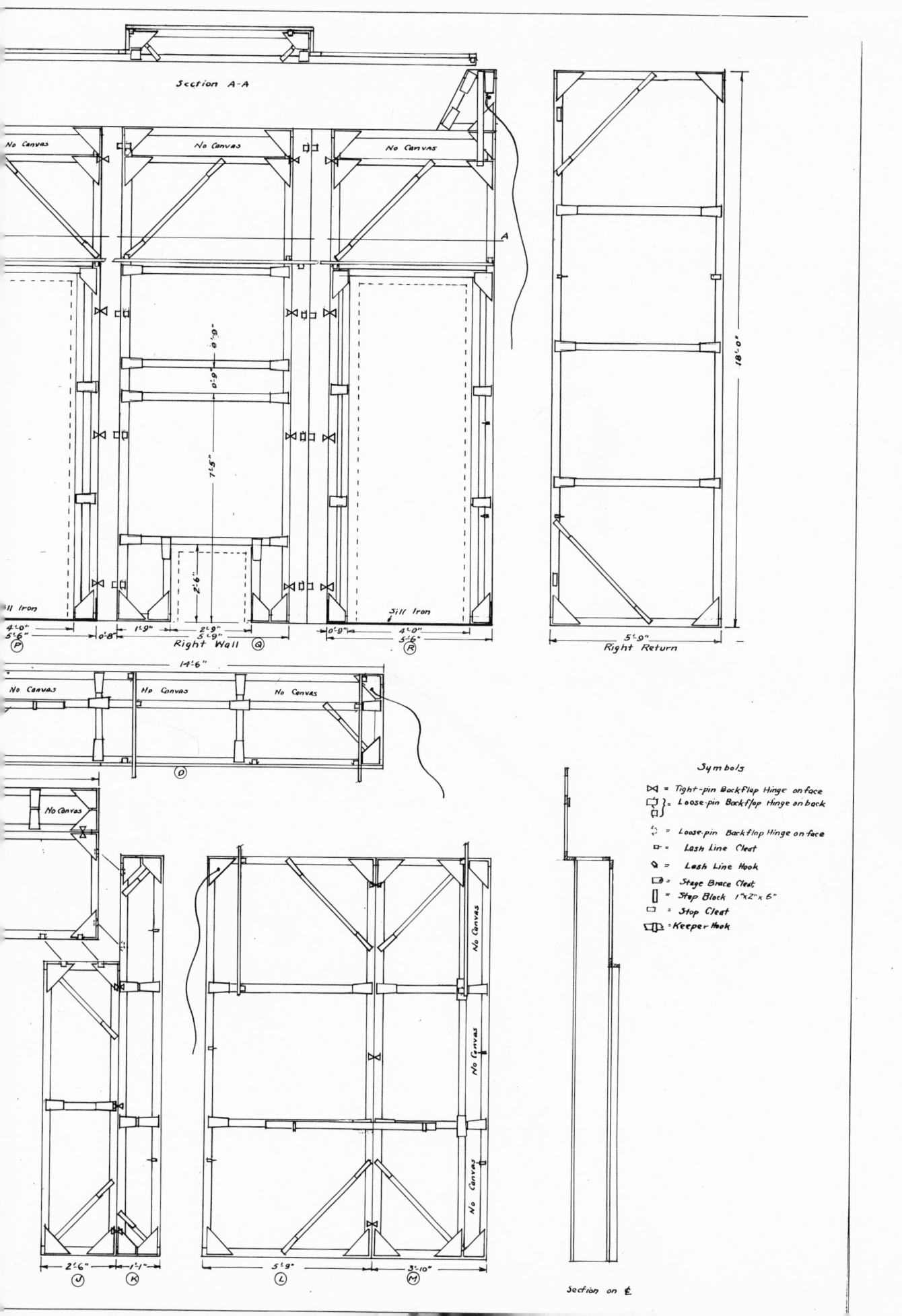

Section A-A

No Canvas   No Canvas   No Canvas

Right Wall

Right Return

Symbols

⋈ = Tight-pin Backflap Hinge on face
⊏⊐ = Loose-pin Backflap Hinge on back
⊏⊐ = Loose-pin Backflap Hinge on face
▱ = Lash Line Cleat
ϙ = Lash Line Hook
▭ = Stage Brace Cleat
▯ = Stop Block 1"x2"x 6"
▱ = Stop Cleat
⊏⊐ = Keeper Hook

Section on ℄

63

ready supply of standard materials and, of great importance, the accessibility of any special materials which are not likely to be carried in stock by local vendors. Quantities of the latter must be calculated and orders placed at the earliest possible time so that they will be in the shop when work on them is scheduled to begin.

working drawings

With the technical analysis complete, it is possible to plan the scenery down to its smallest detail. Working drawings show the size and shape of the scenery, the structural parts of which it is formed, the joining of those parts, and the materials of which all parts are composed. (Figures 4.12 and 4.13).

The technical director, having divided the scenery into units for stage handling and pieces for transportation, makes working drawings of each unit. In a large organization he has draftsmen, or assistant technicians, who make the drawings according to his directions. In a professional scene-building shop this work is done by a layout man. The working drawings for a set of scenery consist of the following:

1. Ground plan to the scale ½″ = 1′ 0″, showing:

• All scenery, including backings, ground rows, drops, and cycloramas, in relation to the proscenium.

• All standing stage equipment to which the scenery is attached or related.

• All curtains, draperies, borders, and other objects hung over the stage, and the battens or line sets from which all scenery is hung.

• The actual thickness of all scenery.

• The division into units and pieces, and the fitting together of all units and pieces.

• The methods of fastening together and bracing.

• The principal dimensions: perpendicular distances of important corners from proscenium line and center line; length of each straight run of scenery; radii and locations of centers of all curvatures; horizontal and vertical dimensions of all platforms; sizes and locations of traps and elevators; horizontal and vertical dimensions of stairs.

2. Rear elevation to the scale ½″ = 1′ 0″, of all flat scenery (Figure 4.13), showing:

• The outline of each unit, faithfully duplicating the designer's outline except as it is necessary to increase or reduce the overall dimensions to allow for fitting against other units.

• All openings in faithful reproduction of size, shape, and location as given in designer's drawings except when openings must be increased to allow the fitting of removable door or window units.

• Openings to be built into the flats for technical reasons, such as for the fitting of cornices, mantel shelves, portraits.

• The division of the unit into flats and their framing and joining.

• All framing lumber, beginning with that which outlines the flats and the openings, and progressing to any other lumber necessary to support, strengthen, or stiffen the flats.

• Devices for joining, bracing, handling, or flying the flats, including the joining of the pieces within the unit, the joining of the unit to its neighbors, the moving of the unit about the stage, and the attaching, if necessary, of the unit to the battens or rope lines of the stage flying system.

• Complete notes on building procedures and specifications of all materials.

3. As many orthographic and isometric views as are necessary to show the parts and the joining of all three-dimensional units, to whatever scale illustrates clearly the smallest details of construction:

• Units of interior architecture, such as doors, windows, fireplaces, bookcases, and wall niches, shown in rear and side elevations, plans, and vertical and horizontal sections to the scale $1'' = 1' 0''$, with intricate details drawn to the scale $3'' = 1' 0''$.

4. Weight-bearing structures, such as ramps, stairs, platforms, practical rocks, shown by:

• A plan to ½″ scale of the whole unit, indicating their relation and fastening to adjacent units, the position and fastening of the frames which compose the units, identification of each type of framing (depending upon shape).

• An elevation to ½″ scale of each type of frame, showing size, shape, position, and fastening of each member with the frame.

• Top view of the flooring to ½″ scale.

• Complete dimensions.

• Specifications of size, kind, and quality of all materials.

• Notes on building procedure.

There are many theatrical producing organizations in which a full and complete set of working drawings of scenery to be built need never be made. A great percentage of the scenery required for modern productions is standard in its form. The requirements of scene shifting, transportation, speed of construction, and available materials, among other factors, have dictated the development of a technique of construction which is applicable, with minor variations, to most scenic requirements. A master scene carpenter, with the amount of experience which rightly accompanies his title, can construct much scenery directly from the designer's drawings. Given a bare outline drawing of the scenery and a simple statement of its materials, he can visualize the required division into standard pieces and the structural conformation of those pieces. With a few pencil sketches and a few dimensions calculated on scraps of paper, he can proceed to construct the set. Although the increasingly exacting demands of American scene designers in response to a rising standard of appreciation on the part of audiences frequently result in such technical mazes as the excellent Aronson settings for *Fiddler on the Roof,* it is doubtful if for even such complex productions complete working drawings are made.

In a closely organized scene shop, either independent or affiliated with a production organization, in which a technique of construction has been developed and a stock of materials is kept, and in which trained workers are employed, it is possible for the technical director to reduce, progressively, the requisite number of working drawings. Parts of the drawings may be eliminated in some such order as the following:

• Specifications of standard stock materials.

variations

- Notes referring to building processes that are standard within the particular shop.
- Detailed drawings of standard types of scenery which have no special parts, such as plain flats with no special internal framing, and door or window flats which follow standard practice. An outline drawing or a schedule of these items, giving their overall dimensions, is sufficient for an experienced builder.
- Construction details which are standard practice or which may be left to the discretion of the carpenters, such as the application of key-stones, corner blocks, or hinges, and the size and shape of mortises and tenons.

Such logical and careful curtailment of the working drawings may reduce them to as little as a ground plan and details of special structures for each set. This minimum can be attained only by an organization with both a complete knowledge of processes and methods, and dependable workmen. Even the most experienced scene builders often require more working drawings than this minimum contains.

In scene shops where there are untrained or untried workers, it is best for the technical director to make complete drawings with complete specifications, until he is cognizant of the abilities of his workers or until many phases of construction become standard practice. Even though working drawings may seem to be a waste of time and possibly money, certain intangible benefits may accrue to the producing organization as a result of their being made: they constitute a visual record of all work that has to be done; they obviate any failure to give or to remember verbal instructions; and they militate against misunderstanding because they have few things that can be *taken as understood*. They are graphic proof that construction is planned rather than haphazard, and errors are more likely to be caught in the drafting room before they are perpetrated in the shop. Reconstruction, which is expensive and time-wasting, becomes redrawing, which is inexpensive and rapid.

In theatre schools the making of working drawings is a desirable form of instruction. The student technicians who make them and the student workers who read them derive training in the medium of mechanical drawing. The student technicians, furthermore, are compelled by the required working drawings to plan all scenery in advance of the builders.

elaborate scenery

Occasionally, scenery may be designed which is so free in form, so detailed in ornament, so complex in its perspective, or so complicated to fit that it would take longer to make working drawings than to do the actual construction. In such a case it is obviously wasteful for the technical director or his assistants to make complete drawings and more practical to make only the drawings needed to establish the basic structure, the division into units and pieces, and their joining, and to finish the work by the cut-to-fit method, referring directly to the designer's drawings or models. Building of this sort is the province of expert craftsmen.

scenery built in place

Certain play-production situations permit building scenery in place on the stage. This obviates dividing the scenery into pieces for transportation and, in the case of a single setting, into units for handling onstage.

Scenery for the plays in active repertory serves the production program most effectively if no takedown and assembly are needed when plays are changed; if in effect, all scenery for the plays in the schedule is designed to be stored *live* onstage and simply recovered from *live* storage either on the floor, below the floor, or in the flies, and set up as if it were the scenery for an act of a single play. Failing this, the designers must observe the maxim: the least amount of scenic changeover when plays are changed is the best.

The technical director has frequent occasion to use a more impromptu form of graphic representation than true mechanical drawing (see Figure 4.14). In making preliminary studies of the technical aspects of the scenery, in working out solutions of problems of construction or rigging, in explaining technical details to assistants, and in laying out work for draftsmen, a method of freehand drawing which makes use of the principles of mechanical projection (orthographic and isometric) is very useful. Fully developed, mechanical sketching may supplant much mechanical drawing. Dimensions may not be scaled from the drawings thus made but must be figured mathematically and applied to the drawings. Cross-section (graph) paper which is ruled horizontally and vertically in ⅛″ divisions provides a convenient dimensional aid to the making of mechanical sketches to ⅛″, ¼″, and ½″ scales.

With the completion of the working drawings, the scenic production becomes a series of separate operations, each operation contributing toward the formation of, first, pieces of scenery, then units of scenery, and finally, settings. Since there may be fifty or more pieces and ten or more units in a single setting, and several settings for a production, it is essential that there be a simple method of identifying the pieces and units so that they may be kept straight in the production process.

Accordingly, the technical director sets up on his work chart a system of identification based on the order of the sets in the production and the position of the scenery on the stage. This system is then used on the working drawings and in marking the scenery as it is built. The same system is used to mark the materials which go into the scenery as they are prepared.

There are currently popular two systems for identifying the pieces of a set:
• Starting downstage on each side, successive flats on the left are marked *L–1, L–2, L–3,* and successive flats on the right *R–1, R–2, R–3,* in progression toward center stage.
• Starting downstage left, successive flats are marked *A, B, C,* etc., in order, from the stage left tormentor around to the stage right tormentor. Doors, windows, backings are marked under either system with the symbol of the flat to which they pertain.

The authors offer yet another system which develops logically from the technical analysis of the scenery into units and pieces and identifies units as well as pieces: Each unit which is handled separately onstage is marked *A, B, C,* progressively, from downstage left to downstage

repertory scenery

mechanical sketching

identification of units and pieces

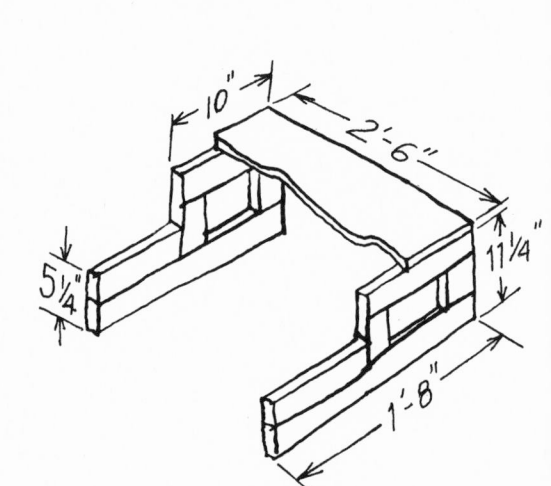

4.14 A mechanical sketch, drawn freehand

CONSTRUCTION ANALYSIS

UNITS	PIECES	MATERIALS	LABOR
Production ~ "FIRST LADY"		*Set ~ Act I*	
Left wall	Flats A, B Stiffener A-B Cornice A-B Door A		
Right wall	Flats P, Q, R Window P Window R Mantel Q Stiffener PQR Fireplace backing		
Back wall	Flats C, D, N, O, L, M Vertical Stiffeners (4) Keepers (3)		
Center door	Flats E, F, G, H, J, K Columns (2) Door track Sliding doors (2)		
Hall backing	Flats S, T, U, V, W, X, Y, Z AA, BB, CC, DD Columns (2) Door track Sliding doors		
Upstage backing Window backing Backing down left Returns	Drop Curved drop Flats (2) Flats (2)		

4.15 Analysis of a set into units and pieces. *First Lady,* Act I

right; the pieces which compose each unit are marked *A–1, A–2, A–3,* etc., in whatever order appears logical. Thus, in a box set for Act I, the flat nearest the tormentor which is part of a sidewall unit would be identified as *I–A–1.*

order of construction

With a complete list of all the units into which each set is to be divided, and the pieces into which each unit is to be divided, the technical director has a clear conception of the magnitude of the work. He can see which units are going to require the most time in construction, painting, and assembly. He then plans the order in which the units are to be put through the production process. This decision is subject to departmental and technical considerations. Departmental considerations are:

• The director may request that platforms be built early and be delivered to the rehearsal stage to facilitate the development of the actors' movements.

• The lighting designer may request that a certain set which presents lighting problems be set up on the stage ahead of the others.
• The painter may request that he be allowed extra time on a set which requires a particularly intricate paint job.
• The large number of properties to be fitted to a set may determine construction precedence.

Frequently all production department heads will have some special demands upon the technical director which he will have to appraise and compromise.

Technical factors which may affect the order of work include:
• Available storage space: Bulky items if built in advance may have to be stored until painted, and again stored until shipped to the theatre.
• Order of assembly onstage: Pieces which fit together to make units, and units which fit together to make sets, must be put through the production process so as to arrive simultaneously at the stage for assembly.
• Efficient employment of carpenters and shop facilities. The work in the carpentry shop must be grouped according to a building sequence. Shop efficiency is best achieved by mass-production methods: measuring all similar lumber at one time; doing all cutting at one time; using an assembly line for the construction of similar flats, etc.

The following normal production sequence for an interior set is given to show the reasoning which underlies the procedure:
• Platforms and steps, if any, built first and delivered to the rehearsal stage to aid in directing the action. To be returned to the paint shop later or painted onstage.
• Ceiling, because it can be built quickly, requires some time in the painting, and is the first unit to be rigged.
• Units which are to be flown.
• Units which are to be handled on the stage floor: those requiring assembly; those requiring no assembly.
• Details of trim which may be set into the units which have been hung and assembled.

The analysis is objectified in a work chart (Figure 4.16) in which each piece or unit is tabulated according to the dates on which it is to be built, painted, hung, set up, trimmed with props, and lighted. The work charts of different productions vary with the complexity of the scenery and the necessity for minute control of the work. A work chart may be made out in terms of sets, if the sets are simple; of units, if the unit is the logical division; or of pieces, if the scenery is complex enough to warrant such meticulous subdivision. The process may be divided into the main divisions of building, painting, etc., or subdivided into separate steps in each process (measuring, cutting, joining, covering, etc.) in the carpentry shop, and priming, laying in, etc., in the paint shop.

The work chart becomes the master schedule for all production departments. The technical director extracts from it the sequence of procedure for each department with the dates of beginning and ending

work chart

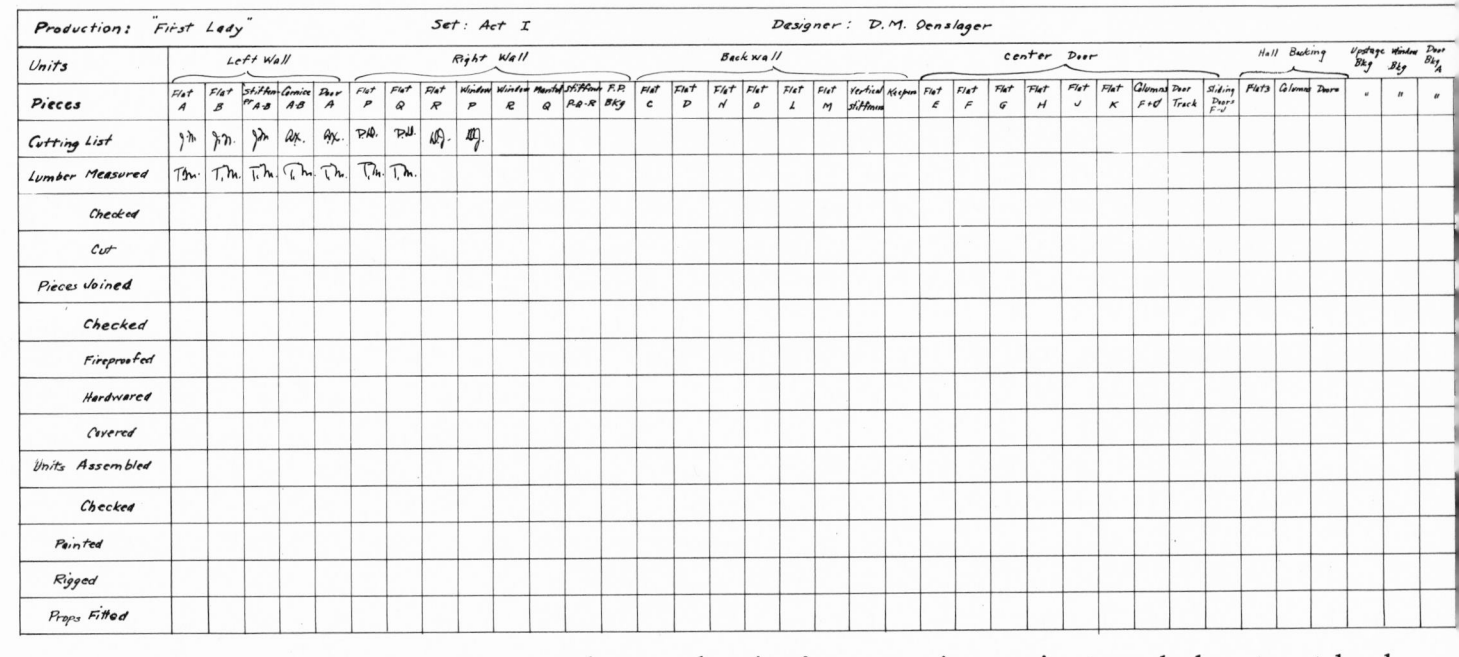

Units	Left Wall					Right Wall								Back wall								center Door									Hall Backing			Upstage Bkg	Window Bkg	Door Bkg A
Pieces	Flat A	Flat B	Stiffen. A-B	Cornice A-B	Door A	Flat P	Flat Q	Flat R	Window P	Window R	Mantel	Stiffon R-R	F.P. Bkg	Flat C	Flat D	Flat N	Flat O	Flat L	Flat M	Vertical stiffenin	Keystone	Flat E	Flat F	Flat G	Flat H	Flat J	Flat K	Columns F+O	Door Track	Sliding Doors F-J	Flats	Columns	Doors	"	"	"
Cutting List	J.m.	J.m.	J.m.	Ax.	Ax.	P.D.	P.D.	Wj.	Wj.																											
Lumber Measured	T.m.	T.m.	T.m.	T.m.	T.m.	T.m.	T.m.																													
Checked																																				
Cut																																				
Pieces Joined																																				
Checked																																				
Fireproofed																																				
Hardwared																																				
Covered																																				
Units Assembled																																				
Checked																																				
Painted																																				
Rigged																																				
Props Fitted																																				

Production: "First Lady"   Set: Act I   Designer: D. M. Denslager

4.16 One form of work chart. Progress is recorded and responsibility for work done is indicated by initials. *First Lady*, Act I

work on each unit of scenery, gives copies to each department head, and controls the work on the whole scenic investiture with the work chart as a checklist.

The department heads assume responsibility for carrying out their divisions of the work within the scheduled time, in order that the entire process may be completed on schedule. If the time in any department proves too short, that department must work overtime to complete work on schedule. Holding the work additional days in construction will cause a pile-up of work toward the end of the production period. The technical director may be able to hold production work to the schedule by using two devices: *intermediate deadlines* by which scheduled work *must* be done even at the expense of overtime, and *cushion time* introduced into the schedules as hours or days into which work is not scheduled but may overflow if necessary.

Throughout this chapter the planning of scenery has been treated as a static operation, performed separately from other steps in the process in an instant of time. This is, obviously, not the case. The planning of the scenery may take place while numerous other processes are in motion. Sightlines may be studied and the fit of each set to the stage checked while the scene designer is still developing the details of the scenery. The working drawings for one set may be well under way before the designer's drawings for another set appear in the drafting room. The last set may still be on the drawing boards after the first set is painted and shipped to the theatre. However, certain basic items of the plan must be disposed of, once and for all, at the beginning of things. The work schedule, for example, is the basis for all later operations. The basic layout of the scenery must be delivered by the designer to the technical director so that the magnitude of the whole job may be clearly perceived. Upon these two items all the other planning may be founded, in its own good time, provided that time coincides with the work schedule.

Strategy is half the battle. Work well planned is half done.

Types of scenery

5

In designing and planning the scenery (Chapters 3 and 4), the scene designer and technical director have divided the sets into units for handling and into pieces for construction and transportation. The division has been governed by the nature of the scenery as designed, the speed of the scene changes, the size of the stage, the available storage space on the stage, the means of transportation, and the openings, such as stage doors and shop, van, airplane, and baggage car doors, through which the scenery must pass. The results of the technical analysis in terms of structural design are the subject of this chapter.

All scenery can be divided into types according to structural characteristics. The types are basically two-dimensional or three-dimensional, framed or unframed, and faked or practical. Further classification depends on the variations necessitated by particular settings. Basic types are treated here in the order of their structural complexity.

Unframed Two-dimensional Scenery

Curtains surrounding the acting area of a stage are the simplest form of scenery. Every school or social hall stage has a set of curtains, probably misnamed a cyclorama. A standard fit-up of curtains for a stage consists of either back curtain and side curtains enclosing the acting area, or back curtain with wing curtains for side masking. Curtains are frequently used in combination with other scenery as masking pieces or backgrounds, or as front pieces in lieu of an act curtain (see "Show Curtains," page 287). Borders of neutral-colored curtains are used as conventional maskings over the stage in place of ceilings or scenic borders. See Figure 5.1.

curtains

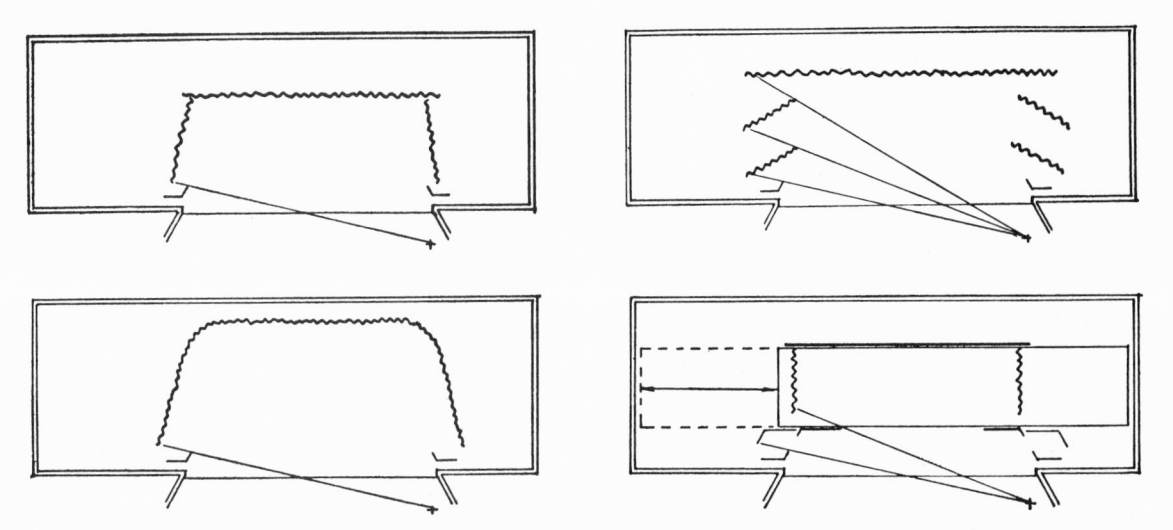

5.1 Uses of curtains. *Top left:* back curtain and side curtains. *Top right:* back curtain and legs. *Lower left:* curtain cyclorama. *Lower right:* side curtains rigged to draw (traveler) or fly (guillotine) to conceal the stage wings but to permit passage of scenery and props on wagon stages

Curtains are made about as high as the proscenium opening of the theatre and in widths to allow the greatest variety of use. Borders are made from 8′ to 20′ high, depending upon the masking problem in the particular theatre, and about one and a half times the proscenium width (see "Sightlines," page 52). Curtains and borders are made either flat or with from 50 to 100 percent fullness pleated in at the top. If flat, any desired amount of fullness may be obtained by tying the curtain to less than its own width on the batten and distributing the fullness evenly.

Curtains are either hung in straight folds or draped, and are rigged to hang in place, to fly, to draw, or to festoon. Curtains may be tied to a regular cyclorama track. Side curtains are a frequent necessity when wagon stages are used. They are hung on single traverse tracks and drawn, or they are flown on spot lines to allow movement of the wagons.

Curtains are made of durable fabrics of high opacity and considerable body, such as velour, duvetyn, Canton flannel, or monk's cloth. If lightweight or semitranslucent fabrics are used, they must be lined or backed with another fabric to render them lightproof and full-bodied. Fabrics for stage curtains must be flameproof or have a backing of flameproof fabric.

Curtains are sewed vertically with face-to-face seams. The top of a curtain is sewed, either flat or pleated, to a strip of jute webbing, into which #2 grommets are set on 1′ centers. Into the grommets 18″ tie lines of ⅛″ cotton line are inserted by half hitches (Figure 5.2). The bottom is finished with a double hem. The lower hem is 3″ deep and breaks on the floor when the curtain is hung. Into the upper half of the hem a light chain is sewed to give weight to the curtain. The heavier the fabric of the curtain, the heavier the chain must be. Chain for weighting curtains varies from 2 to 12 ounces per linear foot.

Curtains of any but the lightest fabrics have a high coefficient of

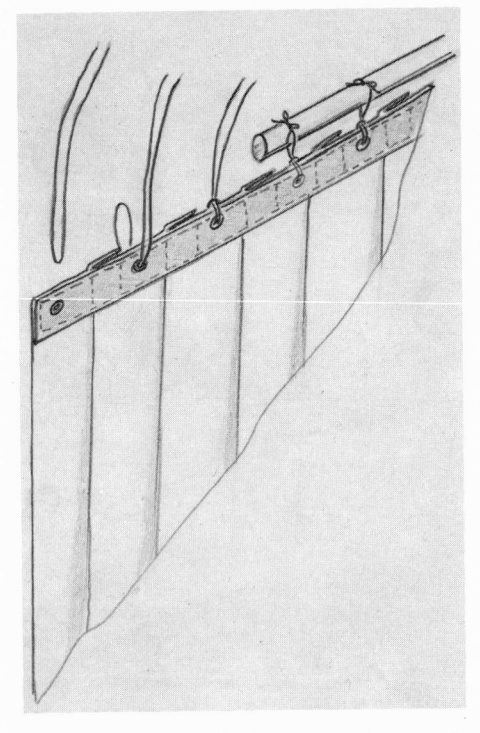

5.2 Detail of the top of a curtain showing hem, webbing, pleats, grommets, and tie lines

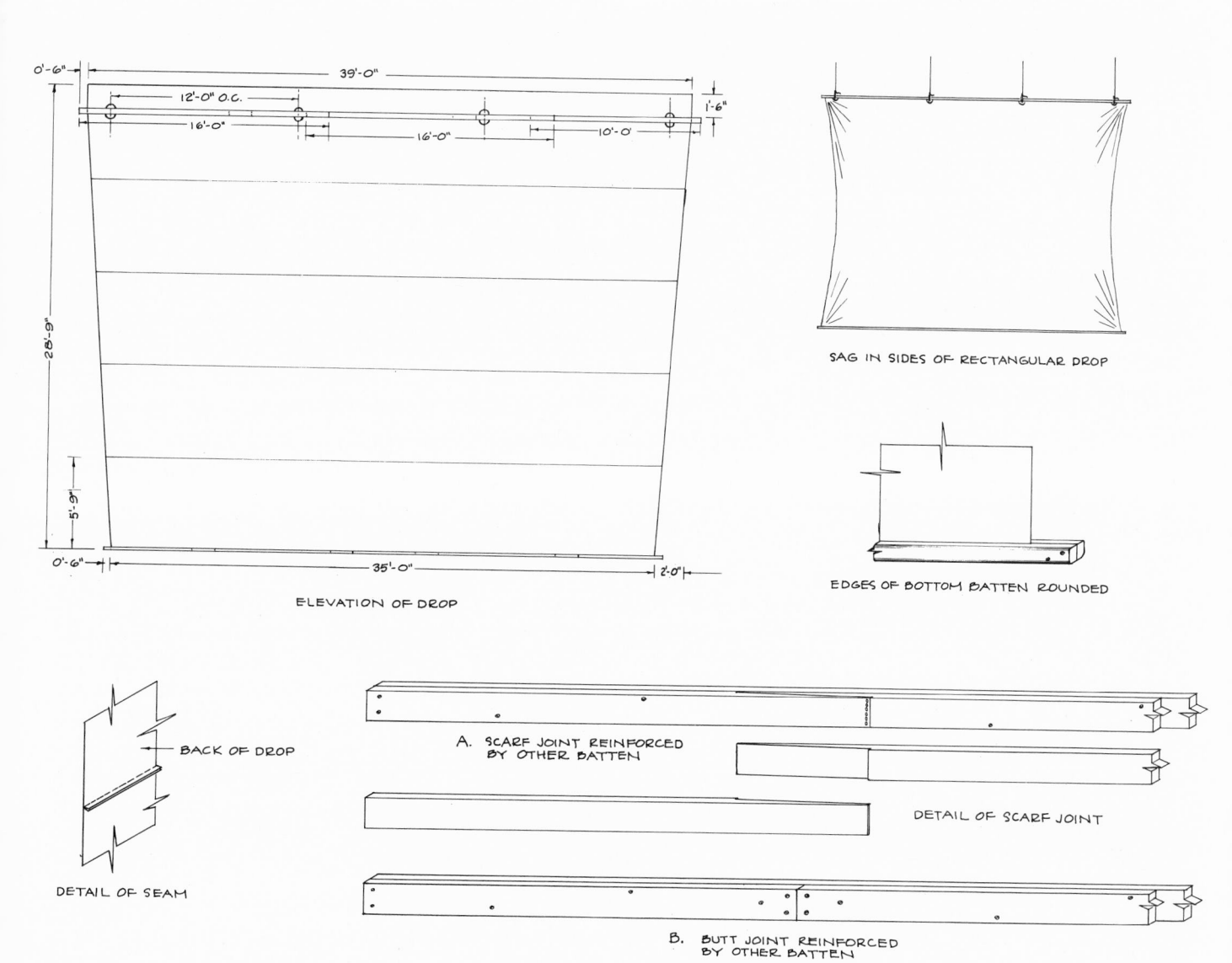

ELEVATION OF DROP

SAG IN SIDES OF RECTANGULAR DROP

EDGES OF BOTTOM BATTEN ROUNDED

DETAIL OF SEAM

BACK OF DROP

A. SCARF JOINT REINFORCED BY OTHER BATTEN

DETAIL OF SCARF JOINT

B. BUTT JOINT REINFORCED BY OTHER BATTEN

ASSEMBLY OF BATTENS
CANVAS NOT SHOWN

5.3 A drop: elevations and details

sound absorption. This characteristic of fabric may operate to the benefit or the detriment of a production. Curtains may be used purposely to minimize backstage noise, to create an acoustically dead stage, or to correct faulty acoustics of stage or auditorium, notably excessive reverberation or focal points. Curtains may, however, absorb sound which should not be absorbed. When the loudspeakers of a sound system are placed behind stage curtains, the cloth will absorb the high-frequency sounds to some degree, depending upon the weight and thickness of the fabric. Heavy velours are particularly sound-absorbent. It is therefore necessary, in order to preserve fidelity of sound, to substitute extremely lightweight open-weave materials for heavy materials in front of loudspeakers.

A drop is a large expanse of cloth. It is made of cotton duck, linen, muslin, velour, or occasionally novelty fabrics. Drops are used as:

• Backpieces for exterior scenes (sky drops).

drops

• Backings for openings in interior sets, sometimes painted light blue, for sky, and sometimes elaborately painted with buildings or landscapes.
• Frankly decorative backgrounds, as in the scene designs of Bakst.
• Backgrounds for vaudeville, revue, or presentation numbers which are played in one while a full-stage change of scene is taking place.

The cloth is sewed horizontally and tacked and glued between double wooden battens, one at the top and the other at the bottom. The battens serve as stretchers for the cloth. The bottom batten is made just heavy enough to impart an even vertical stretch. Its edges are rounded so as not to crease the drops rolled on it. See Figure 5.3.

Drops may have as many variations as the imagination of the playwright and the scenic designer can together demand. A drop may be partly or wholly transparent or translucent, of solid cloth, or cut into strips.

diorama

The diorama (rolling backcloth) travels hanging from a track and is wound on hanging drums left and right. The drums are conical and screw-mounted. They descend as the drop is wound on, and ascend as the drop unwinds to keep the carrying cable level beyond the track. The combination of two or more such moving drops, the front ones cut out, makes the nearest mechanical stage approach to moving landscape. The motion-picture projector is a logical substitute for this clumsy mechanism (Figure 5.4).

gauze drops

These are carelessly named. The so-called gauze drop is made of either bobbinet or scrim, and contributes four effects to the visual repertoire of the scene designer:
• Objects seen through a gauze appear softened in outline and in color intensity.
• A gauze lighted from the front at a sharp angle becomes opaque and obliterates objects behind it.
• Atmospheric effects of snow, rain, or clouds may be projected upon a gauze while a scene remains visible behind it.
• A scene may be painted upon a scrim and be visible only when the scrim is lighted; it disappears completely when the lights on the scrim are put out and the scene behind the scrim is illuminated.

Two or more drops hung close together create an interesting watermark effect.

translucencies

Drops may be of muslin, treated with glycerine, rosin, or glue size

5.4 A rolling diorama on a castered platform. Designed by Peter Larkin for *Goldilocks*

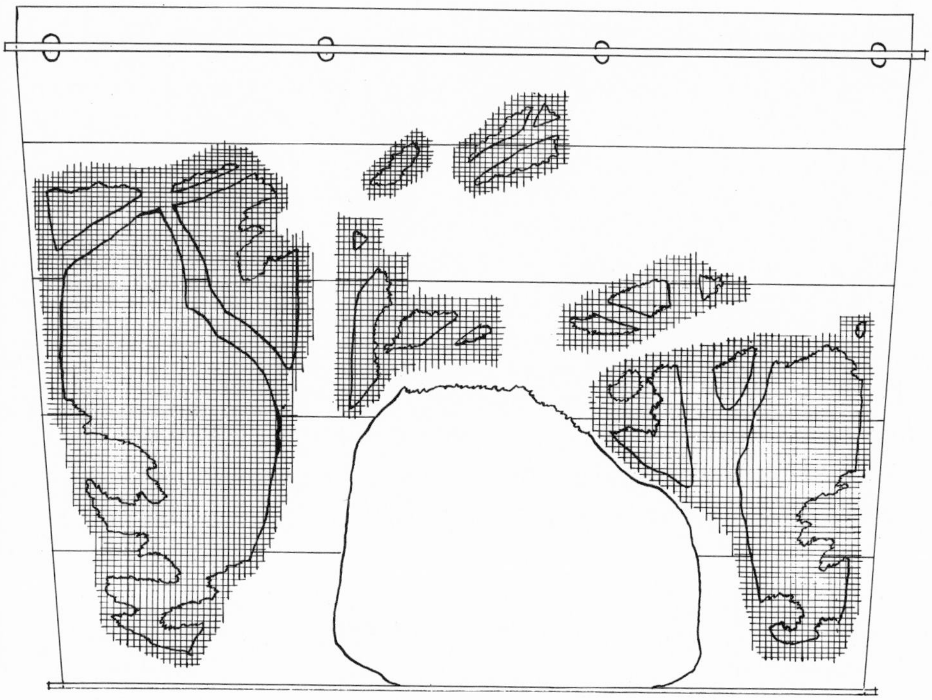

REAR ELEVATION OF CUT DROP

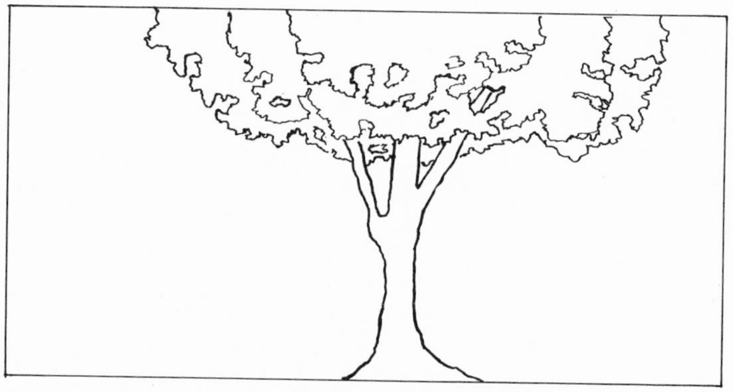

3 CUT BORDERS USED WITH
TREE TRUNK BUILT "IN THE ROUND"

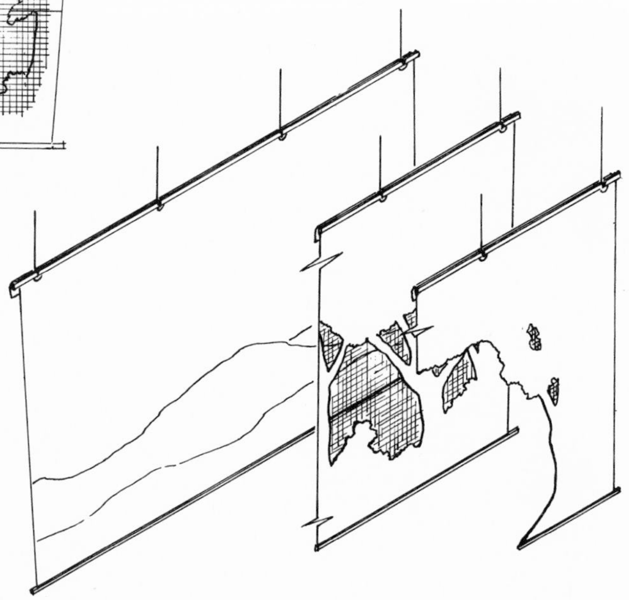

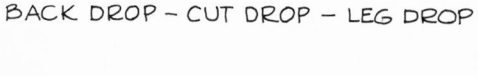

BACK DROP – CUT DROP – LEG DROP

5.5 Cut drops, cut borders, back drop, leg drops, and a scene using drops. *The Forest* by Chekhov, a Drama 140 production of the Yale School of Drama. Phyllis Stohl, designer

5.6 Cut drops and scrim drops with applied cutouts simulate a steamy New Guinea jungle in a scene from *As Mortal Men* by Jack Jacobs, a Yale School of Drama production. Robert MacKichan, designer

to make them translucent. Such drops are forerunners of the Trans-lux motion-picture screen. Translucent plastic sheets, of various trade names, if of sufficient tensile strength and stability (that is, inelasticity), may be made into drops. A translucent drop has numerous uses in the creation of scenic effects. Images may be projected upon it from behind. It may be painted in one part with opaque paints and in another part with dyes, so that varying the lighting from front to back may create two completely different scenic effects. The portion of the drop which is to be translucent must be free from seams or framing.

cut drops

For the creation of a three-dimensional effect in a scene by the superposition of objects, cut drops and leg drops are used. A cut drop is a drop which has been cut after painting, and the cut portion reinforced with net. Thus, in a forest scene, receding trees may be represented by two or more cut drops, set in front of the backdrop: each of the cut drops discloses some of the drops behind it.

leg drops

A leg drop is similar to a cut drop except that the whole center portion of the drop has been omitted; the drop forms an inverted U over the stage and leaves the acting area clear.

borders

These are large expanses of cloth either stretched on two battens as are drops, or chain-weighted and hung flat or in folds from a single top batten. They are hung above the stage to conceal the fly loft from the audience. Borders may be either without scenic significance and used frankly for masking or they may be representational.

Masking borders are either of neutral-toned fabric hung in folds with hemmed and weighted bottoms, or of cloth stretched flat on two battens and painted a conventional color intended to be least apparent to the spectators.

Representational borders range from those painted sky blue or in harmony with the backdrop, to foliage borders, carefully designed, painted, and cut to match trees which are built and placed on the stage floor. Cut borders are reinforced with net to hold the cut portions in place and must be carefully designed to keep the necessary net, which is only theoretically invisible, from being seen.

All the unframed types of scenery so far treated present few problems in construction or transportation. Large drops and borders do, of course, require a large clear shop space for construction and a large paint frame or floor space for painting. For transportation, curtains may be folded and baled, and drops and borders may be rolled on their battens.

All such unframed scenery, however, possesses the essential weakness of instability when onstage. Furthermore, scenery composed of drops must be designed into large flat surfaces.

The scenery space may be partially or wholly enclosed on three sides by a *cyclorama (cyc)* which may be either an item of scenery, if it is portable and installed onstage for a particular show, or an item of stage equipment, if it is built in place onstage or hung permanently on rigging installed for the specific purpose.

cycloramas

A scenery cyc is usually of cloth made like a drop and tied to curved top and bottom pipe battens. Alternate batten arrangements may be curved or they may be straight end sections attached to a straight middle section. Bottom battens may be replaced by chain weights in a bottom hem in the cloth.

Scenery cycloramas may be made in various fabrics, the most common being cotton duck. Cycs intended to represent sky or limitless space should be sewn and hung free from wrinkles. A scrim cyc hung inside the cloth cyc hides any wrinkles that may occur.

A scenery cyc may have pleated and sewn-in fullness like curtains for decorative and abstract, rather than natural, scenic effects, or may simply enclose the acting and scenery spaces and conceal backstage areas.

Cycloramas which are classified as stage equipment are discussed in Chapter 11, page 288.

One step from the battened drop in the direction of rigidity is the framed drop. The canvas is fastened, on two sides permanently and on two sides temporarily, to a wooden frame which is demountable. The drop may be rolled for transportation and may be stretched to remove wrinkles and to adjust the stretch to humidity changes. The weight of the frame tends to prevent movement, and the frame may be planned to allow for door and window openings, into which separate door and window units may be set (Figure 5.7).

framed drops

Framed drops, like other drops, are limited in use to situations which require large flat expanses of scenery, and they are but slightly more stable than battened drops. It is obvious, then, that neither battened drops nor framed drops fill the demand for scenery which may be made to appear as motionless as the architectural works of man or the rocks and earth of nature.

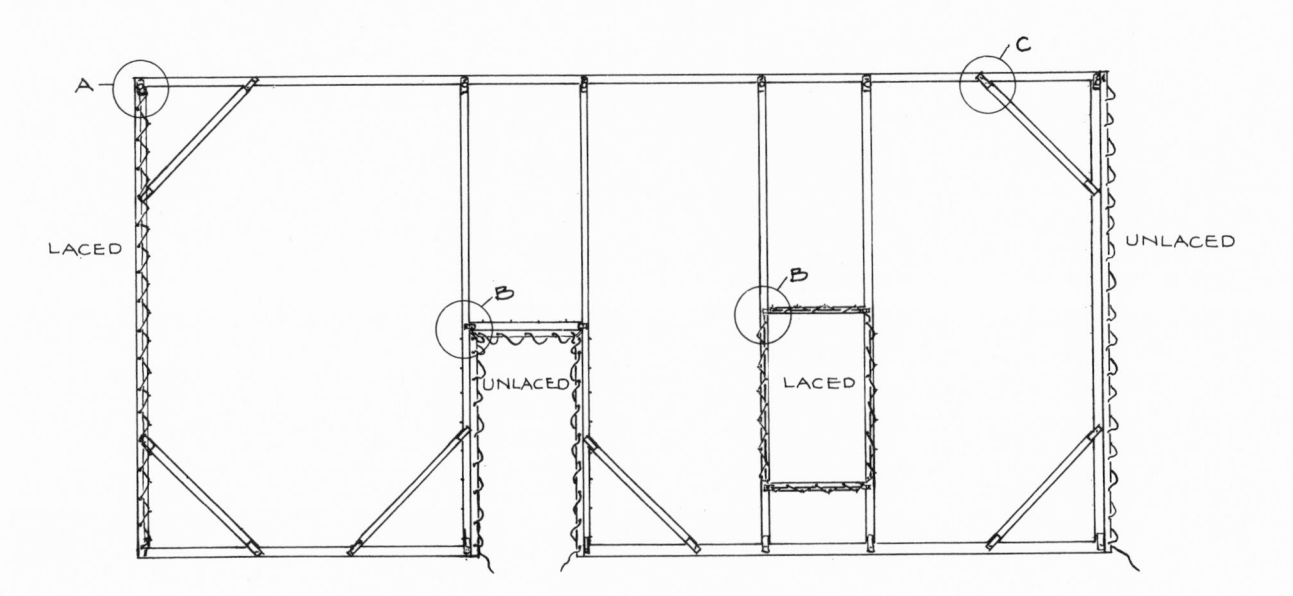

REAR ELEVATION OF FRAMED DROP
W/ DOOR AND WINDOW OPENINGS

LACED

UNLACED

C

A

B

B

UNLACED

LACED

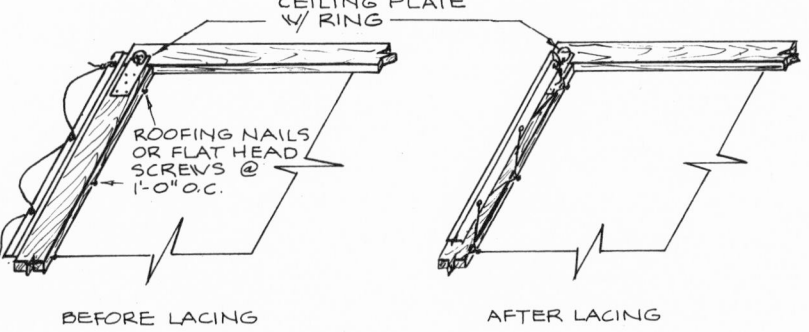

CEILING PLATE
W/ RING

ROOFING NAILS
OR FLAT HEAD
SCREWS @
1'-0" O.C.

BEFORE LACING

AFTER LACING

DETAIL A
JOINT BETWEEN OUTSIDE
STILE AND RAIL

CEILING PLATE
W/O RING

DETAIL C
JOINT BETWEEN
RAIL AND BRACE

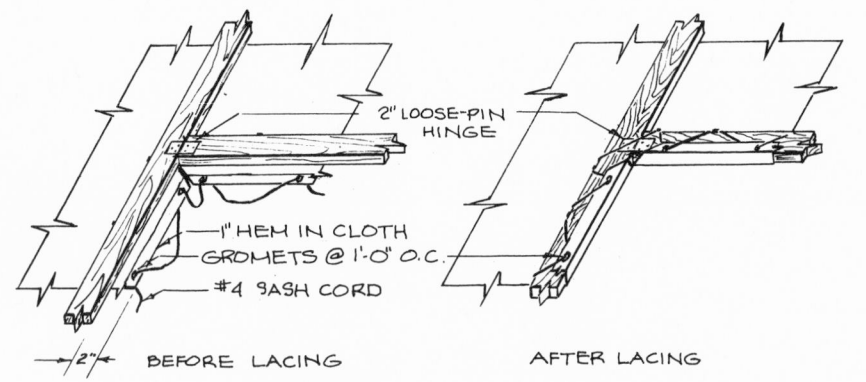

2" LOOSE-PIN
HINGE

1" HEM IN CLOTH
GROMETS @ 1'-0" O.C.

#4 SASH CORD

2"

BEFORE LACING

AFTER LACING

DETAIL B
JOINT BETWEEN INSIDE
STILE AND RAIL

5.7 Details of a framed drop

Ceilings for realistic interior settings usually exceed in overall dimension the sizes of framed scenery which may be transported and must therefore be rolled or folded for shipment and storage.

ceilings

A roll ceiling is substantially like a framed drop. The rectangular frame consists of battens along the two long sides and spreaders set between and at right angles to them, fastened by ceiling plates, carriage bolts, and wing nuts. The covering fabric is sewed into one piece, fastened permanently to the battens and temporarily, by lacing, to the outside spreaders. The ceiling may be rolled on its long battens and the battens lashed to the roll to make one package for shipment or storage. A fault of a roll ceiling is the sag which develops in the expanse of cloth because it is attached only to the outside framing members. It is sometimes necessary to replace the spreaders with others of greater length to restretch the cloth and reduce this sag.

roll ceilings

If the shorter dimension of a rectangular ceiling does not exceed twice the limiting dimension for transportation, a book ceiling may be used. This consists of two permanently assembled frames extending the long dimension of the ceiling, permanently hinged together and permanently covered with cloth. The sag of the cloth is negligible in this type of ceiling.

book ceilings

Very large ceilings may be built to both roll and book, achieving the portability of a roll ceiling and approximating the cloth sag of a book ceiling. The hanging and flying of all types of ceilings is shown in Chapter 15.

roll-and-book ceilings

Framed Two-dimensional Scenery

By far the largest amount of scenery built is framed flat in wood and covered with whatever lightweight material, flexible or rigid, the particular situation demands.

The size of the frame is governed by the limitations which construction, transportation, and handling onstage impose. These three limiting factors are of varying importance in different situations. One scene shop may be limited in work space and be forced to build small individual pieces and hinge them together. Another shop may be restricted in its available raw material to certain sizes of lumber or widths of covering material. Another shop may adjoin the stage and have no restrictions imposed by transportation. Another may have to govern the size of all its pieces by such restrictions. The size of all pieces of scenery built for American commercial production is limited by the established practice of building scenery in one shop, painting it in another, and moving it to one or more theatres during tryouts, run, and tours, and by the absence of elaborate power-driven machinery for shifting scenery onstage.

factors governing size

To the limitations listed are added the size and shape of each particular set and the location of superimposed parts which govern the framing. Doors and windows in a wall, for instance, determine the division of that wall area into flats.

Another consideration, if the organization has a policy of storing

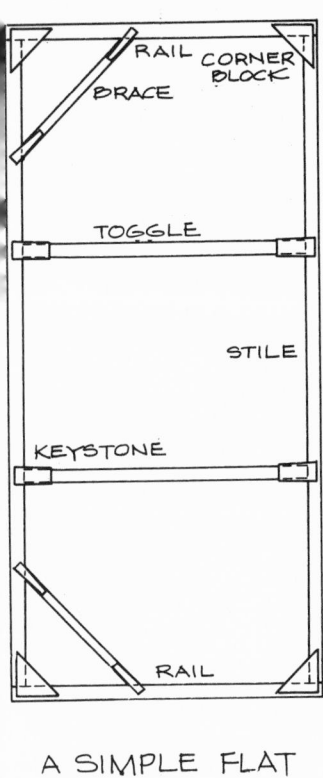

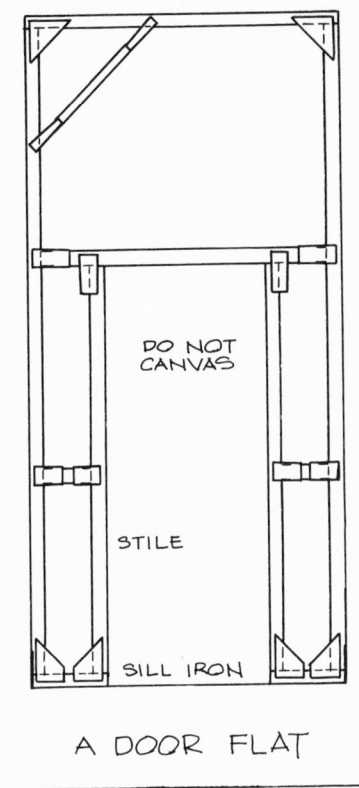

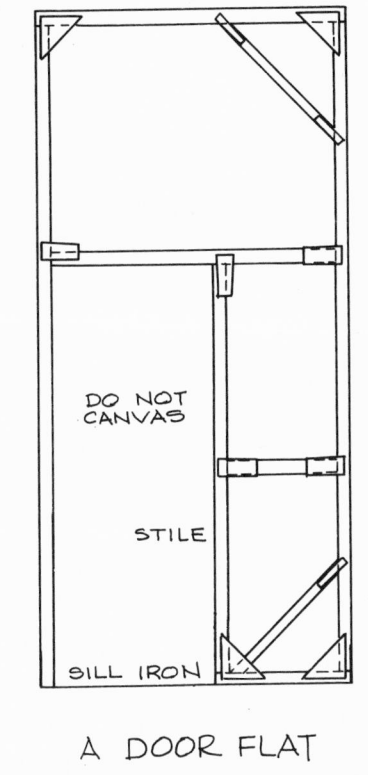

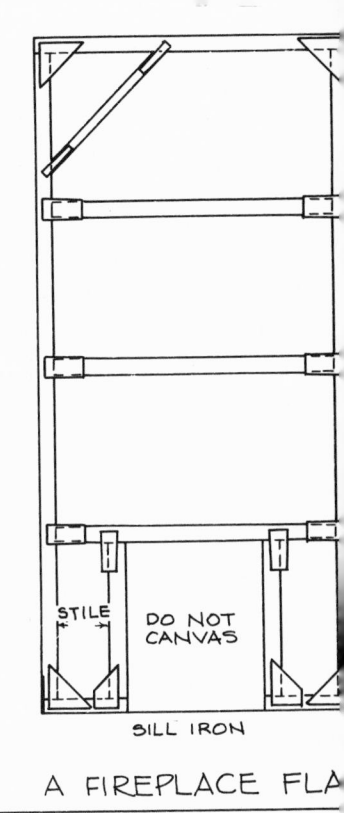

A SIMPLE FLAT   A DOOR FLAT   A DOOR FLAT   A FIREPLACE FLA

5.8 Types of flats

and reusing scenery, is the advisability of building and making use of as many standard-size pieces as possible.

Governing all scene construction and affecting the division of framed scenery into pieces are the basic demands that scenery be strong, portable, economical, built in accordance with design instructions, and suitable to the action of the play. This fivefold statement governing the principles of scene construction has been set forth by Philip W. Barber in his *Scene Technician's Handbook*.

flats   The basic piece of framed scenery is the flat, a rectangular framework of lightweight lumber covered with linen, duck, muslin or other fabric, sometimes over a plywood surface (Figure 5.8). Structural members of flats are as follows:

Stiles: outside vertical members.
Rails: outside horizontal members.
Toggle bars: inside horizontal members.
Braces: inside diagonal members used to keep the flats in shape.
Inside stiles: inside vertical members used to frame an opening.
Sill toggle bars: toggle bars at the bottom of a window opening on which the sills and the windows are to rest.
Lintel toggles: toggle bars at the top of doors or window openings.
Arch toggles: toggle bars at the top of arched openings to which arch sweeps are attached.
Picture toggles: toggle bars to which pictures may be fastened.
Fixture toggles: toggle bars to which wall lighting fixtures may be attached.
Sill irons: pieces of strap iron (band steel) shaped to fit under the rails of door or arch flats.

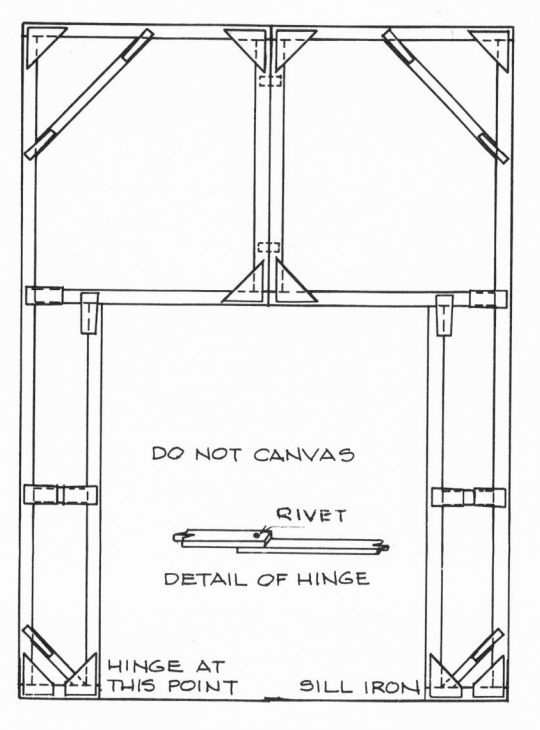

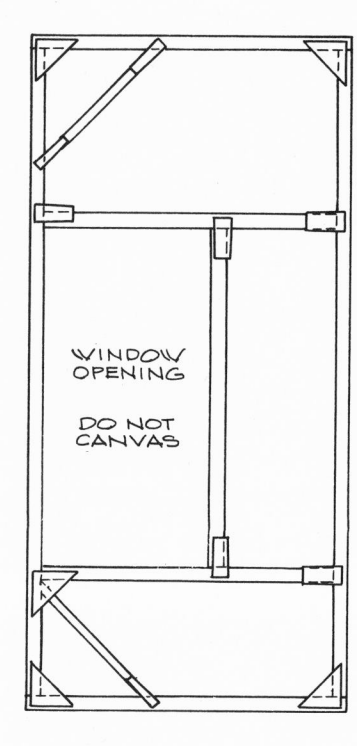

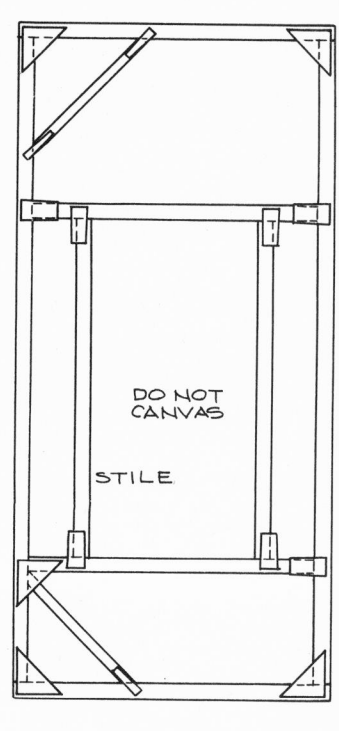

TWO FLATS W/ DOOR BETWEEN   A WINDOW FLAT   A WINDOW FLAT

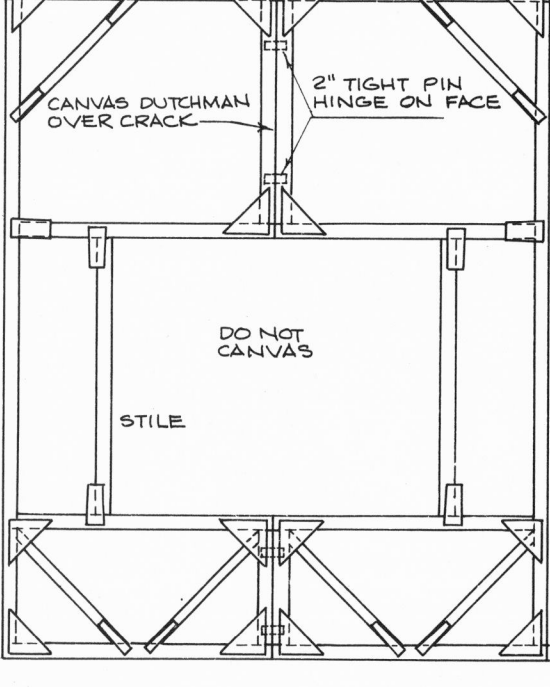

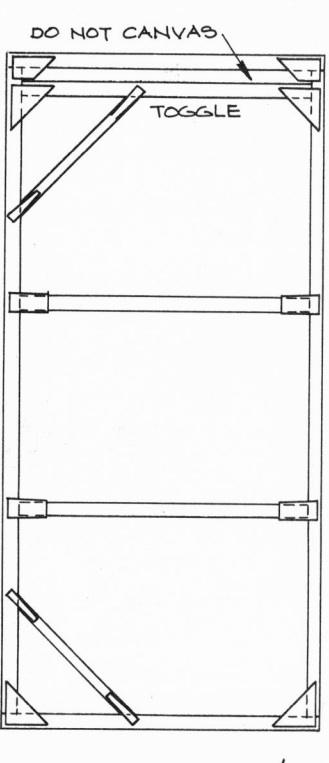

AN ARCH WINDOW FLAT   TWO FLATS W/ WINDOW BETWEEN   A SIMPLE FLAT W/ PROVISION FOR CORNICE

<dl>
<dt>plain flats</dt>
<dd>These are flat areas of scenery of any desired dimension. If the area required exceeds the allowable size of a single flat, two or more flats are hinged together and the joint concealed with covering material. When three or more simple flats are hinged together, strips of wood known as folding battens are hinged between certain of the flats to make folding possible. When folding is unnecessary, the flats may be joined by horizontal battens attached across the backs.</dd>

<dt>flats containing openings</dt>
<dd>For windows, doors, fireplaces, niches, bookcases, and the like, openings are framed into flats to which the window or other architectural parts are attached. When the width of the required opening cannot be framed into a single flat, the opening is framed into two adjoining flats which are hinged together. The sill iron of a door opening constructed in this way is either removable or hinged.</dd>

<dt>curved openings in flats</dt>
<dd>Arches, circular windows, and similar openings require the setting of curved sweeps into the framework of the flat. When no thickness of lumber is required, the framing of the opening may be kept rectilinear and the curves achieved with plywood or composition board, which is applied to the frame before covering.</dd>

<dt>polygonal flats</dt>
<dd>Not all flats are rectangular. Scene designers sometimes create settings in which no piece contains a single right angle. Successful construction of this type of scenery begins in the drafting room. The draftsman who makes the working drawings must supply the builder with accurate overall dimensions and true measurements of the angles between framing members. He can assist the carpenter greatly by planning one or more right angles in the internal framing. He must also plan sufficient triangular bracing to assure rigidity.

Two methods of procedure are open to the carpenter:

• Measure, mark, and cut all framing members according to the heights and angles given on the working drawings; assemble and test the lengths and angles before clinching the clout nails.

• Assemble the frames by lapping and nailing uncut lumber; true up all angles and given dimensions; mark all cuts; knock the frames apart; cut, and reassemble permanently.</dd>

<dt>profiles</dt>
<dd>Flats of very irregular outline are called profiles. They include ground rows, wings, and set pieces.</dd>
</dl>

5.9 Front and rear views of a ground row of buildings. A standard flat is the basic structure and can be salvaged

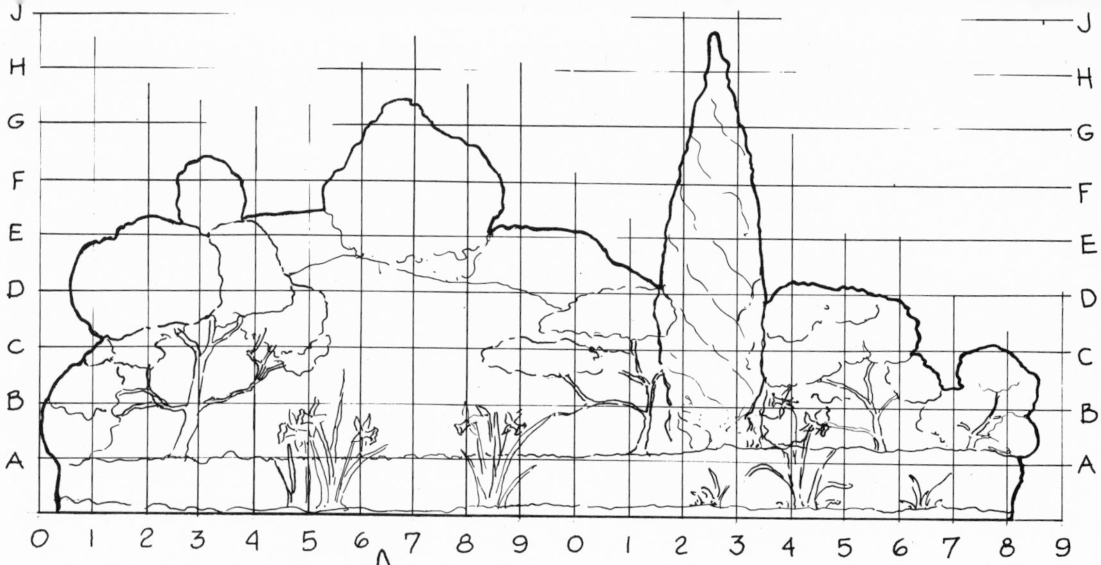

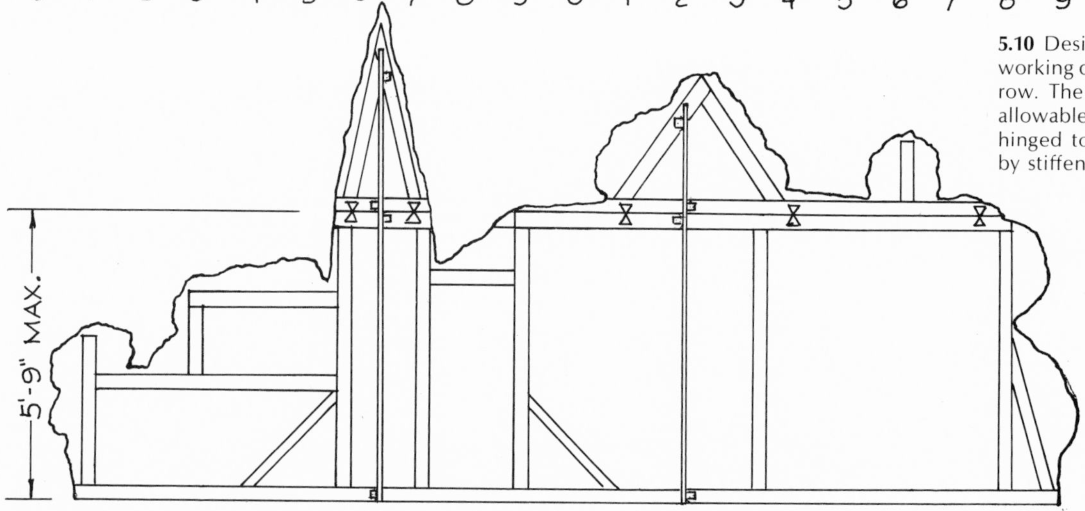

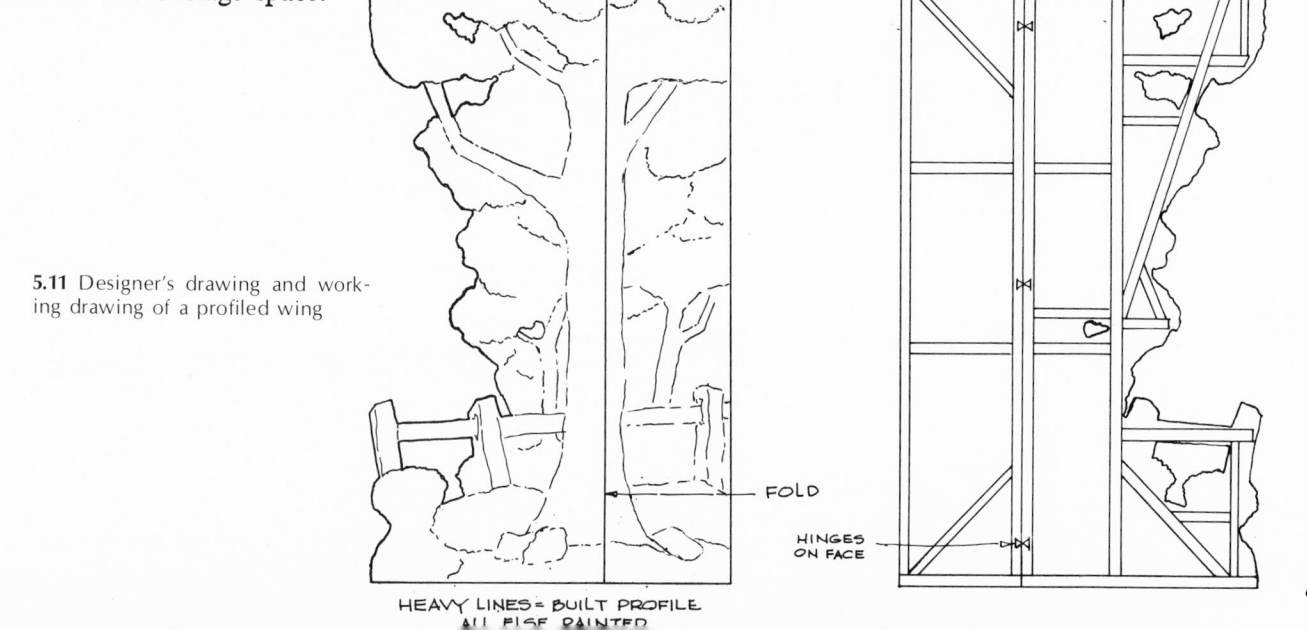

5.10 Designer's drawing (above) and working drawing (below) of a ground row. The parts above the maximum allowable height for touring are hinged to fold and are held upright by stiffening battens

Ground rows are set on the stage floor upstage of the acting area to complete the scenic background and conceal the stage floor, the bottoms of drops, and lights set on the floor. Ground rows are much wider than they are high. When the width exceeds 16', they must be broken vertically to fold. See Figure 5.10.

Wings are stood at the sides of the acting area facing the footlights to conceal the side offstage space.

5.11 Designer's drawing and working drawing of a profiled wing

HEAVY LINES = BUILT PROFILE
ALL ELSE PAINTED

FOLD

HINGES
ON FACE

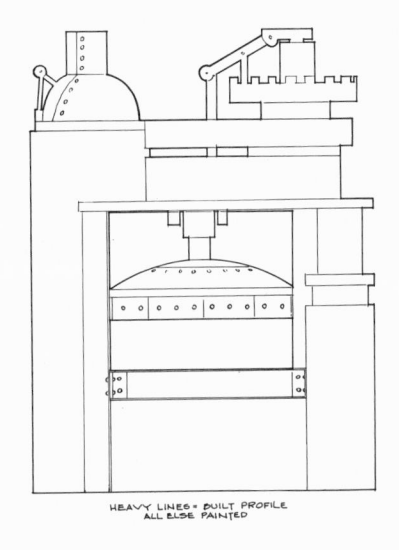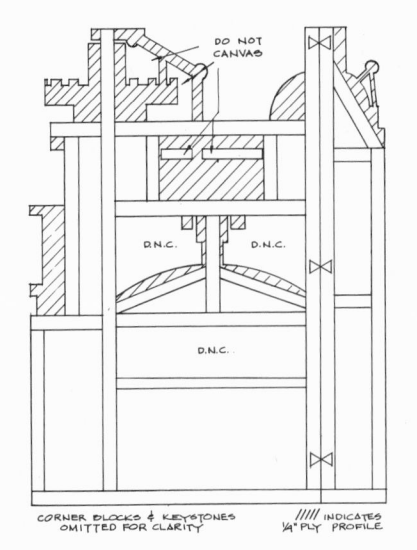

5.12 Designer's drawing and working drawing of a profiled set piece

HEAVY LINES = BUILT PROFILE
ALL ELSE PAINTED

CORNER BLOCKS & KEYSTONES
OMITTED FOR CLARITY

///// INDICATES
¼" PLY PROFILE

Set pieces are placed in or around the acting area to represent isolated objects such as a tree, column, pillar, well curb, or fence post.

The construction of profiles must be governed by the same principles which govern the construction of rectilinear flats. Profiles must be strong and economically built; they must be capable of easy handling and transportation; they must agree with the designs. A profile is constructed like a rectilinear flat except that in most cases the framing members do not follow the outline of the piece. The irregular outline is created in 3-ply laminated wood. The framing members are constructed to follow the outline as closely as is consistent with economy of lumber and sound joinery. The 3-ply is marked from a pattern of the irregular outline, cut with a band saw or a saber saw, and applied to the framing members before covering (Figure 5.12).

Because of the infinite variety in the shapes of profiles, it is impossible to state a rigid technique for planning and construction. It must suffice to give seven general rules which must be observed:
• Bottom rails always carry through the frame.
• External and internal members which are in the longest dimension carry through all other internal members.
• The frame must have a sufficient triangular bracing to assure its keeping its shape.
• The 3-ply must lap completely the outside framing members.
• No more than 6″ of free-standing 3-ply can be left unsupported by framing members.
• Framing members must extend through to the edge of the profile at hinged joints.
• One dimension of a profile, either flat or folded, must be less than 6′. A ground row may be folded either horizontally or vertically. A horizontal fold may be stiffened by brace jacks.

If the time factor is more strategic than the cost or weight factors, time can be saved by cutting the irregular shapes from rigid 5-ply and framing only as required to stiffen and fasten adjacent pieces. Weight can be reduced by cutting out interior portions of the plywood.

Curved surfaces are constructed by bending flexible-board covering materials on wooden patterns called sweeps. The sweeps become the rails or stiles of a frame, depending on whether the curvature is horizontal or vertical, and are spaced along straight members at center-to-center intervals equal to the width of the available materials to allow butting and fastening the edges of the board (Figures 5.13–5.16).

Surfaces curved on a radius of 3' or over may be made of pulpboard ³⁄₁₆" thick.

Surfaces curved on a radius of from 6" to 3' may be made of ³⁄₁₆" 3-ply or of pulpboard which has been softened by moistening.

Surfaces curved on a radius of 6" or less are obtainable ready-made in the form of cylinders and tubes made for nontheatrical uses. Vacuum-molded plastic cylinders of various radii are obtainable.

curved surfaces

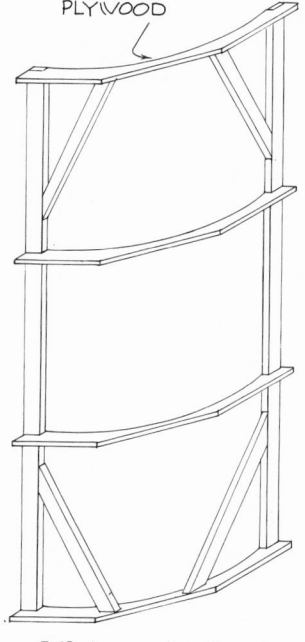

PLYWOOD

5.13 A curved wall section

5.14 A vaulted ceiling with a sky-light built in perspective. Designed by Oliver Smith for *Lord Pengo*

5.15 A simulated Quonset hut for *A Cook for Mister General*. Will Steven Armstrong, designer. The curved sweeps may be either ply-wood in T section or structural steel or aluminum bent to shape. The wall material may be corrugated sheet metal, painted hardware cloth, painted Plexiglas, or painted ply-wood depending upon the visual effect desired

5.16 The prow of a Viking ship for *Song of Norway*. Designed by George Jenkins. Plywood, cut in strips, is bent to fit the compound surface delineated by the horizontal sweeps. A second layer of plywood is glued diagonally over the first. For touring it would be possible to make the stem-figurehead of two identical members, bolted together

superimposed detail

Flats are the basic parts of most sets of scenery, but they are seldom used by themselves. A picture of a play produced fifty years ago discloses that all the architectural trim of the supposed room which was the scene of the play was painted on the scenery. Today a general rule seems to be: build that which must be built to achieve the desired effect; paint that which will achieve the desired effect by painting. The desired effect may not be to produce a convincing realistic effect; it may rather be to produce an effect of *paintedness* or of texture for texture's sake. Assuming, however, that *Mary, Mary* or its contemporary equivalent, is being set in the style of selected realism, and the scenery must *con* an audience into accepting the existence of a bathroom where common sense says there is only offstage space, the reasonable practice is to paint only that portion of the architectural detail which the nearest, most discriminating spectator *cannot* distinguish as *not* being built, and build the rest.

Architectural detail which may have been built in three dimensions for the premiere production may be painted for touring to facilitate setting and striking, and to lighten the scenery load. For historical styles and frank theatricalization, detail may be intentionally painted to *appear painted*.

architectural thickness

In nonrealistic scenery great emphasis is put upon the appearance of solidity and a convincing third dimension. Architectural detail in scenery differs from that which is normal in architecture because of the following considerations:

• Small detail is of no value in scenery because it is not seen by the audience. Small moldings appear as hairlines. To be significant, detail must be selected and emphasized.

• Elaborate decoration must be simplified in terms of mass, line, and proportion for greatest effectiveness.

• Distances measured parallel to the audience's line of vision are fore-shortened and must be exaggerated to be perceived at all. For instance, thicknesses on doors and windows in a back wall, if small, might as well be eliminated; to have value they must be oversized.

• Distances measured across the audience's line of vision have full value and even a little more because of their contrast with the fore-shortening cited above.

The next type of scenery to receive consideration is, therefore, scenery with a three-dimensional appearance caused by the apparent thickness of all walls. The scene designer, when making his ground plan and section, determines by sightline analysis where thicknesses are required and how big they should be. The scene technician determines the methods to be used to build and attach them.

The simplest method of adding thickness to the edge of an opening in a flat is to fasten either a flat or a solid piece of wood at right angles to the flat with loose-pin hinges. If the thickness is less than 1', it can most conveniently and economically be a solid piece of wood; if over 1', it must, because of weight, be a framed flat. The corner blocks and keystones must be held back from the edges of the flat to which the thickness piece is to be attached. Thicknesses 1' wide or over must be braced to a toggle bar in the flat for stability. Thickness around a flat-topped arch opening may be three separate pieces loose-pin hinged to the flat and to each other.

To project a curved opening into the third dimension for an appearance of architectural thickness requires the construction of a curved surface (Figure 5.18).

thickness applied to back of flat

curved thicknesses

5.17 Profiled pieces may be made of whole sheets of plywood in less time than framing takes, but at greater cost. This rustic form is basically flat plywood with the irregular outline which is repeated to give shape to the thickness

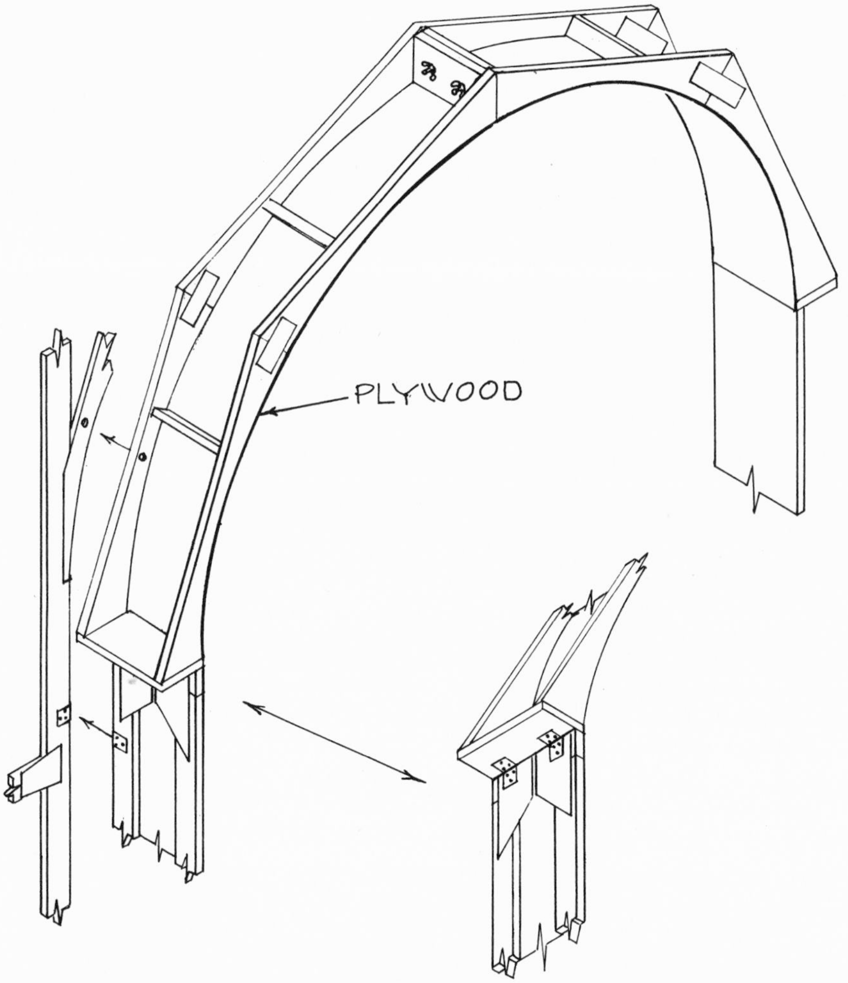

PLYWOOD

5.18 An arch thickness

A thickness for an arch is made in three parts: two sides which are flats or solid pieces of wood loose-pin hinged to the flat, and a top which is constructed as shown. Two sweeps are set out, with radii ¼″ greater than the radius of the arch; they are cut and joined one to the other by short straight pieces. These pieces constitute a rigid frame for 3-ply or wallboard, which is cut, bent, and nailed inside the sweeps. The straight pieces at the ends of the sweeps are loose-pin hinged to the side flats. The front sweep of the thickness piece is fastened to a sweep or toggle bar in the flat by carriage bolts and wing nuts.

irregularly shaped thicknesses

These are built by the same method. When the openings requiring thicknesses are located in the back wall or in out-of-the-way parts of the set, it may be possible to simplify the shape of the thickness by building it larger than the opening for which it is made and reducing the number of planes or curved surfaces. Casings around curved openings are built and handled as separate pieces and are bolted to the flats during assembly of the set.

window and door thicknesses

These are incorporated with the window sash or door and with the casings, if any, to form what are called a *window unit* and a *door unit*. Door or window units without casings are made to the exact size of the opening in the flat to which they fit, and are attached to the rear of the

5.19 An interior setting, c. 1915. All detail and thickness painted. No architectural accuracy

5.20 A portion of an interior setting for *Overlord*, 1929. Frank Bevan, designer. Some detail built, some painted; thicknesses built flat with loose-pin backflap hinges. Door or window units with casings are made slightly smaller than the openings in the flats and are set into the openings from the front of the flats. The width of the casing lumber covers the space allowance between the thickness and the framing of the flats. Methods of fastening in place are discussed and illustrated in Chapter 9. Note particularly the amount of space allowed for fitting a door or window unit which is strengthened with blocked butt joints.

doors

Whenever possible, doors are hinged to their jambs on the upstage side and swing offstage as an aid to actors making exits and entrances. A door which swings offstage, furthermore, need be paneled and painted on only one side. Doors which swing offstage are hinged at the back of the jamb; those which swing onstage, at the front.

TABLE 5.1. DOORS

Material	To Swing Offstage	To Swing Onstage
lumber	1″ stock	1¼″ stock
panels	1 piece rigid board applied on back	separate pieces of board for each panel applied between strips of panel molding or in rabbeted frame
latch	rim latch on back	mortise latch
hinges	strap hinges fastened at back of jamb	regular door butts fastened at front of jamb
paint	applied on one side	applied on both sides

paneled doors

The frame is joined by mortises and tenons throughout. Panels are of rigid board. Screen cloth, muslin, or plastic film is used to simulate glass.

battened doors

To represent planks set vertically and joined on one side with horizontal and diagonal battens: the frame is of 1″ × 3″ lumber joined by mortises and tenons throughout. One or two sides are covered with canvas. Strips of rigid board material are applied horizontally and diagonally to represent the battens. Heavy planking (3″ or more thick) is simulated with rigid plastic foam.

doors with false thickness

For an onstage door, the framing lumber is set on edge and joined with blocked butt joints. For an offstage door the frame is flat, mortised and tenoned throughout, with thickness lumber applied at the edges.

door jambs and casings

A door jamb without casings which is fastened to the back of a flat is constructed of four pieces: threshold, two stiles, and a lintel. The threshold and lintel carry through beyond the stiles and are joined by blocked butt joints in the exterior angles to hold the jamb square. For a door jamb and casing combination, the jamb and casing are first constructed separately and then joined with blocked butt joints. The stiles and lintel of the casing are mortise-and-tenon-joined. The jamb is butt-joined with blocks inserted between the extended threshold and the stiles. The thresholds of all doors must be rabbeted to fit over the sill irons of the flats and beveled front and rear. A small strip of wood is

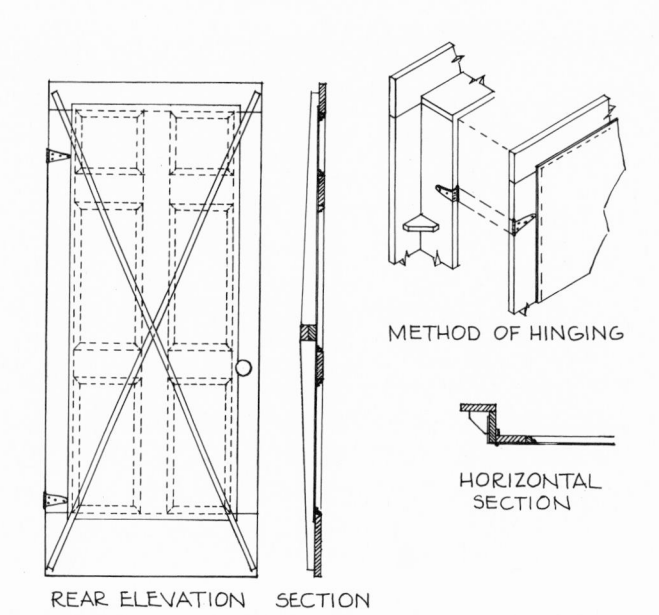

METHOD OF HINGING

HORIZONTAL
SECTION

5.21 A door hinged to swing off-stage

REAR ELEVATION   SECTION

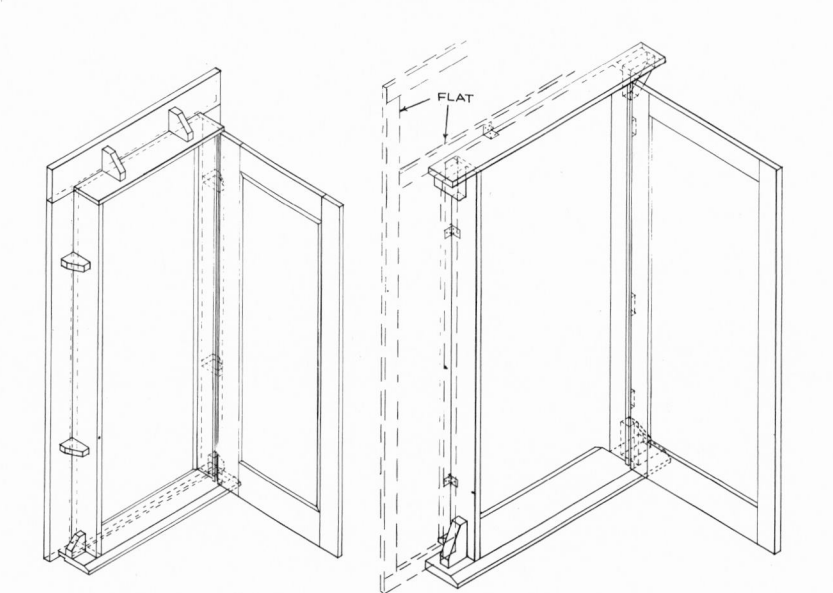

FLAT

5.22 Door frames with and without casings

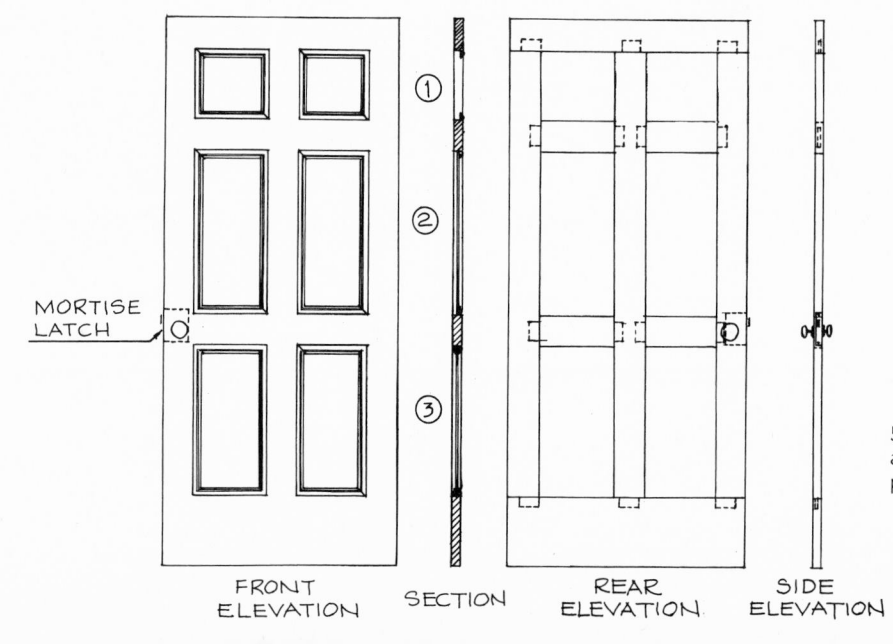

MORTISE
LATCH

① ② ③

5.23 A door to swing onstage. 1, 2, and 3 are steps in building the panels

FRONT
ELEVATION   SECTION   REAR
ELEVATION   SIDE
ELEVATION

fastened around the inside of the door jamb as a stop for the closing of the door. This stop also prevents light leakage around the door.

french windows

French windows are classified as double doors for purposes of scene construction, since the parts and the building procedure are the same for both.

double doors

Double doors present only one problem of construction which single doors do not: to make them close and latch securely without the elaborate latching devices that real double doors normally have. Friction catches set into the top and bottom edges of the doors, or felt strips applied to the top edges, may be used. Stop strips are necessary on both lintel and threshold. An astragal molding must be placed on the face of

5.24 Details of a double door

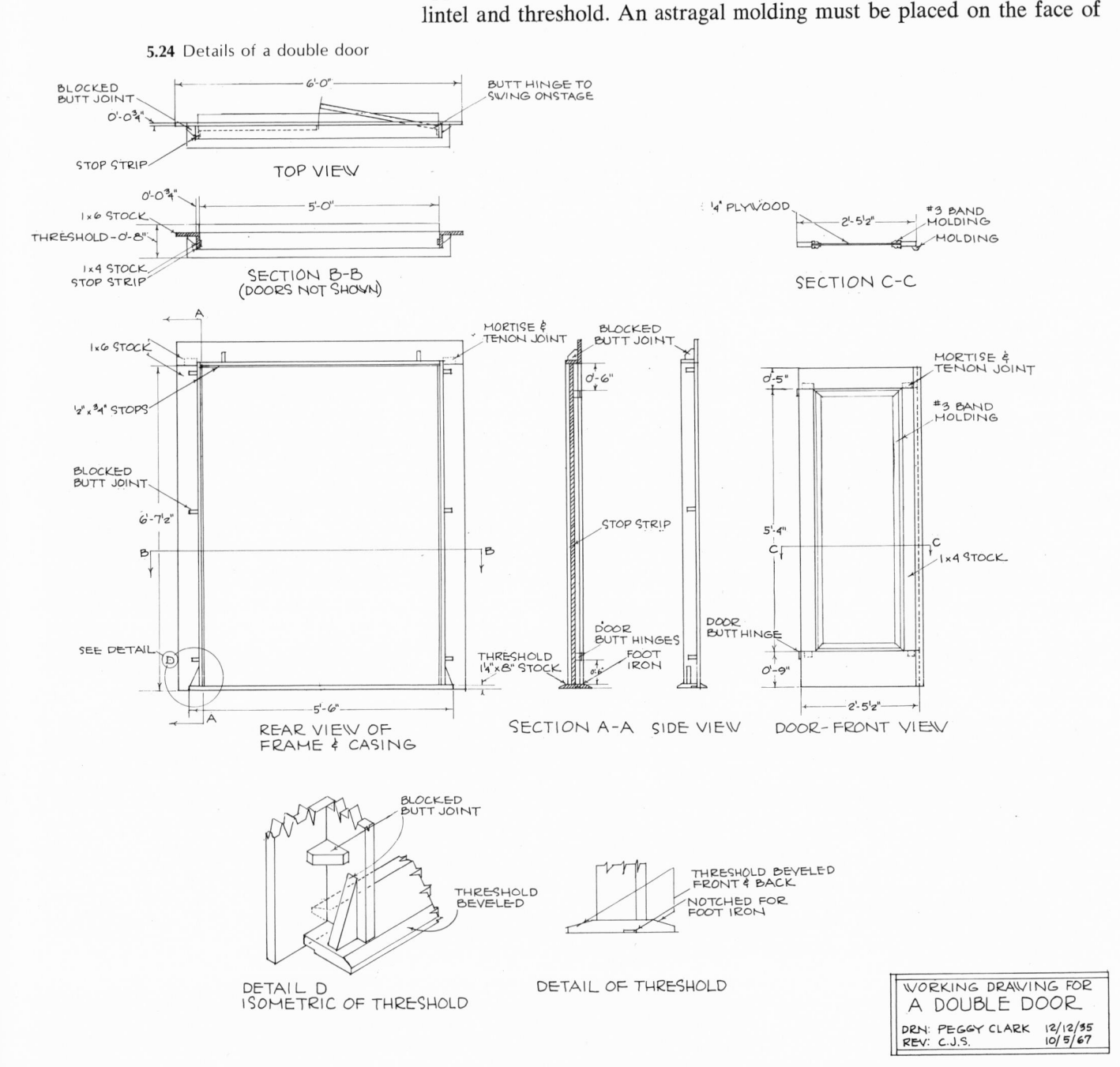

92

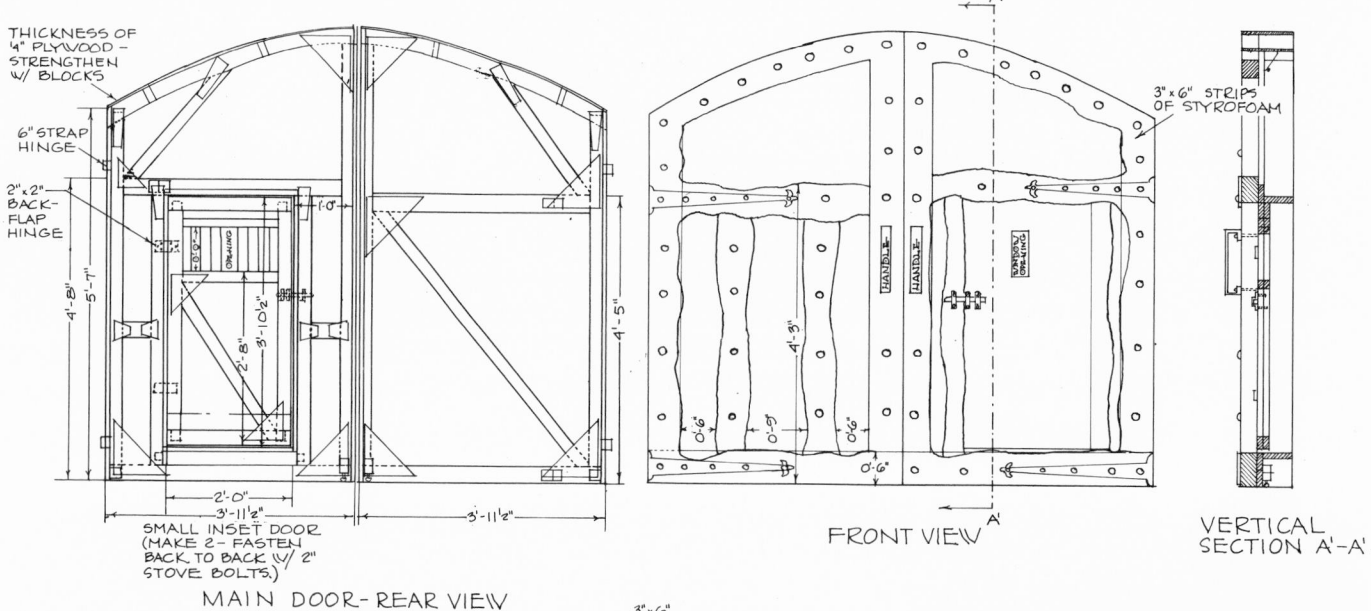

THICKNESS OF
¼" PLYWOOD –
STRENGTHEN
W/ BLOCKS

6" STRAP
HINGE

2"×2"
BACK-
FLAP
HINGE

4'-8"
5'-1"
2'-8"
3'-10½"

1'-0"

2'-0"
3'-11½"

SMALL INSET DOOR
(MAKE 2 – FASTEN
BACK TO BACK W/ 2"
STOVE BOLTS.)

3'-11½"

MAIN DOOR – REAR VIEW

4'-5"

FRONT VIEW

HANDLE
HANDLE

4'-3"

0'-6"
0'-6"
0'-6"
0'-6"

A'

A'

3"×6" STRIPS
OF STYROFOAM

VERTICAL
SECTION A'–A'

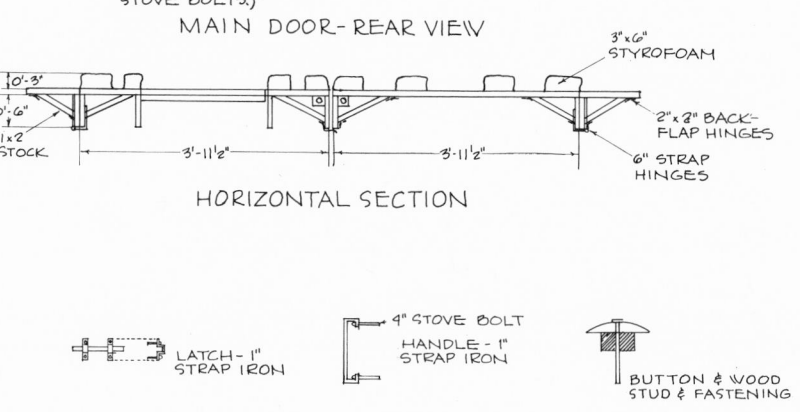

0'-3"
0'-6"
1×2
STOCK

3'-11½"

3'-11½"

3"×6"
STYROFOAM

2"×8" BACK-
FLAP HINGES

6" STRAP
HINGES

HORIZONTAL SECTION

LATCH – 1"
STRAP IRON

4" STOVE BOLT
HANDLE – 1"
STRAP IRON

BUTTON & WOOD
STUD & FASTENING

5.25 Working drawing of an elaborate castle door
and the finished piece

one of the doors to cover the crack between them. Actors must be in-
structed which door is to be opened first and which closed first.

Windows are architecturally of several types, of which double-hung
and casement are the most prevalent. The development of steel casement windows and the use of window walls in modern architecture have
increased the number of window types which the scene technician may
be called upon to duplicate. Double-hung windows have upper and
lower sashes which slide up and down in side guide tracks. Casement
windows are hinged on one side to swing outward. Only windows that
are actually used by actors are built with practical sashes. Double-hung
sash can be imitated by one sash except when the play prescribes the
action of opening or closing the window. See Figure 5.26. French windows are discussed under "Doors" on page 92.

windows

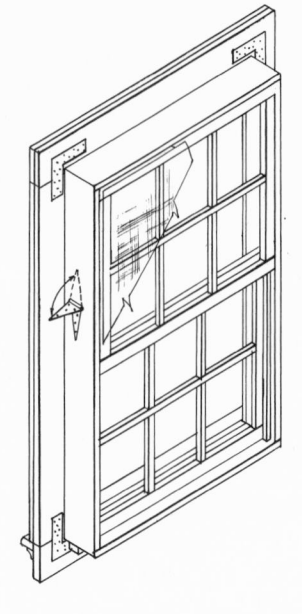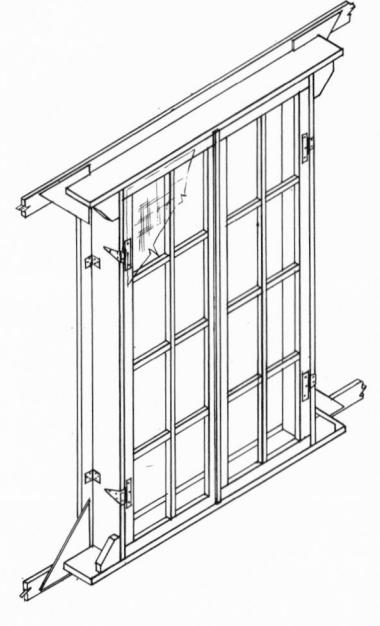

5.26 Left: a double-hung window with a casing. Right: a casement window without a casing

window sash

All types of window sash for scenery are constructed in the same manner. A flat frame of 1″ stock lumber is made with mortise-and-tenon joints, and the window muntins are notch-jointed in place. For quick construction, which is by no means as strong, the muntins may be butted and toenailed to the frame. A variety of window screen as specified by the designer is stapled to the back of each sash to simulate glass.

practical windows

A double-hung window which is to be raised and lowered requires separate upper and lower sashes, with the lower sash inside onstage of the upper, and each capable of being slid over the other. The sliding is made possible by setting three narrow wooden guide strips on each side of the window jamb, to provide a track for each sash. The center strip separates the two sashes enough for clearance.

Practical sashes must be made to stay up when raised. Contrary to practice outside the theatre, no sash weights are used for this purpose. A simple expedient is to set the guide strips so that they bind the sash at a desired height. Simple spring catches which the actor can manipulate may also be used. The stock thriller of making a sash drop at a desired melodramatic moment is effected by having a stagehand withdraw a peg from beneath the raised sash.

elimination of parts of windows

The scene technician can often eliminate window jambs and casings when the windows are, as frequently is the case, covered with considerable drapery material. It is sometimes possible to fake an entire window merely by hanging the required complement of shade, or Venetian blind, under curtains and draperies from a batten attached to an otherwise plain flat.

window jambs

These are rectangles consisting of two stiles butted at top and bottom to lintel and sill. If there is no casing, the lintel and sill boards extend beyond the stiles and the butt joints are reinforced by blocks in the exterior angles. Window jambs with casings are made as are door units: jamb and casing are made separately and the two butt-joined together and reinforced by blocks.

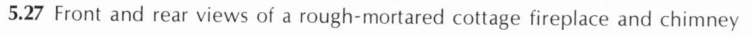

5.27 Front and rear views of a rough-mortared cottage fireplace and chimney

5.28 The mantel for *Mary, Mary*, designed by Oliver Smith. The ornament is molded on a plane surface. See the picture of the trial setup of *Mary, Mary* (Figure 9.4)

To keep door and window units within the size limits imposed by transportation facilities, it is often necessary to subdivide them into parts. Thus the large center door unit on the house in *Mourning Becomes Electra* was divided into four pieces, which were loose-pin hinged together in assembly.

Built-in bookcases, cupboards, niches, and alcoves are all basically variations on the foregoing examples of architectural thickness. A built-in bookcase or cupboard is a set of thickness flats with shelves between and the back canvased. Unless real books are to be used, the shelves are faked by placing 3-ply or wallboard shelves across rails of $1'' \times 2''$ stock. The books are faked unless they are practical (handled by actors) by mounting book backs or half-round moldings on strips of $1'' \times 2''$. The depth of the bookcase itself may be faked, unless the scene is to be brightly lighted, by covering the flat on the back instead of the front, applying book backs, or half-rounds for books and $1'' \times 1''$ strips for shelf edges to the covering material with glue and staples. Painting the exposed covering material flat black gives a satisfactory illusion of depth.

The draftsman must analyze mantels and chimney pieces into structural planes. Flat frames form the foundation upon which the projecting mass and the ornament are applied. All plain surfaces are covered with cloth or board covering material. Support must be provided in the framing for all applied ornament. A mantel that projects less than 6″ from the wall consists of a back frame of flat construction mortise-and-tenon-joined, upon which the columns and entablature are boxed by butting lumber on edge against it. A mantel with a complex arrangement

architectural details
bookcases and cupboards

mantels and
chimney pieces

95

or frontal planes consists of a back frame which fits against the flat and a front frame which forms the basic frontal plane. Horizontal members at top and bottom space these two frames a required distance apart and supply surface for fastening covering material. Minor frontal planes are superimposed on the basic front frame and moldings or ornament applied to them. A chimney piece of the Renaissance type which extends from ceiling to floor can be reduced to an arrangement of flat frames, fastened in proper juxtaposition by horizontal rails (Figure 5.28).

economy of materials

Economy of materials and weight consistent with strong construction is an important consideration in the construction of all applied architectural detail. When two planes of an object meet at a right angle, one plane may be formed by a flat frame, and the other by butting or notching rails into the stiles of the frame. When two parallel planes are separated by a stock thickness of lumber, one framing member may be made the termination of both planes by attaching the surface covering of one plane to the front and of the other plane to the back. This technique is particularly applicable to sunken panels (Figures 5.29 and 5.30).

moldings and cornices

Band and panel moldings are applied to flats by nailing or bolting to stiles and toggle bars. Special toggle bars must sometimes be built into flats to provide support for vertical moldings. Horizontal moldings must be detachable from flats which are to fold. They may be attached with picture hooks and loops or bolts and wing nuts. Composite moldings are assembled on a back piece of 3-ply which is in turn fastened to the flat. Crown moldings are mounted upon small blocks (see Problem 7, Chapter 15) which hold the molding in its proper relation to the piece of scenery. Curved moldings are made by bending straight pieces of molding, or by cutting the molding from a curved piece of wood.

5.29 The side wall of a log cabin set

5.30 A chimney corner created by recessing a flat

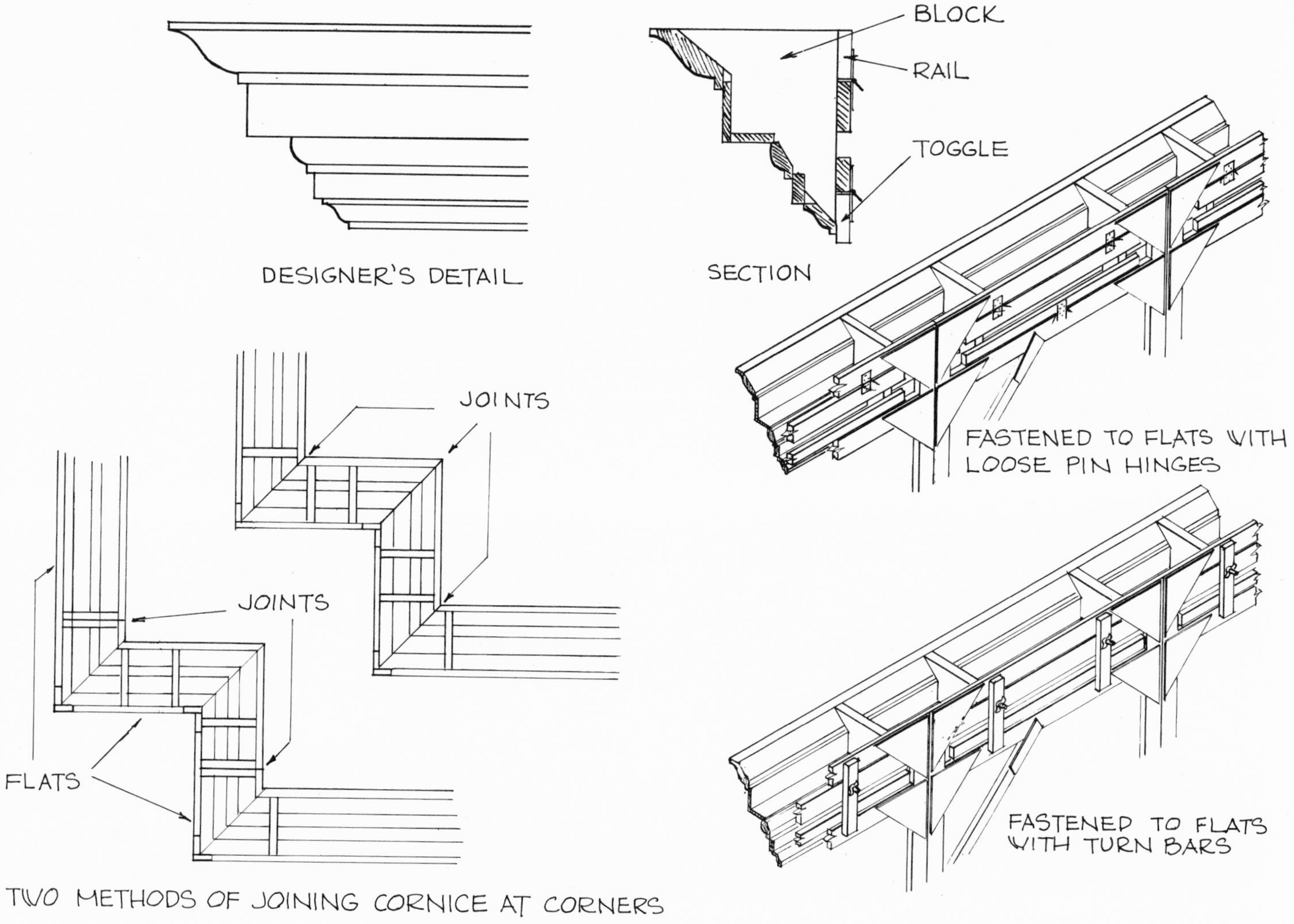

DESIGNER'S DETAIL

SECTION

BLOCK

RAIL

TOGGLE

FASTENED TO FLATS WITH
LOOSE PIN HINGES

JOINTS

JOINTS

FLATS

FASTENED TO FLATS
WITH TURN BARS

TWO METHODS OF JOINING CORNICE AT CORNERS

5.31 Details of cornice construction

Wall panels and wainscots which are built three-dimensional or have
ornament applied to the face are framed separately from the flats to
which they pertain. Raised-center panels are made of thin board materials with framing lumber reduced to a minimum. ½″, ¾″, and 1″ soft-
fiber boards which weigh less than softwoods are used to create the

built panels and wainscots

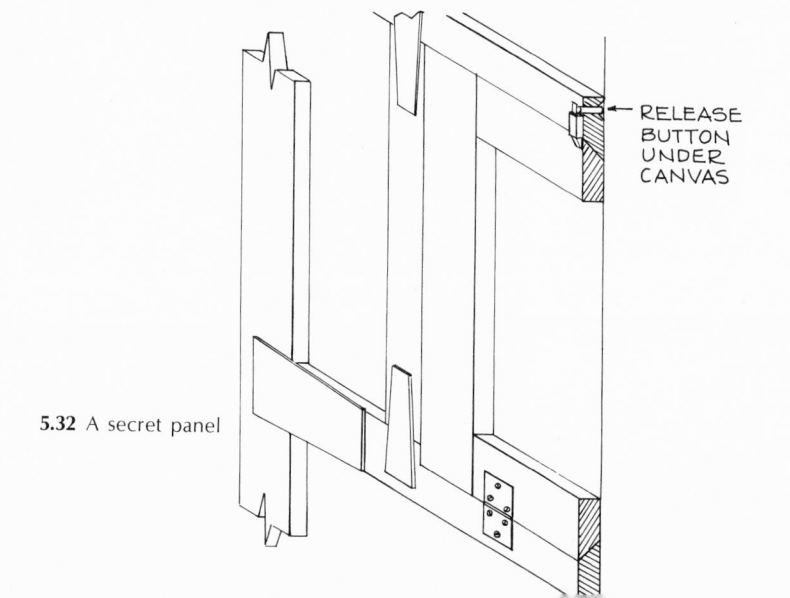

RELEASE
BUTTON
UNDER
CANVAS

5.32 A secret panel

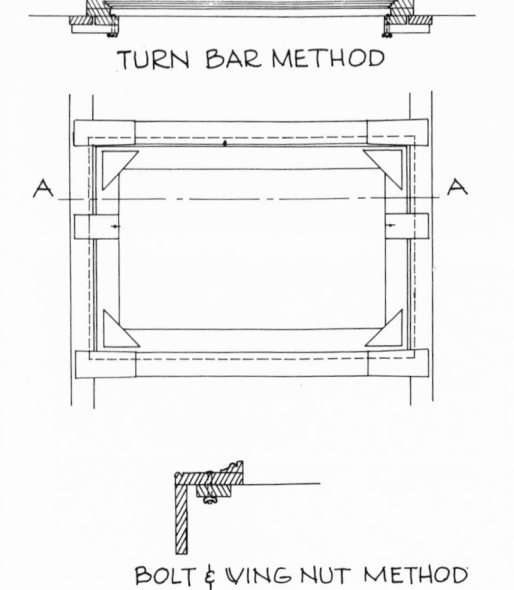

TURN BAR METHOD

A——————A

BOLT & WING NUT METHOD

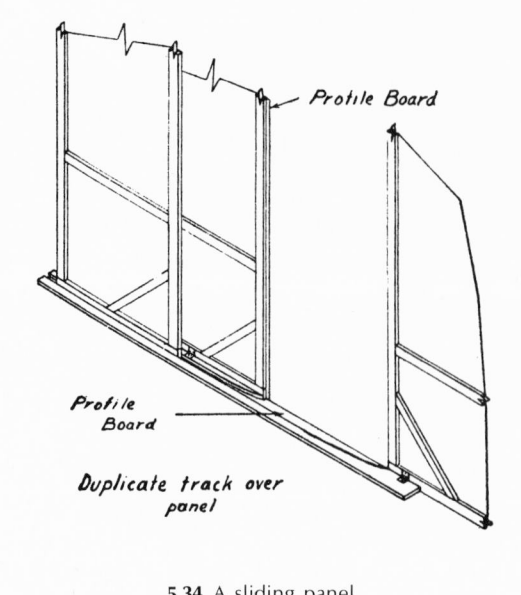

Profile Board

Profile Board

Duplicate track over panel

5.33 Methods of fastening a heavy picture frame or bookshelves into a flat

5.34 A sliding panel

swivel panels

ceiling beams

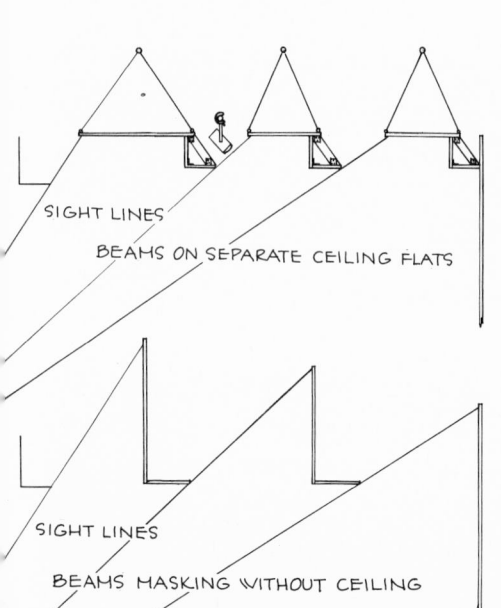

A CEILING BEAM

SIGHT LINES

BEAMS ON SEPARATE CEILING FLATS

SIGHT LINES

BEAMS MASKING WITHOUT CEILING

necessary thickness. Where weight must be avoided, great thickness of architectural ornament is gained by using balsa wood or rigid foam.

Several standard plays involve two aspects of the same setting such as before-and-after alterations, a room shown at two different historic times, or a room before and after paintings have been removed from the walls. The common scenic problem is solved by revolving panels which are set into openings in flats and made to pivot on concentric axial bearings at the top and the bottom of each panel.

Ceiling beams are built separate from the ceiling and attached to it when the scenery is assembled onstage. A beam parallel to the footlights is merely a front flat with an attached thickness flat. The two flats are permanently hinged to fold back to back. Small diagonal braces are set between the two flats on the back at short intervals to establish the angles between them. The front flat must be trussed by internal diagonal framing to prevent sag between points of support. See Figure 5.35.

Ceiling beams parallel to the footlights make possible two or more narrow flats in place of a large ceiling, since a beam will conceal a considerable portion of the ceiling area. This allows suspending light battens in the openings concealed by the beams and obviates the cumbersome rigging and flying of a full-stage ceiling. Disadvantages of such a divided ceiling are the number of battens required to hang the narrow ceiling flats and the number of flying operations in a scene shift. Occasionally, beams parallel to the footlights are so planned and shaped that the ceiling may be eliminated altogether. Ceiling beams perpendicular to footlights are made of two identical flats spaced back to back by horizontal rails and covered. Beams are attached to ceiling spreaders by loose-pin hinges. Preliminary fastening is done before the ceiling is covered with canvas. The bending effect of the beam weight on the ceiling spreaders must be calculated and the spreaders stiffened to prevent noticeable bending (see Graph 4 in the Appendix).

5.35 Ceiling beams

5.36 Steps in the process of forming a baroque door pediment. On a basic wood and plywood armature, the form is built up with cloth and plaster

Architectural decoration of the sort that would in real buildings be cast in plaster or concrete, or carved in wood or stone (corbels, brackets, keystones, pilaster of column capitals, low relief), must for stage purposes be molded and shaped in lightweight, easily worked materials which have considerable strength. The process used must be rapid and the materials inexpensive. Methods of making this type of decorative detail are:

decorative details of irregular shape

5.37 Thermoformed plastic pilasters and column. The pilasters in the left foreground show reinforcing frames of wood

5.38 A vacuum-formed column capital. Four identical sections are fused together and filled with cardboard cylinders and foamed plastic

5.39 Low-relief ornamental tracery, using the anthemion motif, is made on cutout plywood forms using rope, twine, net, paper, beads, and plastics

- Carving in softwood (sugar pine).
- Modeling plastic materials on a shaped wire foundation.
- Making paper replicas in a plaster of Paris cast which has been taken on a clay model of the object, or on the object itself.
- Making Celastic or fiber glass replicas over a positive mold (called a *plug*) of the desired object.
- Vacuum-forming thermoplastic sheets (acetate or vinyl) in a vacuum press.

Figures 5.36–5.39 exemplify these methods.

Wood carving is a craft which requires special tools and machines, and a high degree of technical skill. It can seldom be done by expert scene carpenters, not to mention amateur workmen, and it is customarily let out to expert workers when required for professional production.

Modeling of plastic materials on a wire foundation is an effective method if only a few replicas of one object are required. The scene designer supplies a full-scale front view and section of the object. The scene technician determines the method of fastening the object to the other scenery, and indicates this to the workman.

By a process called **cocooning** or **cobwebbing,** lightweight irregular shapes can be made by spraying vinyl lacquer or synthetic rubber over forms which have been covered with a membrane of wire-mesh netting or scrim.

The process of making **images from plastic casts** is identical with that used for the manufacture of properties and is treated in Chapter 13. A core must be provided within the image, which can then be attached to the set as is applied detail.

Styrofoam, the trademarked name of Dow Chemical Company for rigid expanded polystyrene foam (RPF), and **Urethane,** Dow's trademarked name for rigid expanded polyurethane foam (RUF), are very light in weight and can be worked easily into any desired shape. Polystyrene can also be foamed in place to fill hollow molds. Both the ready-made and the home-foamed RPF and RUF can be coated to produce a protective paintable surface.

Variants

The arena and open forms of stage, partly or wholly surrounded by the audience, challenge the creativeness of designers and the skill of technicians to design and build scenery required by the action which does not obstruct the audience's view of the acting area. Skeletonized representations of realistic architecture or natural forms, as well as outlined abstractions or stylizations, are executed in wood, plywood, or metal, or in combinations of these, strength being introduced by the plywood, and strength and stiffness by the metal. Softwood when used must have metal reinforcements at joints and must be worked and handled carefully to avoid breakage. Fine wire nails, sometimes in drilled holes, must be driven carefully to prevent splitting the wood. Fasteners which tend not to split the wood must be used. Glued notched joints are strong, though exacting and time-consuming to make.

Steel in various shapes affords strength and stiffness. Scenery built entirely of steel is prohibitively heavy; the combination of steel and wood is to be preferred.

Since there is no concealed offstage space where stage braces or brace jacks may be used, stability must be achieved within the scenic structures themselves by angular relation of pieces, by ballasted bases, or by setting downward-extending vertical members into sockets in either the stage floor or in the floor of a platform.

5.40 A Georgian chimney front built in outline scenery. Designed by Robin Wagner for *The Condemned of Altona*

outline (see-through) scenery

Three-dimensional Scenery

So far the discussion of types of scenery has been confined to scenery which is basically flat but which may be given a three-dimensional aspect by the attachment of objects which are themselves flat or built with a slight third dimension. The next category includes all scenery for which

5.41 A rough stone altar simulated in poultry wire and paper. The rear view shows framing and lift jacks for rolling

5.42 The framework for simulating a snowdrift or sand dune has a bent rod joining the peaks of the frames to produce a sharply defined ridge. The piece is mounted on casters

5.44 The armature for a lamppost

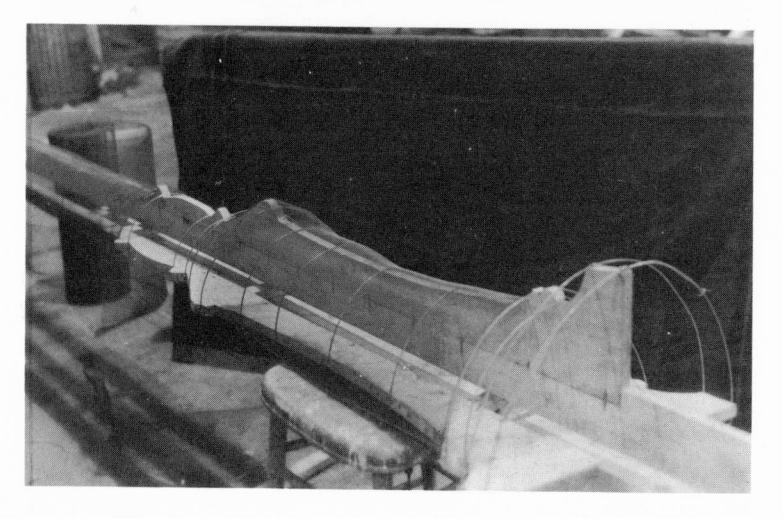

5.43 A column with a square core to set into a socket in a platform. The surface, of asphalt roofing paper and canvas, can be fitted to the tapering entasis in the column

5.45 Close-up of the base of the post. Wire hoops and screen cloth have been applied. Canvas will be the final covering

the third dimension is essential: levels, steps, ramps, rocks, trees, logs, hillsides, and snowbanks. By the nature of its use all such scenery is divided into two categories: that which is not called upon to support weight and is designed and built for effect only; and that which must be capable of supporting a load. The first category is technically called *nonpractical three-dimensional scenery* and the second, *weight-bearing structures.* In most cases the distinction is quantitative rather than qualitative. All three-dimensional structures must have internal frames, the outlines of which delineate their external shape. Members run between

5.46 The framing of a mountain for *Song of Norway*. George Jenkins, designer. Profiled sweeps are of 1¼″ white pine. Identical double sweeps occur where sections are bolted together. The framing at the left side, with cleats supporting the horizontal sweeps and with intermediate vertical members, will support a climbing actor if the surfacing material is molded to supply footholds and handholds

these frames to fasten them in position, diagonals make them rigid, and covering materials give the external appearance specified by the scene designer. In nonpractical units the strength of the members and the joints must be sufficient to support merely the weight of the rest of the structure, and to withstand the stresses of transportation and scene shifting. In practical units the strength or stiffness of all members and joints, and their consequent size, shape, and number, must be based upon the load of actors, properties, and scenery which the units must support with safety and without movement perceptible to an audience. For examples of these types of scenery, see Figures 5.41–5.47.

The scene designer must supply to the scene technician a model done accurately to scale of all irregularly shaped three-dimensional scenery. It is by this means alone that the scene designer can convey completely and clearly the appearance of the scenery which he has designed.

coverings
for nonpractical units

These may be made by any of the processes set forth in Chapter 9 and 15, which will produce the effect desired by the scene designer. Strength and stability are required only to assure that the materials hold together and do not quiver or shake perceptibly. The thickness of the covering will vary with the process used from 6″ for deep artificial foliage to ½″ for chicken wire, paper, and canvas.

for practical units

These must be built to support weight and will have an aggregate thickness of 1″ to 1½″ exclusive of extra padding applied to create an irregular surface. Plywood floors for irregular levels must be laid in

5.47 Locomotive and cars built in perspective for *We Take the Town*. Peter Larkin, designer

monoplane sections, since 1″ plywood cannot be bent or twisted. For units having spherical or cylindrical surfaces or surfaces shaped on a cone, flexible board materials such as ⅜″ fir panel can be bent to fit the curves. Warped floor planes must be built of narrow strips of wood laid separately or of laminations of thin (⅛″) plywood glued and pressed into place with sandbags or other weights until the glue has set. The loads on such floors determine the spacing of supporting frames or beams.

The basic regularity which wood flooring imparts to such units as rocks, stumps, and mounds must be broken up and modified with padding, upholstery materials, or scrap canvas before the final covering of canvas is applied. Only flexible adhesive may be used to fasten padding or covering in areas where actors are to walk, because animal glue when dry crackles underfoot. Cements which remain flexible may be used. Staples must be used only in unnoticeable locations, because the quilted effect which canvas has when stapled has no counterpart in natural forms such as rocks or hillsides.

division of units

The division of three-dimensional units into parts for storing and handling must be done with the appearance of the set on the stage in mind. Cracks in the unit cannot be easily masked and must consequently be in inconspicuous places. Break lines must be, if possible:

- Upstage of a higher part on the unit.
- Across-stage rather than up- and downstage.
- Concealed by foliage, grass, or shrubbery.
- At places where contour changes abruptly.
- In areas of cast shadow.
- In dark-painted areas.
- Coincident or parallel with the lay of actual or painted floorboards.

For touring, all three-dimensional units are made demountable or collapsible. Flooring is battened in sections and nonpractical surfaces are made on flats which may be removed from their supporting frames. Frames which support the flooring or covering are hinged to fold or loose-pin hinged to come apart. Sections of flooring are loose-pin hinged to the frames from below.

parallels

The standard regular three-dimensional unit consists of rectangular frames joined with tight-pin backflap hinges so as to fold. The parallel top is of 1″ 5-ply board. The exposed grain runs the long dimension of the parallel and rests on the four outside frames and on inside transverse frames which are spaced about 2′ 6″ apart. This spacing may be increased for 1¼″ 7-ply (see the loading curves in the Appendix). The inside frames and end frames are parallel and identical, and the two side frames (lengthwise) are identical. Parallel frames are of 1″ × 3″ or 1¼″ × 3″ stock, with all joints preferably mortised and tenoned. Care must be taken to hold corner blocks and keystones away from the places on each frame where other frames will butt and hinge. Parallel frames must have stiles at regular intervals as prescribed in the curves showing spans of beams (Graph 4 of the Appendix), and at least two diagonal braces each. Contrary to regular practice in flat construction, the stiles run through to rest on the floor. See Figures 5.48 and 5.49.

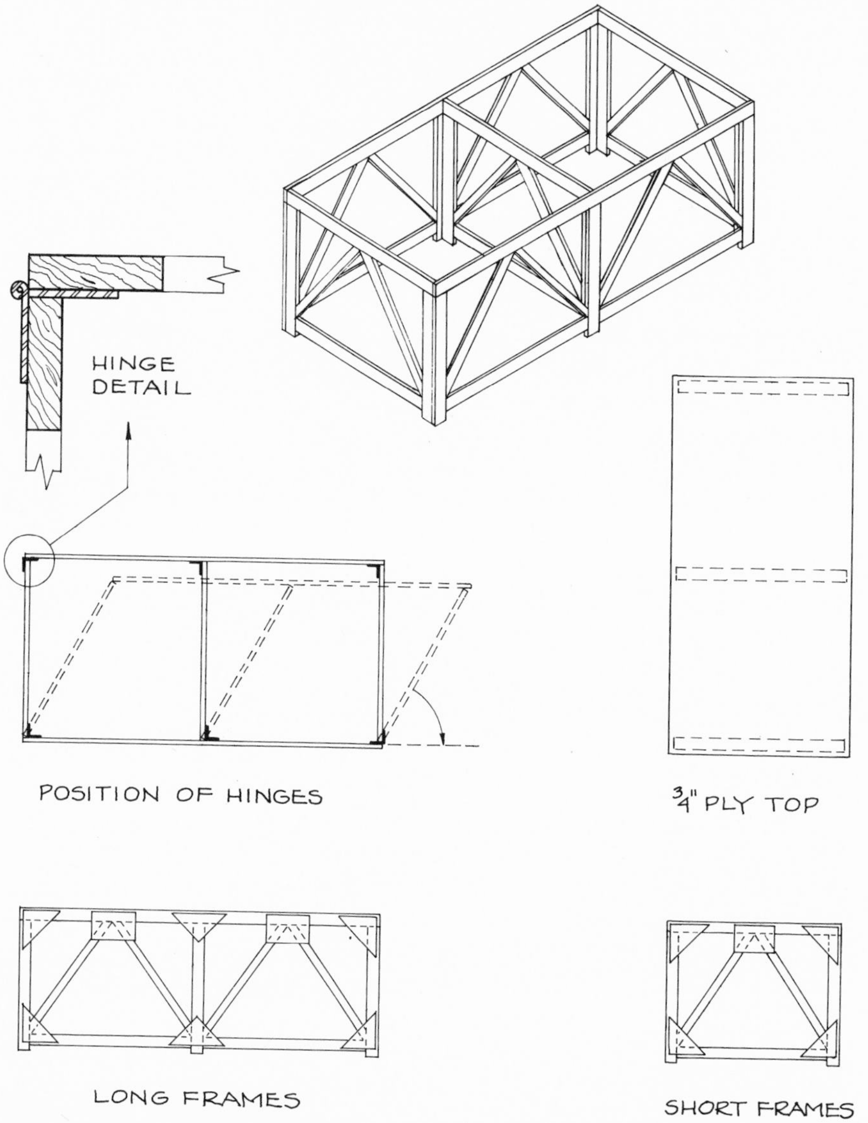

HINGE DETAIL

POSITION OF HINGES

$\frac{3}{4}$" PLY TOP

LONG FRAMES

SHORT FRAMES

5.48 A parallel

5.49 The structure of a platform containing a trap and sockets for square column cores (see Figure 5.43)

5.50 A weight-bearing rock simulated in fiber glass. The process is described in Chapter 15

uses of parallels

Parallels are used to provide any level platform, such as a stair landing; to provide a large, raised, floor level, in which case the parallels may be spaced apart and the flooring made to extend across two or more of them; to provide level support for superimposed three-dimensional scenery which is irregular.

alternate
platforming methods

Parallels are built to established dimensions and are limited as to the sizes of platforms which they will produce in combination; they are prodigal of storage space. Built specifically for a single production, parallels are satisfactory, but the many sizes of parallels required to give a resident theatre even limited versatility in arrangement of platforms justifies recourse to other systems of platforming.

An ideal system is one which permits maximum use of a minimum number of members assembled to produce the largest number of combinations of height, width, and length, based on a reasonable minimal increment of measurement, all related to the load, space, and movement requirements of human actors. The *desideratum* would appear to be a collection of standard-size parts, variable in length, which could be stored in minimal space — on racks or in bins — from which any desired set of members could be assembled into platforms of a variety of useful sizes. However, the work of assembling separate parts into platforms is arduous. Most systems are based not on single pieces but on single frames — sometimes called *gates* — which in some cases are variable in size and in all cases are capable of being assembled into platforms of varying lengths depending upon the lengths of the transverse members which are selected to join them. They are capable of height variation in appropriate increments by the insertion of legs or post extenders. Varying lengths of trusses which may be hung between platforms permit the spanning of open spaces between platforms.

Steel or structural aluminum, both stronger, more stable, and more durable than wood, are suitable for platforming. Patented structural framing systems and standard pipe scaffolding systems have been adapted to scenic uses.

Since designers require latitude in determining the sizes of platforms to comply with composition, the incremental variation permitted by a platforming system is a critical factor in its acceptance by designers.

CANVAS
PADDING
EDGE STRIP
PLYWOOD
MATCHED BOARD
OR PLYWOOD

5.51 Straight stairs

stairs

Stairs consist of *treads,* the horizontal parts upon which a person steps; *carriages,* the slanting notched members on which the treads are set; and *risers,* the vertical members which fill the vertical spaces between the treads. The treads and carriages are weight-bearing members and must be of lumber sufficiently strong or stiff to support the load to be placed upon them. The allowable loads for given sizes of lumber for given horizontal spans are stated in Graphs 3A-3D of the Appendix. The carriages are joined at top and bottom by lateral battens as well as by the treads. The treads are of matched board or 5-ply padded with hair felt. The risers may be of any inexpensive rigid board material nailed to the back of the lower tread and the top or the upper tread in each case. In the best practice each tread is rimmed with ½″ × 1½″ white pine, and ½″ hair-felt padding is set inside the rim to produce square-edged padded treads. The treads and risers are then covered

5.52 A staircase designed by Wolfgang Roth for the Cincinnati Opera. The carriages are bar steel bent and welded to a continuous piece of bar steel, which is bolted to 2″ × 4″ lumber. Sockets are shown being attached to the treads to receive balusters made of square-section metal tube

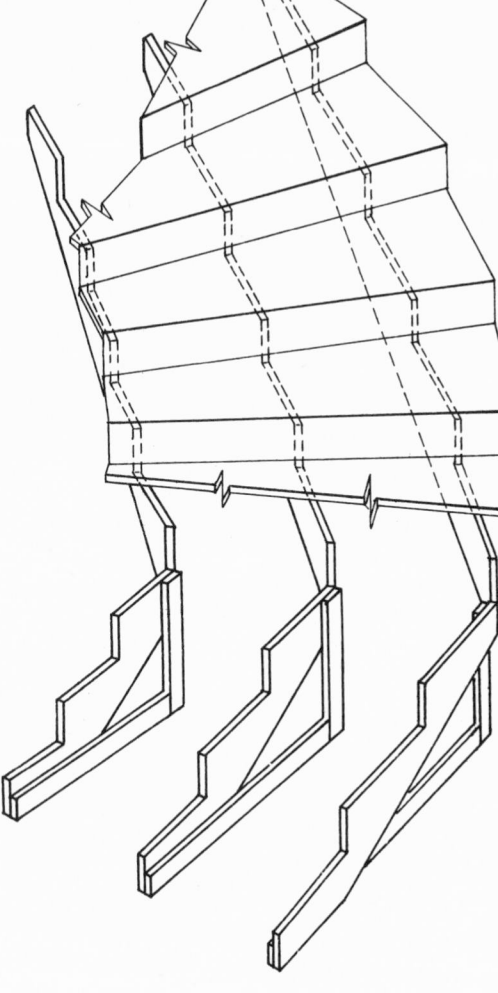

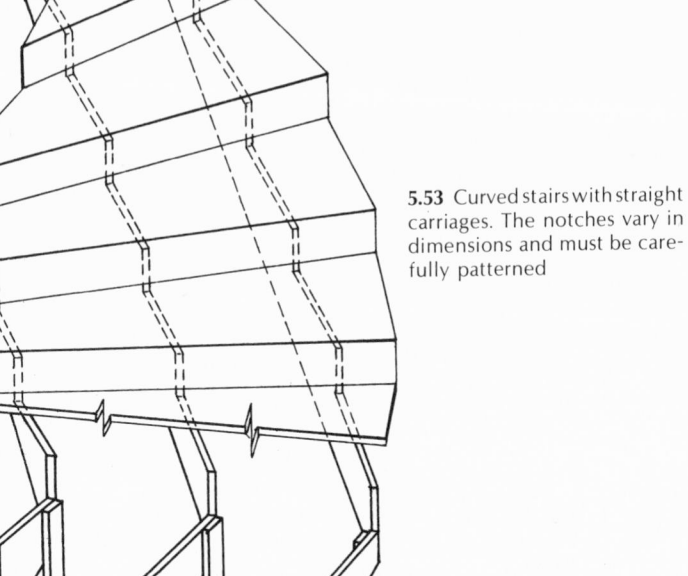

5.53 Curved stairs with straight carriages. The notches vary in dimensions and must be carefully patterned

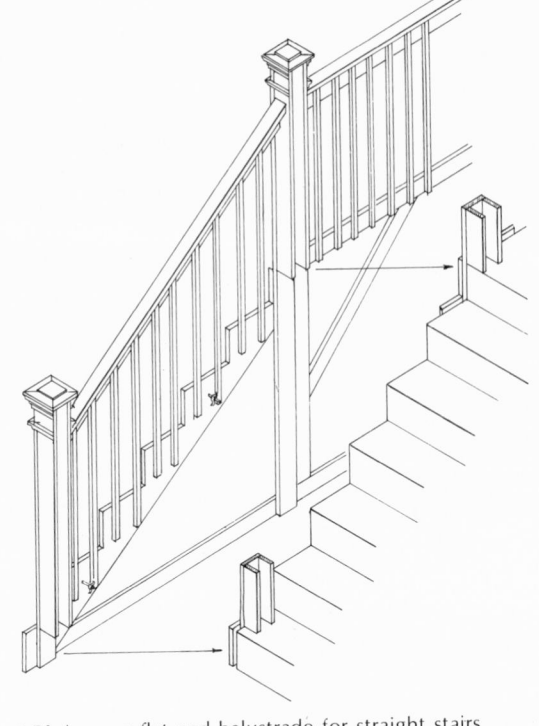

5.54 A cover flat and balustrade for straight stairs

circular stairs

balustrade spindles

metal reinforcement

with a good grade of cotton duck. If a nosing (round projection of the edge of the tread) is required, it is made of half round applied over the covering, and securely nailed to prevent splitting off under actors' feet. Figures 5.51–5.57 give examples of several kinds of stairs.

A stair unit is hooked onto a parallel by means of metal cleats fastened to battens which are set into the upper ends of the carriages. These cleats hook over a batten which is attached to a side of the parallel.

Circular stairs may be made in straight-line construction except that the ends of the treads are cut to the required curves. The circular effect is established by a curved flat behind the stairs and a curved flat set in front of them. The carriages are laid out as chords of the circle, and consequently the notching of each carriage is different from that of all the others and the notch for each separate tread in any one carriage is different from all others. The carriage pattern must be laid out in detail by the draftsman before any building can be started.

These are never notched into stairs as they are in house construction. They are carried down beside the outside carriage and mortise-and-tenoned into a piece of 1″ × 3″ lumber which is in turn bolted to the carriage. The tops of the spindles are lap-jointed to a rail of 1″ × 3″ lumber on which another piece of 1″ × 3″ is set to form the handrail. The lumber sizes may vary and moldings be added according to the design.

If a balustrade has to withstand violent action, all joints must be reinforced with heavy pieces of strap iron bent to fit the angles and bolted to the spindles and handrail. Newel posts are also built as separate units

5.55 A spiral staircase for *The Sound of Music.* Oliver Smith, designer. Plywood sheets, cut to shape by the method shown in Figure 5.57, support the ends of the treads which have been cut to fit the curvature of the stairs, in plan. Laminated strips are fastened to the top and bottom edges of the plywood to form sockets for the balusters. Second sheets of plywood are then attached to form the outer surface

5.56 Designer's model, work in progress, and trial setup of a flying staircase for *Master of Thornfield,* designed by Ben Edwards. Side carriages of plywood support the treads and risers. Sheets of plywood are fitted, bolted in place, marked, and removed; the balustrade design is laid out, marked, and cut. The balustrade is again set in place and another piece of plywood bolted on the outside. When the header of the staircase has been bolted to the landing platform, the temporary supports can be removed. (The cat has faith in the carpenter)

5.57 A form for shaping plywood sides of spiral stairs. The plan is laid down, full scale, on the floor; uprights are placed at regular intervals; vertical dimensions are marked on the uprights; the plywood is set against them, marked, and cut

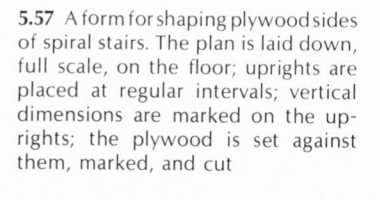

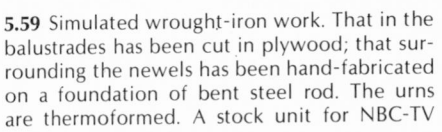

5.59 Simulated wrought-iron work. That in the balustrades has been cut in plywood; that surrounding the newels has been hand-fabricated on a foundation of bent steel rod. The urns are thermoformed. A stock unit for NBC-TV

5.58 A spiral tower. The flooring is tapered planks cut to fit a full-scale pattern. The slope is created with wedge-shaped carriages framed to fit on rectangular vertical frames. Plywood covering is framed to attach to the outside stiles of the vertical frames. Semipermanent fastenings are loose-pin hinges, bolts, and wing nuts. The workman who makes the inside fastenings finally climbs out through the center hole

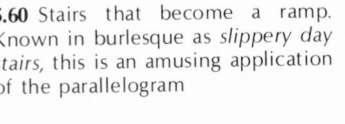

5.60 Stairs that become a ramp. Known in burlesque as *slippery day stairs*, this is an amusing application of the parallelogram

5.61 A scissors lift, hydraulic-powered, for a platform and stairs. The stairs adjust to the changing height of the platform. The Dunes, Las Vegas

of boxed construction. To be rigid enough to withstand violent action a newel must be set securely into a socket in the bottom step and fastened to the stage floor (see "Metal Scene Construction," Chapter 9, and "Metalworking," Chapter 15.)

A staircase is covered on the audience side by a flat which is profiled to fit the stairs. This cover flat conceals the bottom ends of balustrade spindles and the rail to which they are joined.

Certain styles of decoration — Chinese, Gothic, Renaissance, nineteenth-century — are characterized by stair rails supported by tracery wrought in stone, wood, or metal, or cast in metal. These are simulated with cutout plywood or pulpboard. Any desired three-dimensional effect is painted or modeled in plastic materials. Structural strength and stiffness are provided by skeletal metal reinforcement introduced as the design permits. Curved railings have inherent rigidity. See Figure 5.59.

simulated tracery

Stairs by which actors descend from platforms offstage are built in the simplest manner: treads set between carriages by cleated butt joints

escape stairs

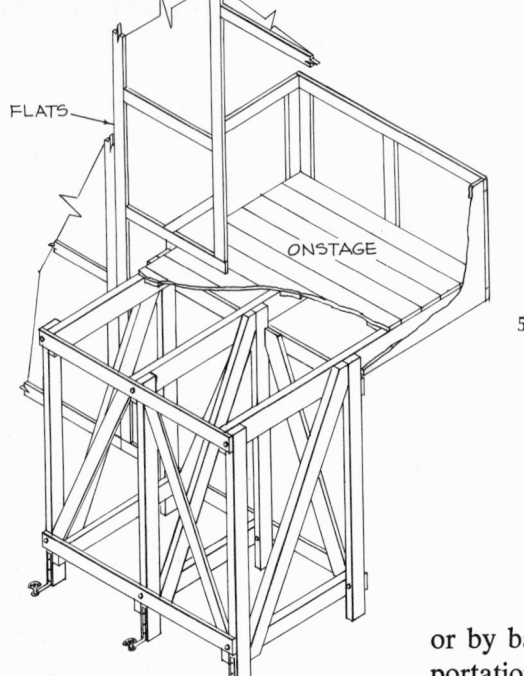

FLATS

ONSTAGE

5.62 A cantilevered balcony

cantilevered structures

or by backflap hinges if the stairs must be folded for storage or transportation. Limited offstage space often dictates the maximum safe pitch, which should never exceed 45° nor have less than 9″ treads. Handrails must be provided.

Balconies, staircases, overhanging cliffs, and other scenic structures which have no visible means of support are actually supported by a structure which is behind the scenery. The mechanical device employed is a simple lever by which a downward force behind the scenery acts on a post fulcrum, also behind the scenery, to balance the weight of the visible structure and the load it carries. The cantilever principle must be employed whenever an acting level overhangs the stage without supporting columns or suspending ropes or cables.

The cantilevered structure is divided into a number of frames, each of which shares the calculated load. Each frame consists of a horizontal beam which extends forward to form the balcony, and backward into the structure behind the scenery, a post on which it rests, and a tension member which acts between the offstage end of the beam and the stage floor. Stage screws or weights are applied to the tension member to balance the load on the onstage end of the beam. A leaning tree may be cantilevered by running a long sloped member from the floor across a post and out into the trunk of the tree.

Scenic Systems

The scenic requirements of multiscene plays may be satisfied by the use of one or another of the many scenic schemes which have been invented through the whole of theatre history. Each embodies a systematic concept; many are so related to particular historical periods that they signify those periods when they are used. It is appropriate to examine several, though not possibly all, of the systems to determine their practical values in modern stage setting.

wing and border

Composed of wings, borders, and drops and sometimes shutters, which are framed pieces propelled in from each side to meet at center

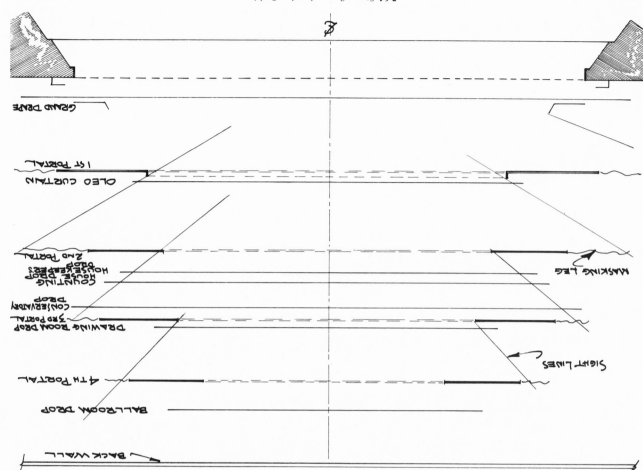

5.64 Stage floor plan for *Fashion*

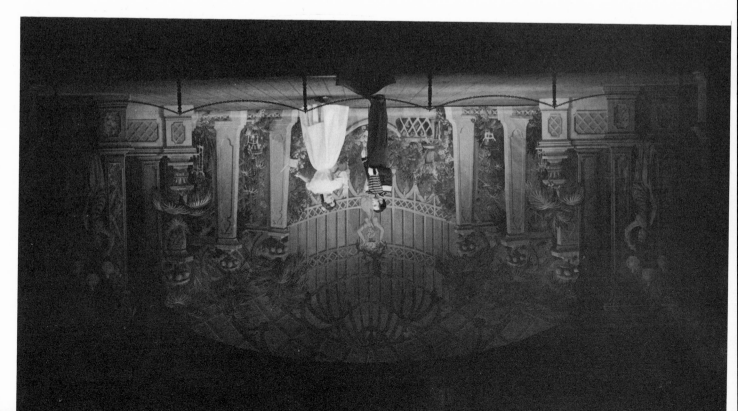

5.63 A wing-and-border setting, *Fashion* by Anna Cora Mowatt, produced in period style by the Yale School of Drama. Robert Darling, designer

5.65 Portal, drops, flown panels, and tracked wagons. *Love in Buffalo,* a musical comedy by Gilbert Leibinger and Peter Gurney, produced by the Yale School of Drama. Richard Casler, designer. Except for a single intermission, all scene changes were integrated with the action of the play and done *a vista.* Neither actors nor stagehands handled scenery or props during the changes

flying and traversing panels

stage to form a wall, this system creates a formal stage setting with many entrances from each side and an upstage entrance through a framed drop or shutter. It permits changes of scene by sliding wings and shutters off- and onstage and flying borders and drops. All architectural and natural detail is painted or profiled on the several pieces. Offstage space requirements are minimal, being limited to the space occupied by the wings that are drawn off to the sides and by any stored properties. Strongly characteristic of seventeenth- through nineteenth-century staging, a wing and border set inevitably bespeaks an antiquarian or archaic style. See Figures 5.63 and 5.64.

This system is a modern adaptation and liberalization of the wing and border system in which flat pieces of any desired shape are flown in and

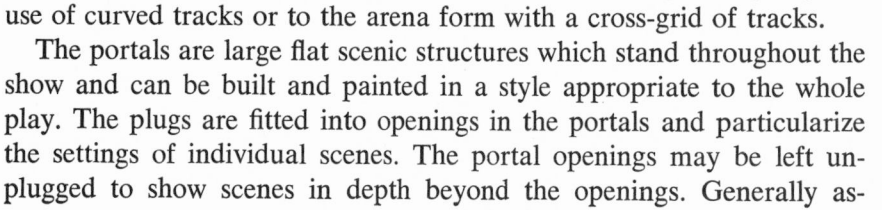

out in any desired position and are moved in from the sides, either sliding in grooves or suspended from overhead tracks, with edges and tops unmasked. The parallelism of the wing and border system is retained but its archaic axial symmetry is disregarded. Freedom of entrance from the sides is kept. This system can be adapted to the open stage by the use of curved tracks or to the arena form with a cross-grid of tracks.

The portals are large flat scenic structures which stand throughout the show and can be built and painted in a style appropriate to the whole play. The plugs are fitted into openings in the portals and particularize the settings of individual scenes. The portal openings may be left unplugged to show scenes in depth beyond the openings. Generally as-

portals and plugs

sociated with proscenium staging, the system is useful as scenic support for performances on open stages, and in skeletalized form may serve in arena staging. See Figures 5.65 and 5.66.

Scenery which is three-dimensional, heavy, difficult of assembly and disassembly, or replete with properties, is generally inimical to flying or to manual shifting and is best moved by the use of casters or wagons. The system to be used depends on the scene plot of the particular show and the size and shape of the stage. The choice between putting the scenery on wagons and on casters is optional according to the particular scene plot and designs. Motion in a straight line is the easiest to achieve and control.

Scenery is set on two wagons (or on one wagon which is at least twice as wide as the acting area) and the wagons are moved across stage parallel to the proscenium to bring one or another set into view. Scenery may be changed on the wagon or on the portion of the wagon which is offstage. The system is effective on stages which have ample wing space.

Scenery is set on a wagon which is stored upstage and rolled into the acting area when other scenery has been cleared. Hung scenery must be flown to permit passage of the wagon.

Wagons or castered scenery, usually of smaller dimension than full-stage sets, are rolled from storage positions surrounding the acting area to onstage positions.

Circular discs, either built into or set on the stage floor, upon which scenery is set, are called categorically revolving stages, or in the vernacular of the stage, *revolves*. Originally used in Japan and later in Germany, they were made big enough to contain two or three full-stage sets, but the limiting size of most American stages has inhibited this practice. Revolves are usually of diameters less than the widths of proscenium

linear-motion systems

traversing (shuttle) motion

up- and downstage motion

radial motion

rotary-motion systems
discs

5.67 Radial wagons and hung scenery. *The Visit* by Friederich Dürrenmatt, produced by the Yale School of Drama. W. Oren Parker, designer. Changes were synchronized with the action and done *a vista*

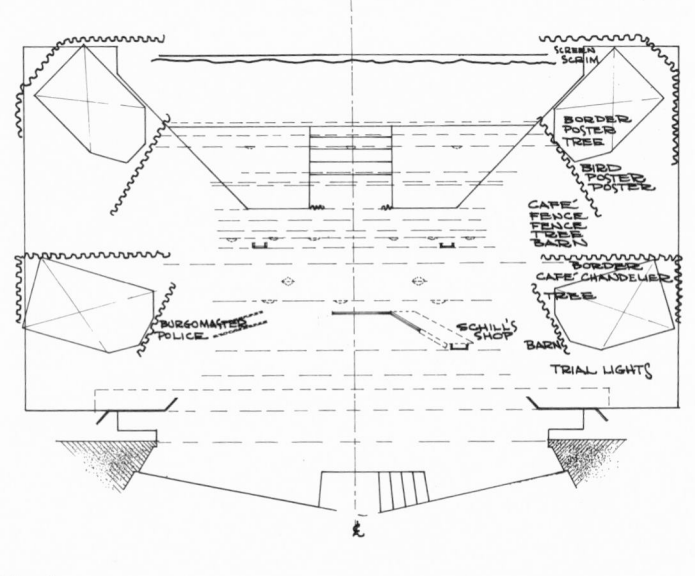

56 Faked perspective. *Beethoven* by Dorothy Bland, produced by the Yale School Drama. Ariel Ballif, designer. All the pieces of scenery except the two door units ere built flat and hung on wires, parallel to the proscenium

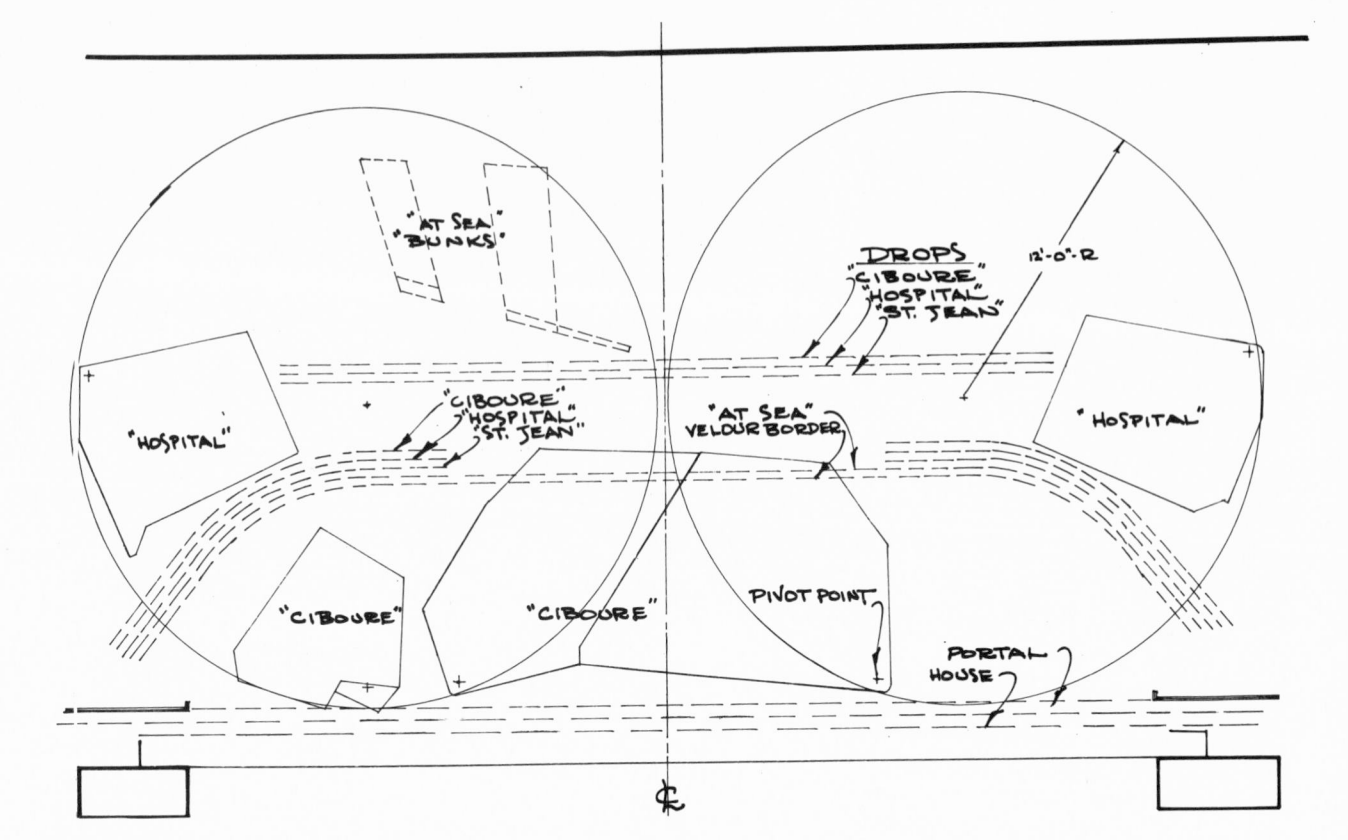

5.68 Stage floor plan for *Gift of Time* by Lael Wertenbaker. Boris Aronson, designer; Garson Kanin, producer. Pivoting pallets on revolving discs with curved and flat drops made rapid changes possible

reciprocating segments

elevating systems

projected scenery

openings and are used singly or in groups, in combination with other scenery, to change parts of sets rather than complete full-stage sets. They are particularly useful for rotating heavy and bulky platforms, staircases, and furniture into the scene.

Rotary motion of less than 360° may be employed in many ways:
- With a very large radius, centered upstage, to change full-stage sets.
- With small radius, pivoted at the side of the stage, to change sidewalls or to rotate platforms into the scene.
- Double-faced flat scenery pivoted about fixed centers in optional locations.
- Double-faced flat scenery edge-pivoted, singly or in groups, to be operated in the manner of vertical Venetian blinds.

Scenery may, obviously, be conveyed to the acting area by elevating it from below stage. Highly developed in Europe, this system occurs infrequently in the United States — at the Metropolitan Opera, Radio City Music Hall, the John F. Kennedy Center, Birmingham Southern College, University of Hawaii — because of the high cost of below-stage building construction and elaborate mechanical installations. Special elevators are sometimes used to raise individual pieces of scenery or properties; this does not constitute a system.

Ever since the development of shadow plays and the discovery of the laws governing the creation of images with light, projection has been looked upon, hopefully, as a possible quick, easy, and inexpensive substitute for built and painted scenery. Though scenic and lighting effects

5.69 Scene 7 of *The Emperor Jones* by Eugene O'Neill. Donald Oenslager, designer. Produced by the Yale School of Drama in November, 1931. Lens projections from the light bridge onto a cloth cyclorama faced by a scrim hung in folds

of many kinds have been and are possible by these means, the creation of entire settings by nothing but light projection on projection surfaces has yet to be achieved. The reasons are simple. In the realistic style, the plot calls for objects and architecture which actors can use: chairs which must be sat upon; doors which must be opened, walked through, and closed with a bang — effects not realizable in light alone. Even in nonrealistic styles, nonrepresentative objects germane to the action must be solid, opaque, and tangible. See Figures 5.69–5.72.

The strictly scenic function is only one of a multitude which belong to projection. Projection apparatus is handled by the electrical department. The technique of producing and using projections is part of stage lighting. Projections of any sort in the theatre demand the skillful use of light on the whole scene, not merely on the area of projection. Only

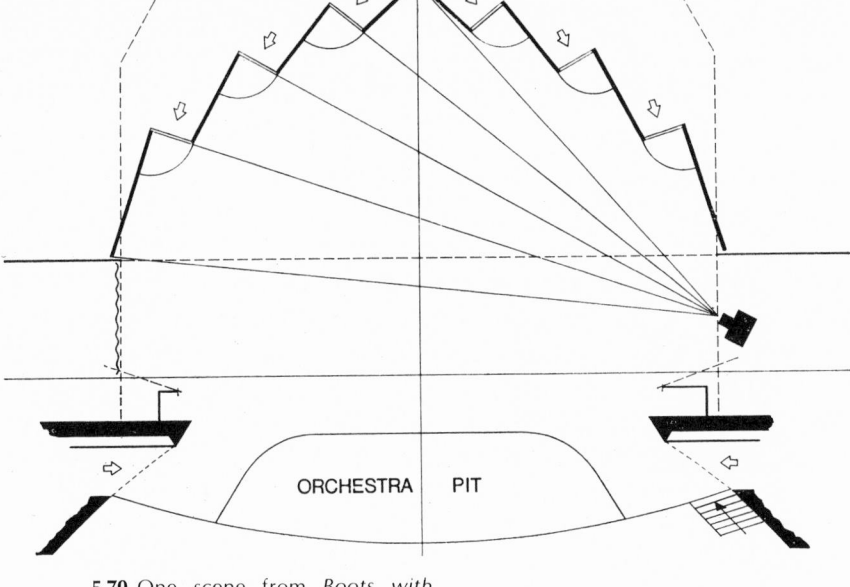

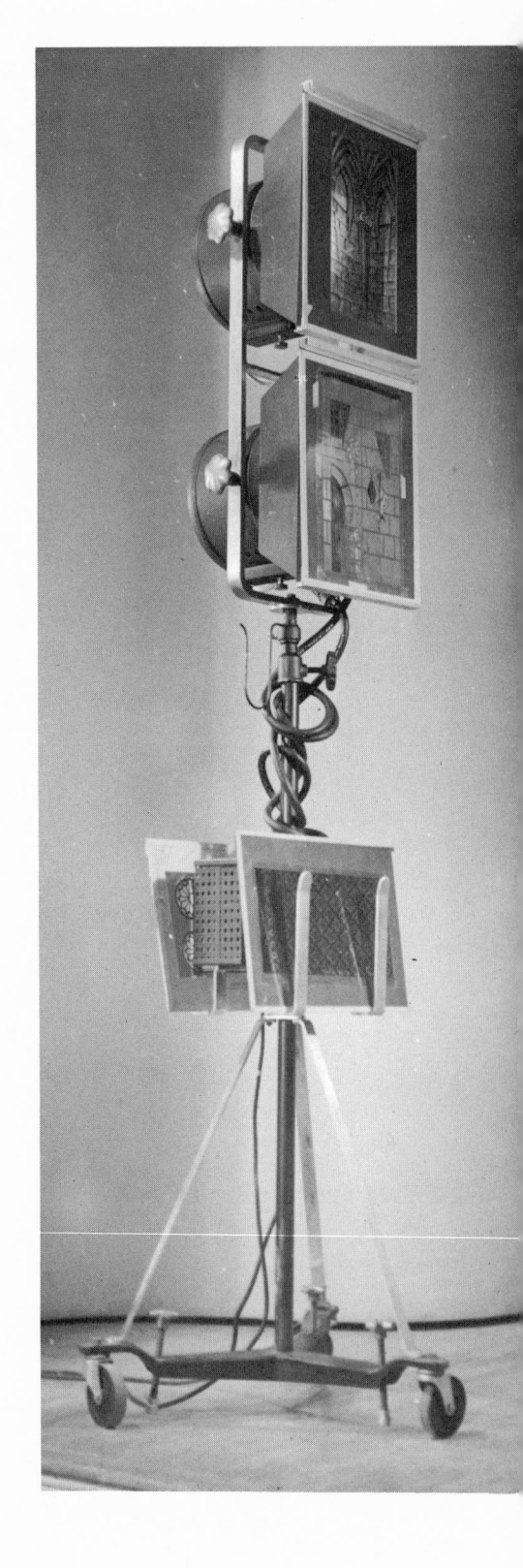

5.70 One scene from *Boots with Strawberry Jam,* a musical biography of G. B. Shaw, produced at the Nottingham Playhouse and designed by Patrick Robertson with slides by Allan Hurst. Images from lens projectors high over left and right first entrances are projected onto flats on the opposite sides. The images are also reflected toward the audience from Mirralite-surfaced flats which stand at right angles to the surfaces which receive the projected images. Scenes are changed by dissolving between projectors

ORCHESTRA   PIT

5.71 A scene from Verdi's *Falstaff* produced by the Hartt College of Music. Elemer Nagy, designer. The columns, stairs, balcony, and frieze are translucent. Scenes are changed and fanciful effects are created by dissolving between only two circuits of rear projectors. A stand carrying a projector (left, on facing page) from each circuit is placed behind each wall panel. Slides are changed manually on each projector when it has been dimmed out

5.72 The slides for *Boots with Strawberry Jam* were made by photographing models of the intended scene from the position, and in the direction, which the actual projector would have, determined by precise scalar reduction

the surfaces on which projections are made visible, and in some cases the projection slides, are the concern of the scenic department.

Since projection by its very nature imposes limitations on scenery, the projection table here presented includes more types of projection than strictly scenic ones. Moreover, in many cases the same projection will be used for scenic and other purposes as well.

TABLE 5.2. PROJECTED SCENIC EFFECTS

Desired Effect	Instrument	Location	Screen or Equivalent	Movement
shadows cast on walls or floors by offstage objects; or other scenery (leaves in moonlight, a gibbet in the setting sun)	slide projector; for large projections where sharp focus not essential, a spotlight and a prop silhouette	first pipe, tower, or stand offstage, shining through door or window if interior set is used	stage floor, walls, or steps; projection most effective when on a light surface, easily seen by the audience	shadow may be moved by moving silhouette; projected slide can seldom be moved
moving light patterns (rippling waves, conflagration, aurora borealis, clouds)	effect machine (spot with moving mica slide, driving mechanism, objective lens)	same as for shadows; water-ripple effect machine sometimes masked by a set piece	water ripple used on painted backdrop (bay, lake, river); sky effects on cyclorama; conflagration on objects presumed to burn, or on walls, etc., if reflection of flames requisite	limited to movement of the mica slide or film; light direction does not change, though various instruments may be faded in or out a various times
moving letter sign (as on Allied Chemical Bldg., New York City)	film of subject in white letters running horizontally through effect head	upstage, completely masked by shadow box	translucent fabric covered by a perforated mask (the perforations make the letters appear to be composed of dots of light)	. . .
outdoor scenic backgrounds in bright daylight	several high-intensity slide projectors	first or second pipe; on flat behind scenery	cyclorama	slide backgrounds are static; extreme contrast impossible if scene is brightly lighted; bounce light brightens dark areas
outdoor backgrounds in dull light or night	Linnebach projector	upstage of cyclorama on floor or tower	cyclorama or Translux sheet	static
constellations, moving moon, twinkling stars	spotlight of appropriate color and beam spread; special star projector or lights built into drop, cyclorama, or dome	bridge or behind cyclorama; bridge from which cyclorama is lighted	cyclorama or dome	direction of spolight beam may be changed; stars twinkle through intensity changes
moving scenery (seen through window of train or airplane), moving background, background with moving figures	motion-picture projector (in fireproof booth unless safety film is used); 16 mm. projector satisfactory for small image or low intensity	upstage (rear projection)	glass curtain or Translux sheet	motion-picture projector may be moved as occasion demands; movement difficult to achieve without image oscillation
projection used as projection	motion-picture or slide projector	projection booth, rear of balcony	sound or silent; screen lowered from flies where and when necessary	movement possible only within the picture
moving foreground	motion-picture projector	projection booth	scrim, set downstage	movement possible only within the picture
translucent projection (ghost, ectoplasm, transparent moving figure)	motion-picture and slide projectors	projection booth	upstage scrim, set in interior sets, or in front of dark background for outdoor sets	projector may be swiveled; motion-picture and slide projectors faded in alternately make variable pauses possible and keep the pace of the scene from being machine-set

combinations of systems   Familiarity with these systems in their pure forms is the take-off point for designers who may combine features of various systems to create appropriate and effective scenic investitures for particular plays.

The technical aspects of these systems are set forth in Chapters 11 and 12, and in the Appendix.

Variants

Some plays require that scenery break or change its form during the action; it is also obviously necessary that the scenery be restored to its opening-curtain condition prior to each performance and that the changes take place under controlled and safe conditions. *The Flying Dutchman, Gold Eagle Guy, The Skin of Our Teeth,* and *The Knights of the Round Table, God Bless,* and sometimes the prologue of *The Tempest* contain examples of these requirements. All such scenery is achieved by carefully tested ingenious adaptations of standard types of joints and rigging devices.

breakaway scenery

A breakaway door panel is used when one must be broken in by raiding police every night of a show's run. The panel is fitted to the door, removed, cut along logical break lines and fastened together on the opposite side with thin muslin dutchmen or adhesive tape. The panel is repaired and retouched with paint between performances.

A breakaway window is one which must be broken realistically. It is obviously hazardous to break panes of real glass. Therefore the glass is simulated by a cast sheet of clear synthetic resin which breaks into full-edged pieces and produces no sharp slivers. It is usually possible to fool the audience without real glass if the sash of the window is built to break. The window sash is built, and then cut along jagged break lines, set in, and fastened with a weak adhesive. A stone thrown against the muntins, from offstage, knocks the cut portion of the sash out of the window, leaving a jagged break.

Breakaway effects within the acting area may be operated by invisible fishline or wire. Large items of breakaway scenery are built in separate parts, which are joined with large loose-pin hinges at the breakpoints. The joints are connected by loosely fastened dutchmen. Cords are attached to the hinge pins and pulled to create the effect. Heavy pieces which must fall to the stage are rigged on wire and controlled by flymen. Differential counterweights, pulleys, levers, and hydraulic checks may be used to cause a fast initial movement, as of falling ceiling beams or wall sections, to be slowed to a safe impact velocity. The fast initial movement is what startles and impresses the audience. The velocity of a falling object may be reduced by letting it fall through a series of slats, each of which breaks noisily in turn. All breakaway effects require thorough testing.

built-in-place scenery

In general, building scenery on the stage is uneconomical for two reasons: the stage is seldom equipped with all the machines, tools, and supplies requisite to efficient work, and while the scenery is being built, the stage cannot be used for either of its primary purposes, rehearsal and performance. However, scenery is sometimes designed which may, under the prevailing circumstances, be better built initially on the stage than built and assembled in the shop, dismantled, transported to the stage, and assembled.

Building in place permits permanent rather than temporary fastening of joints and use of the stage structure for foundation and bracing support; it obviates making scenery which is capable of being dismantled and transported without damage.

Irregular platforms and false floors are the scenic components most frequently built on the stage because of the stability afforded by fastening to the stage structure and the economies effected by the simplified assembly.

The technical analysis of built-in-place scenery is simplified since no provisions must be made for transportation, storage onstage, assembly, and dismantling.

psychedelia and multimedia

The first term may be descriptive of a fad which will expire before this book loses its usefulness; the second is likely to live on. The easy availability of projection apparatus, slides, films, fluorescent paints and fabrics, and the ingenuity of designers and producers of light entertainment have resulted in exuberant presentations that are certainly stimulating, possibly exciting, and sometimes artistic. The presence of motion pictures, slide projection, video tape recording, closed-circuit television, multichannel audio-tape, and electronic music points toward the incorporation of these elements into live productions ranging from musical revue to serious drama and indicates technical areas in which theatre technicians must develop expertness.

band shell

A concert set or band shell is essential for the performance of music in a theatre. Without it, much of the music is dissipated in the fly loft and the wings. Essentially it is a box set: splayed wings, a back wall, and a ceiling positioned to reflect sound to the audience. It has the added requirement of making it possible for the musician to hear his own instrument and those about him.

The shape of the enclosure and the material of which it is made are critical. The shape should be specified by the engineer who planned the acoustics of the theatre.

Cuts for lights and entrances from the wings can be accommodated within the acoustical requirements. The whole set can be rigged to fly. The wings and back wall can roll.

The band shell must have a hard surface. Transite, plaster, heavy-gauge sheet iron, and plywood have been used. Pliable materials are useless, which rules out plastic panels.

Band shells vary tremendously in cost from elaborate machine-operated metal enclosures to simple plywood structures made in the scene shop, than which there are none better. A satisfactory surface material is ⅜″ or ⅝″ plywood, but to maintain the requisite rigidity, the ⅜″ requires more bracing with 1″ × 2″, 1″ × 3″, or 1″ × 4″ on edge than the ⅝″. It is essential that bracing be asymmetrical so that the unbraced areas will vary in shape and size and will therefore resonate at different frequencies.

Use of Materials Other Than Wood

metal

Modern scenery often needs the strength and rigidity that metals possess. Metalworking equipment is available and relatively inexpensive. Metalworking skills are easily learned. Many kinds and shapes of metals

5.73 A sketch by James Newton for a production of *Othello*. Scenery like this is best accomplished in metal

5.74 The model of the setting for *Peer Gynt* designed by John Conklin for the Yale School of Drama production. A dish-shaped, welded web of steel pipe about 30′ in diameter is hung on edge behind bleachers set on a full-stage platform. Ragged projection surfaces of painted burlap are stretched on the pipe web

5.75 A mixture of wood and steel in the structure of a ceiling which contains a skylight with curved tracery. View, from above, of the ceiling being built on the shop floor

5.76 The same ceiling viewed from below when in place on the set. The tracery is painted on sheets of fiber glass which are attached to the wood and steel framing members shown in Figure 5.75. The bent-wire tracery at the right is part of a room divider in the set

5.77 Setting for *The Brig* by Kenneth H. Brown, produced at the University of Delaware. Brooks MacNamara, designer. Metal is obviously the only material for this kind of scenery

are suitable to theatrical uses. Because of its unique properties, metal may be thought of as a substitute for wood in some instances and as a supplement in others. Given knowledge, skill, tools, and machines, one can work metal as easily as wood. Greater cost may be compensated by greater durability, dependability, precise sizing and fastening, predictable load capacities, and greater reuse without deterioration. See Figures 5.73–5.79.

The fiber glass process for making stage scenery and properties has many advantages over other methods of construction. It does, however, have limitations. The principal difficulty is unfamiliarity on the part of the user. When one becomes familiar with the process, which does not take long, he may find it extremely useful.

The process should be called **fiber glass and resin** rather than the commonly used fiber glass. Another name is **glass-reinforced plastics** (GRP). The process involves placing woven glass cloth over a form and coating it with a liquid resin which hardens into a rigid mass. The

fiber glass and resin scenery

5.79 Telespar, another metal framing system

5.78 Unistrut used to frame a platform

hardening is produced by mixing small amounts of a chemical called the hardener with the resin before it is applied to the glass cloth. The hardened fiber glass can be strengthened after removal from the form by the addition of more layers of fiber glass and resin.

The strength of the material makes it ideal for weight-bearing structures, and its lightness makes it useful for building scenery which must be moved. Its setting speed is advantageous as a time-saver when a number of identical objects are to be made. A fiber glass cast can be removed from the mold about an hour after the resin has been applied.

Many types of two-dimensional scenery lend themselves to construction in fiber glass and resin. The fact that this material is strong and lightweight, and is easily cut with a saber saw or compound tin shears makes it ideal for use in set pieces, ground rows, false prosceniums, and other types of profile pieces. It can be formed into thin sheets which, when cut into strips or other shapes and reassembled into skeletal shapes, make excellent impressionistic scenic backgrounds. Silhouette units can be hung on invisible fishline in front of a solid curtain or cyclorama.

Almost any three-dimensional scenic element can be constructed better in fiber glass and resin than by the traditional construction methods such as Celastic, papier-mâché, or burlap. It is best used for

5.80 A Virginia rail fence made in glass-reinforced plastic (fiber glass)

5.81 A fiber glass rock

5.82 This log cabin interior, with logs and chimney in fiber glass, has been in use out of doors for several years

durable lightweight trees, stumps, rocks, log cabins, columns, and the like. The structural advantages of fiber glass and resin construction are most evident when it is used to build weight-bearing structures such as platforms or simulated rock mounds. A platform can be constructed entirely of fiber glass and resin without the use of any framing or supporting materials, and it will weigh one-third to one-half as much as a similar platform constructed by traditional methods. The fiber glass and resin process is excellent for the construction of most decorative elements: column capitals, cornices, moldings, details on period mantels, door and fireplace pediments, and so on. See Figures 5.80–5.83.

Extreme durability and ease of handling make fiber glass and resin ideal for touring scenery. It is practically indestructible, and with a thin coat of transparent resin over the finished paint it is scuff-proof.

For outdoor theatres fiber glass and resin reduces scenery costs drastically. The visual scale in outdoor theatres dictates that three-dimensional detail be built rather than painted to preserve plasticity. This kind of scenery is unaffected by rain, prolonged dampness, hail, sun, or snow; upkeep due to weather damage is eliminated.

5.83 Brick garden walls simulated in fiber glass. The wall to the left forms the stage right proscenium; the one at the right is a rolling unit

5.84 Properties for the monument works seen in *Look Homeward Angel* by Ketti Frings. Designed and executed by Elmer Tangerman for the Port Washington (N.Y.) Players' production

plastic foams

Designers and technicians seeking substitutes for heavy, fragile, expensive, and scarce ornamentation such as balustrades, picture frames, statues, and wall sconces find rigid plastic foams RPF and RUF excellent materials from which such set decorations may be formed. These plastic foams are lightweight, strong, and low in cost, and can be shaped easily. The problems incurred in simulating three-dimensional detail in paint may be eliminated by replacing painted form and texture with actual three-dimensional pieces. Highly dimensional and heavily textured brick, masonry, stone, and stucco can be simulated easily in RPF textured with solvents. RPF may be used by itself or applied to other scenic units. A great variety of stone textures may be simulated with RPF depending on the treatment given the surface. Spattering and lining with a solvent will create natural brick or stone surfaces and dry-brushing with a solvent in a semicircular pattern will produce a stucco effect.

As actual wooden or plaster moldings, cornices, headers, friezes, and railings become more expensive and less available, substitute materials are replacing them. Rather than limiting selections to what is available from commercial molders, technicians may shape plastic foam precisely to designer's specifications.

Many objects that otherwise must be rented, borrowed, or made from papier-mâché, plaster of Paris, or Celastic may be constructed in rigid plastic foams. In preference to other design materials, plastic foams do not require negative molds, layer buildups, or extended drying times. If another material, such as papier-mâché or Celastic, is preferred for certain applications, RPF or RUF may be used as molds or cores. RPF may not be used with Celastic since it is reactive to acetone and methyl ethyl ketone (MEK); however, solvent-resistant RUF may be used without damage.

By combining these plastic foams with wood or metal, chandeliers may be constructed much quicker than if papier-mâché or Celastic are used. Damage-resistant vases and figurines may be carved from RPF in a very short time and at low cost. Plastic foams may be finished in any desired texture.

Constructing substitutes for large heavy objects in lightweight plastic foam facilitates scene changes. Plastic foam may replace lumber, plywood, Masonite, or the relatively expensive balsa wood as thickness. It may be bent, shaped, attached, and trimmed with greater ease than denser materials.

Plastic foam has one critical weakness: lack of compressive strength. This renders it subject to surface damage by impact, which must be prevented by protective coatings.

Realistic or abstract detail and nature forms and properties which have intricate surface modeling and would require many hours to fabricate in wood can be made in thermoplastic sheet, rod, or tube. Door and window casings, cornices, mantels, moldings, balusters, newel posts, columns, pilasters, beams, corbels, wall panels, shingling, bricks, stonework, textured walls, outline forms such as chandeliers, and wrought-iron work may all be simulated in thermoplastics. The saving in time and money is greatest if numerous duplicates of the original image are needed.

thermoplastics

5.85 A gate made of polyvinyl chloride (PVC), with welded joints

5.86 Tree branches heat-molded by hand in polyethylene sheets

6 Materials

The construction of scenery is a manufacturing process: the conversion of raw materials into finished products for a specific use. The so-called raw materials for scenery, however, have already been partially fabricated to a usable condition — rough timber into lumber, iron into hardware — before being delivered to the scene shop. They must be further fabricated to convert them into scenery.

The scene designer and scene technician, who guide this manufacturing process, must therefore have a thorough knowledge of the materials used in scene construction, their properties, and their mercantile facts, such as costs, sizes, package quantities, and sources. This chapter concerns the uses and properties of materials and systems for procurement and issue. Storage of materials is treated in Chapter 7.

sources of information

Manufacturers and dealers in stage supplies issue catalogs which are revised frequently and are available upon request or for a nominal price. These catalogs, listed in the bibliography, contain detailed descriptions of materials, including kind, size, mechanical properties, purchase quantities, prices, and often instructions and precautions regarding use.

Because of the existence of these sources, much information, particularly concerning items whose prices or characteristics vary from year to year, is not included in this book. The information contained here is basic to scenecraft and most useful to the scene technician in planning scenery sizes, dimensions, and load capacities, and in weighing the relative properties of competing materials.

Lumber

required characteristics

Wood is the primary material with which scenery is framed. For scene construction wood must be:

• Easily worked, that is, capable of being sawed, split, chiseled, planed, and drilled without rapidly dulling the cutting edges of tools, and of taking nails and screws without the need of drilling except near ends of pieces. The wood must have even texture and straight grain and be free from growth imperfections. Since it is handled frequently in the play production process it must not be splintery.

• Of medium weight consistent with the requirements of size for strength and stiffness, making scenery easy to handle, fly, and transport.

• Strong and stiff enough to resist the expected stresses from handling, hanging, flying, transportation, and imposed loads. Kinds and sizes must be known to be available when the technician plans the scenic structures to meet design requirements and load specifications. In most cases softwoods satisfy these requirements. If they do not, the technician is well advised to seek additional strength and stiffness in metal reinforcement rather than in hardwoods.

• Straight and free from the tendency to warp or twist, since pieces of scenery must be fitted together to form units frequently and dependably. Kinds of lumber which have this tendency must be avoided. *Seasoned* (dried) lumber has less of this tendency than *green* (wet) lumber, but lumber which has been badly stacked for seasoning can be permanently warped or twisted and therefore not usable.

• Inexpensive, since lumber is the largest single item in the bill of materials for scenery. Because scenery is essentially temporary, the lowest-priced materials, consistent with needed quality, are demanded. The lowest-priced suitable lumber should be used. Kinds will differ in different localities.

• Rendered fire-retardant. It is commonly a legal requirement that wood which is used in scenery on a stage which has a fire curtain or other devices to protect the audience may be rendered flame-retardant by brushed-on flameproofing solutions. Wood used in audience areas or wood used in the structure of the stage must be rendered permanently fire-retardant by an approved pressure process.

• Rendered rotproof if the climate warrants it. In a few instances, chiefly in the scene painting shop and in the storage of scenery in humid climates, replacement of paint frame parts and the loss of scenery may be avoided by the use of fungicides. Temporary applications of water-soluble fungicides or permanent introduction of fungicides by a pressure method are both possible.

Native American woods which satisfy these requirements, in descending order of desirability for scenery (though possibly not of price, which varies with location), are: northern (eastern) white pine, Idaho white pine, western white pine, ponderosa pine, western red cedar, whitewood, redwood. Stronger and stiffer than these and hence useful in weight-bearing structures are Douglas fir and southern pine (longleaf, shortleaf, and loblolly). Their properties are tabulated in Table 6.1.

satisfactory woods

TABLE 6.1. *WOOD FOR THEATRICAL USES*

E = modulus of elasticity[a] e_1 = coefficient for stiffness[b]

Wood	Origin	Appearance	Characteristics
white pine northern (or eastern)	Me. to Ga., Minn., Mich., Wis., Canada	creamy white to light brown	light, soft, not strong
western	Rocky Mt. region, Calif., Ore.	white to brown	somewhat inferior, light, soft, not strong, flexible
Idaho	Idaho, Mont., e. Wash.	creamy white to light brown	light, soft, not strong
yellow pine ponderosa	Ariz., Calif., N. Mex., Colo., Ore., Wash.	light brown to dark yellow	fairly light, not strong
southern longleaf	Atlantic & Gulf states	even dark reddish yellow to reddish brown	tougher, stiffer, heavier than white pine
shortleaf	s.e. N.Y. to Fla., La., Ark., Okla., Mo., e. Tex.	even dark reddish yellow to reddish brown	tougher, stiffer, heavier than white pine
loblolly	Md., Atlantic & Gulf states to e. Tex.	even dark reddish yellow to reddish brown	tougher, stiffer, heavier than white pine
Douglas fir	Pacific coast, w. slope of Rockies	light yellow to red	strongest for its weight of woods listed; tough
redwood	Calif. coast	red	light, soft, fairly strong, brittle; absorbs water
western red cedar	Wash., Ore., Idaho, Mont., Pacific coast to Alaska	dull brown	light, soft, not strong
whitewood (tulip or wh. poplar)[c]	all states e. of Miss. R. and s. of Great Lakes	white tinted green or yellow	very soft, easily bent, light, somewhat rough surface

TABLE 6.1. *WOOD FOR THEATRICAL USES* (*continued*)

Wood	DRY WEIGHT (lbs/ft³)	DRY WEIGHT (lbs/1,000 bd/ft)	E (1,000 psi)	e_1
white pine northern (or eastern)	24.0	2,200	1,240	96
western	27.0	2,330	1,520	117
Idaho	24.0	2,200	1,240	96
yellow pine ponderosa	29.4	2,300	1,260	98
southern longleaf	40.3	3,500	1,990	153
shortleaf	34.6	3,000	1,760	135
loblolly	35.2	3,200	1,800	137
Douglas fir	29.0 to 33.0	2,500–2,900	1,600	128
redwood	26.2	2,100	1,340	107
western red cedar	23.7	1,900	1,120	87
whitewood (tulip or wh. poplar)[c]	29.0	2,400	[d]	[d]

[a] Values for seasoned lumber, from U.S. Department of Agriculture, *The Wood Handbook* (1955), Table 12, pp. 12 ff.

[b] E/12,960, as stated in *Architects and Builders Handbook*, F. E. Kidder and T. Nolan, eds. (17th ed., New York, 1921), p. 665.

[c] Actually the sapwood of yellow poplar.

[d] Not available.

...rain	Resin	Workability	Stage Uses
...e, straight, even, free from ...ots	very little	excellent; takes a high polish; will not splinter	framing, weight bearing, battens
...e, straight, fairly free from ...ots	little	excellent; almost as good as northern	framing, weight bearing, battens, platform flooring, carving, props
...e, straight, even, free from ...ots	very little	excellent; takes a high polish; will not splinter	framing, weight bearing, battens
...e, even, often twisted	some	good	framing, flooring, weight bearing, temporary specials, props
...e, even	much	fair; resin gums tools	framing, flooring, weight bearing, temporary specials
...e, even	much	fair; resin gums tools	framing, flooring, weight bearing, temporary specials
...otty	much	fair; resin gums tools	framing, flooring, weight bearing, temporary specials
...aightest listed, clear, very pro-...unced	very little	fair; splinters easily	battens, weight bearing, framing
...e, even, usually straight, some-...es curly, free from knots	little	good; splits easily; polishes well; holds paint well	props
...arse, straight, even, free from ...ots	little	very good; some varieties very soft	trim, props, framing
...e, even, straight	little	most easily worked of woods listed; takes paint and stain very well	moldings, carved pieces, props

Lumber is grown, not made. The lumber producers cut lumber from logs; they cannot improve upon the natural condition of the wood beyond certain limits. After milling, they sort the cut lumber into grades, and then can improve or damage the wood by careful or careless stacking, drying, and handling.

Only a small amount of lumber can be selected and graded A (perfect). Lumber of this quality is so scarce that for practical purposes Grade A is hypothetical. The highest grade supplied in commercial quantities is known as Grade B and Better, the Better including occasional pieces of Grade A. Grade B and Better is, however, so expensive as to render it prohibitive for any but the finest construction, and hence many lumber dealers stock as their best grade of lumber Grade C Select. This is a satisfactory grade for all general scene construction, and is standard for framing lumber in New York City. Certain scene shops may find it too expensive and try to use Grade D Select or even No. 1 Common.

In any of the grades of lumber below Grade B and Better, there is allowance in the specification of the grade for some imperfections. This is understandable and must be countenanced if the buyer is unwilling to purchase a more expensive and more exactly specified grade. The

quality grades

astute carpenter can use lumber of D Select or No. 1 Common by allotting the better pieces to work requiring them and the poorer pieces to less exacting work.

dimensions

The *board foot* (12″ × 12″ × 1″) is the unit of lumber measurement used to calculate prices. Prices are quoted per thousand board feet. Lumber less than 1″ thick is sold by the square foot; molding, dowel, and lattice by the linear foot.

The actual thickness and width of standard dressed lumber is from $\frac{1}{16}$″ to $\frac{3}{4}$″ less than the nominal dimensions. Dressed dimensions may be more than these minima and must be checked before cutting lengths are calculated. Lumber dressed to other than these dimensions is special and costs considerably more than standard dressed lumber. Standard lengths of lumber used in scenic construction are 10′, 12′, 14′, and 16′. Longer pieces are special and cost more than standard lengths. Douglas fir is easily obtainable in lengths greater than 16′, and structural timbers of various woods may be obtainable over 16′.

sizes and shapes

TABLE 6.2. *STANDARD THICKNESSES AND WIDTHS OF LUMBER* (in inches)

THICKNESS		WIDTH			
Nominal	Dressed Minimum	Nominal	Dressed Minimum	Nominal	Dressed Minimum
$\frac{3}{8}$	$\frac{5}{16}$	2	$1\frac{5}{8}$	9	$8\frac{1}{4}$
$\frac{1}{2}$	$\frac{7}{16}$	3	$2\frac{5}{8}$	10	$9\frac{1}{4}$
$\frac{3}{4}$	$\frac{11}{16}$	4	$3\frac{1}{2}$	11	$10\frac{1}{4}$
1	$\frac{25}{32}$	5	$4\frac{1}{2}$	12	$11\frac{1}{4}$
$1\frac{1}{4}$	$1\frac{1}{16}$	6	$5\frac{1}{2}$		
$1\frac{1}{2}$	$1\frac{5}{16}$	7	$6\frac{1}{2}$		
2	$1\frac{5}{8}$	8	$7\frac{1}{4}$		

Source: U.S. Department of Agriculture, *The Wood Handbook* (1955), Table 19, pp. 115 ff.

The following sizes of lumber are most used in scene construction and may well be carried in inventory:

1″ × 2″ for small framing members and braces.

1″ × 3″ for most framing members.

1″ × 4″ for battens, ceiling members, and parallel framing members.

1″ × 6″, 8″, 10″, 12″ for step risers, treads, door frames, window arches, etc.

$1\frac{1}{4}$″ × 3″ for framing platforms and for road or long-run scenery.

2″ × 4″, 6″, 8″ for large weight-bearing structures.

Other sizes are ordered as needed for special structures.

molding

Molding is made in a wide variety of stock shapes and sizes. Special moldings can be cut in almost any cross section but the cost will include the cost of a special shaper blade.

architectural ornament

Period-style architectural ornament, originally carved and more recently pressed in wood, is available from only a few manufacturers. One scenic studio and a few specialty companies reproduce salvaged ornaments, period moldings, and the like, in thermoplastics.

Dowels are usually made of maple or birch. Standard diameters are ⅛″, ¼″, ⁵⁄₁₆″, ⅜″, ⁷⁄₁₆″, ½″, ⁹⁄₁₆″, and ¾″. Dealers carry on hand or can procure round stock in 1½″, 2″, and 3″ diameters for use as drapery rods.

Board Materials

Board materials are rigid or semirigid materials which have considerable area and little thickness. They are made by laminating and gluing (usually with synthetic resins) layers of wood which have been peeled from logs; compressing wood pulp or paper pulp; mixing wood chips, sawdust, or other chopped fibers with synthetic resins and rolling the mixture into sheets; binding thin layers of wood between outer layers of kraft paper; binding corrugated paper between outer layers of kraft paper; and foaming polyethylene or polyurethane into sheets. Board materials vary greatly in strength, stiffness, workability, uses, effectiveness, and cost.

In architecture board materials are used for wall, door, and cabinet panels; in scenery they are used for: rigid thin edges on irregular flat scenery (profiles); rigid but lightweight surfaces; cutout filigree in simulation of cast or wrought metal; surfaces curved in one plane; surfaces which must bear loads and withstand blows or other rough treatment; and surfaces which must not vibrate when forces are applied to the scenery (for example, when doors are slammed or the action is violent).

Plywood has a multitude of scenic uses. Its lamination, with the grain of contiguous layers crossing at right angles and bonded by high-strength resins, gives it distinctive properties:

plywood

- Strength slightly less than that of an equal thickness of the same kind of wood alone.

properties

- Stiffness, when the predominant grain (two layers of 3-ply, three layers of 5-ply) is in the direction of the span, slightly less than that of wood of the same thickness.

- Flexibility, when the predominant grain is parallel to the axis of curvature, the bendability being, roughly, inversely proportional to the thickness of the plywood.

- Penetrability by nails without splitting.

Flooring. Plywood ¾″ and 1″ thick has largely replaced tongue-and-groove lumber and is standard for flooring platforms and false floors. The commonest stock size, 4′ × 8′, is a useful module which may be divided into sub-modules of 2′ or 1′ 4″ for the spacing of supporting frames, beams, or trusses.

uses

Structural framing. Frames made of ¾″ plywood, lofted (marked full-size) and cut into shapes corresponding to the sectional patterns of irregular three-dimensional scenery, with interior portions cut out to minimize weight, are more efficient than frames fabricated of lumber for making the inside structure for such scenery, whether it is false or practical.

Joining plates. Plywood ¼″ thick is the usual joining plate used in the construction of flat scenery. Beyond the standard corner blocks and keystones, special shapes may be cut to fit any meeting of two or more framing members.

Cornerblocks and **keystones.** Cornerblocks are right isosceles triangles of 3-ply plywood, used to brace frame corners. They may be made of any kind of plywood, and in many shops are sawed out of scrap and salvaged material. In standard practice in America, they are of ⁷⁄₁₆″ or ¼″ stock, have 9″ or 10″ legs, and all edges on one side are beveled.

Keystones (the name indicates the shape), also made of plywood, are used to join toggle bars and stiles. Common keystone dimensions are: length, 8″; width at wide end, 4″; width at narrow end, 2⅔″. When 1″ × 2″ toggles are used, it is well to use keystones whose narrow ends are no wider than the toggles. Beveled edges are desirable.

Straps or half keystones, about 2″ × 8″ or smaller, are sometimes used to join braces to stiles and rails.

Curved surfaces. Plywood ³⁄₁₆″ or less thick is standard for forming simple curved surfaces (curvature in only one plane) such as cylinders, columns, arch thicknesses, and ceiling coves. It will not, however, take the shape of a compound curve like a sphere unless placed under heat and great pressure between male and female molds.

Douglas fir plywood is the kind most used in scene construction. There are two types: *exterior,* which is bonded by hot-pressing with phenol resin adhesive and is not affected by moisture; and *interior,* which is bonded with soybean glue or extended phenol resin, and which will separate if thoroughly wet. Conditions of use determine the type to be selected. It is graded from A–A (clear veneer on both sides) down to D–D (imperfections on both sides).

Other western softwoods, such as ponderosa and sugar-pine plywoods,

---

TABLE 6.3. SIZES OF PLYWOOD (in inches)

Width	Lengths
24	48, 60, 72, 84, 96
30	48, 60, 72, 84, 96
36	48, 60, 72, 84, 96
48	72, 84, 96, 120

Useful thicknesses: ³⁄₃₂, ⅛, ³⁄₁₆, ¼, ⅜, ½, ⅝, ¾, 1, and 1¼.

kinds, types, grades

TABLE 6.4. THE MOST USEFUL COMPOSITION BOARDS

Composition	Appearance	Characteristics	Moisture Absorption
softboards pressed cane fibers	rough; cream or light gray color; may have one smooth, sized surface	weak; easily bent, broken; will not stand abrasion	high; has little tendency to buckle or sag when damp
pressed pulp	smooth; cream or gray color; some kinds have one finished surface	stiffer than cane fiberboard; easily bent, broken; will not stand wear on unframed edges	high; bends, curls, buckles, sags when damp
hardboards pressed pine fibers	one smooth, one rough surface; brown color	quite stiff; not as strong as plywood; brittle	reasonably moisture-resistant; oil-tempered varieties absorb practically no moisture; will not bend, buckle, sag when damp
wood core between layers of cardboard	smooth, sized surfaces; uncolored, red, or tan	very stiff	little; very slight tendency to bend when damp
pressed pine or spruce fibers with enamel, bakelite, or other plastic finish	one glossy, one rough surface; wide range of colors and designs to imitate tile, brick, marble, etc.	very stiff and brittle	waterproof
cement and asbestos	smooth, dull or waxed surfaces; some enamel finishes in many colors; natural color or gray	very stiff and brittle	little

are graded descriptively: *good, sound, solid, sheathing,* and *back* in combinations as *good 2 sides, solid 1 side,* etc.

All other board materials except pulp hardboard and rigid foams are low-cost substitutes for plywood, their use justified by economy when the production situation does not demand plywood's properties.

This board bearing the trade name Masonite, which has become a quasi-generic term, has a hard, durable surface which makes it a suitable covering for platform tops and false floors, especially for dance performances. It is cemented to ¾″ plywood.

Rigid polyethylene or polyurethane formed into sheets is very light-weight and easily cut, shaped, and textured. It provides the readiest means of simulating the thickness of such objects as brick, stone, rough timber, and the like. (See "Rigid Plastic Foams," later in this chapter.)

Fabrics

Fabrics are the most perishable materials used for scenic purposes. They include covering materials; floor-covering materials; draperies; scrim, gauze, and netting; and upholstery fabrics. The choice of fabric depends on a number of variables, of which the most important is the duration of production. For repertory and for touring and long-run productions reliability and economy demand that the materials be in all respects the best that can be obtained. Stock, school, community, and resident productions can use materials which will satisfy appearance requirements but need not have durability beyond the contemplated run. However, even in such productions, the best materials are justified when there is a chance of the scenery's being stored for reuse.

The characteristics of the fibers from which textiles are woven determine to a large extent the characteristics and therefore the uses of the

other board materials

pulp hardboard

rigid foams

Weight (lbs/1,000 ft²)	*Workability*	*Sizes*	*Use*
300–600	easily cut and drilled; leaves rough edges	¼″, ½″, 1″ thick; 4′ wide; 4′–12′ long	applied thickness, sound-absorbent surfaces
570–1,000	easily cut and drilled; leaves uneven edges; can be bent on long radius	3⁄16″, 15⁄32″ thick; 4′, 6′, 8′ wide; 6′–14′ long	trim, props, cheap temporary substitute for hardboard. *Must be framed*
700–850	easily worked; leaves fine, smooth, hard edges	⅛″, 3⁄16″, ¼″, 5⁄16″ thick; 4′ wide; 12′ long	free-standing curved cuts, intricate ornaments, props (table tops, etc.)
830	easily worked; leaves fairly smooth edges	¼″ thick; 4′ wide; 6′–12′ long	large unframed rigid pieces
700+	easily worked; leaves smooth edges	5⁄32″ thick; 4′ wide; 4′–12′ long	tile or marble imitations for surfaces which must stand stresses and impact, particularly props
very heavy	easily worked with metal-working tools	great variety of sizes	heat or electrical insulator for circuits carrying under 100 amps; stone or tile imitations; props

fabric. Length of fiber relates to the strength of a fabric; elasticity relates to the ability of a fabric to stay in place or to recover from stretching; absorbency relates to a fabric's affinity for paints and dyes.

The number of fibers in the yarn, the tightness of spinning, the tightness of weaving (thread count per inch) and the type of weave also determine the theatrical uses. Hard fabrics, tightly spun and woven, do not drape in as fine folds as soft fabrics, but offer better painting surfaces; hard fabrics reflect more light and are more durable than soft ones. Heavy fabrics are more opaque than thin fabrics and when used as draperies will tend to move less when agitated by backstage drafts or personnel than do light fabrics. Pile fabrics are highly opaque.

TABLE 6.5. CHARACTERISTICS OF FABRIC FIBERS

Fiber	Length	Tensile Strength (in grams)	Elasticity[a]	Stretch Percentage[b]	Color Unbleached	Affinity for Dye[a]
cotton	½″–1½″	2–8	3	low	cream, white, light brown	3
linen (flax)	18″–20″	8+	4	lowest	buff to gray	4
silk	1,350′–4,000′	5–28	2	15–20	yellow to gray	1
wool	1″–3″	15–30	1	25–35	yellowish to brown	2

[a] Elasticity and dye affinity, functions of the fiber structure, are rated relatively in descending order, with 1 signifying the greatest elasticity and greatest affinity for dye.
[b] The percentage of the length of a fiber which may be added when tensile stress is exerted upon it.

natural fibers

Linen and cotton fabrics are made from flax and cotton, vegetable fibers of great antiquity. Both fabrics have characteristics which satisfy theatrical demands, but cotton, being less expensive than linen and being readily available in a wide variety of weaves, knits, weights, and widths, is the more commonly used.

Silk, an insect-produced filament fiber, is made into fabrics which are either too fine, too fragile, or too costly for theatrical uses. It has been replaced by fabrics made of synthetic fibers (see below).

Wool, an animal fiber, has strength and durability far beyond theatrical requirements. The cost of woolen fabrics is not competitive with that of cotton and synthetic fabrics.

synthetic and glass fabrics

The physical properties, appearance, and behavior of fibers produced by the synthesis of chemicals vary greatly. Whereas synthetics for specific nontheatrical uses such as stockings, lingerie, and yacht sails, have displaced cotton, silk, flax, and wool, they have not replaced basic cotton fibers in scenery, although they have some usefulness as curtains, draperies, transparencies, and upholstery fabrics.

Glass fabrics, woven of glass fibers, being totally flameproof, are useful for translucent screens and draperies. They lack abrasion resistance.

Called nonfabrics because they are not woven or knitted, chemically synthesized sheets and films are useful for transparent effects and for upholstery. Their flammability must be carefully tested, however, since some kinds are highly combustible and cannot be flameproofed. Certain synthetic sheet materials are thermoplastic and may be molded into rigid shapes.

synthetic sheet materials

Synthetic fabrics, glass fabrics, and synthetic sheets offer designers opportunities to devise novel effects in translucent drops, cycloramas, and draperies, and in upholstery and molded forms. The rapid expansion of the development and manufacture of synthetic materials makes necessary continuing attention to new products in this category.

design opportunities

The stage floor is seldom used bare because the floor, if visible to the audience, must be made a part of the stage decoration, whether the latter is realistic or abstract. Bare floors are noisy underfoot. A floor-cloth or carpet specific to a show is a full-scale portable ground plan, marked with the positions of scenery and props, which obviates measuring and marking each new stage on a tour.

floor-covering materials

Heavy (10- or 12-ounce) cotton duck, usually brown or olive, is double-sewn with flat seams into a rectangle large enough to encompass the largest set. The downstage edge is hemmed; the other three edges are hemmed, then reinforced with jute webbing, and grommeted. All four corners are reinforced with an extra thickness of duck. The downstage edge is tacked or stapled to the floor; the other three are fastened with large-head roofing nails through the grommets. The floor-cloth may be painted as part of the design.

floorcloth

Wilton-weave broadloom carpet may be substituted for a duck floorcloth.

carpet

Linoleums and a variety of synthetic floor coverings produced in widths up to 12′ can make danceable coverings for a stage floor which has been rendered rough by hard use. Unrolled and weighted they will stay in place with few or no fastenings. Most of these floor coverings become stiff or brittle when cold. They must be warm when unrolled or they are subject to damage in the process.

sheet floor coverings

Artificial grass mats, made of raffia woven into a jute fabric may be obtained from dealers in artificial flowers, display (store window) supplies, or mortuary supplies. Small in size, they must be sewn together or glued to a duck backing. Plastic grass, developed for sports fields and playgrounds, is available from dealers in plastics. Green, long-pile carpet may simulate grass.

grass effects

To deaden footfalls on stage floors and on platform and wagon tops, padding may be laid under duck or carpet floorcloths. Domestic carpet padding of hair felt or of various kinds and grades of foamed synthetic rubber are available from carpet dealers. Flameproofing is mandatory. Paper felt, used in house construction as an underlayment for flooring, is adequate as low-cost padding for one-time use.

padding

TABLE 6.6. SCENERY FABRICS

Name	Material	Color	Percent Opacity	Weight (oz/yd²)	Weave	Surface Texture	Available Width	Available Bolt Length (yds)	Use
canvas duck	cotton	natural, bleached, or dyed cloth	59.2	8–22	plain	medium	36″–120″	50–60	covering, floorcloths, sandbags, drops, lining
muslin	linen	natural, bleached or dyed	53.0	8 oz.[a]	plain	harder than cotton	...	...	covering, drops
	cotton	natural or bleached	46.0	3.8	plain	soft	36″–33′	50–60	drops, covering, projection screens, Translux sheets, trail cloths, chafing bags, hems
cheesecloth	cotton	bleached	19.9	1.8	plain	very soft	36″	10–30	glass curtains, glass, drapery
flannel	cotton	any	66.1	4.0	plain, napped	very soft; nap on both sides	27″–50″	35–40	inexpensive substitute for velour
duvetyn	cotton	any	66.1	4.0	plain, napped	very soft, flat nap on one side	36″–50″	50–60	draw curtains, borders, draperies
rep	cotton	any	80.8	10.5	plain, ribbed	trifle softer than canvas	50″	50	curtains, borders, valances, draperies, upholstery
monk's cloth	cotton	gray or brown; can be dyed	73.0	10.7	plain	very uneven, coarse	45″–50″	40	drapery, curtains
velour	cotton	any	99.9	14.0[b]	pile	soft	54″	50	curtains, borders, drops, valances, covering, drapery
velveteen	cotton	any	89.6[b]	7.9	pile	soft	36″	35	props, curtains
plush	rayon	any	82.8[b]	3.9	pile	soft, lustrous	54″	50	upholstery
satin	rayon, silk	any	79.9[c]	5.6[d]	float	hard, smooth	36″–50″	50	props
sateen	cotton	any	69.4[b]	3.5	float	hard, smooth	36″–50″	35	curtain lining, special curtains, drapery
burlap	jute	dark brown	58.4	8.5	plain	hard, rough	36″–72″	50	props, molded forms, three-dimensional trees, etc.
webbing	cotton, jute	brown	no test	no test	plain	similar to burlap	1″–4″	72	side reinforcing for floorcloths; top reinforcing for curtains, borders, draperies
binding tape	cotton	white	no test	no test	twill	same as canvas	½″–1″	100	side reinforcing for scrim, drops, etc.
window shade	cotton with filler and size	eggshell	67.0	no test	plain	hard	...	...	screen, props, temporary projection sheets
felt	cotton, wool & cotton, or wool	any	100.0	12–20	not woven	fuzzy	72″	35	props
gauze	cotton	white, light buff, dark blue, black	0.0	...	$\frac{1}{8}″ \times \frac{1}{4}″$ or $\frac{1}{8}″ \times \frac{5}{32}″$[e]	very soft	30′	any	soft focus, fog; gauze drop usually 30′ high
net	cotton or jute	white	0.0	...	1″ mesh	...	30′	any	support for cut borders and drops

[a] Standard for covering. [b] Considerable variation, as grades vary. [c] If twill weave, 40.7 percent. [d] If twill weave, 2.5. [e] Openings oblong or hexagonal.

Adhesives

Flake or powdered animal or fish glues and casein glues are used to bond joints in wood and to bond plywood reinforcements applied over wood joints. If permanent waterproof joints are needed, epoxy glues are used.

Animal and fish glues, and pastes made from them, require twelve hours to set and dry. This is a determinant in scheduling work.

Fabric covering materials must be bonded to scenery frames with an adhesive which has sufficient strength to hold and to resist shrinkage stresses but is *filled* with an inert substance which will prevent penetration of the glue to the exposed surface which is to be painted. The common components are whiting in suspension in water, wheat paste, and flake animal glue which has been dissolved in water in a double boiler. The proportions are matters of individual preference and occasional disputation. The requirement is adequate holding power without defacement of the painting surface.

Fast setting is a desirable property of synthetic resins and cements. Some of these are available ready-mixed and others require the mixing of two substances to initiate a curing reaction. Commercial contact cements, used in house construction for applying panel board to walls or linoleum to subfloors may serve similar purposes in scene construction.

Contact cement contains elastomers such as neoprene or natural rubber in a solvent. They are added to a long-chain polymer resin to form an extremely adhesive coating which bonds on contact. Pressure, time, and curing under mild heat produce strength in the bond. Contact cement is particularly good when large meeting surfaces are to be joined; it is weakest under shear stress conditions.

Epoxy, the product of complex chemical processes and available in many forms, is capable of bonding almost all materials and can produce strong joints in metal under the manufacturer's directions for use.

These are tabulated and described in Chapter 10 (see Tables 10.3 and 10.4).

wood glues

canvas paste

synthetic adhesives

for metal

adhesives for scene painting

Fasteners

Nails are used to fasten wood-to-wood joints. They hold by one or a combination of several means: tension of the wood fibers which produces friction against the sides of the nail; resin coating to increase this friction; compression of the nailhead on the surface of the wood; clinched (turned) end of the nail against the back surface of the joint; and claw action of one or more nails driven into the wood at oblique angles. Nails must be selected and used with regard for the characteristics of the wood, the locations of the nails, and the purpose for which the joint is made.

Nails tend to split wood, especially when driven near the ends or edges of pieces where tension in the fibers is least. Holes smaller than the nail diameters must sometimes be drilled to prevent splitting. Holes must always be drilled in hardwood encountered in prop furniture alterations.

nails

Clout or **cut nails,** being wedge-shaped, tend to cause splitting when the wedge is inserted along the grain but will cut through the fibers without splitting when driven with the wedge across the grain. Clout nails must be clinched.

Common nails hold joints by the compression of the flat heads as well as by friction.

Box nails, flat-headed but of finer wire than common nails, are adequate to fasten board materials to wood.

Roofing nails, with wide flat heads, hold soft materials in place.

Finish nails, with round narrow heads, may be countersunk and the holes plugged with putty to conceal the nails; hence their use in finish carpentry.

Double-headed nails are used as temporary fasteners and may be easily withdrawn.

tacks and staples

Tacks, either single- or double-pointed, and staples are used to fasten fabric or wire mesh to wood. They are driven by hammer or by spring-powered or pneumatic-powered tackers.

wood screws

Wood screws are used primarily to fasten metal hinges and stage hardware to scenery frames. Corners, angles, foot irons, etc., are drilled and countersunk to receive #8 and #9 flathead screws. Screws of these sizes may be *started* into softwood by hammering. Only near knots or near the ends or edges of wood must holes be drilled.

Intermittent stress on screwed joints causes compression and damage to wood fibers near the screws, loosening them and weakening the joints. Bolts must be used in such situations.

bolts

Holes must always be drilled in the materials to be fastened with bolts, the size of the hole being $\frac{1}{64}''$ to $\frac{1}{16}''$ greater than the bolt diameter depending upon the acceptable tolerance.

threading systems

Two major threading systems apply to bolts used in theatrical construction: *National Coarse,* for almost all uses, relatively large thread size and pitch for threading into mild steel and softer materials permitting rapid tightening and reuse even after slight damage to threads. *National Fine* for tools and machinery where high strength and resistance to vibration are requisite.

kinds

Stove bolts are coarse-threaded their entire length; they have flat, round, and oval slotted heads and are used to join small metal parts or in place of screws in fastening hinges and stage hardware to scenery.

Machine screws are like stove bolts but have fine threads.

Machine bolts are either square- or hex-headed (hexagonal-headed) with threads on only part of the shank and are used to fasten pieces of metal together, the bolt head fitting snugly against the work. Square-headed bolts are adequate for stage uses. Hex heads are used in machine assembly and wherever socket wrenches must be used.

Carriage bolts, which are used primarily in wood, have rounded heads and square shanks adjacent to the head. The squared shank resists turning in hardwood and for a period of time in softwood. A pronged torque washer driven into the wood around the bolt hole will prevent the bolt from turning. If the bolt is used in metal, the head can be similarly held by a square hole in the metal into which the squared shank is inserted.

Lag screws, sometimes mistakenly called lag bolts, have machine-bolt heads but coarse threads on a tapered shank, for insertion either into lead holes drilled in structural lumber or into plugs or shields set into holes drilled in masonry. Their principal theatrical use is to fasten special rigging hardware to stage walls.

Wing nuts are used on bolts when temporary fastenings are adequate to the situation. They may be tightened and unfastened by hand.

Washers are used under bolts and nuts to distribute the compression of the fastener over a greater surface area than is covered by the bolts or nuts themselves.

washers

Lock washers are used under nuts either to keep the nuts from loosening because of vibration or to enable their easy removal.

A **knife-thread insert** or a **T nut** may be inserted in wood to supply threads to receive bolts.

inserts

A variety of inserts — among them, **expansion plugs, expansion shields,** and **toggle bolts** — are available for use with wood screws, machine screws, and lag screws for fastening to masonry, hollow walls, or wooden structures.

This depends upon the physical properties of the material of the fasteners and of the materials fastened. The holding power of nails and screws in softwood is not precisely predictable because of the vagaries of the wood and can only be learned by practical experience.

holding power of fastenings

Steel

Two basic kinds of steel are used in theatrical construction. **Mild** or **structural steel,** sold as A–7 or A–36, is suitable for all structural and scenic uses. **Low-carbon machinery steel** is used for machine parts, shafting, and other parts that may require welding in their fabrication.

Both kinds come in two different finishes: *plain oxide,* which is suitable for general theatrical use; and *oiled* (or *pickled*) — bright steel protected by oil — which is useful for machine parts and when permanent painting is desired.

finishes

Shapes of cross section are specific to the particular ways in which steel is used.

shapes

Channel has a wide central plate or web with two smaller plates called flanges at right angles on each edge and on the same side of the web. *Bar-size channel,* made in nineteen sizes, from ¾″ to 2½″ web and ⅛″ and ¼″ thickness, is useful for strengthening lightweight wooden scenery and for constructing thin-membered outline scenery. *Structural channel,* in sizes 3″ and above, is useful for stair stringers, cantilevered platforms, and long, open spans. Channel is used:

channel

• When the primary stress is across the main axis of the web with secondary stresses against the unflanged side of the web.

• When fastening of other members may be all on one side of the web.

- When an unflanged side of a member is needed to pass other members or to attach flat scenery.
- When channels back to back, though spaced apart, combine strengths to resist stresses against the flanges.

I beam   A cross-section shape similar to the capital letter *I,* the I beam has a web and four flanges, two on each side at each edge of the web. The *regular* type closely resembles its namesake; the *wide-flanged* resembles the *expanded* form of the letter. I beam is used:
- Where the primary stress (P) is parallel to the web but with strong secondary stresses (S) at right or near right angles to the primary.
- Where fastenings must be made on both sides of the web.
- Where flanges are needed to support other members on both sides of the web.

Channels and wide-flanged I beams are the chief structure parts of a stage gridiron.

H section   In an H section beam the width of the flanges equals the width of the web; hence this shape is used chiefly as columns in buildings and seldom in scene construction.

angle   The name describes the shape: two flats (legs) forming a right angle. The legs are sometimes equal, more often unequal, in width. *Bar angles* are available in forty-eight sizes, from $\frac{1}{2}'' \times \frac{1}{2}'' \times \frac{1}{8}''$ to $2\frac{1}{2}'' \times 2\frac{1}{2}'' \times \frac{1}{2}''$; *structural angles* in ninety-eight sizes, from $3'' \times 2'' \times \frac{3}{16}''$ to $8'' \times 8'' \times \frac{1}{2}''$.

Angles are used when there is approximately equal stress along both axes. A tendency to buckle from torsion is countered by using two angles back to back, often with flats or rods between, as in bar joists. Angles are particularly useful for rectangular structures, since other members can be fastened to both legs.

tee   Again, the name describes the cross section. The upright part of the T is called the stem and the transverse parts the flanges. Tees are useful structural members because of the ease of fastening to the flanges and the stem, and because resistance is offered to stresses along both axes. Sizes range from $\frac{3}{4}''$ (stem) $\times \frac{1}{8}''$ (thick) to $2\frac{1}{2}''$ (stem) $\times \frac{3}{8}''$ (thick). Tees serve well as stiffeners for structures which are long and thin, such as ceilings, tormentors, or portal legs, and as guide tracks for counterweights and lifts.

bar   Bar is solid steel of square or rectangular cross section in a great variety of sizes. Sometimes it is used for hangers or posts (if square-sectioned) but most frequently for decorative ironwork such as balustrades or grilles, where it gives strength and rigidity to designs completed in plywood, wire, or other lightweight simulative materials.

rod   Available in diameters from $\frac{1}{8}''$ to $10''$, rod is most useful when in tension as a hanger or in a truss or bar joist. Rod may also be used in decorative ironwork. Rod of C–1018 steel is used for shafts and axles.

plate   Plate is flat steel over $\frac{1}{8}''$ thick, which is used when simulation by a lighter material is not allowable: for instance, in a metal trapdoor which must give an authentic sound when it is closed. Plate is used when extreme loads are imposed upon very thin flooring or clear spans and as a source from which pieces are cut for fabrication.

Sheet is flat steel under ⅛″ thick, with the thickness stated in gauge numbers. The thickness *decreases* by increments of 0.015″ per number as the numbers *increase*. Thus, 14-gauge is thicker than 16-gauge. Sheet is used to make lighting instruments and as surface material when simulation is not possible.

sheet

Pipe is available in three wall thicknesses: standard, extra strong, and double extra strong. The size is given in inside diameter (i.d.); the outside diameter varies with the wall thickness. Commonly used sizes are from ⅜″ i.d. to 2″ i.d., but sizes up to 12″ i.d. are available. Pipe will resist a moderate stress from any direction better than any other shape and is used for beams, columns, and struts in structures, for flying-system battens, and for light mountings. It is also used, with standard fittings, for assemblies which must be demountable. Smaller sizes may be bent into decorative shapes. Widely used in building construction, pipe is the most available steel shape. See Table 6.7.

pipe

Available in many thicknesses and diameters, tubing is used for decorative fabrications and not for strength. With specially shaped dies, tubing can be bent to intricate shapes and can be pop-riveted or welded to make elaborate decoration. Square tubing is used when flat surfaces are required, when easy welding is desired, and when two pieces must be telescoped with easy alignment of bolt holes or pinholes. A system of telescoping square tubing is commercially available (see "Telespar" in the next section). Thin-walled conduit (TWC) may be worked like tubing.

tubing

Unistrut, the trademarked product of the Unistrut Corporation of Wayne, Michigan, is a system of U-shaped channels which when combined with a great variety of fittings can be put to many uses: structures, electrical racks, light bridges, stage lifts, adjustable forestages, or temporary or permanent buildings. All parts are demountable and reusable.

Telespar, also a trademarked product of the Unistrut Corporation, is square-sectioned tubing, in graduated sizes, with the sides perforated by round holes at regular intervals. A piece of one size may be slipped inside the next larger size, telescoped to a variety of lengths, and held in a desired position by bolts or pins through the matching holes.

Dexion (a trademark) is lightweight slotted angle that has circular and elliptical holes punched in each leg so that any kind of fastening can be used to attach it. Like Unistrut, it is useful for demountable bolted assemblies.

Lightweight steel trusses and open-web joists support larger loads over larger spans with less bulk and weight than do wooden trusses and joists. They are fabricated from structural shapes or from Unistrut. Trusses for platforms or bridges over clear spans may be welded from angle and rod. A pair of trusses cross-braced every 4′ can support the weight of four actors, in action, and heavy furniture (see Chapter 15, Problem 59).

TABLE 6.7. WEIGHTS OF STANDARD STEEL PIPE

Inside Diameter	Pounds per Foot
1″	1.66
1¼″	2.25
1½″	2.67

Source: Institute of Steel Construction, *Steel Construction Handbook* (1962).

trusses and joints

Wire Mesh

Window-screen cloth of black iron, galvanized iron, copper, aluminum, fiber glass, or plastic-coated galvanized iron wire is used to simulate glass or is shaped as a support for covering materials on three-dimensional scenery.

Hardware cloth of galvanized iron wire woven into ½″ mesh with welded joints affords stiffer support than window-screen cloth.

Poultry netting in 1″ or 2″ mesh is a moldable subsurface which permits interweaving strips of fabric or stems of artificial foliage.

Wire fence, in various patterns and gauges, woven, twisted, or welded, may be shaped to serve as substructure or actual structure of scenery.

Expanded metal lath is sheet or plate which has been completely slotted longitudinally and pulled out laterally to resemble wire mesh or wire fence. It may be used as surface for scenery or flooring for platforms. It offers possibilities of transparent or translucent effects.

Fiber Glass Fabrics, Resins, and Accessories

Fiber glass fabrics are made in a number of types, weights, and widths, each type having its own particular uses (see "Fiber Glass Construction," page 431).

woven cloth

The most useful type, woven cloth, is plain white and made of glass threads. The 10 ounce per square yard weight is the most generally useful for stage purposes. The lighter weight cloth can be used for fine detail work, and the heavier weight where greater strength is desired.

mat

Mat, the second most useful type, is made by laying short strands of glass fiber over each other in a random interlocking pattern to form a loose layer of fabric that is easily torn apart. The lighter weights are very fragile and can be used only for delicate work. Since the heaviest weights will flatten out any detail, they are useful only in making structural scenery.

loose fibers

Loose chopped fibers are most commonly used as a filler which, when mixed with resin, makes an extremely strong mass with relatively light weight. It can be used where strength or bulk is needed.

substitutes

At some sacrifice of strength, other fabrics may be substituted for the glass cloth. Any substitute cloth should have an open weave which will allow the resin to penetrate (See "Resins" below). Materials such as tobacco cloth and cheesecloth are the best substitutes for the lighter weights of glass cloth, while a material such as burlap is the best substitute for the heavier weights. More closely woven materials do not work effectively because the resin will coat them without penetrating the fabric. Only natural-fiber cloth may be substituted; some synthetic fibers will dissolve in the resin.

resins
polyester

The polyester resins are all heavy viscous liquids with different formulations. Their chemical differences are of little concern to the person using them, provided he remembers that they are available in two general types: *promoted* and *unpromoted*. The promoted should *always* be specified when ordering. The unpromoted lacks a vital ingredient (cobalt naphthenate) without which it will *never* harden. The promoted resin can be obtained with a wide variety of properties, the choice being determined by the intended use.

Most resins ignite easily, but it is possible to obtain flame-resistant types that cost about half again as much.

A few basic types of resin suffice for stage use. If a resin with several different properties, such as fire resistance and impact resistance, is desired, it may be obtained by mixing resins having these properties. The resulting mixture will be less fire-resistant than the pure fire-resistant type, and less impact-resistant than the pure impact-resistant type.

Standard all-purpose rigid resin has average properties, but no particular property is more pronounced than any other. This type is the most useful for stage purposes.

Thixotropic resin is so viscous it will not run; it is therefore useful in making objects with vertical surfaces.

Flexible resins have good resistance to cracking on impact. They resist cracking when walked on and will bend.

Impact-resistant resins are used when the finished object will receive rough use (a shield used in a battle scene or a platform top).

Epoxy resin, while its properties are similar to those of the polyester resins, is much more expensive. Its principal virtue is its ability to bond to *anything*. Its cost requires that it be used judiciously.

In addition to the cloth and resin, other necessary materials are:

Hardener. This is essential in making resins set. The most accessible is methyl ethyl ketone peroxide (MEK peroxide). One ounce suffices for one quart of resin. See Problem 66, Chapter 15.

Cold-weather promoter. Cobalt naphthenate is used to induce the setting of resins in temperatures from 65° F. down to 45° F. It is useful for outdoor work.

Thinner. Liquid styrene is used to dilute resins which are too thick to work and to improve penetration of cloth or mat; it slows the hardening process.

Solvents. Acetone is used to dissolve resin that has *not yet hardened,* to clean brushes, spray guns, and other equipment, and to clean up spillage. It is not to be confused with styrene, the thinner.

Resin Out (trademarked name) dissolves and removes hardened resins from tools and working surfaces, or hardened overflow from molds.

Parting agents. Viscous films, such as vaseline and automotive cup grease, are used only on molds which will not be damaged by oil; they must be washed off the fiber-glass form before painting.

Flexible sheeting, such as aluminum foil, Saran, and polyethylene, may be used if impervious to resins and can be made to conform to the shape of the mold. Dry cleaners' bags, second-hand, may serve and cost nothing.

Rigid Plastic Foams: RPF and RUF

RPF (rigid polystyrene foam, with the trade name Styrofoam) and RUF (rigid polyurethane foam, with the trade name Thurane) are nonporous materials with noninterconnecting cells. This structure gives them great strength relative to low density and light weight, and does not allow absorption of water or sound, or significant transmission of heat or light. Containing nothing of food value, plastic foam will not mold, rot, or attract vermin.

RPF: properties and varieties

Because RPF is a thermoplastic, it reacts to moderately high temperatures but is not adversely affected by extreme cold. Continuous application of 165° F. heat will cause surface distortion of this material and it will melt at temperatures slightly higher than 165° F. Although some varieties are flame-retardant, they will ignite at 690° F., extinguishing themselves when the source of heat is removed.

Of the several varieties of RPF available, Styrofoam DB and FR are currently preferred for scene construction. Styrofoam DB is available in a great variety of preformed shapes from commercial fabricators and from local florist-supply and display-supply outlets. DB must be coated with a flame retardant because it will ignite readily. Styrofoam FR is preferred for most projects because it has a smaller cell structure than DB and is more commonly available in larger sizes.

RUF: properties and uses

RUF is a thermoset and will deteriorate rather than melt when brought in contact with temperatures exceeding 250° F. It is flame-retardant but will burn while exposed to high temperatures and cease burning when the source of heat is removed. Although very similar to RPF, RUF has certain advantages for theatrical applications: It is solvent-resistant and may be used with a greater variety of paints and adhesives (which may be quick-dried if desired in a low-temperature (240° F. oven). But RUF, though available from the same suppliers as RPF, must be special-ordered.

toxicity (warning!)

RPF presents a health hazard in that the expanding agent, methyl chloride, an odorless, colorless gas which is harmful in concentrations of 1 part gas per 10,000 parts air, is trapped in the cells during the extrusion process and is released during the fabrication processes that open formerly closed cells. One cubic foot of RPF contains enough methyl chloride to contaminate 10,000 cubic feet of air to a toxic level.

RUF is not manufactured with methyl chloride or any other toxic gas. However, when the material decomposes as a result of heating, a harmful toxic gas is given off. Hence, efficient ventilation is mandatory when working with both RPF and RUF.

warping and aging

Although cellular rather than fibrous, plastic foam will warp and bow; this is especially true of stock thicker than one inch and of aged stock. Aging also causes plastic foams to become brittle.

protective coatings

Plastic foams are relatively strong, but they may be easily ripped, scratched, dented, and broken when roughly handled. Additional damage will result from exposure to flame, intense heat, direct sunlight, and (for RPF) certain solvents. Satisfactory protection from these elements may be obtained by using protective coatings of one of the following classes:

Damage-resistant coatings provide hard durable surfaces that will withstand moderate impact. Normal handling of any piece of scenery or prop will damage uncoated plastic foams; units that are trouped are likely to sustain even greater damage.

Weather-resistant coatings provide protection from ultraviolet (sun) rays. This is most important in outdoor theatre use.

Solvent-resistant coatings protect RPF from attack by materials containing aromatic or chlorinated hydrocarbons, ketones (including acetones), esters, and high alcohols. Since some paints contain these solvents, care is necessary in their selection and use. Careful perusal of the labels of suspect materials and tests in advance of use are required. Solvent-resistant RUF does not require this protection.

Fire-retardant coatings provide a protective blanket that extinguishes flames or limits their spread. Many commercial fire-retardant coatings are available and many of the coatings for physical, solvent, and weather protection may be used for this purpose.

Thermoplastics

These are orderly chemical arrangements of long-chain polymers which become ductile and can be shaped when heated to slightly above moderate atmospheric temperatures and become rigid in the new shapes when cooled. Kinds which are generally available at prices comparable to those of other scenic materials and which can be easily worked are low-density polyethylene (LDPE), high-density polyethylene (HDPE), cellulose acetate (CA) and high-impact polystyrene (PS). These are manufactured in sheet, rod, and tube shapes in a wide variety of sizes and thicknesses. They satisfy the theatrical requirements of being lightweight and reasonably inexpensive, especially when the time of fabrication is considered part of the cost; workable with low-cost equipment; compatible with most scene paints; and strong enough to withstand the usual stresses of scenery handling. *useful kinds*

Thermoplastics must be stored horizontally under conditions of controlled temperature (safe range: 50° to 120° F.); otherwise, they will become distorted from excessive heat or brittle and even fractured from excessive cold. Tube stock must not be stacked so high that weight will deform the bottom tubes. *storage*

TABLE 6.8. *PROPERTIES OF THERMOPLASTICS TESTED FOR STAGE USE*

Thermoplastic	Forms Commonly Available	Specific Gravity	Heat Distortion Temperature (F.)[a]	Burning Rate	Clarity	Machining Qualities	Molding Qualities
cellulose acetate	film sheet rod tube	1.28–1.32	130–160	slow	transparent translucent opaque opaque	very good	excellent
low-density polyethylene	film sheet rod tube	.910–.925	105–121	very slow	translucent to opaque	fair	very good
high-density polyethylene	film sheet rod tube	.941–.965	140–180	very slow	translucent to opaque	very good	very good
high-impact polystyrene	sheet rod block	.98–1.10	148–200	slow	translucent to opaque	excellent	excellent

[a] Temperatures at which materials lose rigidity and may be reshaped.
Source: Nicholas L. Bryson, "Thermoplastic Scenery for the Theatre," unpublished M.F.A. thesis, University of Wisconsin, 1968.

synthetic rubber   This is useful for making masks, properties, puppets, armor, and architectural ornaments. One brand is Polysar XB–407, manufactured by the Polymer Corporation Limited of Sarnia, Ontario. Although hard and semirigid at room temperature, when Polysar XB–407 is heated two to three minutes at temperatures of 150° to 175° F., it can be shaped by hand, molded over forms, and made self-adhesive. No parting agent is required between the material and a form. It is flexible enough to be cast into undercuts. Edges and surfaces may be made self-adhesive either by dry heating or by brushing on carbon tetrachloride or acetone before joining.

Welding Materials

See the discussion of welding in Chapter 8, page 195.

Materials for Hanging and Moving Scenery

chain   **Welded-steel chain** is used in rigging and hanging scenery when permanence, great strength, and stability are required.

Trim chains of welded-steel **passing link chain** on battens permit adjusting the trim of scenery either by a snap hook into a link of the chain or by a machine bolt through two overlapping links of the chain. **Check chains** between the gridiron and top battens of curtains are of welded-steel chain, with a 100 percent impact factor applied in determining the size of the chain to be used.

Sash chain, stay chain, and single and double **jack chain** are used as continuous weight in the bottom hems of curtains and draperies, the kind and size of the chain depending upon the weight needed to impart the desired *hang* to the fabrics.

wire rope   **Hoisting rope** is used as lift lines in flying systems. It is of 6×19 construction: 19 wires spun into a strand, 6 strands spun into a rope, with a hemp center. Made of plow steel, it is tough and withstands abrasion.

Tiller rope, of 6×42 construction, consists of 6 strands of 42 wires each, spun around a hemp core. Each of the strands is spun as a 6×7 rope on its own core. This construction produces the most flexible wire rope made. Because of the small diameter of individual wires it will not withstand abrasion but it can be flexed around small sheaves.

Wire-centered sash cord, also called tiller rope because it is used in rigging the steering of small motorboats, consists of braided cotton around a 6×7 wire center. It has stability and moderate strength and may be used in motor drives for lightweight curtains.

Airplane cable is made of high-tensile-strength steel in 7×19 construction. It is flexible and is used for invisible rigging, levitation, and lift lines in winch flying systems because it has adequate strength and stores compactly on winch drums.

Galvanized soft-steel rope in 6×7 construction is relatively inexpensive and is used for standing guide wires for counterweights, curtains, and the like.

Nylon-covered wire rope, of 6 × 19 construction plow steel, resists corrosion, is smooth to handle, and provides silent guide wires for act curtains.

Piano wire has high tensile strength and though harder to work may be used in place of airplane cable for invisible flying and levitation.

TABLE 6.9. WIRE ROPE DATA

BS = Breaking Strength   AL = Allowable Load

Wire Rope	Diameter (inches)	BS (pounds)	BS (tons)	AL (pounds)	AL (tons)	Minimum Sheave Diameter (inches)	Recommended Sheave Diameter (inches)
airplane cable	1/32	185		37		1.3	2.2
	1/16	500		100		1.8	2.8
	1/8	1,700		340		4.0	6.0
	3/16	3,700		740		6.0	8.0
	1/4	7,000		1,400		8.0	10.0
hoisting rope	1/4		2.5		0.5	8.0	10.0
	5/16		3.9		0.8	10.0	12.0
	3/8		5.5		1.1	12.0	16.0
tiller rope	3/16		0.65		0.13	4.0	6.0
	1/4		1.36		0.32	6.0	8.0
	5/16		2.13		0.42	6.0	8.0
	3/8		3.05		0.61	8.0	10.0

TABLE 6.10. WIRE SIZES

D = Diameter in in. (thickness). A = Cross-Section Area in in.^{2}

Gauge No.	U.S. Steel Wire Gauge D	U.S. Steel Wire Gauge A	Brown & Sharpe Nonferrous Wire Gauge D	Brown & Sharpe Nonferrous Wire Gauge A	Birmingham & Stubs Iron Wire Gauge D	Birmingham & Stubs Iron Wire Gauge A
1	.2830	.063	.300	.071	.2893	.066
2	.2625	.053	.284	.063	.2576	.052
3	.2437	.046	.259	.052	.2294	.043
4	.2253	.040	.238	.044	.2043	.033
5	.2070	.033	.220	.038	.1819	.026
6	.1920	.029	.203	.032	.1620	.021
7	.1770	.025	.180	.026	.1443	.016
8	.1620	.021	.165	.021	.1285	.013
9	.1483	.017	.143	.016	.1144	.011
10	.1350	.014	.134	.014	.1019	.0082
11	.1205	.011	.120	.010	.0907	.0064
12	.1055	.0087	.109	.0093	.0808	.0051
13	.0915	.0065	.095	.0071	.0720	.0041
14	.0800	.0050	.083	.0054	.0641	.0032
15	.0720	.0040	.072	.0040	.0571	.0025
16	.0625	.0031	.065	.0033	.0508	.0020
17	.0540	.0023	.058	.0026	.0453	.0016
18	.0475	.0018	.049	.0019	.0403	.0012
19	.0410	.0013	.042	.0013	.0359	.0010
20	.0348	.0010	.035	.0010	.0320	.0008

Source: D from American Institute of Steel Construction, *Manual of Steel Construction* (6th ed., New York, 1963); *A* computed by E.C.C.

hemp and synthetic rope
characteristics

The rope most commonly used for stage rigging is spun of hemp fibers. The fibers are spun in one direction to form strands, and three strands are spun in the opposite direction to form a rope. The rope is said to be *laid up,* and the *lay* of commonly used rope is *right-hand* or *right-lay.* An uncommon type of rope for special uses has a *left-hand lay* or *left-lay.* Rope is packed in coils from which it must be carefully withdrawn in order to prevent twisting and tangling. The end to be withdrawn is at the center of the coil and is marked with a tag. When the rope is withdrawn from the proper side of the coil, it will be free from twist. If it twists when being withdrawn, the coil must be remade and inverted. New rope is stiff and hard to handle. Rope for running rigging must be stretched and flexed to render it supple. Rope that is 100 percent nylon is too elastic to be useful in the theatre.

Laid-up rope spins counter to the lay when in tension. For uses where spinning is not tolerable, braided, nonspinning, rope must be used.

kinds

Manila (hemp) rope is the least expensive rope of a quality satisfac-factory for stage use. A vegetable fiber, its cells absorb moisture; it tends to expand laterally and shorten when wet and to reverse this action as it dries. It is also subject to mildew, fiber fatigue, and fiber failure from abrasion and acute flexing.

Dacron rope, made of continuous synthetic strands, costs about three times as much as Manila, but is nonabsorbent, stable, and more durable. Because of its uniformity and stability, it has a higher allowable working load and is preferable for long hard use despite its cost.

Braided cotton rope is inexpensive but is also subject to the imperfections of vegetable fibers.

Braided dacron and **braided dacron-and-nylon rope** are both superior and preferable in stability and durability to braided cotton though they are from three to four times as expensive.

TABLE 6.11.   STRENGTH OF ROPE[a]

BS = Breaking Strength (lbs)   AWL = Allowable Working Load (lbs)

		SPUN ROPE				BRAIDED ROPE				
		Manila		Dacron			Cotton		Dacron-Nylon	
Diameter	Minimum Sheave Diameter	BS	AWL	BS	AWL	Diameter	BS	AWL	BS	AWL
¼"	3"	600	120	1,200	300	¼"	450	90	1,250	350
⅜"	4"	1,350	270	2,600	600	½"	1,000	200	4,500	1,000
½"	6"	1,900	380	4,500	1,000	¾"	1,400	300	10,000	2,500
¾"	9"	4,100	820	9,500	2,000					
1"	12"	7,100	1,420							

[a] The values given are for new rope; for used rope they must be adjusted downward according to the condition of the rope.

signs of weakness

In Manila: dry, short, brittle fibers. In cotton: soft, short, shredding fibers. In synthetic ropes: obvious surface wear. In all rope: the diameter reduced below 75 percent of rated diameter. These signs of weakness indicate the need for replacement. See the note to Table 6.11.

Though rope of small diameter may be adequate for a given load it is desirable to use rope larger than ⅜″ in diameter because of the ease of grasping and hauling.

size

Loft blocks, lead blocks, and **head blocks** are parts of flying systems (see Chapter 11). They vary in strength, noise, and efficiency according to design, materials used, precision of construction, and kinds of bearings. Cheap blocks have common bearings (soft-steel rod in a soft-steel sleeve) and a high friction factor; they are noisy. Friction and noise are reduced and longevity increased by ball or roller bearings and precision of fit and assembly. Flying system blocks are designed to be attached to timbers and structural steel. Kinds are illustrated and sizes and dimensions are given in trade catalogs.

blocks

Floor blocks are attached, either permanently or temporarily, to the stage floor to return curtain operating lines or the purchase lines of free-standing wire guide counterweight sets. A tension floor block allows vertical movement of its sheave to adjust to changing rope tension and has a clamp or lock to fix the sheave in position.

Tackle blocks are used to make up rope tackles to give the workman varying degrees of mechanical advantage in hauling. They are made either with wooden sides (cheeks) bound by steel straps or entirely of steel. A block may contain from one to three sheaves.

Casters are used for rolling scenery on the stage floor. They must be strong, durable, quiet, and of known load capacities. Strength and durability are functions of quality of materials and workmanship and consequently of cost. Quiet operation is dependent on quality of materials, design and workmanship, rubber or neoprene tires, close fit on axles and in frames, roller or ball bearings, and lubrication. Load capacity and ease of rolling are both direct functions of wheel diameter. Casters must never be overloaded for three reasons: caster structure may fail; tires may be so depressed that floor clearance of the unit is diminished, even to zero; movement will most certainly be made difficult.

casters

Selection of the kind, size, and number of casters to support a unit must be calculated, never guessed. Maximum load values are found in caster and stage-hardware catalogs.

Swivel casters are used for universal (multidirectional) movement of scenery, and **stationary casters** for unilinear movement. One type of swivel caster can be locked in various stationary attitudes and swivel casters which have rectangular swivel plates can be blocked into stationary attitudes.

When attaching swivel casters to scenery the circle described by the caster when direction is changed must be kept clear of scenery structure.

Control of Materials

All materials regularly used in scene construction must be on hand or readily available. The technical director must learn the sources in his vicinity, ascertain their ability to deliver specific materials upon order, and the delivery time required for materials which are not carried in stock. He must base his inventory and purchase policy on this information.

The importance of adhering to a production schedule has been emphasized in Chapters 3 and 4. Scenery must therefore be produced on schedule, and, the materials from which scenery is made must be at the place of use in time to be used and in the right kinds, sizes, and quantities. The most costly fault in purchasing and inventory control is for supplies *not* to be available when they are needed.

The objectives of effective purchasing and inventory control are these:

purchasing and inventory control
objectives

- A smooth flow of the right quantity of the right materials into the production process so that the schedule for production will be met and the process will not be impeded either by the arrival of the wrong materials, the arrival of insufficient quantities, the arrival at the wrong time, or worst, failure to arrive at all.

- Purchase of materials at the lowest price consistent with the required quality and with reliable delivery.

- Maintenance of the minimum inventory (entailing minimum tie-up of operating capital) of standard items, consistent with good volume/price purchasing practices and in satisfaction of construction demands.

- Curtailment of wasteful practices and unauthorized buying by using a system of requisitions and purchase orders.

- Accurate allocation of the costs of materials used to the project for which they were issued or purchased.

basic information

Effective purchasing and inventory control require knowledge of:

- All materials that are likely to be needed for scene building, and their sizes, prices, and market units (lbs., cwt., dozens, gross, etc.).

- Dependable sources for these materials: catalogs, directories of local merchants (the Yellow Pages), industrial indexes, trade journals, and reference publications such as *Sweet's Architectural Catalogs* and *Simon's Directory,* all of which must be kept up-to-date.

- The predicted rate of consumption, which is derived from records of past productions.

- Continuous up-to-date information regarding materials currently in stock.

The scene designer and the scene technician must both have a wide knowledge of the materials from which scenery is, or might be, made. They should, in fact, have natural curiosity about new materials and a disposition to experiment with new materials in scenery production.

The tables in this chapter contain basic information about materials which have proved generally useful. They do not contain detailed information on geographic vagaries, such as the need for galvanized hardware in seaside areas, or the relative availability of different kinds of lumber in different regions. The scene designer and the scene technician must supplement the information in this book by visiting local purveyors and gathering catalogs and price lists, especially those of theatrical supply companies.

The lead times for ordering materials from various suppliers must be known so that new supplies may be ordered to arrive before inventory runs out. The predicted daily consumption multiplied by the days of lead time gives the minimum reorder quantity, that is, the minimum inventory quantity which signals the time to reorder.

lead times for ordering

Effective purchasing depends upon successfully performing a series of steps:

steps in purchasing

Determine needs. The technician in charge of a set or show must prepare a *bill of materials* based on the working drawings.

Ascertain availability. The technician must inform the inventory control clerk of the needed amounts of stock materials and he must locate sources of materials not usually carried in stock (see "Stock Materials" and "Special Materials," page 161).

The category of special materials can cause great difficulty unless there has been consultation between the scene designer and the technician well in advance of the time when such materials are to be used. It is within the designer's province to locate and obtain purchase information on such items and to give this information to the scene technician.

It is unwise to plan the use of materials unless and until a reliable supplier has been found who has the needed amounts of the specific materials on hand and ready to ship. Reliance upon a dealer's promise that the material will be ordered from the manufacturer and will be delivered by a certain date can lead to disappointment and expensive last-minute substitutions, with inevitable disruption of the production schedule.

Issue purchase orders. An authorized person (in a small organization, the technical director or business manager; in a large organization, a member of the purchasing department) sends an order to the vendor specifying in detail the materials, quantities, kinds, sizes, prices, date of delivery, method of shipment, place of delivery, and understood terms of payment. This order may be sent in confirmation of a telephone order or it may, if time allows, be the initial order. Information copies of this order are kept in the purchasing department, given to the stock clerk as notification to expect delivery, and to the accounting department as indication of financial obligations incurred by the purchase.

Authorize direct purchase. The purchase order may be given to any authorized representative of the scene shop with instructions to buy materials directly from local merchants according to the terms stated in the order.

Authorize petty cash purchases. To obtain materials from cash-and-carry merchants or when the costs are so small that charging, billing, and the attendant accounting procedures are unwarranted, a representative of the scene shop may be authorized to make purchases for cash and claim repayment upon presentation of sales vouchers, funds for payment being drawn from a petty cash account. This procedure facilitates purchase of highly specialized items which must be selected personally by informed shoppers.

Order No. 48736

To_____

Date

Please deliver to the_____Theatre

_____

Quantity	Description	Price
	Total	

Via_____

On or before_____

_____

Purchasing Agent

6.1 A purchase order form   NOTE: Items purchased without this order form will not be accepted.

Follow up. The purchase has been completed when the stock clerk reports to the purchasing department that the materials have been received in accordance with the details of the purchase order and are in good condition. The purchasing department must be alert to the expected arrival date of materials on order and be prepared to prevent delay in delivery. Suppliers usually acknowledge receipt of an order and send a notification that merchandise has been shipped. If the purchasing department does not receive such documents, it should question the vendor regarding the progress of the order. If the situation is critical enough, it must use every conceivable method, even the threat of cancellation, to get delivery on time. The most efficacious way to achieve dependable service is to select reliable suppliers, maintain cordial but businesslike relations with them, avoid a series of crash, emergency purchases with difficult delivery dates, and pay bills promptly.

Materials delivered in pursuance of purchase orders must be received, their conformity to the requirements of the order verified, and their arrival reported to the purchasing department. The stock clerk does this, then puts stock materials in established places in the stock room, and either delivers special materials to the places in the shop where they will be used or holds them in the stock room until they are requisitioned by workers.

It is the stock clerk's responsibility to account for the use of all materials which have been received. He therefore issues materials only when presented with a materials requisition which contains the details regarding the materials needed, the show or set on which they are to be used, and the name of the requisitioner.

_____ Theatre

Book A - 18

No. 114

Date

Quantity	Description	Cost	Charge to Job

Show   Department   Per_____

6.2 A requisition form

Materials for which there is frequent need in scene construction are maintained in stock, carried in an inventory account, and charged to a show when they are issued by the stock clerk. Since a supply of these materials must always be maintained against possible demand, accumulated data of the rate of consumption and the time required between order and delivery become the basis for determining a *minimum order quantity,* that is, the inventory point at which a standard quantity will be reordered.

Materials for which there is infrequent demand and which could be carried in stock only by the expenditure of large sums of money and the occupancy of large storage spaces are not, therefore, carried in inventory as stock items but, rather, are purchased only as expressly needed. The inventory clerk's responsibility for such items has been described above.

The efficacy of salvage depends on the intrinsic value of the materials, probability of future reuse, the time and space available for the salvage operation, the labor cost of salvaging, and the availability of inexpensive storage space. Salvage, when these factors are favorable, can save a resident theatre company from 10 to 90 percent of the cost of subsequent sets of scenery.

It is logical to salvage stock-size flats, standard-size platform frames and tops, stage hardware, large bolts, long lengths of clean lumber, long lengths of rope and cable. It is illogical to save odd-size flats or platform parts, bulky three-dimensional pieces, low-cost materials like nails or screws, painted canvas, or any materials which cannot be easily and quickly recovered from the scenery being dismantled.

The costs of materials used in scene construction are customarily charged in full to the production or set for which they are used. Salvaged materials, therefore, create an accounting problem which may be solved in several ways. The materials may be returned to stock, their value (purchase price minus any identifiable costs of effecting the salvage) credited to the production from which they were salvaged, their purchase value charged again into the inventory account, and then issued and charged to subsequent shows as if they were new materials. This is the most accurate method of accounting. Its faults lie in the need to keep open the accounts of shows until salvage has been effected, the time consumed in counting, tallying, reporting and recording the materials salvaged, and the inaccuracies in pricing salvaged items because of changes in market prices. This method does, however, record the salvaged materials returned to inventory and gives the stock and inventory clerks an accurate statement of the true quantities on hand thus helping to prevent overstocking.

An alternate procedure is to return the salvaged materials to inventory, store them separately from new materials, and issue them to the new show on requisition but make no charge for them. This reduces the materials cost of the new show in an amount which cannot be estimated in advance.

A third method is to establish a completely separate salvage storeroom and permit the withdrawal of materials for no-cost or low-cost productions, often experimental or laboratory productions, by students.

If the value of salvaged materials is considerable, there is the promise of economies in accounting, as exactly as possible, for the materials salvaged and reused.

supply dumps

The bulk of certain materials for scene construction precludes their being kept in a stock room, unless it is virtually a small warehouse. Such materials are better stored in locations close to the work areas where they will be used: lumber in racks near the measuring, marking, and cutting area; bolts of scene duck near the covering area; plywood near the three-dimensional construction area. Since these supplies are outside the immediate jurisdiction of the stock clerk and he cannot issue them upon requisition, he must use an alternate method of accounting for the materials used: a *running inventory,* in which he records the amount of a material on hand before and after the work on a specific show. He then charges the difference, plus any new amounts received, to the show.

The scene shop 7

A spacious, well-equipped, and well-arranged scene shop is essential to the efficient production of scenery. It must provide space and equipment for all the operations involved in converting its input — the designer's concept and the raw materials — into its output — scenery completed, tested, and ready for the stage — with the least effort by the least number of workers, in the least time and with the least waste of materials.

All too frequently the need for space in which to plan and build scenery has been met by improvisation or the utilization of residual spaces, even in newly planned theatres. Seldom has a plan been brought to completion which has followed a thorough analysis of functions and complete listing of needs for space and equipment without some abridgment resulting from pressure to meet a budget or to conform to site limitations or architectural design.

The functions which must be performed in the scene shop, from the technical planning of the scenery to the transfer of the completed scenery to the stage of the theatre, are described in detail elsewhere in this book. In this chapter it is necessary merely to list them, state the space and equipment they require, and show efficient arrangements.

The facilities for producing scenery may vary according to the quantity and size of scenery to be produced and the number of workers. The scene shop for a stock or repertory program in a known theatre can be planned to produce only the scenery required by the established timetable of scheduled productions, in sizes dictated by the dimensions of the particular theatre, with an employed, competent staff working full-time. A college theatre, having student workers available in large numbers for short periods of time each day requires a more spacious shop. A commercial shop, contracting all kinds of scenery and anticipating profits, must be large enough to undertake several jobs simultaneously and produce scenery of all varieties and sizes.

Limited capital and operating funds may restrict shop space and equipment, and dictate the performance of different functions sequentially in the same space. Ample capital and operating funds permit the separation of different functions in suitable sequential areas, with equipment specific to the functions to be performed. This is obviously the optimal situation in which to produce scenery and is the one which will be fully set forth, after which reductions and compromises will be considered.

location Contracting shops are often located in urban areas zoned for industry, but recently some contractors have fled from urban congestion to rural or suburban areas, where they found ample low-cost space for efficient arrangement of all operations on one level more economical than urban sites. Land or space cost, transportation costs, convenience, and accessibility must be evaluated in selecting a location for a contracting shop.

For all theatres in which productions are prepared *in toto* by the producing organization, the inclusion of the scene shop, along with all other departments, in the same building with the theatre reduces transportation problems and costs to the minimum and renders administration and interdepartmental communication the most convenient possible. Locating the scene shop adjacent to the stage, with adequate sound isolation, will, by the provision of large connecting passageways, permit moving large units of scenery fully assembled from shop to stage and may afford performance storage space for rolling units.

The shop at one side of the stage, rather than behind it, affords the more convenient performance storage space and conforms to the linear-movement principle which should govern the handling of long units like drops and ceilings. Such movement should maintain the direction of the process flow established for the shop.

sound isolation Simultaneous use of shop and stage so interconnected requires that sound reaching the stage from the shop be held below the NC–20 curve, an adequate determinant of sound isolation.

Design and Production Offices

the design studio Though scene designers for commercial production are free-lance contractors who associate themselves with each production separately and work in their own studios, designers in educational and resident professional theatres, are likely to be staff members. The designer in such a situation must have a studio close to the production planning department and the scene shop. This studio must contain a drafting table and stool for each designer and each assistant; a file cabinet for drawings and prints; a resources file; a desk and bookshelves; wall or panel space for pinning up drawings; model-making bench and equipment; a sink and water supply; and possibly secretarial equipment.

the production office To make a thorough analysis of the designer's concept for purposes of determining costs of materials and labor, the technical director needs a drafting table and stool; records and resources files; hand equipment, such as drawing instruments and a slide rule; a desk calculator; wall or panel space for pin-ups; two or three conference chairs; and a conference table.

In the production office are kept the charts, schedules, orders, and reports that are needed for production control.

To accommodate purchasing, inventory control, timekeeping, and accounting, the office will need as many desks, chairs, typewriters, and calculators as there are bookkeepers; inventory control equipment; timekeeping equipment; file cabinets and bookshelves.

This room, in which scenery is analyzed technically, construction is planned, and working drawings are made, must have good-quality drawing tables for the anticipated number of technical draftsmen; the best possible lighting; supply cabinets; files for drawings and prints; resources files; storage for samples; a model-making bench and equipment; a working model of the particular theatre for testing fit and movement of model settings; and ample pin-up space.

the production drafting room

Organization for Scene Construction

There are two basic methods under which scene building may be organized. One employs specialization of work according to the steps in the process, with certain workers doing all measuring, marking, and setting out, others doing all the cutting and working up, others doing subassembly in categories (two-dimensional unframed, two-dimensional framed, three-dimensional framed), and so on through the entire process. This is an orderly procedure which makes good use of particular skills such as accuracy in measuring, dexterity with cutting tools, and so forth, but it tends to reduce the sense of individual responsibility for the finished work.

specialization method

In the second method workers perform all the operations of building units of scenery. This method relates the work to the total process of producing scenery and tends to inspire responsibility in workers: John Doe is careful in measuring and cutting because he is going to join the pieces measured and cut. Certain items of scenery will, by their uniqueness or complexity, demand the craft method: architectural detail, objects built in perspective, objects containing many oblique angles, curved or molded outlines or surfaces, sculptured forms, and the like. With adequate inspection and quality control the method of specialization is more efficient, though less gratifying to workers, than the craft method. A scene shop must be capable of being arranged to permit either method or, on occasion, a combination of both.

craft method

Scenery materials such as lumber and certain pieces of scenery such as flats, drops, and ceilings are so long that they must be moved through the shop in a single direction. Changing direction 90 degrees sweeps an area which either must be kept clear, thereby wasting space, or must be cleared, which interferes with other work. Linear movement of materials and work is the governing principle of shop layout.

materials
flow

There must be easy access for delivery trucks. The receiving door must lead into the storeroom. Lumber requires horizontal storage racks

receipt and storage

for stock sizes in the longest standard lengths; board materials require horizontal storage racks 4′ 3″ wide. Covering materials such as rolled fabrics are stored on shelves. Hardware requires bins for bulk items and storage shelves for boxed items.

control and issuance

It is essential that all materials be stored in lockable rooms and be issued by a clerk who keeps detailed records for cost accounting.

packing and shipping

Scenery which is not durable enough to withstand the strains and abrasions of transportation must be packed. A shop which supplies commercial productions or touring shows must have spaces assigned to this function. Finished and packed scenery is assembled in a shipping area, checked for completeness, and loaded on trucks or into vans.

As within the shop, long pieces, rolled drops, ceilings, battens, and the like, move in the direction of their length. Except in the most spacious of scene shops packing and shipping may occupy the same space, the size depending upon the amount of production and the sizes of the scenery. Special space for packing and shipping is needed only when shipping is a regular activity. Occasional packing may be scheduled into space normally used for other work. Packing and shipping are necessary operations of a resident theatre only if productions are toured to other theatres.

distributed storage

Although the principal supply of materials is kept in stock rooms, there must be storage racks or docks distributed about the shop to contain material and scenery in various stages of fabrication and materials which are used in quantity in specific processes (see Table 7.1).

TABLE 7.1. DISTRIBUTED STORAGE

Between	and	Storage Needed	For Storing	Size of Storage Area
measuring, marking, setting out	cutting	rack	lumber	6′ × 16′
cutting	working up	rack	lumber	6′ × 16′
working up	joining	rack	lumber	6′ × 16′
joining	trial setup	dock	frames	10′ × 10′
trial setup	covering	dock	frames	20′ × 30′
		deck	3-dim. pieces	
		shelves	fabrics	8′ × 10′
		rack	board materials	
covering	packing	dock	frames	20′ × 30′
		deck	3-dim. pieces	
		shelves	packing supplies	8′ × 10′
packing	shipping	deck	packed scenery	30′ × 40′

circulation

The dimensions in Table 7.2 allow for normal movement of workers and staff about the shop. Movement of materials and scenery must be accommodated by assigning additional space to aisles, corridors, or passageways through the shop. Such space, though used occasionally for construction must normally be kept clear for transit of scenery or materials.

TABLE 7.2. SPACE REQUIREMENTS

Material	Process	Equipment	Comment	Length/Width/Height (in feet)
lumber	measuring, marking, & setting out	bench 16′ long × 2′ wide × 2′6″ high or two carpenter's horses	see Chapter 8	16/6/10
	cutting, cross-cutting, & ripping	radial arm or pull-over saw with blade at 8′ in a 24′ bench to cut a 16′ piece to any desired length, to rip a 16′ piece, to cut on any desired angular setting up to 45°	a measuring scale on the backboard of the saw bench with 0′0″ at the blade obviates measuring and marking lumber; if several pieces are to be cut to one length, a stop block may be clamped to the backboard	24/6/10
		table saw on castered pedestal	in ripping, space is needed in front of blade for feeding wood, behind blade for removing it; in crosscutting, space is required at sides of blade	32/24/10
	oblique cuts & curves	band saw on castered pedestal	space is needed in front of and behind blade and at one side for feeding and removing work	32/16/10
		portable powered handsaws, disc saw, saber saw	these require less space than the pedestal band saw since work is kept stationary and saws are moved through it	20/8/10 ea. bench or set of 2 horses
	oblique cuts & curves plus right cuts (rip or across)	man-powered handsaws; cutting benches or carpenter's horses	the scene carpenter must resort to handsawing on occasion; the space is the same as for portable power saws	20/8/10
	working up with hand tools & portable power tools	carpenter's bench 6′ × 2′6″ × 2′6″ high equipped with vise, clamps, bench stops; measuring, cutting, paring, and boring tools from toolroom	space around bench for working lumber 16′ long	20/8/10
	working up with power tools on standards	sander, shaper, drill press, mortiser	simultaneous use of all tools requires space allowance for each; selective use of tools reduces space requirements; tools on casters for removal to storage space	32/6/10 for sander & shaper; 24/18/10 for drill press & mortiser
board materials plywood wallboard Masonite Celotex	measuring, marking, & setting out	bench 8′ × 4′ × 2′6″ high or two carpenter's horses 2′6″ high with top rails 4′ long; measuring and marking tools	space all around bench or horses	14/10/10
	cutting	bench 8′ × 4′ × 2′ high or two carpenter's horses 2′ high spanned by planks; disc saw or saber saw	space all around bench or horses; on bench, work is placed on waste pieces to allow saw clearance	14/10/10
fabrics	measuring, marking, & cutting	table 12′ × 6′ × 2′6″ high with hard surface and measuring scale along one long edge; pipe at one end for rolls of goods	fabric working area to be kept free of dirt from other parts of shop	18/12/10
	sewing	heavy-duty sewing machines		10/6/10 per mach. & operator
	misc. operations (gluing, appliqués, webbing, grommeting)	bench 8′ × 4′ × 2′6″ high	work on large pieces done in trial setup area or paint floor	14/10/10

(Table continues overleaf)

TABLE 7.2. *SPACE REQUIREMENTS* (*continued*)

Material	Process	Equipment	Comment	Length/Width/Height (*in feet*)
two-dimensional scenery unframed	joining (battening drops, ceilings)	hand tools, paste pot, brushes, staple guns	shop floor space must be 10′ longer than longest batten, wide enough for workmen	40–60/6/10
framed & rolled	joining (framed drops, ceilings)	hand tools, portable power tools	requires most floor space of any joining operation; area equal to largest drop plus passage at perimeter	60/40/10 for plays; 100/60/10 for musicals and opera
flats & frames	joining	hand tools, staplers, power hand tools; template benches, each 16′ × 6′, one per two workers	two-dimensional frames constitute large percentage of scene construction as ingredients of flat or three-dimensional scenery[a]	24/14/10 ea. bench
architectural details and the like	joining	carpenter's benches, horses, hand tools, power saws and power tools nearby, portable power drills, sanders, etc.	intricate fitting and joinery	20/14/10 (two units desirable)
three-dimensional scenery	joining	same as for architectural details but a separate space	at least 1 dimension of each piece is limited by transportation requirements; size and weight are functions of portability	20/14/10
	trial setup	flying equipment, hand tools, portable power tools	space large enough to accommodate the largest sets built in the shop with passage and storage at perimeter	50/40/30 for plays; 100/60/50 for musicals and opera
	covering	benches and horses, supplies of covering materials, paste pots, glue, brushes, etc.; paste-mixing area, water, hot plates, sink	covering applied *after* trial setup, check & adjustments	24/14/10 for 2-dim. ea. bench; 25/25/10 for 3-dim.
scenery (all types)	painting on vertical surface	paint frames and paint deck	two frames to work together or separately; must accommodate highest flat scenery; bottom of frame must rise 3′ above paint deck; frame must sink below deck (total height minus 6′); min. deck space behind frame 3′ for back-painting; viewing space in front of frame	40–80/10–15/25–40
	painting on horizontal surface	paint floor	must accommodate largest drop with walk space around perimeter	40–80/30–60/15–30
	paint mixing	counters, stove, sink, hot and cold water, low bench		10–15/15–20/10
	storage of paints & supplies	barrels, bins, shelves, drawers		
		flammable ingredients	fireproofed storeroom; lockable	8/6/10
	packing & shipping	crates built as scenery; canvas covers and pads from fabrics dept.; hand tools; portable power tools	packing necessary for touring shows; shipping in same area; final check on completeness of job	70/50/12 maximum

[a] When no size limits are imposed by shipping, handling, or storage and the shop connects with the stage through a large opening, flat frames larger than 16′ × 6′ may be permanently joined in the space assigned to two-dimensional unframed scenery.

With the exception of the radial arm saw bench and storage racks and shelves, all equipment in the shop must be movable so as to permit arrangement of the space for the construction of unusual types of scenery and for the application of the *craft* method when necessary.

The ideal scene shop arrangement calls for receipt of raw materials at one end of the building process and dispatch of finished scenery at the other end. Site and highway limitations may dictate departure from this arrangement, in which case it may be necessary to arrange the flow of the work along L-shaped or U-shaped paths. The change of direction of long pieces must be planned to cause minimal disruption of operations.

The shops in both Plan A and Plan B (Figures 7.1 and 7.2) can accommodate the largest size of scenery and the materials for making it, and permit its transportation to and installation on the largest stages (see the dimensional scales in the figures). If particular conditions permit scenery of less than maximum size, the following areas may be reduced proportionally: joining and covering large two-dimensional scenery, paint frames, paint floor. Other areas are proportional to the sizes of basic materials and cannot be reduced regardless of the size of the scenery.

Plan C (Figure 7.3) shows further space reduction, achieved by eliminating the table saw and band saw, and relying on the radial arm saw for rip cutting and crosscutting, and upon portable power saws, disc and saber saws, or unpowered handsaws for random cutting. At the sacrifice of simultaneous performance of separate operations, the following combinations are possible: measure, mark, and set out lumber and board materials in the same space; cut and work up lumber and board materials in the same space; join flats, architectural detail, and three-dimensional scenery in the same space; restrict plastic fabrication to sheet materials and include them with lumber and board materials in processing. *(Ventilation is essential.)*

Any reduction of space below that shown in Plan C impairs the sequential process of construction, imposes complex scheduling problems, produces bottlenecks and delays, jeopardizes the production timetable, and tends to make technical limitations stultify the aesthetics of production.

A self-sufficient organization with shop and stage adjoining, one whose production schedule provides for sequential preparation and presentation of productions rather than continuous simultaneous use of both shop and stage may plan to use part or all of the shop for the storage of rolling scenery while other scenery is set up. This system has become popular in American university theatres and has merit provided two factors are considered:

• Since the shop cannot be in operation during technical rehearsals, dress rehearsals, and performances, either the shop schedule or the performance schedule must be curtailed.

• For simultaneous shopwork, rehearsals, and performances there must be adequate sound isolation of the two facilities.

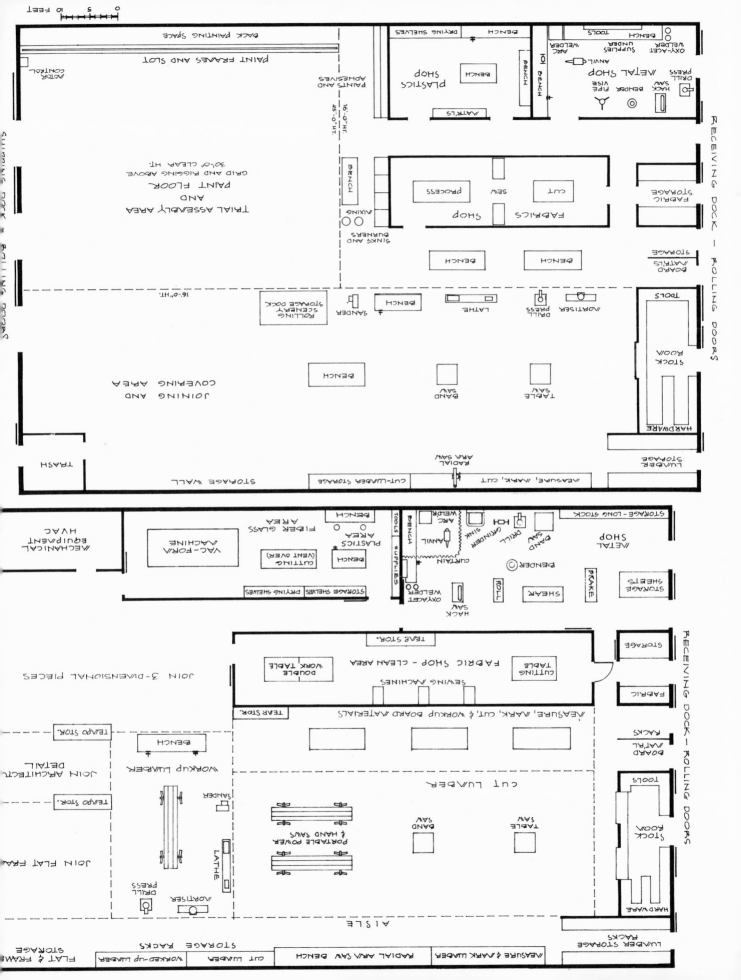

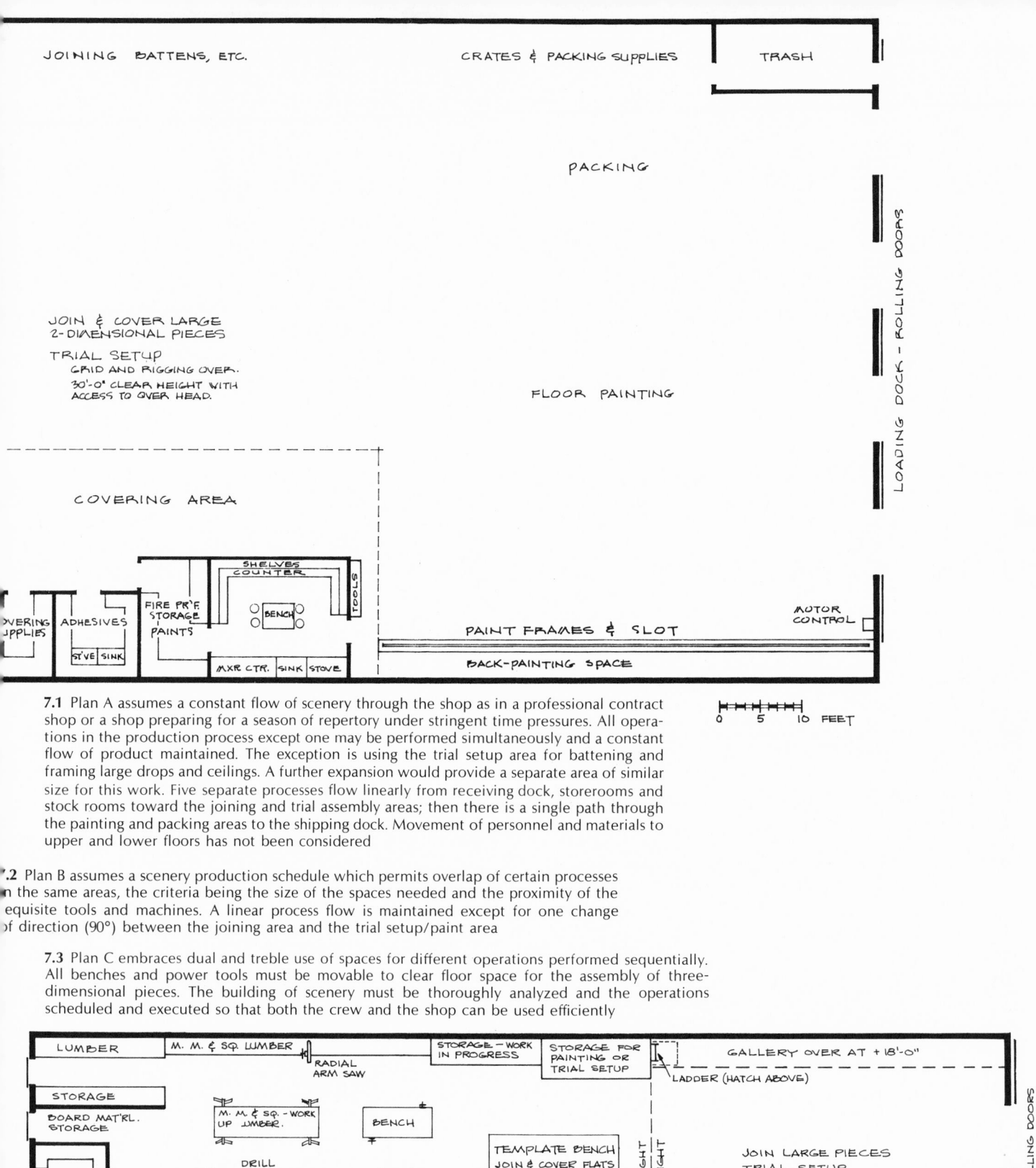

7.1 Plan A assumes a constant flow of scenery through the shop as in a professional contract shop or a shop preparing for a season of repertory under stringent time pressures. All operations in the production process except one may be performed simultaneously and a constant flow of product maintained. The exception is using the trial setup area for battening and framing large drops and ceilings. A further expansion would provide a separate area of similar size for this work. Five separate processes flow linearly from receiving dock, storerooms and stock rooms toward the joining and trial assembly areas; then there is a single path through the painting and packing areas to the shipping dock. Movement of personnel and materials to upper and lower floors has not been considered

7.2 Plan B assumes a scenery production schedule which permits overlap of certain processes in the same areas, the criteria being the size of the spaces needed and the proximity of the requisite tools and machines. A linear process flow is maintained except for one change of direction (90°) between the joining area and the trial setup/paint area

7.3 Plan C embraces dual and treble use of spaces for different operations performed sequentially. All benches and power tools must be movable to clear floor space for the assembly of three-dimensional pieces. The building of scenery must be thoroughly analyzed and the operations scheduled and executed so that both the crew and the shop can be used efficiently

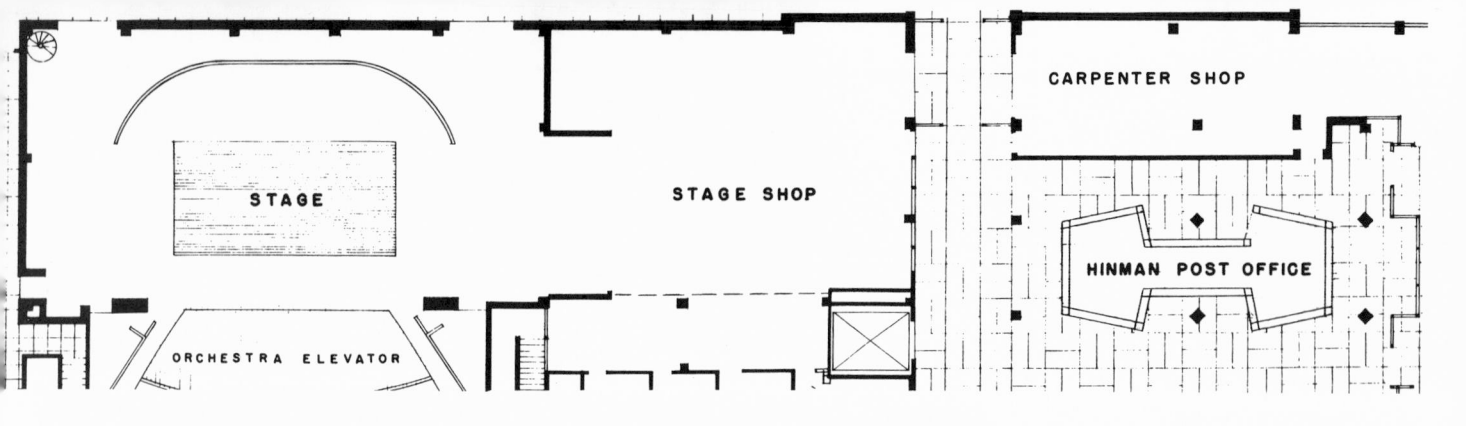

STAGE

STAGE SHOP

STAGE

ORCHESTRA ELEVATOR

CARPENTER SHOP

HINMAN POST OFFICE

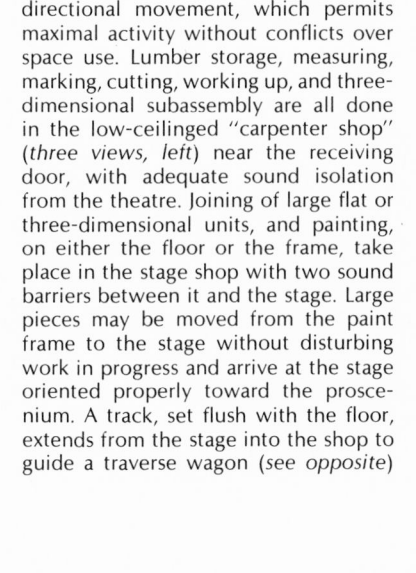

7.4 Floor plan of the shop in Hopkins Center, Dartmouth College. Though small in total area, this shop has unidirectional movement, which permits maximal activity without conflicts over space use. Lumber storage, measuring, marking, cutting, working up, and three-dimensional subassembly are all done in the low-ceilinged "carpenter shop" (*three views, left*) near the receiving door, with adequate sound isolation from the theatre. Joining of large flat or three-dimensional units, and painting, on either the floor or the frame, take place in the stage shop with two sound barriers between it and the stage. Large pieces may be moved from the paint frame to the stage without disturbing work in progress and arrive at the stage oriented properly toward the proscenium. A track, set flush with the floor, extends from the stage into the shop to guide a traverse wagon (*see opposite*)

Heavy-duty outlets for alternating current at voltages of 110 and 220 with 30-ampere load capacity for each outlet and grounding for all equipment must be distributed liberally about the shop, with preference for drop outlets from the ceiling and for wall outlets. Use of the floor for scene construction makes floor receptacles inconvenient.

Compressed air as a power source for tools and machines has many advantages, not the least of which is the incompatibility of pneumatic hand tools with any source of power in home workshops.

Power derived from either hand or electric pumps is capable of supplying high magnitudes (two to twenty tons) of force to the performance of such work as bending pipe and structural metal, punching, cutting, and shearing metal, and lifting heavy objects.

Construction of stage properties involves all the crafts of scenery fabrication raised to the level of cabinetmaking, together with the crafts of drapery making, upholstery, sculpture, wireworking, casting in sundry media, wood finishing, and many others. Hence, if no separate properties shop exists, the equipment and tools of the scene shop may be used. If, however, properties are produced in quantity on a continuing schedule, a separate shop is required, arranged and equipped like the scene shop areas for measuring, marking, setting out, and working up lumber, with additional space and benches for the miscellaneous other crafts.

power requirements
electric power

pneumatic power

hydraulic power

the properties shop

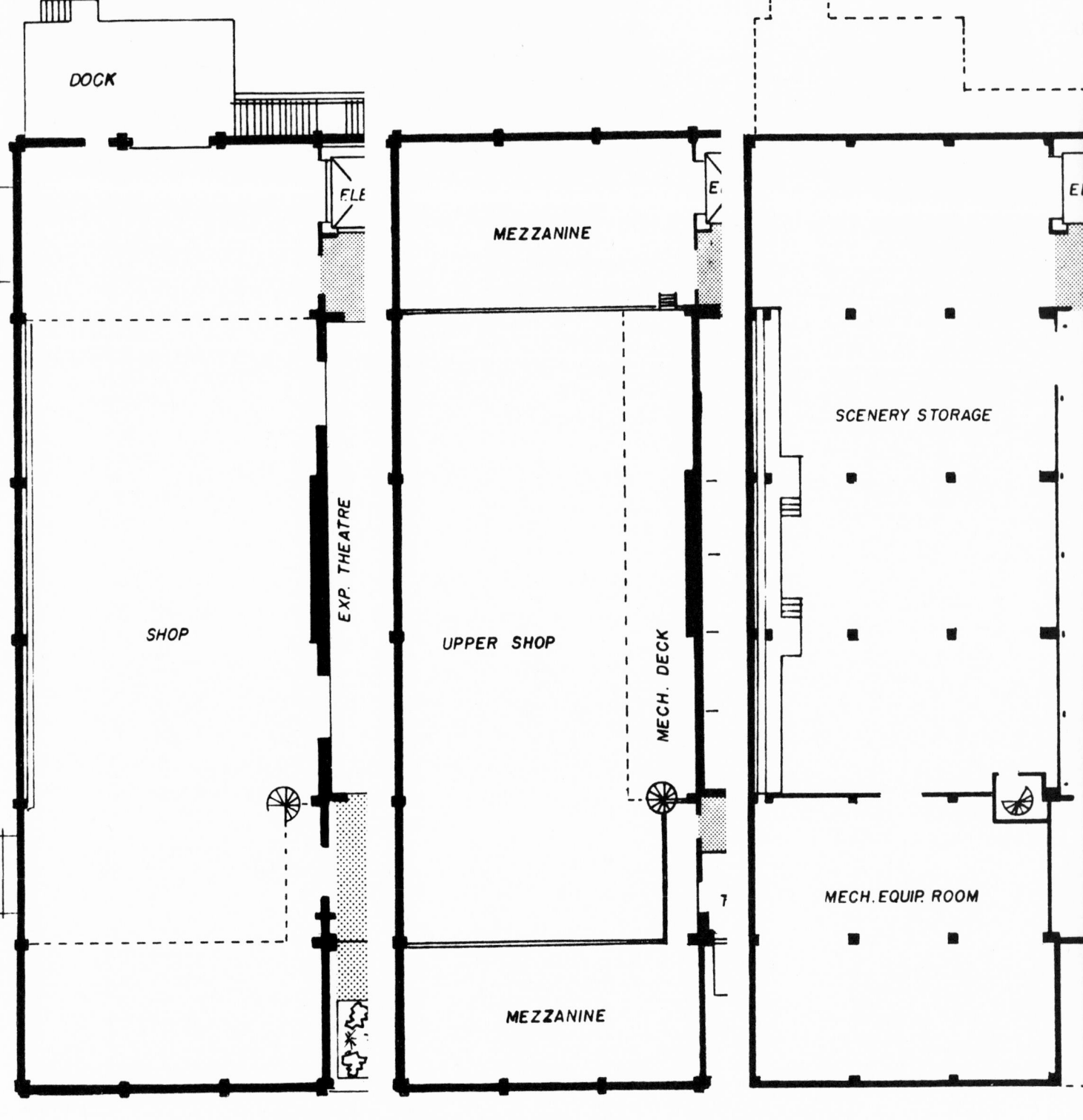

7.5 The shop in the University of Texas Theatre, Austin. Left: the area substantially equals that of Plan C (Figure 7.3), but because of the location of the theatre in the middle of one wall of the shop, the principle of unidirectional movement cannot be applied. When a long piece of scenery is taken from the paint frame to the theatre it must be turned through 90°, interfering with work in progress on the floor. When the shop also serves another theatre, as indicated by the future openings shown in the plan, this condition will be aggravated further. Center: on the mezzanines are the electrical shop and the hand props shop. Supply and tool rooms are under the mechanical deck, which contains storage for drops and battens. Right: a raised deck beside the paint frame facilitates painting at this level as well as at the shop level

7.6 The University of Texas shop

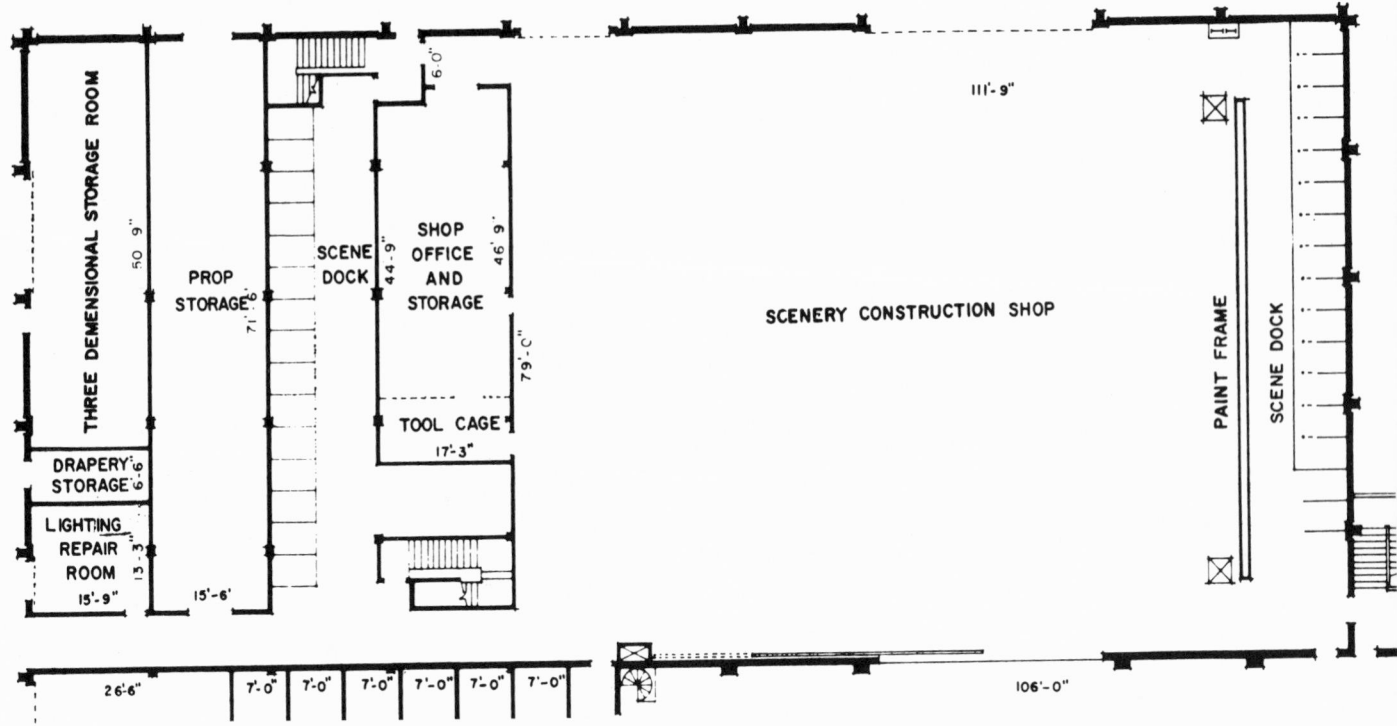

7.7 Shop of the Department of Theatre Arts, University of California at Los Angeles. Generous in area with a large enclosed mezzanine over the storage rooms, scene dock, and shop office, this shop suffers to a small degree from the need to change direction in the flow of work in progress and in the movement of large units from the paint frame to the stage. A drop must be turned through 90° to get the painted surface correctly oriented onstage

the metal shop
space and layout

Metalworking requires, ideally, a large separate shop on the same level as the stage and with adequate access to it, a full complement of tools, separate welding areas, and generous storage space. It must be close to the joining and trial-setup areas, where metal parts are added to the scenery.

receipt and storage of metal

The metal shop must have its own receiving space and stock room since the materials used differ from the usual ingredients of scenery. The weight of metal parts and fabrications dictates short paths of movement and mechanical aids to handling. Convenient storage space is an important adjunct, the amount depending on the amount of work produced. There should be wall racks 22′ long and 2′ wide spaced 1′ apart vertically to a height of 6′ to hold shapes, bars, and pipe; bins for shorter pieces and scrap; a small dock for sheet metal; a moisture-proof cabinet for electrodes; drawers for hardware; and chains to secure extra gas cylinders.

For the average shop, wall racks 22′ long, 2′ wide, and 6′ tall; a bin 6′ long, 3′ wide, and 2′ deep; and a dock to hold five 4′ × 8′ sheets are adequate. If metal suppliers can give twenty-four-hour delivery, this area may be reduced.

special requirements

• No combustible material near the welding area. Fireproof or fireprotected floor and walls.

• CO_2 fire extinguishers.

- One 220-volt, 2-phase, 60-ampere stove outlet for arc welder; four 110-volt convenience receptacles; and 220-volt, 2- or 3-phase outlets as needed for major power equipment.

- Exhaust venting to remove noxious fumes (register intake velocity: 350 f.p.m.).

- Sound isolation. Metal-shop sound levels may be so high as to cause hearing loss from long exposure.

- Adequate light shielding for arc and gas welders.

- Easy access for heavy materials and finished fabrications.

Metalworking requires certain specialized tools, but many are already in the standard scene shop. Electric drills may be used for metalworking with high-speed drill bits, and saber saws can be equipped with metal-cutting blades. The drill press is at home on wood or metal. The grinder used for blade sharpening may be used to prepare welded joints. With the addition of a few special tools, particularly the welder, a scene shop can work metal.

woodworking tools suitable for metal work

Lists of metalworking equipment are in Chapter 8.

Existing scene shops can best accommodate the addition of metal-working in a corner area equipped with a 2′ × 5′ welding bench surfaced with ½″ steel plate, securely fastened to the floor and wall, and equipped with a large swivel-based, pipe-jawed vise in one corner, hand tools and materials stored on wall racks, and castered power tools stored against a wall. When necessary, such a shop can be converted into general scene shop space.

improvised metal shops

Because metalworking tends to be sporadic, a minimal metal shop may be located in space which has other part-time uses, such as the trap room or a rehearsal room. The basic equipment may be placed in a small cage. If large work is done, adequate access to the stage is essential.

The shop must be well lighted and ventilated and should have convenient access to standard woodworking equipment. Plastic foam must be stored flat to prevent warping; hence, shelf or floor space at least 9′ × 2′ must be set aside for storage of new materials. Many plastic foam units may be salvaged and reused.

the plastics shop

If space is limited, forming and finishing plastic foam may be done in areas normally used for other operations if these areas are well ventilated. The only essential item of equipment not found in a well-equipped scene shop is the hot-wire cutter, which may be operated on any workbench and stored in a cabinet with other tools or equipment. Because plastic foams warp, the shop needs clean, flat, unencumbered benches and shelves for binding, coating, texturing, painting, and drying.

The plastic foam shop should be equipped with:

equipment

- A formica-covered workbench 10′ × 3′ × 3′ 3″ high with a flexible hot-wire cutter mounted center and flush with the bench surface.

- A workbench 8′ × 3′ × 3′ 3″ high with a vise to be used for cutting templates, binding, coating, and texturing and painting operations. This bench should be away from the cutting area, accessible from three sides and have a washable surface that will not be damaged by knife cuts.

- A high-speed band saw (220 to 5,000 blade-feet per minute). This item is not mandatory for RPF fabrication, but it is required for cutting RUF.
- A portable sander.
- Hand tools (see Chapter 8).
- Storage for new stock.
- Storage for work in progress.
- A fireproof cabinet for storage of flammable adhesives, coatings, and paints.
- Storage for cutting wires.
- Storage for templates and template materials.

Work with plastic foams must be done as late as possible in the schedule to reduce the chances of damage from scene shop hazards. RPF and RUF fabrication should be completed just in advance of painting.

the paint shop

Space and equipment requirements are discussed below. The techniques of scene painting are described in Chapter 10.

layout and size

The layout of the paint shop should be determined by the relationship of the painting areas to natural light sources (no direct sunlight), the storage and mixing areas, and the convenience for loading in and out. The size of the shop is a direct function of the maximum size of scenery to be painted.

paint floor

The shop must include a floor area for painting scenery laid flat. There are several advantages to painting on the floor: stretching and turning drops is more easily accomplished; snapping lines and drawing large curves is simpler and more accurate; several artists can work on the same piece in widely separated areas; and certain techniques require that the scenery be in this position.

The floor must be clean, level, and smooth, with no depressions in which paint may collect, and must be of wood so that scenery can be nailed, tacked, or stapled to it. The floor is first covered with heavy gray paper which can be thrown away after each job, keeping the wood floor clean and free of spilled paint and dye.

Paint caddies are used to carry paint, pails, and equipment, and the palette table is built very low.

Drops are the largest pieces to be painted and determine the dimensions of the paint floor. The maximum size for drops may be taken as one and a half times the proscenium height and twice the proscenium width. To this must be added adequate space for walking around the drop.

paint frame

A paint frame is a flat structure of wood, or of metal faced with wood, built to supply a rigid plane on which fabrics may be stretched and flat scenery fastened for painting. The wood must be tough but nailable, water-resistant, and so far as possible, rotproof. These specifications indicate bald cypress heartwood 1¼″ to 2″ thick. The frame must be stiffened to prevent deformation. A projecting ledge along the bottom forms a support for flat scenery set upon it.

A rigid structure may be built of standard steel shapes or of systemic

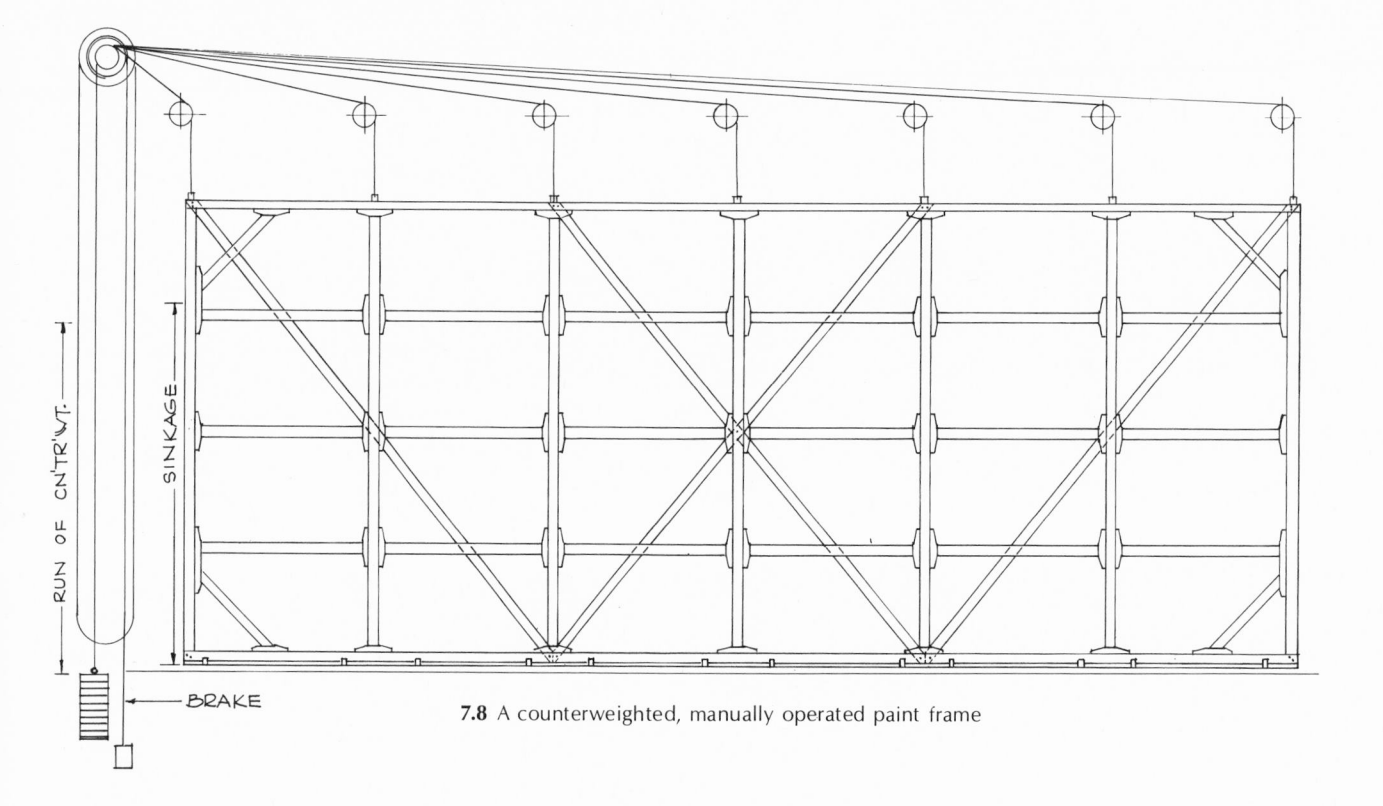

7.8 A counterweighted, manually operated paint frame

metal shapes, such as Unistrut, and faced with wood to provide the required nailing surfaces. The metal must be thoroughly waterproofed.

Dimensions. The height of the frame is, ideally, determined by the height of the largest drop to be painted; the width of the frame, by the sum of the widths of all flats that are to be painted at one time.

Well. The frame is hung in a well or slot in the paint-shop floor close to a long, clear wall. The well is sufficiently deep that when the frame is at the bottom, scenery attached to the top of the frame may be painted by workmen standing on the floor. The frame is rigged to fly. The bottom of the frame, when flown, must be 3′ above the floor to facilitate painting the lowest parts of the scenery.

Operation. Any of the regular systems of hanging, balancing, and operating flown scenery may be applied to the installation, balancing, and operation of a paint frame. A standard system includes wire ropes running from the top of the frame over loft blocks at the ceiling of the shop, then horizontally to and over a headblock and down to a counterweight arbor, which balances the deadload of the frame. This rig is supplemented by a bull wheel geared to the headblock and driven by an endless handline to raise the frame loaded with scenery. A weighted drum brake holds the loaded frame in any position.

Much better than the hand operation is a motor, geared to a traction headblock and capable of raising or lowering the loaded frame and of holding it in any position in response to switches: a pushbutton switch to control UP, STOP, and DOWN, and limit switches at the top and bottom of the counterweight track to prevent overrun.

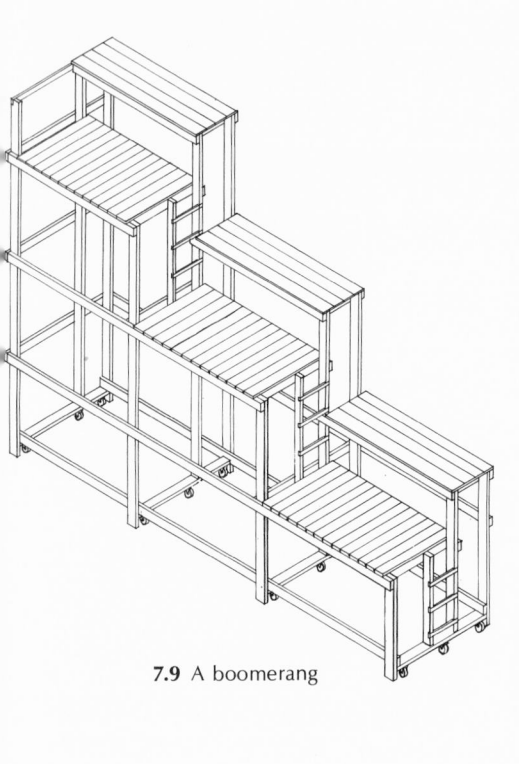

7.9 A boomerang

boomerang

storage area

Fail-safe provision. Whether manual or electromechanical, the operation must be proofed against failure and malfunction from any cause.

Dual paint frames. To lend greater flexibility of use to the paint frame it may be built as a set of dual frames, side by side, each rigged for separate operation and both capable of being coupled for operation as one frame. Different small jobs may be performed simultaneously on each frame or large single jobs may be accomplished on the two frames used as one.

In shops which contract to paint for several theatres the maximum dimensions must apply, but in shops related to specific stages, paint-floor and paint-frame dimensions may be similarly related.

Space around frame. A clear space about 8′ wide along the front of the frame is requisite to accommodate the painters and a movable palette table. A 3′ ledge or shelf at floor level behind the frame is desirable for back-painting. Clear floor space for a distance of 30′ in front of the paint frame is desirable for projecting patterns on scenery. This space may be used for other purposes than painting, but all objects within the area must be removable.

The well and the drain must be easily accessible from the basement for cleaning and recovery of dropped equipment. It is desirable to have the floor of the working area adjacent to the paint frame pitched slightly toward a low curb with drains at the edge of the well. If the frame is hung at a slight angle, the top being several inches further from the wall than the bottom, drips of paint will fall clear of the scenery below the area being painted.

The advantages of a frame include the ability to see the scenery in a vertical position, to use painting techniques that require gravity flow, and to see the degree of translucency or opacity by looking from the back. Disadvantages include the tendency of the frame to shake when two or more people are painting simultaneously, the possibility that spills and drips from loaded brushes may hit lower portions of the scenery, and the difficulty of keeping the whole job in mind while painting the upper portions of the scenery.

Substitute arrangement. A large wall area to which strips of wood 2″ thick have been permanently fastened vertically and horizontally at frequent intervals is used in shops which have no paint frame. The area must correspond in size to that specified for a paint frame. The strips of wood serve as battens to which scenery may be nailed.

A boomerang is a wood or steel platform with two or more levels upon which workmen may stand; it is used to paint scenery fastened to a wall. For each working level there is a shelf for pails, paint, and equipment. The levels are arranged as steps on one side of the boomerang so that two or more painters may work at one time. Two-way casters allow the boomerang to be moved parallel to the scenery.

The paint shop outside the painting area is divided logically into storage and mixing sections. The storage section must have enough wooden containers to hold all the dry colors used. Large containers (at best, 2 cubic feet in size) must be provided for the most-used pigments:

the earth colors, black, chrome, green, cobalt blue, and ultramarine blue. Other colors may be stored in containers of 1 cubic foot content. Working quantities of all colors can thus be kept close at hand.

Dyes are stored either in their original containers or they are premixed in high saturation solutions and stored in one-gallon jugs. Empty plastic bleach bottles are unbreakable.

Binders, both dry and wet, should be stored in their original containers closest to the mixing area.

White vinyl, rubber base, and **casein** are used frequently and in large quantities, and can be purchased and stored in five-gallon drums close to the mixing area.

Brushes, whether with long or short handles, should be hung up to dry with the bristles pointing down. A ventilated cabinet with a lock, near the sink, is convenient. Holes can be drilled in the handles and the brushes hung on finishing nails, or broom clips can be used to support the brushes.

Small accessories such as sponges, rulers, and straightedges are best stored on flat shelves.

Flammable materials, oils, shellac, and the like must be stored in a ventilated metal cabinet.

A locked stock room should be used to store additional supplies of pigment, binders, and dyes, and portable equipment such as spray guns and compressors.

stock room

The mixing section is best located between the storage bins and the water supply, and next to the storage compartments for pails. Its principal items of standing equipment are a large zinc-topped table, a double boiler, and a three-burner stove. The valves or switches of the heating units must be protected from spilled liquids. If the stove is electric, there must be at least four points of heat control for each plate.

mixing area

The sink is an important item of paint-shop equipment because water must be available for mixing glue, size water, and dyes, and all painting equipment must be washed frequently. The sink must be large, at least 10″ deep, of stainless metal or porcelain, and must have an oversize drain and waste pipe. There must be hot and cold water outlets equipped with a mixing valve and a coupling for a rubber hose. There must be sufficient rubber hose to reach from the faucet to the remotest part of the shop. A wide drainboard on one side of the sink serves as a place for drying brushes. A shelf above the sink to hold soap, soap powder, a bracket for paper towels, and droplight complete the equipment.

sink

The paint shop must be well lighted, with high-intensity general illumination so that no parts of the paint frame are more brightly lighted than others and so that a painter will not cast a shadow on his work. Floodlights with color-frame slides may be installed in accessible positions for testing painted scenery under colored lights. Most paint shops are well lighted by skylights and windows. Despite this fact, there is often little necessity for daylight in a paint shop, since it is distinctly advantageous at times to do all painting under controlled artificial light.

lighting

The painting process may be hindered by either too-rapid or delayed

drying control

drying of the paints. Blending techniques require that paint stay moist until the blending is completed, and require slow drying. The application of successive coats of paint, on the other hand, requires that coats already applied be completely dry, and makes rapid drying desirable.

An even circulation of air with temperature and humidity control is ideal for controlling the drying of paint. A battery of electric fans may be used to speed drying.

Shop Maintenance

Tools and machines function poorly or not at all if they are not maintained in good working condition. Loss of productivity can result from misuse or abuse of tools, causing damage or dullness, or from malfunctioning of machines resulting from maladjustment, lack of lubrication, fatigue of the materials of which the machines are made, or parts or connections that have been loosened by vibration.

misuse and abuse

These consist of such practices as using a chisel to lift tacks, using a screwdriver as a prying tool, using a hammer as a mallet, overloading power tools, using the wrong blades in saws or wrong speeds in power machines, and failure to inspect wood for metal in the way of a saw cut.

fatigue of materials

This can show up as breaks in wires or insulation; loose fastenings or electrical connections; crystallization and fracture of metals under impact; wear by friction or abrasion of wooden parts, soft metals, or fabric parts; and deterioration of natural fibers (cotton, hemp, leather) and some synthetic materials (rubber, polystyrene).

maintenance practices

The technical director or shop foreman must be capable of performing maintenance or of setting up a maintenance procedure for designated personnel. Hand tools are their owners' responsibility, embodying the aphorism "A workman is known by his tools"; volunteers in community or educational theatre who use the organization's hand tools are expected to care for them as if they owned them and must be taught proper methods of care.

A trained maintenance man or crew may be part of a shop organization and charged with maintaining all power tools and equipment during shop off-time to avoid downtime during shop hours.

preventing malfunction

Proper function is assured, first, by the purchase of high-quality, warranted tools and equipment from established and reputable manufacturers and by thorough tests of all equipment. Misuse and abuse are minimized by adequate training of workers, either before or during their engagement, in both the correct use and the care of hand tools and machines. Tests and check-outs of personnel are mandatory unless a craft union journeyman's card is presented as evidence of competence. Maintenance of power tools and machines must be scheduled as prescribed by the manufacturer.

Replacement of worn or faulty parts depends on a reserve supply of the parts which are likely to need replacement (saw blades, bits, cutters) and the parts which experience has shown are likely to fail or be damaged or lost. Incipient failure may be detected by test runs with measuring instruments.

Shop Safety

Shop safety results from careful work by skilled workmen, recognition and elimination of unnecessary hazards, recognition and cautious awareness of hazards inherent in the job, and practice of all possible preventive measures. If, despite these precautions, an accident happens, there must be a procedure already established to cope with it.

Common accidents in scene shops are cuts from tools or machines, foot punctures, muscular strains from overexertion, fractures, contusions and abrasions from falls or from falling objects, and minor burns. Uncommon but possible accidents are fires, explosions, inhalation of toxic gases, and electrocution.

Prevention begins with competent administration and organization, orderly procedures, cleanliness, neatness, good space arrangement and use, and effective execution of the following practices:

- Workmen are not given work beyond their capabilities.
- Inherent hazards are recognized (hard hats are worn in areas where objects may fall).
- Workmen are taught safe procedures.
- Work areas are adequately lighted, with particular regard to cutting edges.
- Guards are placed over blades when guards can be used.
- Hazardous machines or areas are color-marked.
- Proper clothing is worn (no loose garments); no machines are operated without gloves; hair is covered; shoes have nonslip, puncture-resistant soles and hard toe caps.
- Adequate masks are worn when indicated.
- Protective devices are installed on stoves and electrical equipment.
- No smoking is allowed.
- Fireproof storage is provided for combustible materials.
- The shop is equipped with sprinklers and fire extinguishers.
- There are adequate, well-marked escape routes.
- Areas where noxious gases may be generated are adequately ventilated.

preventive measures

If an accident happens (and one or more will), the following provisions should be in existence to handle it: At all times a member of the shop crew trained in first aid and certified by the Red Cross must be present. An industrial first-aid kit must be in a prominent place in a part of the shop or an adjacent office where a casualty may be treated in relative isolation and quiet. Instructions for calling a doctor or an ambulance and for reaching and admitting a patient to a hospital, an infirmary, or a clinic must be posted in a prominent place. Procedures should cover all hours of the day and night.

handling accidents

The cause of the accident must be thoroughly investigated. Witnesses must be interrogated and the findings and witnesses' names recorded in anticipation of the report which must inevitably be made and to determine what must be done in order to prevent similar occurrences in the future.

TABLE 8.1. MACHINES AND POWER TOOLS

R = recommended number   E = essential number

Tool or Machine	Type	Small Shop R	Small Shop E	Medium Shop R	Medium Shop E	Large Shop R	Large Shop E
woodworking machinery							
crosscut saw	pull-over or radial arm 10″, 12″, or 14″ depending on shop size	1	1	2	2	3	2
table saw	12″ tilt arbor, 3 hp	1	1	2	2	3	2
band saw	20″, 2 hp (24″–30″ for larger shops)	1	1	2	1	2	2
drill press	15″ min. (larger preferred)	1		2	1	2	2
jig saw	24″, 1/3 hp	1		1		1	1
joiner	6″, 3/4 hp	1		1		1	1
disc & belt sander	3/4 hp	1		1		1	1
tenoner	2 hp	1		1		1	
chain mortiser	2 hp	1		1		1	
thickness planer	12″, 3 hp	1		1		1	1
spindle shaper	1 1/2 hp	1		1		1	1
wood lathe	12″, 3/4 hp	1		1	1	2	1
	24″, 2 hp			1		1	
electric-power hand tools							
circular saw	6 1/2″–8 1/2″	3	2	4	4	5+	5
saber saw	1/4 hp or 2 amps min. (more pref.)	3	2	4	4	5+	5
hand drills	heavy-duty industrial						
1/4″ chuck				2	2	2+	2
3/8″ chuck		2	2	2	2	2+	2
1/2″ chuck		1	1	1	1	2+	2
elec. screwdriver	heavy-duty industrial w/clutch & reversibility	1		2	1	2	2
elec. socket wrench	heavy-duty industrial			1		2	1
disc sander-grinder	7″, 4,000 rpm to 5,000 rpm only	1		1	1	2	1
belt sander	3″ × 21″	1	1	1	1	3	2
finish sander	2 amp motor best	1		1	1	3	2
router	7/8 hp min.; 1 1/4 hp best	1	1	3	2	5	4
Cut-Awl	complete kit	1		1	1	2	1
portable panel saw	heavy-duty only					2	1
elec. hand plane						1	
metalworking machines and tools							
horiz. band saw	1 hp			1		1	1
vert. band saw	14″, 1 1/2 hp, variable speed			1		1	1
bench grinder	1 hp, 10″ wheels, safety glass shield	1	1	1	1	2	1
abrasive cut-off mach.	10″ wheel, 1 1/2 hp					1	
metal-lathe	light-duty industrial					1	
arc welder	180–295 amps	1	1	1	1	2	1
gas cutting torch	gas in rented tanks (o–a)	1	1	1	1	2	1
spot welder	5 kva					1	
power hacksaw	1/2 hp	1					
sheet metal nibbler	12-gauge capacity			1		2	1
portable band saw	variable-speed	1		1		1	
hydraulic pipe bender	sweepbender			1		1	1
manual punch set	7.5-ton cap. (for max. 3/8″ hole thru 1/2″-thick mild steel)	1		1	1	1	1
bench shear	cap. 3/16″ × 3″ bar mild steel	1	1	1	1	2	1
angle iron bender		1		1		1	1
angle iron notcher		1		1		1	1
pipe notcher				1		1	1
standard bender		1		1	1	1	1
pipe cutter		1	1	1	1	2	1
pipe threader		1	1	1	1	2	1
pipe wrench		2	2	4	2	4	4
cable cutter	up to 1/2″ cable	1	1	1	1	2	1
chain & bolt cutter		1	1	1	1	1	1
cable crimping tools	1/16″ thru 1/2″: each size	1	1	1	1	1	1
heavy vise		1	1	1	1	2	1
anvil		1		1	1	1	1

Source: Information supplied by William C. Taylor.

Tools and equipment

8

Scene construction requires the availability of suitable tools and skill in their use. The tables in this chapter list the tools and equipment which should be part of every scene shop. Tools used in scene construction are thoroughly illustrated and described in manufacturers' catalogs which are listed in the Bibliography. The pictures of tools included here are only for purposes of identification by name.

Woodworking Tools

Power-driven saws are divided roughly into two groups: those intended for straight-line cutting and those intended for curved cutting. The straight-line group includes table saws, pull-over saws, and portable motor-driven saws. With each type, crosscutting or ripping may be done.

A table saw may be powered by its own motor mounted in the frame, or by a remote prime mover connected by shafts and belts. The cutter is a metal disc with teeth on its circumference. It is mounted on a horizontal shaft, and revolves through a slot in a cutting table. The work is placed on the table and pushed against the revolving disc. The direction of rotation is toward the work, so that sawdust is taken below the table. T-square guides for crosscutting slide in tracks in the table; fence guides for ripping are attached or clamped in any desired position parallel to the saw disc. Separate interchangeable discs are used for crosscutting and rip cutting. The table may be tilted and the crosscut guide may be set for cuts at angles other than 90°. Table saws are either set permanently in one position in the shop or mounted on caster standards

power saws

8.1 Castered power tools, stored in a bay, may be rolled out when needed

8.2 Behind the four-poster bed (under construction in left foreground): a radial arm saw on a 24' bench, with lumber racks above it. In the rear, a table saw castered

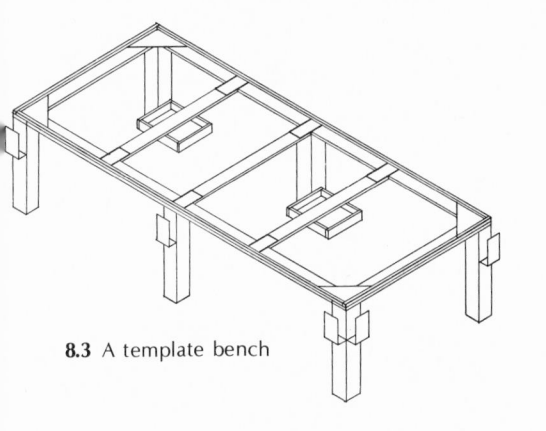

8.3 A template bench

8.4 A template bench with two flats framed and hinged

for moving. If set in one place, a table saw may have extensions for the table to support long pieces of wood.

Pull-over saws are of two kinds. The first has a saw disc mounted directly on a motor shaft and the motor fixed permanently to a rigid metal arm, which is hinged high on the wall and counterweighted to cause the saw and motor to swing back when not in use. This kind is solely for crosscutting. The second kind, radial arm, has the saw disc mounted directly on the motor, and the motor hung to slide on a horizontal track. The track may be swung through 180° in the horizontal plane, and the motor may be rotated in both the horizontal and the vertical plane to make rip cutting or crosscutting at any angle possible. The motor has sufficient power to render the crosscut blade effective for ripping. Both kinds of pull-over saws require bench space on each side of the saw: for crosscutting, a bench equal to the longest stock length of lumber on one side of the saw and equal to one half the length on the other side; for ripping, a space equal to the longest length of the lumber on each side of the saw.

Both table saws and pull-over saws may have dado heads substituted for saw discs, to make possible the cutting of dadoes in one operation.

The direction of rotation of the disc of a pull-over saw renders its operation generally easier and safer than the operation of a table saw. As the disc rotates over the work, the teeth of the saw grasp the wood and pull it into position against the bench stop. In operating a table saw, the work must be thrust against the saw, and the revolving disc tends to force the wood away and to project small particles of wood or broken sawteeth tangentially toward the operator.

Motor-driven handsaws which are portable are used to replace man-powered handsaws for occasional cutting about the shop. They may be used for either crosscutting or ripping and are of value when a large amount of cutting has to be done at the point of construction. They are less useful in scene construction than in other forms of carpentry.

Saws for curvilinear cutting are broadly divided into band saws and jig saws. A band saw has an endless steel blade which passes over two wheels and downward through a slot in a cutting table. One of the wheels is connected either directly or by a belt to a motor. The work is placed on the cutting table and pushed against the blade. Adjustable guides hold the blade in position and take the thrust of the work. Crosscut guides and rip guides may be attached to the table for straight-line cutting. The table may be tilted for angular cutting. Curved cutting must be guided by the operator.

A jig saw is a narrow, straight blade which is stretched taut in a tension bow, as is a hand scroll saw, and moved up and down through a slot in a cutting table, in a reciprocating motion by an eccentric drive. Work is placed on the table and pushed against the blade.

A modification of a jig saw is a machine known by the trade name of Cut-Awl, which has a small tapered blade moving up and down through a slot in the cutting table. The blade is not fastened at its upper end, and it is therefore possible to start a cut at any point in the work by inserting the blade into a bored hole. There is, furthermore, no extension of the standard or frame of the machine above the level of the table, so that pieces of any size may be cut.

A saber saw has short, interchangeable blades which are clamped at only one end and driven reciprocally through a slotted plate. The plate is held against the work. There is a pistol grip, a spring-loaded trigger switch, and a fractional-horsepower motor. The whole assembly is portable.

Band saws, jig saws, saber saws, and Cut-Awls are especially useful in a scene shop for the cutting of thin board materials.

All cutters and moving parts must be encased with grilles or metal guards to prevent injury to the operator.

precautions for operation

Danger zones must be determined and avoided. In general, the danger zone near a saw is in the plane of rotation of the band or disc, since centrifugal force may operate to project bits of wood, broken teeth, or a broken blade outward in that plane.

The working zone must be well lighted.

Blades must be kept sharp. Blades rotated at high speeds through wood develop heat through friction if the teeth are dull. This heat quickly removes the temper of the steel, and blades once heated are of little further use since they are brittle and breakable. To prevent the development of frictional heat, blades must be cleaned frequently of the gummy accumulation of pitch and wood dust which forms in the cutting of softwoods.

Nearly every master scene carpenter has his favorite design for a template bench. Primarily designed to facilitate the construction of rectangular flats, it has established right-angle corner templates, countersunk clinch plates, shelves and racks to carry precut lumber, corner blocks and keystones, fastening hardware, and possibly a glue pot. The top may be either open-framed or solid depending upon preference. If solid it may become a workbench for assembling many kinds of scenery and properties. A template bench may be mounted on casters or set on horses. See Figures 8.3 and 8.4.

template bench

By long-established custom American craftsmen own their own hand tools, each workman possessing and protecting zealously his own preferred variety of hammer, saw, screwdrivers, planes, chisels, rules, pliers, wrenches, etc. This practice is followed in professional scene shops but cannot obtain in the shops of the nonprofessional theatre, whose voluntary workers cannot be expected to purchase complete kits of tools. In school or college theatres a method of lending against deposits or laboratory fees may be used for the issuance of the hand tools most in demand: hammers, screwdrivers, rules, pliers, and try squares.

ownership of hand tools

It follows that whereas the professional scene-construction shop need own only power tools and machines, school and small community theatre scene shops need a full complement of hand tools in sufficient numbers to supply all workers. Table 8.2 lists the hand tools required and the number needed.

TABLE 8.2. HAND TOOLS

Type of Tool	Tool	Quantity
measuring and marking tools	straightedge, metal-bound and metal-ended	1 each 6 workmen
	center square	1 each 6 workmen
	bevel protractor	1 each 6 workmen
	marking point	1 each 6 workmen
	spring curve	1 each 6 workmen
	dividers	1 each 6 workmen
	rule, 6' folding or rolling	1 each workman
	try square (6")	1 each workman
	steel tape (50')	1 each 10 workmen
	metal square (24" × 18")	1 each 4 workmen
	miter square	1
	protractor square	1
	trammel bar and points (beam compass)	1 set
	marking gauge	1
	mortise gauge	1
	spirit level (36")	1
	line level	1
	snap line	1
cutting tools	miter box	1
	crosscut saws	1 each 6 workmen
	ripsaws	1 each 10 workmen
	backsaw (tenon saw)	1
	keyhole saw	1
	compass saw	1
	scroll saw	1
	hacksaw	2
	bolt clippers	2
	tin shears	1
	scissors (4" blades)	2
	canvas knives	1 each 4 workmen
paring tools	chisels (¼", ⅜", ¾", 1", 1½")	2 each size
	spokeshave	1
	drawknives	2
	block plane	1
	smoothing planes	2
	universal plane	1
	circular gouges (¼", ½", ¾", 1")	1 each size
	wood files	2
	wood rasps	2
	triangular files	2
	circular (rat-tail) files	2
boring tools	bit braces (with ratchet)	2
	wood bits (³⁄₁₆", ¼", ⅜", ½", ¾", 1")	2 each size
	expansive bit (1¼" to 2½")	1
	metal countersink (square shank)	1
	wood countersink	1
	hand drills	1 each 6 workmen
	breast drills	1
	drill bits (³⁄₁₆", ¼", ⅜", ½")	6, 3, 2, 1 respectively

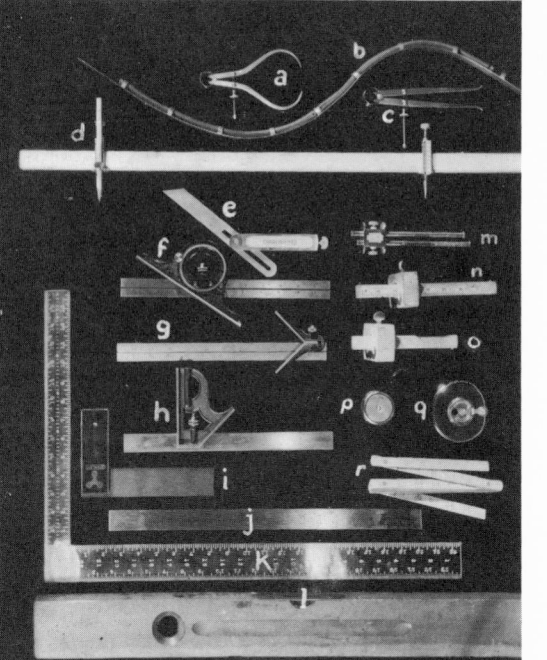

8.5 Measuring and marking tools: (a) outside calipers; (b) spring curve; (c) inside calipers; (d) trammel bar and points (beam compass); (e) bevel set; (f) bevel protractor; (g) center square; (h) combination square; (i) try square; (j) straightedge; (k) framing square; (l) spirit level; (m, o) mortise gauges; (n) marking gauge; (p) rolling rule; (q) steel tape; (r) folding rule

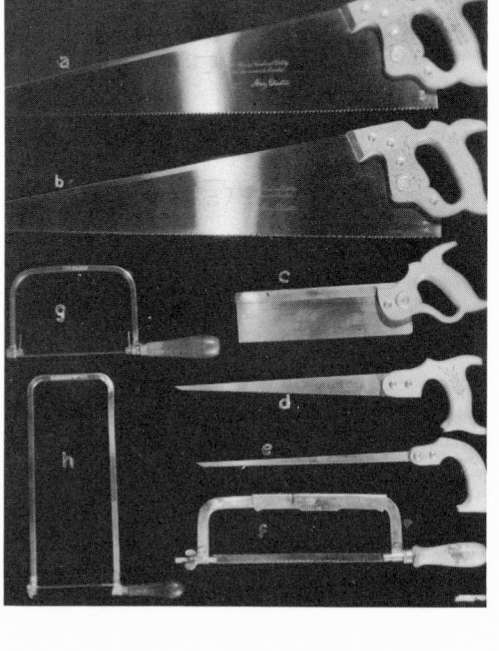

8.6 Cutting tools: (a) ripsaw; (b) crosscut saw; (c) backsaw (tenon saw); (d) compass saw; (e) keyhole saw; (f) hacksaw; (g, h) scroll saws

8.7 Paring tools: (a, b) firmer chisels; (c) mortise chisel; (d, e) gouges; (f) universal plane; (g, h) universal plane cutters; (i) drawknife; (j) spokeshave; (k) triangular metal file; (l) round (rat-tail) metal file; (m) flat metal file; (n) wood rasp; (o) wood file; (p) block plane; (q, r) smoothing planes

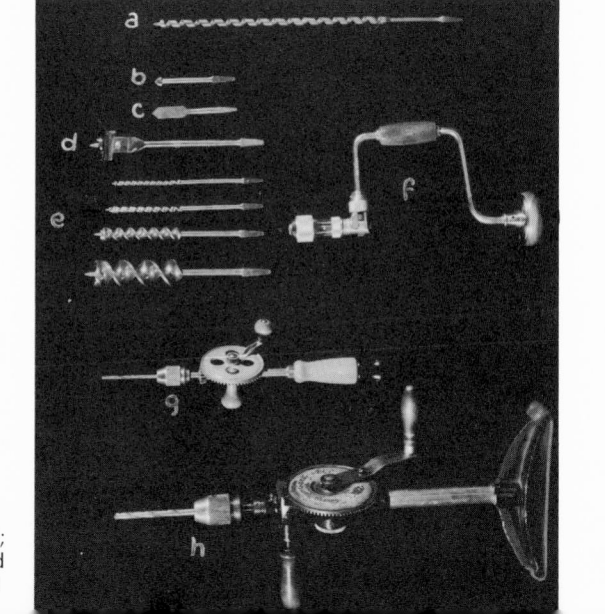

8.8 Boring tools: (a) ship auger; (b) countersink for wood; (c) countersink for metal; (d) expansive bit; (e) wood bits; (f) brace (bit stock); (g) hand drill; (h) breast drill

189

TABLE 8.2. HAND TOOLS (continued)

Type of Tool	Tool	Quantity
driving and holding tools	screwdriver (4″)	1 each workman
	ratchet screwdriver	1 each 2 workmen
	slip-joint pliers	1 each workman
	side-cutting pliers	1 each 4 workmen
	straight claw hammers	1 each workman
	mallets	1 each 6 workmen
	open-jaw wrenches (adjustable 0″ to ¾″)	1 each 6 workmen
	monkey wrenches	2
	Stillson (pipe) wrenches	1 each 6 workmen
	furniture clamps (adjustable up to 5′)	2
	C clamps, metal (3 sizes)	6
miscellaneous	pinch bars	2
	clinch plates, sheet-iron (15″ × 15″ × ⅛″)	1 each 4 workmen
	grommeting tools for #2 grommets	1 set
	emery wheel (preferably power-driven	1
	oil stone	1
	saw set	1

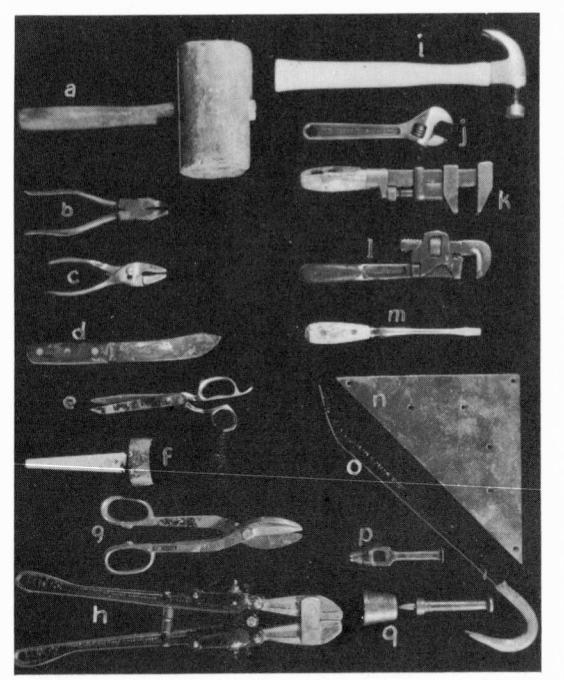

8.9 Fastening, driving, shearing, and canvasing tools: (a) mallet; (b) side-cutting pliers; (c) sheep-nosed pliers; (d) canvas cutting knife; (e) scissors; (f) paste brush (No. 4 round); (g) tin shears; (h) bolt clippers; (i) hammer; (j) Wescott wrench; (k) monkey wrench; (l) Stillson wrench; (m) screwdriver (metal through handle); (n) clinch plate; (o) pinch bar; (p) ring punch; (q) grommet set

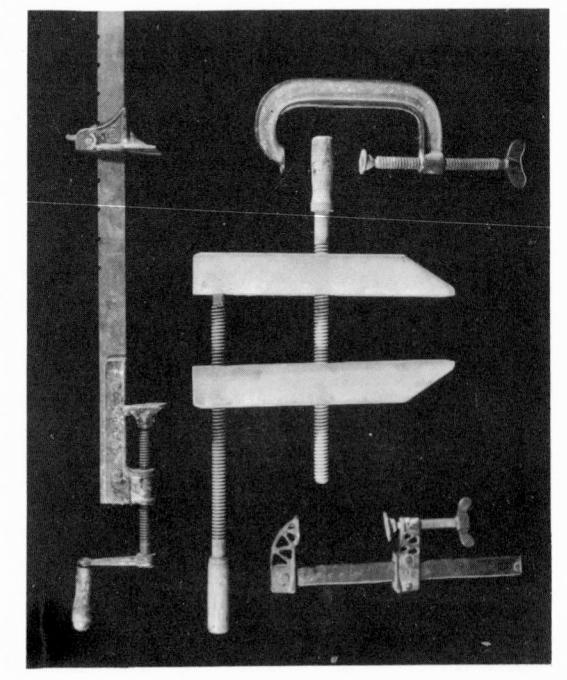

8.10 Carpenter's clamps

These instruments should be those manufactured by a reputable company and as good as the scene shop can afford to purchase. The difference in price between cheap and expensive instruments generally lies in the durability of the materials from which they are made and the amount of time, and resulting care, which is expended in their manufacture. Some instruments have refinements and modifications in expensive models which, when proficiently used, repay the user in accuracy and rapid work.

Saws are made to overcome the strength of the wood fibers either across or in the direction of the grain. The teeth of a crosscut saw are sharpened to points to cut through the tough winter grain. The teeth of a ripsaw are sharpened to flat edges to pare small chips of wood. To allow extra space in the saw cut, in which the saw may move, the teeth of saws are *set* alternately in opposite directions. Crosscut saws can be used for rip cutting, although with slow results. Ripsaws cannot be used for cutting across the grain. Saws which are intended for both rip cutting, and crosscutting are made with crosscut teeth. These saws include backsaws, compass saws, keyhole saws, and scroll saws.

Backsaws are made to supply the need for a stiff saw, which will stay in place without bending, for very precise work. Backsaws are commonly used in miter boxes for the cutting of angles, and for small cuts in cabinetwork.

Compass saws, keyhole saws, and scroll saws are for curved cuts, the choice of saw depending upon the delicacy of the work and the acuteness of the curves. Compass saws and keyhole saws have tapered blades with handles attached to the wide end. Scroll saws are narrow thin blades which are stretched taut in a bow-shaped steel frame.

A hacksaw is used for cutting metal. For general work in soft steel, tempered steel blades of eighteen teeth to the inch are best. For special work on tool steel or on pipe or shapes, it may be necessary to purchase special blades of extra temper or different tooth count.

Handsawing of wood is done with the wood held in position either on a bench, in a bench vise, or on a sawhorse. The reader who is particularly interested in outfitting a shop should consult shop-equipment manufacturers regarding suitable benches.

Paring tools are knives, chisels, gouges, planes, drawknives, and spokeshaves. Powered paring tools are the rotary planer and rotary shaper, in which the cutting edges rotate about a fixed point while the wood is moved past them, in contact with them.

A knife is the simplest paring tool. Although it lacks the possibilities of control which the woodworker must generally have, it may be skillfully used on frequent occasions.

All paring tools and the cutters of rotary planers and shapers have one common characteristic: a cutting edge sharpened in two distinct bevels. The bevel of the edge itself is abrupt to strengthen the edge, and the bevel away from the edge is gradual and wedge-shaped to force the cut wood away from the piece. The sharpening is done entirely on one side of the blade, to minimize the tendency of the edge to bite further into the wood than is required by the operator. All cutting edges,

measuring and marking tools

cutting tools

TABLE 8.3.   HANDSAWS

	Teeth to Inch
crosscut saw	10 or 12
ripsaw	8
backsaw	10 or 12
compass saw	10
keyhole saw	10
scroll saw (narrow frame)	12
scroll saw (wide frame	12
hack saw	18

paring tools

whether in hand tools or machines, are placed so that the sharpened side of the blade comes next to the work.

A **drawknife** is an elongated paring edge with handles at both ends. It is drawn toward the workman to pare the surface of the wood, which is held in a vise.

A **spokeshave** is a small paring edge held firmly in a two-handled frame, designed for paring similar to that done with a drawknife but of more delicate nature. The technique of using the spokeshave is identical with that employed with the drawknife, save that all movements are restricted to the hands and wrists. The work is consequently much smaller and more precise.

The depth of cut of a spokeshave is controlled by adjusting the setting of the blade below the flat bottom of the frame.

Planes are the ultimate refinement in hand-operated paring tools. A plane is basically a chisel fastened securely into a wooden or metal frame (or block) and adjustable for slant of blade and depth of cut. There is a great variety of planes, each of which has particular uses. Of most use in a scene shop are: (1) the block plane for smoothing ends of wood; (2) the smoothing plane for smoothing faces and edges of wood; and (3) the universal plane which because of its numerous interchangeable cutters and its variety of adjustments is useful for a multitude of special cutting jobs, among which are the cutting of rabbets, chamfers, and moldings. The manufacturers of this plane issue a small volume of instructions for its use.

The cutting edge of a plane *iron* is ground to a double bevel, as are other paring tools. The edge, however, is ground with a slight curve at each side so that the paring is done near the center of the blade and not at the sides. This prevents the plane from leaving marks at the edges of each cut.

Gouges are chisels with curved cutting edges, and the technique of using them is similar to that employed with flat chisels.

All types of metal and wood **files** and **rasps** are paring tools. In a scene shop metal files are of chief importance in the sharpening of saws and stage screws. Wood files have occasional use in adjusting the fit of mortise-and-tenon joints, but are rarely useful otherwise. Wood rasps are useful as roughing rather than smoothing agents, in the "antiquing" of furniture and giving edges of scenery a rough appearance.

boring tools These are tools by which cutting edges are revolved about a central axis to remove particles of wood from a progressively deepening circular hole. In this classification are gimlets, augers, bits, spoon drills, and twist drills.

Gimlets, augers, and **bits** have, in common, a lead screw which, when rotated, engages the fibers and pulls the cutting edges into contact with wood. Gimlets and augers are single tools which have the screw-shaped cutter firmly fastened to a handle. Bits are merely cutters which, to be used, must be set into a separate tool, called a bit brace or bit stock.

A **bit brace** is a form of crank by which the workman gains additional power to rotate the bit. The most useful kind of bit brace has an escapement which allows use of the brace in close quarters where a full revolution of the crank is not possible. Standardized square shanks make all sizes of bits adaptable to one bit brace. The combination is called a brace and bit. Bits are manufactured in sizes graded by $\frac{1}{16}''$ differences and the numerator of the fraction is stamped on the square shank. Thus the commonly used $\frac{3}{8}''$ bit bears the number 6 on the shank. An expansive (colloquially "expansion") bit is a bit adjustable to holes of different diameters. One expansive bit with a range of from $1\frac{1}{4}''$ to $2\frac{1}{2}''$ is desirable in a scene shop.

Spoon drills and **twist drills** have no lead screws and are advanced into the wood by pressure of the workman. Drills may be either square-shanked to fit into a bit brace, or straight-shanked to fit into the chucks of either a hand drill or breast drill.

A **hand drill** is a device for obtaining rapid rotation of a drill in metal or wood by a combination of two gears. A handle is provided for holding the drill against the work.

A **breast drill** is operated by the same type of gear system as a hand drill, but has a bow or a strap by which the workman leans his body against the drill to gain greater pressure on the work.

Portable power rotary drills are manufactured by several makers of electrical tools. At least one such drill having capacity up to $\frac{3}{8}''$ is a useful piece of scene shop equipment. It can, furthermore, be mounted in a bench frame to convert it into a drill press.

A metal-cutting **countersink** is a kind of boring tool for cutting a conical depression around a hole bored to receive a screw. It has a V-shaped blade, and a square shank to fit into a bit brace. Examples of the use of paring and boring tools are given in the working up of some of the joints which are set out in Chapter 15.

Metalworking Tools

Metals are worked with special machines and tools and with some of the power and hand tools already listed. In general, even the best-equipped scene shop will not need more than one special machine or hand tool of each type.

The **scriber** is a tool-steel instrument pointed to make scratch marks on structural steel and nonferrous metals.

marking tool

Metal saws are of three kinds:

cutting tools
metal saws

Reciprocating — hacksaw, saber saw, or jig saw. The saw cuts on one stroke; the return stroke is away from the work to allow the sawteeth to be cleaned.

Band, the fastest-cutting. It is used in a vertical, horizontal, or portable frame.

Circular, mounted on a table, in a swing, radial, or portable frame.

Band-saw blades are of three types: *standard pitch,* which produces a fine finish to the cut at relatively low cutting speeds in most metals; *buttress,* or *skip-tooth,* which has a coarse pitch for cutting mild steel

TABLE 8.4. METAL SAW BLADES AND THEIR USES

Teeth to the Inch	Thickness	METAL TO BE CUT
		Kind
14	1″ or more	aluminum, brass, bronze, cast iron, copper, cold rolled steel
18	¼″–1″	tool steels, drill rod, cold rolled steel, medium-weight structural shapes
24	⅛″–¼″	pipe and tubing, BX cable, heavy sheet, metal moldings
32	⅛″ or less	thin-walled tubing, thin sheet

bar and plate stock; and *claw-tooth,* for free-cutting light metals, steel, and plastics.

Whatever the blade used, three consecutive teeth must be in contact with the stock at one instant during the cutting stroke.

A circular saw blade may have teeth or it may be an abrasive disc or a toothless disc which creates melting heat by high-speed friction.

oxyacetylene torch

A cutting torch may replace the welding tip on oxyacetylene equipment for cutting metal. A central stream of pure oxygen consumes the metal, which has been preheated by side jets of acetylene.

paring tools
files

The files listed in Table 8.5 are machinists' files and can be obtained in any of three cuts: *bastard* (coarse), *second* (medium), and *smooth* (fine). There are also special-purpose files for use on particular metals, such as files which cut soft metals without clogging the teeth. A file card is a useful device for cleaning the teeth of files.

TABLE 8.5. METAL FILES AND THEIR USES

File	Use
flat	general
half-round	general
hand (one edge safe)	finishing flat surfaces
knife	corners
pillar (one edge safe)	slots and narrow work
round	enlarging round holes; shaping concave surfaces
square	enlarging holes and inside corners
three-square	making sharp edges; angling corners and notches
warding	narrow work

shaping tools
brake

A brake contains a fixed metal *bed* on which the sheet of metal is placed, a *top leaf* with a changeable *shaping nose* which is clamped down on the sheet by a foot treadle, and a *bending leaf* operated by a lever which lifts the protruding portion of the sheet against the shaping nose to shape it. Various guides, jigs, and nosepieces are available.

roll

A roll is used to bend sheet or bar to a circular curve. Two fixed rollers are opposed by one adjustable roller, located between them. As the work, clamped between the adjustable roller and the two fixed rollers, is moved back and forth by a crank drive to one roller, the adjustable roller gradually reduces the radius of the bend.

bender

This machine bends angle, bar, pipe, and tubing by a movable die acting against two fixed dies. The dies, or forming blocks, are change-able to support the metal as it is bent and prevent deformation. Dies are available to fit standard and special shapes. Benders have varying ca-pacities as to sizes of stock and bend radii. A hydraulically powered bender, by which small amounts of human energy or electrical energy are applied through a hydraulic pump, removes much of the effort from bending metal.

joining tools

The gases are marketed in pressurized cylinders: oxygen in green cylinders with a top-mounted valve with right-hand thread for the regu-lator; acetylene in cylinders with a recessed top, key-operated valve, and left-hand threads to differ from the oxygen equipment. Regulators re-duce tank pressure to working pressure, maintain working pressure as the tank pressure decreases, and adjust working pressure to the needs of different tools. Each regulator has an adjustment screw, a tank pres-sure gauge, and a working pressure gauge. A double hose, green for oxygen and red for acetylene, connects the welding or cutting torch to the regulator. The tanks and hose are stored and moved about the shop on a welding cart.

joining tools
oxyacetylene welding equipment

Filler rods supply the metal for filling the bevels in the material to be welded. They are 36″ long and available in diameters of $\frac{1}{16}″$ to $\frac{3}{8}″$. The alloy of the rod used must match the alloy of the metal being welded.

This consists of a 220-volt, 180-amp, a.c. static welding transformer with secondary taps ranging from 20 amps for thin sheet to 180 amps for 1″ plate, with two connection cables, the negative having a spring clamp for connection to the work and the positive an electrode clamp and handgrip.

arc welding equipment

Arc welding electrodes are rods of steel coated with flux which sup-port the arc and supply filler metal. Diameters vary with the type of joint, its fit-up, and position. The kind of steel varies with the material to be welded:

E6011, for vertical and overhead welding, has a penetrating arc, re-quires a close fit-up, and is coated with white flux.

E6012, with a less penetrating arc than E6011, is used for horizontal and near-horizontal positions, and has a brown flux coating.

E6013, with the least penetration, is used when there is a rough fit-up and for flat and filleted welds; it has a gray flux coating and is the most useful of those listed for scenery applications.

A combination **chipping hammer and wire brush** is used to clean metal preparatory to welding.

accessories

Both a **welding hood** and **leather gloves** must be worn while operat-ing welding equipment. The hood is of fiber glass and has a viewing glass which filters out ultraviolet rays. The gloves protect against burns and abrasions.

Plastic Foam Tools

Like metals, plastic foam is worked with special machines and tools as well as with some of the woodworking power tools and hand tools listed

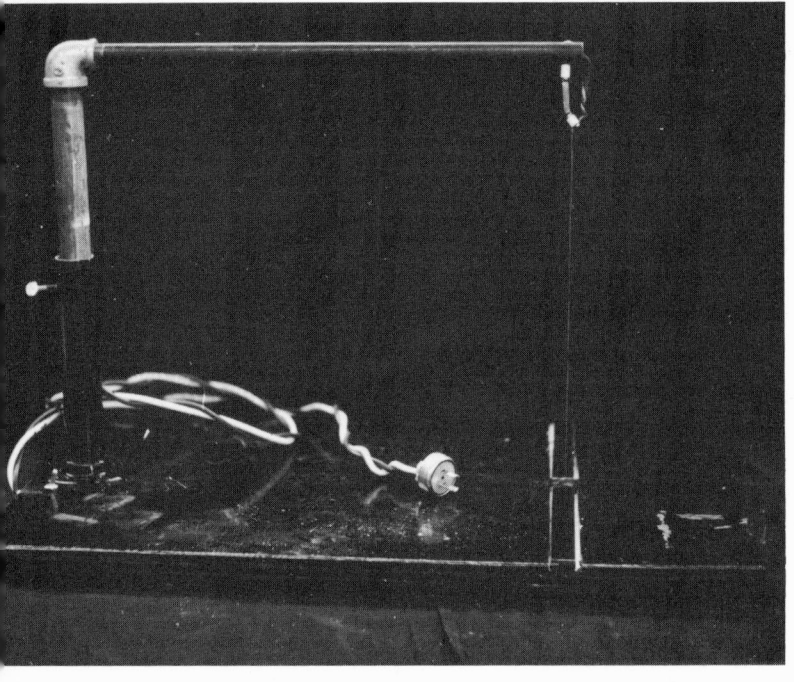

8.11 Simple hot-wire cutter

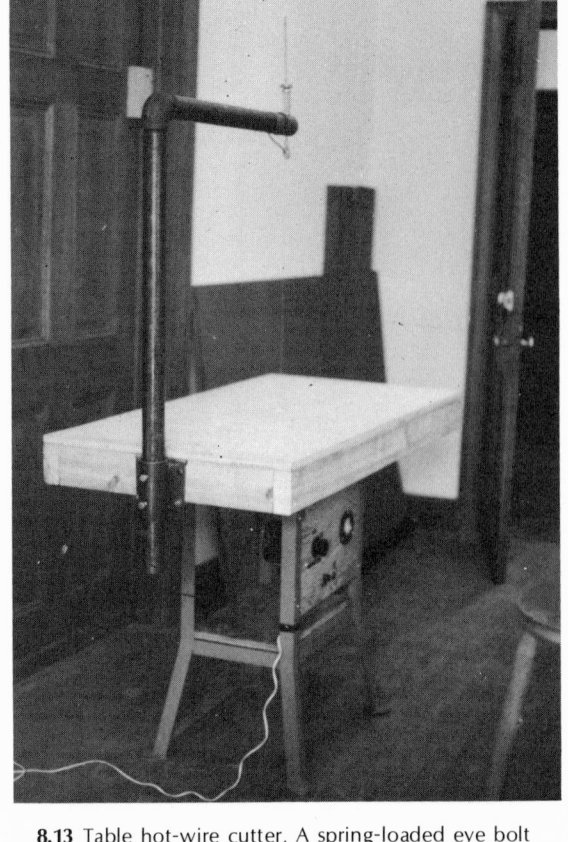

8.13 Table hot-wire cutter. A spring-loaded eye bolt at the top of the wire adjusts for expansion of the wire as it heats up

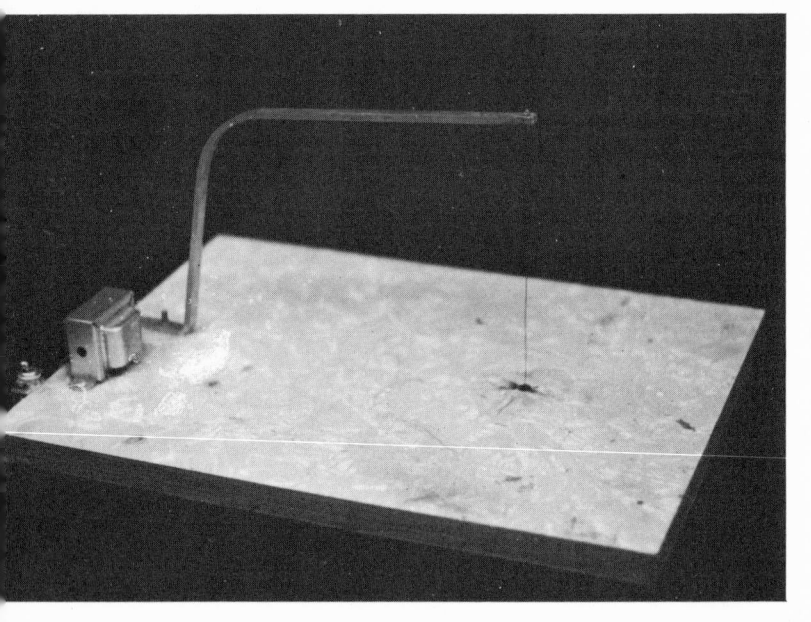

8.12 Flexible hot-wire cutter. Length of wire and angle of cut are adjustable

8.14 Control panel for hot-wire cutter

in Tables 8.1, 8.2, and 8.3. One of each of the following tools should suffice, even for the best-equipped shop:

Simple hot-wire cutter (Figure 8.11)

Adjustable, flexible, hot-wire cutter (Figure 8.12)

Table hot-wire cutter (Figures 8.13 and 8.14)

Flexible-loop, hand-held, hot-wire cutter (Figure 8.15)

Diagonal cutters for cutting resistance wire

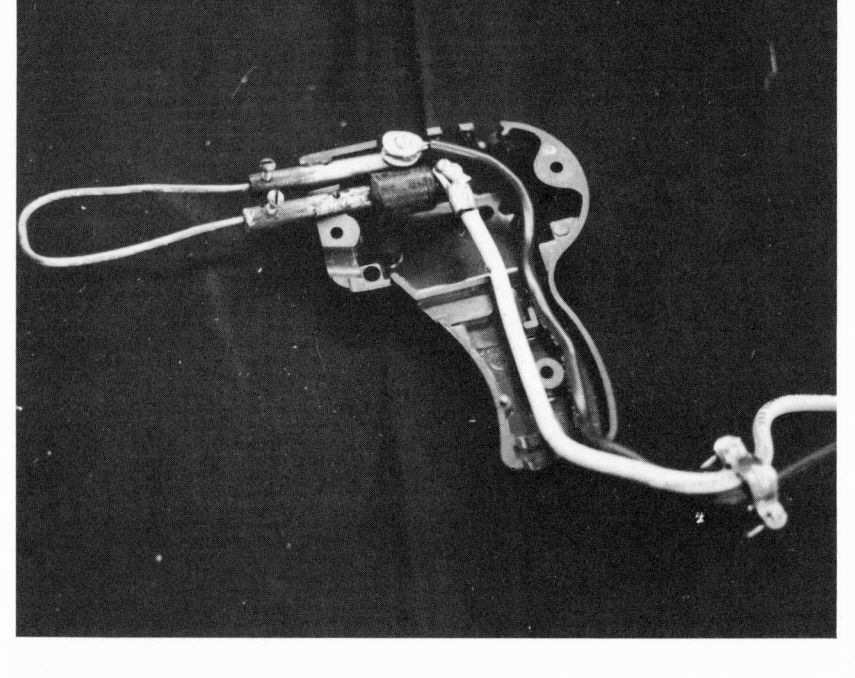

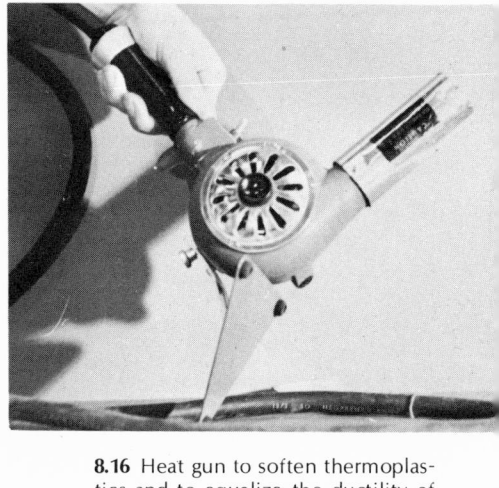

8.16 Heat gun to soften thermoplastics and to equalize the ductility of sheets being heated on the oven

8.15 Flexible-loop hot-wire cutter. Loops of various shapes may be inserted

Carbide-tipped blade for use on a table saw or pull-over saw (to be used only for cutting plastic foam)

Assortment of pliers for shaping resistance wire

Screwdriver, small

C clamps (4)

Assortment of weights of various sizes

Matte knife

Serrated (bread and steak) knives

Propane torch equipped with an assortment of nozzles

Tools for Thermoplastics

For woodworking tools used on thermoplastics, see Tables 8.1, 8.2, and 8.3.

The heat gun is a flameless blowtorch to produce hot air at 750° to 1,000° F. from a turbofan past a ceramic-coated, electrical heating element. Hand-held, its primary use is to direct heated air, under close control, at thermoplastics in order to render them ductile and moldable; its secondary use is to quick-dry scene paint or plaster of Paris casts. The ceramic element will not withstand rough handling. See Figure 8.16.

The hot-air gun is similar to the heat gun but produces heat (400° to 700° F.) in a fine jet of air from a compressor through a valve which regulates airflow: the faster the flow the lower the temperature at the nozzle. Nozzles are changeable to produce various distributions of the heated air. This tool is used like an oxyacetylene welding torch, to direct heat at the seam to be welded and at the welding rod (which in this case is of thermoplastic material) to fill a vee or make a fillet. See Figure 8.17.

heating and welding equipment
heat gun

hot-air welding gun

8.17 Hot-air welding gun

A metal vessel large enough to receive pieces of thermoplastic in boiling water, and at least 25″ × 9″ × 9″ in size. For boiling the water, a hot plate is used under the boiler.

This equipment can be made in any scene shop.

thermoforming equipment
frame

The frame is used to clamp sheet plastic and hold it while it is being heated, formed, and cooled. Small frames can be handled by one person, larger ones by two. Frames large enough for molding columns and pilasters may require suspension rigging or a mechanical lift. To create the necessary air seal, the inside dimensions of the frame must slightly exceed the outside dimensions of the forming table (see below).

heat sources

There are three types: the **heat gun** (see above), the **oven,** and the **infrared lamp cluster.**

The oven is a metal and asbestos box containing gas burners on the bottom. It is open at the top to receive the framed plastic. Gas affords subtle control of heat. See Figure 8.18.

With the infrared lamp cluster, a rheostat and variation of distance between the lamps and the frame afford subtle control of heat. Even distribution of heat is difficult to achieve; power cost is high.

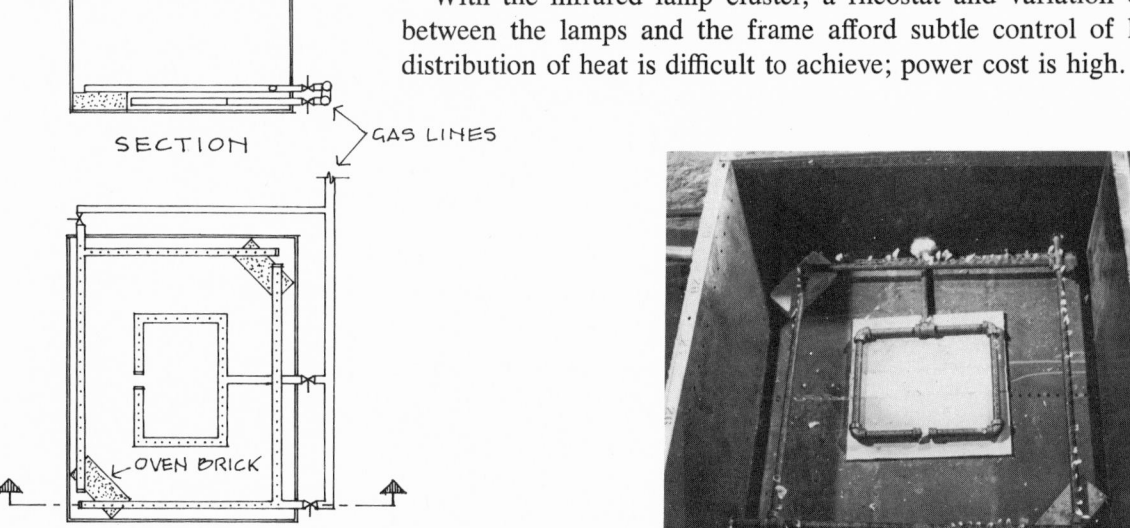

SECTION

GAS LINES

TOP
OVEN

OVEN BRICK

8.18 Gas oven for softening sheets of plastic before placing them on the thermoforming table. Left: schematic of the oven

thermoforming table

The thermoforming table is a sandwich of two pieces of ¾″ plywood on either side of ¼″ masonite strips sealed around the outside edges. The upper piece of plywood is perforated with ¹⁄₁₆″ holes on 2″ centers for even dispersion of vacuum pressure. The lower surface has a through fitting connected to a vacuum tank by a length of pipe; a control valve is placed in the pipe. Molds are placed on this table. A frame containing heated plastic sheet, whose inside dimensions slightly exceed the outside dimensions of the table, is forced over the edges of the table to create the necessary air seal. When the vacuum valve is opened, the air trapped underneath the sheet is displaced into the vacuum tank, which causes the heat-softened plastic to conform exactly to the contours of the mold. The plastic cools and sets within seconds. Forming tables and frames should be dimensioned to take maximum advantage of a standard sheet size. See Figure 8.19.

This consists of a vacuum pump (or compressor altered to reverse the airflow), a reservoir tank, an indicator gauge, and an assortment of nipples, elbows, tees, valves, and pipe to connect the pump to the reservoir to the forming table.

These are worn when pinch-forming and hand-bending.

vacuum system

heat-resistant gloves

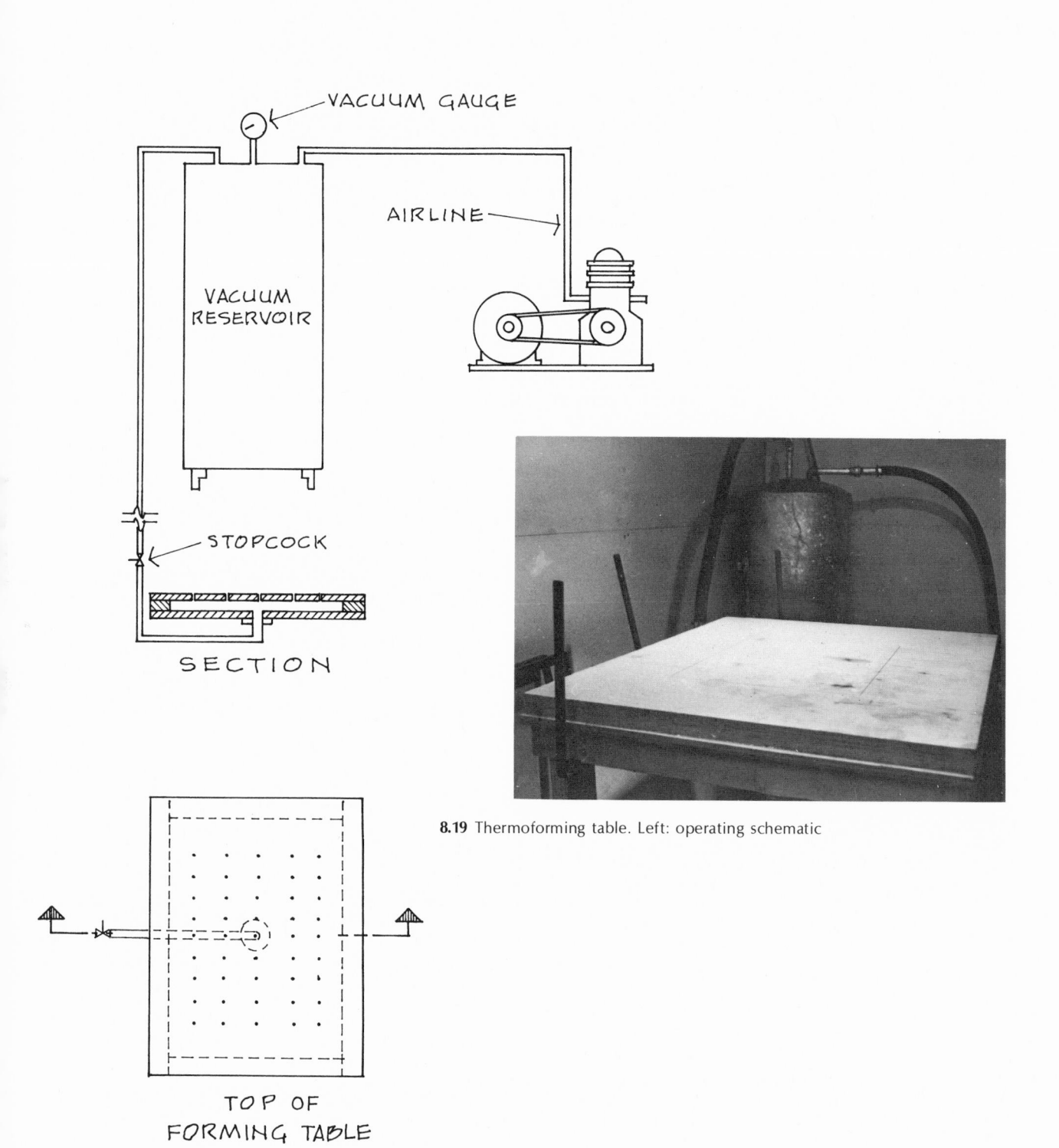

8.19 Thermoforming table. Left: operating schematic

9 Scene construction

Scene construction is chiefly a specialized type of joinery to which have been added metalworking, plastic molding, and other assorted skills. The materials and technique of the woodworker are adapted, and other techniques and materials introduced, to manufacture structures which differ from the product of the carpentry shop, cabinet shop, or woodworking mill. The nature and uses of scenery impose requirements which make scene construction a craft in itself, one with which the ordinary carpenter or cabinetmaker is unfamiliar, though his skills may be adapted and contribute to it.

This chapter offers an analytical approach to the procedure and methods of scene construction and will review the common craft practices which apply to the scene-building shop. The discussion is not intended for the master scene carpenter, but rather for the novice, whose knowledge of woodworking is limited. As an additional help, Chapter 15 contains representative problems with instruction and solutions. To acquire a high proficiency as a woodworker, however, it is necessary to read more specialized texts and to complete training courses or serve an apprenticeship in a shop.

Scene carpentry differs from other forms of carpentry and cabinetwork in several respects:

• The objects built must be demountable and portable, and yet when assembled they must show no evidence of joining.

• Scenery is built for use during a short period of time, as compared with furniture and dwellings.

• Scenery presents only one finished side or face to the audience.

• Scenery is never seen or examined at close range.

Scenery which has to be demountable and portable must be built in pieces which fit neatly together and which are strong enough to withstand intermittent and often rough handling. The frames must hold their shape so that the fit is assured each time they are assembled. There can be no cutting to fit when the scenery reaches the stage. Each piece must be constructed exactly to size and shape as planned. Rebuilding scenery, when it reaches the stage, is costly.

The fact that scenery is used for a shorter period of time than other carpentered objects allows the use of lumber of smaller cross section than is generally used in permanent structures. For the same reasons and for reasons of workability, softwoods are used in scene carpentry.

Scenery which presents only one side to the audience allows the builders liberties in its construction. Joints may be exposed or reinforced on the back of the scenery. Strengthening pieces, stiffeners, and braces may be placed where necessary. Because scenery is always seen at some distance by its closest observers, and is under special lights, it may often be faked, either by substituting one type of construction for another, simplifying construction, or painting details which are built for actual use. The requirements of speed, economy, and portability also make it desirable to replace what would in reality be solid and heavy material with lightweight and quickly joined material.

Standard Procedure

Scenery is built in a series of operations, each one different from the others, and the divisions of the shop personnel accord with this series of operations. A standard procedure which may be followed in the construction of almost all scenery makes a logical outline for this chapter.

Whether the personnel of a scene shop numbers one or fifty, this procedure is effective. It furnishes the checklist by which the progress of a set of scenery can be followed, as well as an analysis by which a scene shop can be departmentalized for efficient operation. It is equally effective when applied to the fabrication of scenery in other materials: metal, fiber glass, rigid plastic foam, and thermoplastics. All of these will be discussed later in the chapter.

The master building carpenter, or boss carpenter, receives from the technical director prints made from the working drawings and the work schedule which governs the construction. He studies the prints to become familiar with the indicated construction and assigns the work to divisions of his shop personnel with the object of completing it according to the schedule. He supervises the process of construction and inspects the work at each step of the process. He manages the routine affairs of shop maintenance.

the boss carpenter

The boss carpenter, having made himself thoroughly familiar with the scope and magnitude of the job, divides the work into logical parts and groups the pieces of scenery into parcels of work which may proceed together through the production process. A group of flats may form a unit; a single door unit may go through by itself. He then uses the work order form (Figure 9.1) which has been designed to suit the

the work order
(work ticket)

SHOW _____ JOB NO. _____

Set _____ Unit _____ Pieces _____

Operation	Start		Finish		Time		Date	Done by	and
	H.	M.	H.	M.	H.	M.			
Cutting List									
Measure & Mark									
Cut									
Work Up									
Join									
Assemble Unit									
Other Work									
Total Time									

Cost:		Total Time each man	H.	M.
Labor ____H. ____M. @____				
Materials				
Other				
Total Cost				

9.1 Work order form

system of operations in his particular shop. The form, known in industrial management as a *work ticket* or *job ticket,* contains a listing of all subdivisions of work to be done on each unit. It is attached to the print and goes from department to department as the work progresses. It is signed and dated by each department in turn and it is returned to the boss carpenter when the scenery is completed. It may be returned to him at the close of work each day for a checkup against the work schedule. The work order may be elaborated to become the form for time-keeping and cost accounting.

the cutting list
A cutting list is made for every parcel of scenery which is to go through the shop as a unit. On it in tabular form are quantity, identification or name, size, length, and notation of special work to be done on each item of material. In the case of lumber, the stock lengths from which required lengths are to be cut are specified.

The cutting list is made by either the boss carpenter or an assistant, working directly from the prints (Figure 9.2 is a representative sample). The prints give the finished overall dimensions. The compiler of the list is familiar with the actual sizes of the lumber carried in stock and calculates actual cutting lengths by deducting where necessary the widths of other pieces which are included in the dimension given on the draw-

					CUTTING LIST		
Production : "Down the Hatch" Set #2 Blueprint #22 Unit F							
Compiled by: J. Doe Measured by: P.X. Cut by: D.G. Date cut: 10/4							

No.	Item	Size	Length	Cut From	Special Work	
2	Stiles	1"×3"	11'-6½"	2-12's	————	✓
2	Rails	1"×3"	5'-9"	1-12	————	✓
2	Toggles	1"×3"	5'-3½"	1-12		✓
2	Braces	1"×2"	3'-0"	Scrap	45° each end	✓
4	Keystones					✓
4	Corner Blocks					✓
4	½ Keystones	2"×8"		2 K.S's		✓
1	Canvas					

9.2 Part of a cutting list

ing. Where necessary, he adds length to be allowed for tenons, halved joints, and scarf joints. He works out the least wasteful way of cutting the required lengths of lumber from the standard lengths carried in stock. He notes as special all work which has to be done to prepare the items listed for joining. He identifies each part with a name, letter, and number, for example, "stile A-1," which he marks on the print and which will be marked on the part for identification during the building process.

Short lengths of lumber tend to accumulate in a scene shop. It is therefore economically important for the compiler of the cutting list to select carefully and specify the stock lengths from which required lengths are to be cut. Short lengths are combined in the cutting list to be cut from one long piece with the least waste. Inasmuch as stock lengths are multiples of 2' from 10' to 16', there need never be more than 1' 11" waste from any stock piece.

With the completion of the cutting list, actual work on the scenery begins. One or more workers, following the directions on the cutting list, select the materials, measure and mark cutting lengths, and set out, that is, measure and mark the materials for all additional woodworking. Setting out may also be done after the lumber is cut.

Measuring lumber can be properly done only by a precise worker with an accurate eye and a steady hand, using dependable measuring instruments and a sharp marking instrument. The worker must, of course, be familiar with the system of measure commonly used in the shop and with the stock sizes and lengths of materials to be measured. A few simple measuring instruments suffice for most of the marking and setting out to be done in a scene-building shop, where neither the allowable error (1/64") nor the detail of the work are as fine as in other kinds of shopwork.

The size of lumber, its width and thickness, is established by the lumber mills, and pieces are supplied in a variety of sizes and lengths. The workman thus has one or two of the three dimensions supplied him, and has to use measuring and marking tools to determine the other two or the third. He has supplied to him, in most stock materials, one or more of the essential reference lines or straight edges from which he can, with his instruments, make the necessary measurements.

measuring, marking, and setting out

cutting and working up

The next step in the process is to carry out the work indicated by the measuring and marking. All materials are cut to exact size and shape. All work that can be done on individual pieces of material before they are joined into a piece of scenery is done at this time. Notches are made into which other pieces will fit later; rabbets, dadoes, and plows are made to accommodate sill irons; mortises are cut for latches in door stiles; mortises and tenons for joints are cut. Bevels, chamfers, and decorative cutting may be necessary. A general rule is that all work which can be done before a piece is joined to other pieces must be done, since it is obviously easier to manipulate and work on a single piece than it is to work on the piece after it has been attached to other pieces to make a frequently large, and always cumbersome, frame.

In this work, speed and adroitness in the handling of woodworking machines and hand tools are requisite. Precision is essential, and governs the success of the later work of joining.

Lumber is cut and worked up either by hand with woodworking tools or with power-driven machines. It has certain characteristics which influence the design of woodworking tools and which must be understood by the workman before he can intelligently select the proper tool for a job, care for the tools, and perform woodworking. The nature of wood underlies the technique of woodworking.

properties of wood

Wood has *density*. The density of wood varies from hard to soft with different species. The worker of hardwoods must work slowly, sharpen his cutting tools frequently, and possess tools of the finest steel, whereas the worker of softwoods may work rapidly, sharpen his tools infrequently, and if forced to economize, get along with inferior tools.

Wood has *grain,* which is an alternate difference in density within the wood caused by the seasonal changes in growth of the tree. The introduction of any sort of wedge between the layers of winter growth tends to split or splinter the wood. Grain, furthermore, is seldom absolutely straight because of conditions of growth, and a split may extend into part of the wood which the woodworker may want to preserve intact. Tools for cutting and working wood, then, are designed to overcome the strength of the winter grain, and nullify the splitting tendencies due to the difference in density between winter and summer grain. The woodworker, furthermore, must pay attention to the condition and direction of the grain at all times.

Wood has *moisture content.* Dry, well-seasoned wood is more easily worked than wet, or green, wood.

Wood from all species of evergreen trees has a *resin content* which varies with the species. This resin may cause the formation of a gummy deposit upon the cutting edges of tools. The presence of resin may cause weak spots in the wood, known as pitch pockets, and in some species of wood may even have a lubricative or a resistive effect. Other properties which do not directly affect the working of wood are treated in Chapter 6.

joining

When cut to correct length and size and completely worked up, the parts of each piece are then laid out on an assembly bench, template bench, or the shop floor, placed in proper juxtaposition according to the prints, checked for correctness of all angles and dimensions, and joined as indicated in drawings and specifications.

Joints are fastenings of two or more pieces of wood so that a surface of one piece is held securely against a surface of another. All possible joints fall into these categories: end to end, end to edge, end to face, face to face, edge to face, edge to edge. See Table 9.1 and Figure 9.3 on the next pages.

kinds of joints used

Because of the demountable and portable requirement of scenery, both *permanent* and *temporary* joints are used. Permanent joints remain until the scenery is destroyed. Temporary joints must be separated when the scenery is reduced to units for storage on stage, and when the scenery is reduced to separate pieces for transportation. Such joints must have strength and rigidity when the scenery is assembled, and must be easily and quickly separated.

The flat is the basic piece of scenery. See Chapter 5 for its development, varieties, and multitudinous uses. There are two standard methods of joining the pieces of lumber which compose a flat:

joints used in flat construction

• A **butt joint** fastened by a piece of 3-ply wood held by clout nails, clinched, is employed whenever economy of time, labor, and materials require it and conditions of use of the scenery allow it. The joint is not a strong one, but is capable of withstanding the stresses of ordinary handling for a short-run production. Butt joints must unavoidably be used when the shop lacks machinery for working up mortise-and-tenon joints since the time required for hand-working mortise-and-tenon joints can seldom be afforded in scene construction.

• A **mortise-and-tenon joint** is usually — but not always — reinforced with plywood. It requires more working up than a butt joint does, and more care and time in assembly. But it is so much stronger that it is universally used by professional scene builders. The mortises and tenons are cut by machine and a quick-setting adhesive bonds the plywood corner blocks and keystones to the lumber.

In conformity with most civic ordinances for the reduction of fire hazards, scenery must be rendered fire-resistive or flameproof. Inasmuch as it is an established custom and practice to use flameproofed covering materials, scenery frames are coated with a flameproofing solution before they are covered. No inexpensive chemicals will render combustible materials fire*proof,* but there are many which will make scene materials slow-burning or *flame*proof.

flameproofing

Theatrical supply houses sell flameproofing chemicals which may be dissolved in water and brushed or sprayed on scenery. A preparation which is approved for flameproofing lumber in many communities consists of 1 pound of borax and 1 pound of sal ammoniac completely dissolved in 3 quarts of water. The theatre technician must be governed by the demands of the fire-department inspector in the particular community in which the theatre is located. Flameproofing solution is brushed or sprayed onto all scenery frames before they are covered. This operation is performed at a time when the frames may be left for several hours to dry, preferably just before closing time.

The hardware which is used to join and brace the scenery is applied

joining to form units

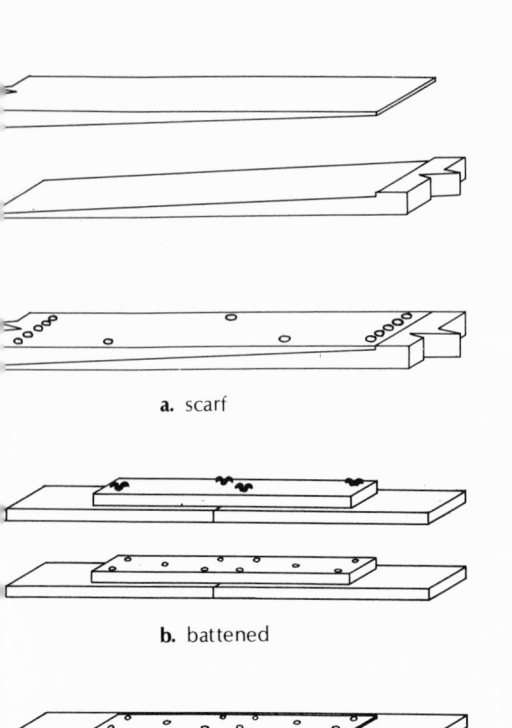

a. scarf

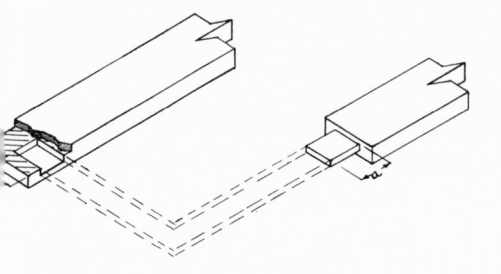

b. battened

c. strapped

d. hinged and battened

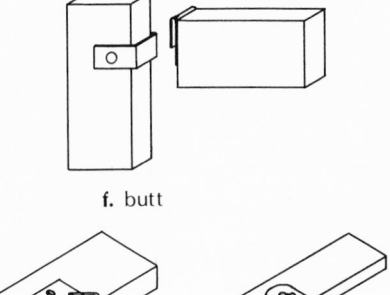

e. mortise and tenon

f. butt

9.3 Joints

TABLE 9.1. JOINTS

(small letters in parentheses refer to illustrations)

Position of Pieces Joined	Name of Joint	Permanent Fastening	Temporary Fastening
end to end	scarf (a)	glue and clout nails	. . .
	battened (b)	common nails, clinched	bolts and wing nuts
	strapped (c)	clout nails or screws	. . .
	hinged and battened (d)	. . .	bolts and wing nuts
end to edge	mortise and tenon (e)	glue and clout nails	. . .
	butt (f)[1]	keystones, corners, or straps and clout nails, clinched	loose-pin hinges, picture hook and loop, or ceiling plate
	shoe with mortise (g)	glue, clout nails, and screws	. . .
	notched butt (h)	finish nails, angled	. . .
end to face	butt (i)	finish nails, angled	loose-pin hinge or picture hook and loop
	tenon and wedge (j)	self-fastening	. . .
	blocked butt (k)	screws and finish or common nails	. . .
	housed (l)	glue and screws or finish nails	. . .
	cleated (m)	screws or finish or common nails	. . .
edge to edge	tongue and groove (n)	glue and battens	. . .
	butt (o)	keystones	loose-pin hinges
		battens	lash line
		tight-pin hinges	. . .
edge to face	butt[2]	nails or screws	lash line
		tight-pin hinges	loose-pin hinges, picture hook and loop, or bolts and wing nuts
	blocked butt (p)	nails or screws	lash line
	housed or rabbeted[3]	nails, screws, and glue	. . .
face to face	lapped (q)	nails or screws	bolts and wing nuts
	halved (r)	glue and nails	. . .
	notched (s)	glue and nails	. . .

[1] Additional illustrations are given in Chapter 15, Figures 15.20–23.
[2] See Chapter 12, Figure 12.39.
[3] Similar to joint l.

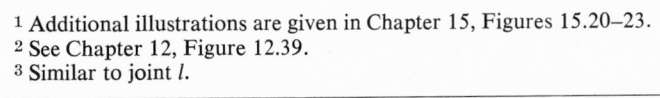

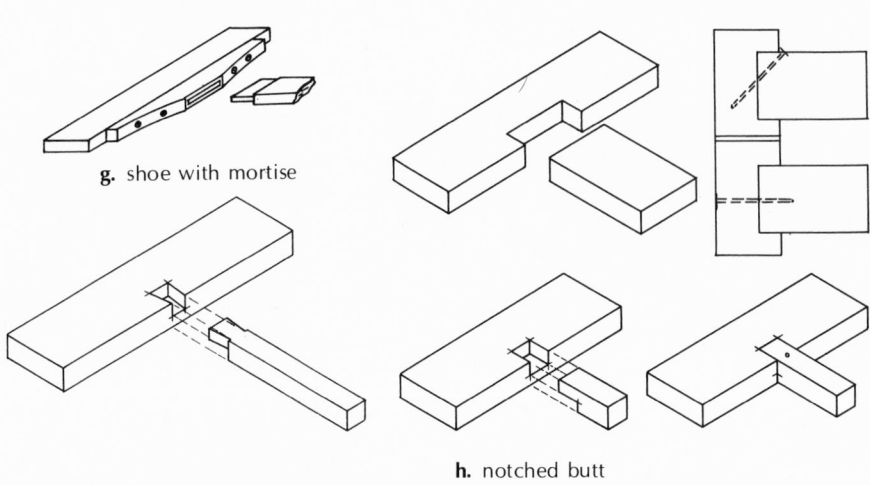

g. shoe with mortise

h. notched butt

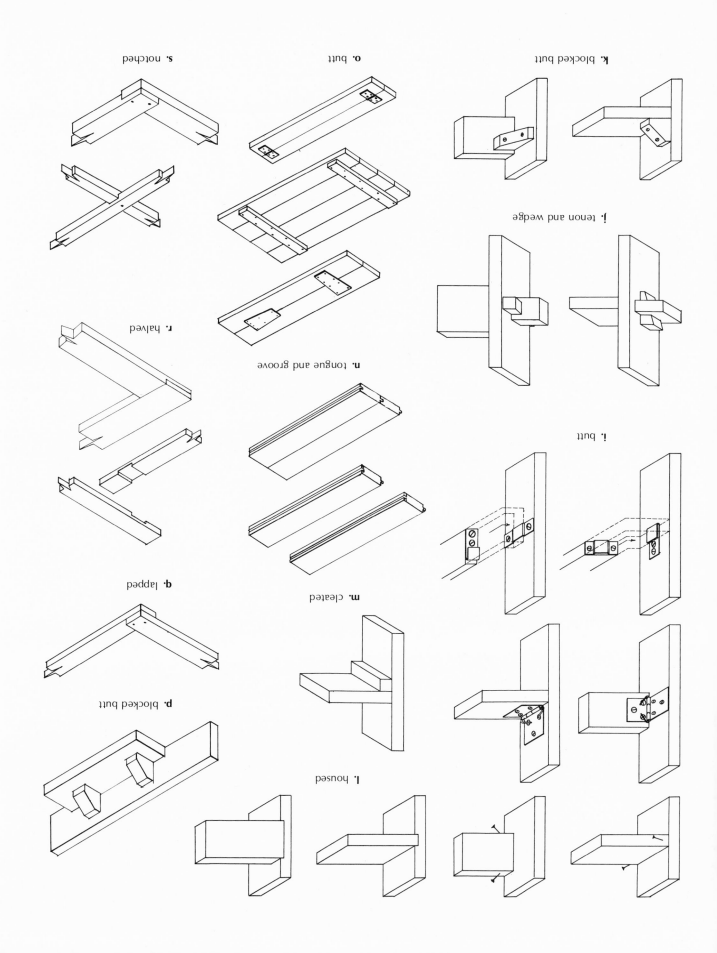

07

s. notched

o. butt

k. blocked butt

j. tenon and wedge

r. halved

n. tongue and groove

i. butt

q. lapped

m. cleated

p. blocked butt

l. housed

9.4 Trial setup of the setting for *Mary, Mary*. Oliver Smith, designer. Left: the stage-right section. Right: the back-wall and stage-left section

according to directions set forth in the prints, and the pieces which go together to make up units of scenery for handling onstage are fitted together. Joints of units which fold up for stacking or shipment are permanent; those of units which must be reduced wholly or partially to their original pieces for shipment are temporary.

trial setup

Concurrently with, or subsequent to, joining the units is a trial setup of the entire set, to assure the correct and easy fitting of all units, one to another. If the set is simple, it is sufficient to test the joining of each two units consecutively, without making a complete setup of the scenery. If the set is intricate, one in which several units may be joined at one or more points to form the set, there must be a complete trial setup. The importance of the trial setup lies in the time saved after the scenery reaches the stage. If errors are discovered in the scene shop, the equipment, materials, tools, and labor are ready at hand for the most efficient remedial work, and corrections are made before the scenery has been painted. If errors are not found until the scenery is being assembled on the stage, the corrections must be made under unfavorable conditions of working space and time, and the altered scenery must be retouched by the painters, to the frequent detriment of the finished paint job.

covering

Cloth covering materials are applied next. A portion of the scene shop is outfitted with benches or horses, reels to contain the most-used covering fabrics, heaters and containers for glue, and glue ingredients.

Cotton duck and linen are the customary covering materials for scenery, although any fiber, fabric, or board materials which are durable enough to withstand wear and rough use may be used. All covering material must be flameproofed.

rigid covering materials

Areas of the scenery which are to be subjected to rough use, whether during transportation or during performance, are covered with a board

9.5 Trial setup of the setting for *Winesburg, Ohio.* Oliver Smith, designer

9.6 Trial setup of the setting for *Destry Rides Again.* Oliver Smith, designer

9.7 Trial setup of a riverboat setting for a General Motors Oldsmobile Show. Ben Edwards, designer

material of sufficient stiffness and strength to resist the stresses put upon them. The panels of doors are made of pulp wallboard, compo board, pressed fiberboard, or profile board. Curved areas of scenery must be covered with a board material which may be bent to the required curve and will hold its shape. Portions of the scenery against which actors lean or bump must have rigid covering.

Board materials when used as covering for flats are themselves covered with the same fabric as is used for the rest of the scenery to provide a homologous surface for painting.

surface textures Smoothly stretched canvas covering on scenery can be painted to resemble almost all artificial surface textures. For the representation of natural surfaces such as turf, gravel, rocks of all kinds, bark, and weathered wood, smooth canvas will not suffice, and the surface must be modeled and fabricated by one of several processes which use a variety of materials.

sizing Commercial scene shops generally give scenery a coat of glue size and whiting before it is sent to the paint shop. Sizing tightens the canvas, gives it a hard finish, and is considered to have some value as an additional fire preventive.

Metal Scene Construction

As with wood, metal may be cut, filed, and drilled with tools made expressly for the purpose, driven at appropriate speeds with adequate lubrication. Both hand and power tools may be used. Unlike wood, metal may be shaped by hammering, casting, and bending.

Metal fabrication is analyzed into the same steps as for wood fabrication: measuring, marking, setting out, cutting, working up, joining, covering, painting, and assembling.

Measuring is done with the same measuring tools as for wood.

measuring, marking, and setting out Marking requires a sharp steel point, soapstone, or a wax pencil which will not rub off the surface of the metal. Carbon pencil can be accidentally effaced.

Setting out is accomplished by scribing around the edge of a pattern which has been cut in hardboard or sheet metal. Layout dye applied to the metal before scribing will make the lines visible. A centerpunch is used in setting out holes to be drilled.

cutting Metal is cut by shears and saws and by oxygen flame.

shearing Shearing is the fastest method of accurate straightline cutting of sheet to produce a fine edge; it is a required technique for sheet-metal working. There are three types of shears: the hand-operated scissorslike tinsnips, the portable power shear, and the bench shear. **Tinsnips** are most useful for cuts in sheet metal that involve few straight lines. A disadvantage is that this bends the edges of the material as it is cut. The **portable power shear** uses a short reciprocating blade that passes through the work beside a resisting supporting edge, and can follow cutting lines with speed and accuracy. The **bench shear** has a wide, slanted, guillotine-like blade which moves through the work past a resisting, supporting edge.

Sawing has the advantage of making cuts without creating internal stresses, deflection, or deformation, as shearing sometimes does. Though not so fast, a saw can cut odder shapes and heavier cross sections than shearing can. The finished cut is cleaner and finer than one made by flame-cutting.

sawing

Flame-cutting offers a quick and easy way to cut steel when a fine finish is not desired. It is particularly useful for cutting odd shapes or for dismantling structures. Only steel may be cut by this process.

flame-cutting

Cutting with oxyacetylene. Red-hot steel will burn when a stream of pure oxygen is directed at it. The cutting torch is fed oxygen and acetylene through separate tubes. Mixed oxygen and acetylene burn at four or six holes around the center of the tip to heat the metal, and pure oxygen, controlled by a separate valve, burns at the center hole to cut it.

Thin and soft metals can be bent cold. Thicker and harder kinds must be heated to be bent. Heating to red heat enables bending without rupture. Slow cooling allows the metal to assume its original characteristics. Sheet metal may be bent on an anvil or in a vise, but for volume work, added power, and time-saving the *brake* is used.

working up
bending

Unique metal shapes may be made on the *anvil*. Flats and sharp bends are pounded on the flat surfaces and sharp edges and curves are pounded on the *horn*. Cold shaping is limited to soft metals. Continued pounding makes metal brittle. It must be repeatedly annealed by quenching in water after alternately heating and pounding. Special molds for shaping metal by pounding may be made from hardwood reinforced by steel strap (concave or female forms) or from steel (convex or male forms).

hammering

Filing removes small amounts of material to bring the work to a desired finish or shape. Correct file selection is important and can only be learned by practice. It is based on the hardness of the metal, the size and shape of the surface, the speed, and the desired finish.

filing

Grinding is the removal of metal by a sharpened abrasive wheel or disc mounted on a medium-speed motor. Grinders are either bench-mounted or portable. Grinding prepares metal for welding, smooths welds and cuts, shapes metal to desired size, and finishes surfaces. Grinding also sharpens and shapes cutting and paring tools.

grinding

TABLE 9.2. *LUBRICANT-COOLANTS FOR DRILLING METALS*

Metal	Lubricant-Coolant
aluminum	kerosene or lard oil
brass	kerosene, lard oil, or none
bronze	lard oil, mineral oil, or none
cast iron	air jet, soluble oil, or none
malleable iron	soda water or none
monel	lard oil
mild steel	soluble oil, mineral oil, lard oil, sulfurized oil
copper	soluble oil, mineral oil, lard oil, kerosene, or none

Drilling requires a high-speed bit ground to a standard point angle of 118°, the proper operating speed, and a lubricant to prevent over-

drilling

heating and consequent dulling (see Table 9.2). Two rules govern speed: the larger the drill, the slower the speed; the harder the material, the slower the speed (for example, aluminum requires high speed; brass, medium speed; steel, low speed).

extruding

Extruding is the process whereby a bar of metal is pulled through a die or series of dies to form a new cross section of metal. Extruding equipment is too costly for a scene shop, but dies may be custom-made and metals extruded for scenery jobs by contract with plants which have the equipment.

joining and fastening

bolts

Pieces of metal are joined and fastened for demountable scenery by bolts having National Course threads: machine bolts when the heads may be exposed, carriage bolts when the heads will not be accessible for wrenching, and stove bolts when the heads must be countersunk flush with the first surface.

A bolt is inserted either through a smooth hole in the first and into a threaded hole in the second piece of two to be joined, or through a smooth hole in both pieces and into a nut on the opposite side of the second piece.

permanent rivets

Permanent fastenings may be made by rivets: pieces of round- or conical-headed metal rod, or of a soft alloy of steel, copper, brass, or aluminum, which are placed in a hole through two or more pieces of metal and the end spread to hold the pieces together.

Bucked rivets are formed by hammering a round head on the inserted and protruding end of the rivet, which is *bucked* with sufficient mass to resist the hammering.

Pop rivets are hollow-tube rivets which are self-heading by means of a ball-ended rod which is inserted in the tube. The rod and tube are then inserted in the hole and the rod drawn backward to cause the tube to spread against the second surface, after which the rod is cut and drops out or is peened.

Pop rivets do not require bucking, being set from only one side of the work. Hence they can be used for blind riveting, to rivet tubular shapes, and where hammering would be harmful to delicate apparatus. Their use is limited to low-stress situations or situations in which stress may be distributed over several rivets in a joint, as in sheet-to-sheet fastening.

welding

Welding is the most effective permanent metal-joining process. The basic principle is complete fusion of the metal from both parts.

In **oxyacetylene welding,** the basis is a flame produced by combustion of oxygen and acetylene at 6,000° F., hot enough to melt all commercial metals. The welding torch permits mixing the two gases in the correct proportion, regulating the size of the flame, and directing the flame conveniently and safely.

Arc welding employs the hottest easily obtainable heat source, an electric arc. A current is produced by a transformer which has one side of the secondary attached to the work by a spring clip and the other connected through the electrode holder to the electrode. Touching the electrode to the work and instantly withdrawing it slightly produces an arc at 13,000° F., which almost instantly melts the metal. As the arc is moved along the joint, it rapidly melts and fuses the metal. The electrode supplies the needed amount of filler.

There are several types and uses of welds:

types and uses of welds

Butt: to join the edges of two pieces in the same plane with no overlap.

Flange weld: to join sheet metal.

Lap weld: to join two overlapped pieces of plate. The welds run along the edges of the plates on both sides.

Fillet weld: to join the edge of one piece to the face of another. Fillets of weld metal are made in the corners formed by the pieces on both sides of the joint.

Plug weld: to join two overlapping pieces when strength requirements are moderate and neatness is requisite. Weld metal is run into holes bored through one piece. When finished by grinding, the weld is hardly detectable.

Tack weld: a short portion of a total weld made to hold pieces in position and to resist distortion.

Stitch weld: a series of tack welds in lapped materials, like stitches, when moderate strength is adequate.

Solder is an alloy of tin and lead which, when melted, acts on metal as glue does on wood: it penetrates the pores of the metal, hardens as it cools, and holds the pieces of metal together. Soldering is a simple technique that requires no elaborate equipment and is used to join sheet metal that would melt under welding heat, to make a temporary joint that can be broken when no longer needed by tapping with a hammer or reheating; for instance, to join intricate detail to a metal prop and remove it after use, to join numerous parts for duplicate machining, and to join wires to each other and to electrical and electronic equipment.

soldering

Brazing joins metals with a binder of brass, silver, or gold (the latter two are not likely in scene construction). It is similar to soldering in that metal cleanliness, the use of special fluxes, and heat transfer still apply. It is different in that the melting points and working temperatures are higher and the strength of the bonds is greater. An oxyacetylene torch is used to produce sufficient heat.

brazing

A glue, or chemical bond, provides a way to repair or fasten metal when the conditions specified by the adhesive manufacturer obtain. Adhesion results from molecular attraction between the adhesive and the work. If the appropriate adhesive is properly applied and allowed to cure, the joint may be so strong that the adjacent material will fail before the bond.

gluing

Construction with Fiber Glass

As a structural material, fiber glass is a product of combining resins which polymerize (form long-chain molecules) around glass fibers. No rigid material exists until the resin and glass fibers have been combined on or in some kind of mold and allowed to cure (complete a chemical reaction).

Prerequisite to fiber glass construction is the design and construction of a mold. The mold may become integral with the fiber glass if a single object is made or it may be the pattern from which several identical images are made.

The process is particularly applicable to scenery which must withstand loads and rough treatment, to rigid panels and plaques which must be translucent or have irregular surface relief, and to scenery for outdoor production. Details of fiber glass construction are set down in a series of problems in Chapter 15.

Construction with Rigid Plastic Foam

Construction in this material follows standard procedures, though with the use of certain specialized tools and with precautions and techniques based on its physical and chemical properties.

cutting and working up
template

RPF may be shaped with any power woodworking equipment, but complex patterns are most easily formed on the hot-wire cutter. When several items are to be produced from the same pattern, a template is made from any rigid or semirigid material such as plywood or pressed wood. After forming, the edges of the template must be sanded smooth to remove all bumps, gouges, and rough spots. Otherwise these, by trapping the cutting wire, would cause excessive melting of the foam around the wire and magnify the irregularities.

blank blocks

When the template is prepared, blocks of RPF, slightly larger than the completed pattern, are cut on a table saw or band saw. Large units often require gluing several pieces of foam together; normally this is done in advance of shaping. The template is secured to the block with staples or nails, or held in place by hand. The block is then placed flat on the cutting table, template on top, and pushed across the wire, guiding around the template. Objects with only one or two cut sides present no special problem, but objects with three or more cut sides should be cut so that only one surface requires special attention.

turning

Objects with circular cross sections, such as newel posts, pillars, and vases may be formed only on a lathe or the flexible hot-wire cutter. The flexibility of this tool allows interchanging straight small-gauge wires with heavier wires (12- or 14-gauge) that have been bent into patterns. When patterned wires are used in combination with a turntable, rounded objects may be formed quickly and simply. Oval and asymmetrical shapes may be formed free-hand, with a traced pattern or with a template in conjunction with a shaped wire.

Cutting wires are formed to the desired shapes by hand, with pliers or in a vise. Twelve- or fourteen-gauge resistance wire is easily bent yet sufficiently rigid to maintain its shape when pressure is applied. Again, the stock is prepared in blocks slightly larger than the diameter of the finished object, then centered and mounted on a turntable base so that the longitudinal axis of the stock is perpendicular to the table of the cutter and parallel with the same axis of the cutting wire. Conical shapes can be cut by tilting a straight cutting wire to the desired angle. By changing the relationship of the cutting wire to the stock, a variety of shapes may be obtained.

The hand hot-wire cutter may be used much like a sculptor's tool for carving or like a saber saw for on-the-job trimming. Various "blades" may be made for this cutter from different sizes of resistance wire, with the heavier wires (10-, 12-, and 14-gauge) giving maximum speed and the lighter wires (16- and 18-gauge) allowing the finest shaping.

Patterns to the depth of one inch may be pressed into RPF by imposing a force of 30 psi to a die made of a rigid material that will withstand this pressure (Figure 9.8). A large-jaw vise may be used for this operation. Thermal molding takes advantage of the low heat-reaction temperature of RPF. Controlled flame from a propane torch can be used to burn patterns and melt dies into the foam. Water should be used as an insulator to control heat distortion where burning is not desired.

9.8 Rigid plastic foam molded by pressure

All power woodworking tools may be used to cut and shape RUF applying the same principles, procedures, and precautions as when working wood. Due to the low density and light weight of the material, which allows it to move freely across any blade, positive control is necessary.

Because RUF is a thermoset and decomposes rather than melts when in contact with a heated wire or die, and because harmful toxic fumes are given off when RUF decomposes, it is difficult to control shaping when using thermo-molding or -cutting techniques. These techniques should not be used on RUF.

Both RPF and RUF can be cut with serrated-edged (bread or steak) knives by using a sawing motion.

reinforcing substructure   In some cases it is necessary to provide a rigid substructure to support the foam. Wood as the core material allows mechanical fastening to other parts and adheres to a variety of binders. A dado head is used to cut grooves within blocks of foam. Wooden substructures may be placed in these grooves to produce well-supported columns, stanchions, chair legs, table legs, and balusters.

fastening   Plastic foam will not grip a mechanical fastening device such as a screw, nail, or staple, nor is it sufficiently rigid to withstand the sheer force of a securely fastened bolt. These methods of fastening may be used only for holding material temporarily; they are not satisfactory for permanent joints.

adhesives   The most effective method of fastening rigid plastic foams to any surface is with an adhesive. Many common scene shop adhesives may be used as well as several industrial adhesives. With all applications, three problems must be considered: heat damage, drying time, and solvent attack.

Some adhesives are melted and applied in a molten state. Care must be exercised to avoid adhesives heated beyond 165° F. for RUF, the distortion point of this material.

Adhesives that depend primarily on evaporation of a liquid for drying present problems when used with nonporous RPF and RUF, especially in conjunction with other nonporous materials such as plywood. In most cases this means that an extended drying time is required for a satisfactory joint. Some adhesives will never dry and should be avoided.

solvent adhesives   All adhesives containing solvents such as alcohol, ketone, ester, aromatic or chlorinated hydrocarbon, or petroleum naphtha, all destructive to RPF, should be carefully tested before actual use to judge the concentration and potential damage to the foam. Solvent-resistant RUF, of course, is unaffected. In some cases, a period of open drying (that is, a period during which the adhesive is freely exposed to air after its application, but before the joint is closed) is recommended and in others it is required. Solvent damage by some adhesives may be reduced by open drying.

clamping   The initial bond of most adhesives is weak so all joints must be clamped. Any standard clamping device may be used, but pinning with resin-coated 6d or 8d box nails or weighting are preferred because they are less likely to scar the foam. In addition, the nails, if left in the materials, provide a measure of mechanical support for the joint. Welder's rods may be substituted for the nails where greater length is necessary.

temporary joints   Although the use of glue is preferred for permanent joints, temporary joints, breakaway pieces, or emergency repairs may be made with nails, screws, bolts, or dowels. Nails and screws must be installed with extreme care to avoid damaging their sockets in the nonelastic plastic. Bolts may not be tightened excessively for they will crush the plastic and wear loose. Wooden rods and welder's rods may be used as dowels. Mechanical fasteners are adequate for temporary joints and very helpful as support for permanent joints, but should not be depended on as independent permanent fasteners.

Careful selection of adhesives must be made with consideration for drying time and possible solvent damage to RPF. Testing is recommended.

protective coatings

Satisfactory protection from impact damage to RPF may be obtained by using protective coatings applied by any standard painting technique as well as by troweling and dipping. Consideration must be given to the type and quality of the protection desired, as well as the added weight and resulting texture of any coating.

texturing

RPF and RUF may be textured in several different ways. Common painting techniques: dry-brushing, scumbling, feather dusting, and spattering will produce their usual results on coated surfaces and other varied results on the raw foam. In addition to these, several special techniques take advantage of the material's reaction to heat, solvents, scraping, and compression. The variety of textures is limited only by the user's imagination and ingenuity (see Figure 9.9).

Construction with Thermoplastics

Thermoplastics are worked with all woodworking tools, some special tools, and four special machines: the heat gun, the hot-air welder, the heating oven, and the vacuum forming table. Cutting, paring, and boring must be done with material at normal temperature (about 70° F.). The standard construction procedure may be followed:

preparation

For measuring, marking, and setting out, the workman uses a pencil or felt marker; or soapstone on polyethylene. He must avoid scratch marks except as a means of scoring to break sheets intentionally.

  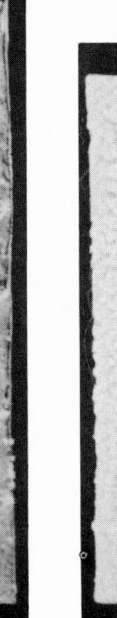

9.9 Textures made in rigid plastic foam. Left to right: by applying a solvent; by using a blowtorch and water; by scraping with a metal comb

| forming | Cutting and working up are accomplished with the usual wood-cutting tools and machines plus scissors, pattern knives, and a paper cutter. |

forming

Cutting and working up are accomplished with the usual wood-cutting tools and machines plus scissors, pattern knives, and a paper cutter.

Forming is uniquely done by heating the material and shaping it either by hand, or in jigs, or in moldless frames by positive or negative air pressure, or over partial or entire male or female molds under partial vacuum (called *thermoforming*). Real objects may be used as male molds, female molds may be made over real objects, and male or female molds may be fabricated to any design which meets a few simple limitations.

joining and fastening

Like thermoplastic materials may be joined and fastened by hot-air welding, by adhesives which are chemically compatible with the materials to be joined, or by the usual types of woodworking fasteners — bolts, pop rivets, staples, tacks, and nails. Butt and lap joints are possible.

strength and stiffness

Strength and stiffness may be gained by incorporating into the design ridges, valleys, steps, or ornamentation. This is particularly important on molds with large, flat, or smooth-surface areas. Undercuts must be avoided. Substructure of wood or metal is sometimes needed to impart strength and for fastening to other scenery.

Scene painting 10

The job of the professional scene painter today is that of a true artist-craftsman. Painting and paint-mixing techniques are to a great extent specialized craft practices which have developed over a long period of time. Painting techniques are as variable as the ingenuity of the painter can make them. The skill and talent of the painter ultimately determine the quality of the job.

The good painter must be able to interpret the designer's elevation in scenic terms, allowing for changes that occur between half-inch and full scale, the effect of distance, the effect of colored lighting, the technical considerations of durability during travel, setup, shifting, and use by the actors, and the relationship between a single unit and the surrounding pieces of scenery and props.

The increased use of three-dimensional pieces and of new materials in recent years makes greater rather than less demand on the versatility and ingenuity of the scenic artist.

The skills required of a capable painter are many. Perhaps for this

10.1 The late Robert Bergman, master scenic artist and owner of Bergman's Studio, at work

reason the quality of scene painting in schools and regional theatres is generally poor. Few schools offer training in scene painting, though they offer courses in the design and technical execution of scenery.

The aim of this chapter is to present the materials, the tools, and the techniques employed by the professional craftsman. It presupposes a basic knowledge of color and some experience with watercolor or oil painting. Scene painting cannot be learned by reading but only by practical application, experiment, and practice.

The requirements, space arrangement, and equipment of the paint shop are given in Chapter 7.

United Scenic Artists

In America, professional scene painting is done by members of the United Scenic Artists, a union to which both scene designers and painters belong. Painters may not work from the designs of nonunion designers. Both designers and painters must pass an extensive examination on their design and painting ability with emphasis in their area of specialization.

paint shop organization

The scene designer is responsible to the producer for the painting of the scenery. He works directly with the shop foreman or chargeman. The division of labor within a paint shop is simple:

The chargeman can do any type of painting and supervises all the work. He is the liaison between designer and crew.

Layout men plan the work and perform all cartooning.

Lay-in men (fillers) do all priming, laying in, and large-scale painting. They are often the new, least-experienced members.

Detail men, the most skilled painters, do all the detailed brushwork.

Paint boys, a separate category within the union, care for equipment, clean the floor, and do the routine work in paint mixing.

In actual practice, all the skilled painters in the shop may do any of the jobs listed, except those assigned to paint boys.

painter's elevations

Union rules prohibit the designer from painting his own scenery. The designer, therefore, supplies the shop with painter's elevations or a painted model, or a combination of both.

The painter's elevation is rendered to a specific scale, usually $\frac{1}{2}'' = 1'$, unless a larger scale is necessary to show complex details without distortion. It is a miniature picture of the finished piece without stage lighting. Painting style and color are indicated precisely. Color samples or swatches of material, photographs of details, or other items may be attached to the side which will help explain more clearly the designer's intentions.

squared elevation

The painter's elevation for elaborate freehand painting such as landscaped drops, borders, wings, and curtains, is divided into 1' squares to scale by horizontal and vertical lines. The designer may, if he wishes to preserve the drawing, cover it with a piece of clear cellophane on which to rule the squared lines. The lines are numbered consecutively to the left and right from the center line and from bottom to top for identification. The squared-off elevation is used as a guide in cartooning the scenery.

designer's model

The painted model as a substitute for the painter's elevation is the clearest method of showing how a complex three-dimensional unit is to be painted. It is usually built to ½″ scale and painted without the effect of stage lighting. It has two major disadvantages: it is difficult to show complex painted detail accurately at this scale, and it cannot be gridded successfully, which makes it difficult to locate details on the full-scale scenery.

The scenic studio is obliged by contract to follow as closely as possible the sketch of the designer. The designer therefore has the obligation to provide the studio with complete, clear, and accurate elevations or models. Thorough communication between the designer and the studio is essential.

relation between designer and painters

As the designer and painters work together over a long period and get to know each others' work thoroughly, the designer may rely more on verbal communication and less on precisely rendered elevations, depending upon the abilities of the artist to interpret rough sketches. This is a dangerous practice unless there is complete mutual understanding. It would, however, be a mistake for the designer not to rely to some extent on the artist's knowledge and experience. The artist can often bring ideas for techniques and methods which significantly enhance the designer's concept.

Preparations for Painting

Before the scenery is delivered to the paint shop, the chargeman in consultation with the designer determines the order and techniques which will be used for the particular job. There is not set procedure for painting scenery; it varies with each job depending on the quality and techniques indicated in the painter's elevation in relation to the surface material, the dimensions, the mounting position (whether on a frame or on the floor), and practical considerations (the show is outside and subject to rain and wind, or the show is touring and subject to hard use). Therefore, the steps of the painting process listed below should be thought of as a general sequence which *may* be followed and *might* be violated for good reasons.

When the scenery comes to the paint shop, the painter checks the set against the designer's drawings and inspects it to see that it is ready to paint. He must see that:

checking the scenery

- All the pieces and the correct pieces have been delivered intact.

- The pieces are numbered in the proper sequence.

- The covering material is suitably stretched.

- There are no protruding tacks or staples or prominent glue mounds on the surface.

- The edges of the covering material are neatly trimmed and completely stuck to the structural members.

- Drops are checked before they are stretched either on the frame or on the floor for dimensions, even hang of cloth, seams all on the same side and sewn in the proper direction.

Wherever flats are mounted, set, or laid for painting, it is essential that they be lined up carefully. If the relative position is not determined

mounting the scenery
flats

by a ledge on the paint frame, if the frame is out of true, if the flats are nailed to a wall or laid on the floor, the alignment can be established by means of a snap line. The flats must be arranged as they are to be assembled onstage, so that gradations of color, repeat patterns, and architectural painting will match exactly at the joints of flats.

Whenever possible, it is best to line up the complete set in order with the back wall in the center and the side walls in their proper position to the left and right. If the frame is too narrow or the floor area not large enough to hold the complete set, the back wall can be painted at one time and the two sides thereafter.

Whatever method is used to rig scenery for painting, it must keep the scenery flat so that its framing members cannot bend while the scenery dries. The flats are fastened to the floor or paint frame with 10*d*. nails which are not driven home so that the nails may be easily drawn and paint can be brushed under the heads to prevent holidays in the finished paint job, but securely enough to resist the pull caused by shrinking of sized canvas and to stay on in the event of a sudden drop of the frame. On the frame, clamps are often used in place of nails, eliminating nail holes and the chance of marring a careful paint job when pulling nails.

The load on the frame must be balanced so that it will run easily.

When flats are painted from a boomerang they are nailed to a cross-grid of wooden battens attached to a wall.

drops

When a drop is to be attached to a paint frame, two special battens are first nailed vertically to the frame as far apart as the width of the drop. The top batten of the drop is then set on blocks attached to the face of the top rail of the frame, spiked securely in place, and the drop is unrolled. The top batten of the drop must be set so that the vertical center line of the drop is plumb. The edges are tacked to the special battens in the same manner as that employed in canvasing a frame, save that the tacks are set closer together and are not driven in all the way. The edges may be tacked over the sides of the battens at wider intervals than is safe on the batten faces. The bottom batten is then lashed to the bottom rail of the frame. If the drop has been made with a few inches of spare material at either side, the painter can staple the edges and cut the sides of the finished drop away from the side battens after painting. When drops are painted on a wall without benefit of a paint frame, weights are hung on the bottom battens to insure even stretch. Drops painted on the floor must be securely fastened with either tacks or staples, starting with the bottom edge. Staples are faster but take much longer to remove. Tacks take longer to set but can be removed much more quickly and are less likely to damage the drop.

three-dimensional units

Doors, door frames, platforms, and other sculptural or three-dimensional units which cannot be broken into flat units are painted standing or lying on the floor. They do not need to be held in place.

sizing or priming

The purpose of the size or prime coat is to fill the pores of the fabric or wood, to tighten the fabric and hold it taut, and to give a suitable working texture to the entire set.

It is called a size coat when only a binder and vehicle are used without the addition of pigment. A prime coat has pigment added and gives a basic color tone approximating the value if not the actual hue of the base coat. Scenery that has been primed will generally require only one coat of base; sized pieces will need two coats of base for a smooth, even coverage.

The size or prime coat is extremely important. It determines the quality of the surface on which all other painting will be done. For example, a painter's elevation which indicates a loose, washy, water-color technique requires a slick, nonabsorbent base so the colors will flow and blend. Conversely, if brush strokes are desirable or if the sur-face is to be *printed* with sponges or stencils, a soft, absorbent surface is necessary.

layout
squaring

To square a drop, measure and mark 1′ divisions vertically and hori-zontally along all four edges of the piece and number these marks for identification to agree with the numbers already marked on the painter's elevation. Make sure vertical lines are plumb and the horizontal lines level. If the piece being marked has horizontal fullness (as in the in-stance of a traveler curtain) and an undistorted effect is requisite, the horizontal measurements are increased in proportion to the amount of fullness in the piece. With the measurements as guides, mark the drop in horizontal and vertical lines by means of a snap line. Two workmen hold the line, which has been coated with charcoal at the top and bottom, or at both sides of the piece; a third worker snaps the taut line near its midpoint to deposit a mark on the scenery. Make the first snaps very light; increase the smartness of the snap as the color works out of the line. Identify with charcoal the horizontal and vertical divisions of the drop to coincide with the markings on the designer's elevation.

cartooning

With the squared lines as guides and the painter's elevation as refer-ence, draw in with stick charcoal the outlines of the objects to be painted, and the outlines of the areas which are to be painted in different colors. A 4′-long drawing stick with charcoal in one end allows the workman to stand away from his work while drawing.

To cartoon a piece of scenery for architectural painting, it is unneces-sary to square the entire surface as in a freehand design, unless the sub-ject is a perspective or intricate design. Measure and mark the main reference lines: base line, center lines of arches, centers of curvature. From these reference lines measure and draw in all subsidiary details. Use the snap line as described above to mark straight lines with full width or full height of the scenery. For vertical lines attach the snap line to a pole. Use a bow snap line to mark short straight lines. Use a large wooden compass with charcoal set into one leg and chalk or rub-ber in the other to describe circles or arcs. Use a large wooden right triangle to establish right angles. Be careful to establish and maintain the true horizontal and true vertical lines which are inherent in archi-tecture. Use as main reference lines the bottom line of framed scenery and the vertical center line of drops.

Pounce patterns are often used to repeat a recurring motif, or, in the case of an extremely complex drawing, to cartoon an entire drop. The design is drawn on heavy kraft paper and corrections and adjustments are made. The paper is placed on a soft board and a pounce wheel run over the design to punch holes in the paper. The paper is then attached to a square wooden frame which is laid against the scenery and registered by measured marks. The pounce bag (a cheesecloth bag filled with powdered charcoal) is rubbed or tapped against the paper to transfer the pattern to the scenery. The paper protects the surface to be painted. Pouncing replaces cartooning when a design motif is to be repeated.

When a design is to be stenciled on scenery, vertical, horizontal, or diagonal lines are snapped on the surface wherever necessary to establish the successive positions of the stencil frame.

A pattern may be **reversed and repeated** by tracing a design with charcoal on tracing paper, reversing the paper, and transferring the design to the proper surface by rubbing the back briskly with a sponge or rag.

projection

If there is sufficient clear space in front of the paint frame to allow long-range projection, a reflecting projector may be used as a guide for the cartooning of scenery. The painter's elevation is placed in the projector, which is adjusted to project the elevation full size on the required area of scenery. The outlines of the image are then traced on the scenery.

When there is not sufficient space or when the drop is on the floor, the elevation can be projected in sections onto kraft paper, the drawing made, and the paper pounced onto the drop.

inking

If there is to be considerable overpainting, make a very weak solution of a dark aniline dye into which a small amount of gum arabic has been melted to keep the dye from running. Determine by experiment the proper dye strength and color. This dye must be faintly visible through subsequent coats of overpainting but invisible when the final coat is completed. Go over the charcoal lines with the dye.

Lines of charcoal which remain on the scenery when inking has been completed may be knocked off by **flogging:** beating the cloth with a flogger, or dusted off with a common hand brush or duster.

texture and appliqué

If all or part of the painting surface is to be built up in relief or textured with other paints or materials, it is generally done at this point, before the base coat is applied.

The Painting Process

In general, the painting process is a progression from the use of the largest (8″ priming) brushes, through diminishing sizes to the smallest lining brushes, all areas of scenery being worked on in each successive step.

base coat

The considerations mentioned in reference to the size or prime coat apply also to the base coat. The color and value of the base must be carefully considered as they determine the entire method of painting that will be used in subsequent steps. There are three general ways in which scenery can be painted: lightest tone first, middle tone first, or darkest tone first.

The chargeman and designer decide together which of the three methods will produce the best result. In some cases, two or all three of the methods will be used in the same drop. The method of application of the base coat must also be decided in relation to the painter's elevation.

The base coat may be laid in as flat painting, by spraying (spray guns should be used for the base coat only if no direct brush coats are to follow) or by sponge roll, rag roll, puddle, or scumble (see "Scene Painting Techniques," page 242). The base coat may be done in a single color or in several colors. Atmospheric effects on scenery may be achieved in the base coat by grading the colors from dark at the top and sides of each flat area of scenery to light in the center. The base coat may be painted in three or more colors or three or more tones of the same color to give the depth characteristic of light, shade, and shadow.

lay-in and detail painting

Lay-in is the painting of other major areas of color and can be simply defined as those areas that can be painted with a 5″ brush.

Detail painting comprises the final highlights and shadows and accents and is usually done with a brush smaller than 3″.

The techniques used for lay-in and detail painting are varied and are elaborated fully in "Scene Painting Techniques," page 242.

back-painting

Scenery which will have offstage light directed or reflected against it from the back will be disconcertingly translucent and show the structural members to the audience unless it is back-painted. Back-painting is best done with rubber-base paint. It will stay on the back surface and not sink through, destroying the front surface. It must be laid on lightly and rapidly and not worked into the surface. Any color may be used for back-painting, but a dark tone will absorb the most light.

paint and dye

Paint and dye may be defined as a combination of three agents: the coloring agent, referred to as *pigment* or *dye;* the binding agent (*binder*) which adheres the color to the surface; and the carrying agent (*vehicle*) which is the solvent for the binder and evaporates as the paint dries. Paint is pigment held in suspension in the vehicle; dye is dissolved in the vehicle.

The combination of binder and vehicle without color is called *size* and determines the kind and name of paint that results from adding pigment (rubber-base, vinyl, casein, gelatin, etc.).

Most paints and some dyes are available premixed, a convenience requiring considerable storage space to maintain a complete stock of colors in each kind of paint. Premixed paints are expensive and limited in color range; unless used frequently, they will deteriorate or dry out. It is therefore better to keep a complete stock of dry pigment and dye with a complete assortment of clear binders and their appropriate vehicles. These will keep indefinitely if tightly covered in a dry room. They afford the artist complete flexibility in choosing the proper medium for the particular job. Premixed paints can be used to supplement the basic supply when a large quantity of a particular kind and color is needed. Frequently used paints (black and, particularly, white rubber-base, casein, and both flat and gloss vinyl) can be stocked and stored in five-gallon cans.

dry pigment

The basic coloring agent of all paints, dry pigment varies widely in manufacturer's name and in quality. Quality is based on purity and the fineness of pulverization. Good-quality pigments are most economical because a small quantity will make as much paint as a larger quantity of cheaper pigment composed of color and filler. The paint will be more intense, have greater clarity, and combine more easily with binder and vehicle. Paint made with dry pigment also has greater intensity and clarity compared to premixed paints. The color range of dry pigment is much greater than that of premixed paint.

mixing dry colors

A distinction must be made between the earth colors (those colors which are natural pigments) and the dye colors which contain a mineral or chemical pigment. Most of the dye colors and some of the earth colors will not dissolve easily in water and must be mixed to a paste in a wetting agent such as alcohol before being slowly combined with a water-base size. Colors generally needing a wetting agent are reds, oranges, magentas, maroons, violets, some blues, umbers, and some blacks. Some rubber and vinyl binders react badly with alcohol and should be tested in sample before large quantities are mixed. Boiling water to which a handful of salt or nonfoaming detergent has been added is a wetting agent which will not react with rubber or vinyl.

Pigments mixed dry and rubbed on a sample of the surface to be painted will approximate the tone of the dry paint.

Binders and the surface will change the tone of colors, usually darkening them. Therefore, to match colors *exactly,* the pigment must be mixed with the binder and painted on a sample of the surface to be used. The sample may be quick-dried with heat (hair dryers) or a fan.

pulp (wet) colors

Pulp or wet colors are dry pigments, commonly those difficult to dissolve, which have been premoistened to the consistency of paste. They are mixed directly with size and are rich and vibrant transparent colors. They must be stored in tightly covered containers. Small amounts of water must be added periodically to prevent drying out. Being water-base, they cannot be used with shellac or oil-base sizes.

bronze powders

Powdered metallic pigments are available in a wide range of colors. High-quality bronze powders cover a larger area more thoroughly and retain their brilliance longer than the less expensive grades, which oxidize (turn dull green) rapidly and cover poorly. Although they can be mixed with any binder, the best binders to use are gloss vinyl, bronzing liquid, varnish, and shellac. All glue binders will discolor and dull the pigment. Bronzes can be added to paint in small quantities and will float to the surface, giving it a metallic glaze when dry.

analine dye

Available by the ounce or pound as a powder, analine dye is either water-soluble (W), alcohol-soluble (A), water- or alcohol-soluble (W/A), or oil-soluble (O). It is indispensable for translucencies and transparencies, and useful for intensifying dry-pigment colors. The water- or alcohol-soluble (W/A) is the most useful type to stock. Except for staining grained woods, oil-soluble has few uses in the paint shop and is rarely stocked.

Dyes are extremely intense and completely transparent. Purity and color vary and, as with dry pigment, the best quality is recommended. Three tablespoons of high-quality powder will make a gallon of full-strength dye. Dyes are first put in solution without binder, then added to a prepared size.

The binder, determined by the surface to be painted and the finished effect desired, in turn determines the surface for the subsequent coats of paint. Some binders (casein, flat vinyl) have a relatively soft or absorbent surface which is excellent for gouache and tempera techniques but is less suitable for watercolor techniques needing a harder, less absorbent surface (gloss, vinyl, rubber-base) on which color can puddle and flow.

Only as much binder as needed to adhere the pigment or dye to the surface should be used in the size. In Tables 10.3 and 10.4 the proportion of binder to vehicle is given, but the resulting size must always be tested for strength before using, to allow for variations in the strength of the binder. Umbers, blacks, and certain other pigments are fluffy and require stronger size to prevent them from rubbing off. Always test the mixed paint or dye on a sample of the surface to be painted. If, when thoroughly dry, any color rubs off, additional binder must be added and another test made.

Charcoal. Available in sticks from ⅛″ to ½″ diameter, charcoal is used for cartooning and can be dusted off with a flogger without marring the surface. It can be inserted into a thin, split-bamboo pole for work on the floor. CAUTION: Avoid the compressed charcoal which has a wax additive and cannot be erased.

Snap line. This can be purchased in a case with a mechanical reeling device or can be simply a 50-foot length of cotton twine tied to a piece of wood. The line is first charcoaled (or chalked for work where only pale tints of color are to be used) and drawn taut by two men between two points. A third man lifts the string straight up and lets go. A straight charcoal line will result. One man can snap lines alone by attaching a safety pin to one end of the line and snapping it himself.

Bow line. This is a cotton line stretched taut between the ends of a bent wooden strip or between the points of cornerblocks fastened to the ends of a piece of 1″ × 2″ scenery lumber. Using a bow line, one man can snap lines, particularly when working on a paint frame.

Straightedges, liners, and **lining sticks** are usually made in the shop from clear pine or maple with beveled back edges to prevent paint from blotting. They have either a screen-door handle (for paint-frame work) or 36″ long handles (for floor work) attached in the center. Hand-held liners are generally 4′ long, floor liners from 6′ to 12′ long. The top is marked off in 1′ sections with twelve 1″ marks at either end. Straightedges should be varnished or enameled to waterproof them and prevent warping. For lining in wet areas, a straight, lightweight board with a large screw at either end, to hold the liner off the wet paint, is used.

A **floor triangle** can be made in the shop from ¼″ plywood, 3′ to 5′ on an edge, with holes cut at random to eliminate excess weight and a 36″ handle attached. The floor triangle is used for 45° angles and for a convenient square.

binders and vehicles

layout equipment

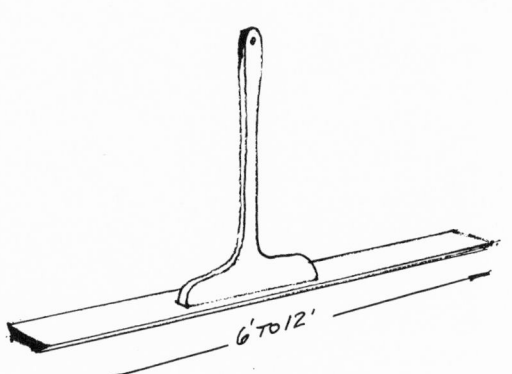

6′ TO 12′

10.2 Straightedge

4′-0″

10.3 Floor triangle

227

10.4 Floor square

10.5 Compass

A **floor square** can also be made in the shop — from $1'' \times 3''$ stock, 12' on a side. It is used to square a drop when it is being laid out on the floor.

Compass. With 2' arms, one with a sharp point and the other able to hold vine charcoal, the compass can be built in the shop or a large blackboard compass can be used. For very large curves, a string with a safety pin at one end and charcoal tied at the desired radius is used.

Trammel bar and points (beam compass). This compass has movable clamps, one with a center point and one with a holder for charcoal, that fit over and slide on a strip of wood. It is more convenient for drawing very large circles or arcs than a very large compass and more accurate than string.

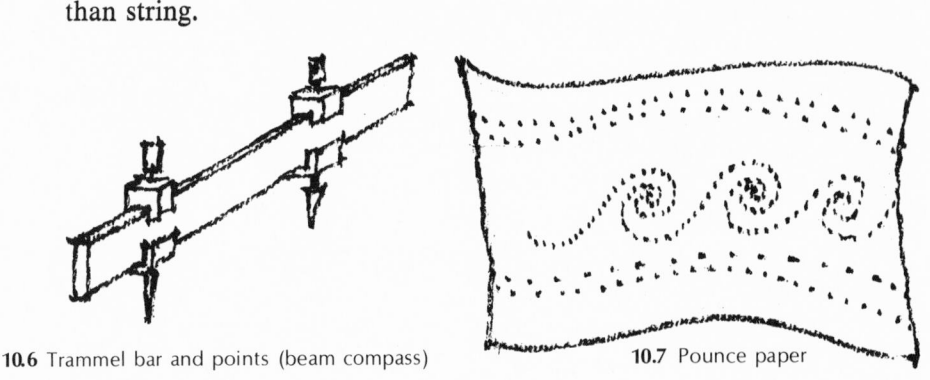
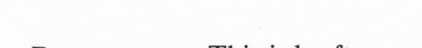

10.6 Trammel bar and points (beam compass)   10.7 Pounce paper

Pounce paper. This is kraft paper on which a pounce pattern is drawn and perforated with a pounce wheel. It is used for transferring a full-scale design to the scenery.

Pounce wheel. A small wheel of sharp points attached to a handle, the pounce wheel is used to perforate the pounce pattern. The drawing is laid on several layers of soft fabric and the wheel run over the lines to be transferred. The back of the paper should be lightly sanded to open the perforations completely. Pounce wheels are available in two sizes. The larger wheel, with longer, more widely spaced points, is used for straight lines and can be run along a straight edge. The much smaller wheel, with many more, very short points, is used for curved lines. CAUTION: Avoid heavy pressure, which may cut rather than perforate the paper.

10.8 Pounce wheels

Pounce bag. This is a bag consisting of five layers of No. 60 to 80 cheesecloth filled with *pounce* (powdered charcoal) and tied around the end of a 36" bamboo pole. When the pounce pattern has been positioned on the scenery and secured in place with tape or weights, rub (*do not pound*) the bag over the perforations to force charcoal through the holes. CAUTION: Avoid heavy pressure, which will force excessive charcoal through the perforations and smudge the drawing.

10.9 Pounce bag

Flogger. Used to erase cartooning lines from fabric, the flogger is made of 1" strips of lightweight muslin tied or taped securely to the end of a 24" to 30" bamboo pole. It beats the charcoal off the surface instead of rubbing it into the fabric.

10.10 Flogger

The **wire whisk,** a kitchen implement, 12″ to 15″ in size, is used for rapidly stirring paint to a smooth mixture.

Strainers. All paint or dye that is to be sprayed must be thoroughly strained to eliminate foreign matter and undissolved particles of pigment which would clog the nozzle. Certain binders should also be strained before using. The strainers with the finest mesh should be used with the addition of several thicknesses of cheesecloth, an old nylon stocking, or screen cloth.

Galvanized garbage pails are used for mixing large quantities of size and for dip-dying nets and other fabrics.

Twelve-quart galvanized pails are used for prime and lay-in colors or for mixing large quantities of paint.

Twelve-quart enamel pails are used for mixing starch, methacel, and dye. They are much easier to clean than galvanized metal and make it much easier to judge color and strength while mixing.

Plastic pails are available in several sizes; they are lightweight, convenient, and easy to clean. Avoid using them with binders, which bond with the plastic, or with solvents, which dissolve the bottoms of the pails.

No. 10 cans are available free from restaurants; they are convenient for mixing moderate quantities of paint; disposable.

Soft drink cans and **food cans** are ideal for smaller quantities of paint.

The **paint caddy** is a small watertight box, holding two to four cans of paint, with a carrying handle and antlers for supporting long-handled brushes. It is used for carrying paint and brushes conveniently as the artist moves over a drop. The box catches drips and splashes that would otherwise fall on the drop. A crosspiece with several broom clips may be used instead of the antlers.

The **priming brush,** 7″ to 12″ wide and with bristles 4″ to 5″ long, is used for priming, laying-in large areas, spattering and dribbling over large areas. Many artists become ambidextrous with priming brushes to avoid overtiring one hand on a large job. Attach to long (5′ or more) bamboo poles for floor work and for reaching considerable distance without moving paint constantly.

The **Dutch priming brush** is like the priming brush but with longer (7″) and thicker bristles which hold a greater quantity of paint.

The **lay-in brush** is a 3″-to-5″-wide version of the priming brush with either blunt-cut bristles or with chisel edges, which are better for cutting sharp, clean lines. The bristles are 4″ to 6″ long and thickly set to hold a quantity of paint. This brush is used for laying-in areas where more control is necessary and for priming and basing woodwork.

Foliage, fitch, and **decorating brushes** are long-handled and come in widths from 1″ to 3″ in ¼″ steps with long, resilient white bristles set to flare slightly from the ferrule and to taper naturally to a thin edge. Most painting after priming and lay-in is done with these brushes. The manipulation of the brush (grasp and contact with the surface) determines the effects achieved.

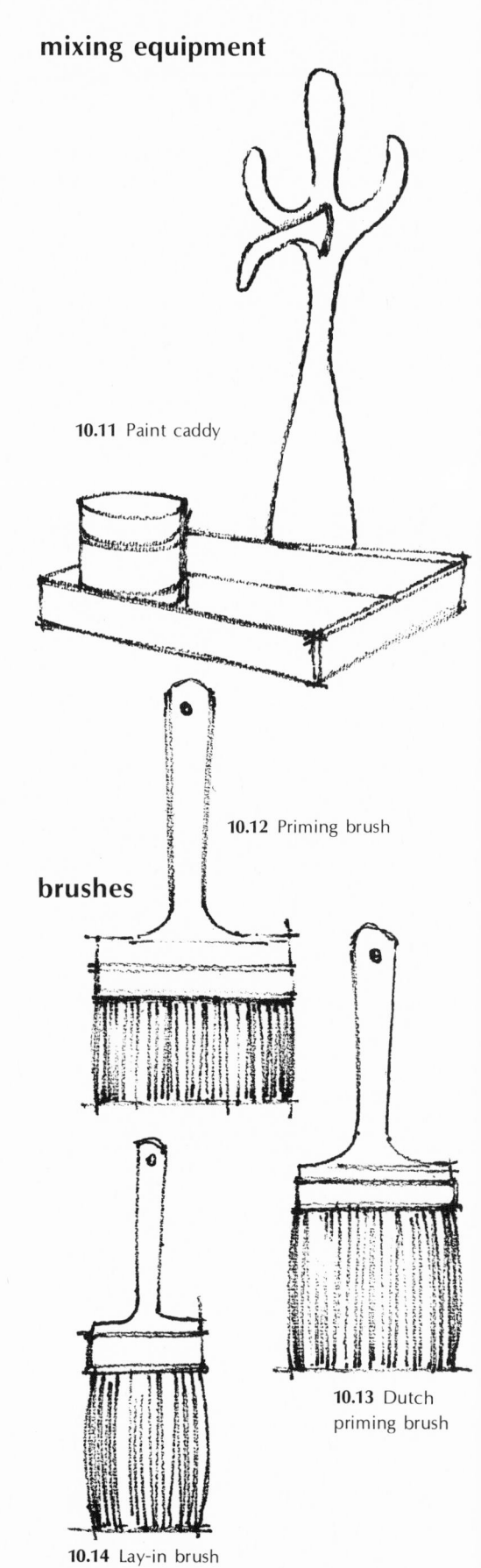

mixing equipment

10.11 Paint caddy

10.12 Priming brush

brushes

10.13 Dutch priming brush

10.14 Lay-in brush

10.15 Foliage, fitch, and decorating brushes

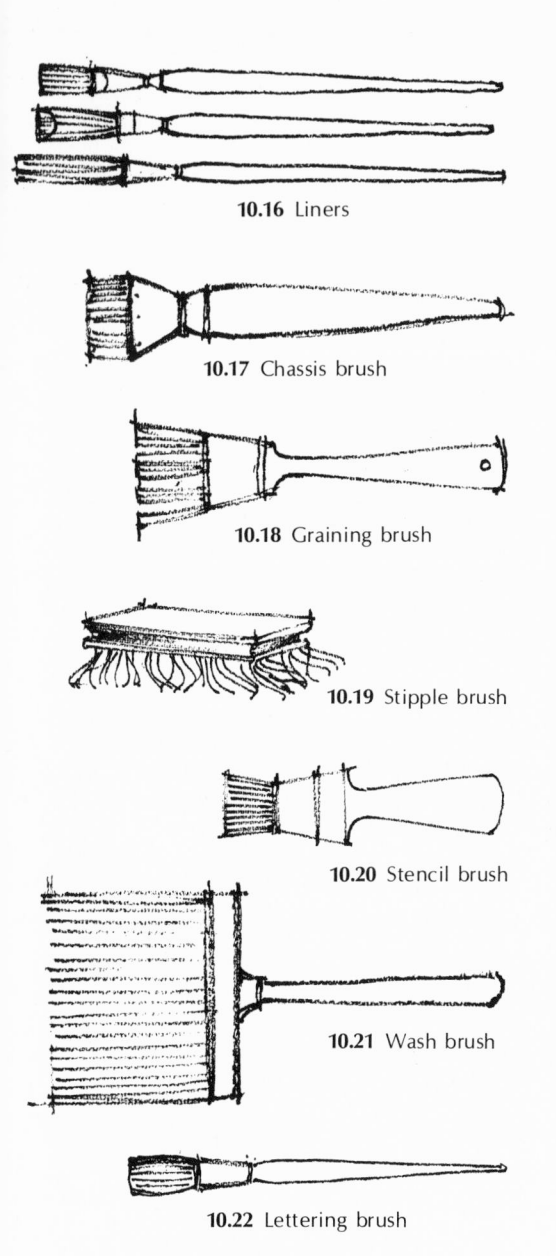

10.16 Liners

10.17 Chassis brush

10.18 Graining brush

10.19 Stipple brush

10.20 Stencil brush

10.21 Wash brush

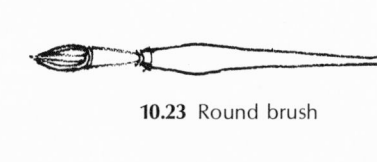

10.22 Lettering brush

10.23 Round brush

Liners are long-handled brushes in widths from ¼″ to 1″ in ⅛″ steps, with either long, resilient white bristles or shorter, stiffer black bristles, used for lining with a straightedge and for painting details. Either blunt-cut or chisel-edged bristles are available.

The **chassis brush** is a short-handled brush with short, stiff bristles which scratch color into the surface; used with dye on scrim or velour.

The **graining brush** is a short, flat-handled brush with 1″, 2″, and 3″ wide bristles set thinly in a very flat ferrule. The bristles separate into clumps and produce a long series of parallel lines (similar to the dry-brush effect) when drawn lightly over the surface.

The **stipple brush** has long, soft bristles set in a block like a scrub brush and used over wet oil paint to blend and eliminate brush strokes. Used in a circuullar motion, it produces an eggshell finish.

The **stencil brush** is a round, hard, stiff-bristled brush with a short handle for the circular, pounding motion used for filling in a stencil pattern. Available from ½″ to 2″ and sometimes larger sizes.

The **wash brush** is a short-handled brush with long, thinly set, soft bristles 5″ wide, used for glazing large areas; allows thin glazes to flow freely without leaving brush strokes; difficult to find; usually imported from Germany.

Lettering brushes, flat, with red sable bristles, are purchased in small sizes from artist supply shops; used for lettering and occasionally very fine detail painting.

The **round brush** is a short-handled brush with long, resilient or stiff bristles mounted in a round ferrule and available from 1/16″ to 1″ at artist supply shops; used to paint detail, ornament, and soft washy effects.

Oil and **shellac brushes.** Because of problems in cleaning oil and shellac from brushes, the least expensive household brushes are used for these paints.

Floor-painting brushes can be purchased with 3′ to 4′ handles. However, any round-handled brush can be made into a floor brush by inserting the brush handle into the split end of a bamboo pole with a diameter slightly less than the handle of the brush and securing the split ends with tape or strong rubber bands. Flat-handled brushes can be taped or tied to a pole.

Rollers are available in widths of 1″ to 15″ and with surfaces varying from short carpetlike pile to long soft pile, each of which produces a different effect. They are used for covering large areas quickly and smoothly and for certain painting techniques in place of brushes. Smaller rollers can be used in combination with a straightedge for soft-edged lining and large rollers to produce the thick and thin veining of marble.

The pile of rollers can be cut away in areas to give a repeated pattern or a repeated texture. These **cut rollers** can also be wrapped with string or masking tape or matted with glue to give other effects.

A **corn push broom** is used for painting large areas and for smoothing sprayed size or prime coats; it is used dry for overbrushing fine spatters to produce the soft grain in wood.

other applicators

10.24 Corn push broom

10.25 Sponges

Sheepswool and **natural** and **synthetic sponges** are used not only for mopping up spilled paint but for a number of painting techniques. Used as-is for painting texture and mottling, for forcing paint through a stencil, and for blotting up areas of wet paint, they can also be cut into chisel shapes and attached to bamboo handles and used like brushes when painting scrim and velour. They can also be cut into shapes and used to print repeated figures, for wallpaper and for large areas of foliage.

All spraying equipment must be cleaned *thoroughly* and *immediately* after each use. It must be completely taken apart and each element cleaned and allowed to dry before reassembling. All paint or dye used in spraying equipment must be thinned to the consistency of skimmed milk and strained to avoid clogging the nozzles.

sprayers
cleaning

These are preferred for jobs requiring a controlled, even spray over moderate-sized areas. The compressor should have adjustable pressure up to 50 pounds for maximum versatility.

compressor spray guns

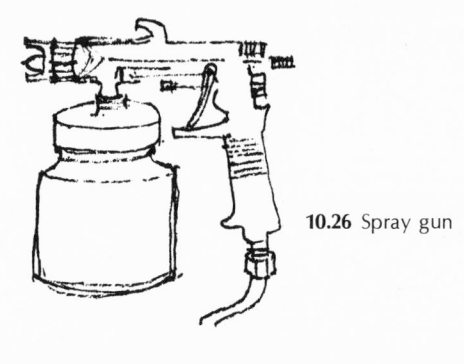

10.26 Spray gun

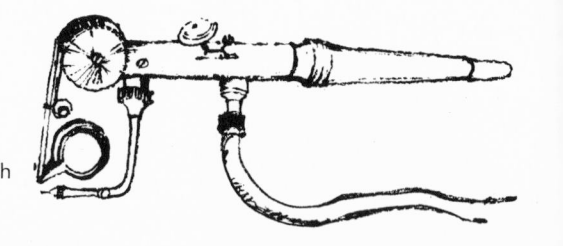

10.27 Air brush

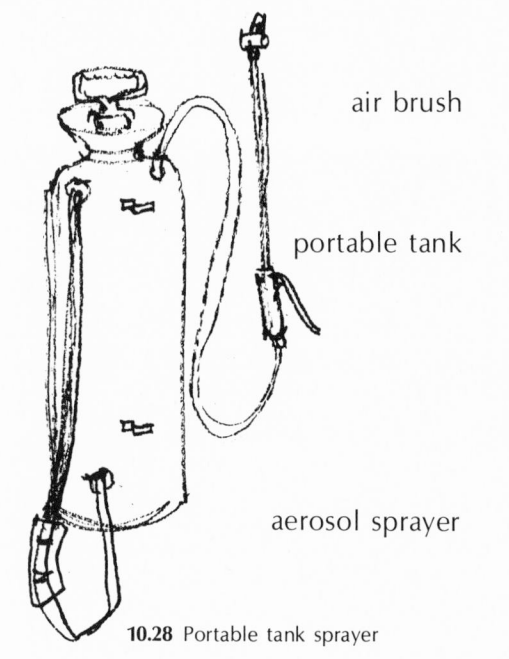

air brush

portable tank

aerosol sprayer

10.28 Portable tank sprayer

Powered by the same compressor used for the gun, the air brush is useful for detailed work and for softening edges that seem too harsh; it is also good for delicate touch-up and for painting very soft shade and shadow as in fluting of columns.

Portable tanks are available in several sizes up to two gallons. The pressure is pumped by hand. A tank can cover a large area with a reasonably even, coarse spray. With practice, the artist can learn to adjust the spray from fairly fine (never as fine as that of the gun) to a very coarse spatter. Two nozzles are available, one for general spraying and a fan nozzle for spraying a wide band. With the regular nozzle, a continuous circular motion of the arm while spraying will produce an even distribution of color.

Available at artist supply shops, the aerosol spray combines a replaceable power unit with a spraying head and a detachable four-ounce jar for the paint. It is ideal for small jobs, for use with stencils, for touch-up, and when spray-painting entirely with translucent or transparent plastics

TABLE 10.1. SOFT PAINTING SURFACES

Painting Surface	Available Weights	Texture (Tooth)	Width
linen	from sheer (theatrical gauze) to heavy (linen burlap); medium canvas weights (8 oz–10 oz) for drops and covering	slubbed (lumps in thread), slightly rough in all weights like quality water-color paper	gauze: 50″, 72″, 160″ canvas: 72″ burlap: 54″
cotton duck	from medium slightly open weave to a very tight, heavy canvas; 8 oz common for scenery	regular, slightly rough with good tooth	72″
unbleached muslin	from thin pattern weight (80 threads per inch) to medium (140 threads per inch)	smooth, regular surface with occasional slight slubbing	36″–33′ (72″ and 108″ most commonly used)
velour corduroy	from medium to heavy	directional pile, somewhat longer than velvet	36″–69″
flannel duvetyn	from light to medium (flannels) to heavy weight (duvetyn)	slightly directional fuzzy surface	36″–54″
burlap jute fabric	from thin, open weave to very coarse and heavy, with many intermediate weaves and weights	rough, slubbed, irregular	36″–72″ (also 9′ and 12′)
silk	from thin China to heavy silk burlap	smooth to heavily slubbed; slight sheen to very glossy	48″–54″
sharktooth scrim Hansen cloth opera cloth	standardized	regular, ribbed, open weave	15′ and 30′
bobbinet net	standardized; nets available from very fine to large fish net	bobbinet: hexagonal weave net: open regular weave	bobbinet: 30′ nets: 72″–216″
cheesecloth	from open #10 to moderate tight #90	open, loose, regular weave	36″

or vinyls, in which case it is useful to have a separate sprayer for each color being used.

10.29 Aerosol sprayer

The **stencil** is used when a design is to be repeated over a large area, **templates** as in painting wallpaper. The pattern to be painted is drawn and cut out of stencil paper, a heavy, waterproof paper. The pattern is laid on the surface, which has previously been painted the background color and texture. Paint is then applied through the cutouts with a stencil brush, a sponge, a roller, or a spray. Stencils should have sufficient borders to protect the surrounding area, especially when spraying. For jobs requiring repeated stenciling, the stencils may be cut from $\frac{1}{8}''$ masonite or from sheet aluminum.

The reverse of stencils, **friskets** are shapes or objects which protect areas of the underpainted surface while a new background color is applied with brush, roller, spray, or sponge. Friskets can be cut from masking tape, from contact paper, or from heavy gray paper which is weighted in place. Materials like gravel, sand, and lace can be placed on the surface and used as friskets.

1969 Price (per ft²)	Shrinkage	Available Colors	Cartooning Media
gauze: .085 canvas: .13 burlap: .35	1″–2″ in 72″	natural unbleached; full range in narrow dressmaker widths	charcoal and dye
.05–.08 depending on quality and weight	1″–2″ in 72″; shrinks to 70″ when flame-proofed	white, blue, black, natural	charcoal and dye
.04–.13	3″–4″ in 72″	natural; white (bleached) has very different properties and cannot be used interchangeably	charcoal and dye; grease pencil or dye and shellac for penetrating through to back as guide for back-painting
.25–$2.25 depending on quality	0–2″ in 69″ depending on degree of saturation	black, white, and full range of colors	charcoal or chalk, used lightly
.05–.10	none	black, white, and some colors	charcoal, used lightly
.06 up	slight	natural; range of colors available in narrower "decorator" widths	charcoal and dye
.13–$2.00 depending on quality	slight	full range of colors	charcoal and dye, used very lightly; surface easily marred; grid with stretched strings, not with snapline
.13–.16	stretchable; edges must be thoroughly secured to hold size and shape	black, white, blue	charcoal and dye with methacel
bobbinet: .13 nets: .13–.16	stretchable; edges must be thoroughly secured to hold size and shape	black, white, blue	charcoal or paint; draw on brown paper and place under the fabric
.01–.06 depending on weight	1″ in 36″	bleached and unbleached	charcoal on the fabric or draw in charcoal, dye, or paint on kraft paper and place under the fabric

(Table continues overleaf)

TABLE 10.1. *SOFT PAINTING SURFACES* (continued)

Painting Surface	Absorption	Size	Prime	Characteristics and Uses	Receives Well
linen (pure flax)	moderate	thin coat of any type	not necessary; paint directly over size	ideal surface for nearly all styles and techniques of opaque and semi-opaque painting	all types of paint and dye
cotton duck	varies with weight from moderate to almost nonabsorbent on the tight weaves	thin coat of any type	light coat advisable	currently the standard covering for wings; the tight weave prevents glue on the stiles and rails from penetrating and destroying the painting surface; the taut surface eliminates the problem of framing members' catching paint as when the covering is a thin fabric like muslin, excellent ground-cloth material	all types of paint
unbleached muslin	moderately high	starch for translucencies; if used as covering, either glue or vinyl size	not necessary over starch size; two thin coats if used as covering	because of great seamless width and translucency, primarily used for drops and other soft scenery; also for covering plywood, masonite, and other hard surfaces	dye, thin color
velour corduroy	colors tend to stay on top of pile; use alcohol with water-bases for deeper penetration; once thoroughly wet, colors will tend to sink through, and should be used thicker than normal	no size	no prime	richest surface possible under stage lighting; range of techniques include soft washy blends and high contrast chiaroscuro effects; dyes used on light tone grounds, japan best on deep tones; paint can be built up in areas contrasting with the free pile in other areas	dye and japan, excellent; vinyl and casein, good
flannel duvetyn	very absorbent; colors sink through fabric unless sealed with size, which destroys surface	vinyl or shellac to seal surface; no size for dye painting	not necessary	rarely used as a soft painting surface; often used for covering carved styrofoam because it is easily molded over intricate surfaces without obliterating the detail; saturated with heavy size, it strengthens the styrofoam and makes an excellent surface for opaque painting; also excellent for low-relief decoration of picture frames, etc.	dye is more successful than paint; even coverage very difficult to obtain
burlap jute fabric	not absorbent	seal surface with vinyl	not necessary	used for drops and other soft pieces; does not show wrinkles after folding; excellent surface on which to build textures; ideal surface for tapestry painting	after sealing; dye and all paints; rubber, excellent
silk	absorbs readily; colors tend to bleed beyond a line	none	not necessary	ideal for flags, banners, draped pieces, and other soft units; framed units should be wrapped and glued on the back to prevent glue destroying surface; usually dye painted which retains the characteristic sheen	dye and thin color
sharktooth scrim Hansen cloth opera cloth	absorbs readily; colors tend to bleed beyond a line	none	none; paint direct	ribbed side is best for painting; avoid heavy paint which will fill openings in weave, decreasing transparency and causing sagging; areas and shapes can be opaqued with iron-on appliqués (available 36″ wide); opaquing with heavy vinyl or rubber-base, which is possible, may pull drop out of shape	dye, casein, and other thin paints
bobbinet net	moderately absorbent	none	none	used to "net" cut drops; in deep colors it disappears under stage lighting; can be cut without hemming into eccentric shapes; often used for appliqué drops with shapes cut from iron-on; for large areas of a single color, net is dipped in vats of dye, rather than sprayed or brushed	dye and thin color
cheesecloth	very absorbent; colors bleed beyond a line	very thin size	very thin prime; with dye, two coats may be necessary for thorough covering	rarely used professionally because it is not sufficiently durable; a good, inexpensive substitute for net or scrim if narrow width acceptable	dye and thin paint

Receives Poorly	Relative Opacity	Reflective Properties	Strength	Remarks
	from transparent to almost total opacity depending on weight	rich luminous color with matte surface	strong, resilient, and durable	once the standard material for drops and covering but now too expensive for general use. NOTE: the preceding remarks apply only to pure flax linen; linenlike fabrics containing rayon or other synthetics have different properties
...ye, unless well primed	depending on weave, from moderate to total opacity	matte surface; color less luminous than linen	strong, durable	used for soft pieces when opacity is needed; seldom for drops
...eavy paint, which alters ...e surface	translucent; must be back-painted for opacity	matte surface	moderately strong; tears and sags more easily than duck	not suitable for covering framed scenery; ideal for drops that are to be stored or transported
...ibber-base	nearly opaque in heavier grades; back with black duck for complete opacity	most absorbent of all surfaces; rich, matte surface	moderately strong; surface is easily marred and must be handled with care	when painting large areas of white velour a single tone, the back should be sprayed before painting the face; this prevents the white backing from showing under the pile
...iost paints, unless surface has been sealed	moderately opaque in heavier grades	matte surface	low durability if unsized; very strong if sized	a useful but temperamental fabric; test techniques thoroughly before attempting large-scale job
...ll paints and dyes except ...ubber unless sealed	translucent to transparent	matte, textured surface	very strong, durable	extremely difficult to flameproof; can be used for scrim effects
...eavy paint, which ...estroys surface	translucent in most grades	luminous and slightly reflective	very strongs, reasonably durable	percale sheeting (which is available in 108" width) is often substituted for China silk; has the same properties
...ibber-base; but can be ...sed if thinly applied	transparent	matte surface	snags and pulls easily	for thorough deep-tone coloring, several coats of paint or dye are necessary; sponges cut and shaped to a chisel edge are better than brushes for lining
...eavy paints, which cause ...agging	transparent	matte surface	snags and pulls easily	avoid nylon and other synthetic nets which are difficult to paint and dye
...eavy paint, which may ...ause sagging	transparent	matte surface	tears and rips easily	should be shrunk before sewing into drops; seams must be vertical; horizontal seams will sag unevenly

TABLE 10.2. HARD PAINTING SURFACES

Painting Surface	Texture	Cartooning Media	Receptivity to Paint	Absorption	Prime (Base Paint)
styrofoam	rough, porous	felt marker before sealing or covering; dye in vinyl after covering	poor unless covered	not absorbent; paint and dye sink through without coloring	white carpenter's glue, plastic resin glue, and combination of vinyl, rubber, and ground asbestos are moderately successful; most paint and all dye will cover unevenly
Masonite	face is extremely smooth and slick, back is rough, regular, pebbled surface	carpenter's pencil, lightly with felt marker	fair on slick side; poor on rough side	completely nonabsorbent on slick side; very absorbent on rough side	face: gloss vinyl or pigment in shellac with very soft brush to avoid streaks; back: spray first with Krylon, then paint with vinyl
plywood	from smooth, knot-free Grade A to rough, knotty Grade D construction grade	charcoal or carpenter's pencil or dye	poor unless covered	soft grain very absorbent; hard grain not absorbent, making it impossible to lose grain	titanium white in shellac or light combination of vinyl and ground asbestos to eliminate grain
vinyl plexiglass most plastics	generally very smooth and slick, though wide variety of pebbled and other textured surfaces are available	carpenter's pencil or very lightly with felt marker	fair	not absorbent	gloss vinyl often with some asbestos to give surface slight tooth
metal	polished, satin, brushed, pebbled, and rough are available	lightly with felt marker	fair	not absorbent	must be thoroughly cleaned of oil and flux; japan for prime; water paints and dyes can then be used
contour board wall board cardboard	from slick to pebbled	charcoal, dye	good	variable: some not absorbent; others with soft surface very absorbent	shellac to seal surface and prevent warping; then any other paints
raw wood	from smooth to rough	charcoal, dye	fair	variable; soft grains like pine are much more absorbent than hard grains like oak	either gloss or flat vinyl; asbestos may be added to eliminate undesirable grain

TABLE 10.2. HARD PAINTING SURFACES (continued)

Painting Surface	Covering	Characteristics and Uses
styrofoam	scrim and flannel cut in easily handled pieces and saturated with strong size made with white glue	easy to carve but difficult to paint unless covered; vinyl and asbestos will seal the surface and create texture, but will not strengthen surface sufficiently, since blue styrofoam bleeds through most paints; use white if available
Masonite	cover rough side with muslin or duck if smooth paint job is desired	used for floor, deck, and platform covering; slick surface makes it ideal (when properly primed) for the flowing and puddling of paints as when simulating marble
plywood	for better painting surface; cover with muslin or duck; duck preferred	grain of plywood is not generally suitable for direct painting with dye or pigment but when covered, it is painted as for muslin or duck; basswood ply or basswood covered ply can be dye-stained directly without prime. CAUTION: all carpenter marks must be sanded off prior to staining; brush strokes, drips, and spatters will show even through subsequent coats of stain
vinyl plexiglass most plastics	rarely covered	to achieve smooth color applications, especially on translucent and transparent pieces, color is sprayed on, as brushing will leave brush strokes; dye in gloss vinyl or acrylic dyes are best; to retain surface gloss on transparent pieces, spray the color on the back side
metal	scrim	paints will tend to chip on very slick surfaced metals; aluminum should be primed with spray lacquer; a final coat of shellac or thin varnish will increase durability
contour board wall board cardboard	muslin or duck; paper covering on back side to prevent warping	used for profiles on framed scenery; should be covered with same fabric as wing to avoid change of surface texture
raw wood	muslin, duck, scrim, and velour	two coats of base for smooth even coverage; antiquing, glazing, and toning over gloss vinyl

Receives Well	Receives Poorly	Relative Opacity	Reflective Properties	Strength
..sbestos and vinyl combi-..ation	all paints and dyes CAUTION: most spray paints contain acetone base which will dissolve the styrofoam	translucent to opaque depending on thickness	matte surface when un-covered; slight to moder-ate gloss when covered	breaks, chips, or dents easily unless covered
..inyls after prime; japan ..nd enamels	thin colors, rubber-base, casein	opaque	slick: glossy; rough: matte	very strong but edges tend to chip; paint surface sus-ceptible to scratches
..inyls and shellac with pig-..ment	rubber-base, casein, scenic paints	opaque	alternating hard and soft grain causes alternating reflections; matte surface if covered	very strong; tends to splin-ter and scar easily
..loss vinyl, acrylics, and ..lastic lacquers; after ..rime, japan and flat vinyl	most paints and dye	variable from transparent to opaque	untextured surfaces are reflective	strong and durable but floppy unless carefully framed
	all water-base paints and dyes	opaque	reflective unless covered	very strong
..ll types of paint after ..rime	dyes tend to streak	opaque	matte to reflective	moderately strong and dur-able; tends to scratch, scuff, and tear at edges
..inyl, and if grain is usable. ..ye in vinyl or shellac	rubber-base, casein	opaque	matte to reflective de-pending on finish and surface	strong and durable; tends to scratch and scuff

---

Remarks

..empered Masonite preferred; untempered chips ..asier and tends to warp

..ght coat of varnish or shellac after painting will ..educe tendency to splinter

..hermoformed vinyl can be filled with foam to in-..rease strength and durability; paints on all plas-..cs should be thoroughly tested for compatibility ..nd durability

..an be textured with vinyl and asbestos to which .. large proportion of cooked glue has been added

..se sponges for painting edges; faster and more ..horough than brushing

..ubber-base may be used on wood, but oil glazes ..re not successful over rubber

TABLE 10.3. DRY BINDERS

Dry Binder	Form	1969 N.Y. Price	Vehicle	To Make Full-Strength Liquid	To Make Working Size	Characteristics
rubber or flexible glue	1 lb. slabs	85¢/lb.	water	cover with water in top of a double boiler and heat until melted	1 part full-strength liquid to 10 parts vehicle	remains flexible after dries; does not discolor pigment
gelatine or ground flake glue	granulated	70¢/lb.	water	cover with water and soak overnight; heat in top of double boiler until all glue is melted	1 part full strength to 10 parts vehicle	pure enough that hues are not greatly affected but tend to darken values
carpenter's or ground glue	granulated	53¢/lb.	water	cover with water and soak overnight; heat in top of double boiler until all glue is melted	1 part full strength to 16 parts vehicle	stronger than other glues a is used where great streng is required
starch	powder	13¢/lb. box	water	½ lb. of heavy cold water starch to 12 quarts of boiling water; add starch to water slowly, stirring constantly; allow to cool completely and strain thoroughly through several thicknesses of cheesecloth	may be used full strength (for sizing) or thinned by as much as 50 percent for use with dye	hard, slick surface which f the weave of muslin to give an even, luminous, trans cent quality
methacel	granulated	$2.75/lb.	water	mix slowly 1 cup granules to 12 quarts boiling water; cool and strain	1 part full-strength liquid to 10 parts water	very strong, completely clea and colorless additive whi prevents bleeding of colo beyond a line
dextrine	powder	32¢/lb.	water	mix slowly 1 part with 3 parts hot water and cook in top of double boiler until clear and completely dissolved	use full strength or dilute slightly for better flow; should be rather sticky	clear thick liquid that is e cellent as a binder for bronz
gum arabic gum tragacanth	powder or globules	$1.00/lb.	water	soak with 3 parts water for several hours, then cook in top of double boiler and strain	use full strength	thick, sticky consistency us primarily as an additive prevent bleeding of colors yond a line

Compatible Additives	Advantages	Cautions	Remarks
ombine full strength with asbestos, ubber-base paint, and whiting to ake an excellent texture paint for se on decks and platforms and her areas of hard wear	flexibility makes it excellent for painting drops and other soft pieces; can be folded or rolled without damage to paint surface	reasonably consistent in strength, but test thoroughly without forced drying	
mbine with other water-base nders to increase strength	goes further than carpenter's glue and dries more slowly than other glues, allowing more time to work wet		relatively uniform in strength
mbine with asbestos and vinyl for xturing metal or for surfaces that ill receive extreme wear	very strong and inexpensive	dries rather brittle, tends to discolor pigment, and does not keep well in liquid form; will bleed through glazes	very inconsistent in strength and should be carefully tested
d glue or vinyl size for surfaces at undergo hard wear; add metha-l or gum arabic to prevent colors' eeding past a line; and rubber-se for greater flexibility and a perb surface for either dye or pig-ent painting	used as a size and binder for dye, it greatly increases the wet working time and prevents the dyes from staining fabric on contact; even when dry, dye can be partially scrubbed out making corrections of tone possible	important that the starch be thoroughly dissolved; undis-solved particles will badly discolor dyes applied over them	stained-glass, wet watercolor, and finger-painting effects can be achieved only with starch
mpatible with all water-base nders and gives added strength	used as an additive to starch to strengthen and prevent bleed; may be used at full strength to build up transparent textures on plastics and plexiglass, and at working strength for use on unprimed metal	somewhat brittle in heavy ap-plications on soft surfaces; does not keep well in liquid form; tends to crystallize	good binder for bronzes
ay be added to any other water-se binder to prevent bleeding of lors beyond a line	stays flexible when dry and will not discolor or oxidize metallic pig-ments as do most glues	*Do not* mix with cold water; undissolved particles will dis-color metallics	methacel and clear gloss vinyl have gen-erally replaced dextrine
mpatible with all water-base ders	remains soft and flexible when dry and is particularly good for use on dye-painted silks and other very soft fabrics		generally replaced by methacel, but better when softness is important as on China silk banners

TABLE 10.4. LIQUID BINDERS

Liquid Binder	1969 N.Y. Price	Vehicle	To Make Working Size	Characteristics
polyvinyl flexible cold-water glue	$5.00/gal.	water	1 part liquid glue to 5–7 parts water	a premixed equivalent of rubber or flexib glue with the same characteristics
clear liquid vinyl	$5.00/gal. gloss $5.50/gal. flat	water	for pigment: 1 part liquid to 5 parts water for dye: 1 part liquid to 8–10 parts water	available flat or gloss finish; does not di color and is reasonably flexible when dr insoluble when completely dry; two th coats are better than one heavy coat
liquid acrylic	$10.00/gal.	water	1 part to 5 parts water	similar to vinyl but dries more slowly ar has a thicker feeling in the brush
liquid latex rubber additive	$5.50/gal. regular and heavy body	water	1 part liquid to 2–3 parts water	very flexible and insoluble when dry; sta on the surface rather than penetrating fa ric unless rubbed in; appearance under sta lighting similar to casein but with sligh more gloss
shellac	$3.30/gal.	alcohol	1 part liquid to 5–10 parts vehicle	available as white (clear) or orange; dri relatively flat and rapidly and can be ove glazed immediately; used as a sealer f cardboard covering and mixed with tit nium white to kill the grain in plywood a raw wood
varnish	$4.75/gal.	turpentine	1 part liquid to 4–6 parts vehicle	hard gloss surface; use with japan to gi gloss and longer drying time; used witho color to give gloss to woodwork and pr furniture; hardest and most durable surfa

TABLE 10.5. PREMIXED PAINTS

Paint	Vehicle	Working Proportions	Characteristics
vinyl	water	1 part vehicle to 2–3 parts paint	available in gloss and flat; colors lack intensity of d pigment or casein; available colors are the basic hu which can be modified by dry pigments and dyes
casein	water	1 part vehicle to 2 parts paste; add water slowly, stirring vigorously with a whisk until free of lumps	available only in premixed form; colors as intense a transparent as dry pigment; insoluble in water wh dry; matte surface suitable for gouache and tempe techniques; the best opaque to transparent paint for on scrim
rubber-base latex	water	1 part water to 2–3 parts paint	fast-drying, insoluble paint that dries very close to color, making it best for touch-up and matching co samples; durable; can be washed frequently, he good for floors, decks, and platforms
poster showcard	water	generally sold at working consistency; if too thick, thin to desired degree of transparency	pigments ground finer than scenic paints and are of purer; colors more intense and can be thinned furt and remain opaque; in theatre used for lettering, paint props, and when intense and day-glow colors needed
japan	turpentine	slowly stir 1 part vehicle into 1 part paste; add additional vehicle until desired consistency and transparency is achieved. For gloss: add 1 cup varnish to 1 gal. paint. For durability with matte finish: add varnish as above and ½ cup flattening oil. To retard drying time: add ¼ cup boiled linseed oil to any of above mixtures. To flameproof: use carbon tetrachloride instead of turpentine as vehicle	in pure state, a fast-drying, flat oil paint that adheres virtually any surface; the amount of gloss can be c trolled by the amount of varnish, therefore extensiv used for painting woodwork and paneling and painting prop furniture
oil-base metallic	turpentine	generally sold at working consistency	not as brilliant as bronze powders but much less exp sive if a large area is to be covered; highlights and cents can be added later with bronzes; bronzes can a be added to the paint to increase brilliance or cha color tone
spray lacquers	lacquer thinner or acetone		will adhere to almost any surface, including synthet metals, and plastic, all of which resist other forms paint; available in wide range of colors and metall both flat and gloss

Advantages	Cautions
saves time and mess	more expensive
gloss: excellent with bronze powders; seals porous fabrics, raw wood, and soft materials producing a hard, smooth surface perfect for watercolor techniques; used at full strength with asbestos to build textures. Flat: used with dry pigments and as a final varnish when no gloss is desired	keep solution thin—even the flat type develops gloss with repeated application; reflection from a glossy surface, especially over closely related deep tones, will render this painting invisible
longer wet working time than vinyl	forms a skin like rubber-base and may be unevenly glossy; brush strokes tend to show
use full strength with asbestos and some vinyl to build flexible textures on drops and other soft pieces; lack of penetration makes it perfect for back painting wings or for opaquing portions of translucent drops	does not adhere to slick or oily surfaces and cannot be overglazed with japan or varnish-based glazes
combines well with pigments and alcohol-soluble dyes, penetrates all porous surfaces, and will not rub up or scar easily; penetration good when cartooning if drawing must be seen on back side as guide to opaquing; used as a glaze mixed with dye it is called French Enamel Varnish or F.E.V.	cannot be used with water-soluble dyes
with oil-soluble dyes it is excellent for staining wood or for glazing painted wood	cannot be used over rubber-base

1969 N.Y. Price	Advantages	Cautions
3.00–$9.00/gal.	dries to a hard, durable surface and is used for painting three-dimensional units and for decks; thinned to make glazes not as transparent as dry pigment; flexible when dry and will adhere to all fabrics and many plastics and metals; gloss dries to a hard, slick, nonabsorbent surface	colors dry a full value lighter than when wet
3.00–$11.00/gal.	extensive range of colors, including some special intense hues with a dye base; compatible with most surfaces except raw wood; resists bleeding	colors dry darker than the wet color and should be carefully tested, especially the deep tones
6.00–$11.00/gal.	does not penetrate fabrics, staying like a skin on the surface; best for back painting; matte surface with slightly more sheen than casein	color range limited and not very intense; thin glazes lack binding properties; washes become grainy; surface is tough but soft and absorbs readily; not suitable for painting on velour; not compatible with oil-based paints and glazes
3.30/qt.	can be overpainted without bleeding	expensive
2.50–$5.00/qt.	can be thinned to palest washes without losing intensity; fairly extensive color range; penetrates well	cannot be used over rubber-base and is only moderately successful over casein; colors dry very close to the wet color
5.00–$12.00/gal.	if strained, it can be sprayed to cover large areas quickly; will adhere to metal and most other surfaces	stir frequently since the pigment sinks quickly
4.80/13 oz.	will cover and seal over paints and dyes that bleed through other paints; most other paints will adhere to the lacquer surface for glazing and overpainting	very expensive if used in large quantities; acetone base may dissolve certain plastics, so testing advisable; assumes surface of material being painted, which makes it difficult to match two different materials that are to appear the same

Scene Painting Techniques

The purpose of this presentation is to show, step by step, how some commonly needed subjects can be simulated with paint. It is not intended to imply that these are the only methods used by scenic artists for painting wood, marble, etc., but rather it is intended as a starting point from which each individual will evolve his own particular method and technique.

selection of examples

The procedures illustrated on subsequent pages are for essentially realistic effects. They are those which rely most on the ability to observe and imitate reality and least on native talent or interpretive skill. The painting of stylistically abstract or painterly subjects would not alter the procedure, but only the color, the degree of exaggeration, or the line quality. As the *design* of abstract subjects must ultimately be based on the realistic, so the *painting* of abstract subjects must ultimately be based on realistic painting techniques.

Artistic considerations and dramatic exaggerations of light and shadow have been eliminated in the interest of clarity.

Each of the examples was painted on a surface primed with white flat vinyl. The mixed colors were painted in flat vinyl except as specifically noted.

color samples

The color samples were painted with the mixed colors actually used on the panels. Color mixing is not a part of this presentation; it is assumed that the apprentice either has this knowledge or can get it from other sources.

The color samples labeled as glazes or transparent paints appear to be opaque. They must be used only as guides to color, not as guides to paint density.

priming and base color

Given a subject to be painted, the first and most important decisions to be made are what kind of paint is to be used for the prime, and what color and kind of paint for the base.

prime

Generally, but not without exception, the painting of subjects with hard smooth surfaces (wood, marble) require hard, slick prime (gloss vinyl, shellac, heavy size) and soft, pliable subjects (foliage, drapery) are best painted over soft, absorbent prime (flat vinyl, latex, casein, light size) regardless of the actual painting surface (canvas, masonite, etc.).

base color

The subsequent technique involved in painting a subject is implicit in the choice of the base color. There are three basic methods from which to choose:

• **Highest value to lowest value.** Match the base color to the lightest tone in the sample and subsequently paint toward the darkest tones (see "Wood Graining," page 249).

• **Middle value.** Match the base color to the middle or local tone in the sample and subsequently paint up to the highest value and down to the darkest value (see "Moldings," page 253).

• **Lowest value to highest value.** Match the base color to the darkest tone in the sample and subsequently paint up toward the highest (see "Foliage," page 252).

10.30 A drop for the Metropolitan Opera's 1966 production of *La Giaconda* being painted in the Metropolitan's own shop by the scenic artist (in the background) and two assistants. Beni Montresor, designer

basic techniques

The brush strokes, textures, and lay-ins that follow on the next dozen pages are fundamental to the craft of scene painting and must be understood and mastered before proceeding to such painting as is shown in the examples.

A-1. Flat of Brush. Hold a thick brush by the end of the handle at forty-five degrees to the surface with only the tips of the bristles in contact with the surface. Lift lightly at the end of the stroke to feather the end. The width of the brush is perpendicular to the lining stick

A-2. Side of Brush—Thin. Same as with flat of brush but with the width of the brush parallel with the lining stick

A-3. Double-Ended Line. Requires at least two strokes: one from left to right, one from right to left. The feathered ends overlap

A-4. Loaded Brush over Feathered Stroke. What *not* to do when a continuous line is desired. This emphasizes the importance of A-3. It also shows the light-dark effect caused by pausing, then lifting a partially loaded brush

A-5. Dry Brush. Shake the excess paint from brush before making the stroke. CAUTION: dry brush does *not* mean dry, thick paint

A-6. Thick and Thin. Creates sense of dimension with a single stroke. Hold the brush, dry or loaded, at a constant angle, vertically and horizontally, during the stroke. Roman brush lettering is ideal for study and practice

A-7. Side Print. Hold the brush, dry or loaded, almost parallel with the surface. Set the brush and pull it lightly up and off the surface in the direction of the arrows

A-8. Flat Print. Same technique as for the side print, but using the flat of the brush, dry or loaded

A-9. Split or Cut Bristle. Brush is prepared either by tying the bristles into clumps or by cutting away clumps of bristles; use dry or loaded

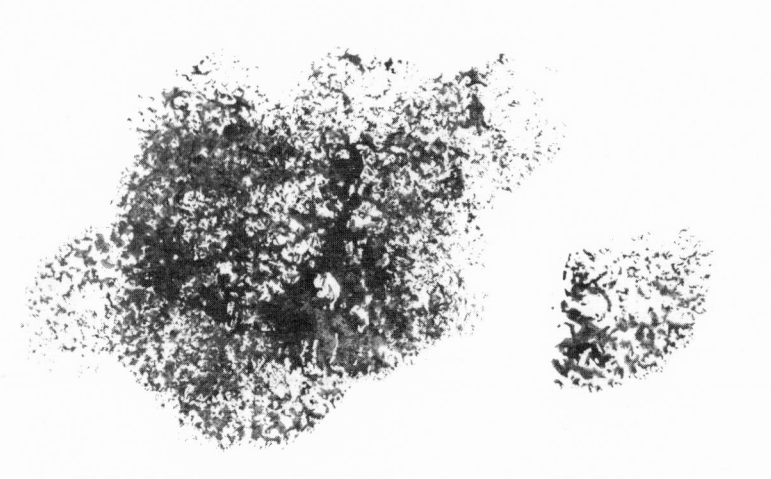

A-10. Sponge Print. Dip natural or synthetic sponges lightly in paint and *print* the surface

A-11. Roller. Loaded or dry rollers of appropriate sizes are used for lining, covering, or texturing

A-12. Thick-and-Thin Roller. Twist the roller from side to side

A-13. Tapestry or Engraving Line. Cut or tape the roller to yield a series of parallel lines; use dry or loaded

A-14. Stipple. Use a light pounding action, with the brush held perpendicular to the surface and with the bristles very dry

A-15. Twisted Brush. With the brush parallel to the surface, twist the brush lightly and turn it on the surface

A-16. Spatter. Before spattering shake excess paint from the brush. To spatter hit the ferrule lightly against the palm of the hand. The length of the bristle, the stiffness of the bristle, and the thickness of the paint vary the results

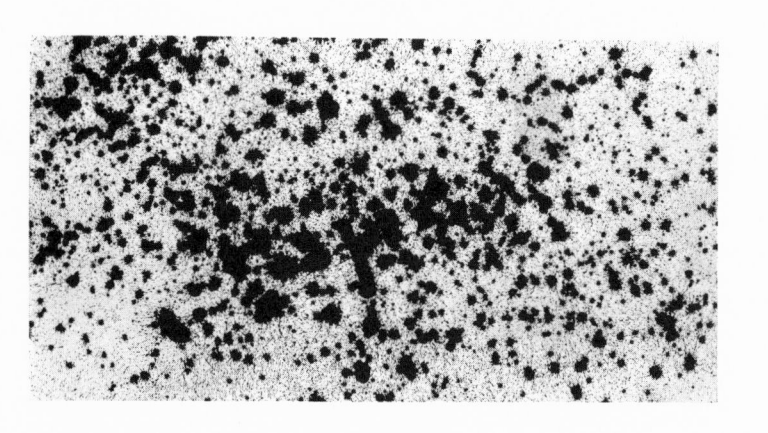

A-17. Dribble. Allow moderately thin color to dribble from the bristles. Hold the brush several feet above and parallel to the surface; while moving the arm up and down and progressing over the surface

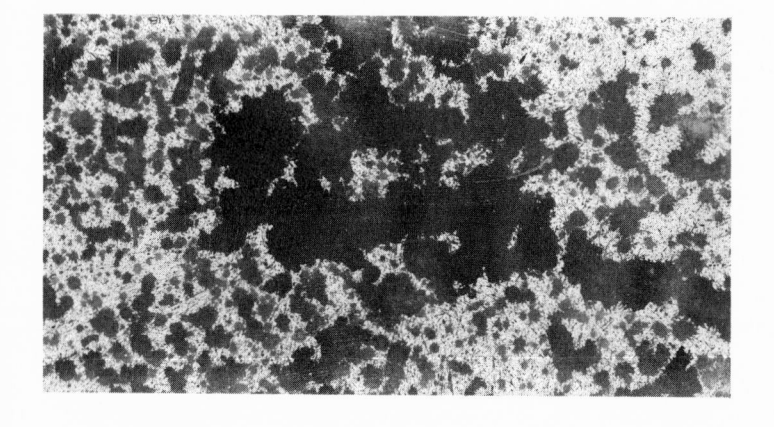

A-18. Splash. Same technique as for dribble but using dye or very thin paint

A-19. Graded Wash. This produces a smooth progression from light to dark or from one color to another. Paint *all* strokes rigidly and smoothly in the same direction. Overlap the last stroke of the first color with the first stroke of the second. Without reloading the brush, paint successive strokes back onto the first color until the brush is dry. Repeat this process for each change of color or value

A-20. Scumble. Paint two or more colors together simultaneously with separate brushes, or with the same brush, dipping back and forth between the colors. Make the strokes in all directions, overlapping colors and feathering edges

A-21. Wet Blend. Blend two or more colors together to form a soft-edged pattern. Make the initial stroke with the second color; overlap the first color while the first color is still wet

brick

B-1. Base Color. Flat absorbent paint matched to the lightest color of mortar

B-2. Brick Lay-in. Matched to middle value. Must be opaque and consistency of cream

B-3. Light Spatter and Highlight. Matched to lightest brick tone

B-4. Dark Glaze and Shadow. Matched to darkest brick tone; transparent with some dye added

B-5. Dark Mortar Spatter. Matched to darkest tone of mortar

procedure

B-6. Steps 1 and 2: Mortar Spatter and Brick Lay-in. Paint the base coat. Thoroughly spatter entire base color area with dark mortar spatter. Increase the density of the spatter gradually until the final mortar tone is achieved; the spatter should vary from very fine to rather coarse. Allow to dry. Place a brick stencil over the mortar and spatter and dribble with the brick lay-in color; for large areas, use a garden sprayer for both steps. Allow to dry

B-7. Step 3: Dark Glaze. With a brush the width of the brick, glaze some bricks solidly, others with a broken stroke or dry brush stroke. Allow to dry

B-8. Steps 4 and 5: Light Spatter, Highlight, and Shadow. Place stencil over brick pattern again and spatter very unevenly with light spatter color. Remove stencil and paint highlights and shadows with broken strokes. Accent the mortar, here and there, with the base color

A-19

A-20

A-21

B-1

B-2

B-3

B-4

B-5

B-6

B-7

B-8

C-1

C-2

C-3

C-4

C-5

C-6

C-7

C-8

C-9

C-10

C-11

C-12

C-13

C-14

C-15

C-16

C-1. Light Base Color and Highlight. Opaque gloss vinyl matched to lightest tone in sample

C-2. Dark Base Color. Opaque gloss vinyl one full value darker than base

C-3. Graining Color. Matched to darkest color of grain and thinned to consistency of milk; slightly transparent

C-4. Spatter Color. Dark base thinned to consistency of water and cooled by addition of blue or green; moderately transparent

C-5. Cut-Line Color. Graining color darkened and cooled by addition of blue or green

C-6. Step 1: Lay-in or Base. Wet-blend two colors in the direction of the grain. Use straight parallel strokes feathered in both directions. Allow to dry

C-7. Step 2: Panel Lines and Cut Grain. Snap lines to indicate each plank. Ink the lines with indelible marking pen. Lightly indicate with charcoal the location of the cut grain. Paint the cut grain with a fitch or graining brush the width of the widest part of the desired cut grain. Hold the brush with the side parallel to the grain; a thick and thin line will result. Paint one area of cut grain at a time. While it is still wet, drag a perfectly dry lay-in brush over the paint in the direction of the grain. This will feather the thick parts of the lines without disturbing the thin. Allow to dry

C-8. Step 3: Long Grain. Paint the long grain with either a graining brush, a split-bristle brush or a cut-bristle brush. Pull the brush in long even strokes, occasionally twisting or lifting slightly to avoid the effect of stripes. Do not overbrush. Dry thoroughly

C-9. Step 4: Spatter and Drag. Spatter the entire surface of one or two planks with a very fine spray of dots. Immediately, before they have a chance to dry, pull a dry brush or push broom firmly over the spatter in the direction of the grain. This produces the fine-lined soft grain. The left plank has not been spattered to show contrast with the two which have. For a pecky or very rough wood the splatter can be coarser (C-11 and C-14); for very fine-grained woods use a fine mist from a compressor sprayer (C-15). For large areas of wood graining use a garden sprayer. Two painters, one spattering or spraying, the other dragging the dry brush, produce the best results

C-10. Step 5: Highlight and Shadow, and Glazing. Following the inked lines which will have bled through the graining, carefully paint the highlight and shadow lines. The wood can now be glazed with dyes or with thin color to correct final tonality, or certain boards may be darkened by glazing to give variety.

C-11. Light Woods. The procedure is exactly the same as in Step 4; the difference is in the colors and in the coarseness of the spatter

C-12. Textured (Weathered) Surface. Using a comb, wire brush, toy rake, or other serrated-edged tool, form the cut and long grain in a dark-colored (C-5) texture paint. Allow to dry. Paint the base coat, matched to the grain color. Dry-brush the surface of the texture lightly with the light base. Steps 4 and 5 remain the same

C-13. Cross-sawed Oak. Only the brush stroke for the cut grain is different

C-14. Pecky Cypress. In addition to Step 4, the surface has a very light dribble, which is dragged and then highlighted to produce the pecky effect

C-15. Long Grain Dominates. Step 2 is eliminated

C-16. Knotty Pine. The knotholes are made by revolving the ball of the thumb in a small drop of paint after step 2

marble

procedure

D-1. Base Color. Gloss vinyl; use two coats and brush out very smoothly

D-2. Warm Veining Color. Transparent; of the consistency of milk

D-3. Cool Veining Color. Flat vinyl; consistency as for warm color

D-4. Steps 1 and 2: Splash and First Veining. Splash either clear water or very thin color over dry base. While still damp, lay in both veining colors with a small roller, twisting, rolling, and scuffing to match sample. The edges will fuzz and bleed. If they seem to bleed excessively, sponge up paint and reroll. If veining fails to bleed enough, splash lightly with additional water. Allow to dry

D-5. Steps 3 and 4: Spatter and Light Veining. Spatter lightly with clear water and apply a third veining color (in this case, white — not shown as a sample) as in step 2. Allow to dry

D-6. Steps 5, 6, and 7: Spatter, Accent, and Glaze. Again spatter lightly with water and reinforce lights and darks as necessary. Finally, glaze the entire surface with either clear gloss vinyl or a color glaze of gloss vinyl with dye

foliage

F-1. Tree-Trunk Base Color

F-2. Background Foliage

F-3. Middle-Ground Foliage

F-4. Highlight Foliage

F-5. Flash-Light Foliage

F-6. Deep Foliage Shade

F-7. Tree-Trunk Highlight

procedure

F-8. Steps 1, 2, and 3: Sky, Cartoon, and Trunk Lay-in. Lay in sky area in graded wash from medium blue at the top to pale blue at the horizon. Ink the drawing with indelible marker and label foliage areas. Paint the trunk with the deepest tone. Paint branches into foliage areas

F-9. Step 4: Background Foliage. Lay in background areas loosely, leaving bits of sky showing through. *Flat print* and *side print* are the basic strokes used throughout

F-10. Step 5: Middle-Ground Foliage. Lay in loosely, leaving bits of sky

F-11. Steps 6 and 7: Deep Foliage Shade and Trunk Highlight. First indications of light and shade. Add additional white to colors to vary the values slightly

F-12. Step 8: Flash Light. Selective place flash lights, brushed in *quickly*. Finish the trunk and leaves with accents of warm and cool tones.

(*Color samples and accompanying text of this section continued on next two facing pages*)

E-1. Warm Base. Flat vinyl the consistency of light cream

E-2. Cool base. As for warm base

E-3. First Splash. Thin color the consistency of water

E-4. First Stencil. Opaque gloss of a consistency for spraying

E-5. Second Stencil. As for first stencil

E-6. Dye Splash. Warmer transparent shade of first stencil; no binder

E-7. Steps 1 and 2: Scumble and Splash. Lay in both base colors in smooth scumble. While still wet, splash the area unevenly with the thin color. Allow to dry

procedure

E-8. Steps 3 and 4: First and Second Stencil. Using a compressor spray gun, spray the first color lightly but thoroughly through the stencil. Continue with the first color until the entire area is stenciled. Begin the second color, spraying less evenly, allowing areas of the first stencil color to show. Allow to dry

E-9. Step 5: Dye Splash. Splash and spatter dye over entire area. Very wet or puddled areas can be sponged up if necessary. Rub the patterned areas with cheesecloth for an antique patina

E-10. Tapestry Effect. Procedure is the same except that following Step 5 the entire surface is rolled with a taped roller in several colors closely related to those used for the base scumble. This example has been stenciled with a color different from the colors in E-8.

variation

For the sky colors, see A-19: Graded Wash

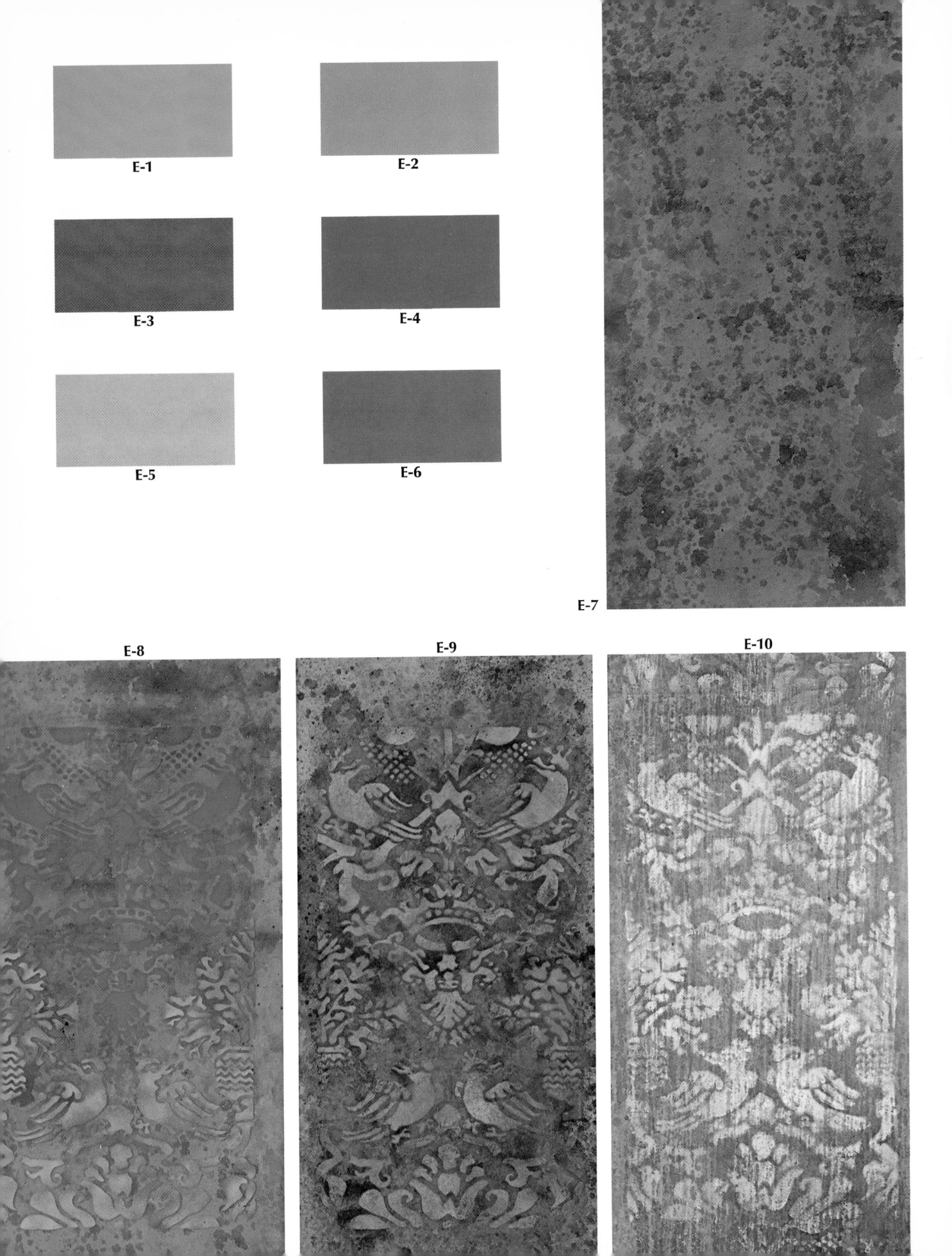

E-1

E-2

E-3

E-4

E-5

E-6

E-7

E-8

E-9

E-10

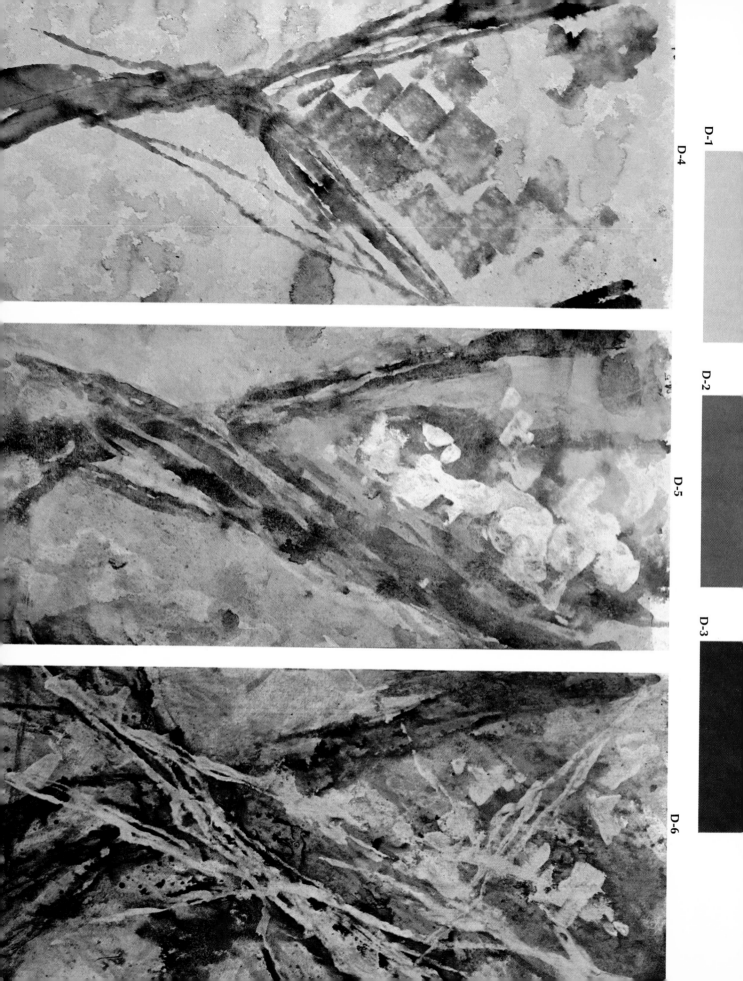

D-1

D-4

D-2

D-5

D-3

D-6

F-1

F-2

F-3

F-4

F-5

F-6

F-7

F-8

F-9

F-10

F-11

F-12

F-13

F-14

F-15

G-1

G-2

G-3

G-4

G-5

G-6

G-7

G-8

G-9

G-10

G-13

G-11

G-14

G-12

G-15

F-13. Foliage with Flowers. The procedure is the same. Introduce a few flowers in shadow tones with Step 4. As foliage tones lighten and move to the foreground, lighten the flower tones. The flowers should appear to be among the leaves, not on top of them

variations

F-14. Foliage with Trellis. As with the tree trunk and flowers, introduce the trellis early and build up with the foliage. Note foliage variation: done with a dry brush and a flat stroke

F-15. Stenciled Foliage. Cut a small stencil of several leaves. Paint in rough background tone for heavy masses. Turning stencil for variation, paint leaves using colors as above

G-1. Base Color on Light Side

moldings

G-2. Light on Light Side. Lighter value of base

G-3. Shade on Light Side. Darker and cooler than base

G-4. Cast Shadow. Cooler than shade

G-5. Reflected Light on Light Side. Very warm, grayed complement of G-4

G-6. Cut Line. Not black, but very cool

G-7. Base Color on Shade Side

G-8. Light on Shade Side

G-9. Shade on Shade Side

G-10. Steps 1 and 2: Lay-in and Cartoon. Ink cartoon lines with indelible marker

procedure

G-11. Steps 3 and 4: Lay-in of Shade Side and Painting of Highlights. Paint highlights with ½″ brush and lining stick

G-12. Step 5: Shade. The shade on the ogee molding has a clean hard edge where it meets the change of plane and a soft dry-brushed edge over the curve of the molding. This involves two strokes, one with a small loaded brush for the sharp edge followed by a dry stroke with a larger brush

G-13. Step 6: Cast Shadow. Line as for Step 4. There is no cast shadow on the shade side

G-14. Step 7: Cutting Line. Line as for Step 4. There is no cutting line on the shade side

G-15. Step 8: Reflected Light. Line with a moderately dry brush and feather off. Use a thin dark-gray glaze in cast-shadow location on the shade side

drapery

H-1. Local Color

H-2. Shade

H-3. Highlight

H-4. Shadow — a Transparent Glaze

H-5. Fringe Base Color

H-6. Fringe Shade

H-7. Fringe Local

H-8. Fringe Highlight

H-9. Fringe Flash Light

procedure

H-10. Steps 1 and 2: Lay-in. Lay in local color and shade in a wet blend. Add clear water to increase transparency in some areas of local color. Lay in fringe, tassel, and rope with fringe base

H-11. Steps 3 and 4: Shadows. Rough in shadows. Strokes are fast and vigorous. Brush in shade and local color on fringe

H-12. Steps 5 and 6: Highlight and Cast Shadows. Paint highlights quickly with a fully loaded brush. Add white to highlight color for a few accents. Note cast shadows and washes of shadow on fringe

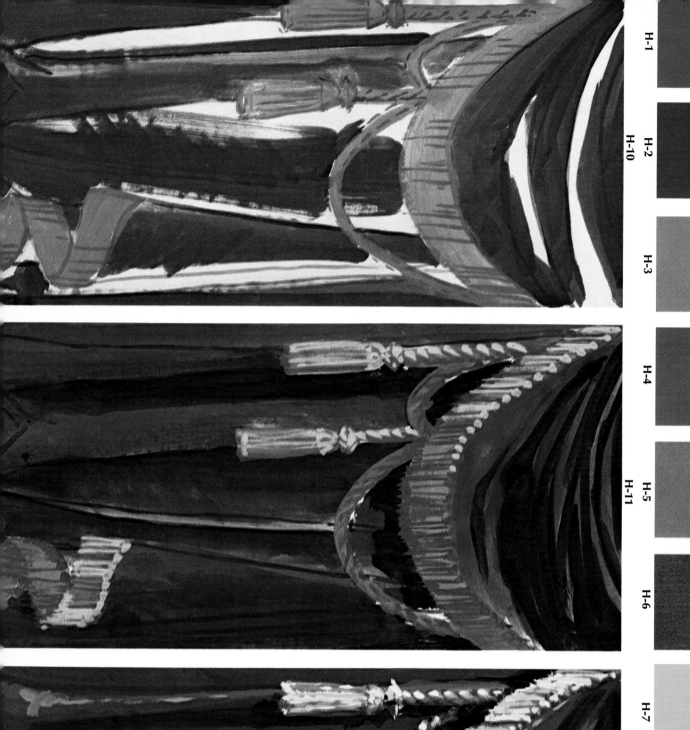

H-1

H-2
H-10

H-3

H-4

H-5
H-11

H-6

H-7

H-8
H-12

H-9

I-1

I-2

I-1, I-2, I-3, and **I-4.** These are combinations of techniques described in the preceding examples

I-3

I-4

The stage and its equipment 11

With scenery built and painted, the next step is to get it on the stage. Before that step can be taken, however, the stage itself merits more thorough discussion than has been included up to this point. The scenery must, so to speak, be fitted into a machine. The machine is the subject of this chapter.

A stage is designed and fitted with machinery for mounting and operating theatrical performances and displaying them to audiences. Its basic characteristics are fixed by its architect. Despite ingenious electro-mechanical installations, the size and shape of the stage building impose the ultimate space limitations on a production. Architectural characteristics of a good stage are to be found in *Theatres and Auditoriums*, second edition, by Burris-Meyer and Cole.

A stage is a space divided into functional subspaces: the *acting* space, the *scenery* space, and the *storage* space. Machinery helps to move scenery, properties, and other objects such as lighting instruments, between the scenery space and the storage space.

Designers and builders of stage machinery have found, in technological developments outside the theatre, equipment and apparatus which they have been able to adapt to stage uses. Research, most of it carried out under academic aegis, has developed applications of servomechanisms, tube and solid-state electronics, telemetering, and improved and new materials, to the solution of problems of setting the stage and shifting scenery. Designers of scenery and users of stage equipment have, at the same time, coped successfully with inadequate stages only by exercising great ingenuity and resorting to stylization and abstraction of scenery.

stage machinery

functions of stage equipment

To conceal and reveal the stage. Curtains, masking draperies, and sliding and flying panels conceal the stage, the scenery, and the actors and reveal them at the discretion of the director. A convention of the theatre has been the heightened theatrical effectiveness of this concealment-disclosure method of beginning a play, an act, or a scene. Arena and open stages, lacking curtains, have accustomed audiences to the new convention of the stage exposed before the performance and during intermissions, and of acts and scenes begun, by dimming houselights and bringing up stage lights. This convention has influenced production on proscenium stages when the acting area and scenery extend beyond the curtain line and in productions which, for stylistic reasons, dispense with the act curtain. This trend does not render the curtain obsolete since many historic styles and modern performance forms still require the concealment-disclosure routine.

To alter the size and shape of the acting area. Machinery is used to change the position of sections of the stage floor to create levels, ramps, and open or sunken portions; to reduce the width of the acting area by moving curtains, panels, or walls; to increase or reduce the depth of the acting area by walls or drops; and to change the height of the stage space and modify its upper aspect by raising and lowering scenery above the stage. Such changes are less applicable in arena and open-stage production because the spaces at the sides and above the stage are not concealed from the audience or are actually part of the audience space. In arenas and open stages machinery may be used to vary the shape and position of the stage floor. There are occasional installations of flying equipment above the stage. Manhandling scenery onto the open stage through tunnels under the audience or through the aisles must be done without the aid of machinery.

To support scenery and facilitate scenery changes. Machinery is used to suspend scenery over the stage and to support it on the stage floor and from below the stage. Whenever scenery or properties are too heavy, too large, too numerous, or too complex for manual handling within prescribed time limits, machinery is used to transport them to and from the scenery space. Machinery is also used when scenery and properties must be set onstage without apparent manipulation by stagehands.

To contribute by mechanical means to the progress of the play. Whether for *a vista* changes of scenery and properties, swinging sailors aboard in a cargo net, or providing moving objects ranging from Jove's chariot to a mineshaft elevator, machinery is essential.

To prevent the spread of fire and smoke. To do this and to assure the audience of its own safety and thus diminish the possibility of panic, a fire curtain of asbestos or steel, with adequate operating machinery, has been a fixture of the conventional theatre. Improved methods of flameproofing scenery, sprinkler systems, and water curtains now render the fire curtain unnecessary. Revision of laws requiring fire curtains in proscenium theatres is overdue and is anticipated. The 1968 New York building code provides for a water curtain as a substitute for asbestos or steel.

Within the infinitely variable context of theatrical production there is little meaning in the textbook definition of efficiency as the ratio of energy produced to energy expended. The output of a theatrical production system is not energy but aesthetic satisfaction, which can hardly be divided by the input of physical energy, be it human or electromotive. We must think of stage machinery not as a substitute for stagehands in an energy conversion cycle in which output-input ratios have significance, but as an aid to the producer, director, designer, actors, and technical staff in achieving effective theatrical results. If a stagehand can execute a required action more effectively than machinery, a stagehand should do it; if a machine can do it more effectively, a machine should be used.

Effectiveness is the valid criterion. Stage machinery is designed to increase the capabilities of human beings in the functions described above by multiplying manpower; enabling manpower applied at one location to be effective at another location; rendering limited manpower effective in moving scenery vertically; replacing manpower with electromotive power, and allowing men to apply electromotive power at points remote from convenient and nonhazardous control points.

If machinery is used effectively, economies of time and manpower result, which in turn contribute in several ways to the economic health of the production: savings in the cost of setup and operation are made; the play opens to paying audiences at the earliest possible moment; and the greatest possible number of performance days, versus setup and rehearsal days, are assured.

There is an opinion held by people who understand little about stage machinery that the installation of anything beyond a counterweight system constitutes overmechanization of the theatre, and that such overmechanization is bad for art.

Machinery must not be blamed for the imaginative deficiencies of theorists, nor for its ability to steal the show when art is weak and technique strong. Stage machinery is an artist's instrument as truly as is the violin. Its limits of usefulness are determined by only two requisites: it must do its job better than the job can otherwise be performed; it must save enough man-hours to earn its keep. Its limits of artistry are those of the creative imagination of its users.

With the best machinery, it is hard enough to stay within hailing distance of the poet's fancy. The world has yet to see an adequately staged producton of *The Tempest*.

The quintessence of effectiveness is the instantaneous shift.

The combined influences of dramaturgy (rapid and frequent changes of locale) and presentation (the desire not to interrupt the performance with scene changes) have generated the truly instantaneous scene shift, one which is integrated with the action so that the actors continue to play in character while scenery is changed around them, under them, and over their heads.

Ten seconds is about the length of time an audience will wait without relaxing attention and concentration; playing time is required to recap-

handling scenery
efficiency

effectiveness

economy

effectiveness of machinery

dramatic effectiveness of shifts

11.1

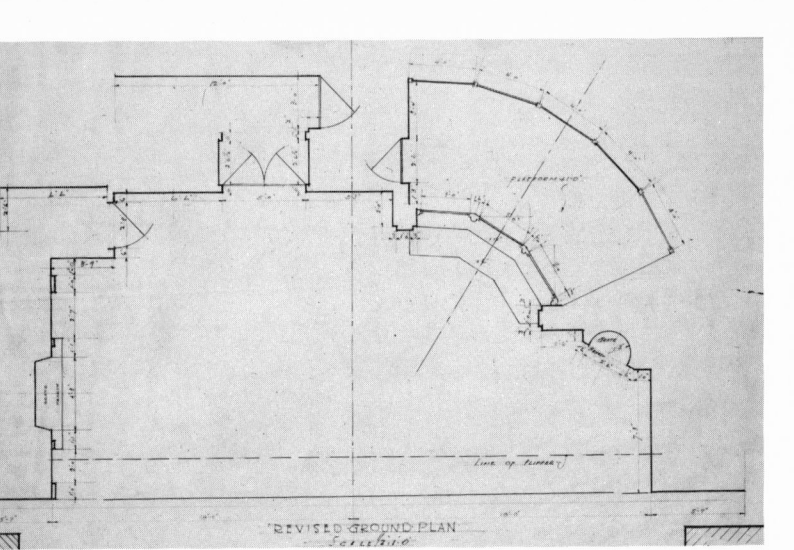

11.2

11.3

Pride and Prejudice. Settings and ground plans. The shift from the first to the third set was made while a scene was playing in the second set (below), which was flown as a unit with the sidewalls folded on the back wall. This is typical of mid-thirties scenery for high-style comedies, which often required rapid changes of full-stage sets. Jo Mielziner, designer

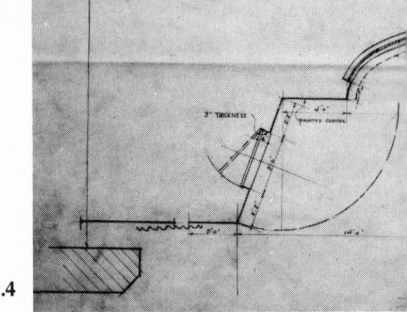

11.4

11.5

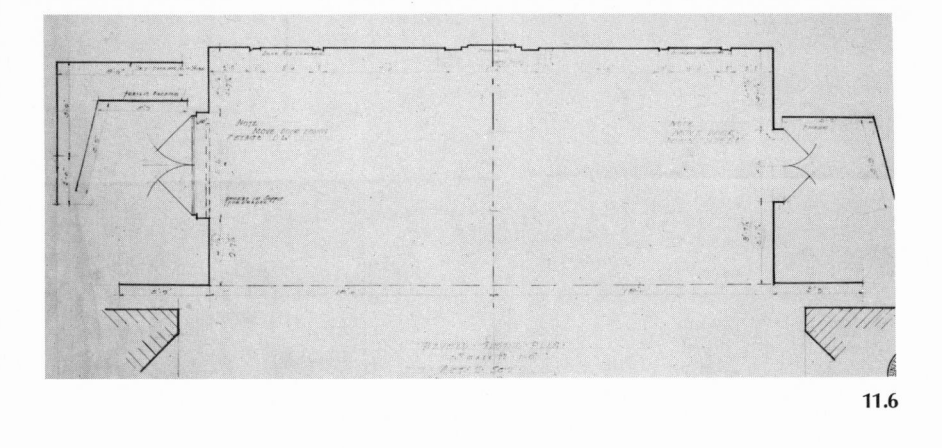

11.6

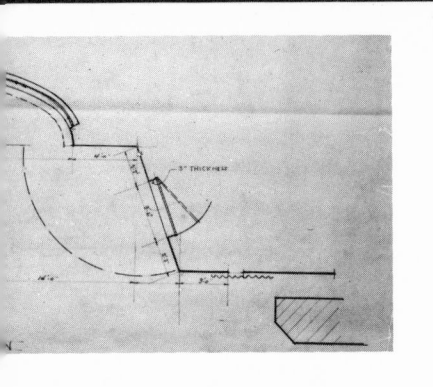

ture them and reestablish the mood of the play. Practically, if a shift must be accomplished in ten seconds or less, which is a trifle longer than the time required to dim stage lights and bring them up again, it is necessary to limit the movement of scenery to one move in one direction, or to as many moves as can be performed simultaneously, that is, one item may be flown while another is moved horizontally. Thus a one-movement shift might consist of revolving a preset disc; shuttling a traverse wagon; raising a two-level stage so that the first scene is up out of sight and the second at stage level ready to use; raising and lowering hung scenery; and rolling or sliding units on the floor.

From this minimum, shifts progress in manual complexity in inverse ratio to the efficiency of the stage machinery, to the wholly manual shift (multimovement) in which the sets are unfastened, separated, and assembled piecemeal without benefit of machines of any kind. Such scene shifts are inefficient. Chapter 14 (page 381) outlines a multimovement shift on a typical American stage.

All scene-changing methods, from full-stage wagons to piecemeal manual transport, assembly, and flying, persist as the plays and styles to which they pertain continue in audience favor. Hence the machinery to facilitate them and the skills to effectuate them are still required.

equipment for repertory

Repertory requires that scenery for sequential shows be changed between performances or that scenery for several shows be installed on the stage for such changes. The minimum available time is that between the matinee and evening performances on the same day. The most demanding situation is that of grand opera in repertory.

If the scenery for each show is designed without consideration for that of the other shows, magnificent quanta of manpower, cost, and frenzy can be achieved. It is reasonable that all the scenery for all the shows that are to be active in the repertory be designed, planned, and built to fit into the available storage spaces — on the floor, in the flies, and below stage — and be ready for setup without dismantling, unhanging, assembling, or hanging any units between performances. Scenery for shows coming into the repertory must fit the scenery which is already installed.

Repertory, therefore, requires the maximum in quantity of storage space and in versatility and efficiency of handling and flying equipment.

the fly loft

The fly loft is storage space above the acting and scenery spaces. All types of flat scenery, of large area, may be most easily set and stored by being attached to overhead machinery, elevated (flown) into the fly loft for storage and lowered to the stage for setting up. The machinery consists of one or more flying systems mounted either on a gridiron or on the structural members which support the stage roof (Figure 11.7).

the gridiron

The gridiron is essentially an openwork floor suspended below the roof of the stage to support rigging machinery and to permit access to it for adjustment and maintenance (Figure 11.8). It has two types of structural elements: primary, which are load-bearing, and secondary, which are bracing and flooring. The load-bearing elements consist of pairs of structural channels set back to back, spaced 10″ or more apart, extending from the proscenium wall to the back wall to form slots (*cable slots*). The transverse distance between these slots is determined

11.7 A bare stage showing the fly loft and a counterweight system

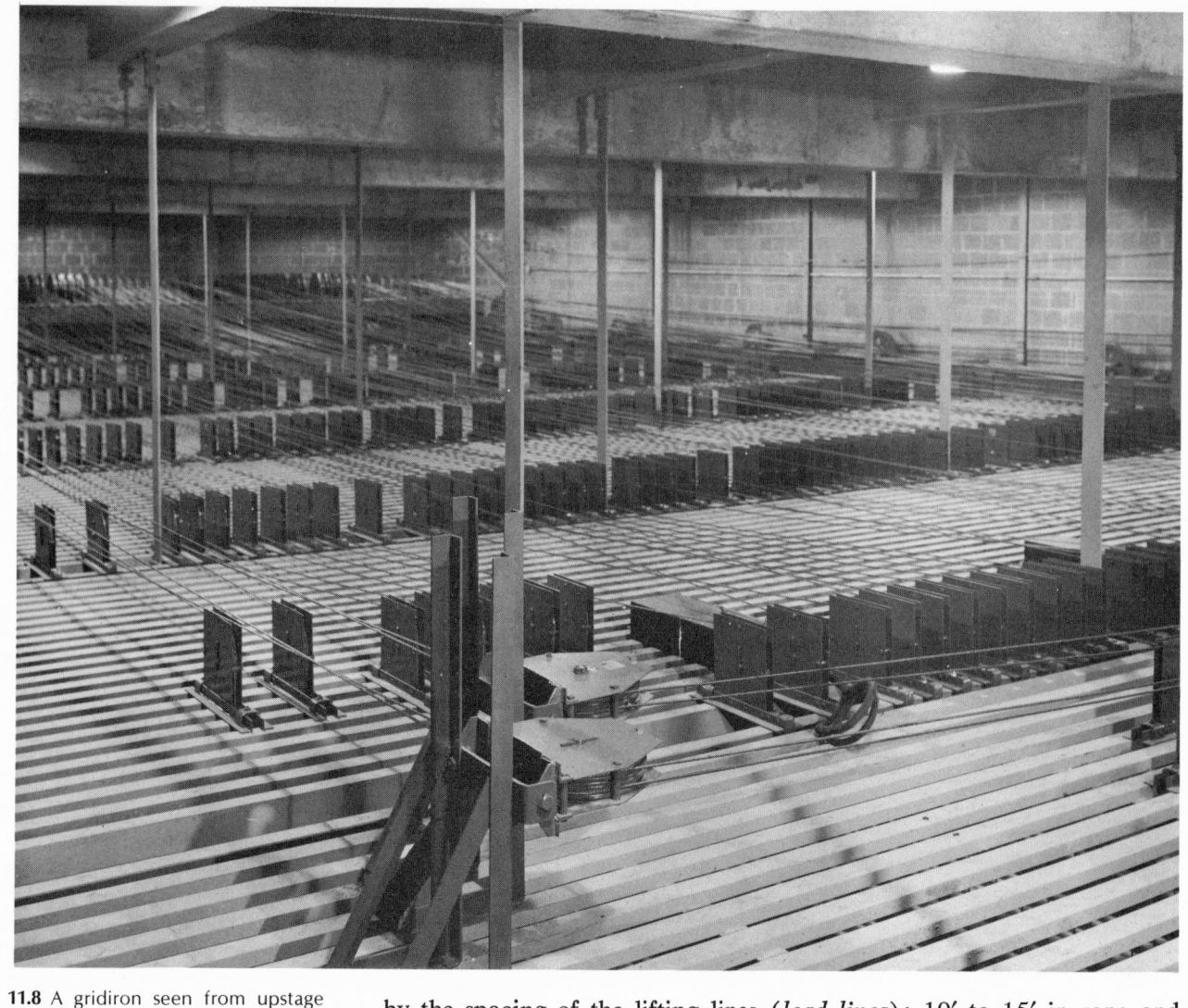

11.8 A gridiron seen from upstage right: standard cable slots supporting loft blocks, and flooring channels supporting spot blocks and, in foreground, muling blocks. Head blocks are at far left

by the spacing of the lifting lines (*lead lines*): 10′ to 15′ in rope and counterweight systems, as little as 4′ in spot-line systems.

The paired channels support *loft blocks* which are clamped to them. The lead lines (hemp or wire rope) pass through the loft blocks and down to battens or other loads at the ends of the lines.

Purlin channels set between the pairs of slot channels support the gridiron floor which is made of 3″ channels, set web up, running from proscenium to back wall, spaced 2½″ to 3½″ apart. This floor serves to support both flymen working on the grid and *spot blocks,* which may be clamped in place to locate a *spot line* no more than 1½″ horizontally from any point on the stage.

The gridiron must be designed to sustain the maximum anticipated loads of scenery and other apparatus, with concentration of loads at the cable slots but with adequate capacity for spot lines over the entire floor. The stage carpenter must know the limits of the gridiron's loading capacity.

double gridirons

Stages in which the maximum use of flying equipment is made have two gridirons, one below the other, which separate different systems and,

11.9 Close view of head blocks
mounted on I beams

with blocks hung under the roof steel, afford three-level separation of
head blocks, loft blocks, and lead lines. Chafing may occur when horizontal and vertical lines cross.

An assembly of heavy steel beams, two upright wide-flange (WF)
I beams, spaced about 24″ apart, coupled by plate diaphragms and
stiffened by an I beam or channel set web horizontal, extends from
proscenium to back wall close to one sidewall of the stagehouse, to support the head blocks, over which the lead lines from the loft blocks
change direction to descend to the fly gallery or to the counterweight
carriages (Figure 11.9). Head block beam assemblies differ for different
flying systems.

head block beams

263

The head block beams bear the combined loads of all hung objects, all counterbalancing weights, and any lifting forces exerted by winches. The stage carpenter must know their safe-load capacity.

loads on equipment and structure

The section "Stage Areas Using Scenery or Scenic Elements" of the *Building Code of the City of New York* specifies the loads as follows:

Scenery battens and suspension system shall be designed for a load of 30 lbs. per linear foot of batten length. Loft block and head block beams shall be designed to support vertical and horizontal loads corresponding to a 4 inch spacing of battens for the entire depth of the gridirons. Direction and magnitude of total forces shall be determined from the geometry of the rigging system including load concentrations from spot line rigging. Locking rails shall be designed for a uniform uplift of 500 per linear foot with a 1,000 lb. concentration. Impact factor for batten design shall be 75 per cent and for loft and head block beams shall be 25 per cent. A plan drawn to a scale not less than ¼ in. equals one foot shall be displayed in the stage area indicating the framing plan of the rigging loft and the design loads for all members used to support scenery or rigging. Gridirons over stages shall be designed to support a uniformly distributed live load of 50 psf in addition to the rigging loads indicated.

stage loft without gridiron

In a stage loft which lacks a gridiron, *underhung loft blocks* and *underhung head blocks* are fastened to roof beams or to the bottoms of roof trusses. Work such as reeving new lines and repositioning blocks can be done only with great difficulty from high ladders, scaffolding, or bosun's chairs. Understandably, stagehands are little inclined to maintain such a system or to attempt novel flying arrangements by moving blocks or installing special rigging.

underhung blocks above a gridiron

There are good reasons for using loft blocks underhung from the roof steel above a gridiron: avoidance of confusion and chafing when two or more flying systems are installed in one gridiron; ease of access for rapid setting and resetting of spot lines; fast, easy, and safe movement of stagehands about the gridiron.

loading platform

For a counterweight system this platform provides a place for loading and removing counterweights into and out of the *arbors* (steel frames which hold them). It is suspended from the stage roof parallel to and diagonally below the head block beams at the level of the bottom of the arbors when the latter are at their highest positions. The stage carpenter must know its loading capacity to control the amount of counterweight stored on it.

fly gallery

The *flies,* meaning the stage loft and all equipment, scenery, and other objects hung in it, are operated from a gallery located directly below the loading platform and eighteen feet or more above the stage floor (Figure 11.11). Counterweight sets are operated at the *lockrail* on the offstage edge of the gallery and rope sets at the *pinrail* on the onstage edge. The location gives flymen a view of both flies and stage floor and removes the flying operation from the stage floor.

vertical traffic

Stagehands gain access to the gridiron, fly gallery, loading platform, and other working areas above the stage floor by a spiral stair, a ship's ladder, a straight ladder, or occasionally a personnel elevator.

The rope system for flying scenery antedates the counterweight system and is still in use in many theatres. Although superseded in modern theatres by the counterweight system, the rope system has many virtues and cannot be completely dispensed with. Stagehands skilled in its use like its flexibility.

Simply stated, one end of a rope is attached to a piece of scenery. The rope is passed through a block or blocks at the top of the stagehouse, and the other end is pulled down to raise the scenery into the flies. As customarily installed, ropes are arranged in sets of three or more; the ropes of each set pass through loft blocks arranged in a row on the gridiron parallel to the proscenium, and over a tandem head block near the junction of the gridiron and sidewall; the onstage ends of the ropes of a set are tied to a piece of scenery to be lifted, and the offstage ends are pulled downward to raise the piece into the flies. The lifting lines are *tied off* on belaying pins in a pinrail which is located on the fly gallery projecting from the sidewall of the stage. When no scenery is flown on a set of lines, the lines are tied together to a small sandbag weight and pulled into the flies. Pipe battens, if required, may be tied to the lifting lines.

In stage vernacular *blocks* are called *sheaves* (pronounced "shivs"). Precisely, a *sheave* is a grooved wheel mounted on a shaft set into an assembly of several parts, the whole called a *block*. In this book a block will be called a block, and blocks will be distinguished by name according to specific uses: loft block, head block, lead block, tension block, etc.

blocks

The pinrail is located on the fly gallery. It is a steel pipe 4″ to 6″ in diameter which is set horizontally on steel stanchions and drilled with vertical holes to receive belaying pins. The stage carpenter must know the upward load capacity of the pinrail and the fly gallery.

pinrail

The lines, in sets of three to six, are named as follows: in a four-line set the line whose loft block is closest to the head block is the *short line,* the farthest is the *long line,* and the lines in between are the *short-center* and the *long-center.* In a six-line set the two farthest lines are the *long-long* and the *short-long.*

names of lines

The head block of a rope set is the *tandem* type, having separate sheaves for each rope in diagonally upward, linear array. The short line runs over the lowest sheave, the long over the highest, etc., so that the longer the passage of a line across the gridiron the more clearance it has to prevent chafing on the gridiron or on loft blocks. A flyman can identify the lines by name according to their entrances into the head block.

tandem head blocks

Manila rope is used, the size — ½″ or ⅝″ — depending upon the anticipated loads. Each line set is tied off as a single line. The tie-off is a lashing, figure-eight fashion, over and under a belaying pin in the rail, secured by a half hitch over the upper end of the pin. Surplus rope is coiled and hung over the pin or over a neighboring pin which has no line set.

rope

If the unit to be flown is light, it is tied on and pulled up by hand without further rigging, and the lines tied to the pinrail. If the piece weighs over eighty pounds, about the maximum weight one man can

operation

lift easily by pulling, the piece is counterweighted by a sandbag tied or clewed to the set of lines. The flown piece is pulled to high trim and tied off. The sandbag is attached to the lines from the fly gallery above the high-trim tie so that it will move only in the space above the fly gallery as the piece is *taken out* or *let in*.

The amount of sand used weighs slightly less than the unit of scenery to produce the condition called *piece-heavy,* meaning that when the unit is released, it will descend to the floor since it is heavier than the sandbag.

advantages

The rope system has greater flexibility in the positioning of lines and line sets and costs less to install than other systems. Makeshift parts and some standard parts and rope can be purchased in local stores and the installation is simple.

disadvantages

The rope system is not satisfactory for flying all kinds of scenery. Sandbags weighing over two hundred pounds are cumbersome, difficult to handle, and dangerous. Manila rope expands and contracts inversely with humidity. Since the lines vary greatly in length, the trim of hung scenery varies unevenly as weather conditions change and all rope sets must be retrimmed often. The rope system requires more manpower to operate, is less certain, needs a longer time in which to hang and balance heavy units, and is generally less safe than the counterweight system.

counterweight system

The counterweight system (Figure 11.10) differs from the rope system in the substitution of durable for perishable materials: fixed-length steel for stretchable hemp in lift lines, iron for sand as counterweight, steel arbors for vulnerable canvas bags to carry counterweight, and pipe battens trimmed level on each set of lines.

head blocks

The head blocks have single multigrooved sheaves, one groove for each lift line and one for the purchase line, set on parallel I beams (*head block beams*) near the sidewall and just under the roof of the stage.

arbors

Against one sidewall of the stage, arbors or carriages (steel frames to carry counterweights) set perpendicular to the wall and parallel to each other, may be moved vertically between the stage floor and the head block beams on T-bar steel tracks or guide wires.

line sets

Three to six lines run from the top of an arbor up and over a head block, across the gridiron to and over loft blocks and down to a pipe batten. The loft blocks are set, and hence the battens hang, parallel to the proscenium. Battens are trimmed parallel to the floor by trim chains or turnbuckles located either at the tops of the arbors or at the battens, the latter location preferred for ease of access. Occasional trimming is necessary to compensate for long-term stretch. Battens must be loaded when trimmed to adjust for the variation in catenary in the lines.

purchase line

A hemp rope ¾″ or 1″ in diameter runs from the top of the arbor up and over the head block, down through a rope lock at the fly gallery, under a single-sheave *take-up* (or *tension idler*) *block,* at or below the stage floor, and up to the bottom of the arbor. It is called the *purchase* (*overhaul, working,* or *endless*) *line* and is pulled to change the position of the arbor and consequently the position of the attached scenery.

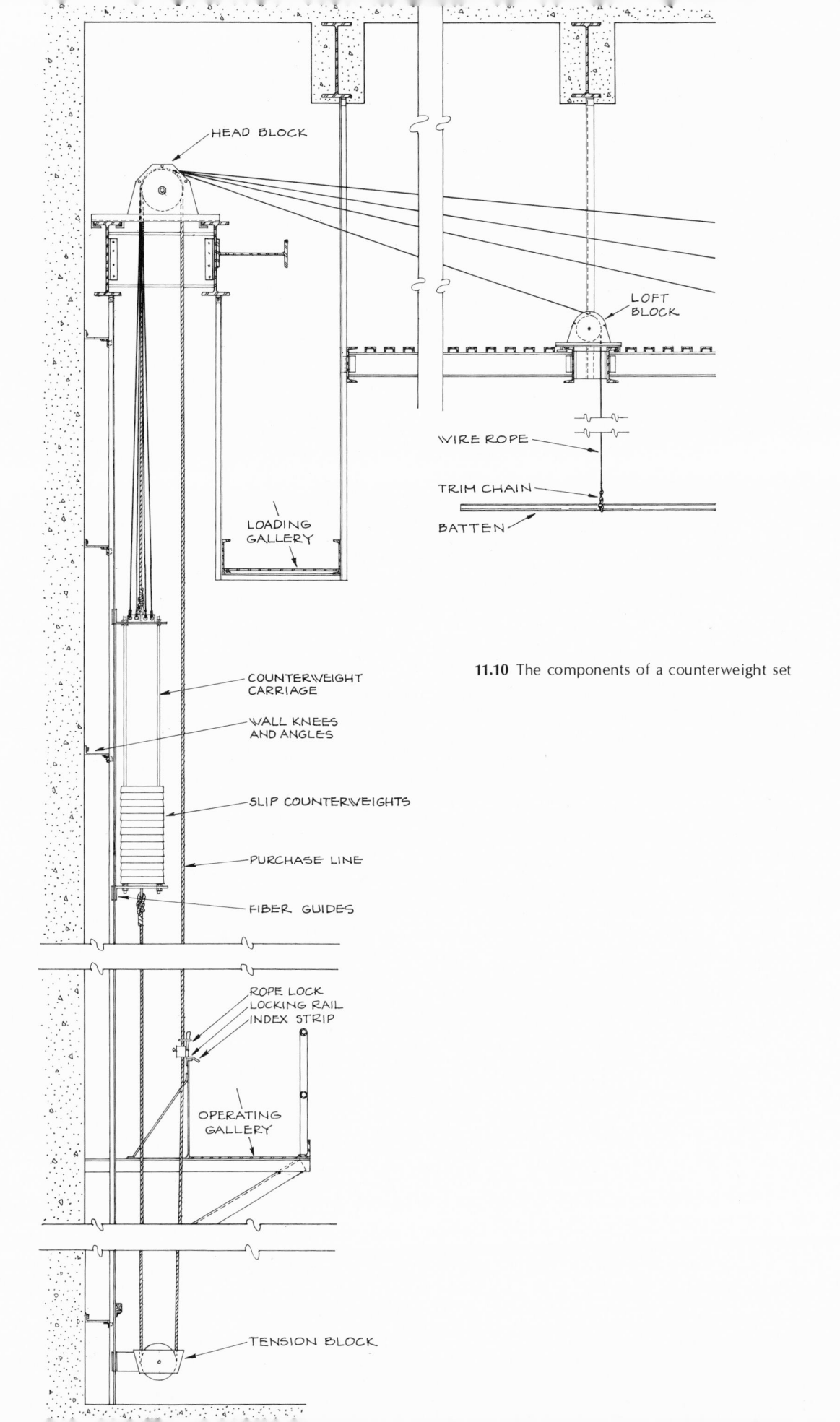

HEAD BLOCK

LOFT BLOCK

WIRE ROPE

TRIM CHAIN

BATTEN

LOADING GALLERY

11.10 The components of a counterweight set

COUNTERWEIGHT CARRIAGE

WALL KNEES AND ANGLES

SLIP COUNTERWEIGHTS

PURCHASE LINE

FIBER GUIDES

ROPE LOCK
LOCKING RAIL
INDEX STRIP

OPERATING GALLERY

TENSION BLOCK

11.11 A lockrail located on the fly gallery

The take-up block compensates automatically for stretch or shrinkage in the purchase line.

lockrail

At the offstage edge of the fly gallery (in older installations at the stage floor) the lockrail runs the full width of the counterweight arbor installation. It supports the locks for all the line sets and must also resist upward stresses imposed by the attachment of checklines, downhauls, and overhauls used in hanging and controlling unbalanced loads (see the problems in Chapter 15). The boss flyman must know its capacity to resist such stress.

rope locks

The locks are intended to hold balanced loads in desired positions or to counter such small unbalance as may result from the weight of the lift lines passing from the counterweight side to the scenery side of the system (Figure 11.12). They are not intended to hold against grossly unbalanced loads. One patented rope lock is designed to hold automat-

11.12 Close view of rope locks, lock-rail and index strip

ically any unbalanced load; it is not operable unless a flyman is standing on a treadle and has a keylock as protection against unauthorized operation.

At the stage floor a unit of scenery is attached to a batten by clamps, chain, rope, or wire. At the loading platform weights are set in the arbor to balance the load of the scenery. Counterweights which fit into the arbors vary in weight according to size and metal (lead being heavier per inch of height than iron) weights ranging upward from ten pounds each. A fixed quantity of weight is left in each arbor to balance the pipe batten. Stop collars on the rods of the arbor are secured tightly against the topmost weight to prevent its being jolted out of the arbor.

The part of the purchase line attached to the bottom of the arbor is pulled down to move the arbor down and the scenery up. The onstage part of the purchase line which passes through the lock is pulled down to move the arbor up and the scenery down.

operation

The counterweight system has the advantages of durable materials, consequent low risk of failure and low maintenance requirements, freedom from retrimming, all sets being permanently assembled from batten to arbor with trim established, easy loading of metal counterweights, and simplicity of operation.

advantages

Its disadvantages are the parallel pattern imposed on the flying of scenery and other items, the fixed lengths of pipe battens which are not easily altered, the inflexibility of not being able to select lines from sets or move either whole sets or single loft blocks easily, and the unsuitability of the head block, arbor, and lockrail for the operation of spot lines.

disadvantages

double-purchase system

Where the counterweights cannot run to the stage floor and the lock-rail and tension blocks must be located above the floor, as where openings into side stages penetrate the sidewalls, the double-purchase counterweight system may be used (Figure 11.13). In this system the lead lines pass over the head block down to and through a block attached to the top of the arbor and up to the head block beam where their ends are fastened. The arbor moves one-half the distance of the scenery and the counterweight must equal twice the weight of the scenery. Friction is increased by this increase in counterweight but is partially overcome and the run of the purchase line made equal to the run of the scenery by leading the upper part of the purchase line over the head block down to and through a block atop the arbor and up to terminate at the head block I beam and by leading the lower part through the tension block up to and through a block attached to the bottom of the arbor and down to terminate at the fly gallery.

The two disadvantages of the double-purchase system — handling counterweight double the weight of the scenery and overcoming added operating friction — are the price of having unrestricted side-stage space at stage-floor level.

auxiliary arbors

Counterweight arbors with purchase lines but without lift lines or battens, one installed between every two complete sets, offer four capabilities: to rig a carpet hoist with any complete set; to add counterweight beyond the capacity of a single arbor to any set; to counterweight scenery hung on spot lines which are run over the head block of the auxiliary arbor; and to add lines to a set by ganging the auxiliary arbor with an adjacent arbor and running the added lines to the auxiliary arbor.

comment: the ideal system

There has been general acceptance of the rope system, the regular counterweight system, and to a lesser degree, the double-purchase system over a period of many years. The rope system affords random selective positioning of lift lines, trimming and grouping them for single application of lifting power and balancing the loads with sandbags, but has the disadvantages described above. The counterweight systems impose limitations of parallel flying, relative immobility, and fixed-length battens. The desideratum in flying scenery is a combination of the random spotting and flexible operating capability of the rope system, the reliability and durability of the counterweight system, electromotive power for hauling, and centralized remote control of flying. This goal has been approached with various items of stage equipment and some flying systems but to date it has not been achieved in its entirety. See Figure 11.14.

winches

Common to all systems is the application of electromotive power through gear trains to winches or windlasses. One or more winches may be installed on a fly gallery to augment or replace manpower in pulling the ropes which move either scenery or counterweights.

bull winch

A smooth-surfaced capstan driven by a motor and gear train is fixed in position at one end of the fly gallery. To it is led a hauling line, which is installed temporarily on a rope set, a counterweight set, a sandbag, a counterweight arbor, or scenery, snatch blocks being used to change

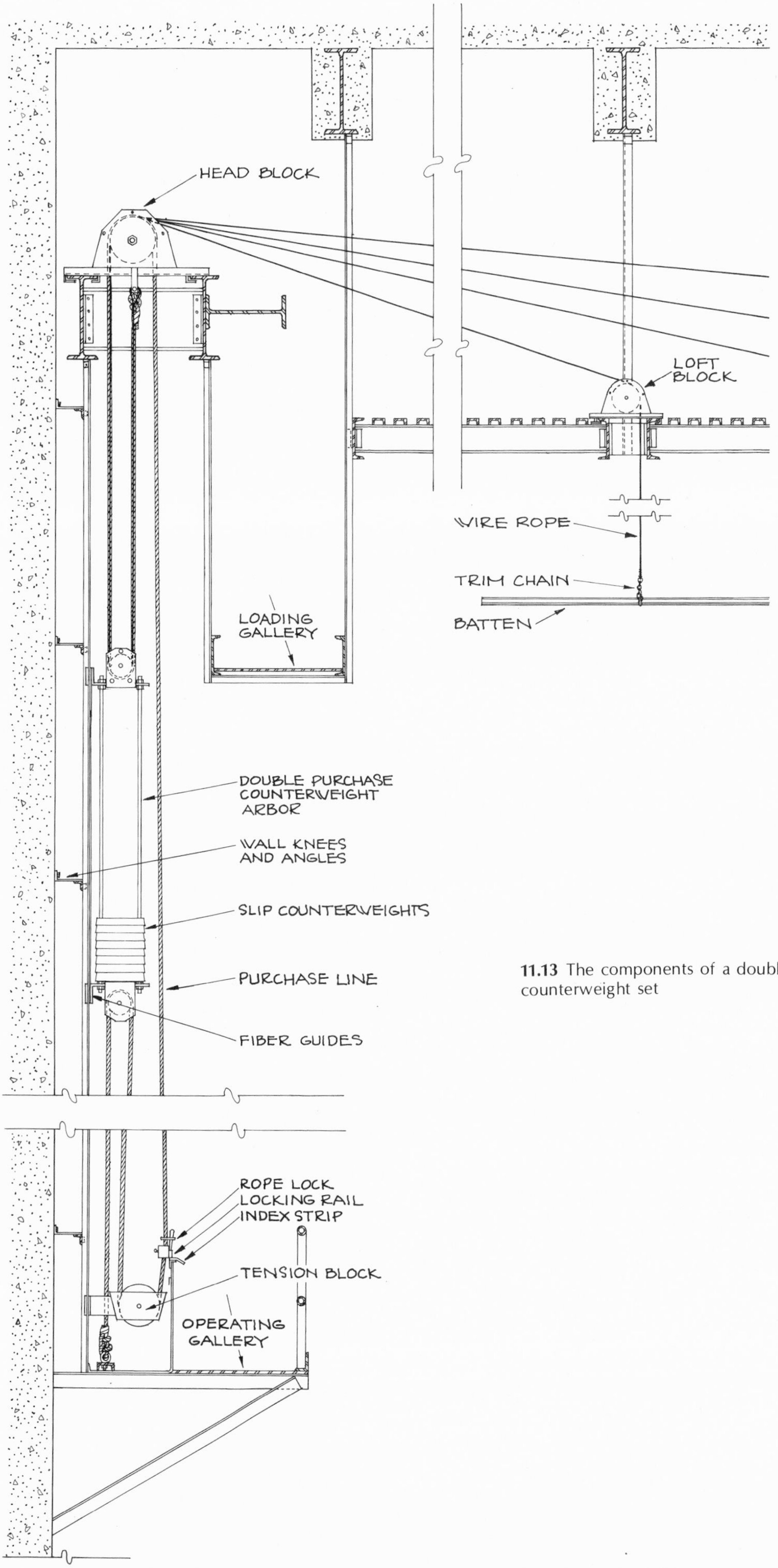

HEAD BLOCK

LOFT
BLOCK

WIRE ROPE

TRIM CHAIN

BATTEN

LOADING
GALLERY

DOUBLE PURCHASE
COUNTERWEIGHT
ARBOR

WALL KNEES
AND ANGLES

SLIP COUNTERWEIGHTS

PURCHASE LINE

FIBER GUIDES

11.13 The components of a double-purchase
counterweight set

ROPE LOCK
LOCKING RAIL
INDEX STRIP

TENSION BLOCK

OPERATING
GALLERY

11.14 A combination of counterweight and rope systems. Each system supplements the other, the counterweight system furnishing the advantages stated on page 269 and the rope system the advantages stated on page 266. Both systems are operated on the stage-left fly gallery, leaving the stage floor clear. A cross-over gallery connects with a second fly gallery stage right, where the picture was taken. Here flying apparatus (*Peter Pan*) and other similar rigging is operated without interference from flymen operating the two systems

direction. The operator makes two or three turns of the line around the capstan, in the direction of its rotation, switches on the power, and by varying the tension in the off-leading part of the line, varies the friction of the line on the capstan and controls the movement of the load. He may release a load under control by slipping the line on the capstan. The boss flyman must know the safe-load capacity of the bull winch.

A device similar to a bull winch is mounted on a castered base and has an arm carrying a sheave which may be inserted between tension blocks of a counterweight system and braced upward against the lock-rail (Figure 11.15). A line attached to either the bottom of the arbor or, through an auxiliary head block, to the top of the arbor, or by a rolling hitch to either part of the purchase line, is rove through the sheave and led to the capstan. The operation is the same as with the bull winch. The off-leading part may be tied off on a rope cleat on the frame of the machine. The boss flyman must know the safe-load capacity of the device and the upward, safe working stress of the lockrail.

A capstan, motor, gearbox, and switch are mounted on a frame which runs up- and downstage on a channel or I-beam track fixed to the floor of the fly gallery, the wheels engaging the top flange of the track to resist load tension on the hauling line. The winch may be positioned next to any flying set, rope, or counterweight, and the hauling line operated as described above.

The purposes of this system are to eliminate the sidewall counterweight installation, the manhandling of counterweights during setup and take-down, and the manhauling of ropes to fly scenery. The outstanding example in the United States is the Metromatic System developed and installed in the Metropolitan Opera House, Lincoln Center, by the Albrecht Corporation. It permits changeover for three different operas performed in one day. It saves the time spent waiting for counterweights to be loaded or unloaded during the hanging and unhanging operation. It gives one man the delicate control over scenery that formerly required many flymen. Its features are 109 fixed-length battens permanently cabled over loft and head blocks to multigroove winch drums, each drum controlling one batten and each motor capable of being jacked into one of thirty control units, these in turn capable of being switched onto one of six master controls. Each winch can move the entire load on a batten (maximum 1,000 pounds) at speeds infinitely variable between 1' per minute and 3' per second, with movement accurate to $\frac{1}{16}$". No counterweights are used and no flymen operate the sets. Paramount in this system is the acceptance of fixed-length parallel battens and the limitations they impose on the design of scenery. There are eight fixed-speed winches for limited selective spotting of lines.

This system is not new in simpler forms and applications, as for the flying of individual light battens and light bridges, but the subtleties of operation posited by opera in repertory require extensive and expensive research and development from which future stagecraft stands to benefit.

The purposes of this system are to eliminate the sidewall counterweight installation, the manhandling of counterweights, and the manhauling of ropes to work the flies, and to enable scenery of any shape

portable winch

tracked bull winch

winch systems
permanently installed battens and winches; no counterweights

11.15 A portable winch which may be used with any counterweight set

randomly positioned spot lines, selective grouping, total-load winches; no counterweights to be flown in random positions over the entire stage. Given adequate load capacities, speeds, precision in operation, and fingertip console control through a patching and mastering network, such a system would be the most capable and versatile possible for hanging and flying scenery — the ultimate flying system.

The closest approach to this ideal is the synchronous winch system developed by George C. Izenour. Spot lines reeled onto individual winches mounted on the front and back walls of the stage above the gridiron and rove through swivel spot blocks hung above the gridiron were capable of random positioning and operation, either singly or in groups of up to four, at varying speeds, controlled from a console at the stage floor (Figure 11.16). However, the system failed to maintain established trims in the repeated operation of groups of lines carrying unevenly distributed loads and to repeat precisely the programmed runs of units of scenery. It is therefore limited in its application to flying movements in which precise trim is not a requirement and in which precise moves of scenery can be visually observed and manually controlled at the console. Perfection of such a system remains a challenge to stage equipment designers.

randomly positioned spot lines grouped and counterweighted; motor driven

The purposes of this system are to achieve random spotting of lift lines, to adjust the trim and maintain it as adjusted, to group lift lines on counterweight arbors, to limit the run of arbors to the upper part of the stage wall to permit side stages below, to apply electromotive power to move the counterweights and hence the scenery, and to control the power application at a console (Figure 11.17).

It is a double-purchase counterweight system modified as follows: the

11.16 The operating console of a synchronous winch system. Individual winches are patched into master drive circuits, which are preset for direction, distance, and speed

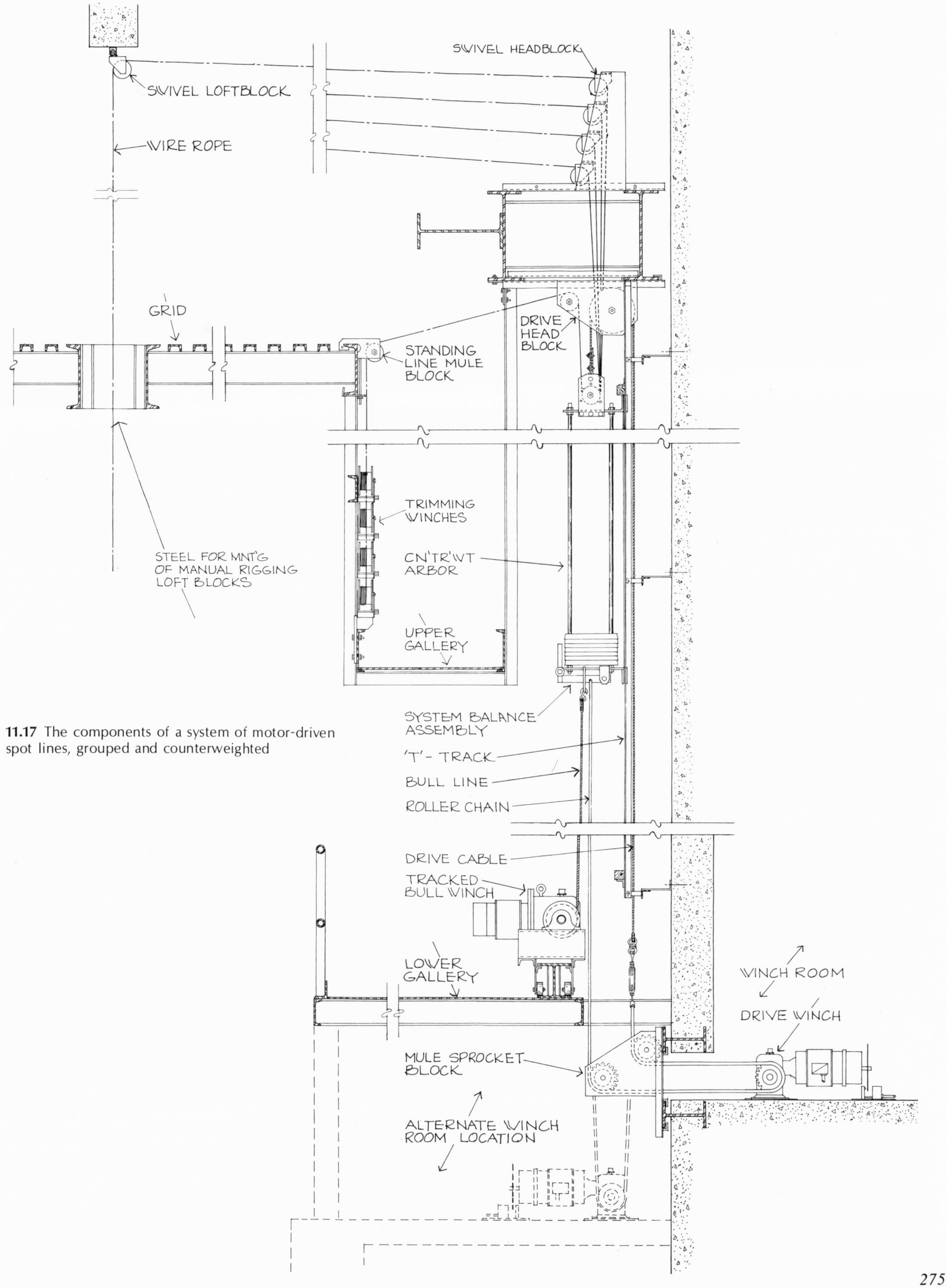

SWIVEL HEADBLOCK

SWIVEL LOFTBLOCK

WIRE ROPE

GRID

DRIVE HEAD BLOCK

STANDING LINE MULE BLOCK

STEEL FOR MNT'G OF MANUAL RIGGING LOFT BLOCKS

TRIMMING WINCHES

CN'TR'WT ARBOR

UPPER GALLERY

11.17 The components of a system of motor-driven spot lines, grouped and counterweighted

SYSTEM BALANCE ASSEMBLY

'T' - TRACK

BULL LINE

ROLLER CHAIN

DRIVE CABLE

TRACKED BULL WINCH

LOWER GALLERY

WINCH ROOM

DRIVE WINCH

MULE SPROCKET BLOCK

ALTERNATE WINCH ROOM LOCATION

lift lines, instead of being fixed in length and terminated at the head-block I beam, are rove through swivel head blocks and made variable in length by being led to and individually reeled onto *trimming winches* located on the loading platform, now called the *trimming gallery*. Thereby, any lift line may be located anywhere over the stage within the limits of its length and its unused part stored on the trimming winch. Groups of randomly located lines may be winched to trim a unit of scenery as designed. The purchase line is a combination of wire rope and roller chain, the latter engaging a sprocket wheel driven by a telemetered motor through a quadrature gear. This driving mechanism may be placed in a sound-absorbent enclosure or located outside the stagehouse, the roller chain being led through an opening in the wall.

Operation is at a console, optionally located on the fly gallery or on the floor. Accurate presetting and telemetered control of movement have been achieved and units of scenery remain in trim during repeated operations.

Manhandling counterweights remains a burden. The system is so designed that a motor will run only when loads are balanced.

The idea of winch-variable lift lines may be applied to a standard double-purchase counterweight system, by some modification of parts, to gain the advantage of random spotting of lines but relying on manpower to move the scenery. In a new installation solely manual operation may be provided as a first phase of expenditure and the motor drives and control devices added at a later time.

A hydraulic-powered system, called the Hydra Float system, has been developed and the first installation planned for the New Orleans Cultural Center (Figure 11.18).

A unit consists of a cylinder 2″ in diameter, equal in length to the maximum flying height, within which a piston is driven by fluid under pressure. The cylinders may be installed horizontally above the gridiron, if the stage width is adequate, allowing one-for-one run of the piston versus the scenery. This location permits open sidewalls at stage level for full-stage wagon storage without recourse to a double-purchase flying system.

Two plastic-coated wire ropes are attached to the faces of the piston, led out through the ends of the cylinder, around direction-change blocks and attached to the two flanges of a U-shaped clew, which is moved in one direction when the piston is driven in the other. The cables from a pipe batten or selectively spotted lines (wire rope) may be run through a head block and attached to the clew.

Hydraulic power to a lifting limit of 2,500 pounds per unit is applied at one end of the cylinder. Fluid under pressure is supplied by either a variable-volume pump or an accumulator (energy storage system) located in a soundproofed room away from the stage, through two main pipes to a position near the cylinders and distributed to the valves which are at the cylinders. Available power is adequate to drive six units fully loaded.

The cylinder valves have infinitely variable control of fluid flow in

hydraulic-powered batten or spot-line system

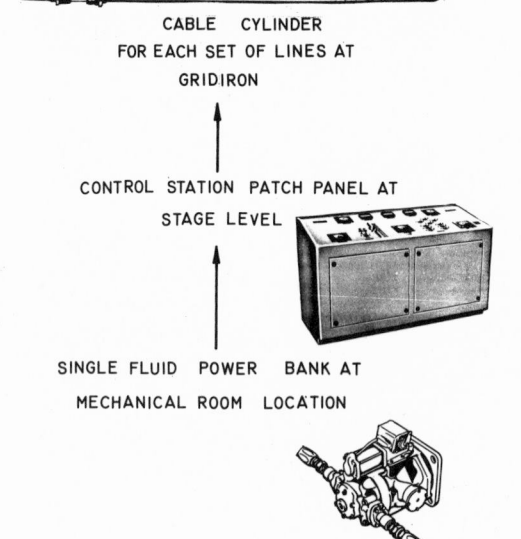

CABLE CYLINDER
FOR EACH SET OF LINES AT
GRIDIRON

CONTROL STATION PATCH PANEL AT
STAGE LEVEL

SINGLE FLUID POWER BANK AT
MECHANICAL ROOM LOCATION

11.18 The pump, the control console and single cylinder-piston unit of a hydraulic flying system (Hydra Float). The accumulator is not shown

either direction and are themselves actuated by a 12-volt current controlled at a remote console, onstage or elsewhere. This console contains selective plug-in, preset, up-and-down travel distance, speed control in the range of 0 to 5 feet per second in zero-plus increments, and a telemetered display of distance traveled in increments of $\frac{1}{16}''$.

Flown loads which are unplugged from the control system are held in position by closed valves and other locking devices. By an optional feature the position of a flown load which is replugged into the control system is located in space for the operator by a visual display called up from a binary memory system.

There are locking provisions against the accidental descent of flown scenery and a device for converting to manual operation in case of failure of the control system.

The predicted operating life of a piston-cylinder unit is 12 million cycles.

It is possible to fly a cylinder unit with its head block and valves on a counterweight set or rope set in a conventionally equipped theatre, supplying the fluid through flexible hoses, and achieve the advantages of hydraulic power under console operation. This makes the system possible and attractive for existing theatres and touring shows. The power and control systems may also be applied to the movement of stage wagons and lifts.

accidents and their prevention

Accidents involving stage machinery are all preventable. The seasonal activity of the theatre provides regular and adequate time for inspection and replacement of worn or faulty equipment. Steel and hemp ropes always reveal weak spots by fraying or reduced diameter. Steel supporting members bend long before they break. Accidents, therefore, result from careless inspection or faulty operation. Unbalanced loads cause most accidents. If a load is removed from a batten before counterweights are taken from the arbor and before the purchase line is released from the clamp, the arbor will fall and may damage itself and the tracks in which it runs, and the batten will be thrown against the gridiron, where it is likely to break the automatic sprinkler system, deluge the stage, and cause considerable water damage. If weights are taken from the arbor while the scenery is in the flies, the flown piece may descend violently to the stage floor. If a load on a rope system is not balanced by a sandbag to within the weight of a man, a flyman may untie his lines and be hoisted aloft and seriously hurt, either if he lets go or if he holds on and hits the head block before the load hits the floor. A leaking sandbag may cause such an accident.

danger zones

Needless to say, it is hazardous to stand or work below loads which are being raised or lowered, or beneath the head locks when weights are being set into the arbors. If traps are opened before the understage structure is in place, falls are invited. Open traps must be fenced or covered between performances. Elevators are operated only when the stage is clear, save for those involved in the operation, or when actors or technicians on or adjacent to the elevators are clear of the edges and know what is going on. Workers aloft carry nothing with them except the tools they need. The cry "heads up" from aloft signifies that something is loose and on its way down. It is standard practice for stagehands to wear hard hats when work is being done aloft.

Proscenium Equipment

The conventional proscenium has certain equipment for the accomplishment of a threefold purpose: to prevent spread of fire from stage to auditorium; to conceal the stage or disclose it to the audience; to determine the shape and size of the opening through which the audience sees the stage. Implicit in the last function are the corollaries: to determine the amount of stage space concealed from the auditorium, and to conceal apparatus directly behind the proscenium from the audience.

automatic sprinkler protection

The *Building Code of the City of New York* provides for automatic sprinkler protection as follows:

Stages in F-1a places of assembly [theatres having scenery] shall be provided with automatic sprinkler protection complying with the construction provisions of Article 17, as follows:

a. Automatic sprinklers shall be placed above all rigging lofts; and above all stage areas, other than those portions of stage areas specifically designated on approved plans as performing areas which do not have rigging lofts above and that are not at any time used for storage purposes. Sprinklers above rigging lofts shall be located so that no gridiron or other obstruction intervenes between the sprinkler heads and the scenery or scenic elements.

b. When any part of a stage is sprinklered in accordance with a. above, or when rigging lofts are provided, such stage areas and rigging lofts shall be completely separated from audience areas by a deluge sprinkler system designed to form a vertical water curtain, with heads spaced to provide a water density of at least 3 gallons per minute per linear foot. The water curtain system shall be controlled by a deluge valve actuated by a "rate of rise system" and "fixed temperature system." The heat actuating devices shall be located on not more than 10 ft. centers around the perimeter of the sprinklered area or as otherwise required for the type of device used to assure operation of the system. In addition to the automatic controls, manual operating devices shall be located at the fire control station as required by (b) (10) below, and adjacent to at least one exit from the stage. Such exit shall be remote from the fire control station. [Additional details of control requirements omitted.]

Emergency ventilation shall be provided for all stages in F-1a places of assembly to provide a means of removing smoke and combustion gases to the outdoors in the event of fire, as follows:

A mechanical exhaust system shall be provided of sufficient capacity to exhaust an amount of air at least equal to the sum of the following: 2 cfm. per sq.ft. of the performing area; 4 cfm. per sq.ft. of that portion of the stage that is not designated performing area; 4 cfm. per sq.ft. of rigging loft area. [Details of control omitted.]

No curtain shall be located between the audience area and the stage unless it is designed to permit air movement required for emergency ventilation (above) to bypass or pass through the curtain without excess billowing.

A fire control station shall be provided, as follows:

It shall be located on or adjoining the stage and shall be manned at all times during the presentation of a performance to an audience. [Details of controls omitted.]

Auxiliary stage spaces such as understage areas, dressing rooms, green rooms, storage rooms, workshops and similar spaces associated with the use of the stage shall comply with the following:

[Abridged and paraphrased:] Maximum 50 ft. to an exit door; two exits from each space; min. 50 sq. ft. per person in dressing rooms; sprinklers; workshop for combustible materials completely separate from stage; noncombustible finishes.

Stage lights shall not develop temperatures on the surfaces of any materials to cause combustion, smoke, or deterioration of the flameproofing.

From the above it can be seen that water and ventilation are the prescribed means of protecting the audience and that instead of a fire-resistant curtain barrier between the stage and audience areas the only curtain allowed is one which will permit the passage of air.

Fire curtains are still required by the building codes of most cities and some time will pass before the new methods embodied in the New York code are generally accepted.

fire curtain

The fire curtain is made either of steel or of fabric woven of metal-bearing asbestos yarn of approved fire-resistive rating. It is hung and counterweighted immediately on the stage side of the proscenium wall. The apparatus for suspending and counterweighting is of fireproof material, and an auxiliary set of chains is installed between the gridiron and the top of the curtain so that the top of the curtain may not descend below the top of the proscenium opening. The sides of the curtains run in steel channels called smoke pockets, which are affixed to or set into the masonry of the proscenium opening. The curtain is held in these smoke pockets by curtain guides which are riveted to the curtain and travel up and down either on steel guide cables or in a steel track.

Steel-framed fire curtains are always mechanically operated because of their weight (Figures 11.19 and 11.20). The power is either hydraulic from a pressure plunger in the basement of the stage, or electric from a motor mounted on the gridiron and geared or chained to a shaft which winds up the curtain lines. Either mechanism is so arranged that the motive power is applied to lift the curtain and the curtain will descend if the hoisting mechanism fails. The curtain is counterweighted to within a few pounds of its whole weight, so that its descent when released is slow but certain.

Controls for the mechanically powered curtain are placed at both sides of the proscenium opening and are in the charge of either the stage manager or the stage fireman. There are additional automatic-release devices which operate when fusible links placed at strategic points above the proscenium melt.

Woven asbestos fabric curtains, the type most frequently used in the United States, are suspended and counterweighted with fireproof materials. The operation is manual, by means of a Manila rope which is

11.19 An asbestos cloth fire curtain stretched on a steel frame

11.20 The motor and chain drive raise or lower the counterweights of the fire curtain. A heat-activated release mechanism disengages the motor drive and allows the curtain to descend in case of fire

attached to the counterweight and pulled at the stage-floor level to raise the curtain, and which is released to lower the curtain. The woven curtain, like the steel-framed one, is slightly heavier than its counterweight, and will descend, if any part of its suspension mechanism fails, until it closes the proscenium opening.

The hoist for the asbestos cloth curtain is at one side of the proscenium, but the curtain may be released from either side of the stage by means of a device called the cut line. The curtain is raised by pulling down on a purchase line. One end of the cut line is tied to hold the purchase line by a simple half-hitch seizing. The cut line has its other end made fast to a cleat in the wall on the opposite side of the proscenium. Thus in an emergency the asbestos curtain can be lowered by releasing the cut line from the purchase line at one side, or by releasing it from the cleat on the other side. In dire emergency the cut line can be cut more quickly than it can be released. Hence the name. A sharp knife is a required item of standing equipment on each side of the proscenium.

The use of the fire curtain follows fairly standard practice. The curtain is kept raised when the house is empty; it is lowered before the doors are opened to the public. It is raised in the presence of the audience just before the overture, and is kept up during the entire performance. It is lowered while the audience is leaving the theatre, and raised again when the house is empty. In London, the law requires that it be lowered once during every performance. The raising and lowering of the fire curtain in the presence of members of the audience is a means of assuring them of its existence and workability.

Popularization of the open or thrust stage has led to a departure from this procedure and from the provision that the curtain must be capable of being lowered to separate stage from house in an emergency. Many productions are presented without using either the fire curtain or the act curtain. Several thrust stage theatres are without both fire curtain and act curtain.

Inasmuch as the assembled audience must look at the fire curtain for some time before it is raised, if one is used, it must be designed to harmonize with the decoration of the auditorium. Many theatre architects and decorators have obeyed mysterious urges to install gaudily painted asbestos curtains. As opposed to these it is probable that a plain curtain of natural asbestos fabric is to be preferred.

To check the speed of the descending asbestos curtain, a hydraulic plunger is sometimes installed. As the counterweight rises to a certain height and the curtain is approaching the floor, the counterweight engages a line attached to the plunger. The resistance of the liquid in the cylinder slows the curtain and allows it to settle slowly to the floor.

act curtain

The act curtain is used as a formal device for beginning the play. The asbestos is raised, the overture is played, the footlights come on, the houselights dim out, the audience becomes quiet, the act curtain is raised. This is a typical sequence, which is, however, varied in many ways by different directors. There may be no orchestra or overture. There may be special lights directed onto the act curtain to supplement or supplant the footlights. The act curtain may rise, part, fold, drape, or sink.

curtain rigs

Today act curtains are customarily of two types: fly curtains which are raised above the proscenium, and draw curtains which part at the center and move to the sides. Other types less frequently used are: the draped or tableau curtain, the contour curtain, and the rolled curtain. Rarely, screens or sliding panels are used to replace the act curtain.

fly curtain

A fly curtain is generally of decorative fabric, processed to render it fireproof and dense enough to be lightproof. Act curtains of thin fabrics are lined to prevent light penetration. The top of the curtain is hemmed, grommeted, and laced or tied to an iron pipe batten, and the bottom has a pipe batten or chain sewn into the upper half of a double hem. The lower hem is intended to break on the floor as the curtain descends, to reduce the impact and prevent spill of light under the curtain. Occasionally fringes, tassels, or flounces replace this lower hem. A fly curtain is suspended by any of the regular methods used to fly flat scenery or drops.

The action of the curtain must be sure. Nothing is more embarrassing than the failure of the act curtain, particularly at the close of a scene. This type of accident is unpardonable; the most complicated act-curtain mechanism is so simple that it permits frequent inspection and easy repair of the few flaws which may develop. Certain precautionary measures are routine in every theatre to insure perfect operation of the act curtain: Sufficient clear space must be provided for the curtain; obstacles must be kept out of this space, or if not, guards must be provided over the obstacles to keep the curtain from fouling them. The position and movement of the curtain must be controlled by attaching the sides of the curtain to guide wires as is done with the fire curtain. The operating rope must be periodically inspected for wear and for loose knots. The counterweighting apparatus and operating rope must be in a position free from interference by other stage machinery, scenery, props, or lights. Only the appointed curtain man must operate the curtain.

A fly curtain, if counterweighted, should weigh slightly more than its counterweight. This makes possible the quick closing curtain so often called for. A quick opening curtain, on the other hand, is seldom required. The operating line for a fly curtain is of braided Manila rope or of braided or twisted cotton rope. Either of these types is better than regular twisted Manila rope, which is hard, splintery, and stiff. The sheaves in the loft blocks and head blocks for a fly curtain are oversize, to reduce friction and prolong rope life.

draw curtain

A draw curtain, also called a *traverse* curtain or *traveler* curtain, is one which is parted at the center of the stage and drawn sidewise in two halves to disclose the stage. This type of act curtain is used when there is insufficient loft space to allow flying the curtain, and when there is an artistic value in having the curtain move horizontally instead of vertically. Some directors dislike having the legs and feet of actors the last parts seen by the audience and prefer to have the curtain close from the sides on the final stage action.

The two parts of a draw curtain overlap at the center. There must be ample (not less than eighteen inches) allowance in the width of each piece to provide for this overlap. The onstage edges of the curtain are faced; that is, the back is finished the same as the front to conceal the lining when the curtain is moved.

The minimum fullness of material for a draw curtain should be 100 percent. The extra material is pleated into the required width of each half of the curtain and sewed to a heavy webbing at the top. Grommets are set into this webbing on 12-inch centers, and tie lines inserted into the grommets. The tie lines are tied to carriers which move laterally on or in a track.

Numerous stage-equipment companies manufacture traveler tracks and carriers whose particular patented features they extol. The requirements for a good curtain track are few and easily fulfilled. An effective draw curtain track is so easy and inexpensive to build in almost any shop and so simple that there is no reason for any producing unit which cannot afford a professionally made track to be without a dependable draw curtain.

The chief requirements of both carriers and tracks are certainty of operation and silence. In instances where side space is at a premium, the carriers may have to be especially small to permit gathering the drawn curtain in small lateral space. One variety of traveler track is made of hardwood or heavy sheet metal shaped to have a continuous slot in the bottom. Balls, wheels, rollers, or sliders, are held on inside flanges and support wire loops which drop through the slot to support the curtain. Another variety of track is an inverted tee iron. The carrier wheels which roll on the flanges are connected by a U-shaped metal loop to which the curtain is fastened. A third variety is made of parallel pipes connected by inverted U irons with ball carriers. Devices which may be adapted to make stage-curtain tracks are metal drapery tracks, obtainable at any large house-furnishing store, or sail tracks used on small sailboats.

Ball carriers and all metal carriers are noisier than carriers made with rubber or leather bumpers. A track for a heavy curtain must be suspended from a pipe or wood batten to keep it stiff and straight as the weight of the curtain shifts. Tracks for very heavy curtains must be fastened securely to wood or steel trusses.

A traverse track is built in two sections, each of which supports one half of the curtain. The two parts are joined to overlap at the center of the stage. There must be sufficient spacing between the two tracks where they join to allow the advancing edges of the curtain to clear each other. Often two stagehands are assigned to the job of walking with the onstage edges of the curtain as it is drawn to prevent it from billowing on the air and to make its closing certain. A draw curtain is operated by means of an endless line which is rigged as follows: The line passes through a single floor block at the working (live) end of the track, through a double block at the same end of the track, and around a single block at the opposite end. Thus, stretching along the track there are two lines which move in opposite directions. The onstage top corner of each half of the curtain is attached to one of these lines in such a way that a downward pull on one of the lines by an operator will cause both curtains to close or to open simultaneously. The fastening of the curtains to the lines must be secure against slipping. The line must be adjusted for length and kept reasonably taut so that it does not sag into view. The blocks through which the line runs must be attached to the

11.21 A curtain track rigged so that vertical panels may traverse, revolve, and trip. Designed by Ben Edwards for a General Motors Pontiac Show

11.22 Roll drops in a curtain set on a stage with no fly loft. Such an installation imposes severe limitations on production

curtain track so that the direction of pull on the lines is horizontal or down, but not up. This prevents the carriers from binding. The track must be firmly supported from above, especially at the operating position. A fixed chain may be used at the point where the downward pull is exerted upon the operating lines.

Draw curtains may be made to operate independently by attaching each to a separate line. Such rigging requires the use of a two-sheave floor block, a four-sheave block on the operating end of the track, and a two-sheave block on the other end. Draw curtains can be run on curved tracks. In such installations the operating rope runs inside the track and the curtain is attached directly to it.

A further variation of the draw curtain is the *backpack,* in which the curtain is hung on one-way carriers. When it is being closed the hangers permit the curtain to run out in the normal manner but when it is being opened the hangers engage the line and the whole curtain moves simultaneously and gathers only when it reaches the end of the track.

A draw curtain may be rigged on a single track to open in either direction and gather at either end of the track.

tab curtain

The tab curtain is made in two pieces which lap at the center as do the halves of a draw curtain. Lines passing through rings sewed to the back of the curtain are attached to the onstage edges near the bottom, and run over sheaves at the upper offstage corners. One line is run across the stage and over another sheave. Both lines are weighted with small sandbags and continue to the stage floor. When the lines are pulled, the onstage corners of the curtain rise diagonally offstage and a draped opening is achieved. The drape is governed by the position of the rings on the back of the curtain and the position at which the lines are attached to the onstage edges.

roll curtain

The roll curtain or roll drop is archaic, but not quite extinct (Figure 11.22). It is flat, usually canvas, and is rolled on a long drum from

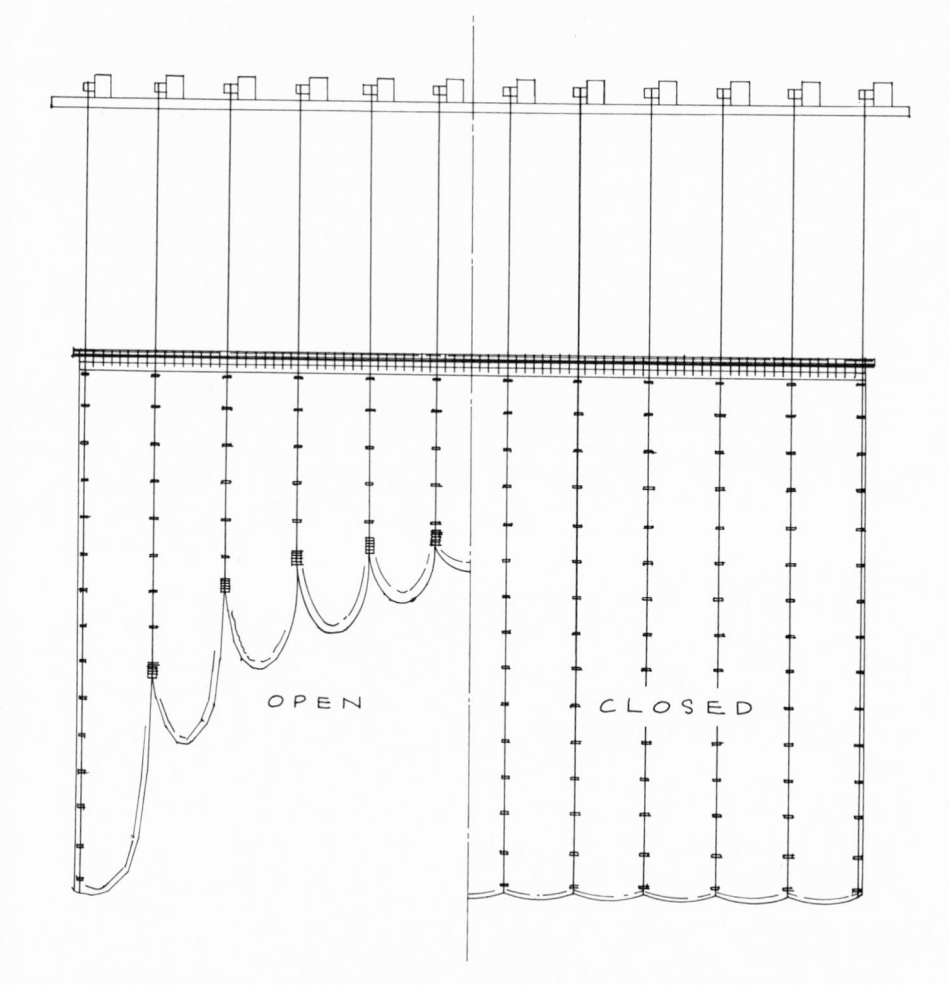

OPEN   CLOSED

11.23 Schematic drawing of a contour curtain

6″ to 8″ in diameter. One edge is attached to the drum, which rests on the stage floor, the other to a flown batten.

A double block is attached to the gridiron or the top batten of the curtain above the operating position, and single blocks above the ends of the roller. With the curtain hung in position and rolled up, lines are attached to each end of the roller so that when the curtain is released and allowed to unroll, the lines wind up on the roller. The other ends of the lines are brought through the blocks to the floor at the operating position. To roll up or raise the curtain the lines are pulled down, causing the roller to revolve and wind up the curtain. A tie-off cleat is installed at the operating position. This method of operation is applicable only if the curtain roller is rigid over its whole length.

A contour curtain is rigged to be gathered vertically (Figures 11.23 and 11.24). It may serve as a fly curtain in a theatre with no fly space or as an *effect* curtain. Made of lightweight fabric in at least 200 percent fullness, it is hung permanently in place, the top edge several feet above the proscenium header. From above, a number of lines, spaced evenly across the curtain, descend through rings attached to the back of the curtain and are fastened to the chain weight in the bottom hem of the curtain. Each line is attached at the top to a motor-driven winch drum

contour (brail) curtain

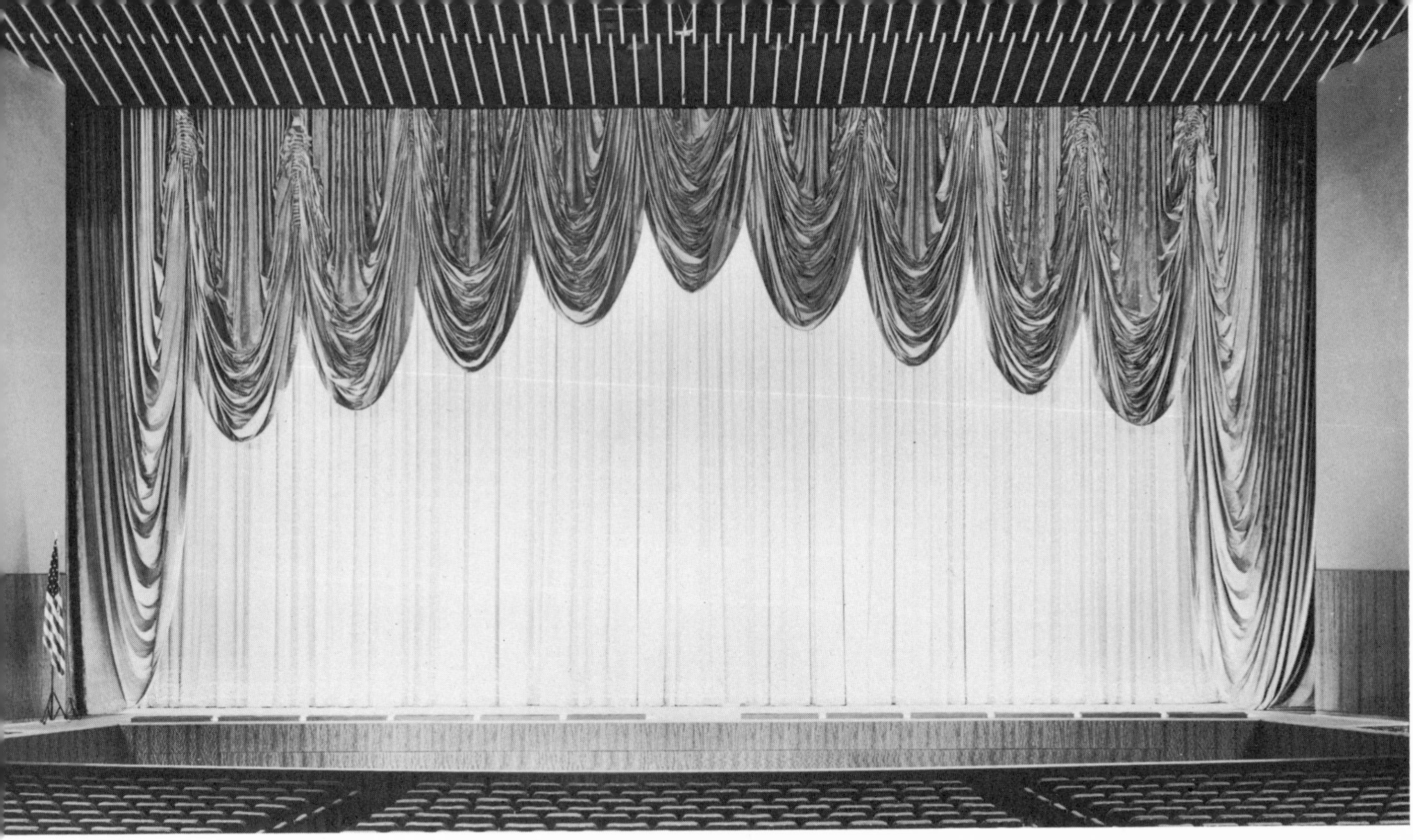

11.24 A contour curtain in a municipal auditorium

11.25 The motor-driven winches for a contour curtain

(Figure 11.25). The motors may be operated together or separately at any speed. With a curtain thus rigged and controlled it is possible to reveal any desired portion of the stage, sections together or in sequence, and achieve innumerable arrangements of valance draping above and to the sides of the acting area.

A device in increasingly frequent use is a special curtain hung directly behind the act curtain, or substituted for it, and especially designed in keeping with the scenery of a particular production. Such a curtain, called a show curtain, may aid in establishing emotional or intellectual values of the production before the action begins (Figures 11.26 and 11.27).

show curtain

11.26 The traverse show curtain for *Chanticler* at the Yale School of Drama. Painted in dye on muslin. Robert Scott, designer

11.27 The flying show curtain for *Yellow Jack* produced by the Yale Dramatic Association. Three canvas panels, slit to simulate bamboo, are hung to be flown singly or together. The permanent set is seen in silhouette through the center panel

cycloramas   Cycloramas which are installed as part of the scenery for a production are discussed in Chapter 5. Cycloramas which are either built as part of the structure or installed with such elaborate and massive rigging, operating mechanisms, and control apparatus that removal is made difficult must be considered as stage equipment.

rigid cycs   These are usually built of smooth plaster and metal lath on steel structure, less frequently of plywood or lumber covered with canvas. They seldom extend very far downstage at the sides but have movable sections which are flown or rolled away to allow the passage of scenery. They must be carefully shaped so as not to cause acoustical echoes or focusing of sound. Their positive values lie in their being an always available background for whatever is onstage and the best possible surfaces on which to create projected effects.

flexible cycs   These are installed for the same reasons as rigid cycs but with an added intention: that they may be moved out to make possible freer use of the stage space. Removal to a storage position may be by flying on specially installed counterweight sets, preferably motor driven, or by drawing sideways on tracks and rolling into vertical cylinders in the least obstructive location. Made of fabric, they are subject to deterioration and must be replaced within relatively short intervals (five to ten years).

Additional information on the types of cycloramas and their design as part of the problem of planning stages may be found in *Theatres and Auditoriums,* second edition, by Burris-Meyer and Cole.

The Stage Floor

traps   Vertical movement on the stage can be accomplished with traps and elevators as well as by flying. Traps are essential to every stage. In arenas and thrust stages they constitute a facility for vertical movement otherwise impossible. The trapped floor is divided into removable sections and set on removable beams. This arrangement makes it possible to open up a small area at almost any place or the whole acting area. Actors can make entrances by climbing up a flight of stairs from the trap room into the acting area, or by being raised (*Iolanthe*) or popped (*Faust*) onto the stage by appearance traps. They may disappear (*Orphée*) by stepping on a modified version of a hangman's trap. Traps for access to storage spaces are usually located away from the playing area.

Opera traps are rectangular traps which may be raised above the stage floor to provide raised playing levels with dispatch and economy. Each trap rests on two vertical frames which are set in vertical tracks below-stage. Each frame is counterweighted to balance the load of the frame, the trap, and any fixed superimposed load. The frames for one trap may be raised together to keep the trap level or independently to slope the trap across-stage.

Stage floors which are trapped in small sections are generally left uncovered except when a production is set up, at which time padding and floorcloth or carpet may be laid. Stage floors which are broken only by large traps or elevators may be covered permanently with linoleum cemented over felt padding.

The accomplishment of the single or simultaneous movement shift, except in the case of very simple or modified unit settings, is possible only by moving the stage floor. The task may be accomplished by double-deck elevators, wagons, discs, or revolving stages, or combinations or modifications of two or more of these devices.

Elevators are generally situated in the acting area and directly upstage of it. The acting area contains at least three, in most installations, and some stages have ten or more in and beyond the acting area. There are only a few double-deck elevators, those in the Théâtre Pigalle, Paris, being the most notable.

Permanently installed elevators are now principally of two types: motor-driven screw-jack and hydraulic. They serve to raise and lower portions of the stage floor or the orchestra pit to positions above or below their normal levels. They serve to raise scenery from a position where it may be set below stage, or to take the place of platforms set on the stage floor. They serve many purposes for which traps may be used.

devices for moving the stage floor

elevators

11.28 A novel hydraulic lifting mechanism for an orchestra-pit cover or a stage-floor trap

The hydraulic elevator is a complex mechanism but it is more flexible than the screw-jack elevator. It is silent in operation and it can move very rapidly, though speeds greater than 6′ per second are seldom used. Good installations have automatic level-maintaining devices which align the top of the elevator with the stage floor and maintain any given relative setting between elevators. The screw-jack elevator is inexpensive, simple, and fast enough for small theatres, although it may be noisy at high speeds.

11.29 The adjustable floor of the experimental theatre at the University of Texas, Austin. The entire floor is divided into sections 10 feet square, adjustable in increments of 6 inches. A rolling lift is placed under a section to raise or lower it. Posts at each corner of the section telescope into fixed hollow stanchions. Steel pins through holes in the posts bear on the tops of the stanchions

11.30 A disappearance trap elevator which, when descending with a person on it, slows to a stop and, ascending without a load, also slows to a soft stop at stage level. The change in the direction of the lifting lines produces this effect

11.31 A trap elevator with a two-man hand-crank drive shaft geared to a cable drum. The cable reels on and off the drum giving the operators control of both up and down movement

Elevators are seldom used alone. In most installations they are combined with discs or wagons, or both, and thereby provide both vertical and horizontal movement of the stage floor.

Besides furnishing a means of shifting scenery, elevators provide quick changes of the stage-floor level. Scenes requiring a raised or tilted stage floor can be set with flexible elevator installations in a fraction of the time required to set parallels and ramps in place.

wagons

The cheapest and one of the best of the devices for moving the stage floor is the wagon stage. It is used on many stages in an infinite variety of ways. For optimum use it requires a stage which has a clear, rectangular floor space, at least three times the acting area, with the proscenium opening in the center of the long dimension. When one wagon is in the acting area, another, fully set, is stored beside it. For the shift, both wagons are moved as a unit toward the unoccupied side of the stage. With additional depth four wagons can be used on such a stage. Set in rotation, as many scenes as there are wagons can be changed with single-movement shifts. For scenes played out of order, repeat scenes, etc., two-movement shifts may be necessary — the first-act wagon moved to one side, the second brought in from upstage. Scenes can be struck from wagons not in the acting area, and other scenes set up while the play is in progress.

jacknife wagons

For small stages the jackknife combination of wagons is popular. Two wagons are set up on either side of the acting area and facing it, their corners pivoted at the proscenium. One may then be swung through an arc into the playing area, swung out, and the other swung in (see Figure 11.32). Scenes may be reset on one wagon while the other plays. Shallow scenes are sometimes set on a third wagon upstage center, which may be run in between the two pivoted wagons when both are swung off. The jackknife stage is a two-movement stage. Resetting of scenes is necessary if more than two, or three in the case of a center wagon, sets are used.

Wagons are best built with steel angle or channel frames and wood floors, and are mounted on casters — on swivel casters if the motion of the wagon is to be in more than two directions. If used on the normal playing floor, they must be as low as possible. On sunken floors or elevators wagons may be as high as structural considerations warrant.

discs and revolving stages

The distinction, often forgotten, between discs and revolving stages is that the disc is shallow and set on the normal stage floor, whereas the revolving stage is built into the permanent floor and has its supporting members and operating mechanism below that. A disc may be put on any stage; a revolving stage is essentially part of the permanent stage machinery.

The disc or revolving stage is set with the downstage edge almost tangent to the curtain line. The larger it is the better. Its diameter may be fifteen feet greater than the proscenium opening. Its center should be at least as far upstage as the back wall of a large set. The most common revolving unit is the disc. Its construction is the same as that of the wagon, save that the center is firmly pivoted and the stage floor around

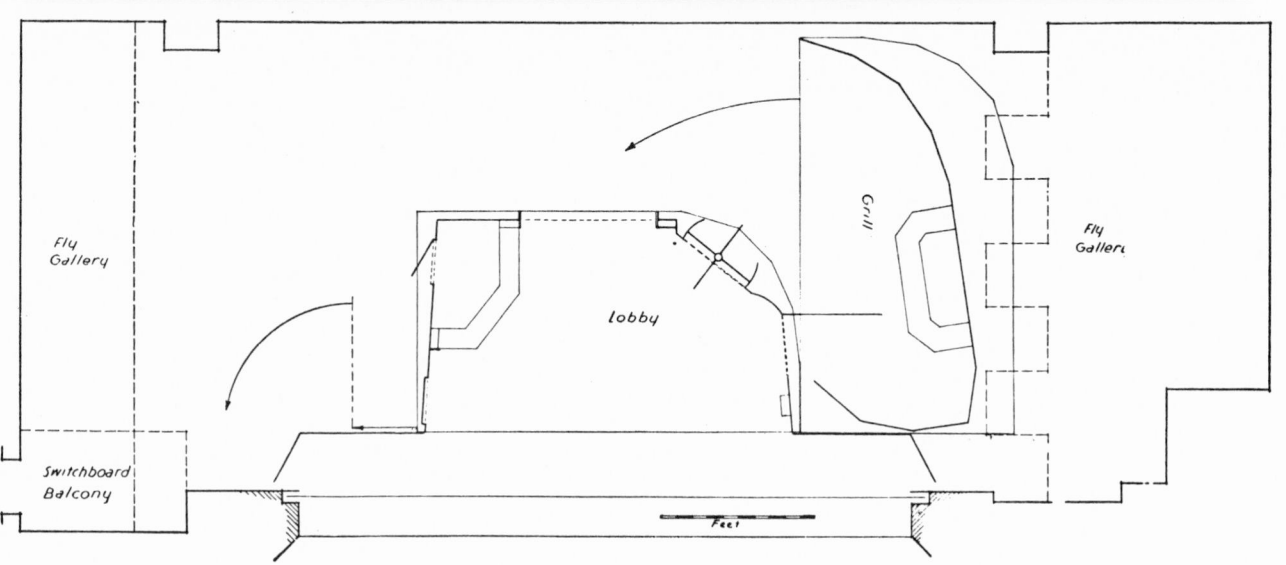

11.32 The lobby scene and floor plan for *Grand Hotel*. Herman Shumlin, producer; Aline Bernstein, designer. The jackknife wagon carrying the lobby must traverse offstage then pivot to permit the full width of the wagon carrying the grill to meet the tormentor

it is built up to the disc level. The supporting casters run on circular tracks. Casters are set at intervals of two to four feet around the circumference, and at similar intervals on as many internal circles as the size of the disc requires. The central pivot is set on a thrust ball bearing.

The revolving stage usually has only one track, deep below stage level, and employs truss construction to support the floor. It is silent and not subject to the troubles (expansion, sagging tracks, fouled drive cables, etc.) which too often beset discs. Discs and some revolving stages are electrically driven by a steel cable which runs in a channel around the circumference, thence to a pulley. Some revolving stages are driven by a motor-driven pinion gear which engages a circular rack attached to the circumference of the disc; others use a gear drive to the center shaft keyed to a spider. Small revolving units are sometimes set up downstage left and right, tangent to the larger unit. They operate simultaneously with it and carry sections of wall, backings, etc., for downstage masking.

The disc or revolving stage provides rapid one-movement shifts. Portions of it may be reset while the play is in progress. Despite its obvious advantages, the disc or revolving stage imposes so many limitations on the design and operation of the show that many theatres which have revolving stages installed alone, not as part of a disc-elevator or disc-wagon combination, seldom use them. On a disc each set must mask all the other sets. It is difficult to combine *plein-air* and interior sets on a disc unless the interiors are built within a hill or large exterior structure and therefore out of sight when the hill or exterior is in playing position. It is difficult to set a large number of realistic sets on a disc or revolving stage, for the floor space allotted to each is shaped like a truncated triangle, an extremely odd shape within which to squeeze realistic rooms. To save space and dispense with backings, entrances and exits must often be made to coincide in adjacent sets, which makes design arbitrary, and renders it almost impossible for all doors to open in the manner desired. In the hands of imaginative and thoroughly competent designers and technicians, however, excellent results are often obtained.

disc–wagon combinations

Combinations of disc and wagon have the advantage of avoiding some of the limitations which are inherent in the disc and of providing efficient horizontal one-movement shifts on small stages. Part of the traverse wagon and part of the disc may be reset while other parts are in the playing area. The floor plan for *Grand Hotel* and the photograph of the hotel lobby show the spaciousness which may be achieved on the disc-wagon stage (Figure 11.33). In construction it is similar to its parent structures. The traverse wagon runs on tracks as does also the inset disc. The drive is electrical; the movement of disc and wagon is simultaneous. In operation the wagon moves from side to side, carrying half a new setting into the acting area, while the disc revolves and brings into position the rest of the setting. The Metropolitan Opera House has a disc-wagon combination as well as elevators.

In European installations, wagons and elevators are used in combination more often than separately. In one opera house four wagons the

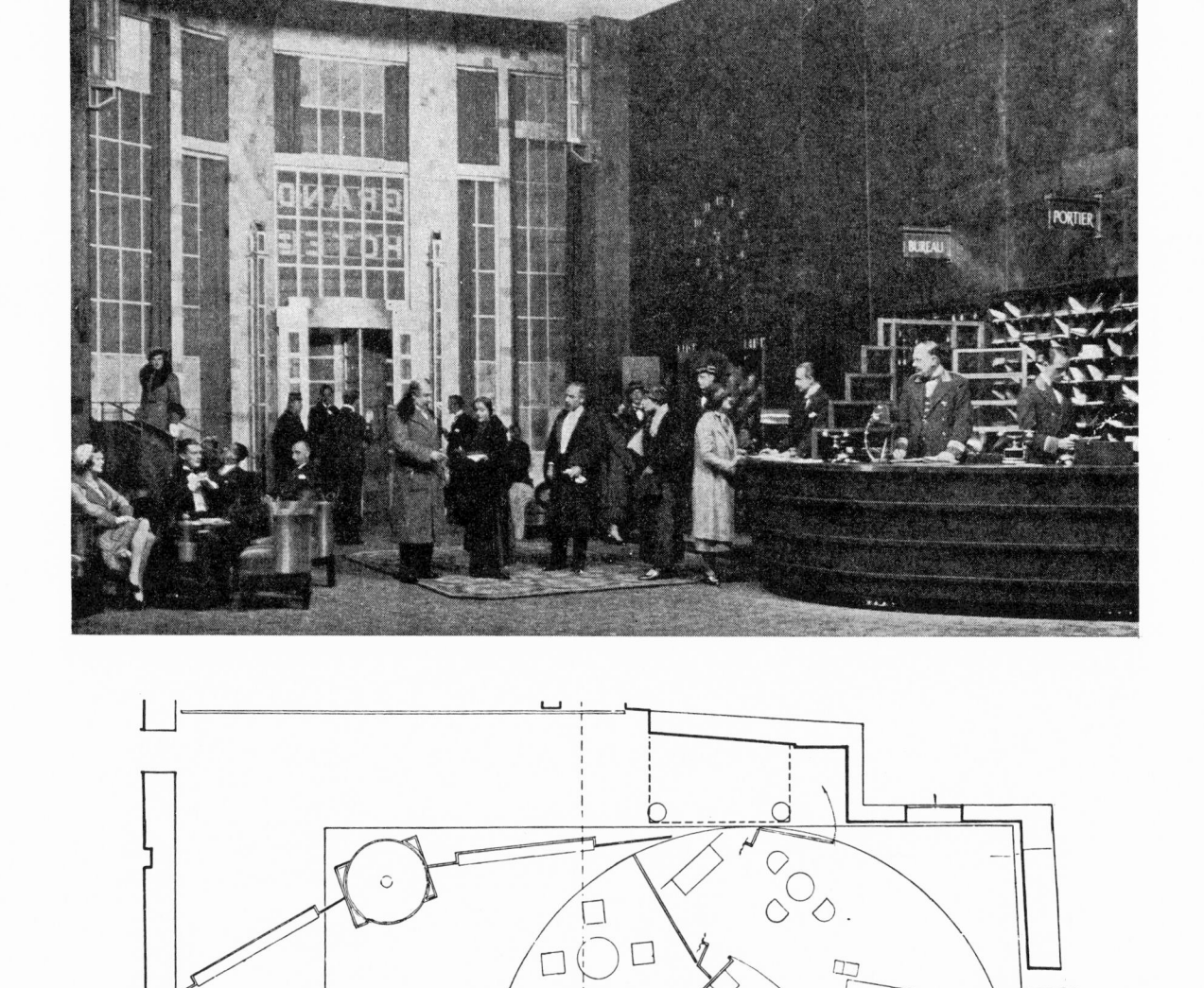

11.33 The lobby scene and floor plan of *Grand Hotel* designed by Max Hasait for the production by Gilbert Miller in London

11.34 Handcrank revolve (left) and handcrank lift (right) for *Starward Ark* impart up, down, roll, and pitch motions to the ark mounted on the disc. The lift requires that the crank be geared to a winch drum to afford adequate power. Ralph Alswang, designer

size of the acting area can be set onstage, and several more below-stage. Elevators in the acting area and directly upstage of it make for easy transfer of wagons from one level to another. One-movement shifts are possible without the use of elevators. For extremely elaborate settings, the elevators fulfill their normal scenic functions as well as serve to keep a large number of completely set stages readily available. Scenes may be set below-stage on elevators while the play progresses above. Elevator-wagon combinations can be elaborated to include discs by simply building a shallow disc into a parallel or wagon and setting it in the acting area.

revolving stage–elevator combinations

Revolving stage–elevator combinations are fairly common (Figure 11.35). The best example is the Radio City Music Hall, in which a single disc is set into three elevators. The revolving unit may be turned when the elevators are at the same height, either at stage level, above it, below it, or in motion. Obviously, such devices are useful for the spectacles they were designed for. In Radio City the orchestra-pit elevator may rise and form a wide stage apron, and the orchestra on an independently powered band car may travel upstage from its own elevator and be raised or lowered on any of the other elevators. It may also travel from one elevator to another below-stage.

A few installations have small elevators set into revolving stages, and revolving stages which are also elevators, capable of restricted horizontal movement.

floor slope

The sloping (raked) stage brings the floor into harmony with perspective used in scenery. Practically, the rake improves sight lines from the orchestra seats of many theatres by elevating the actors. Since most existing theatres have stage floors in the horizontal plane, a raked stage requires placing another floor on the existing one, using a suitable supporting structure.

false floors

A vista scene changes embrace rapid movement: scenery flown into and out of the acting area and scenery space and, what is newer and

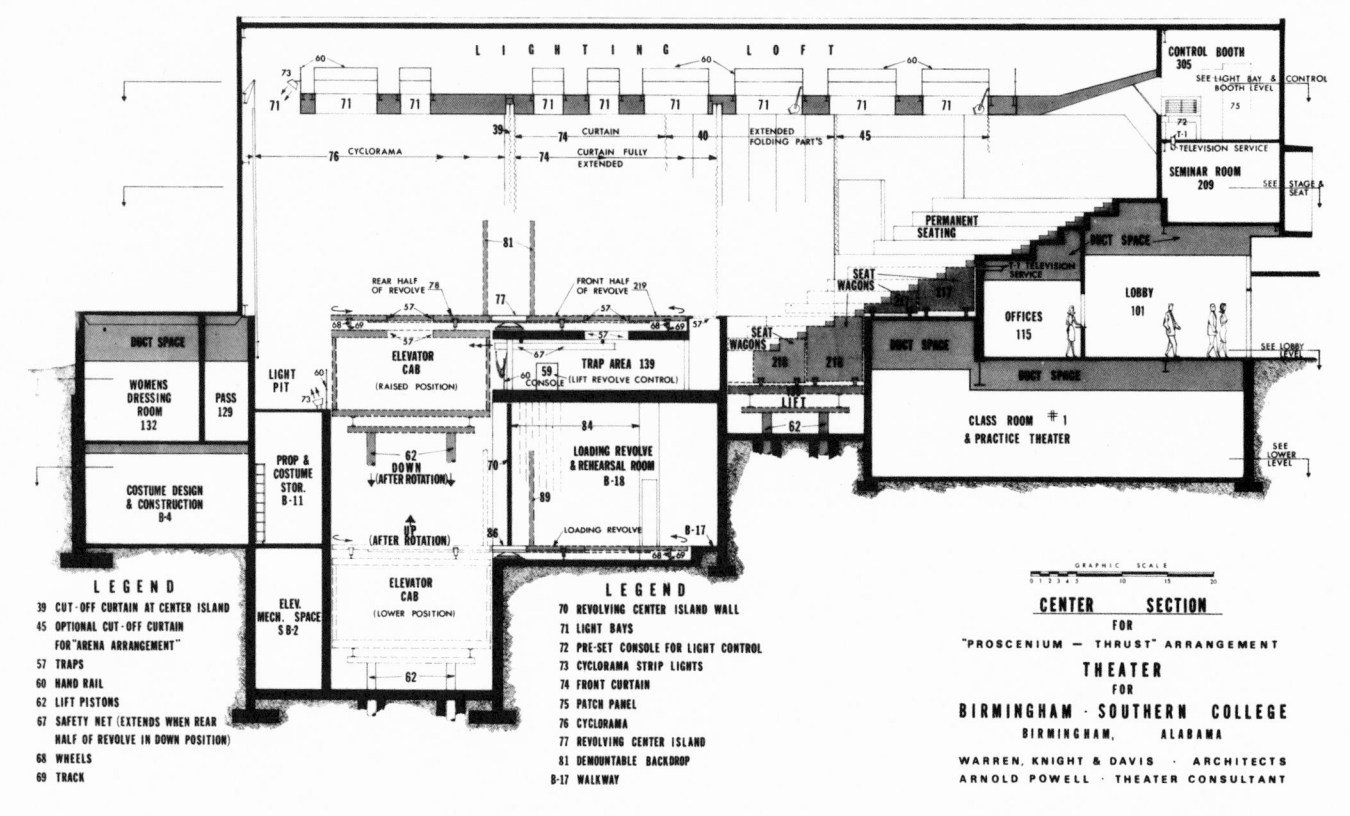

L E G E N D

39 CUT-OFF CURTAIN AT CENTER ISLAND
45 OPTIONAL CUT-OFF CURTAIN
   FOR "ARENA ARRANGEMENT"
57 TRAPS
60 HAND RAIL
62 LIFT PISTONS
67 SAFETY NET (EXTENDS WHEN REAR
   HALF OF REVOLVE IN DOWN POSITION)
68 WHEELS
69 TRACK

L E G E N D

70 REVOLVING CENTER ISLAND WALL
71 LIGHT BAYS
72 PRE-SET CONSOLE FOR LIGHT CONTROL
73 CYCLORAMA STRIP LIGHTS
74 FRONT CURTAIN
75 PATCH PANEL
76 CYCLORAMA
77 REVOLVING CENTER ISLAND
81 DEMOUNTABLE BACKDROP
B-17 WALKWAY

GRAPHIC SCALE

CENTER SECTION
FOR
"PROSCENIUM — THRUST" ARRANGEMENT
THEATER
FOR
BIRMINGHAM · SOUTHERN COLLEGE
BIRMINGHAM,   ALABAMA

WARREN, KNIGHT & DAVIS · ARCHITECTS
ARNOLD POWELL · THEATER CONSULTANT

more significant, rapid movement of castered units in and out from the sides and back of the stage. To assure precise direction, speed, and position, these units must be guided by tracks and propelled by cables, both of which must be sunk below the floor. This kind of scenery requires that a floor specific to the particular production be built and that it be capable of being transported and superimposed on the stage floor in any theatre. For *a vista* changes revolving stages also enjoy popularity among designers. A few have been built into new theatres. However, since most American theatres lack built-in revolving stages, their use in production requires that discs be installed over the existing stage floor and that the surrounding floor be brought up to the same level. For these reasons, then, *false floors* must be built, transported into theatres, and installed. They must be sturdy and smooth, especially for dancers, and they must be capable of installation in the time allowed by the production timetable. Occasionally two false-floor installations have leap-frogged each other to alternate theatres for one production on tour.

Wherever permanent installations of power-driven devices for horizontal and vertical movement of the stage floor are used, control is centralized, usually at or near the stage manager's panel, and an operator whose rank and responsibilities are similar to those of the boss flyman, with the necessary assistants, runs and maintains the machinery and assists in articulating scenic items to the machinery. In the best installations the operator's control panel contains, in addition to control and communication devices, indicators which show the position of elevators, revolving stages, and wagons.

11.35 The system for changing scenery in the theatre at Birmingham-Southern College is intricate and elaborate. All scene changes are made by revolving a divisible disc. When a scene is playing on the front half of the disc, the rear half is lowered on the elevator to the loading level where it is revolved 180° into the loading and rehearsal room at the same time that a third half-disc replaces it on the elevator, which is then raised to stage level. When the scene ends and the set is to be changed the disc is revolved 180°

controls

11.36 The steel frame, take-up drum, and motor drive for a one-way treadmill

Temporary installations may be manually operated or motor-driven. Discs may be propelled by stagehands pushing against bars inserted into the edges of discs, capstan fashion, or by pulling ropes attached to the edges of discs. Discs and tracked rolling units may be propelled by cables attached to hand-crank winches, offstage. Discs, tracked rolling units, treadmills, reciprocating wagons, and jackknife wagons may be driven by motored winches with speed, direction of movement, and stopping position all remotely controlled and possibly capable of pre-setting. Safety features such as slow start and stop, limit switches, and overload switches are essential.

other devices

Stage machinery includes, in addition to the apparatus so far listed, numerous devices which, because of their specialized uses, are not often seen.

The **disc and ring** consists of a disc surrounded by a ring, the two capable of synchronized or separate movement.

The **treadmill** is reminiscent of the chariot race in *Ben Hur*. More recently it has been used in *The Green Pastures, I Married an Angel*, and *Le Bon Soup*.

The **disc segment** has its center of rotation upstage and its circumference tangent to the proscenium line. Its movement is reciprocating. It utilizes the upstage corners of the stage.

Levitation Apparatus

The rigging required to fly an actor or an object in view of the audience is as varied as the sequences in which it is used. Basic levitation methods are as follows:

• A single overhaul line rove through a loft block and a single head block by which a flyman on the gallery provides vertical lift while the actor supplies the force for swinging (pendulum) motion (Figure 11.37).

• Two breast lines with the actor suspended between them, with flymen, one on each line, controlling both vertical lift and sidewise movement between the two lines (Figure 11.38).

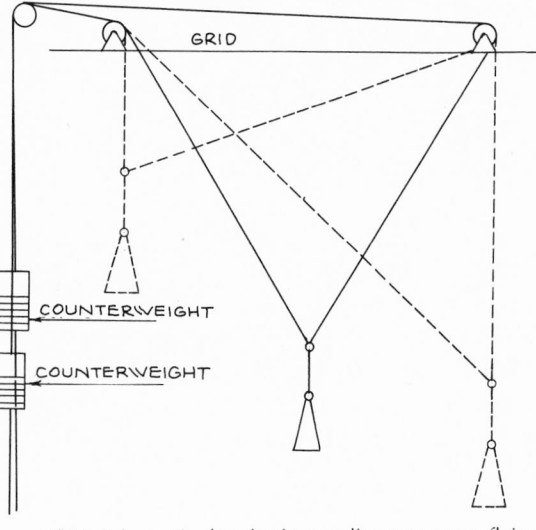

11.38 Schematic sketch of a one-line transverse flying rig in which height is varied by movement of the counterweight and transverse position by the endless lines. The flying actor will rotate freely at the end of the single line

11.37 Schematic sketch of a two-line flying rig

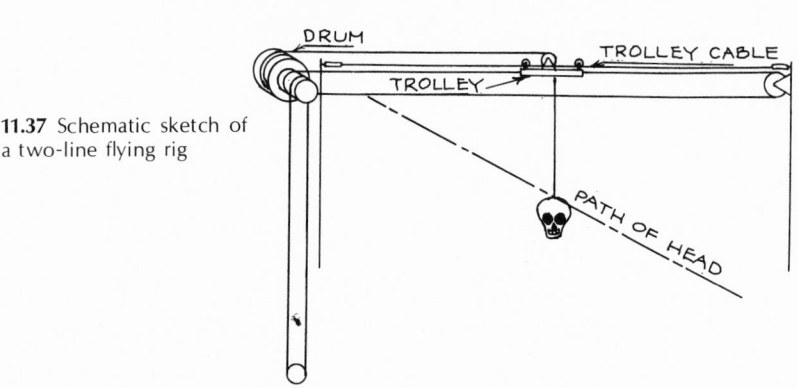

• Three breast lines through loft blocks located on the grid at the points of a triangle so the flymen control vertical, transverse, and up-stage-downstage motion. The more control the flymen have, the less flight control is required of the actor.

The actor is suspended in a harness, designed to provide balance and support with minimal discomfort, to which is attached a single pick-up line of airplane cable. The location of the point of attachment determines the flight attitudes of the actor. The single wire is attached to the single hemp line, or the two or three breast lines, at a point above the vertical sightline. A swivel at the point of attachment allows the actor to rotate and the single strand between the actor and breast lines allows him limited pendulum movement to clear scenery or other actors.

Prop fish in underwater scenes, or items which for dramatic reasons cease to be affected by gravity, may be operated by a flyman with a fish pole on a bridge. Occasionally a javelin or a prop bird must have its line of flight determined by a special wire, stretched in the appropriate position and direction. Such rigging may complicate scenery handling and invites trouble unless it is kept taut and invisible.

11.39 Differential drums are a legacy from Italian Renaissance theatre but are still useful. As the shaft is rotated by the operating line the trolley is moved horizontally and the skull follows the diagonal path because more line is reeled off, or onto, the larger drum than passes around the shaft to move the trolley

Incidental Equipment

• Step ladders in heights varying from 5′ to the largest necessary on the particular stage. Recommended sizes: 5′, 8′, 10′ 14′.

• A-frame ladders (two for setting up temporary scaffolding).

• Bosun's chair in which stagehands or operators may be hauled into the flies to work on rigged scenery or focus flown lights.

• Stage braces (at least twelve) in sizes assorted from 6′ extended to 20′ extended. For small stages the largest sizes are unnecessary.

• Stage-brace rack, brace cleats, or lash cleats set into battens which are fastened to the stage walls, on which stage braces may be hung.

• Rope rack: a rack of pegs, mounted on a caster dolly for movement, on which new and used rope may be stored.

• Tackle rack: a rack on the working side, on which blocks, batten clamps, sandbags, snatch chains, etc., may be stored.

Handling, joining, stiffening, and bracing scenery; hanging the show

12

Scenery is handled numerous times during the process of preparation. Unfinished pieces are moved about the carpentry shop. Finished pieces are transported from the carpentry shop to the paint shop, and from the paint shop to the stage. The pieces of scenery for a production are carried from vans onto the stage and stacked, awaiting assembly. Certain pieces are put together to form units, certain of the units are attached to the stage machinery and others equipped with devices for movement on the stage floor. Finally, groups of units are put together to form sets. This procedure is called variously *setting up, loading in,* or *hanging the show,* and is one step in the assembly of a production as described in Chapter 14.

During the performance of a play, scenes are changed. Stagehands take apart the units comprising one set of scenery, move them to designated storage positions, and bring together the units which make up another setting. This process, called a *scene shift,* consists entirely of handling scenery or operating stage machinery to which scenery is attached (the organization and execution of a scene shift are given in Chapter 14). Or changes of scene are made as part of the play's action, *a vista,* requiring complete coordination of the movements of actors and stagehands, often with accompanying light changes and sound cues. The handling of scenery for a production ceases only when the scenery has been dismantled and either laid to rest in a storeroom, given away, converted into salvaged materials, or scrapped.

The handling of scenery is replete with technical problems. Large expanses of stretched fabric cannot be roughly pushed, pulled, or thrown about without developing wrinkles, sags, indentations, or rips. The wooden frames are liable to warp or rupture if improperly supported,

need for technique

either while stacked or while in motion. Flats are tall and unstable, and will remain upright only when held or braced properly, or firmly attached to other scenery. Painted scenery must be protected from soiling or rubbing. In a shift the units of scenery which comprise a set must be rapidly, precisely, silently, and securely fitted together and as rapidly and silently separated and moved. In *a vista* changes the dramatic values of a performance can be impaired by poor coordination or miscues.

Handling

Chapter 4 states that a determination of the methods to be employed in handling scenery on the stage must precede the making of working drawings. It is self-evident, then, that the scene technician must be fully conversant with the methods and devices employed in handling scenery.

Flats must be stored temporarily at times during construction and on-stage before assembly. Temporary storage of flats is done by stacking them upright either flat against a wall, or perpendicular to the wall in docks formed by pipe stanchions. The first method is the most convenient for temporary storage although it requires considerable wall space. The second method affords easy identification of and access to the flats and makes efficient use of the wall space, but causes the stacked flats to protrude into the floor area.

Floor space for stacking flats is a normal requirement of any shop or stage and must be allowed for in the planning of a theatre building if stored flat scenery is not to cause congestion and inconvenience. It is not unusual for a production with three sets to require seventy-five flats, a third of which might require storing in one place at one time.

The rules for stacking flats are these:

• Stack flats as vertically as possible without danger of their falling.

• Stack uncovered or unpainted frames so that the identification marks are all at the same edge for quick selection.

• Stack painted flats alternately face to face and back to back to prevent hardware and other accessories on the backs of flats from damaging the covering or paint job on other flats.

• Remove a flat from a wall pack by moving the flat laterally (parallel to the pack) as it is taken off the pack. If this is not done, there is danger of dragging the flat next below off the pack by air suction.

• When the show is in performance, store the flats in the order in which they are to be used. Establish two packs, the live pack from which flats are to be taken during scene changes, and the dead pack on which flats are stacked as the scenes in which they are used end. Re-form the packs between performances.

At numerous times in the preparation of scenery it is necessary to raise flats from prone to upright position. As often as flats are raised they are lowered, since much work must be done on flats when they are prone on the floor.

One man can raise or lower a single flat. Two flats hinged together and folded are raised by one man in the same manner as a single flat.

12.1 Raising a flat. The workman puts the flat in a vertical position resting on one stile, moves to the bottom rail, grasps the upper corner with both hands, braces the lower corner with one foot and pulls. When the flat comes upright he grasps the stile with both hands as he would to run the flat. If the flat frame has no covering, it is lowered by reversing this process

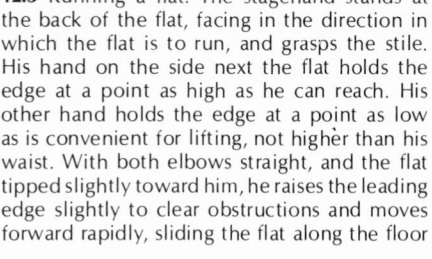

12.2 Floating a flat. If the flat is covered, the air-cushioning effect on the large expanse of cloth is employed to float it down. The workman clears the floor area into which the flat is to be laid, places one foot against the bottom rail to prevent backkick, and releases his hold on the flat, which descends slowly to the floor. This operation stirs up any dust there may be on the floor

Two men are necessary to raise three or more flats which are hinged together and folded. Flat handling is shown in Figures 12.1–12.5.

A different method is used to raise a unit comprising two or more flats which are fastened together but not folded. One or more workers place feet against the bottom rail of the prone piece. Other workers distribute themselves along the top rail at intervals of not more than six feet and opposite stiles. Simultaneously these workers raise the top of the piece and advance under it, handling only the framing lumber, while the other workmen continue to foot it. This operation is called *walking up* a unit.

Flats having large uncovered openings cannot be floated because there will be insufficient air compression to furnish upward support for the descending flat. Such a flat must be lowered like an uncovered frame.

A multiflat unit may be floated down provided it does not have many large uncovered openings or any great amount of heavy ornament. Units which carry heavy items of architectural trim, whether single flats or several flats fastened together, must be *walked down* by a reversal of the walking-up process. If weight is concentrated near the top of a piece, padded poles or stage braces must be employed in either raising or lowering it to prevent excessive bending or possible breaking of the stiles. A convenient pole for this purpose is a bamboo pole with a plumber's rubber suction plunger attached to one end. The other end may be used as a *border pole* to clear pieces fouled in the flies.

Individual pieces of flat scenery are commonly moved in the same position relative to the floor as they have when they are set, that is, flats are moved with the stiles vertical; ground rows are carried bottom rail down. The process of moving a flat by hand is known as *running*.

Twofold flats are grasped at the fold and moved with the fold forward. When one flat of a twofold unit is larger than another, the stagehand holds and moves the folded unit from the side of the larger flat and keeps the small flat leaning against it.

12.3 Running a flat. The stagehand stands at the back of the flat, facing in the direction in which the flat is to run, and grasps the stile. His hand on the side next the flat holds the edge at a point as high as he can reach. His other hand holds the edge at a point as low as is convenient for lifting, not higher than his waist. With both elbows straight, and the flat tipped slightly toward him, he raises the leading edge slightly to clear obstructions and moves forward rapidly, sliding the flat along the floor

running

12.4 Running folded flats. If a threefold or larger unit is heavy to lift, a ⅜" Manila lifting rope, or #8 sash cord, is attached near the bottom of the edge which is to be lifted. A quick method of attaching the rope is to put it through a hole in the stile and knot it on the front of the flat. A lifting iron may replace the rope. The bottom of the iron is so shaped as to slip under the rail of the flat, and the top is bent to form a handle

12.5 When it is not possible to grasp the stile of a unit, metal drawer pulls are attached to the stile

12.6 A chimney piece on trunk casters. Very heavy flats may be slid along the floor with the aid of furniture sliders attached to the bottom rails. Two-way trunk casters or ball casters may be countersunk into the bottom rails of the heaviest pieces. There must be no obstacles in the way of pieces so equipped

For threefold or very large flats, two men are necessary. The second man holds the trailing edge and assists in propelling and balancing the piece. He does not lift. When high (over sixteen feet) flats are run, a third man with a padded pole or stage brace balances the top of the flat. Wood wings, profile trees, screens, etc., are run as are flats.

Flats are seldom lifted entirely clear of the floor for running, since contact with the floor gives stability and reduces the effort required to move them. When it is necessary to lift and carry a flat over obstacles, the piece is grasped in the same way as for running, but more men are required. Flats are kept as erect as possible while being moved because the moment of falling force is zero when the flat is vertical. If balance is lost while a flat is being held or run, the stagehand sets the bottom rail firmly on the floor and regains control by pushing or pulling the flat up into a vertical position. Flats are held, pushed, and lifted only at frame members.

Three-dimensional scenery is either carried, slid, or rolled. Only lightweight pieces of little bulk can be conveniently carried, using furniture movers' technique: all carriers lift, move, and set a piece down in unison, lifting it near the bottom and steadying it near the top at all four corners.

three-dimensional scenery

Lightweight three-dimensional pieces which are to be moved only in a straight line may be slid on the stage floor. Smooth wooden runners with rounded ends may be fastened beneath such pieces.

runners

Heavy units which move in straight lines may be slid similarly if the sliding friction is reduced by applying ski wax or Teflon to both the runner and a track of either $\frac{1}{8}''$ tempered Masonite or hard-surfaced floor covering laid on the stage floor in the path of the movement. Hauling ropes are attached securely to the lower framing members.

Casters are used extensively to aid in moving scenery from storage position to set position, to change the set position, and to rotate scenery in set position. Any piece of scenery may be put on casters, but obviously the use of casters is of most value in the handling of heavy pieces: flats carrying heavy applied detail and three-dimensional units. Caster mountings vary from a single caster inserted under the rail of a heavy door to support it when open, to a full-stage rolling platform, commonly called a wagon, on which a complete set is erected. See Figures 12.6–12.14.

casters

Caster mountings may be for either continuous or intermittent use. For continuous use the scenery is set on the casters and remains on them until the set is dismantled. Continuous-use mountings are permissible only when and if there is no violent action to cause the scenery to move on its casters, the weight of the scenery is sufficient to hold it static under violent action, or there is a means of locking the castered scenery in position to resist movement caused by violent action. When one of these three conditions cannot be satisfied, casters must be mounted on scenery in such a way that their use is intermittent, that is, the scenery when set up rests on the stage floor and the casters are brought into operation only when the scenery is moved.

kinds of caster mountings

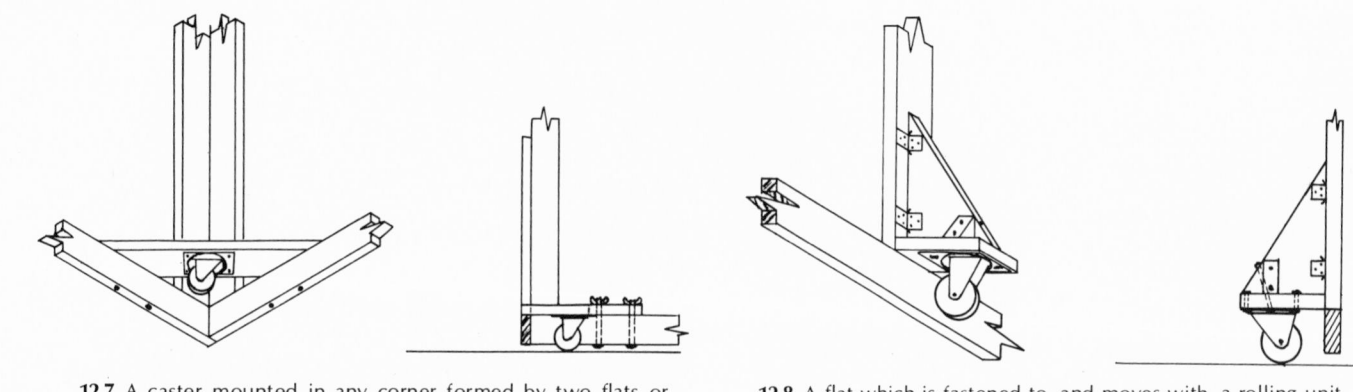

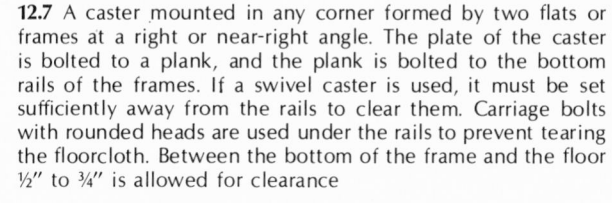

12.7 A caster mounted in any corner formed by two flats or frames at a right or near-right angle. The plate of the caster is bolted to a plank, and the plank is bolted to the bottom rails of the frames. If a swivel caster is used, it must be set sufficiently away from the rails to clear them. Carriage bolts with rounded heads are used under the rails to prevent tearing the floorcloth. Between the bottom of the frame and the floor ½″ to ¾″ is allowed for clearance

12.8 A flat which is fastened to, and moves with, a rolling unit must be supported at its extreme end by a single caster. Inasmuch as this caster is behind the flat, there is a tendency for the flat to fall forward, which must be counteracted by bracing

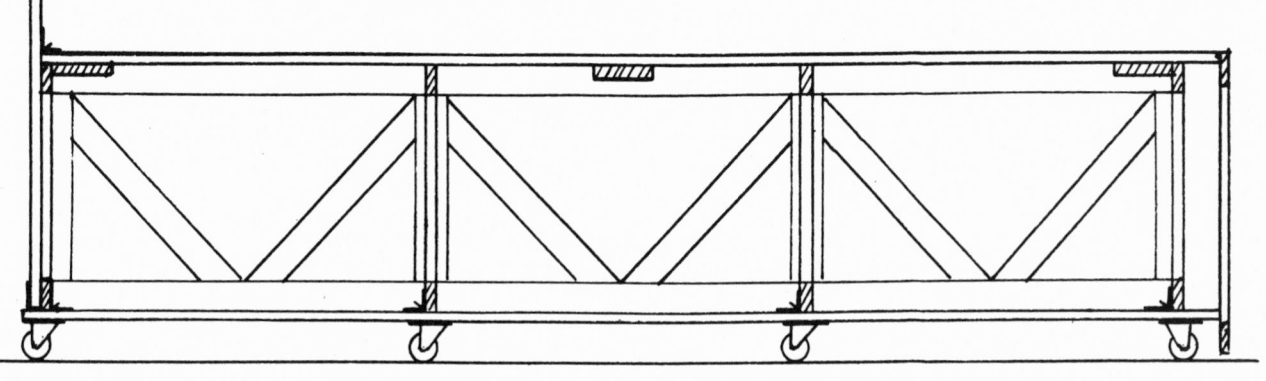

12.9 Multicaster planks set under the frames of the platform, with the casters located directly under the supports. A cover flat is attached to the audience side of the platform

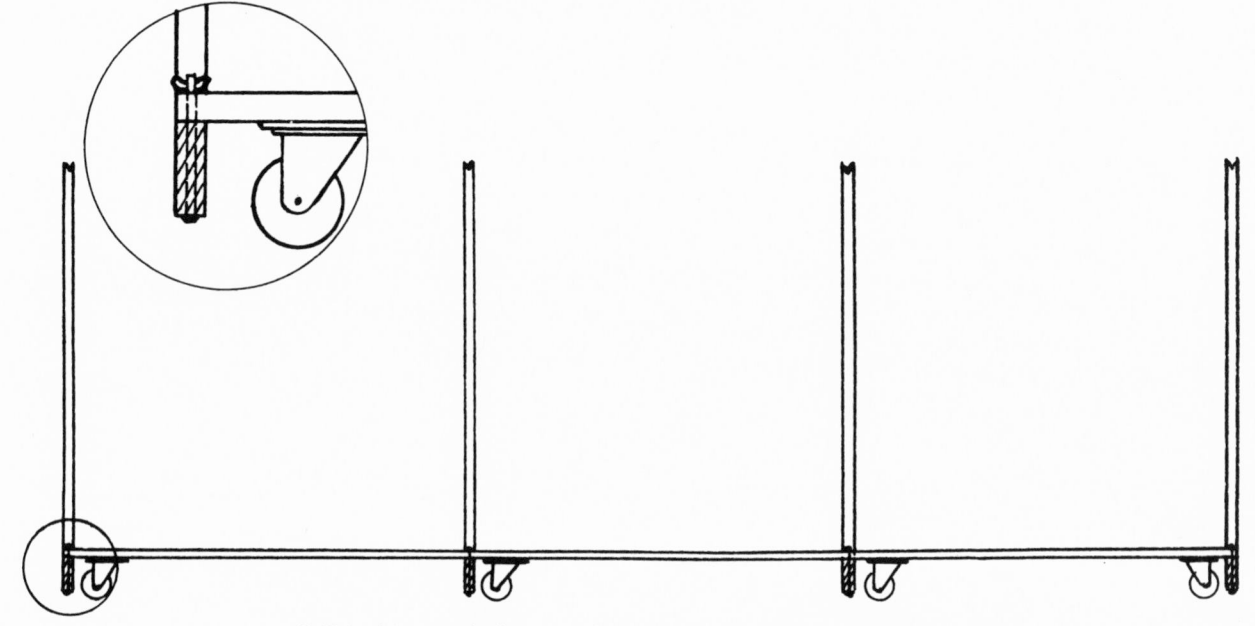

12.10 Multicaster planks inserted above the bottom rails of the platform frames. The front frame of the platform, if covered, serves as the front surface without a cover flat

12.11 Pneumatic wheels under a fiber glass–simulated brick wall

Platforms are mounted on casters either by the corner-caster method or by the use of multicaster planks (Figures 12.9–12.14).

Small sets of scenery and portions of large sets are often mounted on wagons when the production is assembled and kept set on the wagons during the entire run of the production. In scene shifts the wagons are pulled by ropes or cables from storage position to set position and vice versa. Winches offstage on which the cables are wound may be operated manually by stagehands or remotely by switches, speed controls, and position controls located in an offstage console. See Figures 12.15–12.21.

A single wagon may carry two or more sets, which are changed while other scenes are being played.

Wagons which are a permanent part of a theatre's equipment have been discussed in Chapter 11. These wagons are regularly more sturdily built than wagons which are built for use in a single production. The latter type is, however, more prevalent in American practice. A wagon for use in a single production is built to accommodate particular sets or units of scenery. Its area includes only the acting area, entrance space, and space for bracing the scenery. When stage space is limited, the entrance space may be filled by one or more separate small platforms, and the braces may extend to the stage floor. The minimum wagon height is the aggregate of the caster height, the thickness of the caster plank, and the flooring with or without padding.

Loads on wagons determine the spacing of casters and planks, the stiffness of the flooring and the planks, and the choice of casters. Stiffness of flooring and planks may be supplemented by beams fastened on edge to the underside of the flooring, running in either or both directions.

Scenery set on a wagon must be securely braced to resist strains caused by inertia on starting and stopping. Stage braces and brace jacks, which form tension-compression members, must be placed parallel to the line of movement and the bottom rails of scenery must be

**caster mountings
for continuous use**

wagons

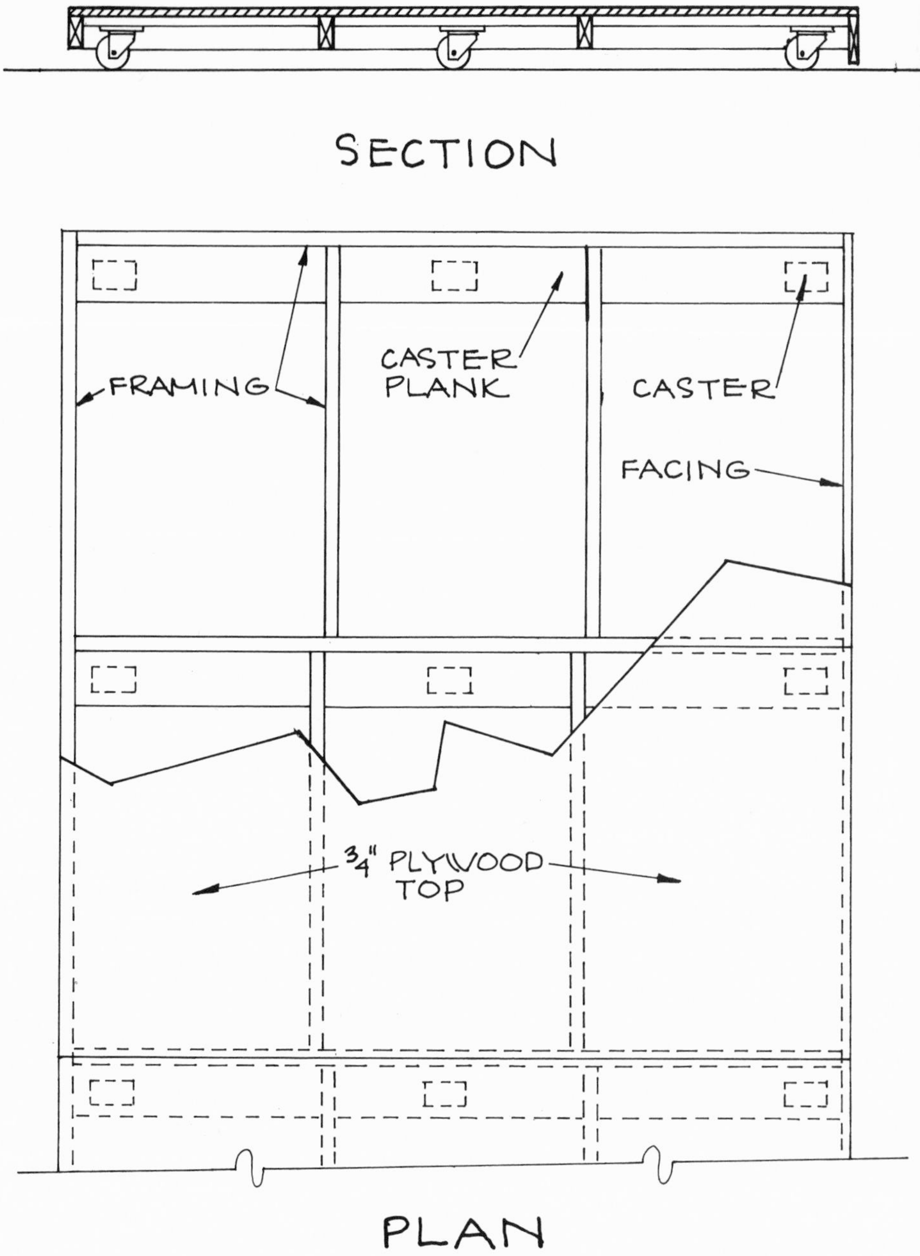

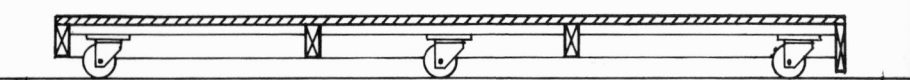

SECTION

PLAN

FRAMING

CASTER PLANK

CASTER

FACING

$\frac{3}{4}$" PLYWOOD TOP

12.12 The simplest wagon consists of caster planks supporting plywood flooring which is stiffened by 2″ lumber on edge, with a cover plank on the side toward the audience

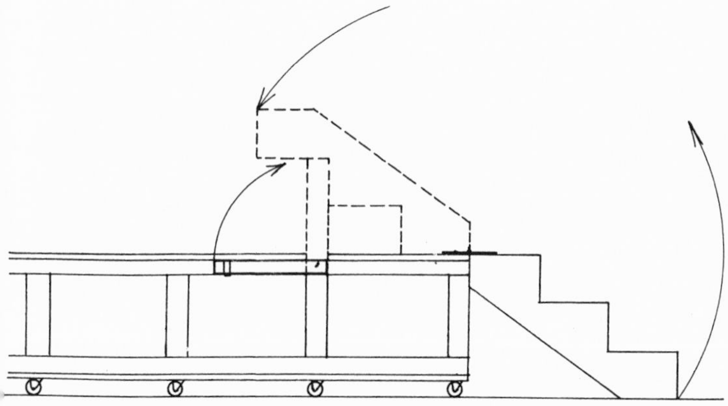

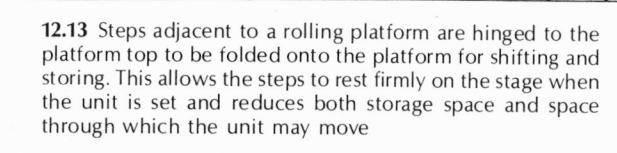

12.13 Steps adjacent to a rolling platform are hinged to the platform top to be folded onto the platform for shifting and storing. This allows the steps to rest firmly on the stage when the unit is set and reduces both storage space and space through which the unit may move

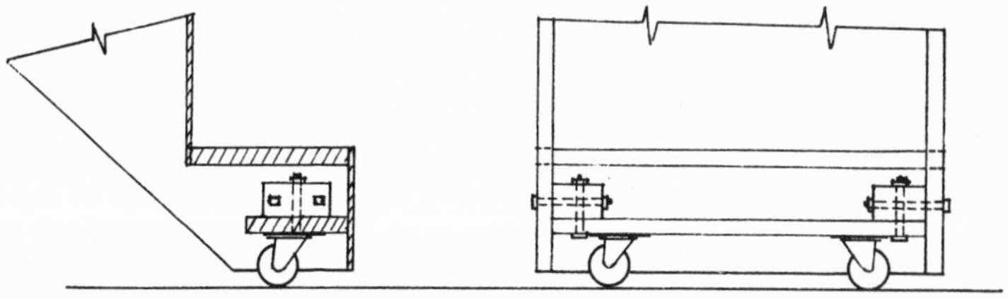

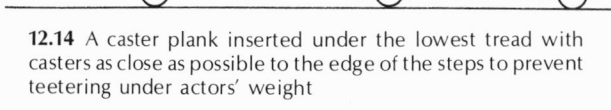

12.14 A caster plank inserted under the lowest tread with casters as close as possible to the edge of the steps to prevent teetering under actors' weight

12.15 The wagon in the foreground is stored in the scene
shop and may be rolled freely
in any direction. The wagon in
the background is in set position onstage and is moved into
the scene shop on a track
which is built into the stage
and shop floors

12.16 A traversing revolve. The motor
drives the chain around the large
sprocket wheel which is attached to
the steel bar. The bar, engaged in a
floor track, prevents the large wheel
from rotating and causes the platform
to rotate oppositely. Rotation is held
to less than one full revolution. The
track guides the traverse motion of
the unit. Swivel casters adjust to traverse motion and rotary motion

foot-ironed or loose-pin hinged to the floor of the platform or set in grooves.

Properties which are set on the wagon must be fastened down or tended by property men if there is any danger of their falling over when the wagon starts to move.

When the path of movement of a wagon must be precise, tracks are necessary, their nature depending upon the kind of wagon, the kind of movement, and the situation in which it is used.

tracks

Fixed nonswivel casters may be guided by two 1″ × 1″ hardwood strips fastened to the floor, but only if the tracks do not invade the acting area. A wagon with fixed casters may be guided by a steel plate, called a *knife,* attached to the wagon and inserted into a slot in the stage floor. Some stages are equipped with slots to guide reciprocating wagons.

When so many wagon tracks are required that if laid on the stage floor they would constitute a hazard for actors or dancers, a false floor is laid on the stage floor. The false floor may consist of as little as one thickness of 1″ plywood or of built-up systems of platforms. In either case it has slots either cut or built into it. The slots, not over ⅜″ wide, receive either the knives or flanges on the wheels of the casters.

Cable drives. Each slot may also contain wire rope — single if for one move in one direction, double for reciprocating movement — attached to a carrier into which the knife of a wagon may be fitted. Several wagons may be interchanged in one slot and on one drive.

propulsion of wagons

Winches. The wire ropes are wound on and off winches (located

309

12.17 A motor drive for linear motion contained in a platform. The platform is tipped on end. (There's that cat again)

12.18 A motor drive for rotary motion contained in a platform, shown with the platform inverted. Drive wheels are in the foreground. All wheels are set tangent to the arcs of rotation

12.19 A trap in the platform top gives access to the machine when the platform is in position for operation

offstage), either by hand crank or by selsyn-motor drives which permit remote control of position.

Manual propulsion. Units of scenery on casters are pulled rather than pushed whenever possible and the pulling is done by means of ropes attached near the floor, if possible to the member to which the casters are fastened. Two men are necessary to handle nearly all caster units; one to lead and guide in front, the other to guide the rear.

special-purpose wagons

For touring. For a production which must tour or must be moved from shop to theatre and theatre to theatre, wagons must be built in sections, loose pin–hinged or bolted together, and of a size and weight convenient for transportation.

For resident stock or repertory. A permanent producing organization will derive economies from owning a set of small wagons of uniform size which may be used individually or in various combinations.

12.20 A handcrank windlass made in a theatre school shop

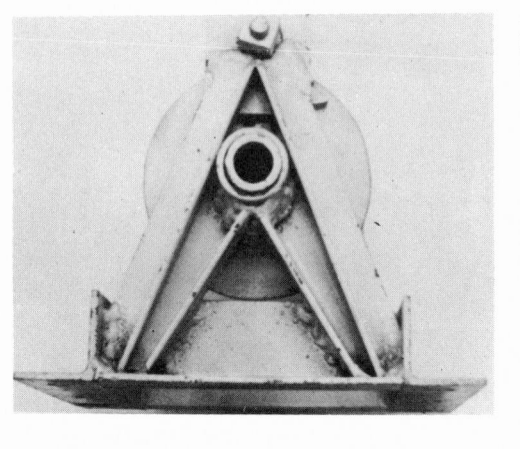

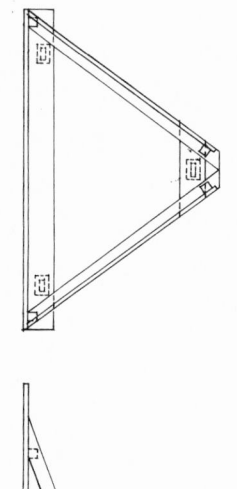

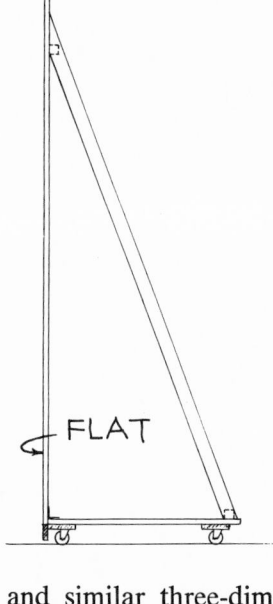

12.21 Centerpin, bearing, and socket for a revolve—homemade

12.22 A single flat on an outrigger wagon

FLAT

12.23 A single flat with a hinged velour wing on an outrigger wagon

Outrigger wagons. Alcoves, bay windows, and similar three-dimensional units comprised of flats may be moved on outrigger wagons. The wagon is merely a framework to hold casters. Its shape follows the plan of the scenery which it is to carry and extends behind the scenery sufficient distance to provide stability for the unit. See Figures 12.22–12.24.

12.24 Bay window on an outrigger wagon. The flats are set into keeper hooks on the front side of the wagon and brace jacks are placed between the backs of the flats and the offstage frame of the wagon. Below: a detailed view of the left corner of the outrigger wagon

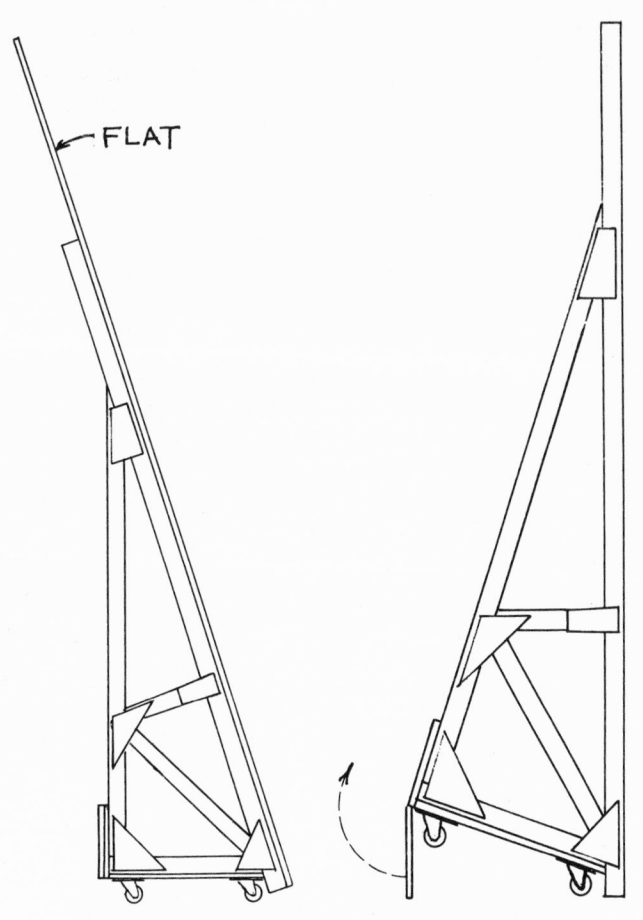

12.25 Tip jack attached to a flat. The unit is laid face down on the floor and the jack attached with loose-pin hinges so that the caster nearest the flat will touch the floor when the flat is stood vertical

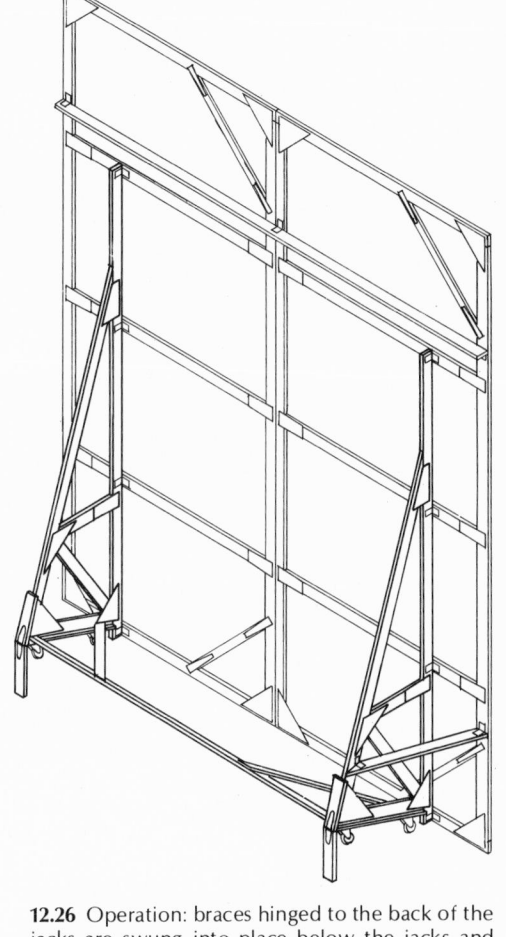

12.26 Operation: braces hinged to the back of the jacks are swung into place below the jacks and foot-ironed to the floor to hold the unit vertical. For rolling, the unit is tipped backward on the near casters until the back casters touch the floor

caster mountings for intermittent use

Casters are mounted for intermittent use when it is necessary for the scenery to be set solidly on the floor. The mounting of the caster allows it to be brought into use when the scenery is moved about the stage. The devices used are called tip jacks and lift jacks (Figures 12.25–12.33).

The **tip jack** is a triangular frame with a caster plank attached to its bottom rail. It is fastened to the back of a flat. A pair of these tip jacks is effective for moving a wide flat unit with much ornament or many props fastened to it.

The **tripod tip jack** may be used for moving small units of scenery which are too heavy for running. Not attached to scenery and with a projecting bottom ledge of steel, it may be used like a stevedore's hand truck for incidental handling of many flats at once.

The **lift jack** is a lever which has one or more casters mounted at the fulcrum. Its short arm is attached to the scenery; downward pressure on the long arm raises the scenery off the floor and brings the caster into operation. One or more lift jacks may be attached to any three-dimensional unit. The applications of the lift jack are as various as the technician's ingenuity can muster and the forms which three-dimensional scenery may take. The illustrations show merely a few.

12.27 Sidewalls of box sets, especially if they have heavy chimney pieces, cupboards, or the like, are conveniently moved on tip jacks. In this example, cantilever beams support loaded mantel shelves

12.28 A wall with fireplace, fireplace backing, and mantel with wheelbarrow lift jacks. To move the unit, stagehands depress the lift jacks, grasp the brace jacks, and lift

12.30 A triangular lift jack under a double-decker bunk. A hinged piece holds the jack in depressed position

12.29 A wall and window alcove with wheelbarrow lift jacks, depressed

12.31 Four lift jacks on a wall with two recessed windows

12.32 A lift jack on a single flat

It is essential that the stagehand have access to the lever and space in which to operate it, but lift jacks can be located under platform floors if a detachable secondary lever can be devised.

Tip-over units. Small heavy units of scenery and properties which must stand firmly on the floor when set up and yet are too heavy for running or carrying may sometimes have casters mounted on a side away from the audience and be tipped over onto the casters for moving and possibly to conserve storage space (Figure 12.34).

powered lift casters

Though some progress has been made in the development of casters which can be forced downward to lift the scenery by the application of electromechanical power, the devices are too complex and expensive

12.33 A fiber glass rock on a wheelbarrow lift jack. The stagehand pulls cords attached to the jack arms to depress or release the wheels. He lifts the opposite end of the rock to roll it

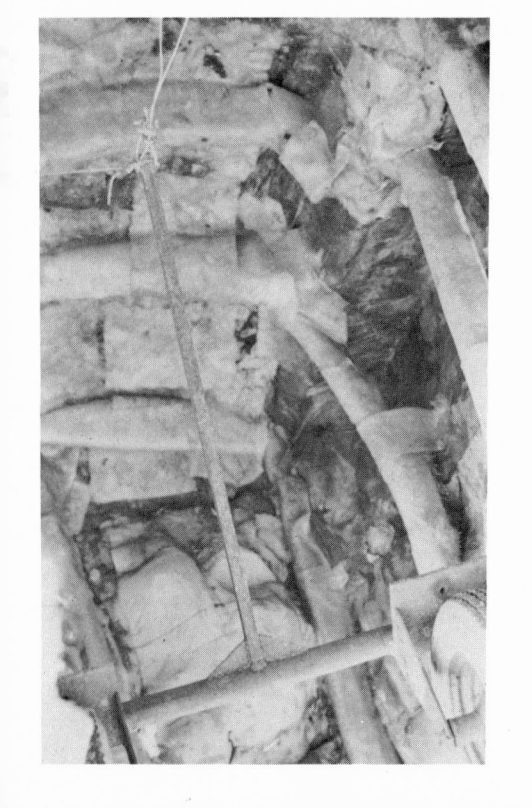

12.34 A tip-over unit

for general use. The use of compressed air to raise scenery above the floor for shifting is an intriguing possibility if the sounds of the compressor and escaping air can be reduced to tolerable levels.

Although the caster mountings, tip jacks, and lift jacks shown are made of wood, steel is to be preferred for long-run productions and when use in subsequent productions is probable.

Joining, Stiffening, Bracing

Scenery must arrive at the theatre complete with all the paraphernalia required for joining, bracing, stiffening, and rigging. Hence, the scene technician must in his plans and working drawings specify the devices and materials to be used and their methods of attachment, and all such devices and materials must be put on the scenery and tested before it leaves the shop.

Devices for joining, bracing, and stiffening scenery may be considered in categories according to their permanence. *Permanent* devices are those which are integrated with the scenery in the shop and remain so until the production is broken up. *Semipermanent* devices are those which are fitted in the shop, removed from the scenery during painting and shipment, but are integrated with the scenery for as long a time as the production remains on one stage. *Temporary* devices are those which are attached to the scenery each time the particular set to which they belong is assembled.

As many joints between pieces as possible are permanent joints, made once and for all by the builders before the scenery is covered and painted. All pieces permanently joined must be transported. Therefore, the joints must be such that the joined pieces may be collapsed or folded to go through or into the least space available to them. The technician of any producing organization must determine to what degree scenery has to fold or collapse, to meet conditions peculiar to his own situation.

Flats are permanently joined and the cracks between them permanently concealed whenever possible, for four reasons:

• The number of units which have to be handled in transportation and setup is kept to a minimum.

• The evidence of joining is concealed.

• The joints are more carefully made under the favorable working conditions of the scene shop than is possible onstage during the setup.

• Flats permanently joined strengthen and stabilize each other.

Scenery may be joined to make nonfolding units under the following conditions:

• The scenery is built onstage.

• The scenery, if not built onstage, is built and painted in shops connected to the stage by passages larger than the largest unit.

• There is ample storage space on the stage for the largest flats or three-dimensional units, thereby reducing the process of joining pieces to its

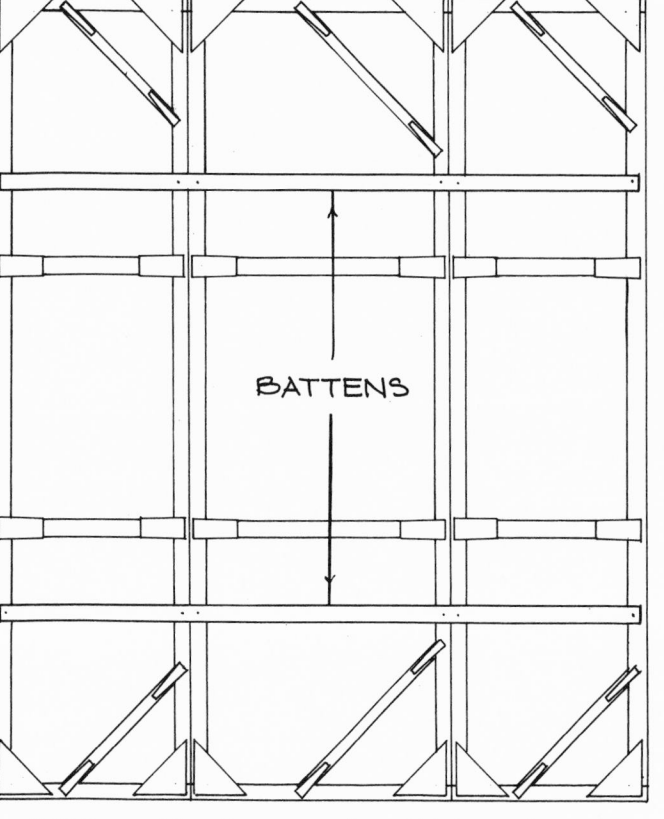

BATTENS

12.35 Battened flats. Two or more flats which form a plane unit and need not fold are joined by wooden battens fastened across the backs of the flats with nails or screws

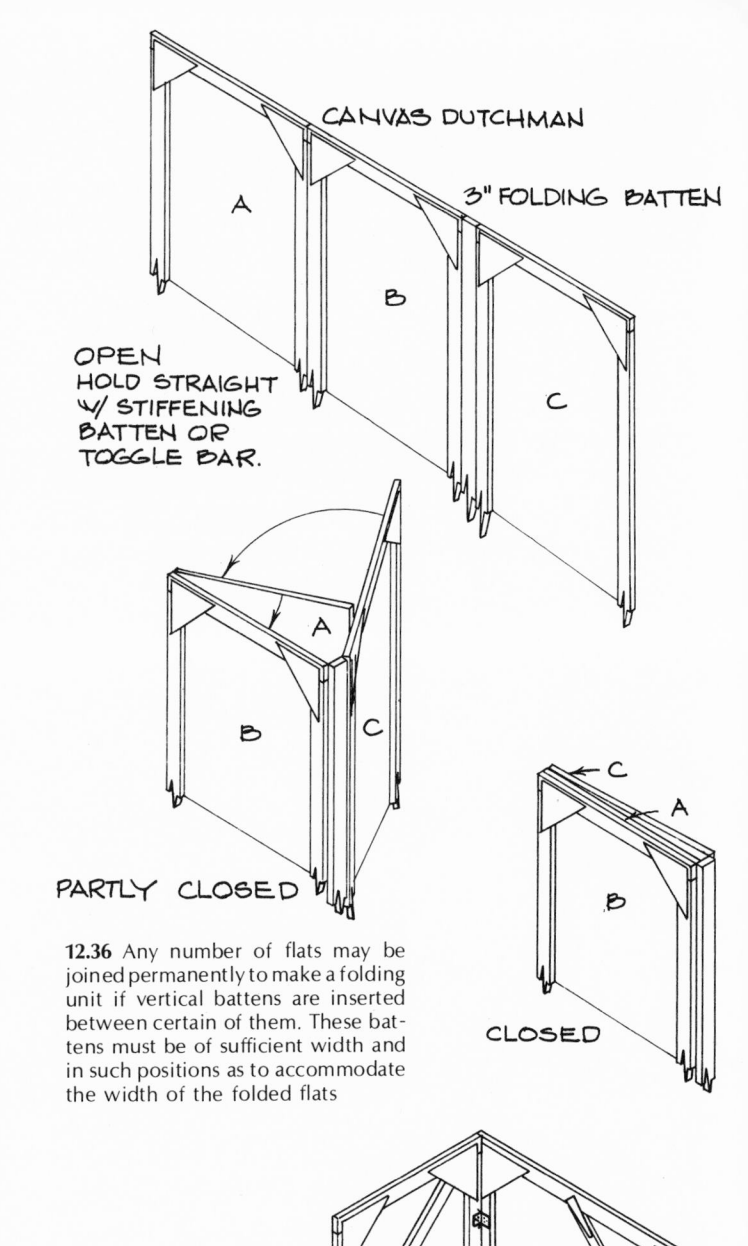

CANVAS DUTCHMAN

3" FOLDING BATTEN

A

B

C

OPEN
HOLD STRAIGHT
W/ STIFFENING
BATTEN OR
TOGGLE BAR.

A

B   C

PARTLY CLOSED

C

A

B

CLOSED

12.36 Any number of flats may be joined permanently to make a folding unit if vertical battens are inserted between certain of them. These battens must be of sufficient width and in such positions as to accommodate the width of the folded flats

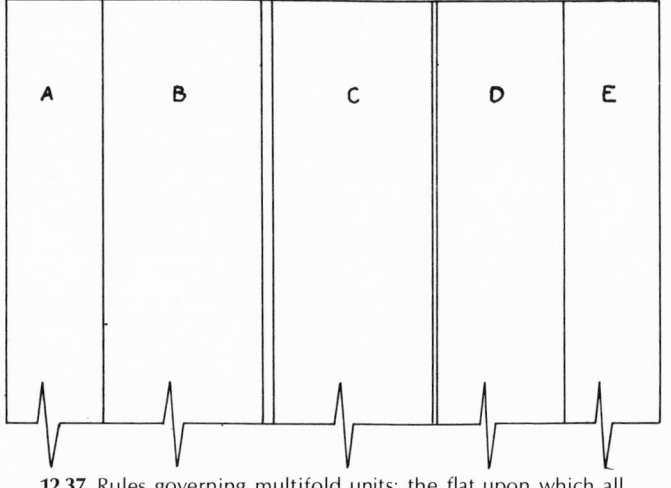

| A | B | C | D | E |

12.37 Rules governing multifold units: the flat upon which all others fold must be the largest; the smallest flats in the unit must be at the ends; the smallest effective folding batten is 1″ × 2″ stock lumber. Anything smaller will not accommodate 1½″ back-flap hinges

12.38 Corner blocks and keystones are held away from the edge of the flat B to clear the edge of flat A. The loose-pin hinges are fastened to flat A, and flat A is fastened temporarily in place with nails through the stile of flat B. The hinges are fastened to flat B, the nails are drawn, and the pins of the hinges drawn to separate the two flats. For convenience in joining thereafter, pin wire is substituted for the regular hinge pins. The pin wire is bent as shown to secure it. If the two flats are to fold back to back, the hinges must be mounted on the corner blocks and keystones

A

B

simplest terms. Flats which form a straight run of scenery may be battened together. Flats or frames which meet at angles may be fastened permanently by the use of nails, screws, bolts, or shaped irons.

flats to fold

Flats or other rectangular frames which must fold are joined permanently by means of 1½″ or 2″ tight-pin backflap hinges applied to the face of the lumber at intervals and in positions to give the greatest strength to the joint. When such folding joints are to receive severe use, the hinges are attached with ³⁄₁₆″ stove bolts. In all other instances, #9 screws are used. Hinges are spaced at intervals of not more than four feet.

concealing permanent joints

Permanent joints must be concealed from the audience. When hinged joints occur in conspicuous places and when the scenery is to be lighted strongly from the side, the hinges used on joints must be countersunk into the flats to prevent the casting of shadows. All cracks between flats, whether the joints are hinged or battened, must be covered by *dutchmen* of the same material as covers the flats.

semipermanent joining

Pieces which for any reason, usually size, cannot be permanently joined to make units for stage handling are joined semipermanently. Examples of such pieces are: thickness pieces, header flats above large openings, all types of architectural detail and applied ornament, door and window units. Semipermanent joints are made and tested in the shop, separated for transportation, remade when the scenery is assembled for production, and remain intact as long as the production runs in one theatre.

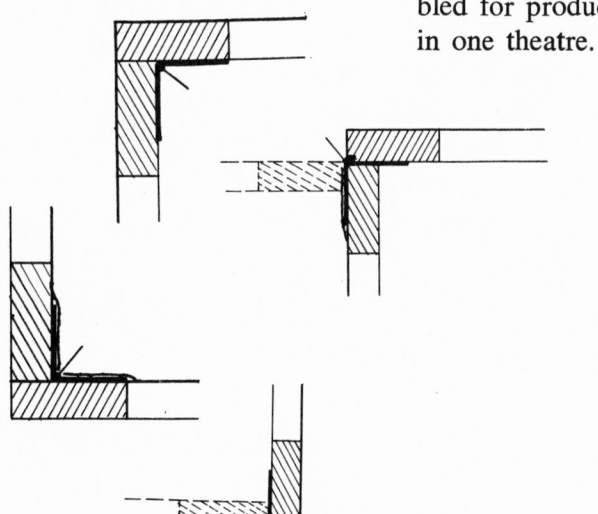

12.39 The loose-pin back-flap hinge is the most useful device for the semipermanent joining of flats or frames

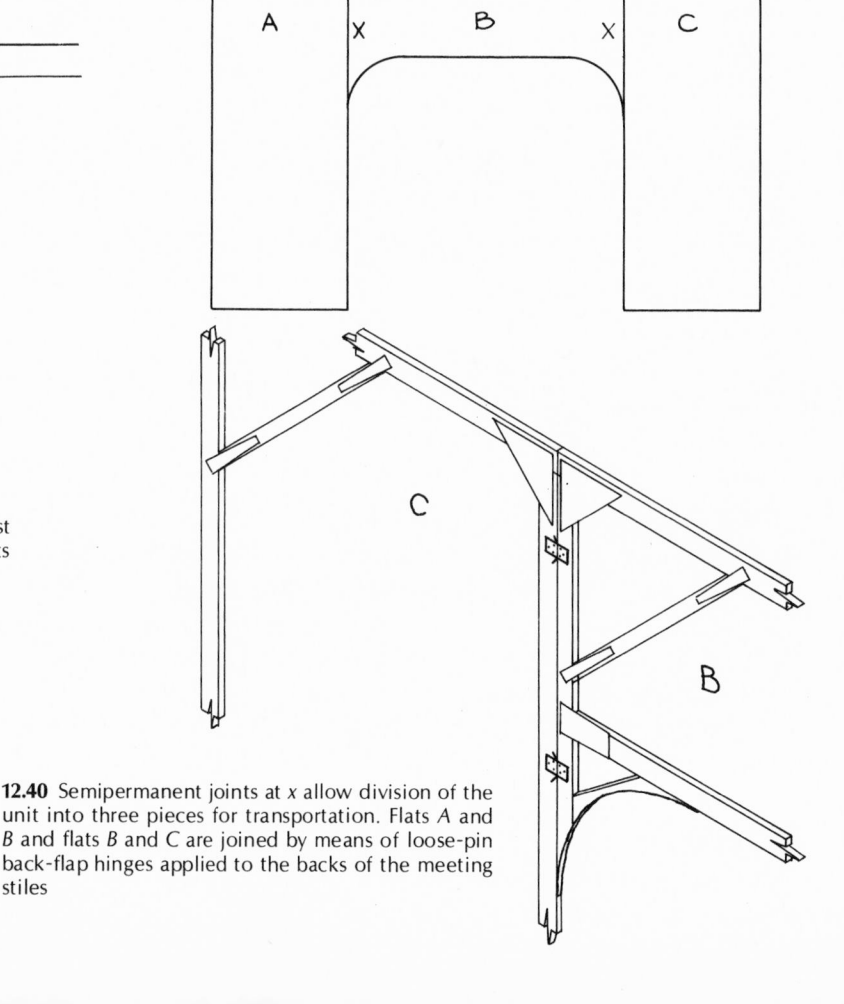

12.40 Semipermanent joints at *x* allow division of the unit into three pieces for transportation. Flats *A* and *B* and flats *B* and *C* are joined by means of loose-pin back-flap hinges applied to the backs of the meeting stiles

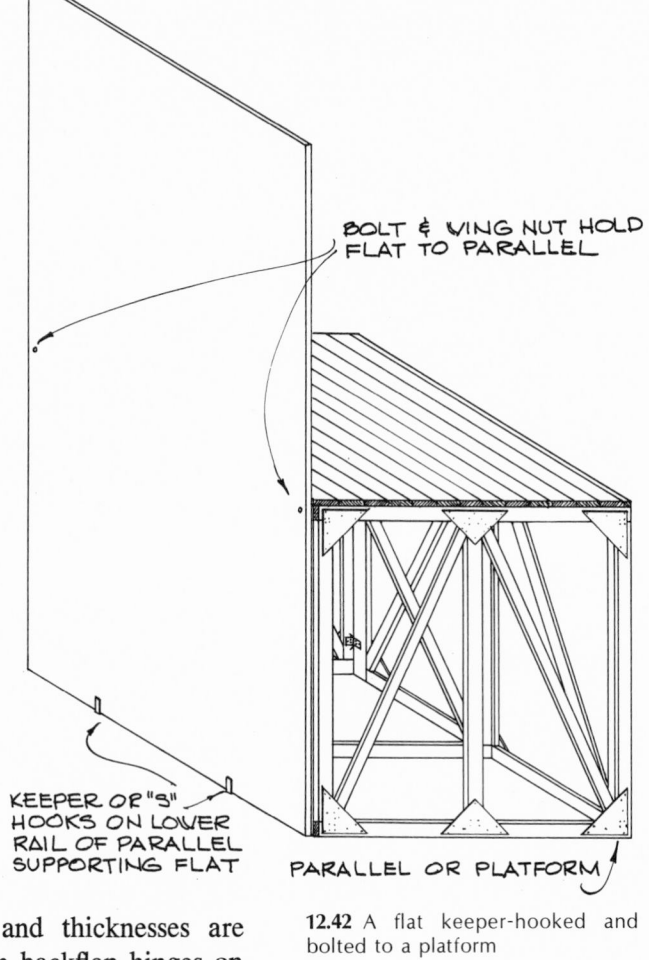

KEEPER OR "S" HOOKS ON LOWER RAIL OF PARALLEL SUPPORTING FLAT

PARALLEL OR PLATFORM

12.42 A flat keeper-hooked and bolted to a platform

12.41 A door casing fastened into a flat with strap hinges and (below) with loose-pin hinges

Flats which form architectural jogs, reveals, and thicknesses are joined to their principal flats by means of loose-pin backflap hinges on the backs of the frames.

Flat expanses of scenery containing large openings can seldom be permanently joined and folded compactly.

Architectural detail and ornament of all types, except that which may be built into flats, are joined semipermanently to the flats. Thicknesses which consist simply of plane flats are joined with loose-pin hinges as shown above. Thicknesses of irregular or curvilinear shape are joined by carriage bolts and wing nuts. Architectural detail which consists of frontal trim and thickness (door, window, bookcase, fireplace) is joined to the flat by inserting the thickness through an opening in a flat until the trim strikes the flat, and fastening it in place by one of the following methods:

• Strap hinges are attached to each side of thickness in such a way that when the thickness is set in place, one half of each hinge drops to a horizontal position behind the stiles of the opening to clamp the stile firmly against the trim. The pivot of the hinge must be put against the thickness of the piece so that the free half of the hinge will fall no lower than the horizontal.

• Loose-pin hinges are mounted on blocks or battens on the back of the trim so that the hinges are flush with the back of the flat.

• Turn bars or turn buttons are mounted on blocks or battens on the back of the trim.

• Carriage bolts are put through the trim and stiles of the flat and held with wing nuts on the back of the flat.

12.43 A staircase spanning between a lower stair unit and a platform. The vertical frame is hinged to the lower unit, folds out and is braced in position. Brace cleats on the batten, top foreground, will receive the stretcher of the *escape stairs*

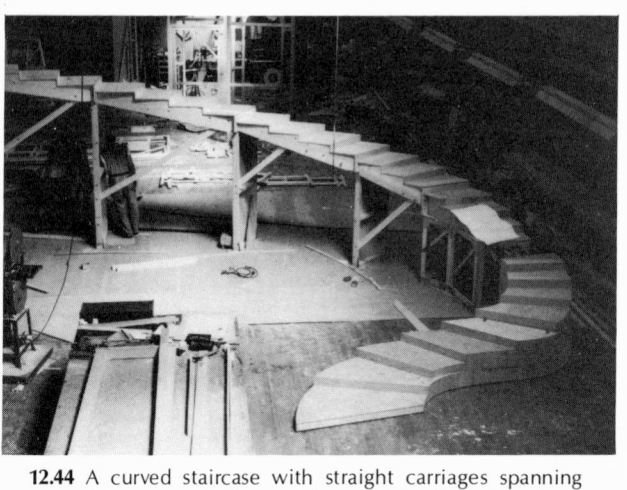

12.44 A curved staircase with straight carriages spanning vertical frames with diagonal braces bolted in place. Stair sections butt each other, and are hinged to each vertical frame. Ford Tractor Show. Ben Edwards, designer

12.45 Dormer windows loose-pin hinged to roof flats and the latter loose-pin hinged to triangular frames. Hanger irons are for flying the unit until the rest of the set is assembled beneath it. Ford Tractor Show. Ben Edwards, designer

12.46 Trial setup with dormers and roof in position

12.47 The façade and roof of a house is ingeniously divided for handling and shipping. Rigid foam is used to simulate rough stone and low-relief carving. Plywood serves as rigid internal framing. Tongues extend downward from the grilles into sockets in the plywood. Steel plates and corner irons are cleverly used. Scenery for *Milk and Honey*. Howard Bay, designer

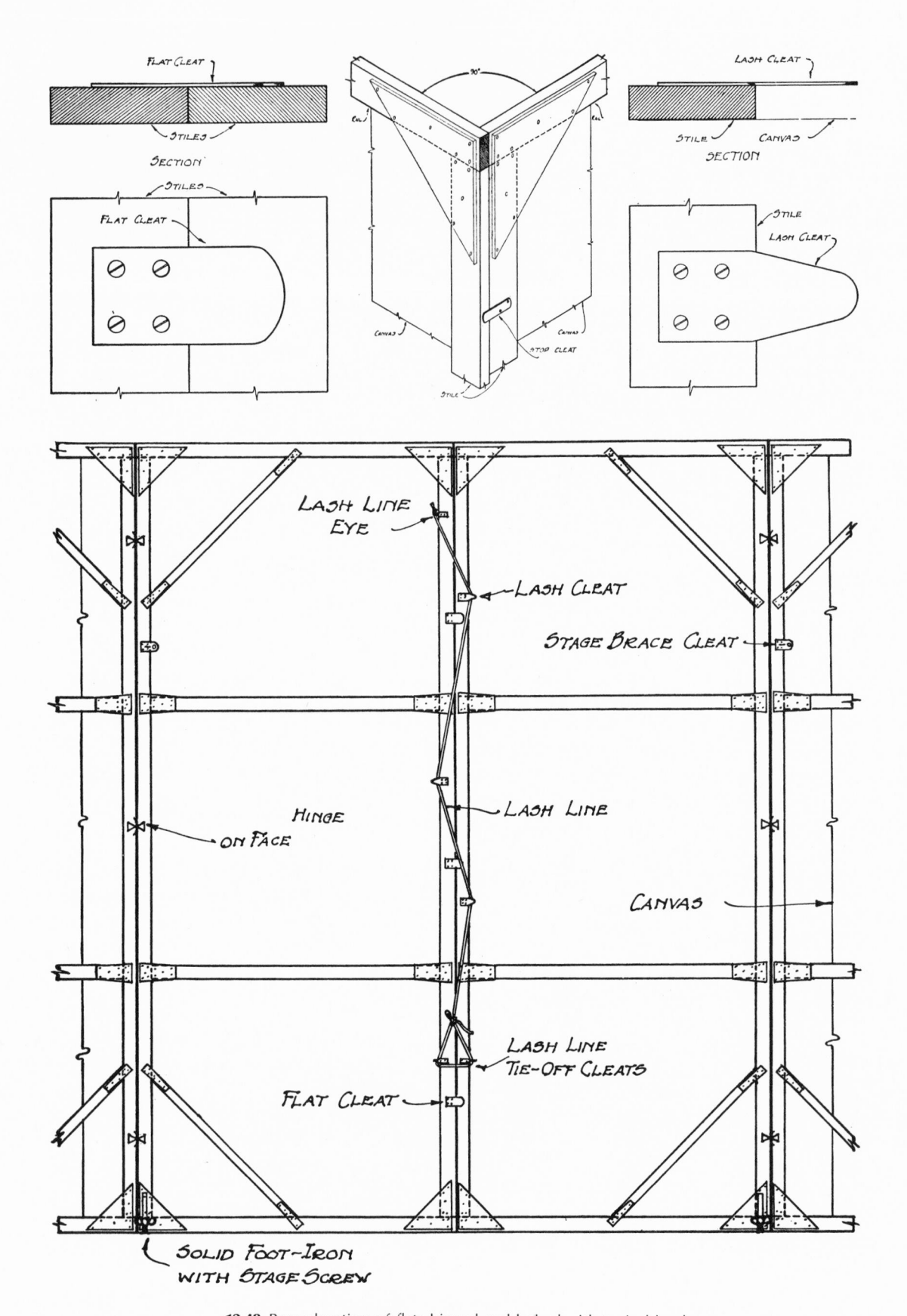

FLAT CLEAT

STILES

SECTION

STILES

FLAT CLEAT

90°

CANVAS

STOP CLEAT

STILE

CANVAS

LASH CLEAT

STILE CANVAS

SECTION

STILE

LASH CLEAT

LASH LINE EYE

LASH CLEAT

STAGE BRACE CLEAT

HINGE ON FACE

LASH LINE

CANVAS

LASH LINE TIE-OFF CLEATS

FLAT CLEAT

SOLID FOOT-IRON WITH STAGE SCREW

12.48 Rear elevation of flats hinged and lashed with typical hardware

The ultimate joining necessary to make separate units of scenery into a set of scenery is temporary. It is done by stagehands before the performance, during intermissions, or while the play is in progress. Its execution must be certain, swift, and silent.

The commonest device for temporary joining of units is a lashing in which a lash line (#8 sash cord) fastened to the top rear corner of the unit is passed behind lash cleats which are placed alternately along the stiles of the two units to be joined. The operation is a simple one but one which admits possibilities of error. Lash cleats badly spaced may render the lashing of two units very difficult. Standardization in the construction of flats to be lashed and of the placing of lashing hardware is a guarantee of effective lashing. See Figure 12.48.

Rules for lashing are as follows:

• Diagonal braces are never located at the edge of the flat which is to be lashed. They are on the edge to which the lash line is permanently attached.

• Lash lines are placed on the right-hand edge of the flat (looked at from the rear).

• Lash cleats are placed not less than 6 feet apart along the lash stiles, thus alternating at 3-foot intervals with the lash cleats on the meeting stiles.

• Lash cleats are never placed within 2 feet of a toggle bar or other brace in the frame of the flat.

• When two units are to be lashed in a straight line, stop cleats are attached to the edge of the flat which carries the lash line.

• When units are joined by lashing, the unit which is set parallel or nearest parallel to the footlights is made to carry through the joint, and the unit which is set perpendicular or nearest perpendicular to the footlights is made to butt the other.

• When two units are to be lashed at an angle of from 90° to 180° on the face, stop cleats are attached to the edge of the flat which is set perpendicularly or obliquely to the footlights.

• When two units are to be lashed to an angle of from 180° to 270° on the face, stop blocks are attached to the flat which is set parallel to the footlights. This type of lash joint is difficult to make and is to be avoided when possible in planning the division of the set into units.

• At least two stop cleats or two stop blocks are necessary whenever they are used, one of either near the top of the flat, and one near the bottom. Occasionally a third of either will be necessary at the mid-height of the flat.

Loose-pin hinges are occasionally necessary for temporary joining. Greater rigidity is obtained by their use than is possible with lashing, but they require more time in joining, since the two units must be carefully aligned in order to insert the pins.

Screen-door hooks and **screw eyes** may serve for temporary joining when little stability is required at the joint.

Rudder pintles and **gudgeons** (marine hardware) are useful for quick and positive hanging and removal of doors, gates, shutters, and like objects that must swing.

stiffening   This is the process of making rigid any unit of scenery that is by its nature or use fragile, supple, or subject to bending stresses. Units consisting of several flats hinged together must be stiffened by the application of battens horizontally across all the flats. Flats which have a superimposed load such as a cornice, a high window, or an attached mantelpiece must be stiffened against bending of the stiles. Back-wall flats to which a ceiling is hinged must be stiffened against bowing caused by the backward-downward thrust of the ceiling as it is being lowered. Ceilings to which chandeliers or beams are fastened must be stiffened against undue bending of their horizontal members. See Figures 12.49–12.54.

Frequently, thickness flats or applied architectural trim serve as adequate horizontal stiffening. A cornice, a chair rail, or a baseboard will hold the flats to which it is applied in a straight line.

Whereas horizontal stiffening is merely a matter of supplying members to prevent movement in the joints, vertical stiffening is made

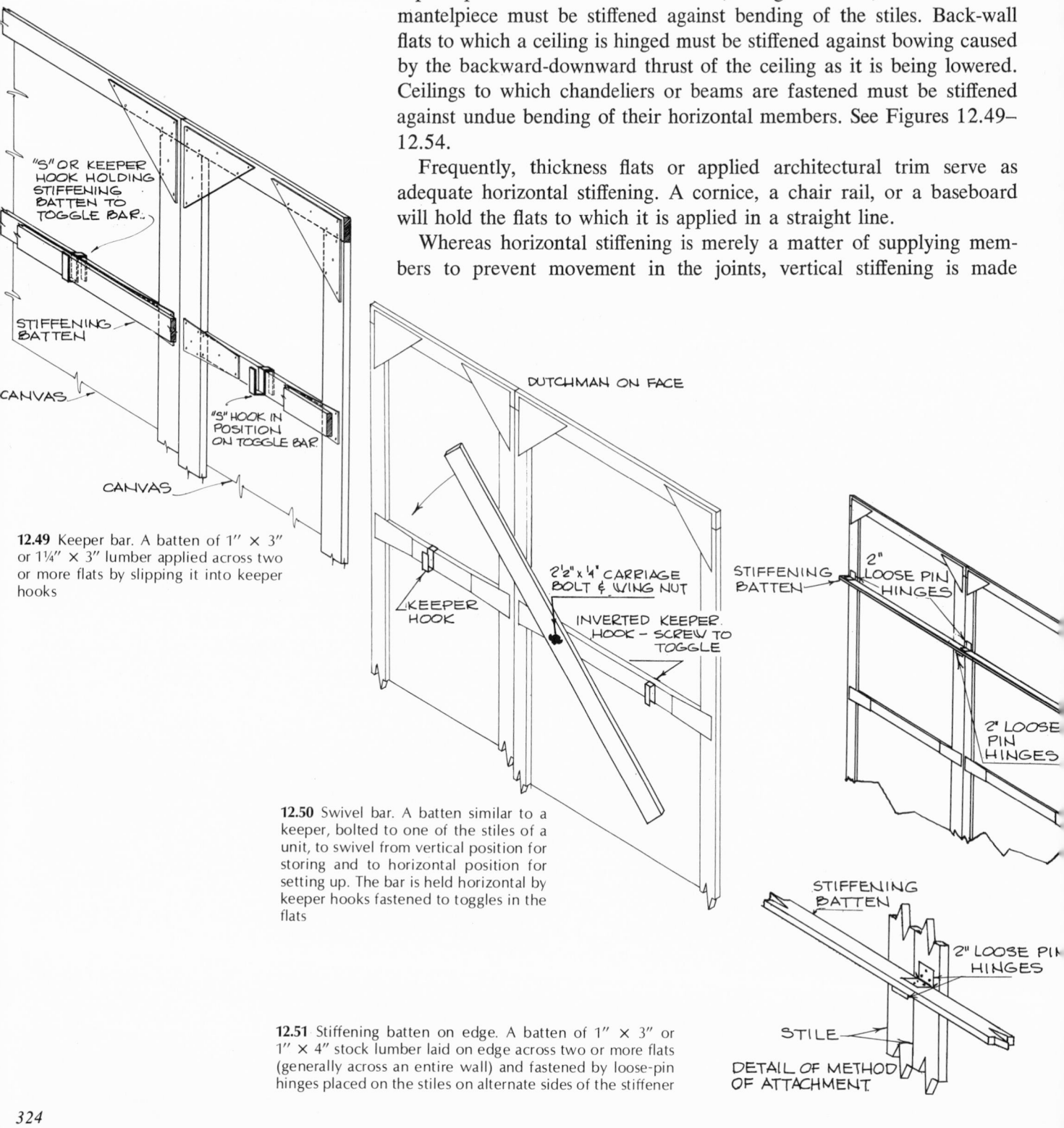

12.49 Keeper bar. A batten of 1″ × 3″ or 1¼″ × 3″ lumber applied across two or more flats by slipping it into keeper hooks

12.50 Swivel bar. A batten similar to a keeper, bolted to one of the stiles of a unit, to swivel from vertical position for storing and to horizontal position for setting up. The bar is held horizontal by keeper hooks fastened to toggles in the flats

12.51 Stiffening batten on edge. A batten of 1″ × 3″ or 1″ × 4″ stock lumber laid on edge across two or more flats (generally across an entire wall) and fastened by loose-pin hinges placed on the stiles on alternate sides of the stiffener

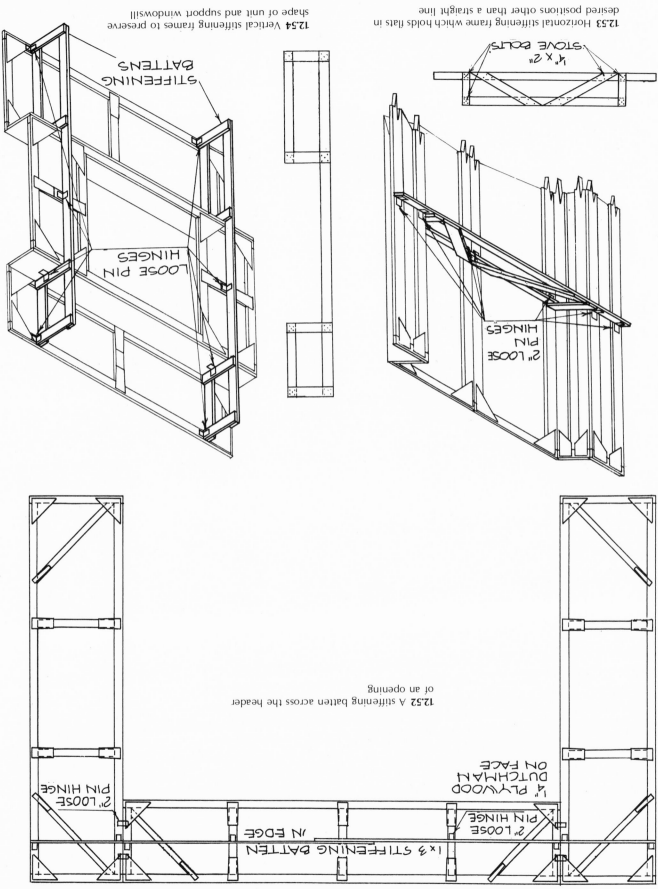

12.54 Vertical stiffening frames to preserve shape of unit and support windowsill

STIFFENING BATTENS

LOOSE PIN HINGES

12.53 Horizontal stiffening frame which holds flats in desired positions other than a straight line

¼" X 2" STOVE BOLTS

2" LOOSE PIN HINGES

12.52 A stiffening batten across the header of an opening

2" LOOSE PIN HINGE

¼" PLYWOOD DUTCHMAN ON FACE

2" LOOSE PIN HINGE

1 x 3 STIFFENING BATTEN IN EDGE

necessary by the presence of definite forces tending to deform the scenery. These forces must be recognized and counteracted by the scene technician when he lays out the construction of the scenery.

A cornice attached to the top of a unit of flat scenery constitutes a force tending to bend the stiles of the flats. There may be no danger of the stiles breaking, but a slight bend may make assembly of the set difficult. Such a bend in the sidewall of a box set is very noticeable from the front. Similarly a window with considerable thickness applied to the back of a flat tends to bow the stiles to which it is attached. Vertical stiffening battens are $1'' \times 3''$ to $1\frac{1}{4}'' \times 6''$ stock lumber, as required by the particular situation, attached to the backs of meeting stiles by means of loose-pin hinges on both sides of the stiffener. The corner blocks and keystones of the flat construction are kept clear of the stiffener position so that it may be in contact with the stiles along the entire height.

Flats 12' high or less seldom need vertical stiffening battens. Flats between 12' and 20' high may need them if loads, as of a cornice, are imposed. Flats 20' high or over need vertical stiffening battens even if there is no load imposed on them, because the weight of the upper portion of the flats is sufficient to cause bowing of the slender stiles.

The front edge of a ceiling on a wagon stage set requires stiffening along its entire length.

Scenery doors subject to slamming must have crossed stiffeners applied to their offstage side to prevent their fragile frames from breaking under the impact of closing. These stiffeners are pieces of $1'' \times 3''$ lumber applied diagonally from the corners, half-jointed at their crossing, and tapered toward the ends.

bracing

Scenery will not stand erect without auxiliary support. Three-dimensional scenery will stand erect only when the center of gravity is within the base. Braces for scenery are seldom permanently attached to the scenery and are most frequently either semipermanent, that is, attached to the scenery for the duration of a run, or temporary, that is, attached to the scenery only while it is set in place.

semipermanent bracing

A **brace jack** is a triangular wooden frame having a stile at least two-thirds as high as the flat which is to be braced, a rail as long as floor space will allow, and diagonal framing to withstand the stresses imposed by use. The members are either mortised and tenoned together or butt-jointed with corner blocks. For extremely rough use the joints are made with corner blocks, cemented and bolted, on both sides. See Figures 12.55 and 12.56.

The stile of the brace jack is fastened with loose-pin hinges either to the toggle bars or to a stile of the flat to be braced. Fastening to the toggle bars is not as convenient and not as rigid as fastening to a stile, since bending of the toggle bars may allow movement of the flat. The brace jack may be fastened to the stage floor by various means:

• A stage screw through a flat foot iron which has been countersunk and attached to the bottom rail of the brace jack.

• A metal strap bent to proper shape and attached to the floor at a point where a flat foot iron will swing under it.

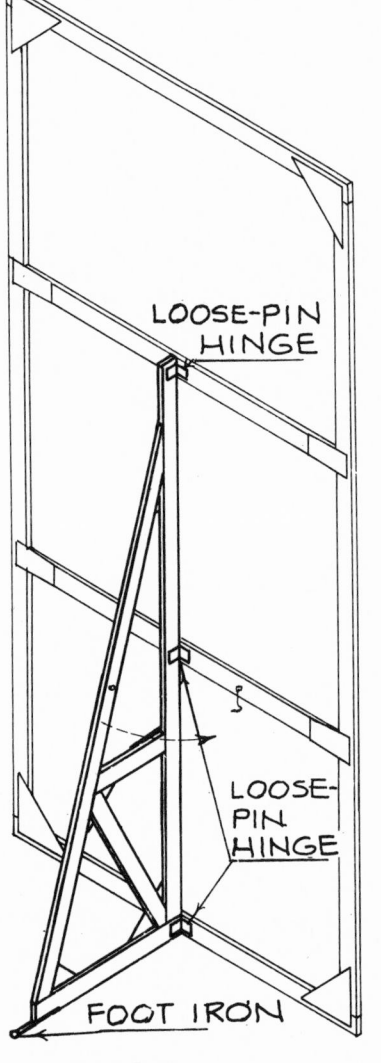

LOOSE-PIN HINGE

LOOSE-PIN HINGE

FOOT IRON

12.55 A brace jack

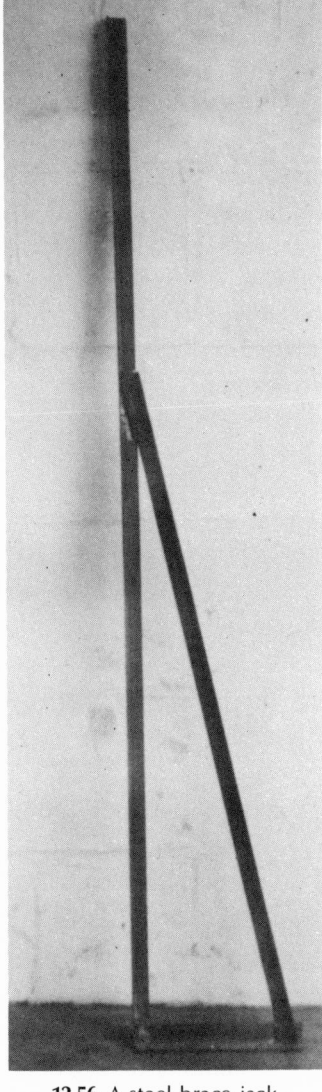

12.56 A steel brace jack

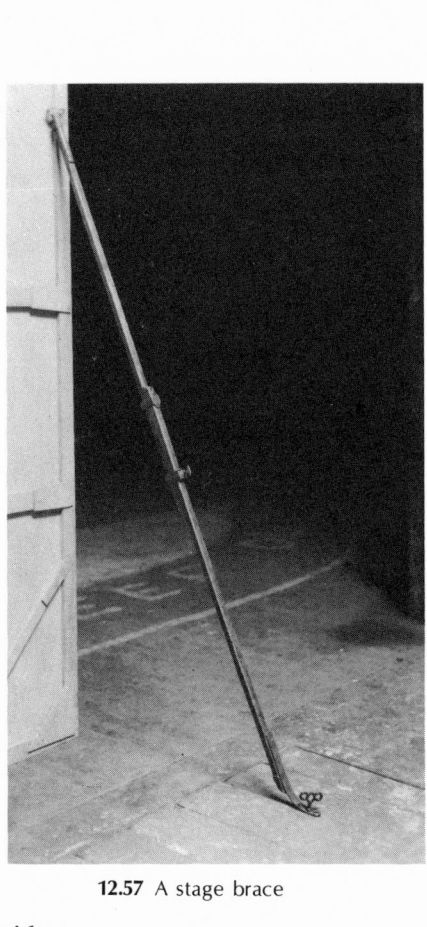

12.57 A stage brace

• A small limp sandbag, of sufficient weight to stabilize the piece, laid over the bottom rail of the brace jack, which in this case is allowed to extend beyond the diagonal member.

• A specially shaped iron weight slipped over the protruding bottom rail of the brace jack.

• An iron weight or sandbags fastened to the bottom rail of the brace jack.

• Construction of the brace jack with the angle between rail and stile less than 90° to let the piece of scenery lean slightly backward. Brace jacks are attached to scenery by loose-pin hinges at points which allow the jacks to be folded and hooked against the back of the scenery when the set is struck. When two brace jacks are used on a unit of scenery, they are hinged to fold in opposite directions, so that when set up, each jack resists sidewise movement of the piece in one direction.

Stage braces furnish the commonest means of bracing scenery temporarily. They are either hardwood (ash or hickory) sticks of fixed

temporary bracing

or adjustable length or telescoping lightweight metal tubes fitted with hardware especially designed for fastening one end of the brace to the scenery and the other end to the floor. The most useful type of brace is an adjustable one which has a hornlike iron at its top end and a rocker iron at its bottom. A stage brace may be attached to scenery by means of brace cleats extending either to left or right of a stile and may be set on the floor at any convenient angle. Stage braces may be wired to hang on scenery and be flown with it. See Figure 12.57.

stage screws

Stage braces, brace jacks, and foot irons are fastened to the stage floor by stage screws (floor pegs). These are drop-forged or wrought-steel screws with shanks $\frac{1}{2}''$ in diameter and large handles; they are sharpened so that turning by hand with a reasonable downward pressure causes them to enter the stage floor. Stage screws must be kept sharp with round files to be effective.

The location of stage-screw holes, once made for a particular set of scenery, must be marked with the same color as that used for marking the rest of the set and care must be taken, when inserting and removing the screws, not to wear the hole in the floor larger than the shank of the screw. Two devices prevent damage to the stage floor from the repeated insertion and removal of the screws:

• A tapped and externally threaded plug which is inserted in a $\frac{1}{2}''$ hole drilled in the floor and which receives a specially made stage screw (the plug can be removed and the hole filled with a dowel).

• A metal plate which is screwed to the floor and which contains a tapped $\frac{3}{8}''$ hole to receive a large thumbscrew.

Both these devices serve well for long runs.

rules for bracing

• Braces or brace jacks are placed at points where the action of internal or external forces tends to impart movement to the scenery.

• An expanse of flat scenery must be braced at one or more places in its width.

• Points where actors contact the scenery must be braced.

• Doors must be braced at their swinging side to counteract the force of closing.

• Neither stage braces nor brace jacks are placed at lashed joints.

• Braces are not used where flats are joined at right or near-right angles, since by this juxtaposition each flat lends support and stability to the other.

Flat scenery of no great height (4' high or less) may be braced by right-angle foot irons attached to the back of the units and fastened to the stage floor (Figures 12.58 and 12.59).

general precautions for handling and hanging scenery

• Keep sets clean by covering the stage floor when units are laid face down and by frequently washing hands if scenery is light-colored.

• Protect painted scenery from rubbing; do not slide scenery which is face down on the floor; do not slide scenery on scenery.

• Depend upon mathematical and graphic calculations and measurements, not on guesses or rules of thumb.

• Know in advance each step of each process.

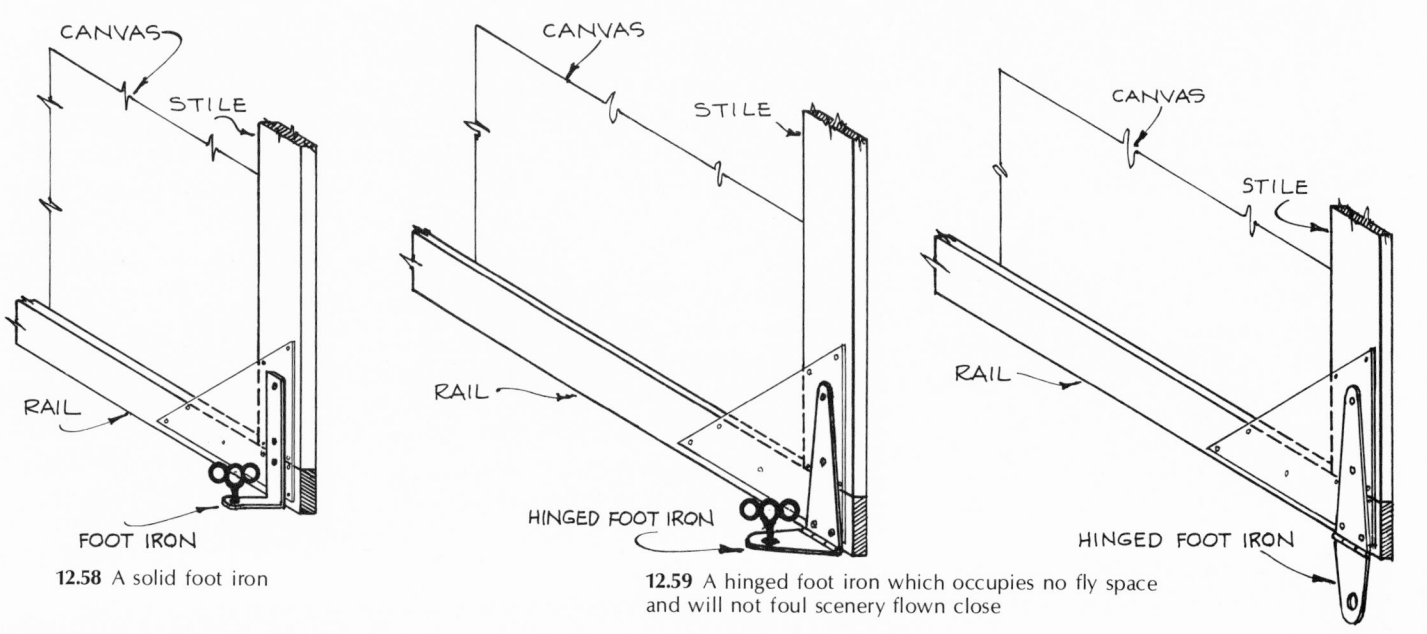

12.58 A solid foot iron

12.59 A hinged foot iron which occupies no fly space and will not foul scenery flown close

Hanging

Hanging is the process of attaching units of scenery to the overhead stage machinery according to the scene technician's plans so that each unit may be readily brought into its exact setting position or taken out to its proper storage position in conformity with the requirements of the scene plot without interfering with any other hung units. The storage position must afford complete concealment from the audience and the means of attachment and operation must be safe. Hanging is in the charge of the stage carpenter (or master carpenter) who has the boss

12.60 A back wall joined, stiffened, braced, and rigged. *Note:* cornice set in with turnbars, vertical and horizontal stiffening battens, brace jacks each side of door, extra battens in flats to support pictures on face, snatch lines from pipe batten to stiles and to door thickness, and battens on the backs of the doors to stiffen the plywood panels

flyman as his lieutenant. The stage carpenter directs the whole operation; the boss flyman directs the operation of the flying equipment and the installation, adjustment, and attachment of scenery to it. The scene designer, the scene technician, and the representative of the scenic studio, who have designed, planned, and built the scenery to fit the stage and to operate according to the scene plot, advise and supervise until the scenery is working properly.

Hanging is interwoven with, or a direct sequel to, the work of joining, stiffening, and bracing: stagehands under the stage carpenter lay out the pieces of a unit, join them, and attach thicknesses, architectural detail, stiffeners, and brace jacks, while flymen under the boss flyman spot loft blocks, let in counterweight or rope sets, and attach them to the unit, and as soon as the floor crew has finished its work, fly it and balance it. All these actions constitute parts of the process of assembly, which is discussed in Chapter 14.

The hanging of any unit of scenery involves a strict sequence of operations which begins with a determination of the suitability of the stage equipment to receive and support the unit.

limitation of equipment

Flying systems, whether rope or counterweight, or combinations of the two, are best suited to units which are hung or set parallel to the proscenium. Special arrangements must be made to hang units which are set perpendicular or obliquely to the proscenium. Any flying system, furthermore, is limited in the location of its lines or battens, but some systems facilitate placing (*spotting*) lines at random pick-up points and selectively grouping these spot lines to fly scenery of any shape, set in any position. When a unit to be hung does not set directly below the installed flying equipment, the technician decides whether to adjust the setting position of the unit to the location of the equipment or move the equipment, or install additional equipment. He must calculate the weight of the unit to be hung and must check it against the load capacities of the equipment, the counterweight arbors, and the gridiron. An exceptionally heavy piece may require two or more counterweight sets or even specially installed counterweights.

Effectiveness in rigging depends upon these measures:

• Careful planning of each step of each operation to make the maximum use of mechanical aids and to avoid hazardous conditions.

• Thorough analysis of each operation so that all necessary accessories of correct size and strength are available.

• Careful adherence to the planned procedures.

• Clear directions to the stagehands and supervision of their work.

planning

Scenery must come to the stage completely prepared for hanging, with drawings and schedules showing its assembly, its set and storage positions on the floor and in the flies, and its means of movement, and with all accessory equipment that is not part of the installed equipment of the theatre. The more complete, detailed, and accurate this information is and the more complete the accessories are, the faster will be the whole hanging process. The more complex the scenic investiture, the more detailed must be this paper work. Even so, one man at a drawing board with a slide rule or desk calculator at hand can visualize scenery set up, hung, and in motion, and can plan the hanging operation and specify the needed accessories in much less time and with greater saving in manpower than can the stage carpenter who thinks out the process as he goes along, with the whole crew standing around while he thinks.

The drawings and schedules must contain the following information, or that part of it pertaining to the particular job:

Drawings: methods of hanging all units and locations of the hanging hardware.

Gridiron plan: location of spot lines, special lead blocks, and direction-changing (*muling*) blocks.

Hanging plan and section:

1. What units are to be hung on what battens.
2. What units are to be hung on what rope sets.
3. New locations of any counterweight and rope sets that must be moved.
4. Locations of specially installed sets and spot lines.
5. Each unit in set position and flown position with
   (a) height of batten above the floor at low trim, and
   (b) height of bottom of unit at high trim.
6. Locations of light battens, light ladders, and booms, and the methods of hanging them.

Schedule:

1. Each unit identified in order from the proscenium.
2. Weight of each unit and the distribution of weight if it is not uniform.
3. Method of hanging each unit.
4. Chain, wire, or rope: number, size, length.
5. Attached hardware and other preparations of each piece.
6. Spot blocks: number, size, location.
7. Batten extensions: number, kind, size, length, method of fastening.
8. Battens to be hung on rope sets: number, kind, size, length, location.
9. Bridle lines: number, kind, size, length, how attached.
10. Breast lines: number, kind, size, length, location, how fastened.
11. Cinch (trimming) tackles: number, kind, size, length, and on what units used.
12. Carpet hoists: kind, load, and on what units used.
13. Guide cables: number, kind, size, length, location, with cross-reference to grid plan and hanging section.

All locations must relate to three coordinates: the stage floor, the proscenium line or other transverse line, and the center line of the stage.

Gravity acts on hung scenery to cause it to descend to the floor if it is not restrained by a tie-off, by sufficient man- or mechanical power, or

flying theory and principles

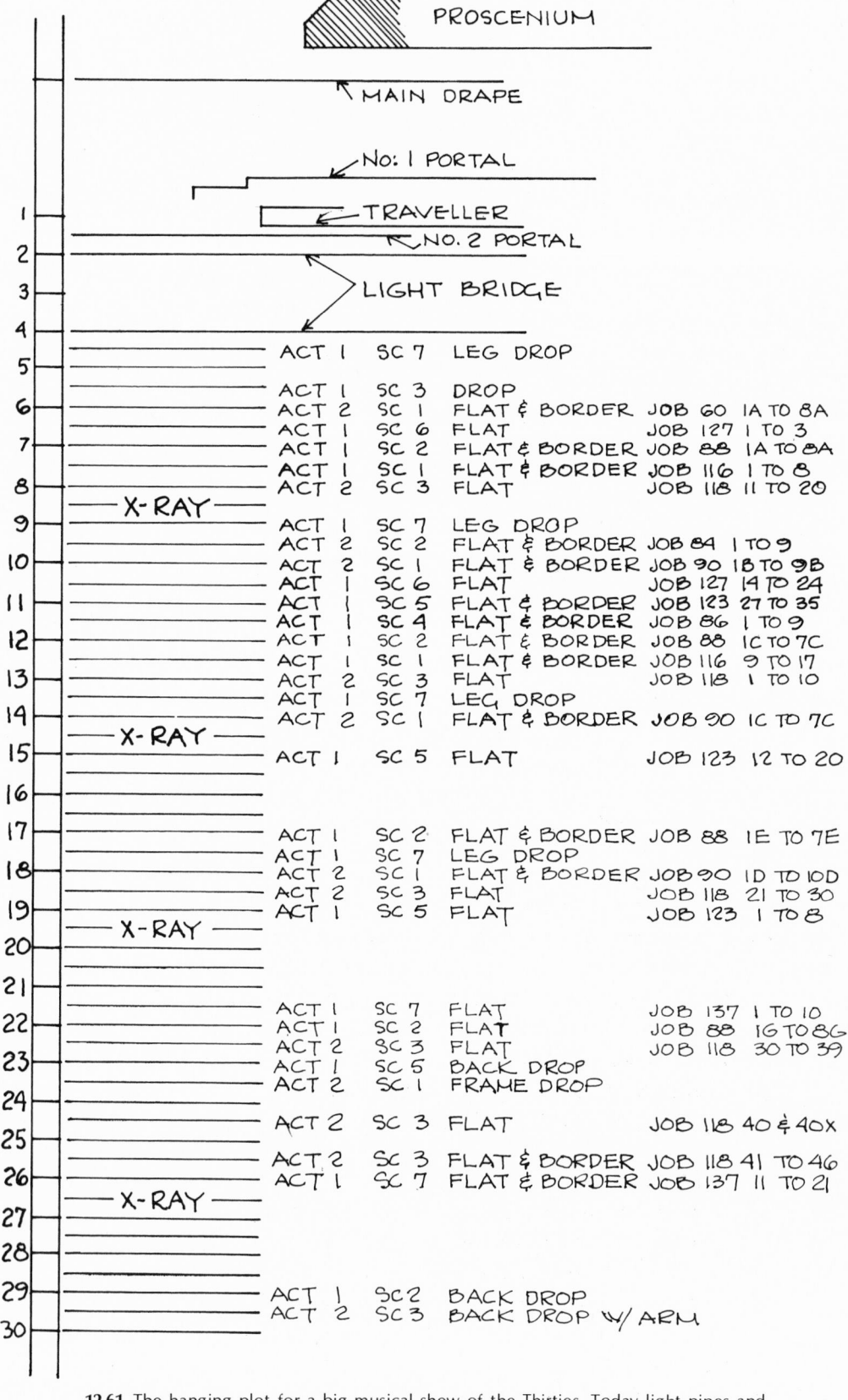

12.61 The hanging plot for a big musical show of the Thirties. Today light pipes and spotlights require more fly space than that allowed here for border strips, colloquially called "X-rays"

by counterbalancing weight, and to descend under acceleration until stopped by the floor, actors' heads, or other solid obstacles, with possible resulting damage. The boss flyman and stage carpenter must therefore be certain that the force of gravity is at all times opposed by strong equipment, adequate tie-offs, and sufficient manpower or mechanical power or counterbalancing weights to keep this from happening.

Gravity acts to determine the positions and locations which hung units will assume when flown, when set, and when in motion. The force of gravity acts along a vertical line. Any departure from this line must be introduced by the technician through engineering design. He must know how much deflecting force he must apply and in what direction he must apply it, and he must make the application within the limits imposed by the stage, its equipment, and other hung objects.

An object hung on a single line will come to rest with its center of gravity on the vertical line directly below the point of suspension.

A unit may be deflected from the gravitational line of action by forces (lines, braces, guides) exerted at any angle to the gravitational line.

The center of gravity of a unit of irregular shape and unevenly distributed weight must be located mathematically to determine the precise hanging position and location it will assume. Other forces (lines, guides, breast lines) may be needed to make it assume a desired position and location.

As an integral part of a show, the rigging must work as planned and rehearsed. It must not fail because of weakness of materials, parts, or fastenings or from inadequacies of personnel. Concerning the last-named, it is desirable that all operating parts be clearly marked and visible, that loads be within human capabilities, and that operating procedures be easy to explain and learn in case of changes of personnel. Hanging must, so far as possible, be fail-safe and foolproof with adequate provision against accident or injury.

The speed at which hung objects must move varies with the requirements of every show, the reasonable range for vertical movement, up or down, being from 1 fps to 10 fps, the latter restricted to light loads.

No technical aid to performance may produce sound which is extraneous to the performance. Sounds of running rigging, motors, gears, casters, or other mechanisms must not be heard by the audience unless they are intentionally parts of the performance.

The fewer the workmen needed and the less time required to hang a show, the less the show will cost to produce and run and the quicker and easier it will be to get ready for rehearsal and performance. On a tour this may enable opening to audiences one or two days earlier in each theatre.

The hanging of many types of scenery presents no problems to any but the veriest neophyte but other scenery, particularly for multiscened productions, which fills the floor and the flies and must be changed frequently and fast, exerts demands of ingenuity and adroitness on the designer, the technician, the stage carpenter, the boss flyman, and the stagehands.

hanging essentials
dependability
and operability

speed

silence

economy

hanging methods

Straightforward hanging and flying consists merely of attaching a unit to a line set or counterweighted batten, setting the low trim, balancing and flying it (or flying and balancing it), hauling it into the flies, and setting the high trim. Complex hanging and flying considers the entire three-dimensional volume of the stagehouse as available space in which hanging objects may be made to move in three dimensions at the command and under control of the boss flyman and his crew. For example, it must be possible to make a unit assume one desired conformation when hanging and another *designed* conformation when set; to have a unit fly into a position which is not directly over its set position; to move a unit horizontally or diagonally in three dimensions in the fly space while changing its conformation; to set a unit, remove its flying lines into the flies, bring them in, reattach them, and fly the unit without risking the descent of unbalanced weights, or to hang units so that their means of suspension are invisible.

hanging problems

To look at pictures or drawings of units hung on line sets or battens, or even to see actual scenery hung is very different from planning and carrying out the operations involved in hanging the units. For this reason a number of hanging problems are set forth in step-by-step analysis in Chapter 15. It is not intended that they cover all hanging problems but rather that the reader, having followed the analysis embodied in the examples, will be able to analyze other problems for himself. Rubrics, precautions, and suggestions for hanging scenery and operating the flies are also stated at that point in Chapter 15.

knots, splices, and tackles

A knowledge of knots, splices, and tackles is needed to hang scenery. Scenery is attached to the standing equipment of the stage by means of knots. Splices must be used to extend and join pieces of rope. Tackles increase the effectiveness of man or machine power in moving scenery. Rope is discussed in Chapter 6. Rope terminology, definitions, and instructions in tying knots and making splices are given in Chapter 15.

Properties, special effects, and sound

13

Properties include all decorative and practical portions of the scenic investiture which are not part of the scenic structure, as well as objects carried or handled by actors and nonelectrical sound or visual effect devices and equipment.

They are planned and built simultaneously with the scenery, and they are physically articulated into the production when it is assembled before the technical rehearsal. Their nature and uses must be understood before the study of scenery can logically proceed further.

distinction between props and scenery

The line which divides scenery from properties is fine, and its position and direction vary. A large tree is scenery. Its sets of foliage which change with the seasons are properties. A fireplace is scenery. The fire is a property. Whether an item is scenery or a property is logically decided by the technical director or stage manager. In commercial production, the designer, the carpenter, and the property man often make the decisions.

In community and school theatres the categories are very flexible. Heavy props are often treated as scenery for expeditious shifting where lack of space or personnel prohibits the use of large or multiple crews.

classification

Properties are divided into groups by size, location on the set, and use:

set props

Set props stand on the stage floor or on other properties. They include carpets, furniture, stoves, and telephones, and for outdoor scenes, anything from the snake in the grass to the coach and six.

trim props

These are set or hung on the walls of the set, and include pictures, draperies, portieres, and the practical apple hanging from the scenery tree.

hand props

Objects which are handled by the actors during the course of the

13.1 A borderline case: a torture machine (a set prop) was built by the prop department and the lift on which it was raised into position (left) was built by the scenery department and installed and operated by grips

play are classified as hand props. They include some costume accessories — a halberd, for example. Hand props are placed onstage in sight, in drawers, behind secret panels, etc., or they are arranged offstage on the prop table to be carried on by the actors. They include cigarettes, books, the stolen pearls, firearms, perambulators, food, and the head of Jokanaan on a silver charger.

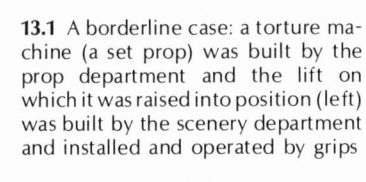
prop sound effects

All sounds created offstage by mechanical (not electrical) means, to further the dramatic purpose of the play, are prop sound effects. They may establish locale (the pounding surf, the passing train), create atmosphere (wind, rain, thunder), maintain a mood (foghorn, tolling bell), or advance the plot (shots, police whistles, sirens).

13.2 A simulated rattlesnake: sand in a painted sateen skin with a plaster head. The sound effect: a real snake's rattle on a doorbell vibrator with the bell removed

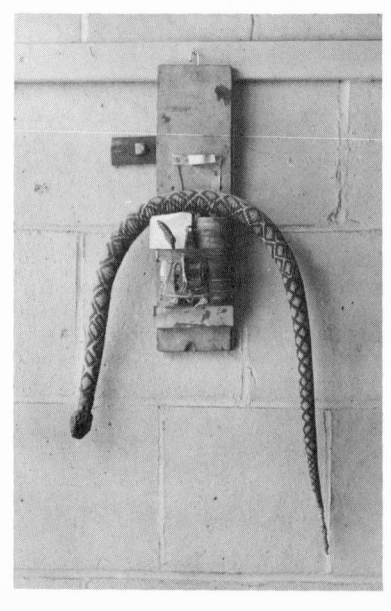

13.3 A fowling piece made in glass-reinforced plastic (fiber glass)

These are effects in which objects, materials, vapors, and the like are made to move into audience vision. They include fire (if not electrical), smoke, steam, rain, snow, and falling plaster.

From the designer, the property master gets designs and specifications for trim and set properties (see Chapter 3). From the director, the costume designer, the stage manager, the technical director, and the script, he assembles a list, together with specifications of all other props. The resultant list is assembled by categories: (1) set, trim, hand, and effect; or (2) lamps, carpets, bric-a-brac, furniture, etc.

The degree to which the scene designer must particularize the specifications for properties is indicated by the following examples:

Tables: a mechanical drawing or perspective sketch showing shape and all principal dimensions, style, historic period, and ornament; notes stating kind of wood, color tonality, finish, covering, and practical requirements, such as drawers, and practical drop leaves.

Chairs: the same as for tables plus samples of covering fabrics and trimmings, and a description of the kind of cover and each particular requirement, including the use of each chair in the action of the play (with particular attention to rough handling, such as sitting on arms, standing on seat, throwing in a fight).

Pictures: a mechanical drawing or sketch showing size and shape, size and kind of frame; position onstage (back-wall picture cannot be glazed); nature of picture (etching, print, still life, oil portrait); name of picture, if known, and appearance of picture and frame (old, new, fresh, battered, faded).

In view of these detailed requirements for props in realistic production it is not unreasonable for designers to hunt props themselves rather than to make drawings and write specifications. Nor is it to be wondered at that current styles of production include pantomiming the use of props.

A similar degree of precise information must be supplied by the stage manager in compiling the list of hand props for the property master, as, for example:

ACT II. PROP TABLE, LEFT

1. Package for George: green wrapping paper, white string, simple bowknot ON TOP. Contains box of candy (1 lb.), soft, NOT CHEWY. Three pieces eaten, fake the bottom layer.

2. Notebook for first student: large looseleaf, gray cloth cover, battered, with large block *X* on one side and fraternity letters on other. Use your own imagination for rest of decoration. Loose yellow papers sticking out at both ends.

The problem of property procurement is handled in a repertory organization by the property master assigned to the show by the technical director. In combination production and stock, the responsibility often falls to the stage manager or to some member of the producer's permanent staff; or the designer may himself shop for props. Organizations with shops and storage space have the necessary personnel and equip-

sources of information

ment for the manufacture of such props as cannot be gotten from storage or bought or otherwise procured more cheaply than they can be made.

The property master's principal problem is not getting props, or getting props that fulfill the specifications, but getting props that the director or designer will not change after the show is set up. To minimize this contingency, which almost inevitably arises, he insists on exact specifications and gets the approval of all persons concerned before and after each property is obtained.

procurement

With list and specifications (material, design, size, shape, function) complete, procurement starts. Properties are taken from storage, borrowed, rented, bought, manufactured. However obtained, they must be seen and approved by the designer before they are contracted or arranged for, or before they are moved to the stage.

from storage

Properties owned by repertory, community, school, and presentation theatres are usually stored when the show closes. In commercial production, they are sold or otherwise disposed of, or may be stored by the producer pending a revival of the play or the production of another in which they may be used. A permanent organization may own or rent storage space and employ a property custodian. If the producing organization has stored properties, the first step in procurement is obviously for the property master to go through the prop storage inventory and select such properties as fill specifications on his list, or can be altered to do so. He takes the designer to inspect the properties when he finds them. Occasionally, the designer changes specifications to fit what is available. The property master sends items to be altered or reupholstered to the shop.

borrowing

School, summer, and community theatres traditionally borrow everything they can until the lender's patience is exhausted by the nonreturn or by the return of damaged properties. Courtesy passes often aid the property man in his pleading. Amateur crews are notoriously hard on properties. Commercial productions as well as school and community productions borrow what they can and acknowledge the loan in the program. Furniture dealers cannot lend new furniture and then sell it as new. Articles such as radios, refrigerators, and sporting goods may often be borrowed from dealers for program acknowledgment. Occasionally items may be borrowed from museums. Valuable items are insured against fire, theft, and breakage, and in some cases a bond is posted to guarantee safe return. Bonds and insurance are arranged by the business manager. The property master must protect the good will of the organization among potential lenders by taking good care of properties.

renting

For short runs (school, stock, presentation), it is cheaper to rent properties than to buy or build them. Property rental organizations and secondhand furniture dealers are the sources.

buying

Articles of mass-production manufacture are generally cheaper to buy than to build, even though the items in question do not have to operate onstage. Exceptions are heavy articles such as stoves and radiators. When such articles are not practical (do not have to function), it is

13.4 A radiator imitated in wood is easier to handle than the real thing

wise to build lightweight imitations, even when imitations cost more than the genuine article, since the imitation can be shifted more easily and with fewer men than the real thing. An antique piano in *The Cat and the Fiddle* was disemboweled to save weight, and the playing faked from the orchestra pit. Many odd articles are purchased from dealers in theatrical properties. These are sometimes purchased in ten weekly payments. If the show closes in less than ten weeks, the articles are repossessed.

Antique dealers sell many items for property use. Trade discounts are occasionally available, especially from firms doing a large volume of business. School theatres may obtain educational discounts.

Manufactured properties include furniture of all periods and styles, draperies, plumbing fixtures and piping (both of which must be faked because of the great weight of the originals), pictures, chandeliers, and interior fixtures, such as cabinets, bookcases, bars, and all other prop-

manufacturing

13.5 A chandelier made of graded balls, mailing tubes and sheet metal

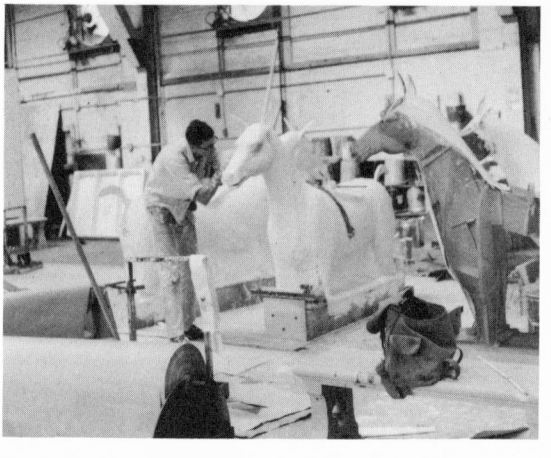

13.6 Saddle horses for *Tenderloin*, Robert Randolph, designer. Each horse is on a traverse wagon. The sculptural armature is mounted on a box which is hung on four coil springs from the corner stanchions. Wire mesh shaped over the armature is covered with padding and plaster-soaked canvas. The sculptor rides a finished mount. A ground row will conceal the unfinished lower portions

materials and substitutes

erties that cannot be procured from any of the sources discussed. A complete list would include any object that has ever been thought of by the mind of man.

The manufacture of properties is ordered according to a plan similar to the one which governs the construction of scenery. A period of experimentation must often be inserted into the procedure. Otherwise, all processes are subjected to analysis and subdivision according to construction operations, the production process formulated, and a work schedule made out.

The crafts involved in property manufacture are cabinetmaking, metalworking, upholstery, dyeing, electrical wiring and assembly, wireworking, pipe fitting, basket weaving, sculpture, plastic molding and casting, painting, and sewing. Most property makers are resourceful and highly skilled in all of these crafts.

Property materials are numberless. They include principally, all materials which are used for structural or decorative purposes. There are many standard substitutes (see Table 13.1).

TABLE 13.1. PROPERTY MATERIALS AND THEIR SUBSTITUTES

Material or Property	Substitute	Technique of Substitution or Use
alcoholic beverages	*see* liquor	
bark, tree	canvas, burlap, or paper	dipped in glue; wrinkled, molded on chicken-wire frames. *Caution:* mold around edges to prevent separation
bones	canvas or paper	same as for bark
books (in case)	binding backs, half-round molding, or book covers	glued in row on cardboard or on plywood nailed in place
branches large	paper dipped in glue over chicken wire on wood frame	paper molded on frame
small	rope or twine	sized, wound with cloth, and painted; stiffened with wire or steel rod
carved wood	*see* wood	
cauldrons	canvas or paper	same as for bark
	fiber glass molded on clay form	
earth	floorcloth	tacked down at curtain line; grommets slipped over carpet pins upstage, right and left. *Caution:* stretch tight
	padding	laid squared side down
	earth	
fabrics, expensive	cheap fabrics	dyed, stenciled, painted, lined, weighted
fixtures, stylized	canvas or paper	same as for bark
floors: wood, stone, tile	floorcloth	painted
	linoleum	glued on stage floor; covered for scenes of different locale
	Masonite	cut in blocks and glued to canvas
foliage, tree realistic	cloth (muslin) cut to leaf shapes	painted or dipped in paint or dye; hung on netting
stylized	feathers	wound on branches
	cellophane	hung from masked battens; artificial foliage on wire stems woven on chicken-wire base
food, nonpractical (roast pig, turkey, cupcake)	fiber glass	molded on clay form
frost on windowpane	Epsom salts and beer	1 handful of salts dissovled in 1 cup of beer, allowed to stand for 3 days; apply with sponge; do not allow to run

(Table continues overleaf)

13.7 Cupcakes (nonedible) simulated in fiber glass

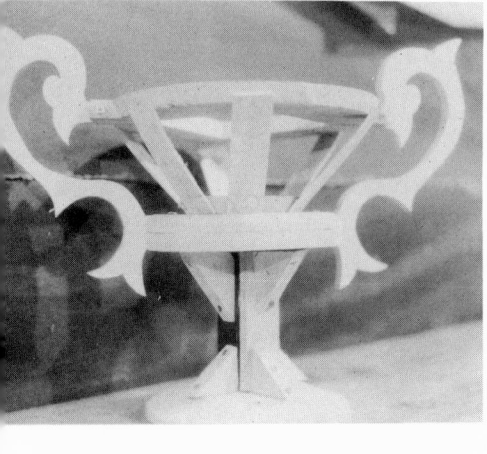

13.8 The wooden frame for an urn

13.9 The frame, now covered with hardware cloth, will next have muslin and plaster of Paris or Celastic applied as the final covering

TABLE 13.1. *PROPERTY MATERIALS AND THEIR SUBSTITUTES* (*cont.*)

Material or Property	Substitute	Technique of Substitution or Use
furniture, marble	*see* marble	
gems	standard imitations plus wire, sash chain, harness studs, cellophane	
gold hollow ware	pewter, tin, wood	gilded or painted
grass	strips of green crepe paper	sized, stippled, glued to canvas, laid on stage floor
	woven raffia or synthetic fiber mats	laid on stage floor
	molded plastic grass mat	
jewelry	*see* gems	
leaves	*see* foliage, tree	
liquor	water, cider, tea, or coffee, carbonated water; beer and light wines preferably genuine	colored for appearance; charged for effervescence; flavored for palatability; in genuine bottles
marble		molded and carved; painted for veins, shadows, cracks. *Caution:* grease molds with heavy grease before introducing or applying plaster
statuary	plastic, plaster	
furniture	wood	painted
metal	*see* gold; sheet metal; silver	
objets d'art, metal	plastic, plaster, papier-mâché	gilded or painted
paintings, oil	burlap	painted with tube oil colors and turpentine; no linseed oil
pottery	canvas or paper	dipped in glue; molded on chicken-wire frames. *Caution:* mold around edges of wire to prevent separation
rocks	fiber glass cast on clay or wire form; *see also* pottery	
sheet metal (for trim)	metal foil or Milar	glued to wood
silver hollow ware	*see* gold hollow ware	
snow		
falling	soap chips or fireproofed paper or mica flakes	shaken from gridiron or from snow cradle above stage (*see* Figure 13.32)
on ground	marble dust and corn meal	liberally laid on white velour; for hard, creaking snow, velour or canvas is heavily sized
statuary	plastic, plaster	molded and carved; painted for veins, shadows, cracks. *Caution:* grease molds with heavy grease before introducing or applying plaster

(*Table continues on page 344*)

13.10 A pagan idol designed by Ben Edwards for *Thirteen Daughters*. Top left: The side view and sections are drawn full-scale. The sections are transferred to plywood, then cut and assembled in two parts, which are clamped together preparatory to inserting bolts and wing nuts. Top right: The upper section covered with hardware cloth and plywood. Middle row, left: The lower section with final covering of canvas and plaster of Paris. Right: Shaping the hardware cloth to form the "feathers." Lower left: Rear view of the upper section with the surface completed. Lower right: The completed idol. The bolted horizontal joint is barely visible below the hands

13.11 A round lamp base turned from RPF

TABLE 13.1. PROPERTY MATERIALS AND THEIR SUBSTITUTES (cont.)

Material or Property	Substitute	Technique of Substitution or Use
steam (from non-practical kettle)	dry ice (solidified CO_2)	placed in dry pot, it gives off continuous visible vapor. *Caution:* do not handle with bare hands
stone floor	*see* floors	
tapestries	burlap	painted with aniline dyes
tile floors	*see* floors	
trees	*see* bark; foliage	
vines	*see* branches, small; foliage	
wines	*see* liquor	
wood		
carved	plastic foam, plaster, or papier-mâché	molded and painted
floor	*see* floors	

cabinetmaking

The property master must be able to repair, restore, and build anew all kinds of furniture. A working knowledge of the cabinetmaker's craft is necessary. The refinements in joinery which characterize good cabinetwork are unnecessary so long as the property possesses the correct appearance and the strength required to withstand transportation and stage use. Numerous woodworking manuals explain the basic technique, which can only be developed into proficiency by practice. The wood joints explained in Chapter 9 are used in the construction of furniture as well as scenery.

Wood for properties is the same as that used for scenery. For framing structures, white pine or similar wood; for decoration and carving, sugar pine or whitewood; for minimum weight in bulk, balsa wood, plastic

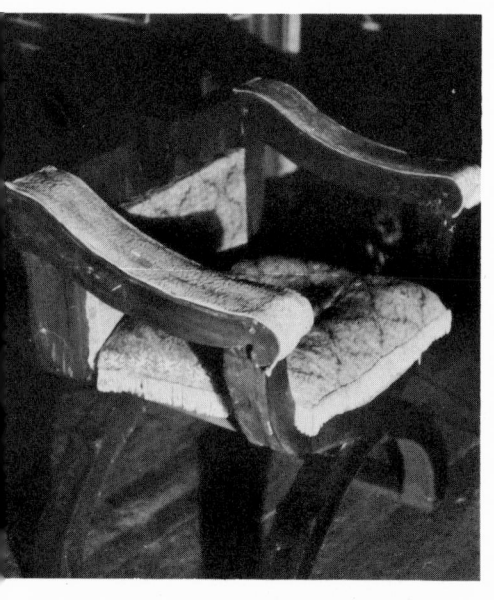

13.12 A Renaissance chair built of ¾" plywood with thickness of RPF

13.13 The frame for an Empire settee, ready to be upholstered

foam, or molded plastic. Wooden properties are stained or painted to give them the desired natural or weathered finish. Oil paint is used on surfaces which are to be handled or sat on, or on which liquids are to be spilled. Since lightness and strength are the prime requisites for wooden properties or properties which are partly of wood, joints in furniture are for the most part mortise and tenon, glued and nailed. Screws are used much more often than in scenery. Thickness, as in a plank-top table, is simulated by making the top of plywood and putting thickness pieces around the edges. Plywood bottoms may be necessary if the bottoms can be seen. An antique effect is heightened by the judicious use of the rasp and drawknife on edges.

upholstery

The craft of upholstery is important to the property maker because he must repair standard upholstered pieces as well as pad and cover pieces of furniture built in the property shop. As in cabinetwork, the demands of stage use upon upholstery differ from those exercised by everyday use. Padding, foam rubber, or even scrap cloth is used in place of springs to save bulk and construction expense. If coil springs are used to repair a piece that is not being completely rebuilt, they must be stiff and securely tied to the frame with heavy twine, top and bottom. The twine makes a rectangular pattern above and below the springs and prevents movement in any direction save that of compression. Overstuffed furniture for the stage is in reality reasonably hard. Seats are made to give only a little so that the actor will not sit in awkward positions and have to struggle to rise. Furniture which is reupholstered seldom has the old coverings removed, so that conversion to original condition is easy.

faking to reduce weight

In the discussion of bought properties, mention has been made of the desirability of manufacturing certain items in preference to buying, renting, or borrowing them. The advantages are twofold: any necessary alterations, finishes, or mutilations may be practiced upon properties owned by the organization; and props which, if real, would be of great weight may be faked in the construction to be very light and easy to handle. Methods of faking to reduce weight are as follows (see Figures 13.14–13.20):

• Simulating pottery, bottles, dishes, and carved stone, casts, metal ornaments, and statuary in paper, plastic foam, thermoplastic, or fiber glass.

• Fabricating in lightweight woods, wallboard, and plywood any pieces of heavy furniture, such as rolltop desks, highboys, and refectory tables. Omitting drawers, drawer rails; simulating drawer fronts.

• Building all planks and table legs hollow by using thin lumber on two sides and plywood on the other two, or by using plastic foam on structural cores.

• Substituting cotton duck surfaces for wood surfaces wherever there is no danger of denting.

• Leaving open and unfinished the upstage sides and backs of pieces which stand against the set.

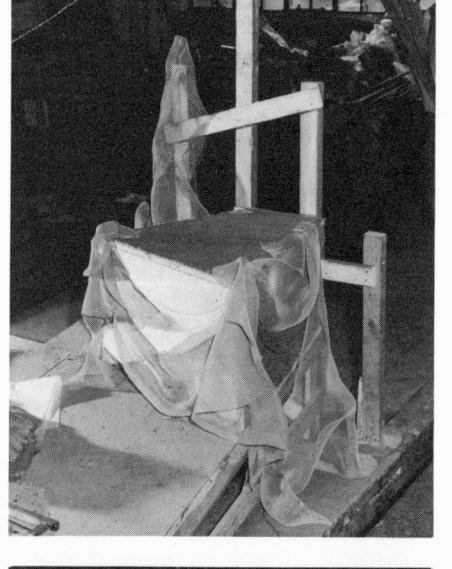
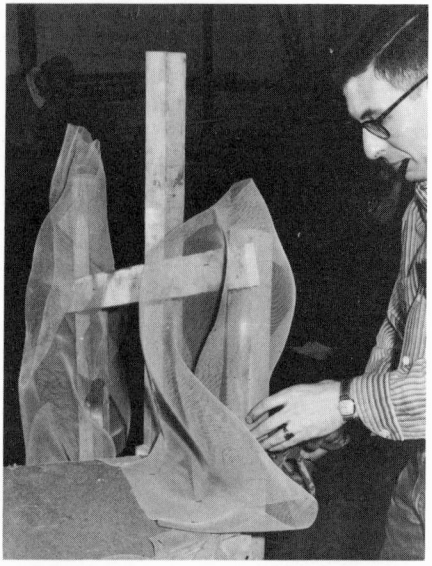

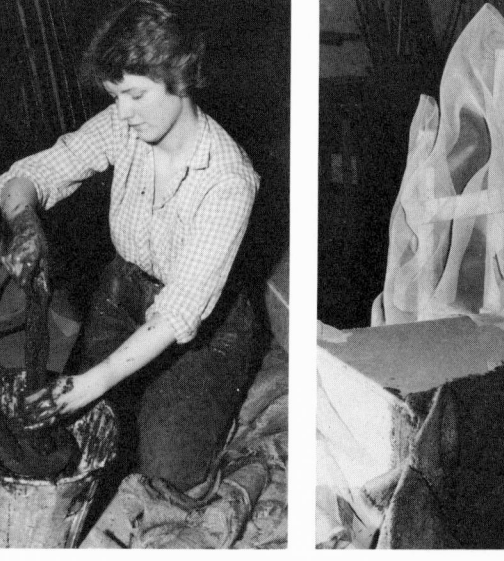
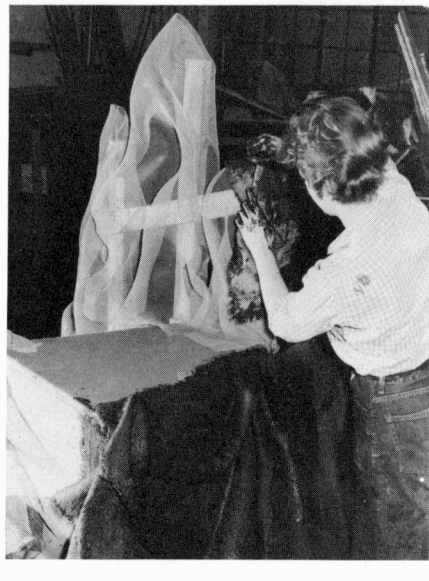
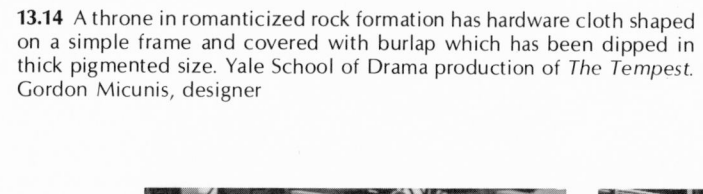

13.14 A throne in romanticized rock formation has hardware cloth shaped on a simple frame and covered with burlap which has been dipped in thick pigmented size. Yale School of Drama production of *The Tempest.* Gordon Micunis, designer

13.15 (*left*) The jeep in *A Cook for Mr. General.* Will Steven Armstrong, designer. Made of wood and plywood for ease in handling, the jeep was mobile but had no engine

13.16 (*right*) A simulated sports car was built in four pieces for shipping

13.17 An ancient cannon: rear view (*left*) and what the audience sees (*right*)

13.18 A half bottle in papier-mâché using a female mold

13.19 Many papier-mâché half bottles fastened to the shelves of a backbar are unbreakable and add little weight

13.20 A giant scallop shell which opens to disclose a human occupant. Designed by Will Steven Armstrong for *Caligula*

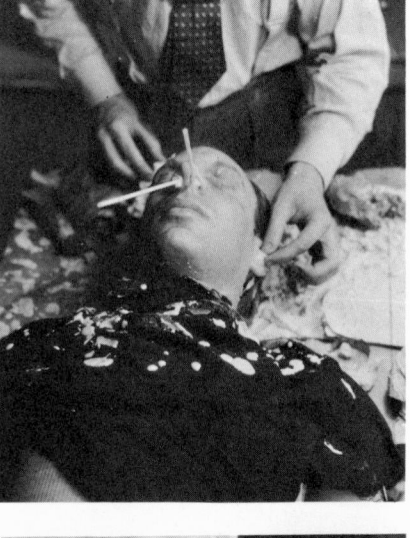

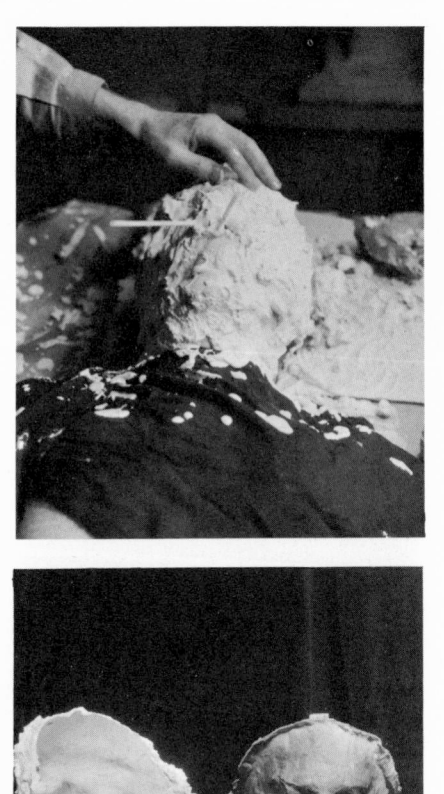

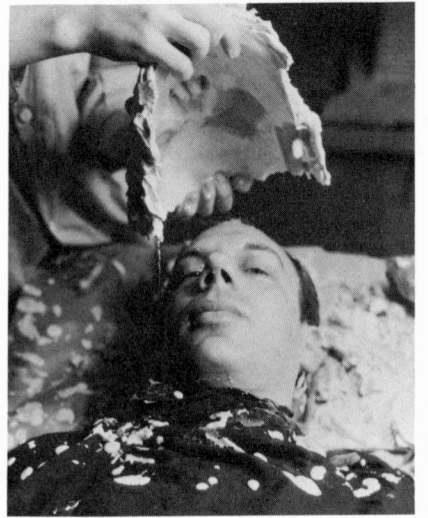

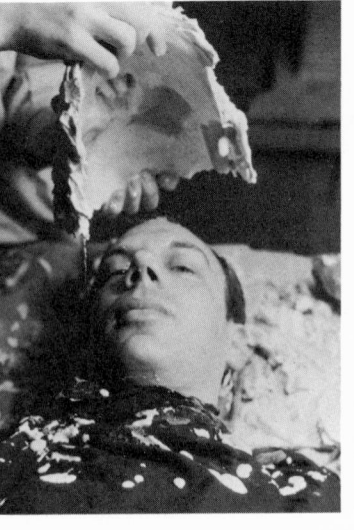

13.21 Making a life mask. Top left: Cotton and breathing tubes in the nostrils; face, eyebrows, and edge of hair greased. Top right: Plaster in place. Lower left: Removing the cast. Lower right: The papier-mâché mask. Other materials which may be used following the same procedure are Celastic and posmoulage—a mixture of plastic and latex

fabrication in paper

A single object is molded on a base of wire, wire screen, chicken wire, or clay as described in Problem 70, Chapter 15. Objects which require duplication are first patterned in clay on which a plaster of Paris cast is made. In the cast several images of the pattern are made. When the required number of reproductions is great, several casts are made on the original pattern, to speed the output. Twenty-four hours' time is required for drying each paper reproduction. Paper is the material of manufacture because of its ready absorption of adhesive agents and because of its cheapness and relative strength. The adhesive may be wheat paste, thin glue, or quick-drying cement. When price is a factor, the wheat paste (which dries slowly) is used. The inside of the plaster cast is coated with soap solution before the paper is put in.

draperies

Window draping is an important part of the property master's work. Full instruction, and specifications of materials are supplied by the scene designer. In combination production, the draperies for the set are sometimes let out on contract to decorators, sometimes made by the property maker under the scene designer's supervision.

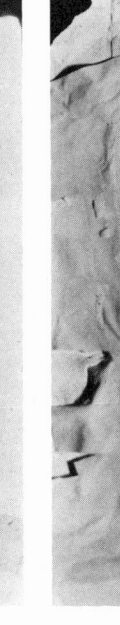

a Clay model　　　　　　**b** Plaster cast from the clay　　　　　**c** Paper in the cast

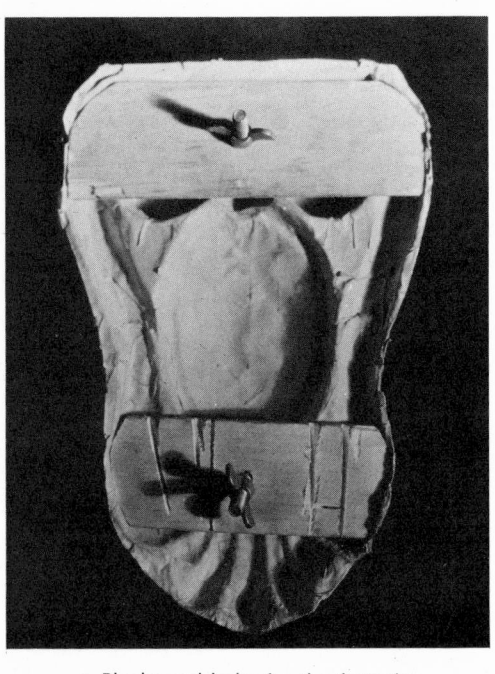

d Paper removed from the cast　　　　**e** Blocks and bolts for the fastening

13.22 A FIREPLACE ORNAMENT

f The ornament in place　　　　*349*

13.23 The canopy of the bed in the first act of *Arms and the Man* upon which Captain Blunschli climbs to hide. It is framed in welded steel pipe

13.24 Blunschli in hiding

Real or substitute materials may be used. Brocades and tapestries are faked by stenciling or painting flat fabrics. Full-bodied materials are imitated with thin materials over heavy, cheap linings. The material is dyed to supply the exact color submitted in sample by the designer. A shrinkage allowance of about 1″ to 1′ of both length and width must be made in estimating material to be dyed. Fabric is dyed in the piece and cut when dry.

The secret of good appearance in draping windows lies in the provision of plenty of extra material, called fullness. The minimum fullness to be allowed is 50 percent, that is, half again the width of the window. Adequate fullness is 100 percent and luxurious fullness is from 200 to 300 percent. The fullness is made into the heading (top) of curtains and draperies by flat pleats or pinch pleats. Curtains with headings exposed to view are finished with pinch pleats and the headings are reinforced with buckram.

The bottoms of curtains are weighted with chain, washers, or dressmaker's tape weights, to make them hang in straight folds. The weights are attached so that they do not rest on the floor. Draperies hung with fullness often have shadows painted on them. They are hung in position as they will appear onstage, and are painted with paint or hot dye. A lining brush is used.

Window curtains and draperies for stage use are seldom affixed to the scenery with standard domestic fixtures, because of the ever-present necessity of removing them and because on the stage attaching devices can be crude and not show. Curtains which are to be drawn are hung on standard domestic tracks, which are attached to battens, which are in turn fastened to the scenery. Wooden curtain rings are hung on wooden curtain poles, but the poles are attached to the scenery with stage drapery hangers, not with interior decorator's brackets.

Whenever possible with curtains which do not draw, the fabric is tacked in gathers to wooden battens, which are then attached to the scenery with flush hangers. Flimsy wire or metal curtain rods are taboo. Curtains hung from valance boards are tacked inside the valance board, and the board is attached to the scenery. Like portraits, cornices, or panels, heavy valance boards may be set into the scenery and fastened with loose-pin hinges on the back.

A few of the conventions governing the use of window curtains and draperies must be mentioned:

• Casement curtains are made of lightweight opaque material and are hung from draw tracks, valance boards, or battens inside the window thickness. They hang to clear the sill.

• Glass curtains (lace or net) are either stretched tight in folds on two battens attached to French windows, doors, or casement windows; or hung in loose folds from a batten inside the window thickness, to clear the sill; or hung loose in folds on battens attached to the face of the window trim. They are long enough to reach the bottom of the window apron or the floor and are made with pleated headings, valances, or cornice boards.

• Overdraperies hang in loose folds from battens, poles, or valances or cornice boards. They may hang straight, be draped in a variety of ways, or be tied back. They may or may not draw across the window. They are long enough to reach to the bottom of the window apron, to touch the floor, or to break and drape on the floor.

The property master puts the bottoms of curtains in protective *chafing bags* (duck bags with a drawstring at the top) when the set is not in use. Curtains which are flown on scenery are tied close to the scenery before flying to prevent their fouling other flown pieces or lights.

pictures

Both real and imitative paintings, prints, and photographs are used for trim. The scene designer decides which type to use. Real pictures sometimes possess too much color and too much attention value; sometimes not enough. Sometimes it is useless to attempt to find the picture the script prescribes, and economical both of time and money to make one.

breakaway props

Breakaway properties must break convincingly, be safe to use, be reassembleable or cheaply and easily reproduced in quantity. Chapter 5 sets forth the principles and technique of building breakaway scenery. Properties follow the same rules. Furniture is taken apart at breakpoints and reassembled with toothpicks as dowels or with thin wood slats under the collapsing seat. The mirror on the dressing table and the whisky bottle with which the villain (or hero) is knocked out are molded-candy glass or resin. The vase is thin plaster of Paris. Not all breakaways sound convincing, so the impact may need a backstage sound backup, a function of prop sound effects.

thermoplastics

When many copies of one design are needed, when the original object is rare, unique, or fragile, or when other handicraft methods of duplicating objects are more time-consuming, multiple images may be thermoformed from one mold or more rapidly from several molds made from one master. Bottles, clock cases, watch fobs, furniture, stoves, plaques, picture frames, spearheads, halberds, swords and daggers, book backs, rocks, plants, trees, in fact almost any artifact, can be simulated in thermoplastic materials.

food

Stage food is seldom what the script says it is, but it must always be palatable and easily chewed. Certain simple rules, if followed by the prop man in charge of food, can save actors uncomfortable and disconcerting experiences and protect the health of the cast. The same rules apply in a measure to drinks served upon the stage.

• Hot foods that are not to be eaten may be as steamy as the director wishes.

• Steaming hot dishes of food may be simulated by a lump of solid CO_2 placed in a shallow warm dish. This obviates cooking and the handling of hot dishes by actors.

• Hot food to be eaten must be tested for temperature before it is taken onstage. It is better for the property man to burn his mouth than the leading lady to burn hers.

• Stage food must never be highly seasoned.

• Stage food must never be dry or hard to chew. Crackers are taboo. Sandwiches of fresh bread and moist jelly can be made up and shaped to represent many types of food. Canned fish is a successful imitation for many other foods and is inexpensive. Canned vegetables are soft, moist, and easily swallowed.

• Potatoes in any form, peanut butter, and any other pasty foods are to be avoided.

• Meat must be tender.

• Odorous foods must not be cooked inside the theatre.

It is not always necessary to supply drinks. If there is absolute as- **drinks**
surance that no one in the audience will know the difference, liquids
should not be used. Pouring from an empty vessel is, however, seldom
convincingly done or completely masked from the audience.

Tea, coffee, light wines, and beer are preferably genuine. Champagne presents a difficult problem to the property man because the
cork must pop resoundingly if the audience is to be convinced. A champagne bottle partly filled with dry ginger ale, tightly corked, and shaken
slightly, gives a good imitation. Other sparkling beverages, especially
those which are highly carbonated, are best opened offstage and re-
capped if necessary, to avoid spilling or too much foam.

Imitation liquor must be carefully concocted and tested for color
under playing lights. The actor's taste must be consulted. It may be
hard enough for him to smack his lips or shudder without having a
mouthful of something which prompts him to do the opposite. Tea,
coffee, syrup of caramel, lemon juice, cider, water, and sugar are the
standard ingredients. Fresh drinks must be made for every performance.

A time has been arranged in the production timetable when each **trimming the set with props**
set is to be trimmed with props. This time ranges from a quarter hour
to six or eight hours, depending upon the quantity and nature of the
trim. When the time arrives, all props for the set must have been
brought to the stage and the stage carpenter must be in attendance to
handle and make any necessary alterations to the scenery. The property
crew places and attaches all trim properties under the watchful and
critical eye of the scene designer. The technical director and property
master work out together the arrangement for attaching trim props to
the sets. The technical director specifies toggles in the scenery for the
attachment of the properties, and for the support of any heavy items.

The property master places hanging hardware on all items in advance of the time that sets are trimmed so that a minimum of time will
be occupied in actual trimming on the stage. Picture hooks are attached
to small pictures and to all other flat or nearly flat hanging objects, and
sockets to the toggles in the scenery. All trim that may be attached
permanently to the scenery is fitted with bolts and wing nuts or loose-
pin hinges. Large, heavy pictures are securely built into the scenery. An
opening, slightly smaller than the picture, is made in the flat to which
the picture is to be attached. Blocks or battens which just fit into the
opening are attached to the back of the picture frame. The blocks carry
halves of loose-pin hinges; the flat framework which surrounds the opening carries the other halves.

If the trim properties are to fly with the scenery, nails are driven into
the frame of the flat just above each one to prevent it from being fouled
out of its socket by other scenery.

Set props must be tested in rehearsal for suitability to the action as
early as possible to allow time for changes and adjustments. But they
must not be used in all subsequent rehearsals for two reasons: they may
become worn and soiled; and property men must be on duty to handle
them. Set props are placed as directed by the stage manager to conform

13.25 A colonial tavern bar (set prop) on lift jacks

13.26 The crystal chandelier is lowered into a castered crate for careful handling onstage

to positions determined in rehearsal. When the positions have been tested in a dress rehearsal, they are marked on the floorcloth.

Heavy properties (chests, stoves, refrigerators) are mounted on concealed dollies or tip jacks. Stage hardware manufacturers make a grand-piano truck for stage use. Piano casters are rubber-tired for quiet rolling. All valuable furniture of any considerable weight should be moved on caster dollies to obviate the hazards inherent in manhandling. See Figures 13.25 and 13.26.

miscellany

Candles must be burned offstage before setting them. Candles previously unlighted ignite with difficulty and burn irregularly for a while. Mica chimneys reduce the fire hazard and promote even burning.

Ash trays are preferably deep and, whenever possible, automatically extinguishing. Smoking butts are to be avoided offstage and on. A little water in the bottom of each tray extinguishes butts quickly.

Cellophane wrappers must be removed from props unless specifically called for. They might delay the act. All packages, bundles, and the like are carefully wrapped and tied to make opening easy.

Properties are to be used only by the actors. The crew must not sit on prop chairs, recline on prop divans, experiment with prop cigar lighters.

maintenance and operation

In addition to the properties themselves, the property master obtains items of equipment needed to maintain the properties and keep the stage clean:

• Prop tables on which hand props are arranged offstage during performance.

- Dust covers and protective pads for furniture and bric-a-brac.
- Trunks for storage of some props onstage.
- Before tour, trunks, crates, and pads for prop shipment.
- Electric heating units, fireless cookers, and a refrigerator for keeping food in proper condition for performance.
- Dishwashing equipment.
- A daily supply of clean table linen.
- Mops, brooms, vacuum cleaners, soap, and towels for cleaning stage and props.

He arranges for the daily purchase of food to be consumed onstage, and purchases adequate quantities of items to be destroyed in performances (vases, statues, crockery, bric-a-brac).

In addition to the tasks listed, the property master is responsible for the cleaning of the stage floor and carpet, dusting and polishing the props, and, in commercial production, for maintaining the seats in the house.

The bird in *The Blue Bird* is a prop and is flown on fishline or wire by prop men. In *Peter Pan* property animals (Nana and the crocodile) are properties when stored but contain actors when they work. Tinkerbell is a light, sometimes operated by an assistant stage manager.

Prestidigitation, necromancy, and legerdemain, when practiced on the stage, have prop apparatus: specially designed cabinets, chests, mirrors, transparencies, equipment for disappearances, flying, and levitation. Some of this apparatus is of secret design and in America may be built and operated only by a registered member of the American Society of Magicians. The property master or technical director often has to contrive workable substitutes for secret apparatus, or by standard stage techniques achieve effects which will baffle the audience.

Special Stage Effects

Modern theatre audiences expect the contemporary stage to present believable phenomena at the proper scale within any visually acceptable environment. Effects must support the dramatic situation. Increased sophistication of effects in other media such as motion pictures and television motivates careful treatment of effects on the live stage, although certain classic production styles such as the Restoration are expected by audiences to employ the stereotyped devices characteristic of their form of the theatre.

Traditionally, the prop man handles effects. However, electronic sound control has bred the sound technician, and several departments may be involved in handling some effects. A fireplace is scenery and so is a funeral pyre, but the fire is a property. An electrician installs the fire light and hooks it up, the prop man supplies the flickering flame (chiffon), and the sound technician supplies the crackle of the burning wood; in television, a special effects man does the whole job.

The visual effect may provide its own sound (live falling rain) or no sound at all (quiet snowfall), or it may require a sound-effects backup

jurisdiction

13.27 A typewriter-missile. When the right key is pressed the machine shoots the carriage off its track to strike an actor sitting at the other end of the desk

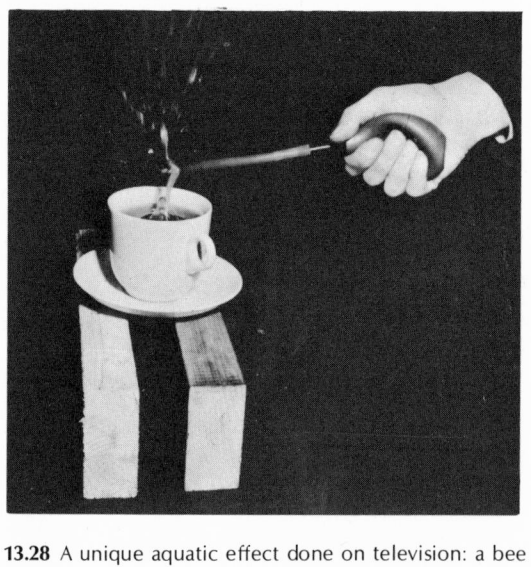

13.28 A unique aquatic effect done on television: a bee diving into a cup of coffee. Trained bees are scarce. The effect involves a sound effect (the buzz of the bee), pantomime by the actor, and the deft squeeze of a syringe by a prop man, off-camera

(a simulated sizable explosion). If an item is not clearly a recognizable prop, scenic element, or regular lighting instrument but must function in a practical manner, it must then be a special effect.

Stage effects may be divided into the following general categories:

- **Atmospherics:** snow, rain, fog, wind or other weather disturbances.
- **Pyrotechnics:** fire, explosions, smoke and allied items.
- **Practical aquatics:** running faucets, garden fountains, pools, etc.
- **Mechanical devices:** items more complex than ordinary props. They must be especially designed and built to order.
- **Lighting effects:** moving or animated effects. Clouds, rain, moving electric signs.
- **Sound:** the voice of the Great Boyg in *Peer Gynt,* the offstage parade, the nightingale.

atmospherics

Fog is probably the most difficult effect to produce because of its volatile nature and because of the critical variables present in the atmos-

13.29 A rain-collecting pan and dry-ice fog

phere. Temperature, humidity, and air currents all affect its production and sustenance. In addition, the lighting of all atmospherics is critical if they are to be visible to the audience. Clouds are essentially identical to fog and are produced and controlled in the same manner.

Two basic kinds of fog — dry-ice fog and oil fog — are produced in theatre and on sound stages (Figures 13.30–13.31).

dry-ice fog

Carbon dioxide in solid, frozen form (dry ice) evaporates when exposed to temperatures above its freezing point. This rapid evaporation produces a cooling effect by condensing the moisture in the air and producing a heavy white vapor. The effect is considerably enhanced by bringing the carbon dioxide in contact with live steam which is at high temperature. This produces the characteristic heavier-than-air white cloud or fog. The same effect may be produced by immersing pieces of dry ice in pails of boiling water. The fog will continue to be generated as long as any dry ice remains and the water temperature remains high.

CO_2 fog is nontoxic and has no objectionable odor. Mains, where available, may permit the piping of live steam into the theatre or self-contained commercial steam generators of 5,000-watt capacity may be used. The steam may then be passed over closed containers of cracked dry ice. Tubes large in diameter may be added and masked onstage to channel the vapor to desired locations.

Dry-ice (CO_2) fog, being heavier than air, hugs the stage floor and is excellent for the effect of walking on clouds. It must be agitated by air currents (fans) if it is to rise above the floor.

oil fog

Oil is vaporized, burned, and passed over dry ice to create a light, gray, smokelike product. The essential parts of the fog machine are a sprayer filled with mineral oil which is directed through the coils of a heating element. The oil is partially burned and converted into smoke at this point. The smoke is blown over a basket of dry ice to cool it and direct it to the desired location. Oil-vapor fog can be made to hang nicely in the air. Temperature is controlled by the heater and by the speed of the fan enclosed in the unit. Compressed nitrogen operates the

13.31 Oil-fog generator controls. Left: nitrogen tank, valve and gauges. Right: heat control (*top*); fan switch (*below*)

13.30 An oil-fog generator

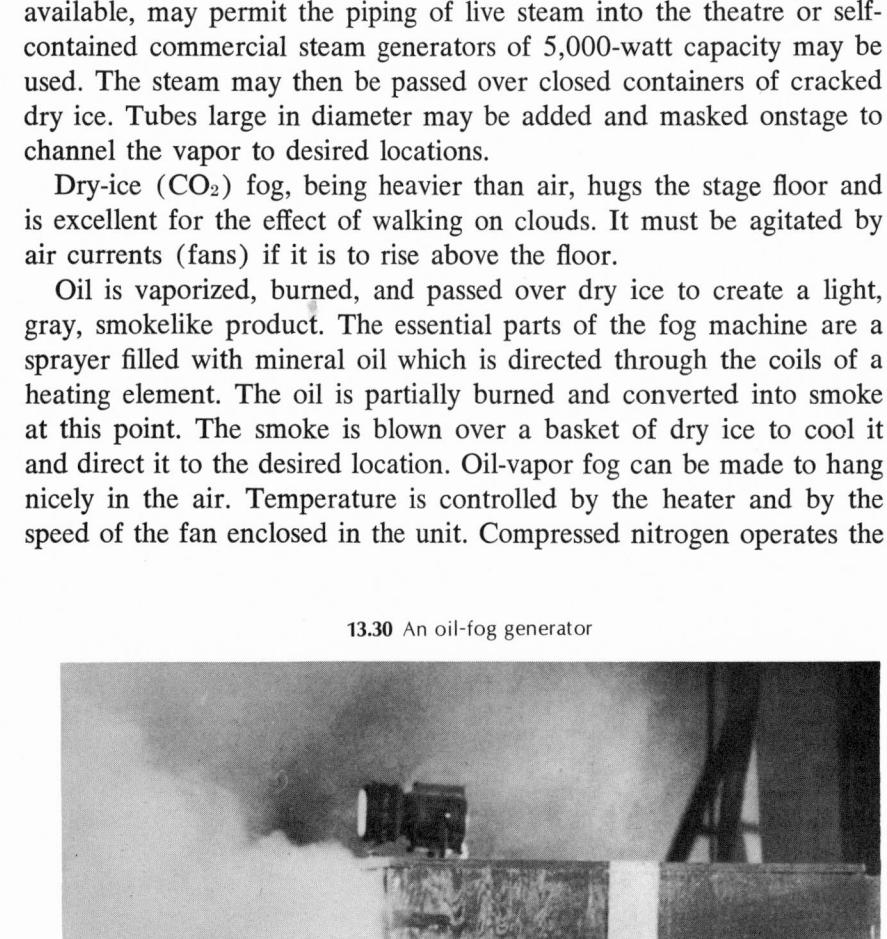

spray gun. This type of fog has an odor and its production must be carefully controlled to be certain that no raw oil is sprayed into the atmosphere where it may be inhaled by actors and cause lung damage.

Opening the smoke doors in the roof of the stagehouse will cause an updraft with two beneficial effects: the fog swirls in the air currents and odorous fog is kept out of the house.

Drafts and major temperature variations on the stage will quickly destroy the production of any fog or render it ineffectual. CAUTION: Don't open loading doors while it is in use!

rain   Rain may be simulated, but there is no substitute for the wet product. The most efficient unit consists of a rain pipe flown overhead which is fed by a sump-type immersion pump. The pump is placed directly in a collecting pan below the rain pipe. This recirculating system eliminates long hoses to sinks and drains, which in many cases are inaccessible to the stage. The trough is lined with hair felt to minimize the sound of the rain striking its surface.

Scenery which may be wet by this effect must have waterproof paint on the good side and plastic covers on the back.

Where an exterior rain must fall, as in a street scene, the collecting pans must be concealed by platforms and covered over with porous material. Rain seen through openings in interior sets does not present this problem since scenic elements conceal the rain apparatus which is outside the door or window opening.

A dry simulation of rain is a drop made of many narrow strips of polyethylene film. When crosslighted and agitated slightly, they give the appearance of rain falling. Polyethylene also simulates a waterfall when it is wound off one horizontal drum onto another, under crosslighting.

Rain of the type suitable for a musical comedy number may be quite satisfactorily of the dry variety. No pumps or hose are required if the rain is projected on the scenic background by means of an effects projector.

clouds   Moving clouds may be created on the sky by light projections. Ripples on water, a volcanic eruption, the rising moon, may be created in similar fashion.

The effects projector usually consists of a spotlight in front of which a large glass or plastic disc is made to rotate slowly by an electric motor drive. A second lens makes it possible to focus the image on the desired surface. The clouds, rain, or other designs are painted or photographed on the revolving disc.

snow   Snow was produced for many years by sifting paper confetti from a snow cradle in the flies (a piece of slotted muslin stretched between two battens) upon little Eva. Today we can do better: pulverized plastic foam is white, lightweight, and three-dimensional. It provides realistic dressing, for it piles up like snow. Snow which will melt consists of shaved ice. It melts appropriately on garments, but it is too heavy to fall realistically. To guide the falling snow, wind is produced by electric fans with deflectors. Large but slow-speed units must be employed to minimize fan noise.

13.32 A snow drum. The flakes escape through the ½″ mesh screen when the drum, flown above the acting area, is revolved slowly by an electric motor. In another snow machine, not illustrated, an endless rubber belt carries snow from a hopper into a breeze made by an electric fan

flames

Cold flames may be produced by setting a spotlight behind an electric fan, which blows plastic or chiffon streamers vertically into the air. The flickering effect of fire on surrounding scenery is achieved by light projection.

pyrotechnics
smoke

The stock, small-scale smoke-producing device for the stage is the electric *smoke pot*. This is a hot plate built into a metal box with a metal top or tray upon which theatrical smoke powder is placed. Conventionally, this powder is a mixture of incense and ammonium chloride or another nonexplosive chemical which produces smoke when heated. Smoke pots may be concealed and turned on from the switchboard in anticipation of the smoke cue.

Smoke machines similar to the oil-fog machine described under "Atmospherics" in the previous pages provide an effect on a larger scale. The devices must be safe, not capable of starting a fire and must produce nontoxic smoke with little obnoxious odor.

fire

Fire laws, practical considerations, and safety dictate what materials may be used to produce live fire on the theatre stage. The most convenient flame-producing fuel, as well as the safest, is jellied alcohol, marketed as Sterno. The only modification it requires is the introduction of an agent to make the flames visible. The readily available agent is sodium chloride (common table salt), which colors the flame yellow. Some fire codes permit bottled gas to be used as fuel in approved burners. The burners and the connecting hose must be concealed. Logs, whether gas burners or fitted with cavities for Sterno must be completely fireproofed. So must adjacent portions of scenery and properties. A man armed with a fire extinguisher and wearing asbestos gloves must stand by every time a live flame is used.

13.33 A jellied alcohol (Sterno) flame made visible by the addition of table salt

13.34 A shell burst

lightning

Lightning units consist of banks of photofloods or other high-intensity lamps wired together so that they may be quickly switched on and off, or of lightning shutters on spotlights, or strobe lights, or a d.c. arc lightning striker.

explosions

Like most items on the stage, explosions are not what they appear to be and are designed entirely for dramatic effect. Some explosions may even be produced without the benefit of pyrotechnics. Spring-loaded dust or dry-powder capsules, breakaway sections of scenery, and debris loaded in traps flown overhead may in combination with sound effects produce a very convincing explosion with no ignition or combustion.

Flash of light. The flash pot consists of a metal box containing an insulated piece of material upon which to place the combustible charge. Fuse wire is connected across the terminals passing through the charge. When a 110-volt current is passed through the wire, it melts, igniting the flash powder. The common photographer's flash powder is magnesium with an oxidizing agent added. When ignited, it produces a flash accompanied with a white puff of smoke. This is the familiar effect used by magicians.

Sparks shower. More realistic explosions may be simulated by adding other elements. Iron filings added to the flash powder will produce a shower of yellow sparks. Partially confining the charge within paper cartridges or lightly sealed tubes will heighten the effect. Lycopodium powder when dispersed in the air will burn spectacularly with a bright yellow flame when ignited. Magnesium, lycopodium, and iron filings are all inert materials and cannot ignite themselves or become chemically unstable. Gunpowder or any other true explosive must not be used.

Shell bursts. Fuller's earth or vermiculite may be loaded on top of charges where a shell burst or similar effect is wanted.

practical aquatics
running water

A sink or tub faucet may be made practical by a simple gravity-feed system. A tank of convenient size is hung on the back of the supporting flat and connected by a rubber hose to the faucet fitting. Fountains may be rented, purchased, or built to meet the particular problem. A small circulating pump and motor, a length of rubber hose, and a suitable jet (or jets) and basin connected back to the pump make up the system.

pools

Small pools of the woodland or garden variety may be built with pans, plastic sheets, or waterproof tarpaulins built into earth mounds dressed with grass mats or with simulated rocks or masonry.

sound

Sound in the theatre, whether live, recorded, or electronically generated, has six general characteristics:

• Intensity: the amount of sound energy measured at a given moment; often called volume and confused with loudness. It is measured in decibels (db).

• Frequency (pitch): ranging from subsonic sounds, which are felt rather than heard, to ultrasonic sounds, which are too high to be heard by the human ear. The audible range, roughly from 20 to 16,000 cycles per second, is slightly greater than that of the piano.

• Quality: the relationship in intensity and frequency between fundamental tones and their harmonics.

• Direction: the apparent direction, fixed or moving, from which the sound comes.

• Distance: the apparent distance from which the sound comes. It is a function of intensity, frequency, quality, and direction. (Direction and distance changes are illustrated in the Doppler effect.)

• Form: the real or apparent reverberation or lack of it.

required knowledge
of sound

The director must understand the production and distribution of sound, and its psychological (therefore dramatic) uses and limitations if he is to stage his play well. The technical director, actor, musician, electrician, sound technician, and property man must know the characteristic capabilities and limitations of their sound-producing and distributing apparatus, to give the director what he wants. Technical director and sound technician must understand the acoustical characteristics of house, stage, and settings, or they will encounter difficulties in many productions. Generally speaking, at the time of this writing, theatre designers are not specialists in acoustics, and the personnel of producing organizations, even those devoted exclusively to opera, know little about the science of sound. In the theatre the conventionalized sound is standard. Nonrealistic but artistically appropriate sound is seldom attained.

For conventional realism in sound, that is, recognizable sound, which is the type most often required, two principles must guide all efforts: there is no substitute for high fidelity (in the strict, not the commercial sense); and sounds with characteristics other than what seem in the auditorium to be natural are not convincing.

Traditionally, the property master makes and operates sound-effect machines. In commercial production, these machines are obtained from property-manufacturing concerns. Some companies which make stage-lighting instruments also make prop sound apparatus.

Table 13.2 lists the most common mechanical sound effects.

TABLE 13.2. MECHANICAL SOUND EFFECTS

Effect	Apparatus	Technique of Operation
airplane	*see* automobile	
animal noises	made vocally by a specialist in the craft; wind instruments sometimes used for frogs, cattle, poultry; special whistles for bird calls	
	for sound of bull, dog, lion, etc., a bull roarer; a can, piece of sheet metal, wood, fiber, or drumhead, to which is attached a resined string or thong; materials vary with sound required	draw thong taut; rub with resined cloth
artillery	*see* thunder	
automobile	snare drum	roll
	metal barrel with calfskin stretched tightly over one end; calfskin is struck by a buckskin thong which is attached to the shaft of a variable-speed motor; knotted ends of thong describe a circle when motor is run; circle slightly intersects plane of drum; different motor sounds are produced by varying the impact of the thong on the drum and by varying the speed of the motor	run motor
bells	bells, pipe chimes, lengths of pipe, automobile brake drums, or any suitably pitched piece of metal hung free in a frame	strike
bombs	where fire regulations permit: smokeless powder bombs made up in heavy cardboard, plus squibs, batteries, wire, metal barrel	set squib in bomb, wire to current source; place bomb in barrel; to fire, close circuit. *Caution:* disconnect both wires from current source and firing switch before wiring squib; one man only does all wiring
	metal barrel, 12-gauge double-barreled shotgun, blank shells	fire shotgun into barrel; both barrels may be fired simultaneously if necessary. *Caution:* piece is loaded just before firing by man who fires; shells are kept in his, and only his, possession
	heavy padded weight	drop on reverberant floor
chimes	*see* bells	

TABLE 13.2. MECHANICAL SOUND EFFECTS (*continued*)

Effect	Apparatus	Technique of Operation
crashes, wood	a spiked drum mounted in a frame; slats are fastened in one end of frame and rest snugly against drum at loose end	rotate drum with crank
	slapstick and lattice (thunder board)	strike a number of boards with one stroke of the stick
	laths set up in a slotted plank like an open picket fence	break laths with hammer
door slam	door in frame	fairly obvious
	wooden chest	slam lid
	3' piece of 1″ × 3″	place end on floor, press downward on that end with foot; hold other end away from floor; release
elevated	*see* train of cars	
explosions	*see* bombs	
fire	crumbled piece of cellophane held in hand; sound system	manipulated near microphone to produce crackling sound
gas, escaping	compressed air	valve
	tacks and small metal chute	pour tacks down chute
glass crash	box of broken glass	drop the box. *Caution:* when glass is broken onstage, prop men wear gloves and tight-fitting goggles; a cloth is laid to catch broken glass where practical
hail	rain drum (*see* rain)	revolve rapidly
hoof beats, cavalry	coconut shells	strike together or against a flat surface in cadence; padded surface used to simulate footfalls on earth; various materials give different pitches
horn	*see* whistle	
industrial noises	chain run through blocks, ratchets, riveting machines, electric hammer, etc.	operate in conventional manner; pound pipes, floor, pinrail, etc.
locomotive	snare drum, wire brushes	beat or rub the side, rim, or head of the drum with the brushes
	sandpaper mounted on blocks	rub two pieces together
	trombone	remove mouthpiece; blow in cadence
	sheet metal, 2' × 2'; wire brushes	beat sheet with the brushes
	shot in dishpan covered by another pan	shake
machine gun	*see* crashes, wood (1)	

(*Table continues overleaf*)

TABLE 13.2. *MECHANICAL SOUND EFFECTS* (*continued*)

Effect	Apparatus	Technique of Operation
marching feet	a square frame, 2′ × 2′–4′ within which is stretched a string net of 1½″ mesh; a ½″–1″ dowel stick, 4″–6″ long, is hung from each string intersection	raise and lower frame in cadence, so dowel ends strike a surface of whatever reverberant characteristics are desired
	bass drum or kettledrum	strike in cadence with a number of padded drumsticks
metal crash	a metal barrel, can, or tub full of scrap hardware	drop can or tub, or pour scrap from one container to another
	junk chute; a rough metal chute, 60° to horizontal, 10′–30′ long	pour junk metal down chute
motorboat	*see* automobile	
music	offstage musicians or orchestra	
rain	shallow metal plate containing handful of dried peas or rice	oscillate plate
	perforated pipe over trough equipped with drain	run water through pipe
	rain drum: a barrel or drum mounted on a frame on bearings, so it can revolve on its long axis; longitudinal slats set 2″–6″ apart on inner surface; dried beans, peas, or rice placed in barrel	revolve barrel
	rain chute: dried beans in bag which tapers to 1″ opening hung over hopper; hopper opens into chute 4′–15′ long and 6″–12″ square; top and bottom of chute are of canvas; sides, of wood; bottom canvas crossed by slats placed inside, 4″–10″ apart; tub at bottom of chute to catch beans; chute 45°–60° to horizontal	hold small end of bag in hand; release grasp to allow beans to run into hopper
shots	pistols, shotguns; some stage weapons are constructed to fire blank ammunition only	*see* caution under "artillery"
	leather-covered chair cushion, suitcase, or stretched hide; switches	beat cushion, suitcase, or hide with switches
sirens	the genuine articles when possible	operate by hand power or electrically. *Caution:* make certain correct current is used
steam, escaping	*see* gas, escaping	
subway	*see* train of cars	
surf	*see* thunder drum and barrel; rain	
	teeter trays: similar to goldwashing cradles; dried beans or peas placed in tray	rock floor of tray through 100°
	rain drum (*see* rain)	rock slowly

TABLE 13.2. MECHANICAL SOUND EFFECTS (continued)

Effect	Apparatus	Technique of Operation
thunder	16- to 24-gauge galvanized sheet metal, 30″–36″ × 6′–14′, battened top and bottom hung offstage	shake bottom batten, beat sheet with mallet or hammer; pitch varies with gauge, area, and violence of shaking
	sheet profile board, hung offstage	shake or beat like sheet metal above
	thunder drum: hide stretched on rigid wooden frame, about 3′ × 4′, with resonant chamber underneath	beat with padded mallet (must be heated before using; an electric light bulb will suffice)
	drum-ended resonating barrel; pitch varies with diameter and length	beat with padded mallet; pitch varies with distance of blow from center of drum; intensity varies with power of blow
	rumble wagon: a small wagon with hexagonal wheels, heavily weighted	roll on reverberant floor
	thunder board: a number of boards made up like a Venetian blind, hung offstage on one line	release the line
train of cars	four metal-tired casters mounted on the ends of a 3-foot 2″ × 4″ X-frame; center of X-frame pivoted above a box on which is mounted a circular metal track, $\frac{5}{16}″$ thick, split at two places, 110° apart; casters run on the track	rotate X-frame; box may be modified to give different reverberation characteristics of subway, surface car, or elevated
underbrush	burlap sack filled $\frac{2}{3}$'s full of white flake glue and securely sewed or tied shut	walk on bag
	open tray of flake glue	walk on the glue
whistle	the genuine article when possible; or organ pipes	blow by lung power, bellows, mechanical or electrical blowers, or compressed air
wind	slatted drum mounted on bearings; sheet of cloth fastened to mounting frame, passing over drum, and battened at free end; pitch varies with texture of cloth; canvas generally used	rotate drum toward free end of cloth; pull canvas taut; pitch and intensity vary with speed and canvas tension
	strips of bamboo or umbrella ribs fastened to shaft of variable-speed electric motor	run motor; speed governs pitch
	blower	run motor

Except when actual rather than substitute sources are used, the effects listed in the table are unconvincing unless carefully operated and intelligently rehearsed by the director. The sounds they emit have fairly correct pitch, but they are of incomplete or incorrect quality. The direction of the sound is limited by the placing of the apparatus. Distance

13.35 Three time-honored sound effect devices. Background: a rumble cart produces varying sounds as its cargo is changed. Left foreground: subway train, trolley cars, or railway cars according to the loading on the revolve and the speed of rotation. Right foreground: a bull roarer which produces various animal sounds as operator varies the tension in the cord with one hand and varies the way he strokes the cord with a rosin-coated glove on the other hand. He stands on the base to which the boiler is fastened

and intensity are restricted only by the number and size of the pieces of apparatus, by the vigor with which they are operated, and by the acoustical conditions of the auditorium and stage. The formidable-appearing field piece which fires with a pitiful pop and emits a lone wisp of smoke will get a snicker from the audience. Better have an adequate bang offstage!

electronic sound control

At best, with currently available equipment, it is possible to produce in the theatre any sound from any apparent source, or a moving source, or no source, and with any apparent intensity, direction, distance, form, or reverberant quality. Essential characteristics of such a system are:

• Microphone pickup at any location where the sound to be controlled may be located (stage, trap room, pit, prop room).

• Pickup from tape reproducers in the control room.

• Centralized control, so that the operator can see and hear the show as the audience does. (NO GLASS in the face of the control booth.)

• Loudspeaker positions in the theatre walls, ceiling, and proscenium, and on, above, and below the stage.

• Multiple channels. Three is the minimum to provide movement; the audience cannot unscramble more than three different simultaneous auditory presentations.

• Tape reproducers.

Equipment must be of broadcast quality or it will reveal itself for what it is. If the audience thinks it is listening to a sound system, the distraction thus introduced militates against the acceptance of the episode which the effect was supposed to support. See *Sound in the Theatre* by Burris-Meyer and Mallory.

playback from audio-tape

If the sound system is adequate in response (30 to 16,000 cycles flat) and power (110 decibels undistorted through the audience area), almost

13.36 A sound control console and equipment rack. Two phono inputs, two tape transports, and a patch panel facilitate making complex show tapes, though the system may also be used for playback in rehearsal and performance

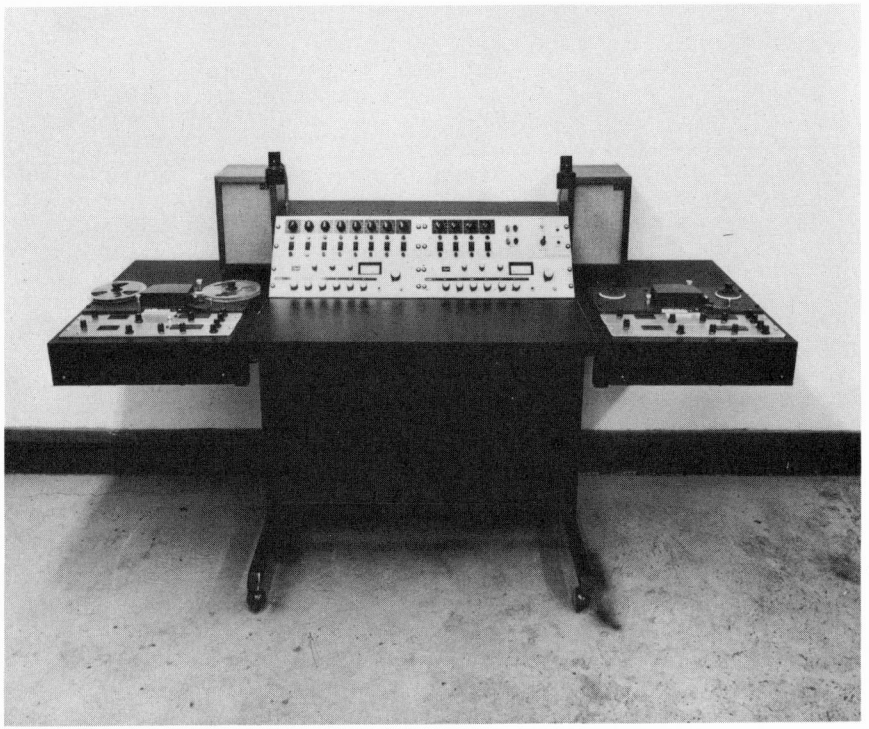

13.37 A sound control console designed primarily for rehearsal and performance playback of tapes made on the two-unit system (Figure 13.36)

all sound effects can be reproduced from audio-tapes. The tape recorder-reproducer can be used to make records of sounds from life from electronic music synthesizers, electronic music instruments, and from all sound-effect machines previously listed except loud crashes close at hand. It can make tape recordings from disc, music, or effect records.

The edited tape can be precisely cued. The operator, and only one is needed, can hear the effect as the audience does. Therefore, the good sound system eliminates the use of most mechanical sound-effect devices except when they are used to make tape effect records. WARNING: disc records must *not* be used in performance; a speck of dust can spoil the show.

The title "Sound designer" has been proposed to designate a person who develops the sound plan from the script and the director's requirements, plans and supervises the installation and operation of sound equipment for the production, directs the making of special recordings, and integrates the sound planning, assembly, and rehearsal with the director, musical director, and the technical departments.

Assembling and running the show; post-production procedures

14

This chapter describes the procedures and personnel involved in taking the scenery into the theatre, assembling it onstage, operating it, both in the requisite technical and dress rehearsals and in performance, dismantling it after the production is over, and disposing of it.

Assembly includes preparing the theatre and stage, installing scenery, properties, and lighting and sound apparatus, hanging the show, as described in Chapter 12, integrating the various elements into sets or working units, and developing the mechanical, lighting, and sound effects as designed.

The technical rehearsal comprises the organization and practice of all stage maneuvers, both in and out of the action of the play, with actors and backstage personnel taking part as required.

The dress rehearsal is the final melding of actors, costumes, makeup, lighting, sound, properties, music, and other elements into a smoothly running entity ready for performance.

These procedures require a form of organization different from that which prepared the show. Whereas the preparing, or manufacturing, organization practices different crafts simultaneously in separate shops (even though within the same building), the organization to assemble and run the show must function with a close interrelationship of crafts, sometimes simultaneously and sometimes sequentially, in the same space — the stage — on a tight schedule, to fit all the productional elements of the show together.

Just as knowledge of how the scenery was planned to fit the stage is helpful to the builders, so knowledge of how the scenery was built is helpful in assembling it onstage. Ideally, the same persons take the scenery from the drawing board through the shop to the stage into per-

the stage organization

formance and down and out of the theatre. But this is seldom possible, for a variety of reasons: specialization of crafts, geographical separation of shop and stage, overlapping schedules, separate contracts with unions and individuals covering separate parts of the production process, and differences in corporate purposes, policies, and procedures.

In a small organization with limited staff, whether for a single show or stock on a relaxed schedule, the same people may prepare the scenery, assemble and operate it onstage, dismantle it, and dispose of it.

In multiproduction situations such as stock on a tight schedule or revolving repertory, different personnel *must* perform separate parts of the process: overlaps in the schedule prevent one crew from being in two places or doing two jobs simultaneously, thereby making division of labor (for example, shop crew and stage crew) necessary.

In commercial production geographical separation, craft specialization, unionization, and differences in organizational purpose impose the division of functions and separate organizations to prepare and present the show. The shop in Brooklyn, the Bronx, or New Jersey is contractually committed to produce scenery for a number of producers in rapid sequence; the single producer on West Forty-fifth Street is concerned about a single show with its own schedule, and must have a unique organization to take in, assemble, and run it, and ultimately to strike it.

In any production situation, refinement of artistry and skills, some requiring lifetime training and practice, separates the functions of preparation from those of presentation and generates separate organizations of specialized workers.

authority and responsibility　　Lines of authority and responsibility are shown in Figures 14.1 and 14.2. The working staff — department heads and their crews — are responsible for creating the designed effect, executing the work according

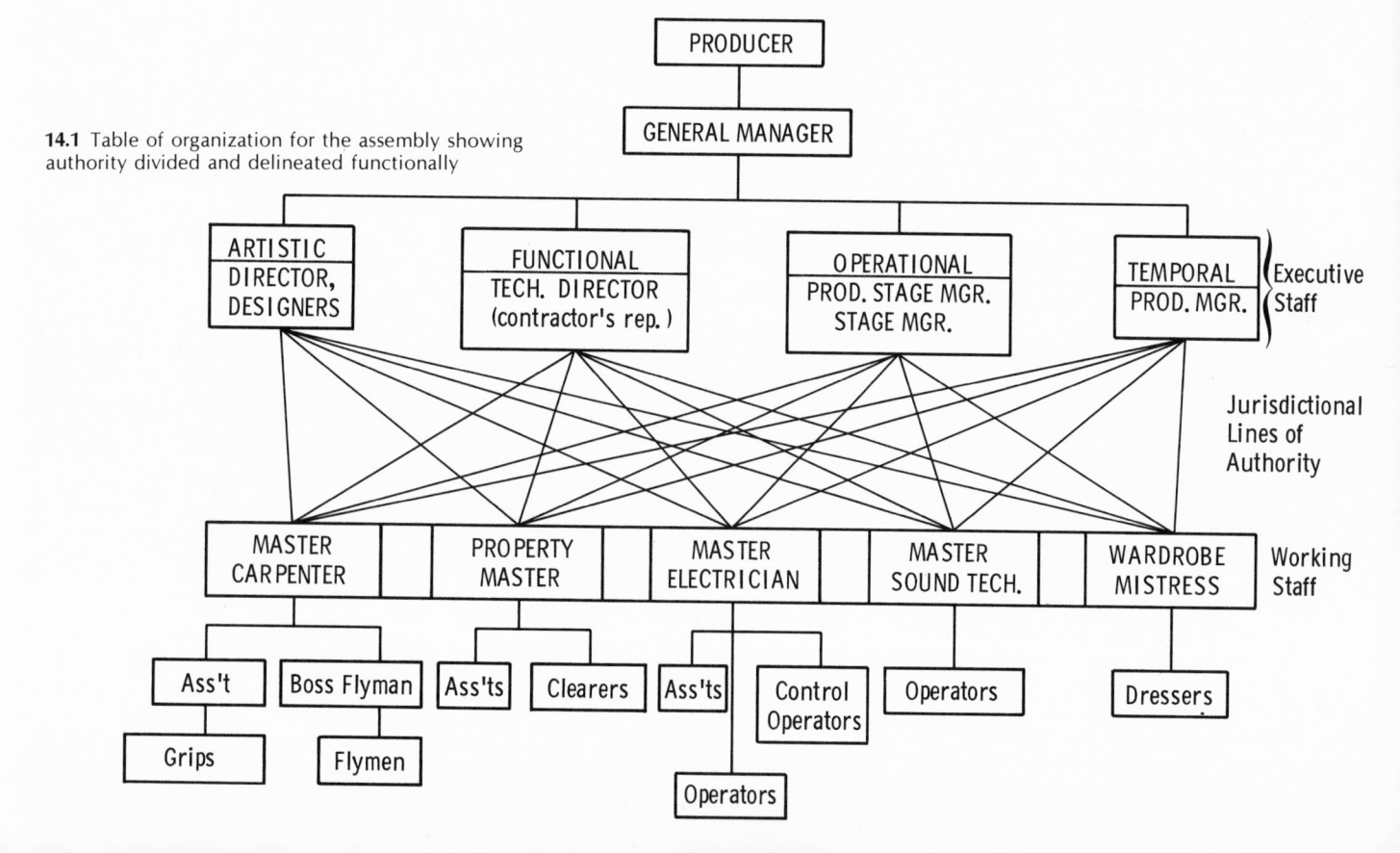

14.1 Table of organization for the assembly showing authority divided and delineated functionally

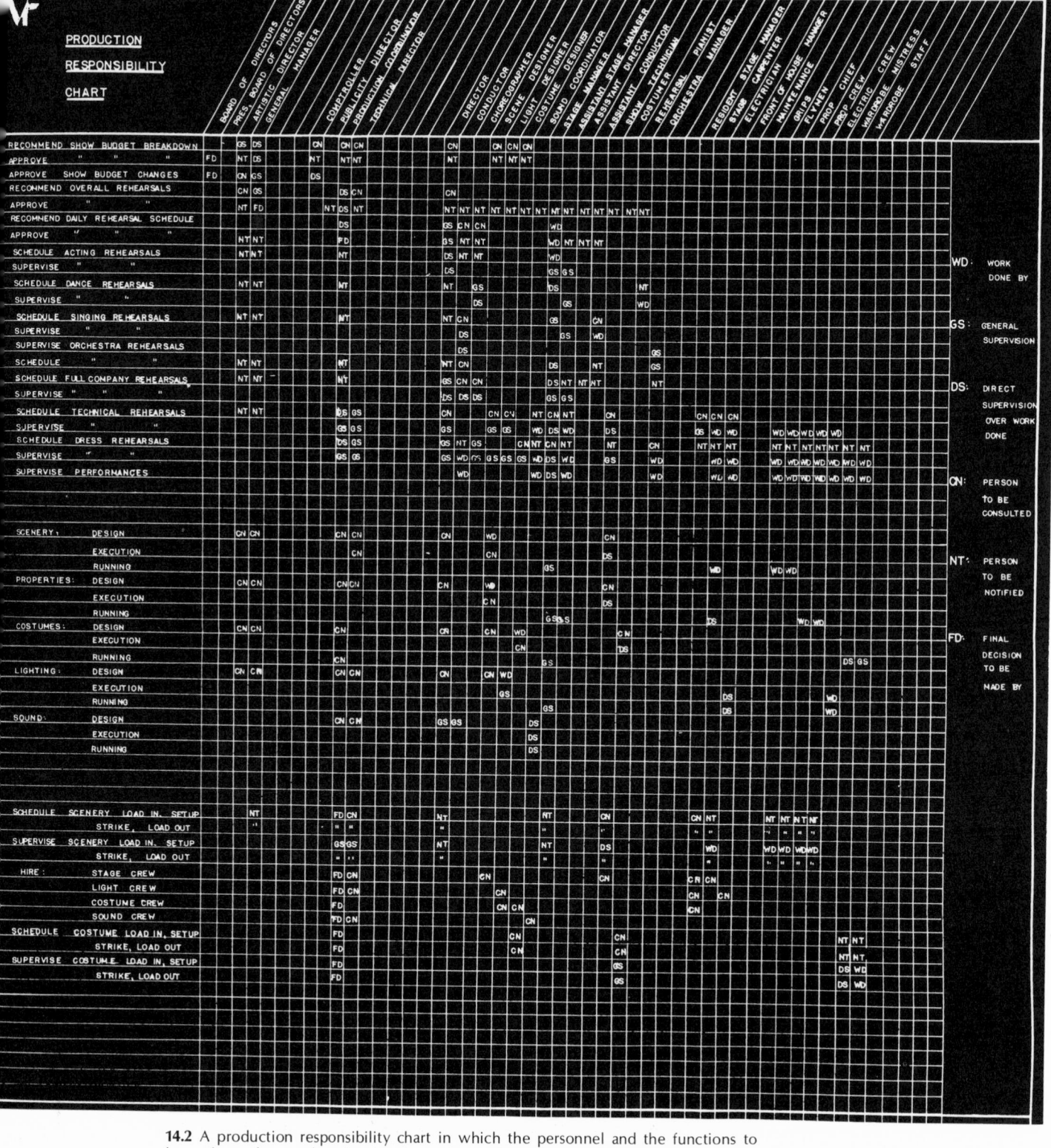

14.2 A production responsibility chart in which the personnel and the functions to be performed are analyzed and each member of the organization is assigned his specific and appropriate part of each function. A chart like this one, if thoroughly done, prevents failure to assign all the steps in a process to the appropriate member of the organization and delineates to each member both the scope and the limits of his responsibility. The chart can only be made by a production manager who is totally familiar with all the divisions and details of the production process. This chart and those in Figures 14.3, 2.4, and 2.5 are parts of a total plan for the organization and operation of a large and full-scheduled theatre-concert-opera festival in two theatres. The plans were prepared by Ann Farris

to a planned schedule, and achieving effective operation of the production. The executive staff has authority divided along the same lines: the several directors and the designers, who with the producer and the playwright have planned the theatrical artistry of the production. They are the ones who must be satisfied by the work of the technical departments.

producer

The final source of decisions is, of course, the producer. The general manager is his executive assistant.

director and designers

As the artistic authority, the director does not attend all the work of the assembly, but he is present at technical rehearsals containing effects which contribute significantly to the theatrical artistry and attends the final technical rehearsal with the actors. The designers (scenery, costumes, lighting, and sound) attend assembly sessions pertinent to their own areas and observe effects and correct errors.

production manager

As the temporal authority, the production manager schedules the use of the theatre by the departments, including the sequence and time of preparing the stage, take-in, setup, tests of working parts, rehearsals, light and sound sessions, dress parades, work periods, technical rehearsals, dress rehearsals, and any other activity in the theatre before opening night. To do this he must have detailed knowledge of all elements of the production, equally detailed knowledge of the theatre, the stage, the stage equipment, its capabilities and its limitations, an acute ability to estimate the time required for the various operations, close liaison with the director, the stage manager, the designers, the technical director, the costumer, the musical director, and any other persons who are concerned with parts of the production as they exert demands for time in the theatre. He maintains continuous supervision of the work as it progresses and is prepared to negotiate adjustments in the schedule when unforeseen and unforeseeable occurrences make these necessary. An important part of his work is to maintain a system of communication whereby all responsible persons know the schedule as planned and subsequent changes in it.

stage manager

As the operational authority, the stage manager is in complete charge of the production on opening night and thereafter, and must see that the elements of the production all operate and coordinate as the director and designers intended and that the routines are assimilated by the crews. To do this he uses the detailed knowledge of the production he has achieved by being with it from its earliest tryouts and rehearsals. He is responsible to the producer.

production stage manager

The tables of organization (Figures 14.1 and 14.3) show the production stage manager over the stage manager. Experienced and very capable stage managers are sometimes hired to combine the jobs of stage manager and production manager, sometimes simply to perform stage manager's tasks until a show is running smoothly, and, in repertory, to direct and supervise the separate stage managers of individual productions. Sometimes, on a production difficult to manage, the job of stage manager is dignified by the title production stage manager; men capable of stage-managing are hired to assist him but are called stage managers rather than assistants. Salaries match the titles.

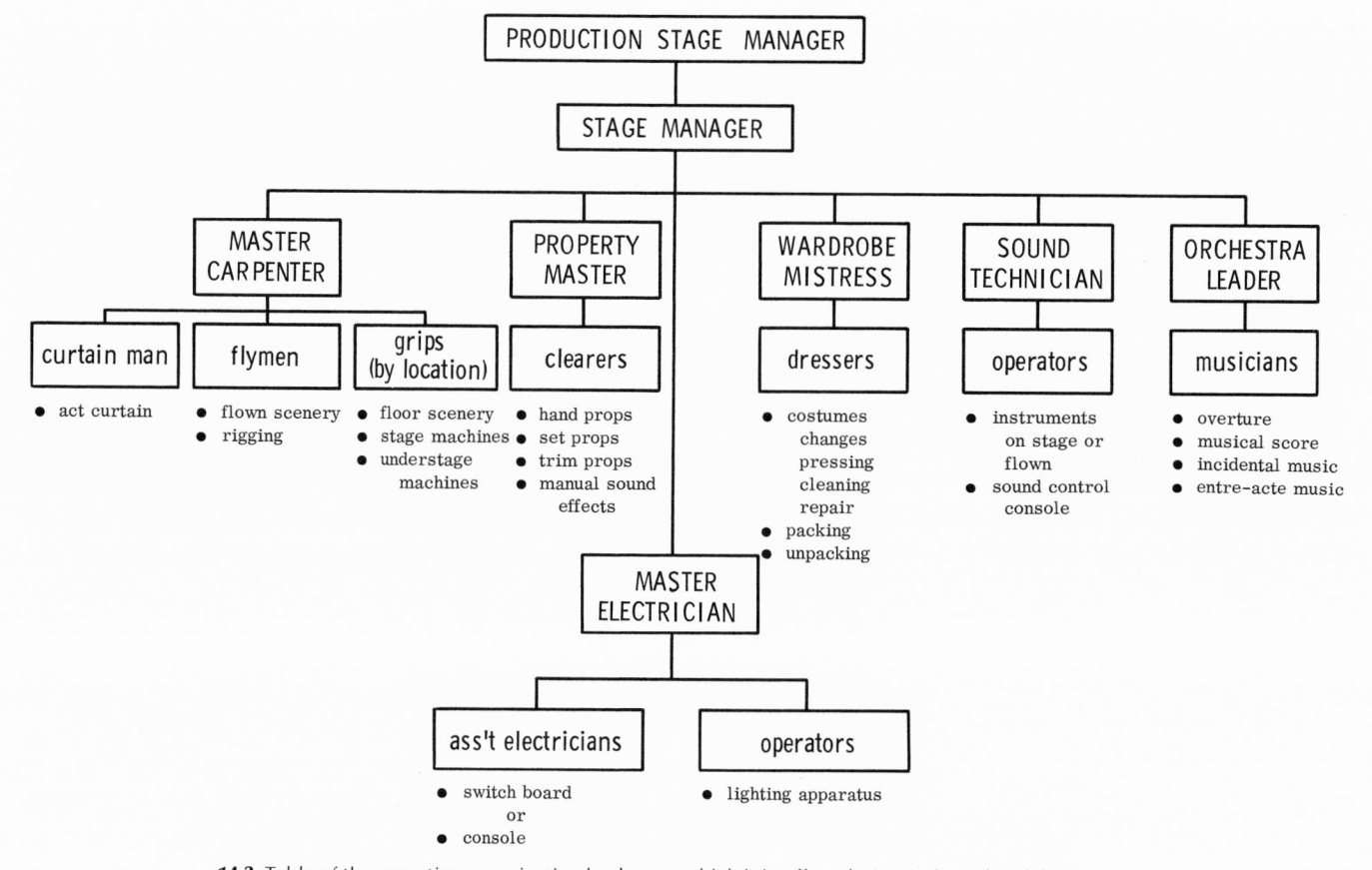

14.3 Table of the operating organization backstage which is in effect during technical and dress rehearsals and during performances. The functional authority of director, designers, and production manager continues in matters within their jurisdictions, but all orders pertaining to running the show come from the stage manager

As the functional authority, the technical director has planned the scenery, properties, lights, sound, and other elements to come together on the stage and work effectively. He directs and supervises the assembly. His job is ended when everything works as planned. He is responsible to the producer, through the general manager. In commercial production, for technical director read contractor's representative.

technical director

The master stage carpenter, property master, master electrician, and master sound technician direct the crews which assemble, hang, and work the show. They take orders from the technical director during the assembly and from the stage manager during rehearsals and performances. The stagehands are divided into groups according to the nature of their tasks: *flymen,* who attach scenery to the rigging and operate it along with other machinery for raising scenery into the overstage space; *grips,* who assemble and move scenery on and below the stage floor; *clearers,* who handle properties and manual sound effect apparatus; *operators,* who install and manipulate lighting equipment; and *sound operators,* who install and operate electronic sound apparatus.

department heads

The Assembly

The production manager, the technical director, the stage manager, and the department heads plan the assembly according to the amount of time available, and the complexity of the job. The process of assembly

planning

and the time required for it vary with each production. A drama in one realistic interior set may be moved onto the stage, set up, trimmed and set with properties, lighted, and dress-rehearsed in a twelve-hour period, whereas an elaborate musical show or an opera with many scenes, with mechanical, lighting, and sound effects, in elaborate, frequently changed costumes, and with songs and dances to an original score played by a pit orchestra, may require two or more weeks of work by crews, cast, and finally the orchestra to prepare for the first showing to an audience.

The assembly of the technical elements of a production is best planned when the plan provides for completion in a minimum number of regular eight-hour working days. Unavailability of the theatre, out-of-town opening, last-minute change of theatre, advance of opening date, or delay in delivery of the scenery often necessitate overtime work in assembly.

The shorter the time available and the more impossible it seems to get the show ready, the more necessary it becomes to make and adhere to a planned program of work. The frenzy and fatigue of constant, un-planned plugging away to get the job done are somehow associated with the traditional show-must-go-on attitude. However, division of the work so that groups of men work in four-hour shifts, get rest and refreshment between, and are constantly fresh on the job is a better guarantee that the show will get on than is the unrelenting drive through thirty or forty consecutive hours (at overtime pay), which is frequently reported, and often recalled with unexplainable pride.

Properly organized and with sufficient time allowed, the installation of the scenery can be an orderly, efficient procedure, economical of money, time, and tempers. Improperly planned and hastened, it can be chaotic. Chapters 12 and 15 set forth in detail the special techniques involved in assembling the scenery onstage.

assembly sequence   Whether the show comes into the theatre from the contractors' shops or from baggage cars or vans, or from a scene shop in the same building, the assembly sequence is the same. And with one exception (step 6), it is the same for one-set and multiset shows. Touring (*package*) shows are asked to supply information (Figure 14.4), plans, and plots which will allow a resident production manager and his staff to begin step 1 in advance of the show's arrival.

1. Prepare theatre and stage

The master stage carpenter, boss flyman, master electrician (and stage engineer if stage machinery is involved), and their crews make changes and adjustments in the permanent equipment of the stage according to plans made by the technical director (see Chapters 3 and 4) to prepare for the arrival of the scenery, properties, and lighting apparatus. Typical tasks are:

• Remove items of standing stage equipment which are not needed for the show and would be in the way.

• Clear unwanted lighting equipment and run additional cables as prescribed.

• Install special lines and line sets in the flies and reposition flying equipment to conform to the hanging plan of the show.

14.4 A form sent to the company manager of a touring company to returned in advance of arrival. This, together with plans and plots, perm the staff to assign and hire personnel, schedule space use, accomplish much makeready of equipment as time allows

PACKAGE SHOWS - PRODUCTION REQUIREMENTS

SHOW _____ CONTACT _____ PERF _____
ADDRESS _____ DATES _____

ARRIVAL SCENERY _____ VIA _____ PROD. MANAGER _____
         COMPANY _____   STAGE MANAGER _____

DEPARTURE SCENERY _____ VIA _____ SHOW CARPENTER _____
           COMPANY _____

PRODUCTION REQUIREMENTS

I. REHEARSAL

NO. OF REHEARSAL ROOMS
AND TIME REQUIRED   BOOK _____   CHORUS _____
                           DANCE _____   ORCHESTRA _____
TECHNICAL REHEARSAL REQUIRED _____   TIME REQUIRED _____
DRESS REHEARSAL REQUIRED _____   TIME REQUIRED _____

2. TECHNICAL

NO OF CREW REQUIRED / AMT TIME REQUIRED

	LOAD IN	SET UP	PERFORMANCE	STRIKE	LOAD OUT
CARPENTERS					
FLYMEN					
ELECTRIC					
PROPS					
SOUND					
COSTUME					

3. SPECIAL REQUIREMENTS

I. SOUND   NO. OF SPEAKERS _____   PLACEMENT _____
               MICROPHONES _____   OTHER _____

II SCENERY   BUILDING _____   REPAIRING _____
               PAINTING _____   PROP BUILDING _____
               SPECIAL MASKING _____   OTHER _____

III ELECTRIC   LIGHT PLOT _____   INSTRUMENT SCHEDULE _____
               SPECIALS _____   OTHER _____

IV COSTUMES   NO OF COSTUMES _____   CLEANING _____
               REPAIR WORK _____   WIG WORK _____
               HAIRDRESSERS _____   OTHER _____

MISCELLANEOUS

- Adjust forestage elevator, if any, to meet the show's requirements.
- Set the inner proscenium, if any, at the prescribed height and width for the show.
- Clear the trap room for such platforms, stairs, and trap elevators as the show may contain, and render understage machinery adequate to the show's needs.

Structural alterations to the theatre are not done by stagehands but by contractors and workmen from the building trades.

2. Load in

Equipment and scenery must be delivered to the stage, hence shipped from their sources in time to reach the stage, in the sequence required by steps 3 to 10 below. Transit time is a factor which the production manager must consider in ordering shipment. Specific items must reach the stage just in time, neither earlier nor later, to be assimilated into the production; otherwise either clutter or delay may result.

3. Mount lighting equipment and sound apparatus

The master electrician and his crew hang and cable all stage lighting instruments: on first pipe or bridge, on other pipes, booms, and ladders. (Pipes, booms, and ladders are show equipment.) This work is done most efficiently now, when the stage is clear. Provision must also be made for access to these instruments after the floor has become encumbered by platforms, traps, or fixed scenery. The sound technician similarly hangs overstage loudspeakers and microphones, and runs cables to the sound control console or to connection points at the stage floor. Lighting and sound equipment may be mounted in positions away from the stage: house ceiling slots, sidewall slots, box booms, and balcony fronts, and on floor-based stands and towers, at times when the stage and prop crews are working on the stage. The carpenter will appreciate it if the sound technician sets up one channel and gives him a microphone for giving directions in hanging the show.

4. Prepare the stage floor

The master carpenter and crew cut or open traps, if any, and rig them to be opened; the property master and crew lay padding and floor-cloth or other floor covering; the carpenters close the traps; the master carpenter measures and marks key points on the floor cloth for reference in hanging and setting the scenery.

5. Hang flown scenery

The boss flyman and his crew, working the flies, and the master carpenter and his crew, working the floor, hang, trim, and fly all scenery which must go into the flies before floor-based scenery is set up or assembled into units (see Chapter 12). They test the operation of all flown units.

6. Install floor modifiers

The master carpenter and crew install fixed platforms, ramps, and false floors. In multiscene shows they also install stage wagons and pallets, their associated guide tracks, and revolves with their attendant tracks and pivots, cables, and driving mechanisms.

7. Assemble floor-based scenery

The same crew then assembles the floor-based scenery into units which will work the show and sets up all this scenery, installing, testing, and familiarizing themselves with the fitting and joining of the units.

8. Trim with props; place floor-based lighting instruments

The property master and crew place the set props and trim props in and on the set under the supervision of the scene designer; the master electrician and crew place floor-based lighting instruments under the direction of the lighting designer. The master carpenter and crew look for and mask light leaks through scenery caused by the instruments.

9. Light the show

The lighting designer, the control board (or console) operator, with the master electrician and crew making necessary adjustments, focus lights, set the dimmer readings, establish and record presets and cues, and practice them.

10. Test the sound equipment

The sound technician and his crew, working at a time when there is no noise to impair the test situation, run sample effects through the sound system, judge them, and make required adjustments.

At the end of this sequence, unless there is some extraneous reason for striking the set, it is left standing, covers are put on the properties, a pilot light is left in the middle of the stage, and the production is ready for technical rehearsal if there are light changes and sound or visual effects. If these are not requisite, or are very simple, the technical production is ready for the dress rehearsal.

multiset shows

For the play of two or more separate sets, steps 1 through 5 are the same as for the one-set show, except that more than one set has to be provided for, and certain parts which would be fixed and permanent for a one-set show may have to be adjustable, for example, the tormentors and teasers, traps, and floorcloth. Step 6 is different, of course (q.v.).

Steps 7 through 10 are repeated as sequences for each scene of the show.

repairs and alterations

Ideally there should be no interruption in the assembly sequence, either for the one-set show or for the show of more than one set. Actually, however, repairs, alterations, or additions often have to be made. These, if minor, are made immediately; if extensive, in overtime periods so that the regular schedule is not retarded.

Technical Rehearsals

The show is ready for technical rehearsal when the assembly of the technical elements is completed, and all elements function as planned. The stage manager assumes command onstage. The designer attends technical and dress rehearsals, to see that the scenery and lighting remain the same as planned in the assembly, or to discuss with the director or producer any changes which they all think should be made to suit the action of the play. In commercial production, the designer is contracted to be available for conference on the scenic production until the metropolitan opening.

Two sets of plans are compiled, the first by the stage manager and the second by the heads of stage departments. The stage manager's job in connection with the technical rehearsal is to run it on the same schedule as is to be used in performance, to cue the light control and curtain man, to check the scenery, props, and lights before beginning each scene, to cue all effects, and to call and supervise scene shifts.

While the technical elements of the production have been in the process of construction and assembly, the stage manager has been primarily concerned with the rehearsals. He has followed the developments, has noted all action and business related to the technical production, has kept the scene designer and technical director informed of any alterations in the technical elements made necessary by changes in the action as rehearsals have progressed.

During rehearsals, the stage manager has accumulated information concerning the way in which the technical elements must fit with the action. He knows and has marked on small stage plans, one for each scene, the location of the scenery and details about the scenery that have special relevance, for instance, the fact that a certain window must be half open and a certain door slightly ajar when the curtain goes up. He has also marked on the same plans the exact location of all furniture, with special notes such as that the space between a sofa and a table must allow passage of a person, or that the leaf of the dropleaf table is down at the rise. He has listed in sequence from left to right around the set all the hand props and trim props and their exact positions. He is particularly concerned with the hand props since they tie in with the action of the play: cigarettes, matches, writing paper, pen, the book lying open on the table, the pearls in the secret compartment. He has listed the hand props which are to be set on the prop table offstage, to be carried onstage by actors during the scene.

His plot of the lighting he compiles from two sources:

• The rehearsals of the play, from which he gets the condition of the lights as specified by the play itself ("Stage dark at curtain") and the light cues which arise from the action ("Digby enters, pauses, strikes a match, hunts for light switch, finds it, turns on the light").

• The lighting sessions during the assembly, from which he ascertains the visual aspect of each scene: the areas lighted, the instruments used, their position, color, intensity, and direction. Although the lighting is watched carefully by the designer during both technical and dress rehearsals, the stage manager becomes solely responsible for it when the production is in performance and must be thoroughly familiar with the light plot.

During rehearsals he records in the prompt script the warning and dead cue for each technical effect which arises from the action, for example, a blackout of lights when an actor throws a fake switch on the wall, a clap of thunder, a drum roll, a waltz, an angry mob, or the beginning and end of a downpour of rain visible through the windows. He must also observe during rehearsals or get from the director as detailed a characterization of the effect as he can: long or short, slow or abrupt, loud or soft, constant or intermittent, crescendo or diminuendo, or any other appropriate description of each particular effect. Such descriptive matter, along with the plot of the effects, he conveys to the sound technician. The stage manager must select records of sound or music, and approve trials of manual sound effects.

Whether the stage manager cues the effects from the prompt script in which he has them completely annotated, or from a cue sheet, is a matter of his own preference. If he is following the actors in their lines, he will use the prompt script for cues as well. If he has an assistant to do the prompting or if no prompter is needed, he will choose to excerpt the cues into the smaller, more easily handled cue sheet.

In practice, prompting is unnecessary after the first few performances. If an actor cannot remember his lines, it is wise to get an actor who can, unless he is an aging but great star for whom it may be necessary to place prompters wherever concealment permits. Moreover, the use of cue sheets becomes progressively less as the run continues, and it is not uncommon to have very complicated shows running without a single sheet in evidence backstage. In one production, an eighteen-page sound setup and cue sheet of the most complex character was discarded by the operators after twelve performances. Technicians learn their parts as do actors. Their plans, setup, and cue sheets, however, are at least as essential, and they must be more detailed, specific, and closely adhered to than the actors' sides.

Finally the stage manager must get the actual running time of the show: length of time for overture, time of curtain, estimated playing time of each scene, and times allowed for each scene change.

Below is a summary of the information which the stage manager must have for each scene in order to run technical and dress rehearsals and performances:

Drawings: Arrangement of scenery
               Arrangement of properties
               Lighted areas

    Lists: Props on stage at opening
               Props on offstage prop table
               Lights burning; their colors, intensities,
                  direction
               Actors ready before opening
               Beginners
               Crowds
               Running schedule of entire show

The second set of plans incidental to the technical rehearsal is the set made up by the heads of the technical departments. They have to do primarily with changes in scenery, props, and lighting.

planning the scene shifts

When planning the scenery, the technical director has made a basic division of the offstage space for the storage of scenery, props, and floor-based lighting instruments. The master carpenter, following the technical director's general scheme for storage and handling of scenery, works out a detailed plan for each scene shift. The plan includes a plot of the storage positions of each piece, analysis of the moves necessary to accomplish the change, and assignment of the moves to his crew.

In planning the movement of the scenery, props, and lights he must think like a computer programmer; all moves *must* be listed and in their proper order. If a move is omitted or out of order, the following moves will be affected or even arrested. He must visualize, the more accurately the better, each stagehand performing each detailed operation, each object in motion and clearing other objects, and each object occupying its own allotted space.

Very often no actual paper work accompanies the planning of the shifts by the master carpenter. In many cases without benefit of technical rehearsal, he gathers his crew about him during the first act of the dress rehearsal, and says in effect: "You grab that and take it over there. You take out that brace, you unlash that flat and take it there . . . " and so on. Then, at the end of the act, the crew tries the shift, muddles through it, and has another conference to clear up difficulties. This may not necessarily be called an unplanned shift. Working with experienced stagehands who are acquainted with the paraphernalia of the stage and know how to handle scenery, a carpenter who has worked from twenty-five to two hundred shows can tell very rapidly what the shift procedure must be. Good stagehands, furthermore, readily notice details of the shift which have been overlooked in the verbal instructions and assume responsibility for their execution.

It is only for scene shifts by inexperienced workers, for very complicated scenic arrangements, or for very rapid shifts that a detailed analysis is needed. For the sake of completeness, the most elaborate method of planning a scene shift is given below. The master carpenter in the particular situation will eliminate the parts he finds unnecessary.

analysis   **Offstage storage.** The master carpenter, property master, and master electrician make a basic division of the offstage space for storage of scenery, props, and lights. A customary division is: scenery to the side-walls and upstage corners; props directly up center; lights to the side downstage. This division is modified according to the scenic scheme of each show and according to the plan of each stage. In certain theatres a workable division of storage space has been designed into the stage by the architect, as when space has been provided downstage in each wing to receive props taken off wagon stages. In well-designed stages, adequate offstage storage space, properly located, is provided and the shift problem is minimized; it is not eliminated because no two productions are alike in their scenic requirements, and designers' concepts tend to equal and occasionally exceed the cubic capacity of the stagehouse. Large three-dimensional units of scenery, planned by the designer to store in certain positions, may be the items around which the entire storage scheme is planned. Storage positions for heavy pieces are planned to provide for the most direct movement through the shortest distance.

The master carpenter's plans. The master carpenter draws a series of ground plans, each one showing a different set onstage, and the units of the other sets disposed in their storage positions. He must make certain that he has drawn all fixed obstacles in their correct sizes and positions, and noted the limits of overhead vertical clearance. If the storage problem is a complicated one, these plans may be drawn to scale, to make sure that the scenery proposed to store in a certain position will actually fit. A variation of this procedure is to test on the plan small cardboard cutouts of the major items for fit and movement in restricted spaces.

On each plan, one scene is shown completely set up. For each scene the carpenter marks every item which will require attention in the shift. He may used a code of initials for this: *L* marked at the junction of two flats indicates Lashing; *B* means Stage Brace; and *SS* may mean Stage Screw. The objects above the stage floor such as chandeliers, borders, ceilings, and light pipes, are drawn in broken line.

The moves. With the plans of two consecutive scenes before him, the carpenter lists each job in the order of performance and checks it on the plans as he does so. The moves to be made are classified as *first moves, second moves, third moves,* and so on. First moves are, obviously, those which can be made as soon as the stage manager calls "Strike" or gives a silent cue, for example, removal of chandelier, backdrop, borders, and ceiling (when there is no chandelier). Removal of certain braces and stage screws may be included as first moves. Second moves are those which may be made when passageways are cleared by first moves and include removal of ground rows, entrance backings, and their attendant braces. In listing the moves, the carpenter notes the number of men necessary.

The setting up of a scene approximates the reverse of the strike of that scene. Variations occur when storage positions are changed. When variations occur, it is necessary to analyze carefully the strike of a scene that has been previously set, or vice versa.

Crew assignments. The master carpenter now assigns to the crew individually each movement or operation in the shift. The crew is divided into groups by locations: flymen on the fly gallery or at the locking rail, stage-left crew, stage-right crew, and center crew. The moves are assigned on a cross-ruled schedule, from which assignment cards for the individual stagehands are made up. The schedule is either posted for reference, or kept by the carpenter for checking the shifts.

A similar type of analysis is made by the property master for the handling of properties, and by the master electrician for the movement of lights, although in these latter cases the shifts are rarely complicated enough to require such elaborate treatment.

The technical rehearsal without actors serves the purpose of integrating in performance sequence all the technical elements of production. It is, to all intents and purposes, a performance without actors. In order to make the technical rehearsal of maximum value, the pro-

the technical rehearsal without actors

ducer, director, designer, and their assistants must be present. Much of the chaos proverbially attendant upon dress rehearsals results from the omission or slighting of the technical rehearsal. No department of a production can profit much by a rehearsal in which the stage carpenter cannot work on scenery because the set is being lighted, where the actors cannot be heard because of backstage noises, where cues go awry because the person who should receive them is elsewhere making adjustments. With department heads all simultaneously giving orders and trying to get their elements of the production into shape, integration of those elements becomes impossible.

The technical rehearsal starts under conditions duplicating those which exist before a regular performance. The stage is clear and the scenery in its proper stored position, except in the case of a one-set show. Working toward a predetermined curtain time, the house is lighted, the act curtain lowered, the fire curtain raised, the stage swept, the first act set up, properties set in position, floor-based lights placed, the stage lights put on readings, and the lobby call made. Then, simulating the start of a performance, the houselights are dimmed and curtain lights brought up, the act curtain raised, curtain lights dimmed, and front lights brought up. If the show has no curtain or is on an arena or thrust stage, the opening routine is run through. The stage manager gives all cues, including orchestra cues and dressing room calls even though musicians and actors are not present, so that he may practice and test the workability of his own complete routine. If his routine proves unworkable, he assigns parts of it to the assistant stage manager.

As soon as the curtain is up, the set is checked by the designer for position, trim and set properties, and lighting. The stage manager inspects all entrances and exits for suitability and accessibility; all working parts of the scenery (doors, sliding panels, traps, windows) for operation; platforms on- and offstage for strength, size, position, and noise; and furniture and hand props for position relative to the business of the play. All errors, unless they are so extensive as to cause unwarranted delay, are corrected at once and appropriate notations made on plans, schedules, cue sheets, and the prompt script. The department heads note and mark positions for all items in their charge (for example, high and low trim on lines, dimmer settings).

The scene is then run by the stage manager, who skips all parts of the play except those with which effects are integrated. He gives line, light, phone, signal, or buzzer cues in sequence, reading lines when the cues must time with them, and all light, sound, and mechanical effects are performed on the appropriate cues. Errors on the part of any of the backstage personnel call for immediate correction and repetition of the whole sequence in which the error has occurred. Failure to repeat the sequence as many times as are necessary to eliminate the error invites repetition of the error in dress rehearsals or performances. Such changes in scenery and properties as are made by the actors in the scene are made in their stead by the stage manager and the property master.

When the first scene is finished, the stage manager reads the curtain line or blackout line or mimes the final action, the act curtain is lowered or the lights blacked out, and the first shift takes place. The stage manager times the shift. Heads of departments check all items in their charge and report to the stage manager, who runs through his complete routine of checklists and calls and cues the start of the next scene. In an arena stage or on an open stage the shift is made by neutrally uniformed stagehands, under houselights, in an orderly unobtrusive manner. Objects having surprise value may be set in blackout just before a scene begins.

Designer, director, stage manager, and producer then go over Scene 2 in the same manner and with the same purpose as those employed in checking Scene 1. Corrections are made, recorded, and marked, the scene is run, the next shift made, and the cycle repeated for each scene in the play. When the final curtain is down, the set is struck and stored, and the stage is cleared. Scenery, properties, and floor lights are arranged for availability in the proper sequence, and storage positions marked if restricted space makes it necessary. Any remaining repairs and adjustments (torn canvas patched, lines retrimmed, touch-up painting done) are made. This ends the technical rehearsal, and from a backstage point of view all subsequent rehearsals and performances follow the routine established in the technical rehearsal.

Even if the technical planning of the production has been thorough, some errors or delays usually occur in technical rehearsal. The curtain routine is seldom right the first time it is run; the houselights are dimmed too fast or too slowly; the curtain lights come on at the wrong time or in the wrong manner, or the curtain moves late. The curtain routine can be rehearsed and set for the beginning and end of each scene as soon as the scene has opened and while the set is being checked.

Shifts seldom run according to schedule the first time they are tried. The pace of the crew is slow, the sequence of moves is often broken because one operation takes more time than was estimated, and another takes less. If the assigned moves prove too few or too many for the stagehands, they must be changed and the shift rerouted and repeated. Occasionally it develops that the paths of movement of properties or scenery, or both, cross and cause a traffic jam. Such jams are cured by a change of pace in the movement of certain pieces, change of storage position, or change of the order in which pieces are handled. Corrections are expedited by interrupting the shift at the instant of confusion and stopping all movement until the corrective changes are effected. In any case, shifts must be repeated until they are made within the time allowed. The stage manager discounts unfamiliarity of the crew with the scenery, and if the sequence of the shift is right, it is speeded by repetition. It is not unusual for three rehearsals to reduce the time of a shift by 90 percent. The technical rehearsal is, incidentally, the proof of the technical planning of a production; one item overlooked in the planning may add hours to the rehearsal.

Although the technical rehearsal outlined may seem to apply to the average American stage, the process and the purpose is the same, no matter what the setting or how the stage is equipped. If the stage has wagons, a disc, elevators, or any combination of them, or if the shift takes five seconds and not a thing is moved by hand, the technical rehearsal is no less important.

When shifts have to be accomplished in a very short time, or during the action of the play, the stage manager dispenses with the cue for the shift and the crews move on dead cues taken directly from the lines, the lights, or stage business. Their actions are as carefully timed and as precise as if they were visible to the audience. Final setting of these shifts cannot be accomplished without rehearsals in which both the cast and the crews participate.

The shift plan described is for a production in two or more conventional realistic interior sets. Though there will probably always be plays staged in this style, the current trend is away from realism toward more imaginative uses of stage space and more ingenious uses of the stage apparatus, with increased use of machinery, sometimes remotely controlled and at least partially automated. Scene shifts are more frequently *a vista* and integrated with the stage action. They must be rehearsed with the action to perfect the changes. The same is true of both light and sound plots. It may therefore be necessary to plan the assembly of the production so that the moving parts of the stage, the scenery, the lighting effects, and sound effects, separately or together, may be rehearsed with the actors prior to what would usually be the first technical rehearsal. Indeed these special or partial technical rehearsals may render a full technical rehearsal unnecessary. The director decides how he wishes to introduce and integrate the technical effects with the stage action, and the stage manager becomes the planner and coordinator, working with the technical director and the department heads. Such rehearsals, of course, entail added crew calls, which increase the production's cost.

The technical rehearsal without actors never gets all the kinks out of the performance routine, particularly those which relate technical effects and stage action. Especially is this true in lighting and sound. Electronics has placed subtle and easy control of changes in lighting in the hands of the console (no longer the switchboard) operator and encourages both director and designers to call for more frequent light changes precisely executed. Tape recording of sound has given wider scope and variety to the application of music and other sounds to theatrical production. The degree of complexity of lighting, sound, and mechanical effects will determine the need for a technical rehearsal in which the whole physical production is operated with the actors walking through the show, skipping dialogue which does not relate to effects, and playing precisely only those parts of the play which do. Thus, actors adjust their action and dialogue to the technical requirements of the show: setting, light, sound, and scenery-movement cues are timed; scenery movements and actors' movements are coordinated; and malfunction of any part of the technical production is corrected.

It is essential that all functions of all departments be tested and adjusted in this rehearsal. Extraordinarily light or dark makeup, or costumes which might cause difficulty in movement over platforms or stairs, should be worn.

Time is consumed in the technical rehearsal with actors in making technical adjustments and repeating actions and cues to get them right. The actors should not feel that they are in a performance or even in a serious rehearsal, but they should take care that lines given to time cues are read at the correct tempo and that lines which are cues for effects are correctly given. The object of the rehearsal is to render actors at ease with the technical elements of the show in subsequent dress rehearsals and performances.

About three to six days before the first dress rehearsal the costume designer and costumer must see all the actors wearing all their costumes in the set and under stage lights. The dress parade is scheduled by the stage manager to take place when the production has been assembled and sufficiently ahead of the first dress rehearsal to allow the costumer time for the alterations which the parade has shown to be necessary.

dress parade

At this time also, the stage manager must schedule a photography session (picture call) for the taking of publicity pictures. This involves actors, costumers, stage personnel, the show's press agent, and the photographers whom he has assembled. The stage manager runs the call to give the photographers preselected scenes and poses. Effective management is required to accomplish scene and costume changes without costly and annoying delays.

picture call

In musical shows and operas the first rehearsal with orchestra follows the technical rehearsals. The emphasis of the rehearsal is upon integrating the orchestra into the performance, with adjustments made either on the stage or in the pit as feasible.

orchestra rehearsal

Dances, rapid movements over levels, manipulation of properties, the entrances, movement, and exits of the chorus, lighting and mechanical stage effects, and all potential trouble areas require time and attention. It is the rare musical director who, during rehearsals with piano, anticipates *all* the difficulties in relating stage action and effects to the music. The rehearsal with orchestra removes these difficulties, usually minor but numerous, which might interrupt dress rehearsals and distract performers, musicians, director, and musical director from the chief purpose of dress rehearsals — the achievement of artistic excellence. A long rehearsal should be anticipated and scheduled by the production manager.

Dress Rehearsals and Performances

The dress rehearsals are, as far as the backstage organization is concerned, regular performances, and the routine which governs performance is followed. Crews report one half hour before curtain time. If technical rehearsals have revealed the need for further work on the technical elements or additional rehearsals, this work is done in separate calls earlier in the day. The stage is swept by the property crew. Grips and flymen inspect and put in order all scenery onstage and in the flies and test the operation of all machinery. The electricians and sound technician check out all circuits and equipment and preset opening lighting and sound. Properties are uncovered and put in order; the properties

daily routine

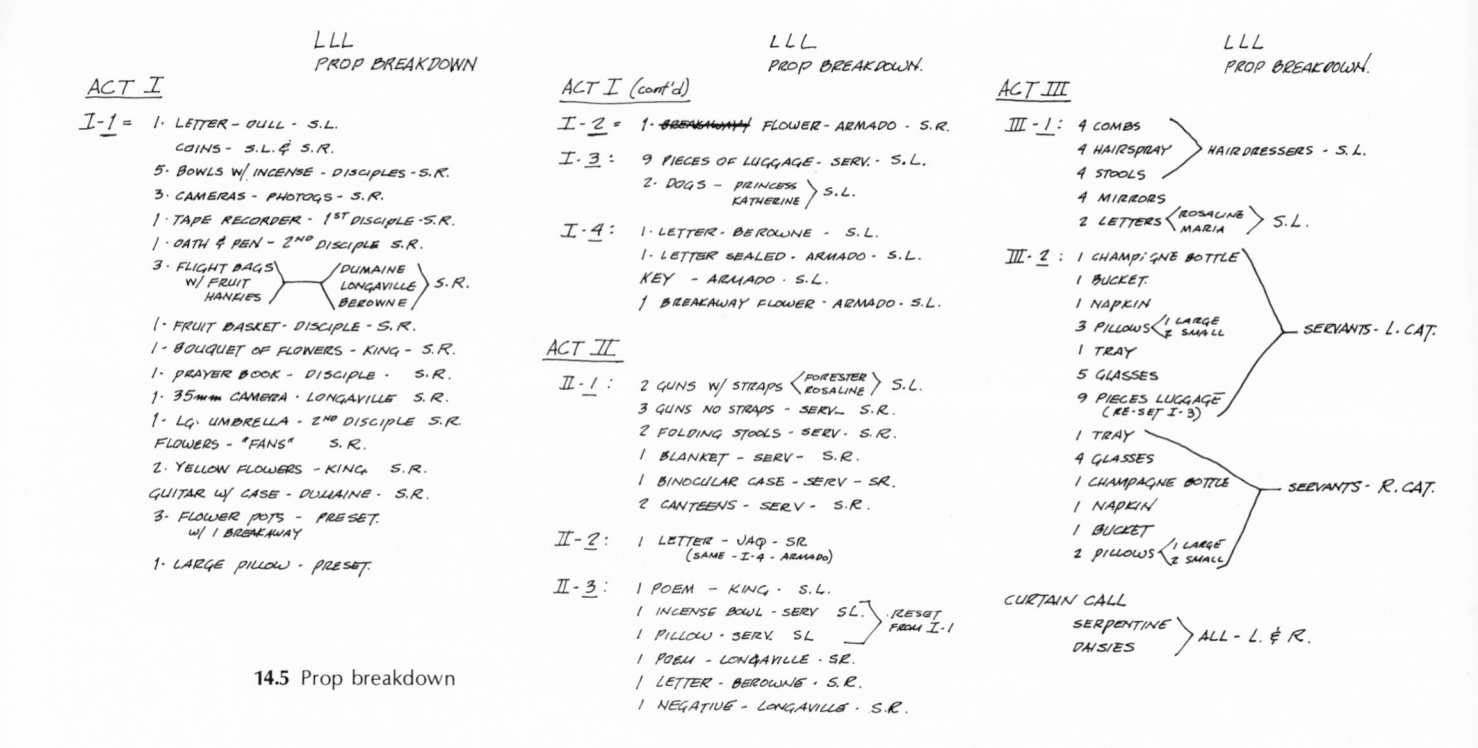

LLL PROP BREAKDOWN

ACT I

I-1 =
1. LETTER - OULL - S.L.
   - COINS - S.L. & S.R.
5. BOWLS W/ INCENSE - DISCIPLES - S.R.
3. CAMERAS - PHOTOGS - S.R.
1. TAPE RECORDER - 1ST DISCIPLE - S.R.
1. OATH & PEN - 2ND DISCIPLE S.R.
3. FLIGHT BAGS W/ FRUIT HANKIES } DUMAINE / LONGAVILLE / BEROWNE } S.R.
1. FRUIT BASKET - DISCIPLE - S.R.
1. BOUQUET OF FLOWERS - KING - S.R.
1. PRAYER BOOK - DISCIPLE - S.R.
1. 35mm CAMERA - LONGAVILLE S.R.
1. LG. UMBRELLA - 2ND DISCIPLE S.R.
FLOWERS - "FANS" S.R.
2. YELLOW FLOWERS - KING S.R.
GUITAR W/ CASE - DUMAINE - S.R.
3. FLOWER POTS - PRESET. W/ 1 BREAKAWAY
1. LARGE PILLOW - PRESET.

ACT I (cont'd)

I-2 = 1. ~~BREAKAWAY~~ FLOWER - ARMADO - S.R.

I-3 : 9 PIECES OF LUGGAGE - SERV. - S.L.
2. DOGS - PRINCESS / KATHERINE } S.L.

I-4 : 1. LETTER - BEROWNE - S.L.
1. LETTER SEALED - ARMADO - S.L.
KEY - ARMADO - S.L.
1. BREAKAWAY FLOWER - ARMADO - S.L.

ACT II

II-1 : 2 GUNS W/ STRAPS / FORESTER / ROSALINE } S.L.
3 GUNS NO STRAPS - SERV. - S.R.
2 FOLDING STOOLS - SERV - S.R.
1 BLANKET - SERV - S.R.
1 BINOCULAR CASE - SERV - S.R.
2 CANTEENS - SERV - S.R.

II-2 : 1 LETTER - JAQ - S.R. (SAME - I-4 - ARMADO)

II-3 : 1 POEM - KING - S.L.
1 INCENSE BOWL - SERV S.L. } RESET FROM I-1
1 PILLOW - SERV. S.L.
1 POEM - LONGAVILLE - S.R.
1 LETTER - BEROWNE - S.R.
1 NEGATIVE - LONGAVILLE - S.R.

ACT III

III-1 : 4 COMBS / 4 HAIRSPRAY / 4 STOOLS / 4 MIRRORS } HAIRDRESSERS - S.L.
2 LETTERS / ROSALINE / MARIA } S.L.

III-2 : 1 CHAMPAGNE BOTTLE / 1 BUCKET / 1 NAPKIN / 3 PILLOWS (1 LARGE 2 SMALL) / 1 TRAY / 5 GLASSES / 9 PIECES LUGGAGE (RE-SET I-3) } SERVANTS - L. CAT.
1 TRAY / 4 GLASSES / 1 CHAMPAGNE BOTTLE / 1 NAPKIN / 1 BUCKET / 2 PILLOWS (1 LARGE 2 SMALL) } SERVANTS - R. CAT.

CURTAIN CALL
SERPENTINE / DAISIES } ALL - L. & R.

14.5 Prop breakdown

STAGE MANAGER'S WORKING SHEETS FOR *LOVE'S LABOUR'S LOST* AT THE AMERICAN SHAKESPEARE FESTIVAL THEATRE
(continues on next five pages)

RE-SET: PILLOW C. PLATFORM
1' UP. ORANGE SIDE UP
3 FLOWER POTS BREAKAWAY FLOWER O
L.L.L. PROPS MS

STAGE RIGHT:
5 BOWLS W/ INCENSE (2 STICKS PER)
3 CAMERAS (PHOTOGS)
1 TAPE RECORDER
1 OATH W/ PEN
AIR BAGS W/ 3 HANKIES 3 FRUITS
1 FRUIT BASKET
1 BOUQUET FLOWERS
1 PRAYER BOOK
1 35mm CAMERA
1 LARGE UMBRELLA
FLOWERS - (FANS TO THROW)
COINS
2 YELLOW FLOWERS - LARGE
GUITAR W/ CASE
1 RED FLOWER STEP
3 GUNS - NO STRAP
2 STOOLS - FOLDING
1 BLANKET
1 BINOCULAR CASE
2 CANTEENS
1 POEM - LONGAVILLE
1 LETTER - BEROWNE
1 NEGATIVE (ROLL)

9 PROGRAMS
POLE W/ CURTAIN
1 COPPER TRAY W/ 4 GLASSES
1 CHAMPAGNE BOTTLE NAPKIN BUCKET
2 PILLOWS 1 LG. 1 SMALL
SERPENTINE
GINGER-ALE

STAGE LEFT
1 BREAK-AWAY RED FLOWER
9 PIECES LUGGAGE
1 LETTER - (BEROWNE)
1 LETTER - (OULL)
COINS
2 GUNS W/ STRAPS
1 POEM (KING)
INCENSE BOWL
PILLOW
4 COMBS HAIRSPRAY STOOLS MIRRORS
2 LETTERS (ROSA. MARIA)
SERPENTINE DAISIES
L. CAT.
1 CHAMPAGNE BOTTLE NAPKIN BUCKET
1 TRAY W/ 5 GLASSES
3 PILLOWS 1 LG. 2 SMALL
GINGER ALE
KEY
1 LETTER SEALED (JAQ/ARM)

14.6 Prop lists

LLL PERS. PROPS

PRINCESS - BINOCULARS - II-1 / BRACELET - III-1
MARIA - PEARL NECKLACE - III-1
ROSALINE - PEARL RING - III-1
KATHERINE - GLOVE - III-1
JAQUENETTA - BUBBLE GUM - THRU-OUT.
2 DIPLOMATS LUMISH GLENN / BRIEFCASE / HANDCUFF / UMBRELLA } III-2
NATHANIAL - NAPKIN - III-1
COSTARD - FLOWER - THRU-OUT / CIGARETTES - I-3 / SWORD - III-2
FORESTER - PIPE - II-1
DUMAINE - SHEET MUSIC - II-3
ARMADO - SCARF - ALL THRU.
BEROWNE - CIGAR / LIGHTER } THRU-OUT.
BOYET - FANS

SOUND CUES — Love's Labour's Lost

ACT	CUE	SOURCE	DESCRIPT.	TAPE	LOCATION	VOL.	SPKR.
I-1	#1	S.M.	CROWS	LLL·ASFTA COPY "A" 5/24/68	DECK #2	2½	LEFT RIGHT COVE
	#2	S.M.	"	"	" #2	2½	"
	#3	S.M.	"	"	" #2	2½	"
	WIND AHEAD TO LONG CROWS #2					—	
	#4	S.M	LONG CROWS	"	" #2	2½	"
	#5	S.M.	X FADE CROWS OUT HORNS UP	" TILL COPY B 3/24/68	DECK #2 DECK #1	"0" ↘ 8 ↑	BOX SPKR
	#6	S.M.	FADE HORNS	"	DECK #1	"0" ↘	
I-4	#7	S.M.	MIKE-ON	——	AMP #1	4½	BOX SPKR
	#8	S.M.	MIKE-OUT	——	AMP #1	"0" ↘	
II-3	#9	S.M.	MIKE-ON	——	AMP #1	4½	BOX SPKR
	#10	S.M.	MIKE-OUT	——	AMP #1	"0" ↘	
	#11	S.M.	MIKE-ON	——	AMP #1	4½	BOX SPKR
	#12	S.M.	MIKE-OUT	——	AMP #1	"0" ↘	
	#13	S.M.	MIKE-ON	——	AMP #1	5	BOX SPKR
III-2	#14	S.M.	VOL.-UP	——	AMP #1	7½ ↑	"
	#15	S.M.	VOL.-DOWN	——	AMP #1	5 ↓	"
	#16	S.M.	MIKE-OUT	——	AMP #1	"0" ↘	"

14.7 Sound cue sheet

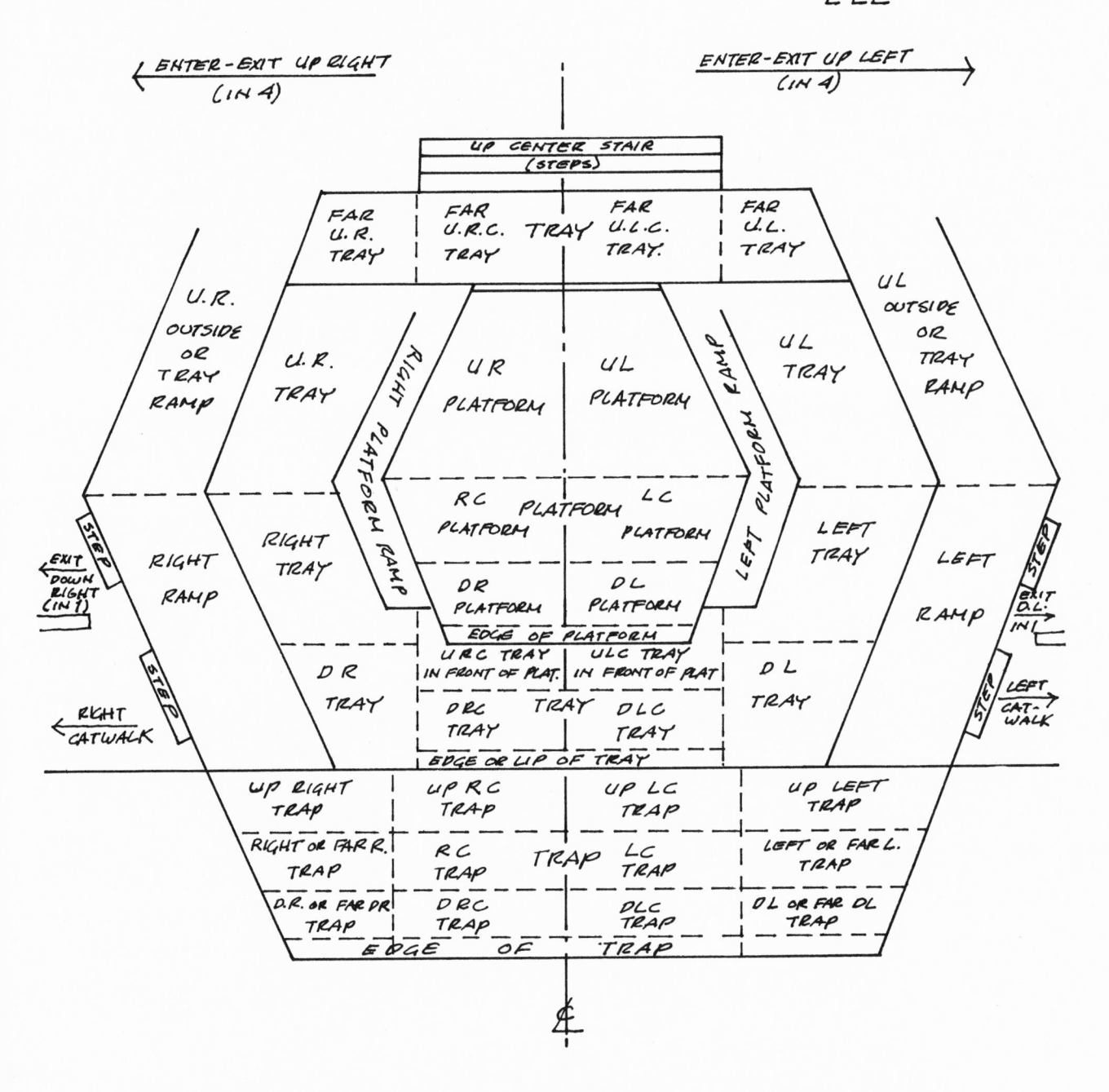

14.8 Master floor plan

SITARIST ENTERS FROM DOWN RIGHT IN "1"
HE CROSSES TO DOWN CENTER OF PLATFORM
& SITS ON CUSHION. HE BEGINS TO PLAY.

AT 20 MIN. 2 GUARDS & 6 DISCIPLES BEGIN
Entering From stage right. They
enter at their own pace in the
following order: 1 Mr. LAWRENCE
                 2. BOTH GUARDS
                 3. MR. RUSSELL
                 4. MR. SELIGIN
                 5. MR. ELLIS
                 6. MR. LUMISH.
                 8. MR. LEVEROTT.
They assume the positions indicated
at the left on this page.

AT PLACES THE FOLLOWING PEOPLE
move to the Front of the House:
GROUP 1 { KING
          2 MONKS { DANIELS
                   WORSNOPP

GROUP 2 { DUMAINE
          LONGAVILLE
          BEROWNE
          3 TEENY-BOPPERS (FEMALE)
          4 PRESS REPS (3 men, 1 WOMAN)

ACTORS ENTER THRU BACK OF HOUSE.
Groups 1 & 2 enter simultaneously
Group 1 led by King come down
          aisle on stage right.
     He is followed by
          Daniels w/ oath
     & Worsnopp w/ umbrella and
                   tape recorder.
          NAVARRE is holding flowers.
     They ascend stage:
          King crosses to Down
              Center of Platform.
     Worsnopp crosses Left of King.
     Daniels crosses left of Worsnopp
                   on tray in front of
                   Platform. He takes
                          OATH.
     ELLIS crosses Right of KING
              taking umbrella from
                   Daniels in cross.
GROUP 2 enters thru AISLE stage LEFT.
     Leading are Dumaine with guitar
          Longaville w/ camera & Berowne.
     ALL 3 Have FLIGHT Bags.

14.9 Action and cues prior to opening

388

AT:

12 MIN. —————————— CUE PROPS: LITE 1 INCENSE

13 MIN —————————— CUE SITARIST ON STAGE

18 MIN. —————————— PLACES FOR GUARDS AND DISCIPLES
CUE PROPS LITE REST OF INCENSE

27 MIN ———————— PLACES

| WARN |

SOUND #1

↓

28 MIN. ———————— MUSIC #1
SOUND #1

28:45 MIN ——————— | WARN |

SOUND #2

↓

29 MIN. ———————— SOUND #2

29:45 MIN ——————— | WARN |

SOUND #3

↓

30 MIN. ———————— SOUND #3

31 MIN. ———————— | WARN |

HOUSE TO ½
AND OUT
STATUE LITES OUT
ELEC #1
SOUND #4
#5

↓

32 MIN. ———————— HOUSE TO ½
STATUE LITES OUT

↓

HOUSE AT ½ ——————— HOUSE OUT

HOUSE OUT ————————— ELEC #1

↓

+:15 SEC. ———————— SOUND #4

↓

+:15 SEC. ———————— SOUND #5

IMMEDIATE FOLLOW. ———— | WARN |

SOUND #6

389

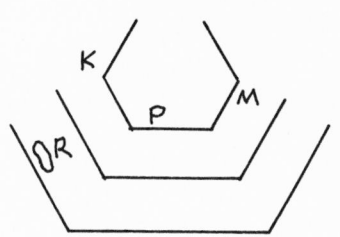

LADIES MOVE QUICKLY AWAY FROM PRINCESS
MARIA CROSSES LEFT OF PLATFORM ON TRAY
ROSALINE CROSSES TO SCOOTER ON DOWN RIGHT RAMP.
KATHERINE CROSSES TO UP RIGHT CENTER TRAY RIGHT
OF PLATFORM.

BOYET ENTERS DOWN RIGHT (in 1) & CROSSES
RIGHT OF PRINCESS

PRINCESS STANDS & CROSSES TO DOWN CENTER TRAY

KATHERINE CROSSES TO UP LEFT OF PRINCESS AT DOWN
RIGHT CORNER OF PLATFORM ON TRAY
MARIA CROSSES RIGHT OF PRINCESS

PRINCESS CROSSES TO DOWN LEFT TRAP
BOYET COUNTERS TO DOWN CENTER TRAY ON UP.

KATHERINE MOVES LEFT OF MARIA
ROSALINE DRESSES ONE STEP IN
GENERAL REACTION, TO THIS PRONOUNCEMENT, OF SHOCK

ENTER FROM DOWN RIGHT (in 1) KING CARRYING FLOWERS FOLLOWED
BY BEROWNE, LONGAVILLE, DUMAINE, 2 MONKS

BOYET CROSSES TO UP RIGHT OF MARIA

STAGE IS POSITIONED AS INDICATED ON DIAGRAM.

LONG PAUSE — "LOVE AT FIRST SIGHT" ♡

PRINCESS WHEELS – CROSSES UP TO LADIES – CROSSES TO
UP LEFT CORNER OF TRAP BELOW TRAY
PRINCESS TURNS TO KING

14.10 Action with dialogue

PRINCESS

God bless my ladies! Are they all in love(X)
That every one her own hath garnished
(With such) bedecking ornaments of praise?

~~LORD~~ *MARIA:*

Here comes Boyet.

(Enter BOYET)

PRINCESS

(Now,) what admittance, lord?

BOYET

(Navarre) had notice of your fair approach;
And he and his competitors in oath
Were all addressed to meet you, gentle lady,
Before I came.(X)Marry, thus much I have learnt;
He rather means to lodge you in the field,(X)
Like one that comes here to besiege his court,
Than seek a dispensation for his oath
To let you enter his unpeopled house.

(Enter NAVARRE, LONGAVILLE, DUMAINE, BEROWNE,
and ATTENDANTS)

(Here) comes Navarre.   *MUSIC:*
                                              SITAR CHORD
KING

(X)Fair princess(X)welcome to the court of Navarre.

PRINCESS

"Fair" I give you back again; and "welcome" I have not yet.
The roof of this court is too high to be yours, and welcome
to the wide fields too base to be mine.

KING

You shall be welcome, madam, to my court.

PRINCESS

I will be welcome, then. Conduct me thither.

KING

Hear me, dear lady -- I have sworn an oath.

PRINCESS

(Our) Lady help my lord!(X)He'll be forsworn.

KING

Not for the world, fair madam, by my will.

PRINCESS

Why, will shall break it, will, and nothing else.

As You Like It

CAST	CHARACTER	I 1	2	3	II 1	2	3	4	5	6	7	III 1	2	3	4	5	IV 1	2	3	V 1	2	3	4	Pre	U/S
LARRY PRESSMAN	ORLANDO	✓	✓					✓		✓	✓	✓					✓				✓		✓		DEVREN BOOKWTR.
DICK MATHENS	ADAM	✓						✓		✓	✓														
BILL DE VANE	OLIVER	✓										✓						✓		✓	✓				
ANDREW WORSNOPP	DENNIS	✓																							
REX EVERHART	CHARLES	✓	✓																						
DIANA VAN de VIIS	ROSALIND		✓	✓				✓				✓		✓	✓		✓	✓		✓		✓		✓	
MARION HAILEY	CELIA		✓	✓				✓				✓		✓	✓		✓	✓				✓			
REX ROBBINS	TOUCHSTONE		✓					✓				✓	✓									✓	✓		
TONY MAINIONIS	LE BEAU		✓																						
TOM RUISINGER	FREDERICK		✓	✓	✓							✓													
CHARLES CHIOFFI	DUKE				✓						✓										✓				
DEVREN BOOKWALTER	AMIENE/HYMEN				✓				✓		✓										✓				
RICHARD KLINE	1st LORD to DUKE				✓																				
ANDREW WORSHOPP	2nd LORD to DUKE				✓																				
IAN TUCKER	1st LORD to FRED.					✓																			
BOB LAMISH	2nd LORD to FRED					✓																			
	CORIN							✓				✓		✓	✓		✓								
TED GRAEBER	SILVIUS							✓							✓		✓		✓		✓				
STEPAN GIERASCH	JAQUES						✓			✓		✓	✓				✓	✓			✓				
	3rd Lord to Duke										✓														
ZOE KAMITSES	AUDREY													✓			✓			✓	✓	✓			
REX EVERHART	SIR OLIVER MARTEXT													✓											
JANE FARNOL	PHEBE															✓		✓		✓	✓				
	4th Lord to Duke																	✓							
IAN TUCKER	WILLIAM																✓								
ANDREW WORSHOPP	1st PAGE to DUKE																					✓			
JAMES DANIEL	2nd PAGE to DUKE																					✓			
	HYMEN																						✓		
TONY M.	DE BOYS																						✓		
BOB LUMISH	DEER KILLER																								
	ATTENDS to FRED.	✓	✓		✓						✓														
	ATTENDS to DUKE			✓				SING		SING								SING				✓			

14.11 Stage manager's cast list for *As You Like It*

which have to be replaced for each performance, such as food, or crockery which is broken in the show, are arranged. The prop table is set up. The first scene is set. The stage manager makes dressing-room calls at thirty, fifteen, and five minutes before curtain, personally checking the cast at the half hour (he must *see* each actor inside the theatre), calls the cast onstage, gives all precurtain cues, receives the "go" signal from the house manager, and cues the opening routine as it has been rehearsed. Traditionally, the show starts seven minutes after the advertised curtain time. Some theatres which have well-trained audiences ring up on the minute. Delays irritate the audience and have a bad psychological effect on green casts. Except when speed is essential, the shifts do not start until the actors are off. The stage manager and the crews follow the routines established in the technical and dress rehearsals.

Small repairs and necessary replacements in technical apparatus are made after each performance or before the next, depending on the nature of the work and the time available. The house carpenter maintains the house equipment (rigging, etc.), the show carpenter the scenery. The periodic repainting of the set is done over Sunday, usually at the scenic studio which painted it originally, or it may be done onstage by scene painters brought in for the purpose. If the show is moved, the stage carpenter supervises removal and installation of scenery. A theatrical transfer company does the trucking.

The master electrician maintains the lights, the stage telephone, and the cueing system. The property man purchases the perishable props daily, and is reimbursed on the weekly payday. The stage manager makes a daily or weekly report to the producer covering the immediate performances and the general state of the production. He also posts notices on the call-board, including calls for the next day, for special rehearsals of sections of the play, understudy rehearsals (usually once a week), and any other communications affecting the personnel.

In all systems of production except combination, a week is about the longest continuous run a show will have. In repertory it may alternate with other productions for many years. The tedium of a run is thereby avoided and the show is spared progressively less-inspired performances, the curse of continuous-run productions. Good repertory productions do not run downhill. The director is present from time to time to see that the roles are played as originally conceived or even developed and enriched further, that the performances do not lose quality, and that the production runs smoothly.

Long-run productions of a single play, however, often become tedious to the actors after the first few weeks, and that tedium shows in performance unless the stage manager, on whom the complete responsibility for a smooth-running performance rests, is able enough to preserve the freshness of the first week. While the producer, in Montego Bay or Cannes, awaits the weekly report of the gross, the stage manager must keep the show good enough to make the weekly report satisfactory.

Even in the most reputable producing organizations, after a show is successfully launched, the producer often institutes economies such as cutting out props to reduce the crew, changing gelatines every four instead of every two weeks, reducing the chorus or the crowds, and recasting minor parts at lower weekly salaries. Such practices hurt backstage morale.

As the show runs on, actors forget lines, drop cues, lose laughs, change pace, often as a result of sheer boredom. The muse is satisfied when the part has been created. Further creation is inhibited by the system under which the actor works. The stage manager, in addition to keeping the technical end of the production running smoothly, must observe every detail of every performance and allow no error to be repeated. He must rehearse the whole show if necessary when there are replacements in the cast, must rehearse understudies at least weekly, and must maintain the morale of the organization. This makes the stage manager's job increase in difficulty as the run continues. If he relaxes his attention or loses his sense of perspective or fails in any particular of his arduous task, the show will degenerate into a travesty of its original self, as have some notable productions which have had very long runs. The best presentation of the duties and responsibilities of the stage manager is in *The Stage Manager's Handbook* by Bert Gruver.

out-of-town openings

In commercial production in America, when a show opens out of town prior to a Broadway run, it is often moved into the theatre on Sunday, rigged, set up, lighted, and rehearsed before a Tuesday evening opening. Complex productions are generally given a trial assembly of scenery in the New York scenic studio before shipment and sometimes take a week to assemble, light, and rehearse in the out-of-town theatre before opening there. The crew sometimes works straight through from the time the show arrives until after the opening performance. A four-day stubble on the face of the master carpenter on opening night is not an unusual sight. The ordinary complications attendant upon working against time are augmented by the fact that the theatre may be a strange one; the resident crew may be unfamiliar with the scenery; the road city may be far from the purveyors of theatrical apparatus and accessories which may be found lacking.

Few productions break even financially on out-of-town openings. A musical comedy which later became an outstanding hit in New York played to standing room for a full week of tryout in a large (1,880 seats) theatre not far from Manhattan, yet lost money on the week because of the costs germane to the out-of-town opening. Many plays and musicals in recent years have switched from out-of-town tryout tours to series of pre-opening performances, called previews, in New York, the exceptions being musical productions which book tryouts in huge new theatres (2,500 seats or more) in a few cities and reap golden pre–New York harvests.

touring

There are still, in a score of cities in the United States, theatres which book plays and musicals on road tours either after successful New York runs or with a so-called national company during the continuing New York run. In recent years one professional repertory company has made the broad continent its theatrical home and New York City its final roadstop each year. A number of university theatres have instituted limited regional tours into high schools and community halls. Tours of plays, vaudeville units, and musicals to defense installations overseas have continued from World War II to the present time. The fascination of touring still outweighs its rigors for many theatre folk and it appears to be increasing.

Whereas touring theatre has customarily traveled by railroad in first-class accommodations, two other means of transportation have become increasingly popular and feasible: air travel by chartered passenger and freight planes, and by bus-and-truck (highway motor coach and trailer van). Speed and routing flexibility have combined with financial economies to encourage the adoption of these modes of travel.

preparation

Preparation of the show for touring involves, first, assembling the plans and specifications of the theatres in which the show will be played. The technical features of the production are then planned as closely as possible to conform to all the limitations that will be encountered. If a new set of scenery is not made for the tour, the one in existence may be cut down or strengthened. The prime requisites for touring are simplicity and ruggedness. Occasionally scenes will be cut or telescoped to save shipping costs and congestion on small stages. One show, played in New York on jackknife stages, was changed to a hung show, with two scenes telescoped and one cut, for the tour.

If the scenic scheme includes complex structures or floor modifiers that cannot be set in the time available for setting up in each road theatre, these parts are built in duplicate so that one copy can be sent ahead of the show and set up in anticipation of the arrival of the company and the rest of the scenery. duplicate parts

If the scenic scheme involves structural alterations to theatres, the tour must be booked so that they can be made during a dark period preceding engagements of the show. alterations

The planning and alterations of scenery for a tour are done by the original designer and builder, unless the changes are very minor, in which case they are planned by the stage manager and done by the show's crew under the supervision of the department heads.

The stage manager forwards to the theatres of the tour the hanging plot and a set of ground plans for the house carpenter. The show's master carpenter sends to the business agent of the IATSE local for each theatre a *yellow card* which states the number of stagehands, prop men, and electricians required to load in and hang, to run, and to load out the show. The local which receives the yellow card is obligated by its contract with the theatre to furnish the men specified. The company manager may receive, fill out, and return a form like Figure 14.3. information sent ahead

For the protection of scenery in transit, the flats may be crated. Set pieces are packed in special crates. Draperies and curtains are removed from battens and packed in trunks. Backdrops, gauzes, and arm cycloramas are rolled on their battens and wrapped in cotton covers. Scenery with fragile surfaces is wrapped in quilted pads. packing

Plastic foam units must be carefully padded and packed securely, preferably in crates, for touring. Plastic foam may be made into lightweight protective packages by carving or heat-molding containers for fragile objects. Scrap foam may be shredded or cubed and used as filler for packing fragile items such as lamps, chandeliers, vases, or antique furniture.

Ceilings are rolled on the long battens after the spreaders have been removed. Curtain tracks are unbolted in the center and the sections lashed side by side. Battens are tied together. Floorcloths are rolled on battens or packed in trunks. Properties are loaded into trunks or crates, laced into padded coverings, or covered with pads (similar to those used by furniture movers) tied on with webbing belts. Hand props are packed in trunks made with trays or individual compartments. Electrical sound equipment goes into special padded trunks, and lights go into crates and boxes. Light battens, with instruments clamped in place, sometimes travel with the show; if so, they are uncoupled into short sections.

Moving from stage to express cars or planes is done by a theatrical transfer company. Two types of trucks are supplied: for long loads (20′ and over), and short loads (under 20′). Long loads include battens, ceilings, floorcloths, travelers, and carpets. Flats, most properties, lights, sound equipment, set pieces, and parallel structures make up short loads. The removal from the theatre and the loading of the cars is done by the crews. A show on tour usually has its own baggage cars and sometimes its own Pullman cars. Passenger and cargo planes are contracted to be available for each hop. Highway coaches and vans are usually contracted to stay with the touring show since most bus-and-truck tours consist of many short engagements, split weeks, and one-night stands.

The department heads and a portion of the crew travel with the show and operate it with the assistance of additional local men, except when the show is simple enough to be handled by a local crew. In that case, only heads of departments travel. When the baggage cars or planes arrive, the local theatrical transfer company has trucks waiting, arrangements having been made by the advance man or company manager, and the department heads supervise the unloading of the cars. In general, the show is assembled onstage immediately. Any changes necessitated by the structure or equipment of the stage are made, new men routined into their jobs, and a technical rehearsal run if time permits. When the stage manager has checked the set, properties, lighting effects, and arrangements for shifts and storage, the show is ready to open.

When the tour stand is finished, the set, properties, lights, and so on, are usually moved out of the theatre into the baggage cars at once. The transfer trucks are waiting when the performance ends, and occasionally some easily portable items leave the theatre before the show is over.

Summer touring companies which are organized on a modest scale often play in tents, out of doors, and on the stages of high schools, country clubs, town halls, converted barns, or lodge halls. They usually travel by automobile or bus and move technical equipment by truck. Several companies which play in city parks or on streets use specially designed trailer stages. Because of the inadequacy of the stages on which they perform, sets for touring companies must be so built that they can be set up anywhere and can be altered to suit almost any set of conditions. When preparing a show for transportation by truck, the scenery must be designed and built for the limitations of the truck as well as the stages. It is also well for the advance man to travel the route of the show and to send back information on road conditions, particularly clear heights under railroad bridges.

Intercommunication

Communication among the various persons in charge of parts of the production during assembly, technical rehearsals, dress rehearsals, and performances is of critical importance. Actions of numerous people widely separated must take place precisely on time. Information must be conveyed clearly and reliably.

There are five situations which have differing intercom requirements:

Makeready. The stage manager, stage carpenter, and boss flyman in locations remote from each other (gridiron, trap room, stage floor, side stages, machinery room, fly floors) communicate about arranging permanent equipment of the theatre to receive the scenery; and the chief electrician and his assistants in such locations as the control room, the patch panel, the dimmer bank, the perches, the ceiling slots, light bridges, and the gridiron, communicate as they inspect, test, and arrange all permanent circuitry and apparatus.

Assembly. The stage manager, stage carpenter, boss flyman, and master electrician, remote from each other, resolve problems of installing the scenery on the stage; and the members of the lighting and sound departments, variously located, resolve their problems of installing and testing equipment.

Technical rehearsals. The director and the stage manager must talk to all members of the company by loudspeaker and to department heads by two-way phones. The light designer, seated near the director, must talk to the light-control operators, two-way, and to the operators of lighting instruments, two-way and common-talk; and the sound designer, seated near the director, must talk to the sound-control operator, two-way.

For makeready, assembly, and technical rehearsals, therefore, at least three separate clear two-way channels are needed plus one multistation common-talk channel and one public-address system.

Dress rehearsals. The stage manager must give cues, call actors, talk with personnel at any location where any action related to the show occurs. The director must be able to cut in on the stage manager's input circuit to talk to the same persons; when the light designer must talk to the console operator and instrument operators, the console operator must talk to instrument operators, and the sound designer to his console operator. Three channels are needed.

Performances. The stage manager must talk (Figure 14.12) to the house manager, the company in dressing rooms, and greenroom, and give cues and calls to all persons involved in running the show. Circuits which are used only in makeready, assembly, technical rehearsal, and dress rehearsal are no longer needed unless emergency repairs and adjustments call them into use. In performance it is essential that the stage manager be the originator of all communication and that talk-back and cross-talk be eliminated. Therefore a single channel common-talk system, with signal lights replacing buzzers as calling devices, or open channels with stage personnel wearing earphones is the desired system. Separate two-way channels can be energized as emergencies arise.

The optimum in operator mobility is afforded by a wireless system such as the 60 KHz inductance loop, which transmits to individual pocket-sized receivers with single earplug phones, the single input being the stage manager's microphone.

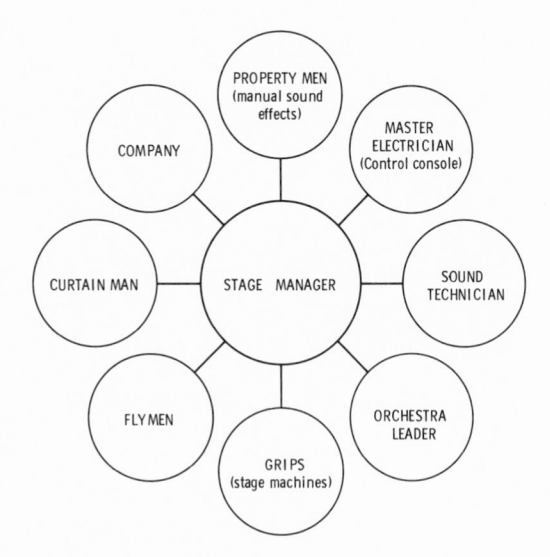

14.12 Schematic diagram of the stage manager's communications network during a performance

Postproduction Procedures

final disposition
of equipment

When a show closes, the following operations take place:

• The scenery, props, lights, sound equipment, and costumes are removed from the theatre.

• The stage and its permanent equipment are restored to the condition they were in when the show came in.

The theatre is thus restored to an intershow condition. When the closing show is moving to another city or another show is coming in next day, the moving trucks or vans are at the theatre by the end of the first act, and the crew can often strike sets and props into the vans as the scenes which required them end.

If the theatre is to remain dark for a few days or longer, the take-out starts the morning after closing and proceeds by a sequence of tasks which is exactly the reverse of the take-in.

The take-down is performed faster than the setup because precision is not a factor. However, the caution which safety demands must be observed. Counterweights must not be removed until scenery has been detached from battens; a piece of sandbagged scenery which has been unweighted must be lowered to the floor under control by snubbing the lines around a belaying pin or snubbing an overhaul on a winch drum. Special care is needed if floor traps are open or if stage or forestage elevators are above or below stage level. Thus far, the procedure is the same for both single- and multiple-production organizations. If the run is ended, the fate of the scenery is determined by a wide variety of considerations which differ as producing organizations differ: the scenery is sold, destroyed, salvaged for reuse, or stored for revival.

Economic and political rather than theatrical considerations are often responsible for the last two methods of disposal. American customs regulations provide that scenery built abroad must be shipped out of the country or destroyed at the end of the run. The transient character of commercial production, the small size of theatres, the high cost of trucking, and the lack of good inexpensive warehouse facilities all induce the producer to get rid of the scenic investiture before it becomes a large liability. He is lucky if he can sell it.

sale

There is little market for used flat scenery. Cut borders and fabrics which are worn out or are of no value in the market are sold as rags.

Curtains, except those which are dyed or painted for a specific production, find a fairly active market. Black and neutral-colored velours, draw curtains, teasers, borders, legs, and the like are fairly durable and are sometimes sold by one producer to another. Such items, when baled, are not bulky and may well be stored pending advantageous sale.

Items of stage machinery, if not too specialized, can often be sold. A good disc will find a buyer in almost any season. The market for used travelers is quite active.

Lighting equipment which is not repossessed or repurchased at the close of a production by the company which originally furnished it, often finds its way into the hands of dealers in used lighting equipment. Such dealers generally have in stock, at reasonable prices, equipment ranging from orchestra music stands to water-ripple effects.

Properties, if they are genuine, are sold to dealers in secondhand furniture, bric-a-brac, and the like. Sundry items of furniture in producers' apartments were practically new when taken from the stage.

Community and stock theatres and schools buy considerable amounts of secondhand scenery, lights, props, and mechanical equipment. They purchase direct from the producer whose show is closing, from the theatrical transfer or warehouse who may be acting as agent for the producer, and from the dealer in used equipment. Such purchasing, if intelligently done, involves considerable exploration and long-range planning, and is usually possible only when time is no factor in the transaction. Advantageous purchases are seldom accidental or opportune. The buyer must look over shows before they close and keep the theatrical transfer companies and equipment dealers informed of his needs and what he is willing to pay. Many standard items can be bought at a great saving if the buyer is willing to hunt and wait. Twenty percent of the list price of the new item is a fair price to pay for the same item used. Prices, of course, vary with supply and demand, locality, the total amount of the purchase, and the imperative on the producer to dispose of the material.

junked scenery

What the commercial producer cannot sell he is often happy to give away to any organization that will come with a truck from a theatrical transfer company, load it with a union crew, and cart it away. What cannot be given away goes to the nearest dump. The commercial producer cannot afford the labor necessary to salvage hardware. The school or community theatre can, and may find it profitable to accept a whole show, salvage what it wants and dump the rest.

salvage

Between one fifth and one half of the cost of noncommercial production is represented by the scenery. The materials and labor of scene construction constitute a large percentage of this cost. Producing organizations with limited budgets may therefore save a considerable amount by salvaging and storing sets when productions close.

The salvage of hardware and rigging materials effected at the time the set is struck will result in an appreciable saving in the cost of these items in the course of a theatrical season.

School and community theatres may often effect substantial savings in scenic budgets by salvaging junked scenery from commercial productions. With cheap labor, hardware can be salvaged from abandoned flats. One school theatre which runs a fairly heavy production schedule salvaged in a day enough hardware to fill its needs for several years. Occasional flats, parallels, and once in a while an entire set, may thus be obtained.

It is true that not all scenery has future value if salvaged. If an established producing organization can standardize the size and shape of much of its basic scenery, it can make appreciable savings by salvaging those pieces of standard sizes and shapes. Flats, of course, are the most obvious type of scenery in which savings are possible.

The procedure for their salvage (which applies to other types of scenery) is as follows:

• Build the flats to standard sizes, particularly standard height, as far as possible, consistent with the designer's requirements. Build odd-shaped flats so that they include standard shapes in their structure.

• In striking the set, select only standard sizes and shapes for salvage. The odd sizes are reused only with great difficulty. Remove all hardware.

• Mark each flat with an index number according to a storage catalog. The marking should be such that it is readily distinguishable in whatever position the flat is stored and not easily effaced. Numbers die-stamped into the edges of the lumber soon fill with scene paint. Numbers stamped into narrow brass strips which are tacked to the four edges of the flat are lasting and easy to find and read. The numbering system can be developed so that the number itself is indicative of the type and size of flats.

• Store the flats in the manner described in the next sections of this chapter. A good warehouse layout often has as much space allotted to aisles as to storage.

storage

The decision whether to store or discard scenery can be based primarily on the expected frequency of reuse, which in turn depends upon a number of factors:

• The number of shows per season.

• The general nature of the scenery: realistic interior sets use more standard pieces in a limited number of sizes than do exterior sets or abstract sets; abstract sets may make frequent use of standard-sized platform parts; imaginative designing inclines to nonstandard and non-reuseable parts.

• The amount of available storage space and its consequent value. Decisions based on these factors are not difficult for the experienced technical director.

active storage

To warrant the capital investment in space, storage of scenery and properties must contribute in reduction of costs an amount equal to or greater than the interest on the cost of building and the direct cost of operating the storage facility. The pieces stored must have enough intrinsic value and be used with sufficient frequency to pay their way.

The establishment of standard sizes of flats, doors, windows, platforms or platform parts, and stairs tends to keep nonstandard parts from being built and limits the variety of scenery stored; hence it renders storeroom operation easier than otherwise and tends to increase the use frequency of the pieces stored.

inventory,
index, and catalog

A memory and use system which will tell the owner or potential user what scenery is stored, where it is, and its characteristics is essential to efficient storeroom operation. Each piece must be represented by a card in a card index, bearing the index number for the piece, a written description of the piece, and a dated record of each use of the piece.

If a piece is altered structurally or its dimensions changed, a new card is substituted when a piece is taken out of storage for use. The use is recorded on the card, which is then placed in a file box titled with name of the show for which the piece is to be used and held there until the piece is returned to storage. This affords a method of charging costs, if any, to the show, of preventing another user from taking the piece from storage without authorization, of knowing what pieces are out of the storeroom, and of following up when pieces have not been returned.

Scenery for repertory is stored at the end of each season as long as the play of which it is a part is in the program. It may be kept in storage for a number of years while production of the play is suspended. It often wears out and has to be replaced, usually according to new designs, before the play is dropped. Repertory storage is unique in that scenery and properties for a show must be stored as an entity, kept readily available for recall when the show is revived, and stored until the show is dropped from the repertory. repertory storage

Community and school theatres save their scenery for alteration and reuse, seldom for revival of the same play. Units thus saved lose their identity as parts of a show and are grouped according to types when they reach the warehouse. Scenery from stock productions is altered for the next show. community and school storage

Community and school theatres need storage space as badly as repertory theatres do, but it is seldom provided for in the design of the plant. Whatever space is available is generally inadequate in size and shape, and inconveniently placed. In a college theatre in New York, scenery is stored in the basement, carried up a flight of stairs to a yard, and raised four stories by outdoor block and tackle to stage level. This is a difficult and, for inexperienced students, a dangerous operation, and it depends upon favorable weather.

The prime requisites for scene storage are: storage requirements

Accessibility. All items must be placed so as to make possible easy inspection and removal of any one item without moving other items. The warehouse must be in or near the theatre building if trucking costs are not to reduce the potential savings.

Safety. Scenery must be stored where fire hazard is minimal and where there will be no damage from dampness. Woolen fabrics must be protected from moths, and objects made with wheat paste, from rodents.

Order. It is generally more economical of space and time to store similar units rather than whole settings together.

Under excellent conditions, to be found in some European theatres, scenery is stored in a brick or concrete building, adjacent to the stage. Large units are stored on the ground floor. Elevators are of sufficient capacity to carry loaded scenery trucks to the upper floors.

Flat scenery is best stored vertically, at right angles to a wall. Wooden or metal separating members project from the wall at intervals to keep flats upright and divided into groups of from five to ten. Flats may be easily slipped out for inspection. Under this system it is possible to store more than one hundred flats per fifteen feet of wall.

Three-dimensional scenery is collapsed and racked as flat scenery whenever possible. When it cannot be collapsed, it is stood on whatever side or edge will occupy the least floor space. Units are set in rows, and aisles are left between alternate rows to facilitate inspection and removal. Occasionally, three-dimensional units are hung from the ceiling.

Drops packed in trunks are best stored on shelves against a wall after the manner of trunk storage used in some railroad terminals. Rolled drops, carpets, and the like, are stored in racks. Drop racks, wood or metal, consist of upright members from floor to ceiling, to which are attached two- or three-foot horizontal cross members at intervals of one or two feet. The upright members are placed in parallel lines, at intervals of not more than four feet, with all horizontal members parallel. Rolled drops, rolled ceilings, and travelers are placed on the horizontal members, and tagged at the ends for identification. Where a high narrow space is available, drops may be raised to any height on a flying bridge and stored on wall brackets. Such a drop storage space located at one side of the stagehouse is common in continental repertory theatres.

Property storage is best achieved by storing according to categories: furniture, lamps, bric-a-brac, etc., and by the methods employed in industrial or commercial storage within the categories. Open, accessible shelves for small props are indispensable. Trunks are to be preferred to drawers for the storage of draperies and other fabrics, and small boxes are used for the linen, laces, etc.

Stage lighting equipment, when not rigged, can usually, by virtue of its lack of bulk, be stored in the theatre. For warehouse storage, units are put into crates and boxes. Since lighting equipment is noninflammable, it may be stored in locations forbidden to properties and scenery.

storage onstage Scenery is seldom stored onstage unless it is to be used, as in repertory, within a short time. Scenery on the stage is divided into two categories, live and dead. Live scenery is for the show currently running (within the show, for the scenes still to be played) and dead scenery, for the show which has closed (or acts which have played). Flat scenery is stacked against the walls in the order in which it is to be next used, or is flown. Three-dimensional units, standing or rolling, are stood on the stage floor in the order of their next use. No objects may be stored onstage in such a position as to interfere with shifting or the movement of actors, or free access to any doors.

Flown scenery such as drops is best stored in the flies. When the flies are full, it is sometimes racked in rooms adjacent to the stage. Properly designed theatres have rooms adjacent to the stage for live and semilive property storage.

variations Under the combination system of production, warehouses are not usually owned by the producing organization but by a theatrical transfer company. Shows are stored in rented warehouse space pending the start of a road tour or revival, or sale of the scenery. In the warehouse, scenery is usually stored or grouped by shows, flat scenery laid on the floor, drops, three-dimensional pieces, properties, and sometimes cases of lights piled on top of the flats. This system, wasteful as it is, keeps shows owned by different producers reasonably well separated, but scenery thus stored is inaccessible for inspection. Unless the producer files complete sets of drawings, he has no convenient way of keeping track of what he has stored.

Processes and techniques 15

It has seemed logical to write the following exposition of processes in a form of direct address, on the assumption that the builder, like a chef with a cookbook, seeks specific instructions for the performance of work. In place of recipes, this chapter contains problems, numbered serially for easy reference. The person addressed is a composite of all the workers in a scene shop. The master craftsman, whether carpenter, property master, charge painter, or master stage carpenter, is of course familiar with each step and detail of the process and the time required for it, so that he may plan and assign the work, and supervise and assist in the execution of any part of it.

Carpentry

The premise of this presentation is that competence in elementary woodworking is basic for all other skills required in scenecraft. Some simple processes and exercises are described in detail in the first part of the chapter. Processes and exercises in the working of metals and plastics are presented in less elementary fashion with the assumption that the trainee brings to this work skills acquired in woodworking.

Standard sizes and lengths of lumber are kept in stock in the scene shop. The cutting list specifies the number of pieces, sizes, lengths, and stock lengths from which they are to be cut.

selecting lumber

Select stock lengths and sizes as called for in the cutting list. All lumber, except the finest grade, contains flaws. For long lengths, and for any lengths which are to be fitted against other scenery, select lumber free from warp or twist. For pieces which are to be subject to transverse strain, select lumber free from knots, short grain, and pitch pockets. For cutting into short lengths which are not to be used for outside framing members, long lengths having slight warp or twist may be used. For pieces which are to undergo little stress, lengths weakened by knots, pitch pockets, or short grain are acceptable. For pieces which are to be worked into special shapes, select clear (free from knots and other imperfections), straight-grained lumber.

- When a number of pieces are to be marked uniformly, clamp them together in parallel alignment and make one measurement for all pieces.

- When marking a number of pieces uniformly with instruments which are set (protractor, dividers, compasses, mortise gauge, marking gauge), mark all pieces with one setting of the instrument at one time.

- Be sure that the measuring instruments are true, both the graduations into feet and inches, and the established angles. Wooden rules should have metal-sheathed ends to prevent wear.

- Use a steel stylus rather than a pencil for all points and lines. Some measuring instruments contain a scriber inserted in the head. An improvised stylus may be made by grinding a large nail or a short length of steel rod to a sharp point. Lines made with a stylus are called scratch lines. *Do not mark with felt pens and ink.*

- Protect steel instruments from corrosion with a thin coating of fine oil. Rust pits the edges and disfigures the graduated marks.

- Roll or fold all tapes or rules and leave them in protected places if only for a few minutes.

- Protect all instruments from falling or other damage by inserting them in cases or racks when they are not in use.

1. To test a try square.

With the try square held tightly in place, scribe a line perpendicular to the straight edge of a piece of wood. Reverse the square. If the edge of the square coincides with the line, the square is accurate (Figure 15.1).

2. To measure a required length on a stock-sized piece, and to mark for square-cut ends.

EQUIPMENT: try square, rule or tape, marking point.

PROCEDURE: select a piece of lumber of the proper size and of the standard length next longer than the required length. Place on a bench or pair of horses. Select an end that is free from check or split. Square the end. Do this by holding the head of the try square firmly against an edge of the piece (Figure 15.2), and scribing a line across the surface, with the edge of the blade as a guide. Square the end far enough back to produce a square cut and avoid imperfections in the wood. Lumber with ends guaranteed square and perfect is produced by certain lumber companies at a slightly increased price. The carpenter must decide whether the saving in labor, time, and waste material warrants the additional cost of square-ended lumber.

Place the zero of the folding rule or rolling tape exactly on the scratch line just made, and extend the tape tightly along one edge of the wood. At the required length on the rule or tape, mark the edge of the lumber with the marking point. Place the try square exactly on this mark, and

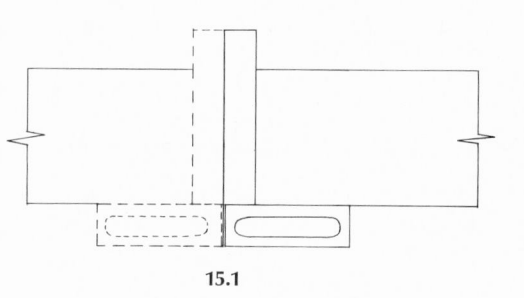

15.1

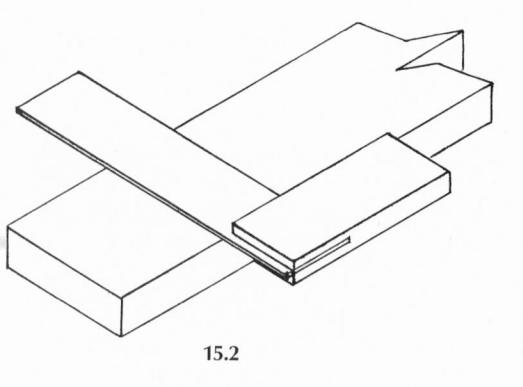

15.2

holding it firmly as before, scribe a line across the surface. Mark X on the waste portions of the piece. When the piece is cut, the saw cut will be made on the waste side of the scratch line. Mark the full identification and the length on the piece in large figures.

3. To measure a series of small lengths on a standard-length piece, and mark for square-cut ends.

EQUIPMENT: rule or tape, square, marking point.

PROCEDURE: select a piece of lumber of proper size, free from objectionable flaws, and of the standard length next greater than the sum of all the short lengths to be cut. The cutting list indicates the necessary standard length. Square the end and measure the first length as in Problem 2. Mark a saw-kerf allowance (the amount of wood removed by the saw) at the end of the first length. From the second mark of the saw-kerf allowance, repeat the measuring process for the other required lengths. Avoid objectionable flaws by starting the measurements for subsequent lengths beyond them. Avoid having a cut mark coincide with a knot. Mark X on waste portions and full identification and measurement on each good portion.

4. To set out, on a standard piece of standard length and size, a required length of lumber for oblique-cut ends.

Oblique ends form any angle with the edge of the board between 0° and 90°, except 45° and 90°.

EQUIPMENT: rule or tape, bevel protractor, marking point.

PROCEDURE: select a piece of lumber with a clear end. Set the bevel protractor at the desired angle. Hold the bevel protractor firmly against the edge of the wood, the blade firmly against the surface, and scribe a line along the blade (Figure 15.3). From the apex of the angle just made, measure the required overall length along the edge of the piece. Reset the protractor for the second required angle, hold as before, and scribe the second line. If the apex of the second angle is on the opposite edge of the wood from the apex of the first, scribe a square line across the wood and hold the protractor against the second edge. Mark the identification of the piece and the *identification of or number of degrees in each angle* on the measured length.

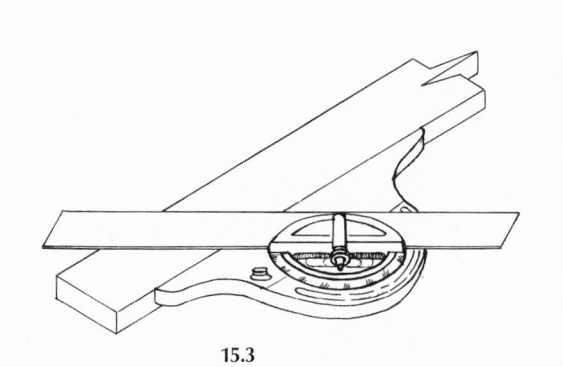

15.3

5. To measure and set out a series of required small lengths with mitered ends.

A mitered end forms an interior angle of 45° with the edge of the piece.

EQUIPMENT: rule, miter or combination square, marking point.

PROCEDURE: select a piece with a perfect end, or if the end is imperfect, start measurements at the nearest possible point to the end. Measure and mark the overall length (from apex to apex along one edge) as given in the cutting list. Hold the miter, or the miter side of the combination square, against the edge of the piece at the points marked, and scribe lines across the surface of the board. Scribe, parallel to these lines, the allowance for the saw kerf. See Figure 15.4. Proceed to measure other pieces, letting the marks serve for the ends of two pieces. When the lumber is reversible, a series of lengths may be set out with the angles matched so as to cause no waste of lumber. When moldings or other

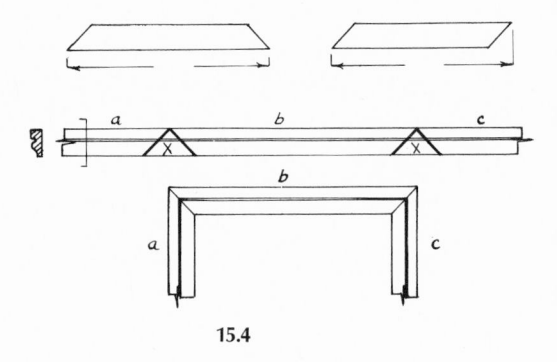

15.4

stock are being mitered for cornices or panels, make sure the first end has the correct miter mark, before measuring the length. For panels and picture frames, the miter must be reversed and a small amount of material wasted between pieces.

6. To set out, on a piece of wood, a number of blocks for block-butt joints, each block to be an isosceles right triangle.

EQUIPMENT: rule, miter or combination square, marking point.

PROCEDURE: select a piece of wood of good quality and required thickness (generally 1¼″) and as wide as the perpendicular distance from the right angle to the hypotenuse of the block. At a point *a* on one edge of the piece, with a miter as a guide, scribe two lines which form an angle of 90°. Move the miter to the intersection of one of the scratch lines and the other edge, *b,* and scribe another line. If the blocks must meet precise dimension requirements, scribe at each point the saw-kerf allowance. See Figure 15.5.

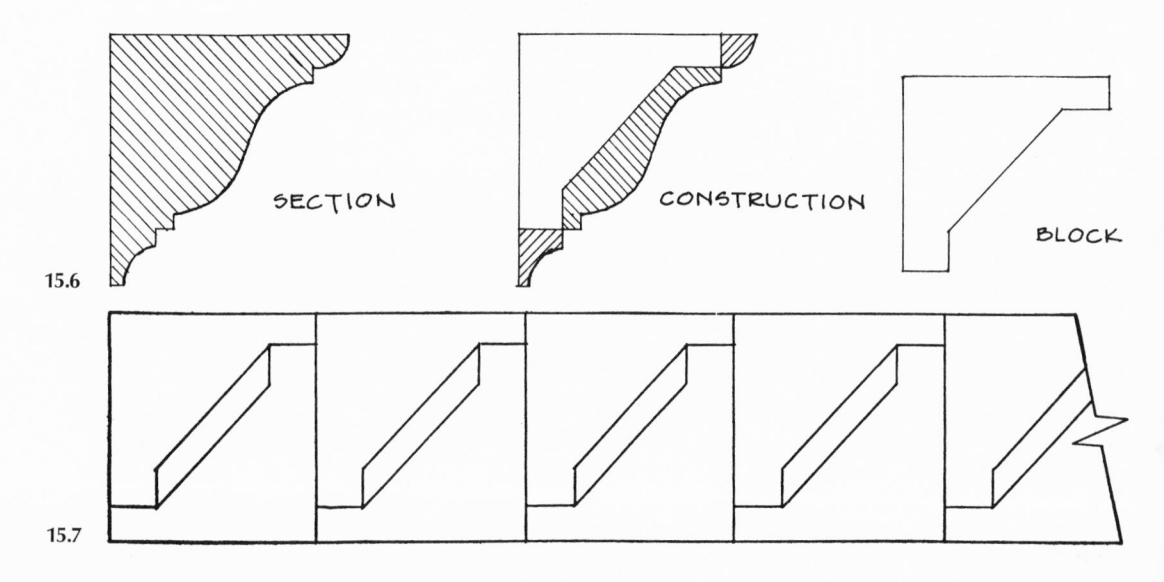

15.5

Blocks set out in this way have the grain of the wood running in the best direction to resist any stress put upon the block. Small triangles may be cut from the corners of the blocks to reduce the side dimensions and allow a large block to be used to reinforce the joint of narrow boards.

7. To set out a series of cornice blocks.

EQUIPMENT: marking point, pattern of block.

PROCEDURE: the pattern of the cornice block is developed on pattern paper by the draftsman, cut out, attached to the blueprint, and sent to the shop.

Test the pattern on various widths of wood (generally 1¼″ thick) to determine which width allows cutting with the least waste of wood. Examine the pattern to determine if a certain direction of the grain of the wood is better than any other for the strength of the block. Be governed by this in setting the pattern on the wood. Take advantage of mill-cut straight edges of the wood where possible. Provide, in setting out the pattern, for occasional through cuts to aid the sawyer. See Figures 15.6 and 15.7.

SECTION   CONSTRUCTION   BLOCK

15.6

15.7

8. To measure and mark for a rip cut.

First Method

EQUIPMENT: marking gauge.

PROCEDURE: place the piece on a bench or horses. Set the block of the marking gauge at the distance from the spur equal to the desired width of the piece. Turn the thumbscrew up tight to hold the block in position. With the block of the marking gauge set against a straight edge of the lumber, make two or three rolling strokes of the gauge, thus scratching a line on the face of the piece. See Figure 15.8.

Second Method

EQUIPMENT: rule, marking point.

PROCEDURE: this method is to be used only after considerable practice. Grasp the rule with thumb and forefinger at the desired distance from the end. Place the stylus firmly against the end of the rule. Guide the rule perpendicular to the edge of the piece, with the forefinger under the rule and against the edge. With several strokes, the first very light, and with later ones increasing the pressure on the marking point, scratch a line on the face of the piece (Figure 15.9).

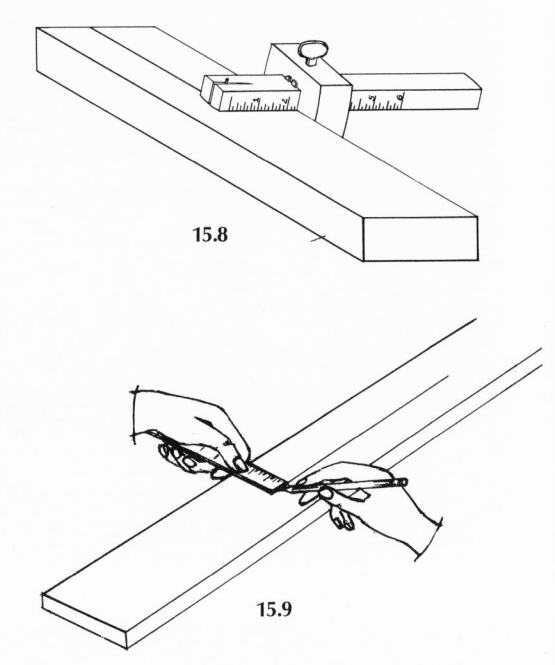

15.8

15.9

9. To set out an open mortise-and-tenon joint between two pieces of wood, end to end, at right angles.

EQUIPMENT: mortise gauge, marking gauge.

PROCEDURES

For hand cutting: cut pieces A and B square to required length. Set the marking gauge for the width of A. Scratch lines on both edges and both faces of B, guiding gauge against the end. Set marking gauge for the width of piece B. Scratch lines on the edge of A, guiding the marking gauge between the block and first spur, and the distance between the two spurs equal to one-third the thickness of A. Scratch lines on both edges and the end of A, guiding against the face. With the same setting of the mortise gauge, scratch lines on both edges and the end of B. Mark ends M and T for the benefit of the cutter. See Figure 15.10.

For machine cutting: mortise machines and tenon machines are equipped with adjustable guides, fences, and gauges, which, although differing in operation with the makes of the machines, work basically in the same way to regulate the depth and shape of the cuts. Machines may be so completely equipped with guides and gauges as to require no marking of the lumber beyond the notation of the positions and dimensions of the mortise and the tenon.

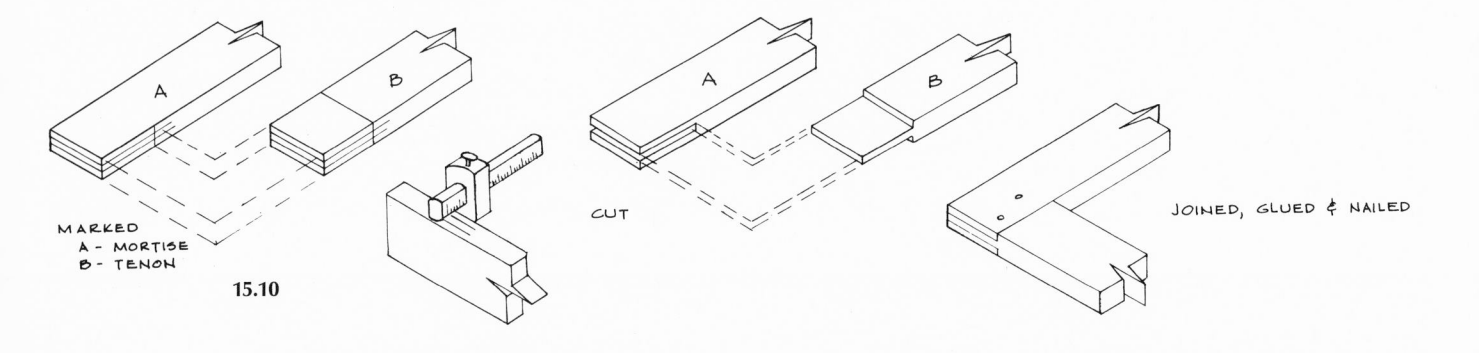

MARKED
A - MORTISE
B - TENON

15.10

CUT

JOINED, GLUED & NAILED

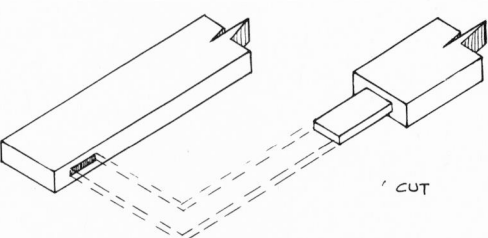
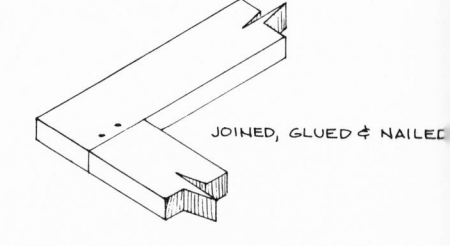

MARKED
A- MORTISE
B - TENON

' CUT

JOINED, GLUED & NAILED

15.11

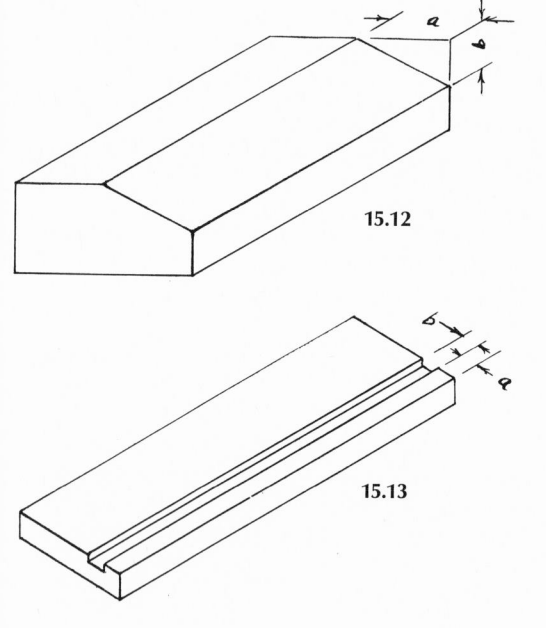

15.12

15.13

10. To set out a closed mortise-and-tenon joint.

EQUIPMENT: mortise gauge, marking gauge.

PROCEDURE: set the mortise gauge with the first spur at a distance *a* from the block, the second spur at a distance *b* from the first spur (Figure 15.11). Guiding against the end, scratch two lines on the edge of the piece to be mortised. With the same setting, guiding against the edge, scratch corresponding lines on one face of the piece to be tenoned. Reset the mortise gauge so that the spurs divide the thickness measurement of the piece in thirds. Guide against the face of the mortised piece and scratch two lines on one edge. With the same setting, guide against the face of the tenoned piece and scratch lines on both edges and end. Set the marking gauge for a distance equal to the width of the mortised piece, on the tenoned piece, guide against the end, and scratch lines on both edges and both faces.

For a stopped mortise, either open or closed, which does not extend entirely through the piece, the depth of the mortise is indicated by a scratch mark on the face of the piece, but the depth must be measured by the cutter with a depth gauge or by a setting of the mortising machine. The tenon is not so long as for a full mortise.

11. To set out a bevel on the edge of a piece.

EQUIPMENT: marking gauge.

PROCEDURE: if the required bevel is indicated in degrees in the working drawings, make a full-scale section drawing of the piece and measure the amount of the bevel in inches on the face and edge of the piece. Set the marking gauge for the distance *a*, guide against the edge of the piece, and scratch a line on the face. Reset the gauge for the distance *b*, guide against the face, and scratch a line on the edge. See Figure 15.12.

12. To set out a lengthwise dado, or plow, on the surface of a piece.

EQUIPMENT: mortise gauge.

PROCEDURE: set the mortise gauge with first spur at a distance *a* from the block, and second spur at a distance *a* plus *b* from the block (Figure 15.13). Guide against the edge and scratch two parallel lines on the face of the piece.

13. To set out a circular sweep.

EQUIPMENT: square, trammel points and bar (beam compass).

PROCEDURE: establish a right angle on the bench or wooden floor (whichever will accommodate the radius of the required curve). Fasten a straightedge to the bench and lay out a line perpendicular to it at its center (Figure 15.14). Fasten the piece to be marked against the straightedge. Set the trammels on the bar for the required radius. From

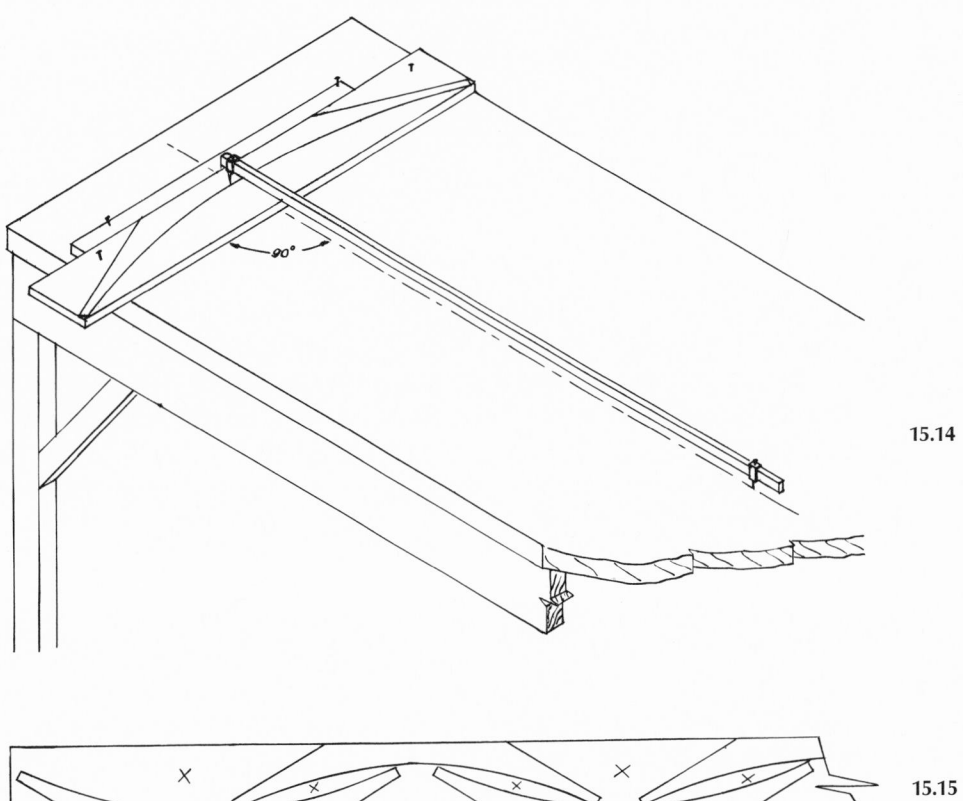

15.14

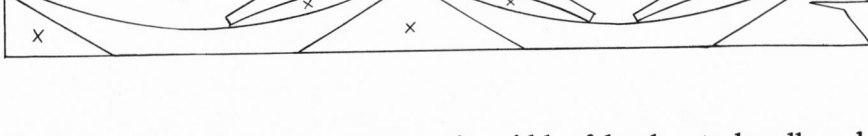

15.15

the back edge of the piece, measure the width of lumber to be allowed at the narrowest point when the arc is cut. Set the marking point of the trammel or compass at this point and at the center point on the line. Swing the bar and scribe the required arc. Set out the straight cuts as required at the ends of the arc for fitting to other pieces (Figure 15.15).

14. To set out a stair carriage.

EQUIPMENT: 24″ × 18″ metal square.

PROCEDURE: select a piece of lumber 1¼″ or 2″ thick as specified in the drawing, of sufficient overall length to accommodate all the treads. Determine the cutting dimension of the tread and riser. Measure the distance of one riser from the end of the board as a safe allowance for the beginning of the first tread. Place the square on one edge of the board at this point with the right angle on the wood, so that the tread measurement on one side of the square and the riser measurement on the other side of the square coincide with the edge of the wood. Trace around the edge of the square. Move the square along the board and repeat the process until all the cuts are marked (Figure 15.16). At each end, mark for a square cut, and at the bottom end, mark to cut off the waste under the bottom riser. Make sure that the bottom riser height is one tread thickness shorter than all other riser heights. If the stair is to be mounted on casters, deduct another ¾″ from the height of the bottom riser. Cut one piece, check it against the measurements, and if it is correct, use it as a pattern for the other identical pieces.

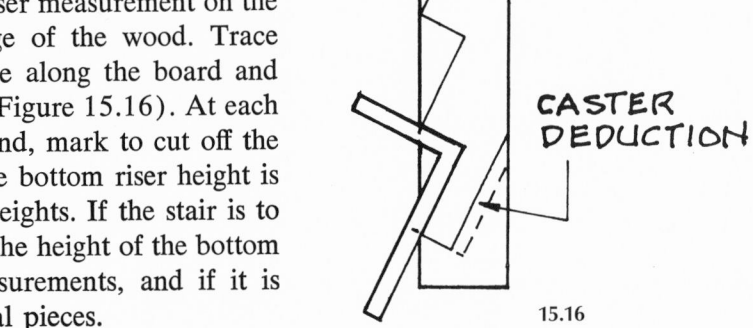

CASTER DEDUCTION

15.16

15. To work up an open mortise-and-tenon joint.

EQUIPMENT: backsaw and chisels (¼″, 1″, or 1½″), mallet, ¼″ wood bit and brace.

PROCEDURE:

The Mortise (A): clamp the piece end up in the bench vise. With a backsaw cut *inside* both scratch lines to the depth indicated by the line scratched across the edge. Reset the piece horizontally in the vise, edge uppermost. With a ¼″ chisel pare across the grain until the mortise is cleaned out. Reverse the chisel and cut directly along the wood at the bottom of the mortise. *Alternate method of cleaning out the mortise:* With a ¼″ wood bit, drill a series of contiguous holes into the mortise from one edge of the piece. With 1″ and ¼″ chisels smooth the inside surfaces and square the corners of the mortise.

The Tenon (B): fasten the piece in the vise on the bench top face up. With the backsaw cut along the scratch line on each face to the depth indicated by the scratch lines on the edges of the piece. With a broad chisel (1″ or 1½″) split off the waste, cutting from the ends. With the same chisel pare down the tenon to fit the mortise. Follow the same basic procedure for working up closed or stopped mortise-and-tenon joints.

16. To work up a beveled edge.

EQUIPMENT: drawknife, smoothing plane.

PROCEDURE: clamp the piece in a vise or nail it on the bench with the marked edge protruding. With a drawknife pare the bevel down to within ¹⁄₁₆″ of the scratch marks. With a smoothing plane pare the wood down to the marks.

17. To work up a lengthwise dado on the face of a piece.

EQUIPMENT: 1½″ chisel and other chisel as required.

PROCEDURE: Fasten the piece face up to the bench. With a 1½″ chisel (see Problem 18 for the proper technique) cut along both scratch lines to the depth required. With a chisel as wide as the dado, split and pare out the waste. In splitting, make a series of short splits rather than a few long ones.

In the carpentry problems that follow, equipment is not listed since it is assumed that the apprentice now understands that before he starts work he must read the problem and assemble the tools specified. Each solution will consist of the recommended procedure supported by appropriate precepts.

use of paring tools
pointers and precautions

• Propel paring tools along the wood with the grain (that is, in the direction in which the grain runs up and out).

• Keep all paring tools under control while in use. Propel the tool with one hand and simultaneously restrain the forward motion of the tool with the other hand.

• A slight slant of the cutting edge across the wood, as in whittling, makes all paring easier.

• Spend time in sharpening paring tools in order to save time and damaged work when using them.

• Take good care of the cutting edges of paring tools. Avoid striking nails or screws or other metal. Place tools in guarded places when not in use.

- Chisels are not screwdrivers or tack lifters.

18. To use a chisel.

A chisel is used to remove the waste from beveled joints, notched joints, and mortise-and-tenon joints. The technique of its use falls into four divisions: splitting with the grain, paring with the grain, cutting across the grain, and paring across the grain.

To split: secure the wood in a vise or on top of the bench with the end to be split projecting. Ascertain direction of grain. Place the chisel against the end of the wood so that the split will not extend into the portion of the wood to be used. Tap the end of the chisel handle lightly with a mallet. If the grain of the wood is straight, the split may be the final cut.

To pare: place the chisel with the ground side toward the wood and pointed with the grain (Figure 15.18). Grasp the handle firmly in one hand and propel the blade forward; at the same time control the direction and depth of the cut by pressure of the fingers of the other hand near the cutting edge.

To cut across the grain: with the wood secured in a vise, hold the chisel at right angles to the wood with the ground side toward the waste portion of the wood. Tap the end of the chisel handle lightly with a mallet.

To pare across the grain: with the wood secured in a vise, place the chisel at a steep angle to the wood with the ground side toward the wood. Control the depth and direction of the cut by holding the chisel near its cutting edge with one hand. Propel the chisel into the wood by light taps of a mallet.

19. To use a plane.

A plane is used to smooth the ends, edges, or surfaces of wood which have been roughly cut by other tools, such as a saw or drawknife.

Secure the piece to be planed in a vise. Check the piece for smoothness with a straightedge. Check it for squareness with a try square. Plane the areas which are not smooth or square. Push the plane in the direction of the upward slant of the grain. If the grain is wavy, it may be necessary to reverse the direction of the plane on different parts of the surface being planed. Set the depth of the cut according to the degree of roughness to be removed. Make several strokes with a deeply set blade ($\frac{1}{100}''$) and make finishing strokes with the blade set to remove the thinnest possible shaving ($\frac{1}{200}''$ or less). If the uneven surface of a piece is long, use a long smoothing plane, since a short plane will ride into the depressions of the surface without smoothing it.

20. To use the drawknife.

Secure the wood horizontally in a vise. Stand at the end toward which the grain slants out of the wood. Place the drawknife with its ground edge toward the work. Slant the blade slightly across the work and draw the tool in the direction of the grain. Control the depth of the cut by varying the angle between the blade and the wood. Long gentle strokes are more efficacious than short hard strokes.

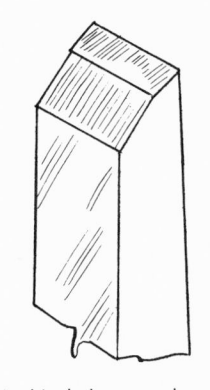

15.17 A chisel sharpened correctly

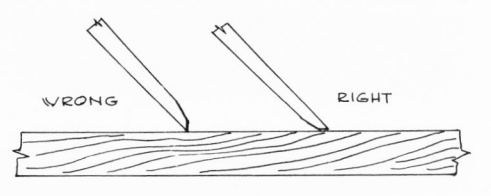

15.18 Wrong and right ways to pare with a chisel. Note the grain of the wood

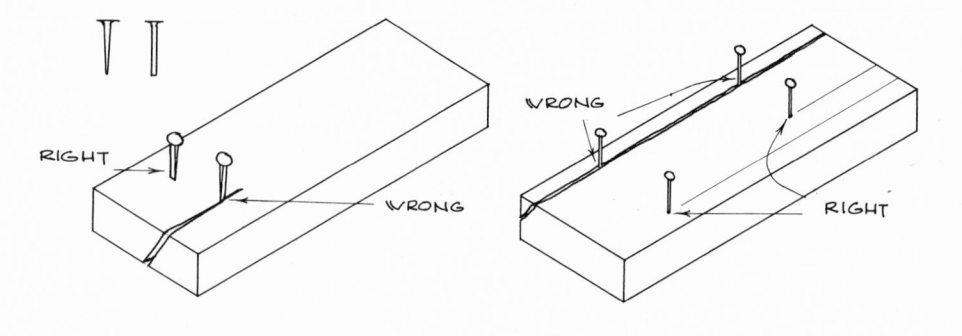

15.19 The right ways to use clout nails: the end of the nail across the grain; no two nails in the same grain

RIGHT

WRONG

WRONG

WRONG

RIGHT

construction of flats
precautions

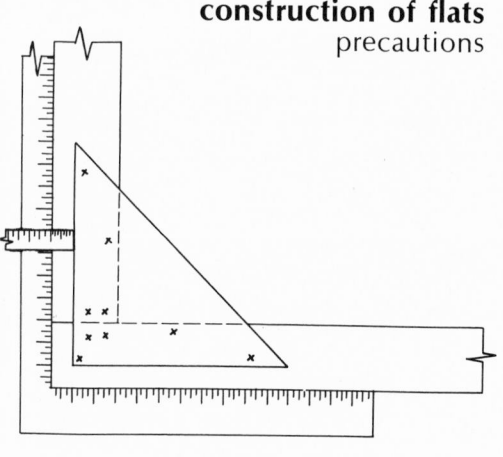

15.20 Stile and rail

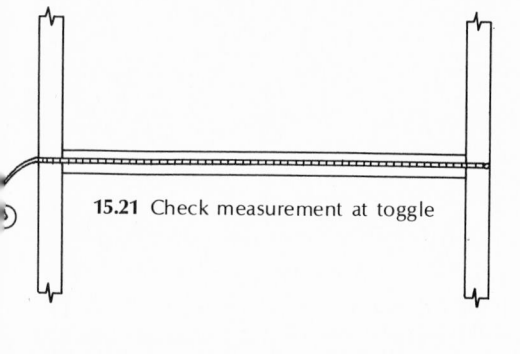

15.21 Check measurement at toggle

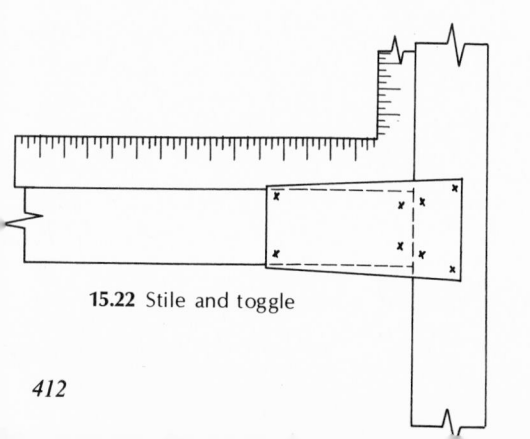

15.22 Stile and toggle

- Lay out the work on a level surface.
- Fasten the work firmly in place until it is joined.
- Use established angles: a true right angle or a template bench.
- Join right angles first.
- Do not clinch any clout nails or apply glue to mortise-and-tenon joints until the accuracy of the whole frame has been checked.
- Keep all glued joints fastened in position or in clamps until the glue has set.
- Round the edges of toggles and diagonal braces to prevent brush contact in painting.
- See Figure 15.23 for the steps in building a flat.

21. To make a butt joint between stile and rail, fastened by a corner block and clout nails (Figure 15.20).

Fit pieces into an established right angle (24″ steel square or template) and set the rail to carry past the stile. Tap the far end of the stile to tighten the joint. Place a corner block on the joint with the exposed grain running at right angles to the joint. Set clout nails of a length at least ⅛″ greater than the total thickness as shown, two on each side of the joint close to the joint, one in each remote corner of the corner block. Drive nails halfway to hold joint until all joints are made and the frame is tested and found to be square. Place an iron clinch plate under the joint and drive nails completely into wood. The assembly of the flat with others may require that a corner block be held back from either or both edges of the frame. Flats which are to become part of the permanent equipment of a theatre are assembled regularly with corner blocks held back 1″ from all edges, to allow greatest flexibility of assembly with other flats.

22. To make a butt joint between stile and toggle bar, fastened with a keystone and clout nails.

Locate the position of the toggle by measuring from the bottom rail and marking the stile. Set the toggle bar in position at the mark on the stile. Make a check measurement of the overall width at the point of the toggle bar to make sure that inserting the toggle bar has not sprung the stile outward (Figure 15.21). Place the keystone over the joint and drive nails halfway into stile. Square toggle against stile by placing a square in the angle between toggle and stile (Figure 15.22), and drive nails halfway into the toggle. When the whole frame is checked, clinch the clout nails.

15.23 BUILDING A FLAT→

a The materials

b The frame laid out

c Squaring a corner

d Clout nails half driven

e Checking the diagonals

f Clinching nails on clinch plate

g Checking measurement at toggle

h Placing the keystone

i First four nails in keystone

j A half keystone in place

k Boring a hold for the lash line

l Overhand knot in lash line

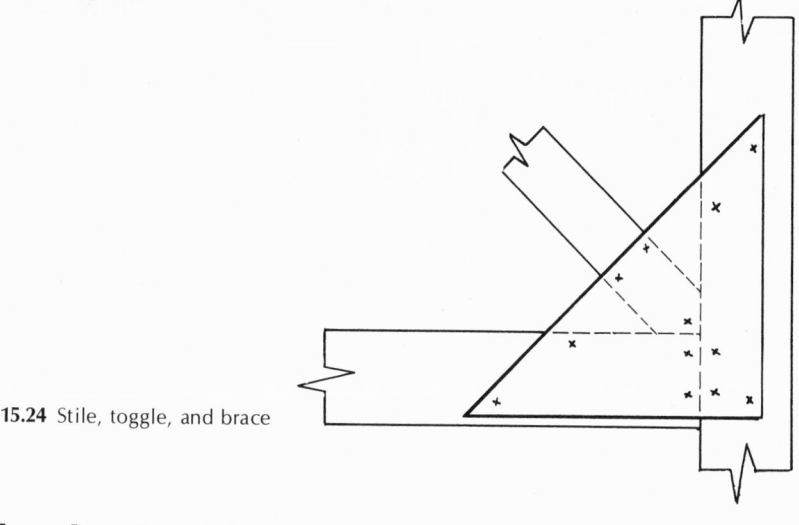

15.24 Stile, toggle, and brace

23. To make a butt joint between stile, toggle, and diagonal brace, fastened with a corner block (Figure 15.24).

Fit all three pieces together at the measured point to check size and position. Nail the corner block to the stile. Square toggle to stile and insert nails halfway. Set the brace under the hypotenuse of the corner block and drive nails in halfway. When the entire frame is checked, clinch the nails (note the position of the nails).

24. To make butt joints between a diagonal brace and stile and rail, fastened with half keystones and clout nails.

Cut a keystone in half the long way. Set the brace in position so that the ends bear completely against the edges of both stile and rail. Place a half keystone over each joint to cover as much of the stile and rail as possible. Set nails halfway into the stile and rail and into one end of the brace. Make sure the corner of flat is square. Set the nails in the other end of the brace and clinch all nails. (See Figure 15.25.)

Portions of keystones or corner blocks may serve to fasten minor butt joints in scenery frames as follows: half corner blocks (cut diagonally) for joints between stiles and rails of flats less than 2′ wide and less than 10′ high; half keystones, cut the long way, for joints between braces and stiles or rails; small pieces (straps) of 3-ply wood to fasten miscellaneous minor butt joints.

Full-sized corner blocks are used to fasten as many pieces simultaneously as is possible consistent with the general rule governing the direction of the exposed grain. Special pieces of 3-ply may be cut to fasten unusual joints. Scraps of plywood left from the cutting of profiles may be saved and cut up for use as corner blocks and keystones. (See Figures 15.26 and 15.27.)

15.25 Stile, rail, and brace

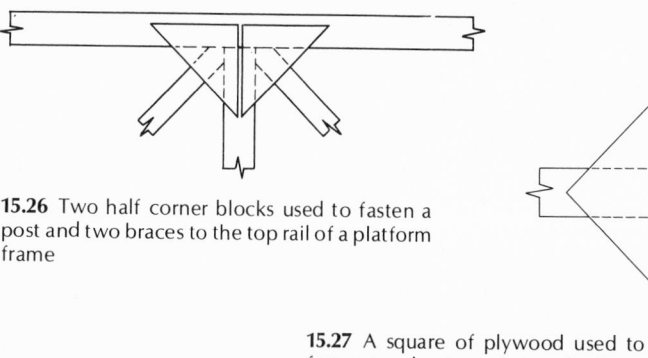

15.26 Two half corner blocks used to fasten a post and two braces to the top rail of a platform frame

15.27 A square of plywood used to fasten toggles to an internal stile

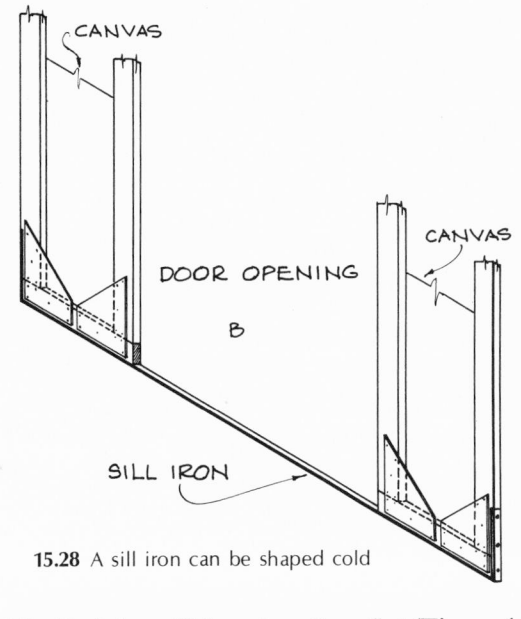

15.28 A sill iron can be shaped cold

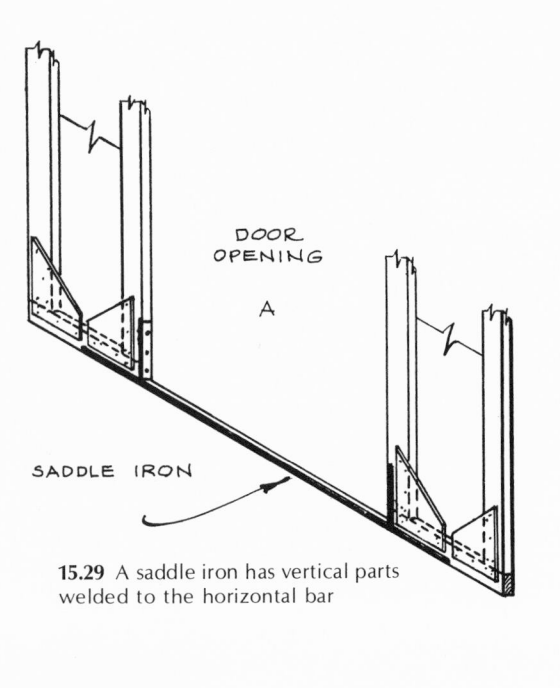

15.29 A saddle iron has vertical parts welded to the horizontal bar

25. To join a sill iron to a door flat (Figure 15.28).

Measure and cut all stiles for door flats $\frac{3}{16}''$ shorter than stiles for flats which have no sill irons. Rabbet the outside edge of the outside stiles of the flat $\frac{3}{16}'' \times 9''$. Use a marking gauge, a chisel, and a ripsaw. Join the frame of the flat. Nail a temporary batten across the door opening in the flat to establish the correct width. Select a piece of strap iron $\frac{3}{16}''$ thick and as wide as the lumber is thick ($\frac{3}{16}'' \times \frac{3}{4}''$ for $1''$ stock lumber). Measure, mark, and cut (with a hacksaw) a length $1'\,6''$ longer than the flat is wide. Measure for right-angle bends $9''$ from each end. Before bending, drill and countersink eight $\frac{3}{16}''$ holes, two well spaced in each of the $9''$ ends, and two which coincide with the bottom rails on each side of the door opening. Bend on the $9''$ marks so that both right angles are on the same side of the iron, and the countersinks are on the other side. Fit the iron to the bottom of the flat and fasten with $1\frac{1}{4}''$ #9 flathead wood screws.

A removable sill iron to go across an opening in a pair of hinged flats (Chapter 5) is fastened with $\frac{3}{16}''$ flathead stove bolts and wing nuts. The sill iron in this case does not bend around the corner of the flat. The bolts are $\frac{1}{2}''$ longer than the sum of the thickness of the sill iron and the width of the bottom rail. A hinged sill iron is attached permanently when the flats are joined to form a twofold unit.

26. To join a curved sweep into an arch flat (see Figure 5.8h).

The sweep has $1''$ width of lumber at each end and a minimum of $2''$ at the middle. Notch the inside stile to house the sweep so that the curved edge of the sweep is flush with the edge of the stile. Set the toggle above the arch $1''$ above the height of the arch opening. Drill two $\frac{3}{16}''$ holes in each end of the sweep through the width of the lumber. Set the sweep in place and fasten with $2''$ #9 wood screws through the drilled holes. *Do not* join curved sweeps with corner blocks or keystones. Driving clout nails into the short grain at the ends of the sweep is sure to split the wood.

27. To assemble a mortise-and-tenon-joined frame (Figure 15.23).

Lay out all the members of the frame in proper juxtaposition on the bench or floor. Set tenons into mortises, making certain of snug fit. Tenons should enter mortises under light taps of a mallet. Square the entire frame and verify measurements and angles. Take apart, apply glue to the tenons, insert wedges where the tenons are too thin for the mortises, and reassemble. Square the frame as before and nail through each joint. Clinch nails thoroughly. Apply corner blocks and keystones over the joints, and nail in place.

To check the construction of a scenery frame against the working drawing, inspect the following:

• The layout of the entire frame for agreement with the layout shown in the drawing.

• Overall dimensions at as many points as there are different dimensions.

• Internal dimensions wherever there is internal framing which is to be exposed or to fit other pieces of scenery.

• All structural angles.

• Squareness of framing, according to either of the following propositions: (a) the diagonals of a symmetrical figure are equal; (b) the square on the hypotenuse of a right triangle is equal to the sum of the squares on the other two sides (if the sides of a right triangle are 3 and 4, the hypotenuse must be 5; the larger the unit of measurement, the more accurate the result).

• Observance of all construction notes, such as "hold back corner blocks 1″ from edge."

• Corner blocks and keystones held back 1″ from edges.

• Lash lines — length and location.

• Lash cleats spaced for easy lashing.

• Lash-line hooks where lash cleats are ineffective.

• Tie-off cleats 30″ from floor and opposite each other at each lash joint.

• Stop cleats or stop blocks.

• Hinged joints to fold completely.

• Folding battens proper width and in proper places.

• Easy fit of all loose-pin hinges.

• Profile dutchmen on loose-pin hinge joints.

• Keeper batten cut and fitted.

• Fitting of proper hooks.

• Swivel stiffeners: length, bolts, wing nuts.

• Flat stiffeners (nailed or screwed): lengths measured, cut, and fitted.

• Stiffeners on edge: length measured, cut, and fitted. Loose-pin hinges bolted to alternate sides of stiffener.

• Brace cleats bolted.

• Brace cleats in position for easy insertion of stage brace hook.

- Brace cleats at two-thirds the height of the flat.
- Brace jacks loose-pin hinged securely. Hinges bolted. Easy fit of pins.
- Brace jacks to fold completely against back of flat. Screen-door hooks to fasten.
- Brace jack on stile on each side of every door opening.
- Thicknesses applied from rear: corner blocks and keystones held back from edges. Loose-pin hinges. *applied detail*
- Door and window units applied from front: bolts and wing nuts.
- Swing of doors.
- Fit of doors in jambs.
- Operation of all door latches and window catches.
- Operation of secret panels and breakaway parts.
- Fit of cornices, chair rails, and baseboards at corners.
- Rectilinear alignment of all parts. Attention to vertical, horizontal, and parallel elements.
- Special toggle bars for pictures, curtains, and lighting fixtures.
- Top and bottom hanger irons where specified. Bolted. *rigging*
- Foot irons where specified. Bolted.

Every item of scenery or accessories identified according to the system established in the working drawings. Name of play, act, scene, and piece identification on each part. *identification*

28. To cover a flat frame with canvas (Figure 15.30). **covering flats**

Place the frame on two horses or benches. Unroll sufficient cloth from the bolt or reel to cover the frame, allowing about two inches of overlap at each end, and tear the piece from the bolt. Place the selvage edge of the cloth even with one side of the frame and set the staples along the inside edge of the stile at 6″ intervals. Stretch the selvage edge lengthwise of the flat. Set staples along the stile opposite the selvage edge, starting in the middle of the stile and working both ways to the corners. During this operation stretch the cloth diagonally toward the unstapled corners. Staple the ends last. Adjust any wrinkles or sags by removing staples and restapling. Stretch cotton duck or linen smooth but not as tight as possible; painting will tighten it further. Muslin should be quite loose because painting shrinks it considerably. Lay back the cloth from each stile and rail in turn and apply to both wood and cloth a liberal even coat of scene paste. Fill the pores of the cloth with the paste. Do not allow any paste to get on the front surface of the cloth. Pat the glued cloth firmly in place with a flat piece of wood. Set staples along the outside of the frame, ¼″ from edges, at intervals of about 18″. Set three staples in the outside edge at each corner. Allow the paste to dry. Trim waste cloth from the edges by running a short convex blade along the face of the lumber, guiding the movement with the thumb against the side of the frame, or by running a small butcher knife along the edges of the frame, meanwhile pulling the waste canvas away with the other hand. The first method is the better.

a Fireproofing

b The canvas

c Inside tacks (or staples) set

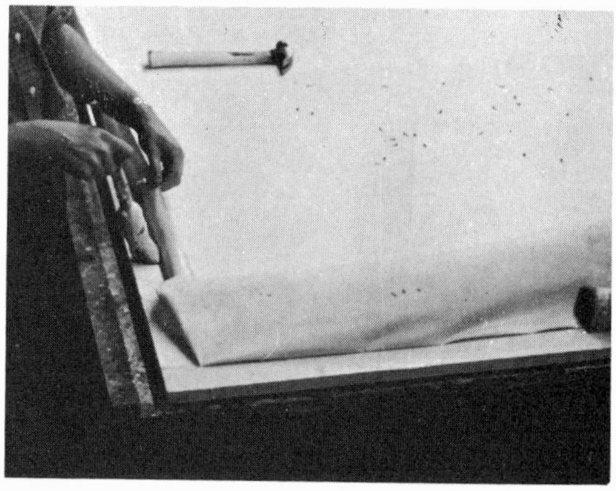

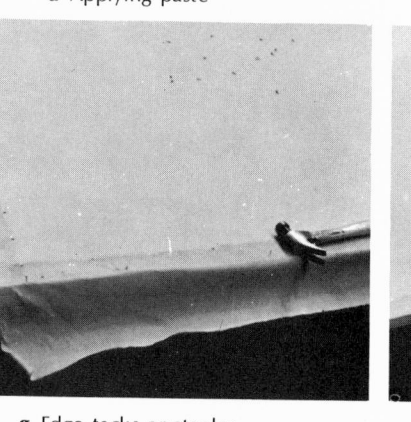

d Applying paste

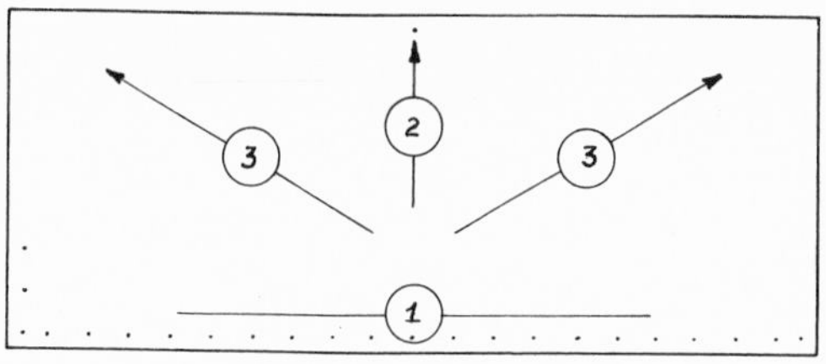

e Order of operations in stretching cloth

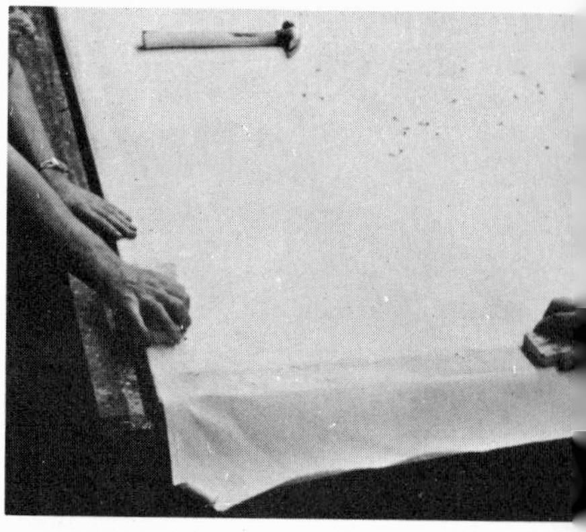

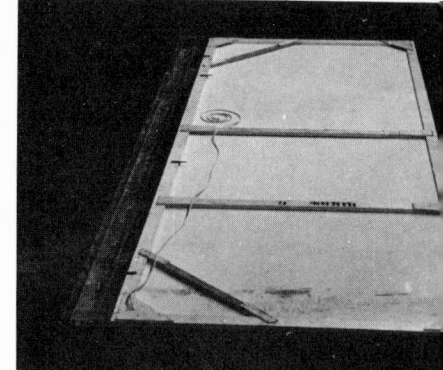

f Patting down cloth

g Edge tacks or staples

h Trimming the edge

i Hardware applied

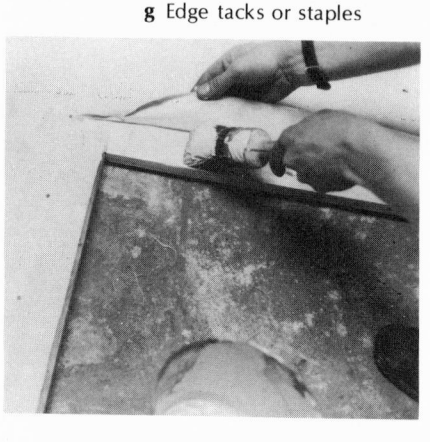

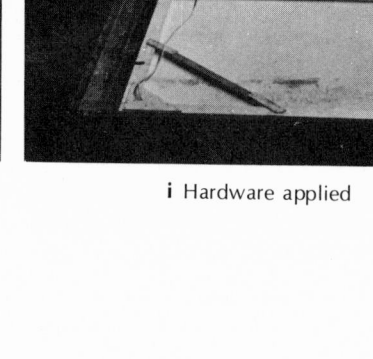

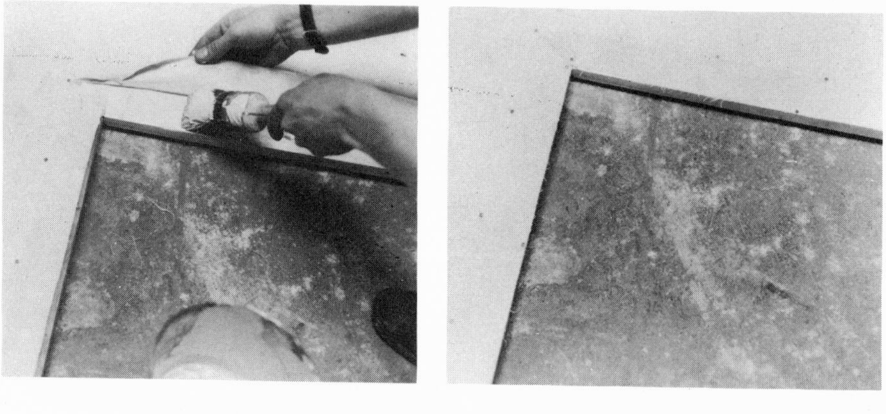

15.30 COVERING A FLAT WITH COTTON DUCK. The illustrations show tacking; stapling is faster

j,k Applying canvas to an inside corner

29. To attach cloth around an opening in a flat.

Cover the entire flat with cloth as described in Problem 28. On pieces of lumber which frame the opening, staple along the edges away from the opening. Cut out the waste cloth. At the corner of the opening make a diagonal cut in the canvas to allow folding back for paste. Paste, pat down, and staple as in Problem 28.

30. To fasten cloth to frames with plywood edges.

Staple the cloth to all regular framing members. Staple it to the inside edge of plywood which is fastened to framing members. Paste and edge-staple the cloth to the regular framing members but paste the cloth without edge-stapling to the plywood. Use more paste on the plywood than on the framing members because plywood absorbs more of it. Allow the paste to set, then trim the cloth around the edges of the plywood with a razor blade.

31. To cover frames with velour or other fabrics which are not to be painted.

It is assumed in this problem that the cloth has sufficient body to resist penetration of scene paste to the front side. Stretch the fabric, making it as tight as possible consistent with its strength. Set in all tacks halfway on the inside edges. Turn back the edges, apply paste, and pat the fabric down without tacking or stapling the outside edges. When the paste has set, trim the edges and remove all tacks.

32. To cover flats with cloth through which scene paste will penetrate.

Carry the cloth over all edges and staple and paste it only on the back side. Unflameproofed covering may be put on scenery only if the frames are first covered with a flameproofed fabric.

33. To patch torn canvas.

The patching piece must be of identical material and identical condition as the cloth to be patched: patch new canvas with new canvas, patch painted canvas with painted canvas, patch washed canvas with washed canvas. Apply scene paste liberally to one side of the patch, to the unpainted side if painted canvas is used. For quick repair use prepared vegetable glue. Apply the patch to the back of the torn canvas. With an assistant holding a board against the front of the canvas, press the patch firmly into place with a block of wood.

If only standard sizes of scenery are stored, the technician, in planning a set, can lay out his flats and drops to include as many stored pieces as possible. It is only necessary then for the builder to remove the pieces from the storeroom, make any alterations shown on the working drawings, and build the new pieces to complete the set.

reuse of salvaged flats and drops

• Inspect for accurate agreement with the requirements, shape, and size indicated in the drawings.

• Wash all painted surfaces of items which are to be reused (see Problem 34).

• Remove all covering material which is not usable. Scenery paste may be softened with hot water to make removal easier.

• Rebuild as required in the drawings.

• Avoid alterations which will require time or labor approaching that necessary to build a new piece.

• Do not convert a standard-sized piece into a special shape. Build the special-shaped piece new.

• Three-dimensional units can seldom be altered with less labor than is necessary to build a new unit. A system of standard-sized parallels which will minimize the necessity of manufacturing new levels each time they are needed can be designed to fit any particular stage. With such a scheme, only specially shaped units need be constructed to fit into and upon the standard units. There is no such system which is truly suitable to all stages, since the dimensions of the stage constitute a factor in the design of the parallels.

34. To wash flats and drops.

EQUIPMENT: hot and cold water supply with good pressure; mixing fitting attached to faucets; ample length of ¾″ high-pressure hose; hose nozzle with adjustable force and with pistol grip and trigger valve; fiber-bristled scrub brushes, ordinary and long-handled.

WHERE TO DO THE JOB: flats and drops are washed on the paint frame or on the wall which is used for painting. They are left fastened in place until they dry. They cannot be washed on the floor since the paint and water must drain off during the washing process. Flats may be washed out of doors against the side of a building. They must be blocked up off the ground during washing, to allow the paint to run away from the edges, and must be nailed to a wall or floor to dry so that the frames will not bow. Drops, hung and washed out of doors, must be stretched and securely fastened to a wall or floor while they are still wet, or they will shrink unevenly and become useless.

THE TECHNIQUE: soak the flat with warm water, until the paint begins to flow; scrub it with brushes to loosen the paint; use a strong stream of warm water for rinsing; use hot water to soften glue or very thick paint.

PREPARATION FOR NEW PAINT: some pigments impart a stain to canvas which cannot be removed by washing and which may show or bleed through subsequent paint jobs. Canvas thus stained must be glazed with an alum wash before repainting. Back-painting which tends to bleed through must be washed off and the face of the canvas given an alum wash.

Flats which are properly painted with properly mixed scene paint require only infrequent washing. Scene paint properly mixed is not thick, and properly applied it is brushed out on the scenery to a very thin covering. It is so thin that a complete job of several coats of paint will not obliterate the texture of the canvas. Certain techniques of scene painting, however, do depend for final effect upon paint thickly applied. It is generally possible to repaint flats for several productions before washing is necessary. A wash of alum and water applied quickly to old scenery will set old paint and prevent it from brushing up and mixing with newly applied paint.

WHEN TO WASH: scenery which is to be subjected to very little handling (transportation or shifting) may be given more consecutive coats of paint than scenery which is to be frequently shifted or toured. The accumulation of several paint jobs adds weight to the scenery. More important, however, the accumulated paint forms layers which, because of the vagaries of painting conditions (humidity, drying, thickness of application, glue content), do not adhere uniformly to the fabric, and are likely to crack and flake off. A piece of scenery should be washed:

• If it has so many layers of paint that a faint cracking sound is made when the paint is touched.

• If there is any visible sign of cracking and flaking.

• If the texture of the cloth does not show through the paint.

• If the piece is painted with brilliant or strong colors, particularly those colors having dye in them, which will bleed through subsequent coats of paint.

35. To alter flats.

Salvaged flats are altered in external dimensions and shape, and are cut to provide openings for doors, windows, fireplaces, inset bookcases, and the like. When flats are to be altered to conform to a new design, the following technique will fulfill the requirements and prevent the sagging or stretching of the canvas:

• Wash the flat.

• Insert new framing members before cutting either the existing frame or the covering material.

• Cut down flats only in one dimension.

• Enlarge flats, not by inserting new stiles or rails, but by framing the necessary addition separately and battening it on or attaching it with plywood to the original structure. Remove existing internal framing members after new members are inserted near them, to keep down weight.

• Examine all points in the existing structure for weakness, and strengthen with corner blocks, keystones, corner plates, or corner irons where necessary.

• Check all reused flats for squareness and freedom from warp. Brace, trim, and stiffen them as necessary.

Metalworking

36. To shear metal.

cutting

Clamp the sheet to the shear table with the cutting line at the edge; lower the blade by depressing the foot treadle.

37. To cut metal with a circular saw.

EQUIPMENT: circular saw, liquid coolant (cutting oil or kerosene), or stick lubricant, goggles. *Caution:* put on the goggles before beginning the work.

PROCEDURE: feed the work at an adequate speed for continuous cutting, but not so fast as to jam the blade. Use liquid coolant or apply stick lubricant to the blade every two or three minutes while cutting.

See that the specified blade speed agrees with the speed of the saw spindles (in rpm).

38. To saber-saw sheet.

EQUIPMENT: saber saw, layout die, scriber, coolant (cutting oil or kerosene), goggles. *Caution:* put on the goggles before beginning the work.

PROCEDURE: scribe the cuts by tracing around the die. Hold the saber saw frame tightly against the surface. Use the coolant.

39. To band-saw sheet.

EQUIPMENT: band saw, coolant (cutting oil or kerosene), goggles. *Caution:* put on the goggles before beginning the work.

PROCEDURE: select the correct blade for the metal to be cut, the speed of the saw, and the finish of the cut. Advance the work toward the blade fast enough for continuous cutting but not so fast as to jam the blade. Use the coolant.

15.31 Cutting the end of a steel angle with an oxyacetylene flame

40. To cut metal with an oxyacetylene torch (Figure 15.31).

EQUIPMENT: soapstone or scriber, straight piece of scrap steel, clamp, oxyacetylene torch.

PROCEDURE: mark the line to be cut with the soapstone or scriber. Clamp the piece of scrap steel to the work to guide the cut. Attach the cutting torch to the oxygen and acetylene tubes. Light the preheat flames (O-A at the six side holes) and adjust to a neutral flame. Holding the tip about ½″ from the metal, heat the steel. When red heat has occurred, lift the torch away slightly and push the oxygen-valve lever in full. When the pure oxygen has burned a hole through the plate, slant the torch in the direction of the cut and move it along the cutting line at a speed which gives a smooth cut. Too-fast movement stops the cutting; too-slow movement results in a wide, messy cut with unnecessary slag.

Oxygen pressure must be about four times the acetylene pressure. Equipment specifications give correct pressures according to the thickness of the steel to be cut. Smooth the cut with a coal chisel, files, or the grinder.

41. To cut and thread pipe.

EQUIPMENT: pipe vise, files, wheel cutter, die, stock, cutting oil.

PROCEDURE: clamp the pipe in the pipe vise. Measure the length to be cut and mark the cut with a file. Set up the wheel cutter on the mark, make a turn, tighten the cutter; repeat this process until the cut is made. Place the die, correct for pipe size and thread, in the stock. Place the die against the end of the pipe, press while turning the stock until the cutting begins. Apply cutting oil frequently. For each full turn reverse a quarter turn to clear chips. Continue this process until the desired amount of thread has been cut. Reverse and remove the die. Use kerosene to clean the thread.

42. To calculate the length of metal allowing for bends.

For soft steel, brass, or aluminum, add ⅓ the stock thickness for each bend; for hard metals, add ½ the stock thickness.

43. To bend metal with the bender.

bending

Place the correct dies in the bender, place the work in it. Pull the lever until the bend is made. Make large bends in several stages.

44. To bend metal with the brake.

Attach the desired shaping nose to the top leaf. Place the sheet on the bed with the center line of the bend at the edge. Clamp the sheet with the foot treadle. Push the lever until the bend is made.

Filing is accomplished in steps beginning with the bastard file (the coarsest), then using the second-cut file, and lastly the smooth-cut file. Use the file card occasionally to clean the file teeth. Before filing soft metal, fill the teeth with chalk to keep them from becoming clogged.

filing

45. To push-file metal.

Fasten or hold the work securely. Grasp the file handle in one hand, the end of the file in the other. Press the file to cut on the forward stroke; lift it slightly on the return stroke to clean the teeth.

46. To draw-file.

Hold the file at both ends and draw it toward you, pressing on the draw stroke. Draw-filing produces a rougher finish than push-filing but removes material faster.

15.32 The workman is grinding a steel pipe on the left wheel of a two-wheel grinder. He has swung the spark guard aside but he is wearing shatterproof goggles

grinding

47. To grind metal (Figure 15.32).

Put on goggles. Resting the metal on the guide bar, move it slowly against the rotating wheel or disc and hold it under pressure until the desired amount of metal is removed. Control frictional heat by applying water to the wheel by drip or jet devices.

drilling

48. To drill metal.

EQUIPMENT: center punch, twist-drill bits, drill press or portable hand drill, lubricant.

PROCEDURE: at the center point of the hole, dent the surface of the metal with the center punch to start the drill. For large holes ¾″ or more in diameter, bore a small lead hole through the metal. Mark the intended circumference with two or more center-punch dents as guides to accuracy.

Use twist-drill bits in either the drill press or the portable hand drill. A drill press affords accuracy and variable speed: the larger the drill, the slower the speed; the harder the metal, the slower the speed. Lubricate the drill.

49. To join metal by riveting.

Joints must be designed and rivets specified for the type of joint (*butt* which uses a joining piece, or *lap* in which two pieces are overlapped). The rivet diameter must be 1.2 to 1.4 times the metal thickness and the rivet length should be the thickness of the joint plus the rivet diameter.

50. To head rivets.

Having inserted the rivet, hold a *bucking bar* against the head while a second person hammers the inserted and protruding end to form a second "head," which overlaps the edges of the hole; or hold a bucking bar, shaped like a hollow die of a rivet head, over the inserted and protruding end of the rivet, while a second person, using a riveting hammer (pneumatic or electric), drives the rivet into the die.

51. To set a pop rivet.

Insert the ball-ended rod in the hole in the metal to be riveted and slide the tubular rivet onto the rod. With the setting tool, grasp the rod on the first side of the work and squeeze the tool, pulling the ball into the rivet and expanding it. When the ball comes against the second surface of the work, thereby spreading the tube, snap the rod, leaving the rivet in place. See Figures 15.33 and 15.34.

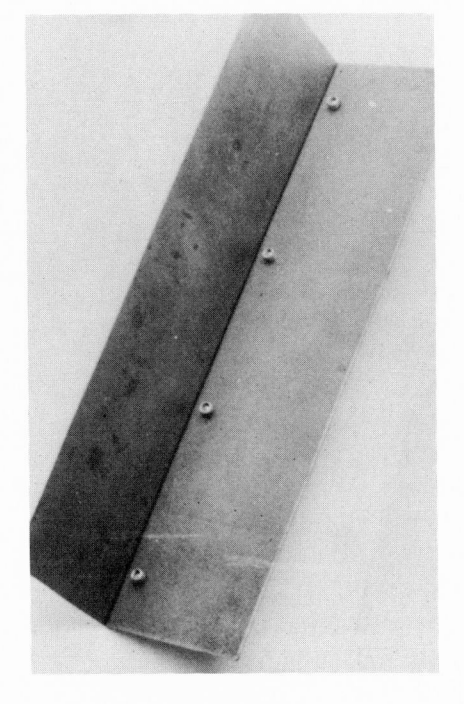

15.33 (*left*) Pop rivets set in place: the working, or exposed, side

15.34 (*right*) Pop rivets in place: the blind, or enclosed, side. This side can be totally inaccessible. The ball of the rivet rod is on this side and is drawn into the rivet tube by one workman on the exposed side

52. To light the torch.

Turn all torch valves to OFF. All connections must be tight. Set the regulator screws in the *screwed-out* position. Open the acetylene tank valve 1½ turns. Open the acetylene torch valve 1 turn. Screw in the acetylene regulator screw until the gas escapes at the desired working pressure (on the gauge) and shut off the acetylene torch valve.

Open the oxygen tank valve all the way. Open the oxygen torch

oxyacetylene welding

valve 1 turn. Screw in the oxygen regulator screw until the working pressure gauge shows the desired pressure and then shut off the oxygen torch valve.

Open the acetylene torch valve slightly. Using a flint striker, light the torch. Open the acetylene torch valve until the flame is not producing free carbon and is making a slight roar. Open the oxygen torch valve slowly until the torch is producing a neutral flame. Start heating or welding.

53. To weld.

Clean the metal of all impurities (oil, grease, paint, rust scale, and dirt) by sanding, grinding, or using chemical cleaners. Prepare the edges of the joint so that the heat will completely penetrate the metal.

The working pressures of the two gases are stated in equipment specifications, but the general rule is equal pressures of acetylene and oxygen.

STEEL SHEET: *flange weld:* on the brake upset the edges to be joined, making flanges equal to the thickness of the metal. Butt them and apply torch heat to fuse them together (Figures 15.35 and 15.36).

STEEL ¾₁₆″ THICK: *butt weld:* allow a slight crack between the pieces; the torch will melt both edges and make a sound joint.

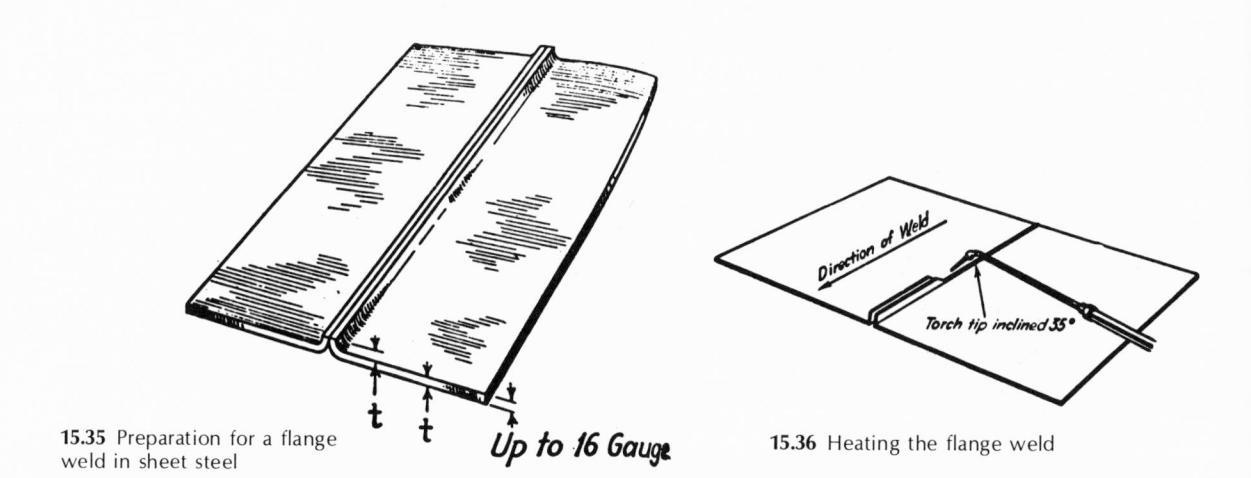

15.35 Preparation for a flange weld in sheet steel

15.36 Heating the flange weld

STEEL ¾₁₆″ TO ½″ THICK: grind a single 60° bevel on both edges to be joined and fill the vee thus formed with molten metal from the welding rod (Figure 15.37).

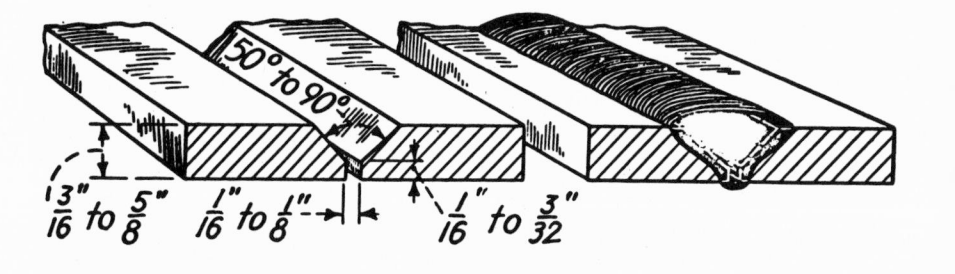

15.37 Left: a vee groove ground and in position for the weld. Right: the weld completed

STEEL OVER ½″ THICK: grind a vee on both sides of both edges to be joined and weld it on both sides.

PLUG WELDS: make plug welds in lap joints by drilling holes through the top piece; heat and fill the holes with molten metal (Figures 15.38–15.40).

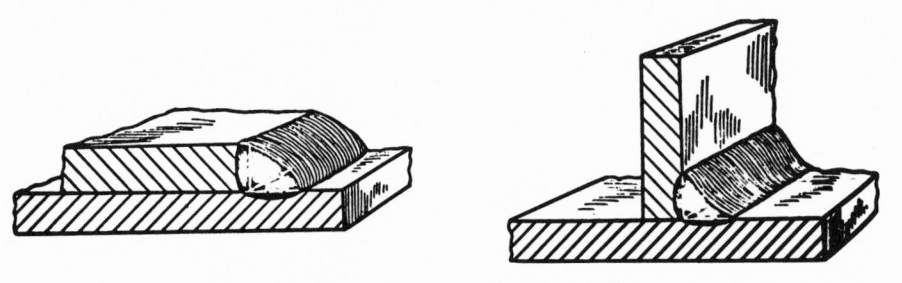

15.39 Lap welds to join overlapped pieces

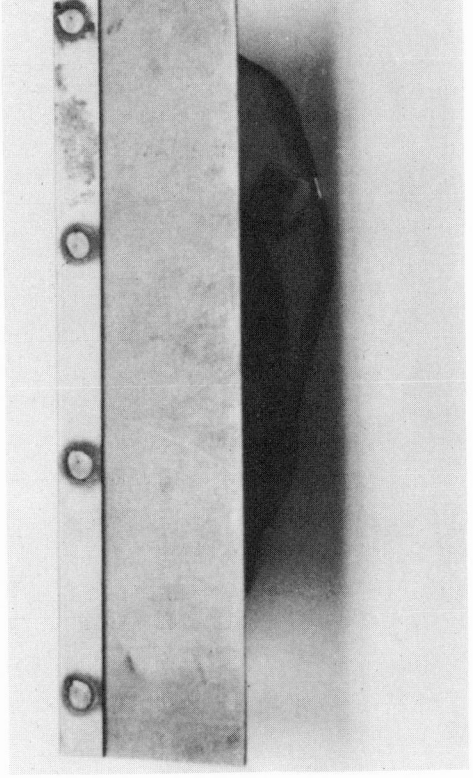

15.40 Left: fillet welds to add thickness for stiffness or strength. Right: to make a tee-joint

15.38 Four plug welds joining a piece of sheet to a flange

welding techniques

54. To shut down the welding equipment.

Turn off the oxygen torch valve, then the acetylene torch valve. This is sufficient shutdown for a few minutes' break. To shut down for a longer time: turn off both tank valves; open the oxygen torch valve until both oxygen gauges read "O"; unscrew the oxygen regulator control and turn off the torch valve; open the acetylene torch valve until both acetylene gauges read "O"; unscrew the acetylene regulator screw and turn off the torch valve; coil the hose neatly and clean up.

In the following examples assume that the weld is a single-bevel, flat butt joint in ¼″ steel plate. Vertical and overhead welding are variations of the process. The following procedures are for metal up to ⅜″ thick, for sheet metal, and for brazing.

55. To weld forehand.

Hold the lighted torch in one hand, the welding rod in the other. Hold the torch ½″ above the end of the joint and vertical. When the metal melts, tip the torch 45° in the direction to be welded. Holding the rod in front of the flame, oscillate both torch and rod to heat the metal evenly. When the walls of the beveled vee are melted evenly, fill the bottom of the vee with molten rod metal to half its depth and ½″ long, making a puddle. With rod and torch in the same position build the puddle to the top of the vee, hold it there with the rod, and heat the next ⅛″ of vee with the torch. When this is heated, bring the puddle ahead to fill it and repeat as before to complete the joint.

Pointers: complete penetration of the weld is essential. The inner core of the flame must not touch and carbonize the rod. The rod metal must fill the bevel completely and must be evenly deposited.

56. To weld backhand.

Easily producing complete fusion and penetration of material ¼″ or more thick, the backhand weld requires a narrower vee than the forehand weld and produces a more ductile joint, since the flame prevents oxidation of the molten metal.

Hold the lighted torch in one hand, the welding rod in the other. Hold the torch ½″ above the end of the joint. When the metal melts, tilt the torch 45° away from the direction to be welded. When the metal is melted, form a puddle in the vee to fill it; hold the puddle in place with the rod and heat the next ⅜″ of vee; with torch and rod extend the puddle along the vee, adding rod metal to fill it, and heating ahead of the puddle to complete the joint.

Pointers: obtain complete fusion between the edges of the vee and the weld metal. Use a more plastic (hotter) puddle than in forehand welding. Direct the flame at the edges of the vee without sidewise motion by rotating the wrist.

57. To braze with oxyacetylene.

Use flux-coated brazing rod and have flame slightly carbonizing (less oxygen). Heat the steel only red-hot, then add rod metal. Make a puddle and continue as in forehand welding.

safety checklist for oxyacetylene

- Keep all oil away from oxyacetylene equipment to prevent explosion.
- Keep cylinders away from heat sources.
- Keep acetylene working pressure below 15 p.s.i. Above this pressure, it is unstable.
- Wear leather shoes, leather or asbestos gloves, flameproof clothing, and goggles of proper density.
- Test all equipment for leaks periodically.
- Allow no flammable materials in the welding area.
- Protect floors and benches against molten metal.
- Have a CO_2 fire extinguisher ready at hand.
- Use a striker or candle, *never a match,* to light the torch.
- Have adequate ventilation.
- Do not cut or weld a container that has held flammable materials except after thoroughly cleaning and ventilating it.
- When cutting be wary of falling pieces.

arc welding
distortion from heat

The arc produces intense heat in a localized area, which causes expansion of the metal in that area. All parts to be welded must be clamped securely and released only after the weld has cooled. To reduce distortion, tack-weld both ends of a long joint before completing the entire seam, and design welds in which counterdistorting forces are generated as in a double-veed butt weld.

58. To weld with an arc (Figure 15.41).

Assume the weld to be in ¼″ veed steel plate. Use electrode E6013 ⅛″ in diameter; set the transformer at 120 amps. Clamp the electrode in the holder and the negative cable to the work. Hold the electrode perpendicular to the work, ½″ away from the end of the vee. Lower the hood. Touch the electrode tip to the work with a quick scratching mo-

15.41 Arc welding. The welder wears a hood to protect his face from heat and hot metal and his eyes from the U-V content of the arc. The helper shields his face with a gloved hand but might better wear U-V protective goggles

tion. As the arc starts, raise the tip ⅛″ above the work to maintain the arc. If the electrode sticks to the work, quickly twist it free. Holding the electrode perpendicular laterally but inclined slightly in the direction of the open vee, move it along the vee with a slight circular motion, depositing a rippled beaded weld. Continue to the end of the vee. If a single pass did not fill the vee, chip away all slag, wire-brush the weld, and deposit additional rod metal where needed.

From this example the welder may progress in complexity and skill by practice.

- Use electrodes of the proper kind of metal and the proper size.
- Clean the metals to be welded.
- Select the proper amperage as specified on the equipment to achieve the correct heat.

arc welding checklist

- Use the correct arc length.
- Be sure the speed of movement along the vee is neither too fast nor too slow.
- Feed the electrode to the arc at the right speed.
- Clean the metals before rewelding.

- Have no flammable gases or liquids in the area.
- See that the area is dry and well ventilated.
- Wear welding hood with adequate filter glass.
- Wear gloves and full-cover protective clothing.
- Maintain the equipment, especially electric cables and fittings, in good condition.
- Weld containers which have held combustible materials *only* after a thorough cleaning and ventilating.
- Do not touch the electrode when *you* are grounded.
- Allow no spectators without ultraviolet-filtering goggles.

59. To make a truss or joist for a platform.

Mark two pieces of ¾″ × ¾″ × ⅛″ angle every 8″. Align them parallel with ends even. Weld rods ¼″ in diameter and 8″ long perpendicular to the angles at each mark. Weld diagonals of ¼″ rod between the cross-rods. Weld another, identical, piece of angle back to back with one of the first two to make the top chord of the truss.

60. To make a bridge.

Align two trusses built according to Problem 59 and cross-brace them every 4′ with similar small frames. Apply a plywood floor with contact cement.

soldering

There are two methods of soldering: by iron, and by torch. The iron technique is used when the parts to be joined would be damaged by the torch and when the solder must be shaped. The torch technique is used when the metal to be joined can be heated to soldering temperature without injury to itself or other parts, and when the work is too big and heat-conductive for a soldering iron to be effective. It is excellent for *sweat-soldering* and when hard-to-solder alloys require greater heat than the soldering iron can generate.

The metal to be soldered must be clean metal or a good bond will not occur. Clean with sandpaper and use a *flux* to dissolve oxides, to prevent further oxidizing when the metal is heated, and to aid in alloying the solder with the metal. The metal to be soldered must be heated to a temperature that will melt the solder (about 535° F.). At a lower temperature the solder will not penetrate the metal and a weak joint will result.

61. To solder with an iron.

Clean the cool tip of the iron to the bare copper; coat it with flux, heat it, and coat it evenly with solder to prevent oxidation of the copper which would destroy the affinity of the copper for the solder. Load the hot iron with molten solder and touch it to a fluxed clean joint. When the metal has conducted sufficient heat from the iron, capillarity will draw molten solder off the iron and into the crack of the joint, and the solder will penetrate the heated metal.

62. To join a seam.

Run the iron along the seam, heating the metal and applying solder, thus joining the pieces and making a fillet of solder. The fillet provides reinforcement and completely fills the seam. When cool it may be ground to render the joint invisible after finishing.

63. To solder with a torch.

Clean the parts; place them in the desired positions, clamped if necessary, and flux them. With the torch, a hand-held propane type, heat the metal around the joint. Keep the flame away from the immediate area of the joint so as not to burn the flux and oxidize the metal. When the metal is hot enough to melt the solder, withdraw the torch and apply fluxed wire solder in a quantity sufficient to fill the joint.

64. To sweat-solder.

With the torch, heat and *tin* (coat with solder) both pieces of metal at the actual surfaces to be joined. Recoat them with flux, place them in contact, and reheat until the solder melts and joins.

Observe the following rules when using structural adhesives: **structural adhesives**

• Surfaces must be chemically clean.

• Etch the surfaces, by chemical or mechanical means, if a strong bond is needed.

• Follow mixing directions carefully.

• Keep resins and catalysts free of foreign substances.

• Avoid skin contact with the adhesives. If skin contact occurs, wash with soap and water.

Fiber Glass Construction

Fiber glass can irritate the skin. It can also be injurious if particles of   **precaution**
it are inhaled, including dust sandpapered from hardened resin. Avoid excessive skin contact with glass fabric. Wear rubber gloves and discardable clothes or coveralls reserved for this work. Wear a sanitary mask when sanding hardened glass and resin objects.

The first step in the process is to construct a form over which the   **forms**
fiber glass cloth will be placed and a cast made. Many different forms are possible.

The most obvious is the familiar chicken wire on a wooden frame.   chicken wire
It has only to be strong enough to hold its shape under the first layer

15.42 A log: glass fabric and resin on a chicken-wire form

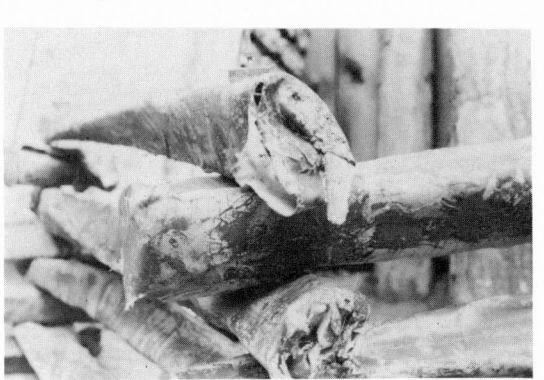

15.43 A Virginia rail fence: split rails of glass fabric and resin on chicken-wire forms

15.44 A STUMP

a Top and bottom profiles and a single post

b Part of the fabric in place

c Resin, with extra hardener added, being applied

d The resin has set

e A second coat of resin followed by a mixture of resin and sawdust

f The stump ready for painting

of fiber glass and resin. It is possible to make one-of-a-kind rocks, platforms, and the like, by merely draping chicken wire over a cardboard box, shaping it as desired, and applying the fiber glass and resin. After the first coat has hardened, the supporting core — wood, cardboard box, or whatever — is removed, and the object retains its shape. The resin forms a permanent bond with the chicken wire and the wire becomes a part of the final product. It will not show through the fiber glass and resin after a second coat has been applied. See Figures 15.42–15.45.

a Metal foil on the floor

b Applying resin to the glass fabric laid on the foil

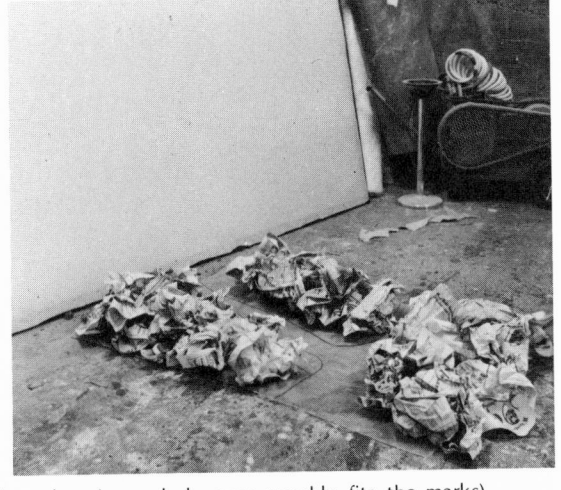

c Rock outlines marked on the newly made sheet of fiber glass (crumpled paper roughly fits the marks)

d Applying resin to the glass fabric laid over the paper

e The finished section of wall

15.45 A ROCK WALL

Clay can be easily worked to the desired shape. It can be a solid mass or it can have a wooden armature to reduce the amount of clay used. A rough shape may be made of lightweight wood and the clay placed over this and sculptured to the final form. This method is useful if the object to be made is very large; for smaller objects it may be easier to use solid clay. Relief should be exaggerated slightly to compensate for the flattening effect of the cloth. Lighter cloth is used when the mold has fine detail.

One of the easiest methods is to use the original object and cast the fiber glass and resin over it, making certain that the object can be removed from the cast without damage.

65. To part a fiber glass cast from a clay mold or original object.

A parting agent must be used between the fiber glass and the clay mold or original object to prevent the resin from forming a permanent bond with either when it hardens. There are two types of parting agents: viscous films such as vaseline or automotive cup grease, and membranes such as polyethylene sheet or aluminum foil. Films work well on clay molds but will not work on rough surfaces. Membranes are universally applicable and leave the mold clean after the removal of the cast, an advantage when an original object of value is used as the mold.

The membrane must be impervious so that the resin will not penetrate it and bond with the mold and it must conform to any shape. Aluminum foil meets both these requirements. Lightweight foils conform to fine details of the mold better than the heavier weights. Thin plastic sheets like Saran Wrap or dry cleaners' bags will serve as parting agents.

66. To mix polyester resin and hardener.

Proportions may vary from 1 part hardener in 200 parts resin (0.5 percent) to 1 part hardener in 50 parts resin (2 percent), depending upon two basic relationships: (1) Reaction (setting) time varies directly with the percentage of hardener; the mixture should never be more than 1 part hardener to 20 parts resin nor less than 1 part hardener to 400 parts resin. (2) Reaction time varies inversely with temperature. The normal working temperature should be about 72° F. The reaction time can be controlled by adjusting the amount of hardener in relation to the temperature, more hardener being added as the temperature drops below 72° F. and less hardener as the temperature rises above that figure. Cold-weather promoter must be added if resin is to be used in temperatures below 65° F. No work should be done in temperatures below 45° F.

Increase proportion of hardener with care. Over 2 percent speeds setting in the container as well as on the cloth. Excessive percentage of hardener crazes the surface of the cast and may generate reaction heat to the combustion point.

AMOUNT OF RESIN TO MIX: Mix only as much resin as can be used before it hardens in the container. Start with one pint and increase the quantity as experience dictates. Resin sets in the container before it hardens on cloth.

67. To mix epoxy resin and hardener.

The normal amount of epoxy hardener (a different substance from polyester hardener) is 1 part hardener to 4 parts epoxy resin. Working temperatures must be slightly higher than for polyester resin.

68. To cast an object in fiber glass.

casting

There are three steps in casting a fiber glass and resin object after the resin has been mixed and the mold covered with a parting agent:

APPLYING FABRIC: apply the fiber glass fabric to the mold in large areas before the resin has been mixed or in smaller amounts or pieces as resin is applied. The complexity and shape of the object will determine the choice of method.

APPLYING RESIN: apply the resin by either brush or spray gun.

STIFFENING THE CAST: apply additional layers of fabric and resin to impart additional strength and stiffness. Particular sections of the object which must withstand loads are strengthened by applying on the inside additional layers of resin and glass mat, or ribs or struts made of fiber glass and resin.

cleaning the
equipment

Clean brushes promptly with acetone. If resin hardens in a brush, the brush is ruined. Resin gels just before it hardens; this is a warning sign.

Clean spray guns with acetone immediately after using them. Avoid time intervals between uses.

69. To make a flat sheet of fiber glass.

Cover an area of smooth floor slightly bigger than the desired sheet with overlapping strips of aluminum foil. On this, lay glass cloth to the desired size and brush or spray on resin (see Problem 68). When the resin has set, add more layers of glass cloth or glass mat and resin to produce the desired thickness or stiffness.

70. To build a wood and chicken-wire form.

Subtracting from overall dimensions to allow for the chicken wire and the fiber glass thickness, build contoured wooden frames as for a tree or three-dimensional ground row and assemble them on cross members with enough strength to maintain the shape but capable of being easily dismantled (nailheads left upstanding, etc.). Mold chicken wire over this framed core to the desired shape but do not fasten it to the wood. When the cast has set (see Problem 71), the resin will have bonded the cloth and the chicken wire. The wooden core may then be dismantled and removed.

15.46 Evenly spaced planks are the temporary form for making a log cabin wall. When the fiber glass has set, it may be removed from the planks and attached to a lighter-weight frame of 1″ × 3″ lumber

15.47 A fieldstone chimney; log wall in background

15.48 The junction between chimney and log wall

71. To apply glass cloth to a chicken-wire form.

Cut the cloth into conforming shapes and lay it over the form. On vertical or near-vertical surfaces, fasten the cloth with U-shaped pieces of soft iron wire (about 20-gauge) punched through both cloth and chicken wire and twisted together on the inside of the form. See Figures 15.47 and 15.48.

72. To apply glass cloth to vertical or nearly vertical surfaces of solid molds when wiring is impossible.

Apply a thorough coat of viscous film parting agent, apply thixotropic resin and let it get tacky, then apply glass cloth and another coat of resin.

73. To cast fiber glass over a clay mold.

For small objects such as jugs or bottles, sculpture modeling clay to the desired shape, cover with a parting agent, apply glass cloth and resin, allow to set, and remove from the mold. For larger objects, construct a core of wood, wire, or other material with supporting strength adequate to the shape, sculpture clay over the core, cover with a parting agent, apply glass cloth and resin, allow to set, and remove from the mold.

If multiple copies are to be made from any mold, the design must provide for removal of the cast without destroying the mold.

74. To cast fiber glass over a real object.

Cover the object with a parting agent, apply glass cloth and resin, allow to set, and remove. Make certain that the object can be removed from the mold without damage before starting. Avoid this process with fragile originals.

75. To apply glass cloth to finely detailed surfaces.

Use 4 oz./yd. cloth cut into strips of suitable size, but not less than 3″ square; after applying parting agent to the mold, laminate the strips to fit the surface, working with cloth and resin simultaneously. See Figures 15.49–15.51.

15.49–15.51 A castered garden wall unit may be cast over real brick laid on a floor, or over brick-shaped pieces of wood nailed to plywood. The joint between a column and the wall is made with glass cloth and resin

436

76. To apply resin to glass cloth with a brush.

Using a short-bristled brush with an unpainted handle, apply the first coat of resin with a direct dabbing motion to make it penetrate the cloth and make the cloth conform to the mold. Apply additional resin with a stroking motion, flattening any frayed edges of the cloth.

77. To reinforce weak parts of a fiber glass cast.

After the cast has been removed from the mold, apply resin and either glass cloth or mat to the inside surfaces where reinforcement is needed. Additional layers will add strength.

78. To stiffen weight-bearing parts of fiber glass casts (Figure 15.52).

Dip pieces of fiber glass mat in resin, shape them into ribs, and apply them inside the parts to be stiffened. Increase the size and number of ribs until adequate stiffness has been achieved. Or cut ribs of rigid poly-styrene foam (RPF) to fit snugly inside the structure to be stiffened, wrap in parting foil to prevent the resin from dissolving the foam, and fasten in place with layers of glass cloth and resin. If polyurethane foam (RUF) is used, omit the foil wrapping.

15.52 Stiffening ribs inside a weight-bearing rock

79. To prevent scuff damage to painted fiber glass.

Spray a thin layer of transparent resin on the surface.

80. To remove gloss or shine from hardened resin.

Rub with steel wool or sandpaper.

81. To correct a coat of resin which does not harden.

Thin some resin with liquid styrene, add 3 percent hardener, and brush this mixture on the recalcitrant resin surface.

82. To prepare a fiber glass and resin surface to receive water paints.

Rub the surface with sandpaper or steel wool.

Rigid Plastic Foam

The following problems exemplify scenic uses of rigid plastic foam described in Chapter 5 and methods of working the material discussed in Chapter 9. Specific kinds of rigid foam are named and described in Chapter 6 and specific tools and equipment listed in Chapter 8.

83. To make several ornaments of the same design from RPF.

Lay out a full-scale pattern of the finished ornament on a piece of ¼″ plywood. Using a band saw or saber saw, cut out this template and remove all distortions with sandpaper and files. On a band saw or table saw, cut blocks of foam ⅜″ larger than the template in all directions. Holding the template firmly on top of the foam, guide the material across the hot wire, following the outline of the template at a slow, steady rate. Do not distort the cutting wire by excessive pressure on the material. Two or more items of the same pattern may be formed simultaneously by pinning several layers of foam together with the template on top.

84. To make several ornaments of the same design that require interior as well as exterior shaping.

Prepare the template and cut the exterior shape as described in Problem 83. Then, with the template still in place, drill a hole through the plastic foam within the interior pattern. Disconnect the cutting wire, thread it through this hole, then reconnect it. Cut the interior shape by guiding the foam by the template as before. When this operation is completed, disconnect the wire, withdraw it from the stock, and reconnect it to the cutter.

85. To make a rectangular ornament 12″ long and over 4″ thick by following a full-scale drawing and using the simple hot-wire cutter.

On the table saw, cut two 8″ × 12″ blocks of 4″-thick RPF for each ornament. Coat one 8″ × 12″ surface of one block with full-strength casein glue, put the two blocks together, apply pressure by weights, and allow to set for at least twenty-four hours. While the glue is setting, prepare a template as described in Problem 83. Using two 4d. box nails attach the template to one surface of the glued-up stock. Following the outline of the template, move the stock across the hot wire. Repeat this operation for each side of the block, cutting one side at a time in counter-clockwise rotation. See Figure 15.55.

86. To make a rectangular ornament by following a full-scale drawing and using the flexible hot-wire cutter.

Prepare the stock as described in Problem 85. While the glued material is drying, prepare a cutting wire for the flexible hot-wire cutter. From the drawing, determine the required length of 12- or 24-gauge resistance wire and add 1½″ for attachment to the upper and lower terminals of the cutter. Cut the wire and shape it to the desired profile using pliers, finger pressure, and a vise. Attach the wire to the cutter. Stand the stock on end and move it across the wire of the cutter. Repeat this process for each side of the form.

87. To make a round ornament of RPF from a full-scale drawing.

Prepare the stock as described in Problem 85 and prepare the flexible hot-wire cutter as described in Problem 86. Mount the prepared stock, centered, on the turntable base of the flexible hot-wire cutter and move the base into cutting position next to the wire. Turn the foam block on

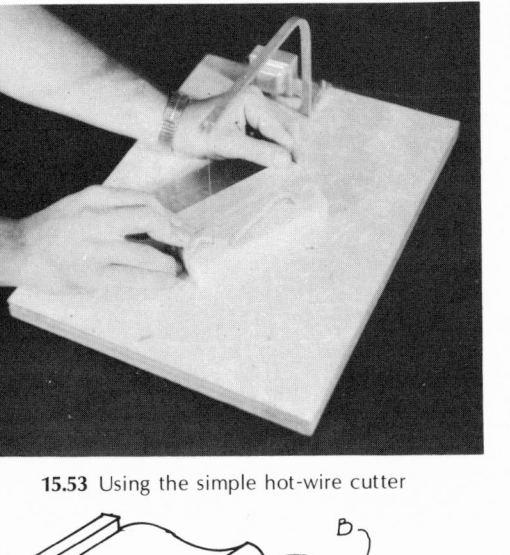

15.53 Using the simple hot-wire cutter

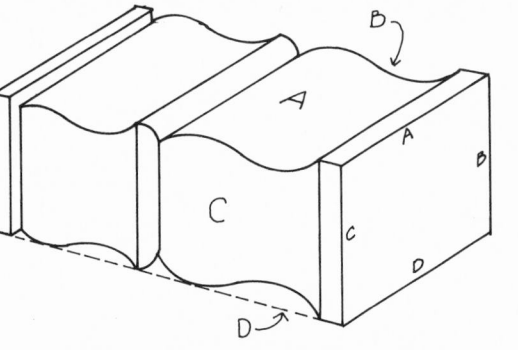

15.55 A rectangular pedestal or lamp base made on the simple hot-wire cutter

15.54 An ornament cut with a hot wire

15.56 A cone cut on the flexible hot-wire cutter by tilting the wire and rotating the block of RPF

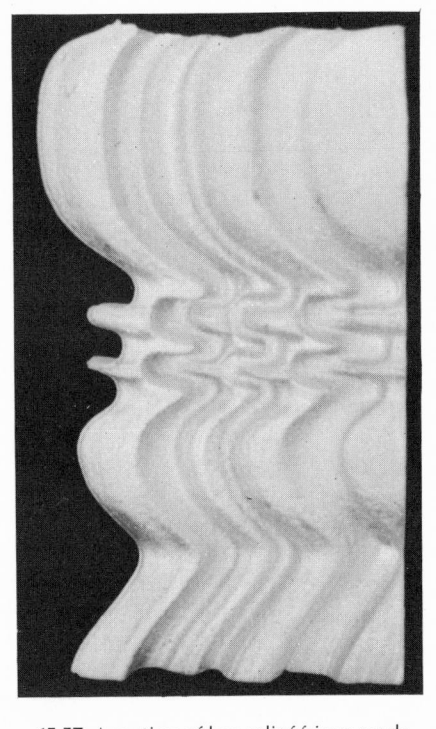

15.57 A section of bas-relief frieze made on the flexible hot-wire cutter

439

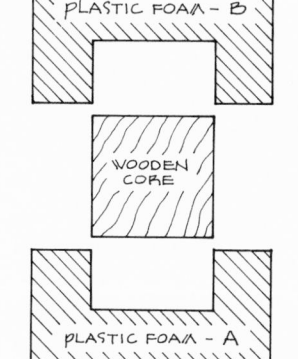

PLASTIC FOAM – B

WOODEN CORE

PLASTIC FOAM – A

15.58

the base at a slow even speed until the unit is formed. Be very careful not to distort the cutting wire by excessive pressure. See Figure 15.56.

88. To fabricate a table leg from RPF following a full-scale drawing.

Prepare the foam by ripping two 32″-long planks of 3″-thick stock 6¼″ wide. With a dado head, cut grooves exactly 2″ wide and 1″ deep down the center of one 6¼″ side of each plank. Cut one piece of 2″ × 2″ (actual dimension) white pine exactly 32″ long. Coat the grooved sides of the RPF planks with full-strength casein glue. After 5 minutes of open drying, place the 2″ × 2″ in the groove of one of the planks and cover it with the other grooved plank. Apply pressure and allow to set for 24 hours. Form the leg, using one of the techniques described in Problems 85 or 86. See Figures 15.58–15.60.

15.59 A finished table leg

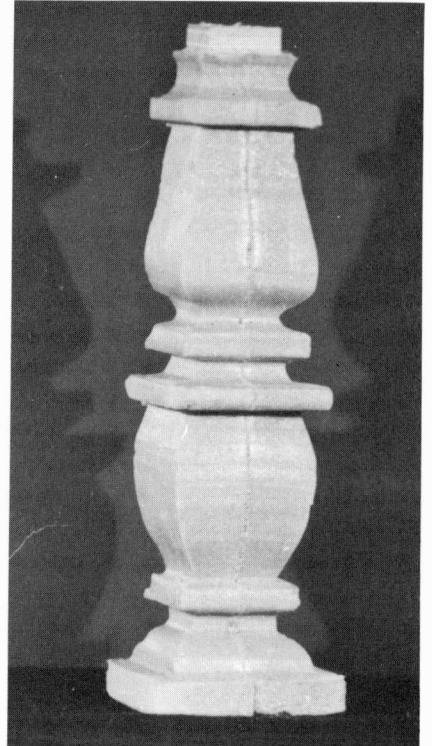

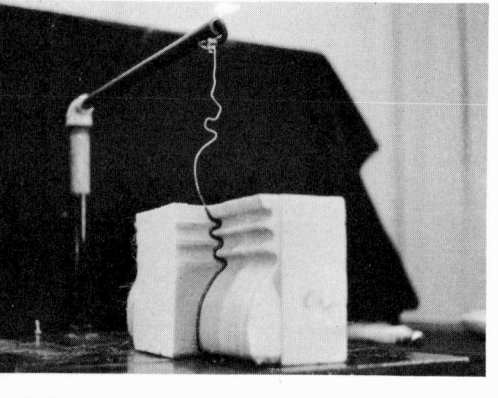

15.60 A table with legs of RPF

15.61 A molding is shaped by guiding a block of RPF against a fence past the bent hot wire

89. To make a specially designed profile molding according to a full-scale drawing.

Using a table saw, rip the required quantity of RPF to the exact height of the finished molding. Prepare the cutting wire for the flexible hot-wire cutter as described in Problem 86. Mount a fence to guide the stock in a straight line across the wire. Guiding against the fence, move the stock across the cutting wire at a slow steady rate. See Figure 15.61.

90. To make a natural rock wall from RPF.

Construct the wall flat using standard techniques. Cover the wall with plywood instead of canvas. Keeping in mind that each rock should be different in size and shape, cut several random-shaped pieces of foam on the band saw, keeping one flat surface on each piece so that it may be easily and securely attached to the wall. Mount each fake rock with an acceptable adhesive (Tuff-Bond #9) and at least two 6*d*. or 8*d*. rosin-coated box nails inserted from the rear of each piece. Allow 24 hours' drying time, then paint as desired.

91. To make a bas-relief plaque from RPF or RUF.

Using the desired thickness of plastic foam, cut the outline of the plaque with a band saw or saber saw. Lay out the desired relief work with chalk or charcoal. Using a high-speed router, set to the desired depth, cut out the recessed portion of the plaque. This work must be done in a *well-ventilated* area, for toxic concentrations of methyl chloride build up rapidly when a router is used on RPF. Sandpaper any rough spots. See Figures 15.62 and 15.63.

15.62 A bas-relief plaque in RPF

15.63 Cutout ornament in RPF applied to a flat surface

92. To construct a statue from RPF from a scale drawing.

On the scale drawing, divide the statue into general planes and 2"-thick layers. Label each section of each layer. Using a table saw, cut rectangular blocks of plastic foam to correspond with the blocks of the statue. Label each block to correspond with the designated labels of the sketch. Assemble the blocks in the proper order using an acceptable adhesive (Tuff-Bond #9), apply pressure, and allow to dry for at least 24 hours. If thicker blocks of RPF or RUF are commercially available, this layering process can be reduced or eliminated. As the adhesive is setting, sketch the design of the finished unit on the rough stock. Use chalk or a felt-tipped marker. With a hacksaw, hacksaw blades, and a keyhole saw, hew out the rough shape. If necessary, resketch the design before beginning the detail work. Detail work may be done with saws, serrated knives, and the hand hot-wire cutter with tips shaped as required. The saws and knives are faster but much coarser and will not

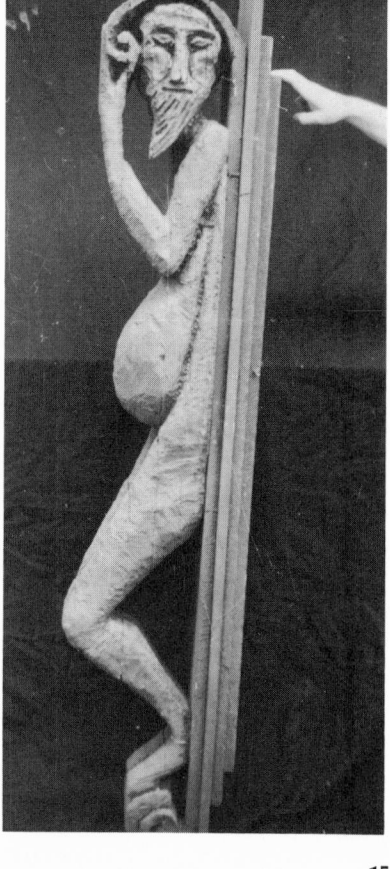

15.64–15.66 A statue made in RPF. Center: Detail of the leg showing layers.
Right: Detail of the head

do as fine detail work as the hot-wire cutter. If the work is too rough
when forming is completed, the entire unit may be sanded by hand or
with a power sander. For a polished wood or marble finish, coat the
entire unit with latex-modified Elmer's Glue-All, allow to dry, then paint
as desired. See Figures 15.64–15.66.

Thermoplastics

cutting and pinch-forming

93. To cut sheet stock by scoring.

With a metal straightedge placed on the measured marks, score one
side of the sheet with a matte knife. Fold the sheet to break it at the
scored line.

94. To cut and pinch-form sheet stock in quantity (e.g., to make leaves).

Cut polystyrene sheet to uniform-sized pieces larger than the leaf
pattern. Make stacks of twenty or thirty pieces with edges even. Mark
the top piece from a prepared pattern with a felt pen. Gang-cut the stack
on the band saw. Place the cut leaves in boiling water. In 20 seconds
remove the leaves one by one and immediately form each one by hand
as desired (wear heat-resistant gloves). The leaves may be stapled to
twigs or branches. See Figures 15.67–15.70.

15.67 Cutting multiple leaf shapes on the band saw

15.68 Softening the cut leaves in boiling water

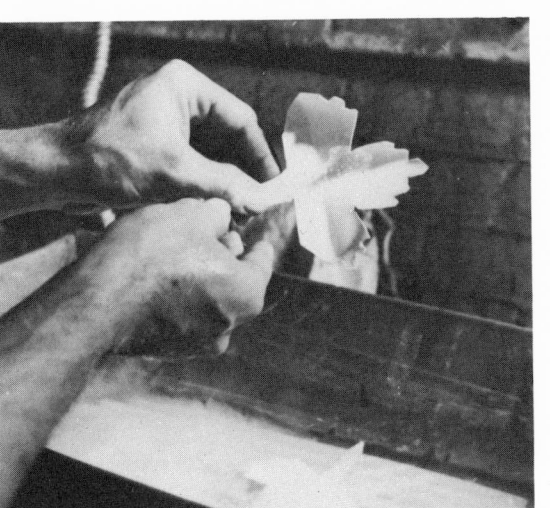

15.69 A leaf after being shaped by hand

15.70 Stapling polystyrene leaves to real twigs

95. To make tree branches and twigs by using dry heat and pinch-forming.

Cut polystyrene sheet (cellulose acetate if an icy effect is desired) into long tapered pieces to suit the design. Suspend them by stapling the wide ends to a batten at working height. Connect the heat gun to an adequate-load circuit, switch it to HOT, and allow 10 seconds for heating. Control the output heat by regulating the intake of air to the turbo-fan. Heat the area near the top (wide end) of a piece for about 5 seconds, remove the heat, and crush the plastic with the *gloved* other hand. Hold this for a few seconds until the plastic cools in its new shape. Repeat this process to the tip of the branch. When all forming is done or when process is interrupted, switch the gun to COLD to force-cool the ceramic element before cutting the current. See Figure 15.71.

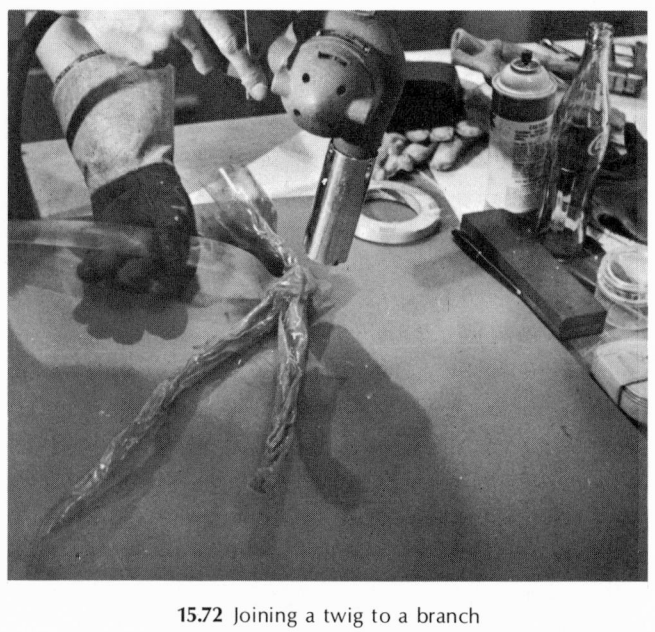

15.71 Pinch-forming a twig in cellulose acetate film

15.72 Joining a twig to a branch

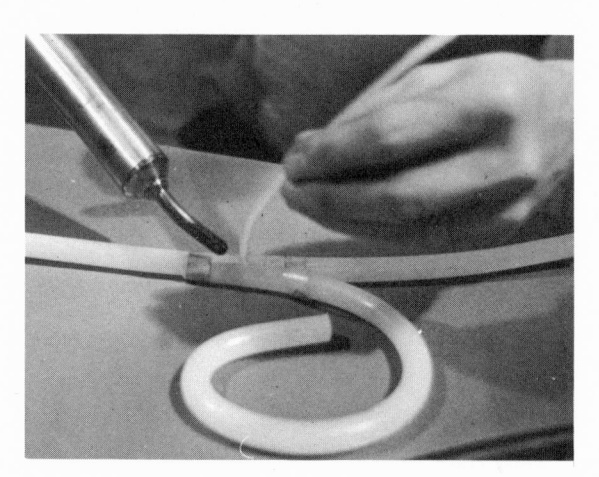

15.74 Welding bent rods together

15.73 A chandelier in which polyethylene rod, flexible conduit, and chain are combined

15.75 Shaping the fit-up of PVC tube for welding

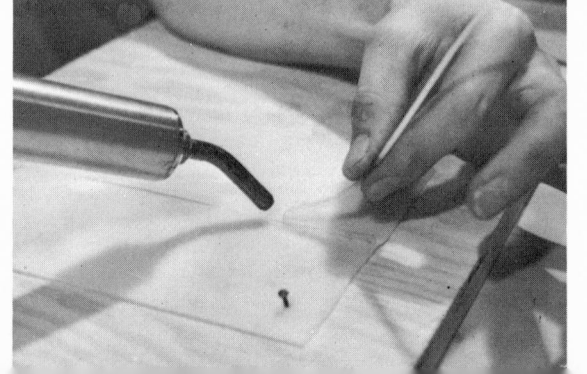

15.76 Butt-welding two pieces of sheet plastic

96. To join a formed twig to a formed branch (Figure 15.72).

Heat a strip of plastic 2″ wide and when it is soft, wrap it around the joint. Hold it until it is cool.

97. To make icicles.

Follow the process for twigs, using cellulose acetate and avoiding curves.

98. To bend thermoplastic rod.

bending

Heat either low-density polyethylene rod 8 minutes in boiling water, or high-density polyethylene rod 12 minutes. Remove and shape by hand, or bend around a jig or between and around nails driven into a board. Place in cold water until it is set. The limit of curvature is 2½″ radius for ½″ rod and proportional for other sizes. See Figure 15.73.

Follow the techniques described under "Oxyacetylene Welding" (page 425) but use the hot-air welding gun and filler rods of the same plastic as that being welded and use only the amount of heat needed to soften the base material and the rod. Push the softened rod lightly into the weld seam or vee, if there is one. Snug fit-ups produce the best welds. See Figures 15.74–15.76.

99. To start the hot-air welding gun.

welding

OPEN the air supply valve. This *must* be done before the gun is connected to electricity. Set it for 6 psi pressure. Connect the gun to a 110-volt circuit and preheat for 3 minutes. Vary the output air temperature inversely by adjusting the input air volume. DO NOT TOUCH the metal cylinder around the heater element. Do not handle the welder roughly.

100. To shut down the hot-air welder.

Disconnect heater but keep air flowing for at least 5 minutes at maximum volume to cool the ceramic heating element slowly.

101. To form rough shapes without air pressure or vacuum (ridge-forming).

ridge-forming

Place some object or form which approximates the desired shape on a flat base. Clamp a piece of polystyrene in a frame. Heat the sheet to ductility and press down over the form; hold or clamp the frame in place until the sheet cools.

102. To form three-dimensional shapes (domed or bubbled) entirely by the use of air pressure differentials — vacuum or positive pressure — without the use of male or female molds.

bubble-forming

Construct a vacuum pot or box with an air hole in the bottom of sufficient depth to draw the shape desired. Match the box with a frame constructed of plywood whose inside contour is the outline of the base of the finished product. Place the plastic sheet in the frame; heat it to ductility and clamp the frame to the top of the box. Exhaust air from the box through the air hole (vacuum or negative pressure) and maintain the vacuum until the sheet has cooled. Or, send compressed air through the hole (positive pressure) until the plastic has assumed the desired shape; maintain the pressure until the sheet has cooled. Even if the contour of the frame is square or triangular, the plastic will tend toward a spherical shape, since a sphere has the smallest surface area of any shape for any given volume. As the box and frame are special to the shape, this process is only efficient if several forms with identical frames are needed.

15.77 Equalizing the heat on a sheet of polystyrene

drape-forming

103. To replicate objects by drape-forming over a male mold by vacuum.

Place real objects or designed molds executed in wood, clay, or plaster of Paris on the forming table. Limiting specifications are given below. Close the vacuum valve to the forming table and start the vacuum pump to reduce the pressure in the vacuum tank to about 26″ mercury. Clamp a polystyrene sheet into the frame and heat it over the oven. Use the heat gun to equalize heat differences which are indicated by buckling (Figure 15.77). When the sheet is uniformly limp (rubbery) from heat (practice is the only preceptor in this matter), position the frame over the forming table and press it down until all edges of the frame are slightly below the upper surface of the table. This forces the soft plastic into contact with the forming table and creates the necessary air seal. Immediately open the vacuum valve and the air trapped underneath the sheet will be displaced into the vacuum tank. Keep the vacuum constant for 10 seconds to allow the plastic to cool and set in its new shape.

specifications for male molds

- The mold height must never exceed the least width.
- The width at the bottom of a mold depression must never be less than the depth of the depression.
- There must be no double or locking undercuts.
- There must be no sharp edges or 90° bends.
- There must be holes $\frac{1}{32}$″ in diameter drilled through the molds at or near all low points so that the sheet will be sucked into these depressions.
- See Figures 15.78–15.82.

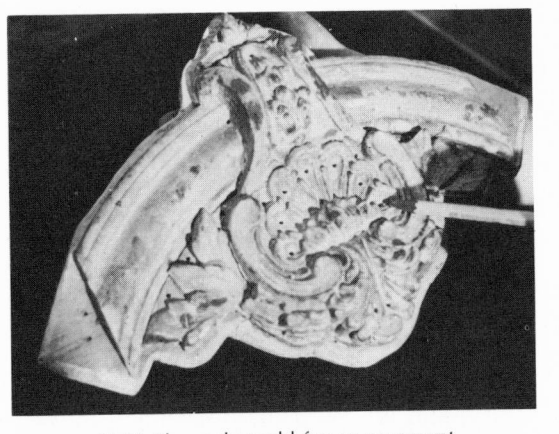

15.78 The male mold for an ornament

15.79 Three images of the ornament: one on the frame, one roughly cut out, and one trimmed

15.80 The mold for a ceiling panel on the forming table and a completed image in the frame

15.81 Sections of a thermoformed cornice aligned for joining

15.82 A large thermoforming table with a mold for the quoined corner of a building. The heating component and the forming frame are on overhead tracks. The frame is lowered onto the mold

Basic Rope Skills

terms

Standing part: that part of the rope which is between the finished knot and the other end of the rope, which is generally made fast to some distant object.

Running part: the end of the rope which is free and is manipulated in tying a knot.

Strand: a twist of fibers, three of which are laid up together to form a rope.

Bight: a loop formed by grasping the standing part in one hand and bringing together the parts of the rope on each side of the point grasped.

coiling

104. To coil right-lay rope.

Grasp a free end in one hand, palm up. With the other hand moving in clockwise circles, form loops, placing the top of each loop in the first hand. Sailors call this *coiling with the sun*. Rope coiled in this manner will lie smoothly in the coil; rope coiled in the reverse direction will form twisted coils which are hard to handle.

105. To make a gasket (Figure 15.83).

When a rope which has been used is to be stored, it must be neatly coiled and the coil secured against coming apart until it is to be used again. The fastening, furthermore, must be easily taken apart. Coil the rope as described above. When about 6′ of rope remains to be coiled, wrap it around the middle of the coil to force the coil into the shape of an 8. When 3′ remains, pass a bight through the upper half of the coil and back over the coil on the outside. Draw the free end taut.

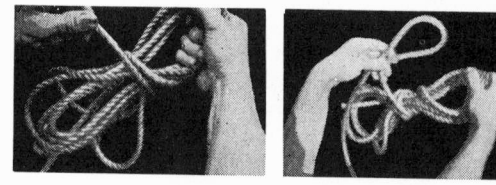

15.83
To make a gasket

106. To gasket the end of a rope which is too long (Figure 15.84).

Coil the rope at the point where the gasket is to be made. Pass one hand through the coil and seize the rope beyond the coil. Draw the rope through the coil, thus making a bight; slip this bight over the coil on the outside.

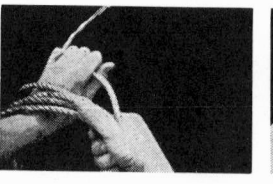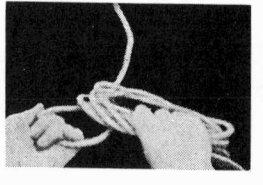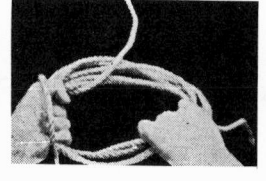

15.84 To gasket
the end of a rope

107. To store a coil of rope on a cleat or pin.

Coil the free rope close to the pin. Pass one hand through the coil and grasp the rope between the coil and the pin. Draw a bight thus formed through the coil and lay the bight over the pin. The coil is thereby suspended from the pin in a manner which permits releasing quickly.

108. To prepare a rope to pay out freely without fouling or snarling.

First method (flaking): starting with the free end, lay the rope in lazy eights (overlapping) so that each successive complete figure is offset slightly from the preceding figure.

Second method: starting with the free end, overhand the rope, letting it pile up as it falls. *Do not disturb this pile.*

With either method a rope, when released, will pay out rapidly without fouling.

Knot is the generic term applied to the joining of two rope ends together or the joining of one rope's end to other objects. Usage has loosely differentiated knots into hitches and bends, although there is no logical order to the established nomenclature. The following discussion treats only knots that are useful to the stagehand.

OVERHAND KNOT (Figure 15.85): the basis of many other knots, it is of little use by itself except to make bumps in a rope, frequently undesirable when they occur by accident. Turn the running part through a complete circle to form a loop. Pass the running part around the standing part and through the loop. Draw out the running part in its original direction.

15.85 Overhand knot

109. To allow adequate length of rope for knots.

When calculating the length of a snatch line ⅜″ in diameter, allow for knots and bends as follows:

Bowline to a ring	1¼′
Clove hitch to a 1½″ pipe	2′
Fisherman's bend to 1½″ pipe	2′
Fisherman's bend to a ring	1½′
Cinch tackle, two-part	5′
Cinch tackle, three-part	8′

For a larger rope, increase the allowance in proportion to the rope diameter, except for cinch tackles.

110. To join two ropes' ends.

SQUARE KNOT (Figure 15.86): pass the running part of one rope once around the standing part of the other in the manner of an overhand knot. Reverse the direction of both ropes' ends and repeat the process. Make certain that the end and standing part of each rope are parallel and contiguous when the knot is completed. Secure the ends to their respective standing parts with tape or twine. A square knot is most effective when two ropes of the same size and stiffness are being joined.

15.86 Square knot

SHEET BEND (Figure 15.87): make a bight in the end of one rope, pass the end of the other rope through this bight, behind the two parts of the first rope, and under its own standing part. The end does not return through the bight. A sheet bend is effective for joining the ends of ropes of unequal stiffness or size; the bight is made in the stiffer or larger of the two ropes.

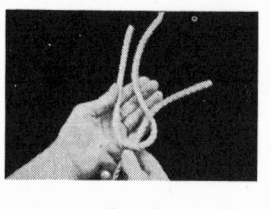

15.87 Sheet bend

SPLICES: the short splice and long splice described in Problem 118 are still other methods for permanently joining two ropes' ends.

111. To join a rope to a ring.

BOWLINE (Figure 15.88): pass the end of the rope through the ring. Lay the end across the standing part at a point which will make a loop of desired size. With the other hand grasp the rope within the loop just formed, between the end and the ring. Pass the point grasped around the end, thus making a second smaller loop with the end inside it. Hold this loop slightly open, draw the end through it to take up slack, pass the end behind the standing part, and return it again through the small loop.

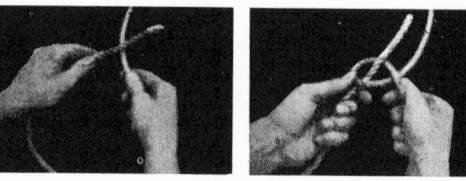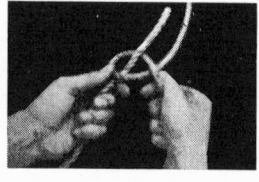

15.88 Bowline

A bowline is useful to form a loop of fixed size in the end of a rope for any purpose. It is particularly useful for tying a safety line to secure a rigger who is working in a precarious position. A stagehand must be able to tie a bowline in any position. A bowline will not slip and may be untied quickly.

112. To join a rope to a hook.

BLACKWALL HITCH (Figure 15.89): pass the rope behind the shank of the hook. Lay the end in the bight of the hook, and pass the standing part over it. Make sure that the standing part is binding the end against the hook. Secure the end by (1) tying two half hitches around the standing part; (2) whipping the end to the standing part, or (3) tucking the end through the standing part as in splicing.

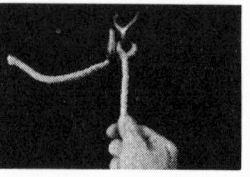

15.89 Blackwall hitch

113. To tie off the lash line by which two flats are joined.

TIE-OFF HITCH or LASH KNOT (Figure 15.90): when the lash line has been taken around the lowest lash cleats, which are opposite each other on the adjoining stiles of the flats, make a bight in the free end of the line. Pass this bight behind the standing part above the lash cleats, a distance of about 4 inches. Grasp this bight, turn it back over the standing part, and pull the line taut. Form another bight in the remaining free end and slip it through the first bight. This knot is of no effect unless the line is kept taut when it is being tied. To untie, pull the end of the line.

15.90 Tie-off hitch or lash knot

114. To join a rope's end to a batten or timber.

CLOVE HITCH (Figure 15.91): make a turn of the rope around the batten. At the completion of this turn pass the end over the standing part and make another turn. At the completion of the second turn, slip the end between this turn and the batten. The direction of the end around the batten is always the same. When the hitch is completed, the end and the standing part are parallel, contiguous, and leading in opposite directions, and they are bound against the batten by the turn or the rope.

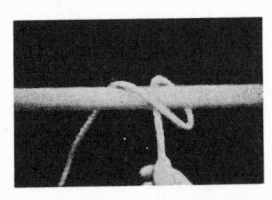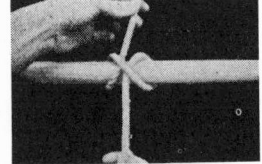
15.91 Clove hitch

TIMBER HITCH (Figure 15.92): pass the end once around the batten and around the standing part. Reverse the direction of the end and twist it several times around the part of the rope within the loop just formed.

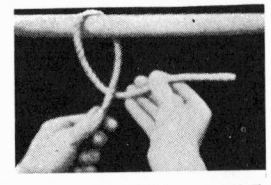
15.92 Timber hitch

TWO HALF-HITCHES (Figure 15.93): pass the end once around the batten, and then twice around the standing part in the manner of a clove hitch.

15.93 Two half hitches

FISHERMAN'S BEND (Figure 15.94): pass the end twice around the batten, inserting the fingers of one hand between the first turn and the batten. Pass the end around the standing part and through the loop which is held open by the fingers. Draw the knot taut and make another half hitch around the standing part. The fisherman's bend provides two parts of rope around the batten and has very little tendency to bind, so is not difficult to untie. Furthermore, it allows adjustment by slipping rope through the knot when it is partly tied. It is the recommended method of tying snatch lines to battens.

15.94 Fisherman's bend

Any of these knots for joining a rope to a batten is subject to slipping and ultimate untying if the tension upon it is intermittent rather than constant. To guard against this, the rope's end must be made fast to the standing part by whipping with cord, or with friction tape, or by tucking the end under one strand of the standing part. The latter method is the simplest because it requires no materials and can be done quickly.

115. To join the end of one rope to the standing part of another.

STOPPER HITCH (Figure 15.95): pass the end three full turns around the standing part exactly as in a clove hitch, making the third turn identical to the second of the clove hitch. This hitch is useful to tie off the purchase line of a counterweight unit when the load on the unit is temporarily unbalanced. Short ropes, known as checklines, are fixed permanently into the lock rail for this purpose.

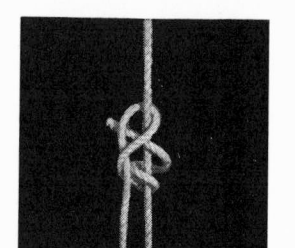

15.95 Stopper hitch

ROLLING HITCH (Figure 15.96): with a long end of rope tie a clove hitch around the standing part, passing at least 3′ of the end through the hitch. Roll this 3′ along the standing part with the lay of the rope. Tape or whip the end securely to the standing part. The friction of the rolled rope is ample to withstand a pull up to the capacity of the rope used.

15.96 Rolling hitch

A rope's end may be spliced into the standing part of another rope for permanent joining by the method employed for an eye splice, below.

SPLICES: splices are made by interweaving (tucking) the strands of one or more ropes or by laying the strands of one rope into the space vacated by unlaying strands of another rope. Splices which are tucked are thicker than the rope in which they are made and consequently will not run freely through blocks. Splices intended to be run through blocks must be little if any thicker than the rope itself.

116. To make a permanent loop or eye in the end of a rope.

EYE SPLICE (Figure 15.97): this is used to join a rope's end permanently to a pulley, ring, or shackle. Unlay the end of the rope a distance equal to about four complete turns of one strand around the rope. Bend the rope around a thimble which has been previously inserted in the ring or pulley. Open up the standing part at the point where the splice is to be made by twisting against the lay of the rope or driving a marlin spike under one strand. Insert one of the unlaid strands under one strand of the standing part where the opening has been made, and draw it through as far as the thimble will allow. The strand must be inserted at right angles to the lay of the rope. This is called a tuck. Similarly insert the other unlaid strands each under separate strands of the standing part, *at the same cross-section point,* each tuck being at right angles to the lay, and under only one strand. There must be no progression along the standing part until the three strands have been tucked. When this has been accomplished, pass each unlaid strand over the standing part strand next to it and tuck it under the one beyond. Thus, tucking becomes a process of weaving each unlaid strand over and under strands of the standing part until the unlaid strands are completely tucked. Frayed ends may be trimmed off and the splice pounded or rolled to give it shape.

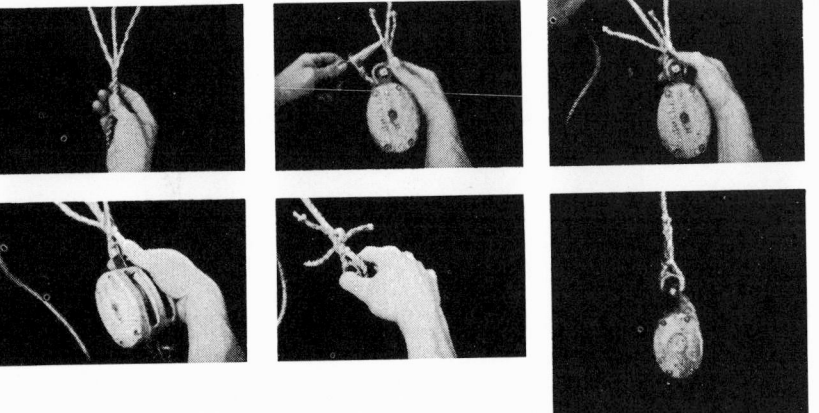

15.97 Eye splice

117. To make an eye splice in the standing part of a rope.

At the desired point in the rope, twist the rope against the lay to make the strands separate and twist upon themselves. When the twisted strands are long enough for at least two tucks, lay them against the standing part to form a loop of the desired size and tuck.

118. To join two ropes' ends permanently.

SHORT SPLICE (Figure 15.98): unlay the end of each rope an amount equal to four full twists of the rope. Separate the unlaid strands and place the ends against each other so that the strands of the two ropes alternate. Fasten the three strands of one rope to the standing part of the other temporarily, to hold the ropes together. With the other three unlaid strands tuck over and under as in an eye splice. Complete one side of the splice, remove the temporary tie, and complete the other side.

Both eye splice and short splice may be tapered by trimming out some of the hemp from each strand before the final tucking is done.

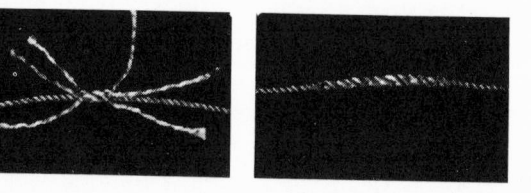

15.98 Short splice

LONG SPLICE (Figure 15.99): This is used when the spliced rope must run freely through sheaves or blocks. Endless lines are made with long splices. Unlay one strand from each rope's end at least 15 complete turns of the strand. Place the two ropes together at the points where the unlaid portion ends. By unlaying still further one strand of one rope and laying in its place one strand of the other, join the two ropes. Repeat this process with another pair of strands in the opposite direction, leaving, at the original point of joining, two strands unlaid but in contact. There are now, at three points in the joined rope, pairs of strands. Trim each strand to a length equal to two twists of the rope. Tie each pair of strands with an overhand knot so that the knot may be pulled snugly into the rope, and continue each overhand knot to the end of each strand. Roll and pound the joined rope to smooth out unevenness.

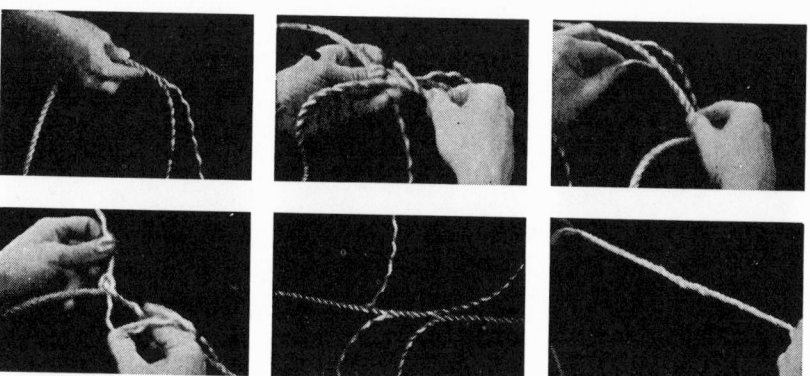

15.99 Long splice

Hanging Scenery

All hanging consists of attaching scenery or other objects to flying equipment for the purpose of hanging it as part of the scenic investiture and of elevating it into space above the stage (*flies*) for concealed storage, there to stay until it is needed in the scene or taken from the theatre. The kinds of rigging systems are described in Chapter 11 and the principles of rigging in Chapter 12. The use of the systems and the application of the principles are set forth here in rules and precautions followed by a series of exemplary problems.

hanging on rope sets
rules governing
hanging on rope

- Sandbags must underbalance the units so that the scenery will go to low trim if the high-trim tie is released, except that if an overhaul is attached to the sandbag, the bag may balance the scenery and the overhaul used to pull the bag up and let the scenery in to low trim. Low trim and high trim are defined in Problem 119.

- A safety factor of 10, breaking strength versus load, is mandatory.

- On a double rail the low trim is tied on the upper rail and the high trim on the lower. This facilitates attaching and detaching sandbags.

- The low-trim tie is never released except to retrim the lines and to strike the show.

- Lightweight units (drops, cut drops, leg drops, and borders weighing under 150 pounds) which are low-trimmed to clear the floor may be let in by *pulling the pins* from the high trims if the lines have been carefully coiled or flaked to run without snarling.

- Keep all rope, whether dead or in use, neatly coiled and ready to be paid out.

- Keep all rope sets which are not in use in condition for immediate use.

- Do not allow uncoiled rope to accumulate on the fly floor. The hazard is twofold: tripping, and getting one's ankle caught in a rope which is paying out toward the grid.

- Replace any rope the condition of which is doubtful. The specified strength is accurate only when the rope is new. After use, its strength is dependent upon the use and care it has received. Stiff rope is strong. Supple and splintery rope is old and weak.

- Keep all sandbags in good repair to prevent sand leakage. For signs of wear, look particularly to the points where the rope or webbing of the sandbag is attached to the top and bottom rings.

- The larger the sheave, the less the wear on the rope and the longer its life.

- When lines are being sandbagged, keep personnel outside the area below the fly gallery.

- Allow no one but the regular flymen to work any flying equipment.

- The direction of any rope must never be more than 5° from the plane of rotation of the sheave, lest the rope jump the sheave or be subject to excessive frictional wear. Muling and lead blocks must be used to establish this direction if necessary. Swivel head blocks make possible wide angular separation of several lines in one set.

Variations in hanging with rope sets are infinite. Units which set perpendicularly or obliquely to the footlights are flown on one or more lines from various sets. The unwanted lines are weighted and taken out, and the lines to be used are grouped together either before they enter the head blocks on the gridiron or before they are clewed to the sandbag.

A small box set may be flown within a large box set, by hanging the sidewalls of the large box set on the long lines and the short lines respectively, the back wall and ceiling on a complete set of lines further upstage, and hanging the small box set on short-center and long-center lines of the sets used otherwise for the large sidewalls.

auxiliary counterweights

Iron counterweights may be employed on rope system sets for the balancing of heavy loads such as lighting border battens, by installing steel cables between gridiron and fly gallery as guides for counterweight arbors.

drops

119. To hang a drop on a rope set, the drop to be centered on the stage (Figures 15.100 and 15.101).

Place the drop, rolled, on the floor parallel to the footlights *with its center line on the center line of the stage.* Be sure that the painted side will face downstage when it is unrolled. Remove the jacket or cover. Bring in to the floor the set of lines on which the drop will hang nearest its setting position. If no rope sets are located at the prescribed setting position and precise hanging is necessary, the loft sheaves must previously have been relocated to make precise hanging possible. Such precision is seldom necessary. Tie each line to the top batten of the drop with either a fisherman's bend or a clove hitch. Make a short horizontal cut in the cloth directly beneath the top batten to receive the rope. Tuck each free end once under one strand of the standing part of each line to secure it. Drop holders may be used. Trim all lines to equal tension. Stagehands stand on the top batten at the points where the lines are tied, and the flyman equalizes the tension of the lines. Fly the drop until the bottom batten clears the floor. This is the setting position of a drop and is referred to as the *low trim:* the lowest point to which the drop will be brought. Adjust the low trim at the pinrail so that the drop hangs level, plumb, and free from wrinkles. If the drop is painted with architectural features, it is important that vertical lines be vertical. Tie the low trim permanently. Fly the drop to the height indicated in the hanging section. This is called the *high trim:* the highest point to which the unit need be flown. Tie off the high trim at the pinrail on top of the low-trim tie, or on an adjacent pin if one is available. If there is a double rail, the low trim is tied on the upper rail, the high trim on the lower. Mark high trim on the ropes by inserting a piece of rag with a marlin spike at a point even with the top of the pin. The drop is now properly hung unless it weighs

15.100 A drop holder

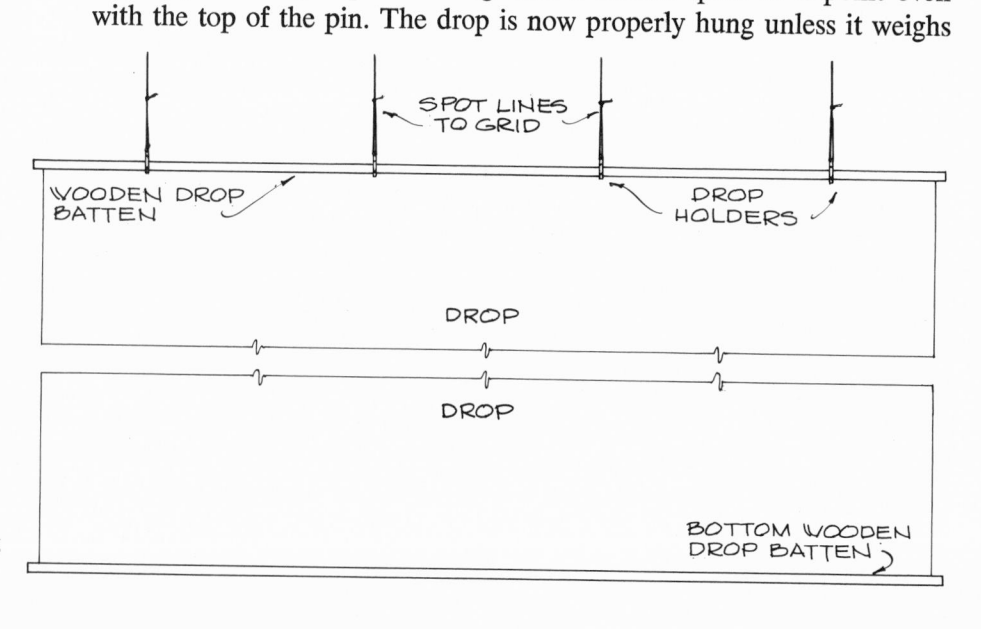

15.101 A drop on a rope set using drop holders

more than one flyman can hoist conveniently. If the drop weighs over 80 pounds or so, attach a sandbag weighing slightly less than the drop to the set of lines by means of a clew or a *Sunday* at a point above the high-trim tie. Check the trims of all pieces hung on rope lines at least once before the show opens to correct stretching in new rope or slippage caused by tightening of knots. Thereafter check the trims periodically and particularly after abrupt changes in humidity.

120. To stretch a drop or to secure it against side-sway.

Let the drop in to the floor. Fasten floor stays over the projecting ends of the bottom batten with stage screws. Put a slight tension on the set of lines and tie off. See Figures 15.102 and 15.103.

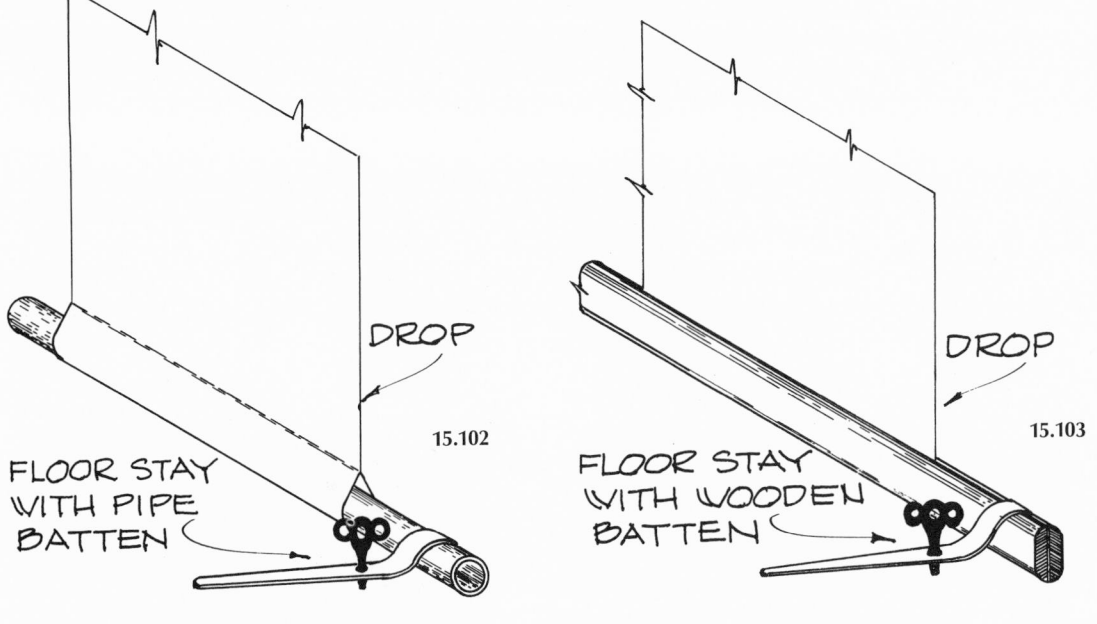

DROP

15.102

FLOOR STAY WITH PIPE BATTEN

DROP

15.103

FLOOR STAY WITH WOODEN BATTEN

121. To unroll or roll a drop.

A drop is unrolled and rolled in the arms of stagehands rather than on the floor. The stagehands, facing upstage, hold the drop on their forearms and roll or unroll it at arm height and at an even rate of speed. In rolling, take care to avoid rolling wrinkles into the drop.

122. To shorten a drop temporarily.

Attach snatch lines to the top batten of the drop at 10′ intervals. Roll the drop on its bottom batten to its required length. Slip drop hooks under the rolled portion and attach the snatch lines to these hooks by cinch tackles.

123. To hang a drop which is not centered on the stage, on a rope set.

On the hanging plan locate the point on the top batten of the drop which coincides with the center line of the stage. Measure from this point the distance of each line from the center line of the stage and tie the lines to the top batten of the drop at these positions. Repeat all other operations of Problem 119.

If the drop requires only two lines of the set, tie a sandbag to the extra line or lines and fly and tie them separately.

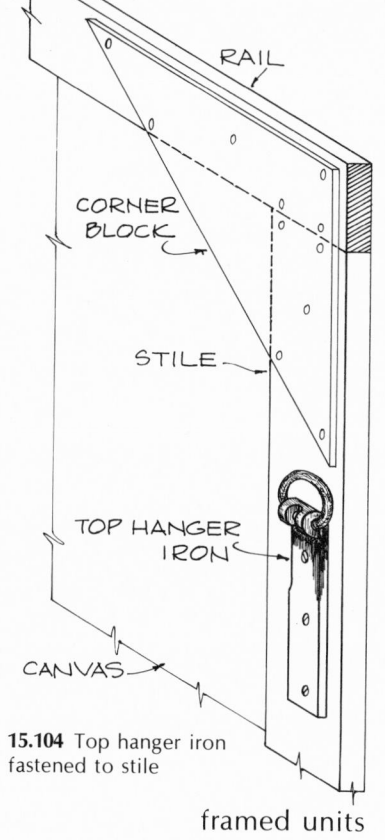

RAIL

CORNER BLOCK

STILE

TOP HANGER IRON

CANVAS

15.104 Top hanger iron fastened to stile

framed units

sandbagging

124. To trip a drop.

Fly the drop as in Problem 119 or 123. Attach the next upstage line set to the bottom batten of the drop. Fly the drop, flat, to high trim, then haul on the *trip set* to take the lower part of the drop above sightlines. Mark the trip set for reference in future operation. If the drop is heavy enough to require bagging, use not more than half the weight on the lift set and less than half the weight with an overhaul on the trip set.

125. To trip a drop in thirds.

ASSUMED: tie lines are sewn to the horizontal seam material on the back of the drop at one-third of its height.

Attach the specified line set — the *lift set* — to the top batten of the drop. Attach the next upstage line set — the *trip set* — to a pipe or wooden batten and attach the tie lines also to this batten. Fly the trip set until the top and trip battens are even or until the bottom batten and the fold in the drop are even. Then fly both sets together. If the drop must be counterweighted, allot weight equal to the top batten and one-third of the cloth to the lift set, and weight equal to the trip batten, the bottom batten, and two-thirds of the cloth to the trip set, with an overhaul which will be used to lift the latter weight and let the drop hang from its top batten.

126. To hang a framed unit on a rope set.

ASSUMED: the unit comes to the stage equipped with top hanger irons (Figure 15.104).

Lay the unit face down on stage floor in the same position relative to the center line of stage as it will have when hung. Bring in the set of lines to be used. If the positions of the lines coincide with locations of the hanger irons, proceed to tie lines to rings in hanger irons with bowlines. Trim and fly as in hanging a drop. If the positions of the lines do not coincide with the positions of the hangers, attach blocks to the lines which are offset and run bridle lines through the blocks to the hanger irons.

Alternate method: Attach a pipe batten with snatch lines (see Problem 138). Take a low trim for the unit which allows the bottom rail to rest firmly on the floor. Fly the piece to high\ trim by man power. Tie off the lines at the high trim and clew on a sandbag of almost the weight of the unit and the pipe batten, if a pipe batten is used.

127. To use a sandbag to aid in initially flying a piece to high trim.

From the fly gallery clew a sandbag to the empty lines to be used, at a point approximating the high-trim tie. Raise this sandbag by means of a double luff (four-part) tackle previously affixed to the gridiron over the fly gallery. When the unit is tied on and ready to be raised, release this sandbag and allow its weight to aid in raising the unit. Detach the double luff from the sandbag when the sandbag descends to the fly gallery and keep it in position to aid in striking the unit.

128. To use an overhaul and bull winch to raise and lower a sandbag.

ASSUMED: an electric bull winch mounted on the fly gallery; a cheek block on the head block, or a block tied under the gridiron, through which is rove an overhaul, that is, a piece of ¾″ or 1″ rope with both ends at the fly gallery.

Attach óne end of the overhaul to the sandbag. Lead the other end through a snatch block at the pinrail to and around, with at least two turns, the drum of the winch. Start the motor and put tension on the end of the overhaul to engage the drum by friction and raise the sandbag. When the scenery has been attached to the lines, ease the tension on the overhaul to allow the sandbag to descend, aided by a flyman, thus raising the scenery. Detach the overhaul from the sandbag. When striking the show, reverse this procedure, using the winch drum to snub the sandbag down to the fly gallery after the scenery has been detached from the lines.

129. To fly an unbalanced unit to initial high trim with a double luff, prior to sandbagging.

With empty (sandbagged) lines at high trim, clew the moving block of a double luff onto the lines at the pinrail. Attach the fixed block to the pinrail. Let the lines in to the floor by paying the double luff upward toward the gridiron. When the unit is tied on, fly it to high trim by hauling downward on the tackle. Tie off the lines at the high trim; then attach a sandbag to the clew and disengage the tackle from the clew.

130. To fly an unbalanced unit to initial high trim with a down haul and a bull winch, prior to sandbagging.

Substitute a piece of ¾″ or 1″ rope for the double luff in Problem 129, attaching one end of the rope to the clew on the empty lines and running the other end through a snatch block at the pinrail, to and around the winch drum. Proceed as in Problem 129.

131. To slack off a set of lines on which a unit is hung and sandbagged when the unit is resting on the floor.

This operation is performed when the unit is a backwall and a separately hung ceiling that is to be set on it; when the unit must set obliquely to the proscenium line; and when a ceiling is hinged to the unit and must be lowered forward onto sidewalls.

ASSUMED: at low trim the sandbag is sufficiently below the head block to provide the required slack in the lines when it is raised; an overhaul is attached to the sandbag and rove through a cheek block on the head block or through a block hung under the gridiron.

At the gallery lower the unit to the floor; at the floor set the unit on its marks; at the gallery pull on the overhaul to raise the bag (man power if the bag weighs under 200 pounds; bull winch, if over) and tie off the overhaul.

132. To hang a unit which must be detached from its lines when set up (carpet hoist) (Figure 15.105).

At the fly gallery slip a strong iron ring on two lines of the set to be used to hang the unit. At a point approximating the high-trim tie, but below the ring, attach a clew or trim clamp to all the lines. Attach a sandbag, weighing slightly less than the unit, to the ring, and an overhaul to the sandbag. With the overhaul raise the sandbag to the gridiron, thus letting in the set of lines.

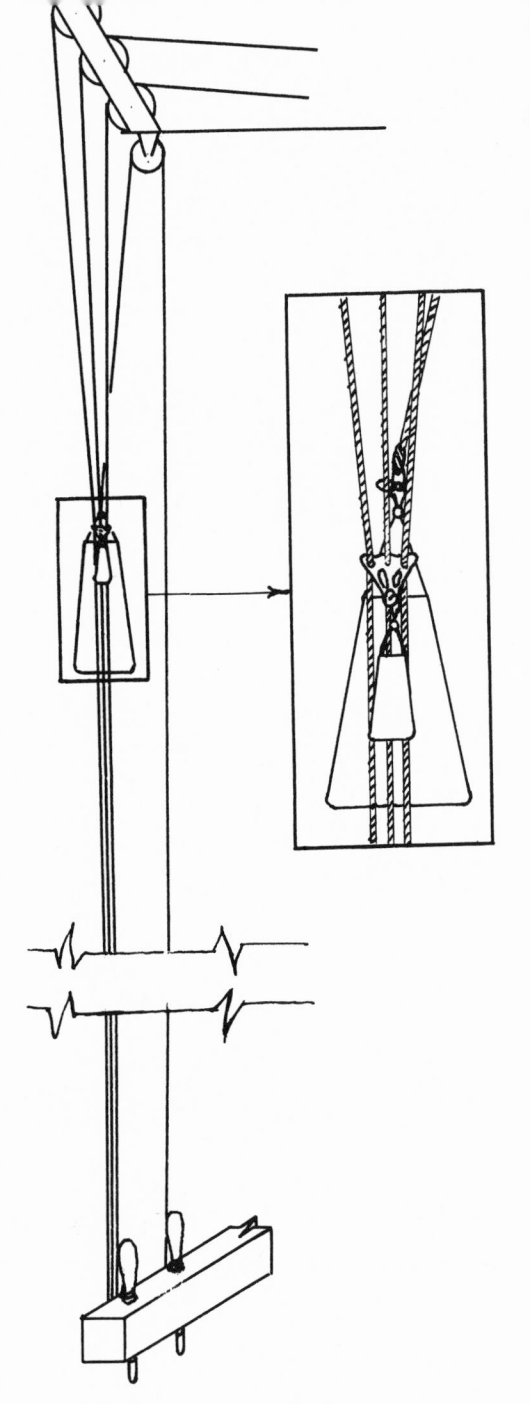

15.105 Carpet hoist rigging

carpet hoists

At the stage floor, attach snatch lines to the hanger irons on the unit, equal in length to the height of the unit and equip each with a snap hook. When the line set is let in, detach the deadweight bag and equip each line with an iron ring and a sandbag of sufficient weight to bring the empty line in. Snap the snatch lines from the unit to the rings on the line set.

At the fly gallery raise the piece to high trim by releasing the overhaul and bringing the sandbag ring to bear on the clew, applying any necessary additional force on the line set.

133. To set a unit hung on a carpet hoist.

At the fly gallery release the line set and raise the sandbag by the overhaul, thus letting in the unit. At the floor, set and brace the unit as it comes in, detach the line set from the snatch lines on the unit. At the gallery, tie off the sandbag at its high position and take out the line set, pulling the lines through the sandbag ring.

134. To fly a unit hung on a carpet hoist.

At the fly gallery, let in the line set by gravitational pull on its deadweight bags. At the floor snap the snatch lines from the unit to the rings on the lines. At the gallery release the overhaul to bring the sandbag to bear on the clew. Add manual power on the lines to fly the unit. Tie it off at high trim.

weighting empty lines

135. To weight empty lines.

Line sets: tie the onstage ends of all the lines of the set through the ring at the top of a sandbag. The bag must have sufficient weight to overpower the weight of the lines as they cross the grid and descend to the pinrail.

Single lines: tie a bag of sufficient weight (see above) to the single line.

Carpet hoists: snap-hook a small bag to the end of each line as it is detached from the unit or slip a pipe sleeve of sufficient weight onto each line and fasten it with a line clamp when the piece is being hung.

hanging on counterweight sets

Counterweight rigging enables loading the counterweight at the loading platform with the batten at the floor. This method of loading eliminates the necessity of hauling the unbalanced scenery into the flies for loading at the floor or fly gallery, but it presupposes careful calculation of the scenery loads. In many instances the counterweight load, once put on the arbor, cannot be altered without considerable difficulty because the run of the arbor may be limited by the nature of the particular scenery. When a power hoist is available, the scenery may be attached and hauled to the gridiron, to permit loading of the arbor at the floor. For this purpose, a downhaul line is attached below the arbor.

Units of scenery which are hung so close together in the flies as not to clear each other when taken in or out are equipped with guards to insure clearance. Metal straps attached to units above projecting thicknesses will prevent other units from fouling them. Vertical stiffeners on the back of one unit, tapered top and bottom, serve as runners for the unit next upstage which may have a frontal projection such as a picture frame.

Basic procedure: attach the unit to the batten; load the counterweight; fly the unit to low trim and adjust if necessary; fly the unit to the grid and adjust counterweight if necessary; bring in to high (storage) trim.

Basic rule: *avoid unbalanced loads.* If a hanging procedure inevitably requires a temporarily unbalanced load, provide adequate restraints in the form of man power, overhauls, downhauls, or check lines, using tackles or bull winches if necessary.

Check lines: Check lines are attached to the locking rail and to the line which supports the unbalanced load. Use one new ⅜″ Manila check line for each 100 pounds of unbalanced load. Replace check lines at least once a year and oftener if signs of wear develop.

Loading: perform all loading at the loading platform or at the stage floor. Allow no work under the loading platform while loading is being done. Never load counterweights until scenery is attached to battens. Top off every loaded arbor with the heaviest weight which is used to make up the load, or fasten with stop collars to keep the weights from bouncing.

Attaching architectural trim: avoid work on stepladders. In planning, anticipate such work and provide for it to be done either when the scenery is flat on the floor or when it is partially flown to an angular position which permits work to be done on its face by stagehands standing on the floor. Examples: attach light-masking dutchmen when scenery is face down on the floor; attach cornices when the top of the scenery has been lifted to a convenient working height.

The importance of computing counterweights: occasionally after a unit is hung, the condition of the flies or the setting render it impossible to get the counterweight arbors either to the loading platform or to the lockrail. Changing the amount of counterweight then becomes an arduous task of climbing up or down the wall and transferring weights under precarious circumstances. This must be avoided by careful calculation of the amount of weight to be put into the arbors when hanging the unit.

136. To hang a drop centered on the center line of the stage (Figures 15.106-15.109).

drops

Place the drop as in Problem 119. Bring in the pipe batten nearest to the prescribed hanging position. At points not more than 10′ apart attach drop holders to the batten and adjust all of them to equal length by snap hooks fastened to links of their trimming chains. Measure the distance of each drop holder from the center line of the pipe batten. (Center lines are marked with paint on regularly installed pipe battens.) From the center line of the drop, measure the corresponding distances and attach the drop holders at the points thus located. At the loading platform, place counterweights equal to the weight of the drop in the arbor of the set. As the load in the arbor increases, workmen on the floor must hold the batten down, since the weight of the drop is still resting on the floor and the counterweight consequently tends to raise the batten. When the arbor is loaded, release the batten and allow the loaded arbor to descend *under control* until the drop is clear

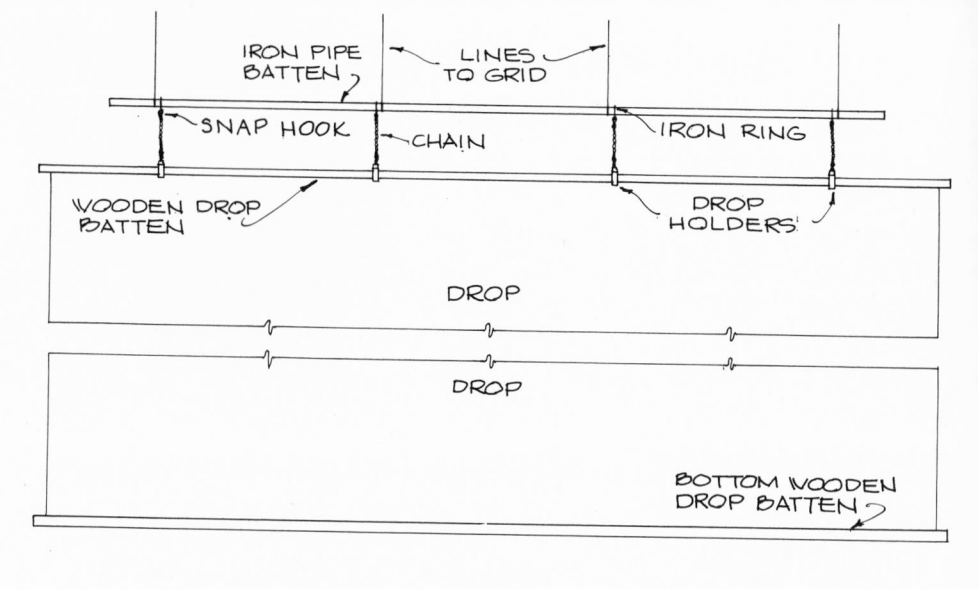

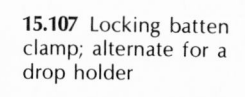

15.106 A drop hung on a counterweight-set batten using snatch chains and drop holders

15.107 Locking batten clamp; alternate for a drop holder

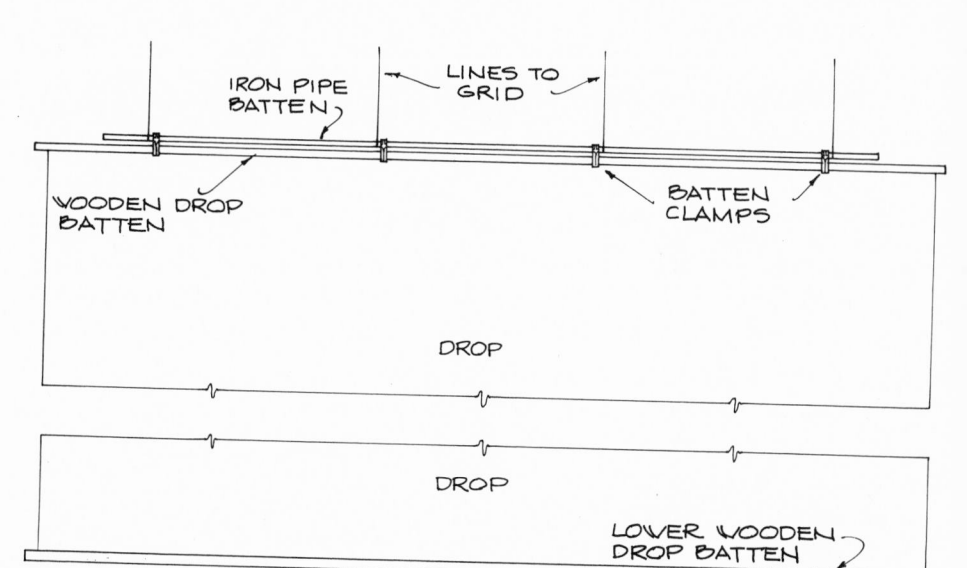

15.108 A drop hung on a counterweight set using batten clamps which are permanently installed on the batten

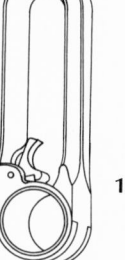

15.109 A batten clamp

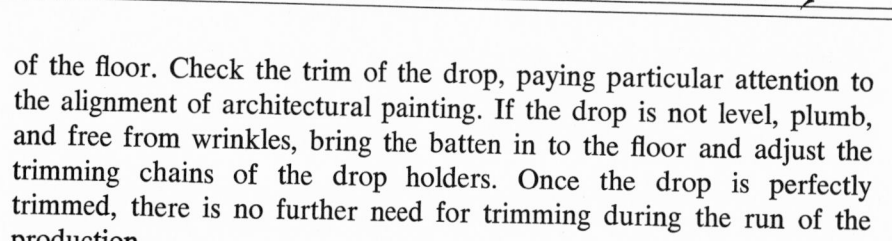

of the floor. Check the trim of the drop, paying particular attention to the alignment of architectural painting. If the drop is not level, plumb, and free from wrinkles, bring the batten in to the floor and adjust the trimming chains of the drop holders. Once the drop is perfectly trimmed, there is no further need for trimming during the run of the production.

137. To hang a drop not centered on the stage.

Repeat the procedure of Problem 136 except: determine from the ground plan of the set the point in the top batten of the drop which coincides with the center line of the stage. Let this point thereafter be the reference point from which points are measured for attaching drop holders.

framed units **138. To hang parallel to the footlights any light, framed unit which has no concentrated load other than that inherent in normal flat construction.**

ASSUMED: the scenery is already fitted with top hanger irons by the builders.

462

Determine from the ground plan the vertical line in the unit which coincides with the center line of the stage. Determine from the hanging section of the set the required height of the batten from the floor when the unit is set. Calculate the length of the snatch lines, deducting the height of the hanger irons from the batten height and adding length for each knot to be tied. (When snatch lines of special length are unnecessary, the piece may be hung on snap chains which are standard equipment on pipe battens.) Measure and cut as many snatch lines as there are top hanger irons. Bring the selected batten in to the floor. Measure the position of the hanger irons on the unit in relation to the center line of the stage. Make similar measurements on the batten in relation to its center line. Do not approximate or guess these measurements because the precise position of the unit depends on them. Tie the snatch lines at the marks with fisherman's bends with ends tucked. Arrange the pieces of the unit face down on the floor in correct relationship to the center line of the stage and with top toward and parallel to the proscenium. Complete all joining, stiffening, and bracing. Tie the snatch lines to their respective hanger irons with bowlines. Make all lines equal in length from batten to hanger iron *by actual measurement*. With stagehands holding the batten down, load the arbor with weights equal to the weight of the unit. The calculated load must include all items of scenery and trim which are to be fastened to and fly with the unit. Before the unit is raised to vertical, attach to it all such items of scenery or properties as are to be permanently attached and cannot be attached by workmen standing on the stage floor after the unit is erect. This procedure eliminates the awkward and inefficient use of stepladders.

139. To hang a framed unit which has a concentrated load such as a heavy door, a jamb and door, an attached mantelpiece, or an inset bookcase.

ASSUMED: the builder has supplied top hanger irons and, additionally, bottom hanger irons at points of concentrated loads.

Proceed as in Problem 138 except that at points of load concentration supply snatch lines long enough to extend from the batten to bottom hanger irons plus an extra allowance of 6′ for a cinch tackle at the bottom. When the short snatch lines are tied to the top hanger irons, reeve the long snatch lines through their respective top hanger irons and fasten them to the bottom hanger irons with cinch tackles. Fly and trim so that the lines carry the load and relieve the strain on the flats. See Figure 15.110.

140. To support heavy thickness pieces attached to the back of a flat unit.

The projection of a thickness piece (door, window, alcove) backward from a hung unit adds a concentrated load to the unit and locates the center of gravity of the unit so as to cause it to hang aslant in the flies and thus occupy fly space greater than the actual thickness of the piece. If fly space is at a premium, as is often the case, run auxiliary snatch lines adjustable by cinch tackles from the batten to the bottom of the thickness piece and trim them to level the unit.

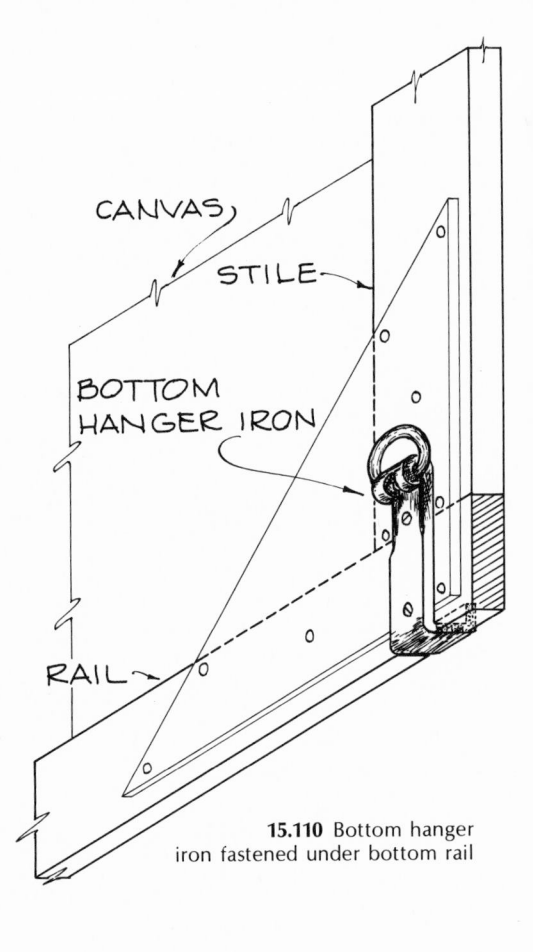

15.110 Bottom hanger iron fastened under bottom rail

141. To slack off the snatch lines of a back-wall unit to allow a flat ceiling to rest on it.

With the unit on the floor (low trim), affix an eye splice by a rolling hitch to the downhaul purchase line of the counterweight set at a height from the locking rail determined by the amount of slack required. Hook the moving block of a double luff into the eye splice and the stationary block into an eye bolt set into the locking rail. Take up the double luff, thus raising the counterweight arbor and lowering the batten to give the slack required.

ceilings

142. To hang a flat ceiling and back wall to fly as one unit.

Select a batten slightly downstage of the setting position of the back wall. Lay the ceiling on the floor face down, in correct alignment with the center line of the stage, and attach the front edges to the batten. Use sufficient snatch lines to support adequately the load of ceiling, back wall, and attached objects. Load the counterweight arbor for both back wall and ceiling, meanwhile supporting the unbalanced load in the arbor by a check line rolling-hitched to the downhaul purchase line. This check line may be snubbed around a bull winch or it may be a double luff to the locking rail. Do not depend on the rope lock to control this unbalanced load. Lower the counterweight arbor under control of the check line until the ceiling is vertical and clear of the floor. Lay out the back-wall unit, face up, with the top upstage and aligned with the bottom edge of the ceiling. Fasten back wall and ceiling together with loose-pin strap hinges, which have been attached to the top rails of the back-wall flats, and to the under side of the ceiling spreaders by the builder. Lower the counterweight under control of the check line, while stagehands swing the back wall upstage into position under the ceiling.

143. To lay out a roll ceiling.

ASSUMED: a roll ceiling built as stated in Chapter 5.

Unroll the ceiling face downward on the stage floor with battens parallel to the footlights. Insert the spreaders and join to the battens with $\frac{3}{8}'' \times 1\frac{1}{2}''$ carriage bolts and wing nuts, the wing nuts on the top side. Lace the sides of the covering material to the outside spreaders. Draw the lacing tight to eliminate sag and wrinkles in the covering material.

144. To hang a roll ceiling (Figure 15.111).

Determine from the hanging section (Chapter 4) the battens on which the ceiling is to be hung. The section shows the position of the ceiling on the set. The ceiling must be hung on two battens so that when raised it will clear other scenery in the flies and when lowered it will come to rest in the proper position with relation to the set. Any two battens may be selected which are equidistant from a vertical line drawn through the center of gravity of the ceiling. Lay the ceiling face down on the stage floor. Locate the line on the ceiling which corresponds to the center line of the stage. Let in the battens to be used. Measure the position of the ring ceiling plates from the stage center line and measure the corresponding tying positions on the battens. (If the ceiling is to be hung on rope sets, some of the ceiling plates may

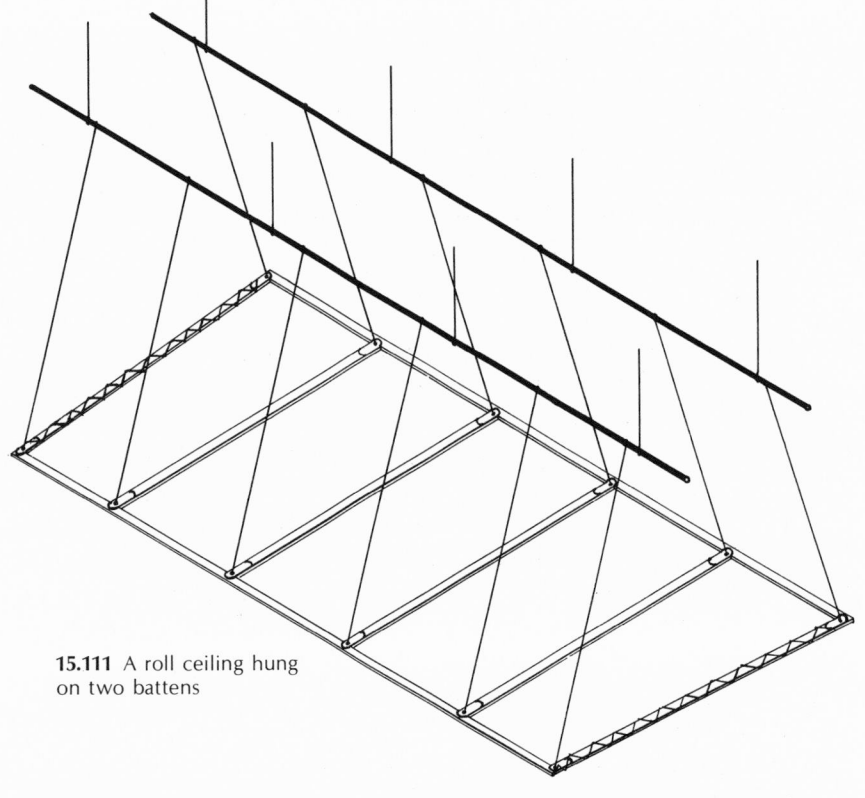

15.111 A roll ceiling hung on two battens

be placed in positions to correspond with the positions of the lines.) Set the batten snap chains in the measured positions; fasten them in place with a turn of friction tape. Snap the chains into the rings of the ceiling plates. Counterweight each batten with one half the total weight of the ceiling.

145. To operate a roll ceiling.

Two flymen are necessary. The battens or sets of lines on which the ceiling is hung are called the *front line* (downstage) and the *back line* (upstage).

To fly: raise the ceiling by the front and back lines together until it clears the floor (or the set, if the ceiling has been resting on it). Hold one line stationary and raise the other. The decision which to hold (front or back) and which to raise depends upon the location of other objects in the flies. If the flies are congested upstage, the front line is raised. If there is danger of the ceiling's fouling the first border or bridge lights, the back line is raised. Continue to raise the selected line until the ceiling is as nearly vertical as necessary to clear other hung pieces. Raise both lines together until ceiling is high enough to clear the sightlines or to permit bringing in other scenery.

To bring in: bring in both lines together until the lower edge of the ceiling just clears the set. Hold the line which supports the lower edge and continue to bring in the other line until ceiling is level a few inches above the set. Bring in both lines simultaneously until the ceiling touches the set. Slack off the back line slightly to bring the ceiling firmly in contact with the top of the flats. Keep the counterweight load effective on the front line to prevent the ceiling from sagging across the front of the set. If there is a stiffening batten, flipper, or truss across the front of the ceiling, the front line may also be slacked off to make the ceiling rest firmly on the downstage ends of the sidewalls.

Ceilings must be operated smoothly by the flymen. If a ceiling is allowed to start swinging in the flies, it cannot be brought to its exact setting position with dispatch and precision.

146. To hang a book ceiling (Figure 15.112).

ASSUMED: the book ceiling has ring ceiling plates on front and back battens and on one of the middle pair of battens, which are hinged together.

Select three adjacent pipes which will suspend the ceiling directly above its correct position on the set. Locate the positions for tying snatch lines by the process described in Problem 144. At each tying position on the middle pipe attach two single blocks by short lines and a snatch line as long as half the ceiling width. At each tying position on the front and back pipes tie snatch lines twice the length of those tied to the middle pipe. Reeve these lines through the blocks on the middle pipe. The longer the snatch lines from all three battens can be, the easier will be the operation of the ceiling: as the lifting angle of the front and back lines approaches the vertical, the force required to raise the edges of the ceiling is reduced.

Lay out the ceiling face downward on the floor, aligned with the stage center line, with the long battens parallel to the proscenium. Tie the snatch lines from each batten at the corresponding hanging points on the ceiling. Trim all lines to exactly the same height by measurement. Counterweight the center batten to support half the weight of the whole ceiling, and the front and back battens to support half the weight of their respective sections. If both sections are structurally

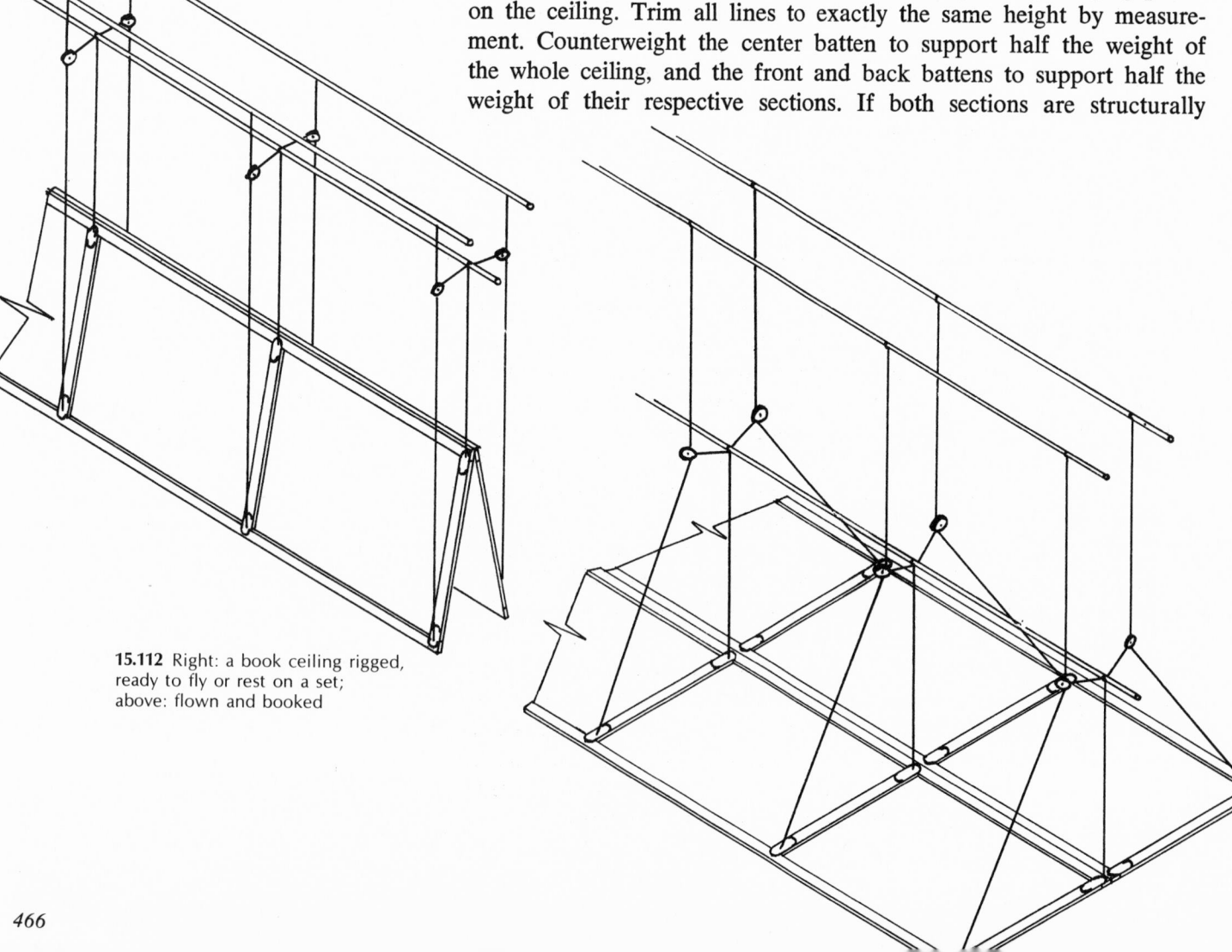

15.112 Right: a book ceiling rigged, ready to fly or rest on a set; above: flown and booked

equal, the front and back lines will each be counterweighted to support one-fourth the weight of the ceiling.

147. To operate a book ceiling.

To fly: fly all lines together until the ceiling clears the floor or the set. Hold the front and back lines and continue to fly the middle lines until the ceiling is folded. Fly all lines together to high trim.

To bring in: bring in all three lines until the edges of the ceiling clear the set about 6". Hold the front and back lines and bring in the middle lines until the ceiling is flat. Bring in all lines simultaneously until the ceiling rests firmly on the set. Keep a slight tension on the front lines to prevent sag in the front edge of the ceiling. Vertical battens may be attached to the downstage ends of the sidewalls to stop the ceiling from swinging forward to hit first border lights.

148. To hang a unit whose width exceeds the lengths of the installed pipe batten (Figures 15.113 and 15.114).

Insert extensions of small pipe into the ends of the batten; fasten these with wooden wedges or nails driven into the ends of the batten.

extra-wide units

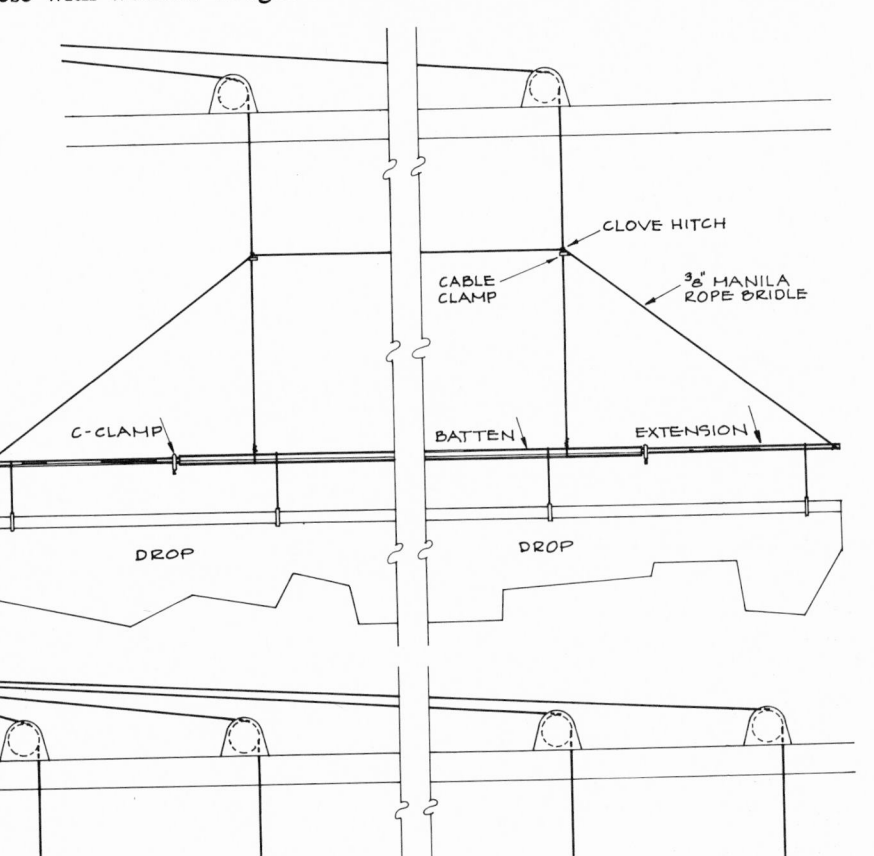

15.113 Batten extensions and bridles rigged to hang on extra-wide drop

15.114 Additional lines, loft blocks, and head blocks (not shown) installed to hang an extra-wide unit

467

Alternate for permanent alteration: extend the batten with pipe of the same diameter fastened with internal sleeve reinforcements held by machine screws.

Support the extensions with a bridle, preferably of wire rope, running between the ends of the extensions diagonally up and across all the batten cables, and fastened to all of the cables with wire rope clips. This bridle reduces the uprun of the batten by the height of the clips above the batten.

Alternate for use when the batten run may not be reduced or for a permanent alteration: install additional loft blocks and a two-groove head block; run wire rope between the ends of the extensions, through the loft and head blocks, to trimming turnbuckles attached to the arbor related to the batten.

Attach the unit to the batten, counterweight and fly it.

149. To hang a unit of scenery which is set in three dimensions and which is flown flat (Figure 15.115).

three-dimensional units

When a portion of set such as a deep bay window with a ceiling has too great a third dimension to permit it to be flown as an assembled piece, it is necessary to fold the piece out to a flat plane for flying.

ASSUMED: ceiling spreaders placed to coincide with the principal stiles in the back wall; ring ceiling plates attached to the spreaders at the downstage edge of the ceiling; top hanger irons attached to the outer stiles of the sidewalls; loose-pin hinges at the joints between back wall and sidewalls and at the joint between back wall and ceiling; pins at the back of the scenery; a stiffening batten which extends the full width of the backwall plus the sidewalls; lash lines or lines with idler sandbags at the outer stiles of the sidewalls; snatch lines prepared in two lengths — batten to edge of ceiling, and batten to top of sidewall, with allowance for knots; a predetermined flying set downstage from the set position of the back wall.

Bring in the batten; measure and tie the snatch lines to the batten only; fly the batten. Lay the scenery, face down, on the floor, the downstage edge of the ceiling toward and paralleling the proscenium. Pin the joints and attach the stiffener. Bring in the batten, swing it downstage, and tie the snatch lines to the hanging hardware, making sure the lengths are as planned.

Load counterweights equal to the weight of the unit while stagehands hold the batten down or the arbor is held up by an overhaul and winch. Fly the unit slowly with stagehands lifting at the ceiling–back wall joint to ease the strain on the hinges. When the unit is vertical, check the trim of the snatch lines. If properly measured and tied, no adjustment should be needed. Lash the sidewalls to the stiffener or rig the idler sandbags and fly the unit.

To bring in: lower and set back wall on its marks; swing sidewalls downstage to their marks; connect a tackle or winch to the downhaul purchase line and raise the counterweight until the ceiling rests on the sidewalls.

If a stiffening batten on the back wall is extended at each end to

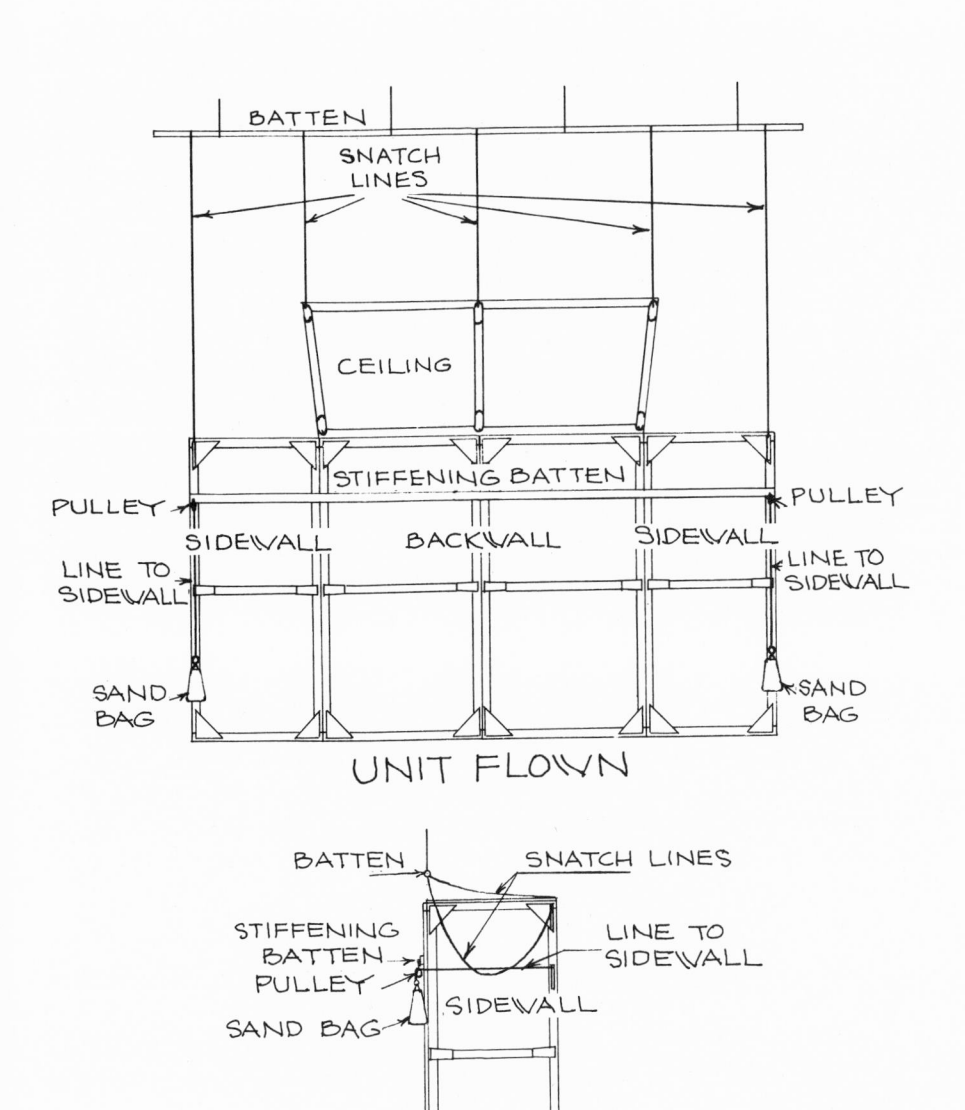

BATTEN

SNATCH LINES

CEILING

STIFFENING BATTEN

PULLEY   PULLEY

SIDEWALL   BACKWALL   SIDEWALL

LINE TO   LINE TO
SIDEWALL   SIDEWALL

SAND   SAND
BAG   BAG

UNIT FLOWN

BATTEN   SNATCH LINES

STIFFENING
BATTEN
PULLEY   LINE TO
                      SIDEWALL
SAND BAG
              SIDEWALL

UNIT SET UP
SIDEVIEW

15.115 Idler sandbags on lines attached to the sidewalls pull the sidewalls against the stiffening batten when the set is flown

carry a block, lines from the outer stiles of the sidewalls, rove through the blocks and sandbagged, will hold the sidewalls in straight alignment in the flies.

150. To hang a flat set piece on wire rope.

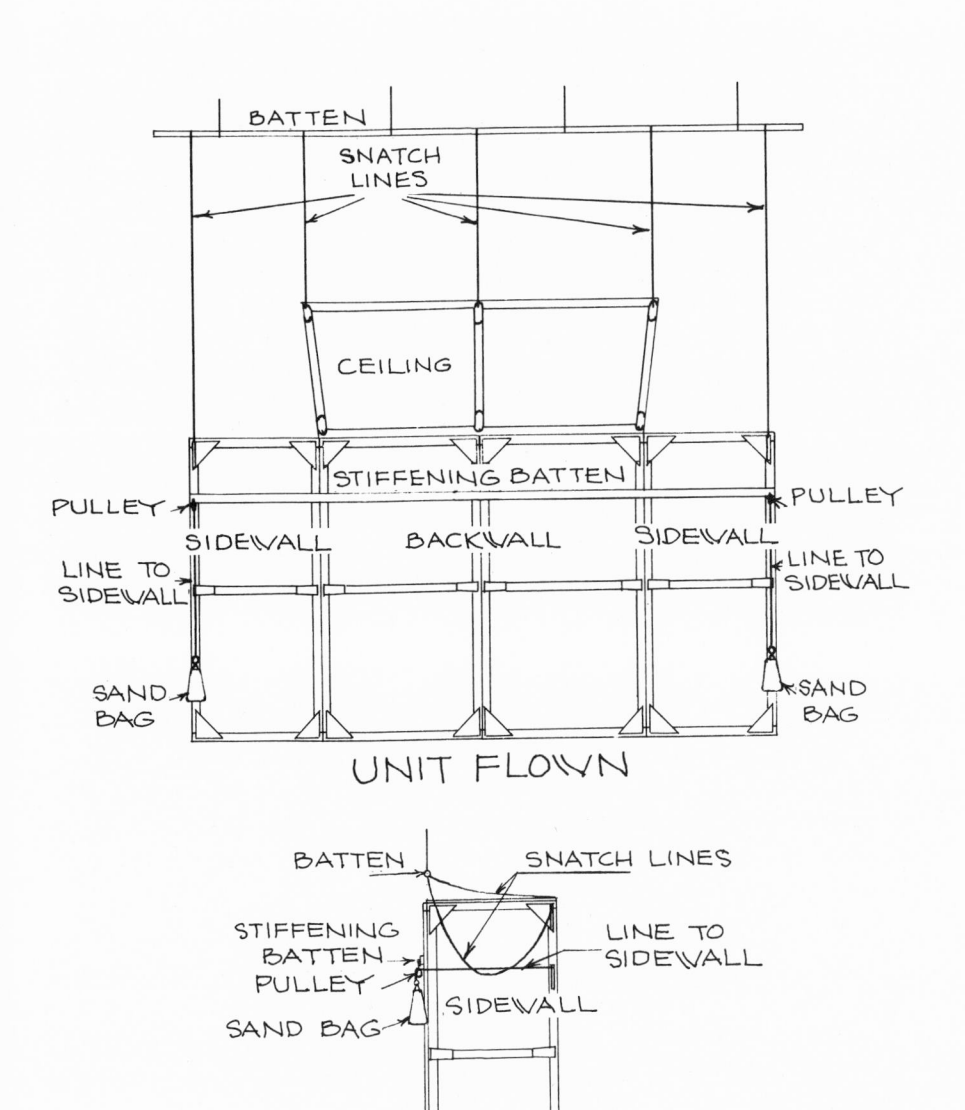

hanging on wire

ASSUMED: a unit equipped with top and bottom hanger irons at an adequate number of stiles.

Determine the height of the batten from the stage at low trim. Cut the required number of pieces of wire rope equal in length to the height of the batten, minus half the height of the unit, plus 3 feet for knots. CAUTION: whip the wire rope both sides of the mark before cutting. Bring in the batten. Measure the pick-up points on the batten and tie a wire at each point. Wire rope may be tied into knots with the aid of pliers. Fly the batten while assembling the unit, with small deadweights on each wire to prevent fouling. With the unit face down on the floor and aligned with the center line, remove the deadweights, reeve the wires through the top hanger irons, and tie them to iron rings (of adequate strength). Tie Manila rope to these rings with bowlines and to the bottom hanger irons with cinch tackles. Load the counterweight and lower the arbor under control until the wire is taut. Fly the unit to low trim and adjust the cinch tackles.

151. To rig a counterweight carpet hoist (Figure 15.116).

Lower the arbor adjacent to the one to be used to fly the unit. Detach the batten cables, lift them clear of the head-block grooves, and dead-tie them clear of all rigging, with the batten dead-tied at the grid. Raise this arbor (the *load arbor*) to the loading platform and tie it off, using an eye splice rolling-hitched to the purchase line and a double luff to the lockrail. Fly the batten until its arbor (the *running arbor*) is just below the load arbor. Place two **Z**-shaped iron bars in the bottom of the running arbor extending to receive the bottom of the load arbor. Hang the unit on its batten and load counterweights into the load arbor to balance the scenery.

152. To breast a unit to set it in a position not directly below its flown position.

This is necessary when other objects occupy fly space over the set position of the unit. The rigging must not foul or disturb these other objects; for example, it must not start lighting instruments swinging or knock them off focus.

ASSUMED: the flown and set position of the unit and of the other objects to be shown in the hanging plan and section.

Determine from the drawing the best possible directions in which breast lines may lead from the top of the unit, *clearing other units and equipment,* with the possibility of attaching to (or reeving through blocks attached to) the grid, the galleries, or stage walls and of leading the free ends to operating positions on the fly galleries or the floor. Cut and prepare lines of adequate size and length, or let in suitable flying lines, and attach them to the tops of the unit when it is being hung. Lead and fasten or reeve the free ends. If the breast lines are to be worked to control the unit's movement (*running breast lines*), install rope cleats for tying off.

Dead-tied breast lines: breasting may be done with breast lines tied to the gridiron, to the side, front, or back walls or the floor of the stage and of such fixed length that when the flown unit is let in, the breast lines assume part of the load and cause the unit to swing into the desired set position.

Running breast lines: these afford the possibility of adjustment, even though they are treated as fixed lines and not handled while the piece is being set or flown. Running breast lines may be lines selected from other line sets (the loft blocks relocated to keep the lines clear of other flown objects). They may be operated by flymen on the gallery to control the unit at a desired instant and to a desired extent to set its

a carpet hoist

breast lines

15.116 A counterweighted carpet hoist

position. Running breast lines may also be special lines rove through blocks, which are affixed to the walls or (rarely) to the floor of the stage, and let to a convenient operating location.

Breasting large equipment: breasting to change the position of a cyc or light bridge for the duration of a show may be easier than repositioning the loft blocks and retrimming the flying lines of such large equipment.

Guide wires: stranded cables or tiller rope stretched between gridiron and floor may be used to guide flown scenery into precise set positions. Lightweight curtains which tend to billow when descending and to foul the upper parts of rigid scenery may be let in on guide wires which are installed to slant away from the scenery. Vinyl-coated cable is quiet.

153. To prevent an object hung on a single line from spinning.

spin prevention

ASSUMED: a chandelier hung on a line which passes through a ceiling spreader.

Slip a tapered square (truncated pyramidal) block on the conduit which passes through the spreader and shape the hole in the spreader to receive the block.

ASSUMED: an object hung on a batten in clear fly space.

Run two invisible lines (black nylon) from the sides of the object diagonally up to the batten.

- Have adequate working light without spill onto the stage. Use a red filter on lights for seeing best in low-intensity illumination.

aids to operating the flies during a show

- Identify all line sets by acts, scenes, and sequence of operation, e.g., *1–1–1* or *11–1, eleven* meaning act I scene 1 and *one* meaning the first *operation*.

- Put position markers on each operating line: tuck coded fabric markers *through* the lines. Markers tied around or adhesive tape wrapped around the lines will slip and jam in rope locks.

- If apparatus is jammed, it must be unjammed by discovering the cause and remedying it. Application of additional force will either intensify the jam or exceed the strength limits of some part of the apparatus and cause damage and further difficulty.

- One or more cue sheets, posted where the operators can see them, should contain warning and dead cues for each operation, details of the operation, timing, and by whom done. The cue sheet for a winch-system control operator must add heights of high and low trims (unless preset) direction of run, speed, and mastering.

- The load on a single line must not exceed the allowable working stress of the line.

loads on flying systems
loads on a rope set

- The weight of a unit hung on a set of lines must not exceed the total allowable working stress of the set.

- The load on a line must not exceed the rated capacity of the loft block.

- The load on a set must not exceed the rated capacity of the head block. (Strength of a block embraces the strength of all parts of the block including fastening to grid steel.)

- The weight of the hung piece before bagging must not exceed the rated, concentrated, upward working stress of the pinrail and the fly gallery.
- The weight of the scenery must be balanced by sandbags or other counterweights to within 50 pounds of equality.
- The sum of the weights of all scenery and all counterbalances must not exceed the designed allowable working stresses of the gridiron structure.

loads on a counterweight set

- Scenery load must not exceed total allowable working stress of the snatch lines, trim chains, airplane cables, or other connections between the scenery and the batten. Concentrated loads in scenery must be supported by proximate lines, chains, or cables of adequate load capacities. Loads imposed on battens by snatch lines, trim chains, airplane cables, or lighting equipment must not cause deflection of the batten exceeding $\frac{1}{360}$ of the batten length between supports.
- Battens must be loaded so that no lift line is slack and therefore likely to jump out of a sheave. The total load on a batten must not exceed the total allowable working stress of the lift lines. Concentrated loads on battens must not exceed the allowable working stress of the proximate lift lines.
- The allowable working stress on a lift line must not exceed the rated load capacity of its loft block. The load on the lines of a set must not exceed the rated load capacity of their head block.
- The weight of scenery on a batten must not exceed the rated load capacity of the counterweight arbor.
- The sum of all loads of scenery, counterweight, and load forces exerted by lifting machinery must not exceed the designed allowable working stresses on the gridiron structure.

loads on a winch set

- Assuming that a batten and a set of lift lines are integrated with a motor-driven winch as a designed system and that all parts have allowable working stresses compatible with the allowable load capacity of the winch and the motor, the limits applying to loading a counterweight batten, lines, and loft blocks apply, plus the following:
- The load on a set must not exceed the allowable working load on the winch and its motor and the allowable working stresses of their fastenings.
- The sum of the loads on all winch sets must not exceed the allowable working stresses of the structure supporting the winches.

loads on winch lines

- Assuming that a winch line has an allowable working stress equal to the working capacity of its winch and motor, the load on a line must not exceed the allowable working stress or the allowable working load of the winch, whichever is smaller.
- The sum of the loads on a group of winch lines must not exceed the working capacity of the power source which is driving the group.

loads on the gridiron

- The total load of all hung scenery and equipment and counterweights must not exceed the rated loads for which the gridiron was designed and built. In new theatres the allowable loads may be obtained from structural drawings; in existing theatres they must be derived from engineering analysis of the gridiron structure, its fastenings to the supporting structure, and the supporting structure itself.

• The New York City building code of 1968 requires that this information be displayed onstage in a scaled drawing of the gridiron structure.

Appendix

Mechanics and Mathematics as Aids to Construction and Rigging

Mechanics is the branch of physics that deals with the action of forces on material bodies. It is pertinent to designing, planning, joining, stiffening, hanging, and operating scenery because the forces of gravity, forces generated by movement of actors, and forces exerted to move scenery are all in effect at times during the production process. "Scenery must be strong" is interpreted to mean: scenery must be strong and stiff enough to withstand all forces acting upon it at all times during its preparation and use.

A sense of the mechanics of a particular scenic situation is often all that is necesssary to indicate the correct action: If a flat is left standing vertically, without lateral support, it will fall to the floor. The action: support the flat. Experience supplies practical mechanical knowledge often sufficient to render precise calculation and computation unnecessary; for example, an installed counterweight unit which has been maintained in good condition will support and fly a unit of scenery which weighs no more than the capacity of the counterweight arbor. Even in this case, the technician planning the scenery and the stage carpenter hanging it must compute the weight of the scenery and must know the capacity of the arbor.

Certain easily learned quantitative facts like the safe loads on selected kinds and sizes of wood, pipe, rope, and wire rope, and easily learned physical principles like those of leverage, power ratios in simple machines and tackles, moments and vectors, and a few pre-calculated tables and graphs supply the technician, carpenter, and flyman with the mechanical knowledge to plan, execute, install, and operate most scenery. This small amount of practical knowledge must be possessed and applied in all theatrical situations requiring it, and these situations must be recognized if accidents injurious to scenery, equipment, and persons are to be avoided. *There can be no guesswork.*

This appendix cannot substitute for a text in mechanics, nor is a thorough course in the subject needed for the solution of the mechanical problems normal to scenery. However, an understanding of the physical principles underlying mechanics and the basic formulas which express the application of these principles in structures and rigging, access to sources of the pertinent data, the ability to recognize mechanical problems when they occur, and sufficient acumen in mathematics to solve them are necessary to successful technical production.

Allowable Loads on Wooden Structural Members and on Steel Pipe (Battens)

loads on scenery structures

It is a common phenomenon that structural material will bend before it will break. Bending causes deflection, which in scenery may cause displacement of parts which must fit together, loss of trim of hung scenery, or visible movement of parts of scenery under forces generated by violent movement of actors or dancers. Hence it is good practice to compute scenic structures and rigging to withstand loads which will cause deflection only within an acceptable limit: not more than $\frac{1}{360}$ of any span, or 1″ in a span of 30′.

lumber sizes

Since load tables in reference works for building construction do not include lumber sizes commonly used in scenery, fourteen graphs of loading curves are supplied here which show allowable loads on sizes commonly used in scenery computed for adequate stiffness.

All load values in the curves are computed for minimum actual sizes of yard lumber as given in *The Wood Handbook* (see the Bibliography). Curves are labeled with the corresponding nominal sizes, the usual nomenclature.

loads on floors, false floors, platforms, and ramps

Whereas building codes of various cities give between 40 and 60 lbs/ft² as acceptable minimum loads on floors of dwellings and from 75 to 100 lbs/ft² on floors for public assembly areas, the dynamic action of a dance company or a chorus line may create impact loads of the magnitude of 200 lbs/ft². The floor of a stage must therefore be built to withstand such a load with deflection not more than $\frac{1}{360}$ of the span of any member — flooring, joists, or beams.

Loads on scenery platforms, false floors, and ramps may vary with production requirements from minimal residential loads to the maxima stated above. Hence the technician for a show with *known* load limits may design the structures to carry only such loads. But the technician planning structures for repeated use under unforeseeable future production requirements must build weight-bearing structures to withstand maximum loading.

conversion factors
for woods other than white pine

The values in Graphs 2, 3, 4, and 5 are computed for white pine. To obtain equivalent load values for other woods, apply the appropriate conversion factor from Table A-1.

TABLE A–1. CONVERSION FACTORS FOR WOODS OTHER THAN WHITE PINE

Wood	Conversion Factor
white pine	1.0
ponderosa pine, hemlock, spruce	1.0
redwood	1.1
loblolly pine	1.4
Douglas fir, longleaf yellow pine	1.6

To determine the required size of a structural member of one of these woods, divide the known load by the appropriate conversion factor and enter any of the graphs with the quotient.

To determine the load capacity of a known structural member of one of these woods, enter any of the graphs with the dimensions of the member, read out the applicable values for white pine, and multiply them by the requisite conversion factor.

Plank and beam loads given in Graphs 3 and 4 are stated as being concentrated in the middle of the span. To convert to a load concentrated elsewhere in the span, apply the appropriate factor from Table A-2.

for loads concentrated elsewhere than middle of span

TABLE A–2. CONVERSION FACTORS FOR PLANK AND BEAM LOADS

Load Concentrated At	Conversion Factor
0.5 span (middle)	1.00
0.4 span	1.07
3.0 span	1.42
0.2 span	2.44
0.1 span	7.80

Example: a load of 500 lbs. is concentrated at 0.25 span; find the equivalent load concentrated at the middle. From Table A-2, use the conversion factor for 0.3 span (rather than 0.2 span — to be on the safe side). Divide the load by this factor: 500/1.42 = 350 lbs. Enter Graphs 3, 4, or 6 with this quotient.

The conversion factors in Table A-2 also apply to loads on pipe battens or metal beams.

Beams of Single Span. Values in the curves for wooden beams (Graph 4) are computed for beams supported at both ends. (*Supported* means that the beam is resting and bearing on the supports but that there are no fastenings of the ends which would tend to resist movement under flexural loading.)

For beams fixed or restrained at both ends, the values in the curves are multiplied by 4. (*Fixed* means that the ends of the beam are secured against movement under loads up the allowable limit of deflection.)

Since it is difficult to calculate the strength of fastenings used in scenery

for structural conditions of beams

and impossible to predict the effects of use and handling on the strength of the fastenings, it is best to limit loads to those allowed for supported beams. Conversion factors for various conditions of loading are given in Table A-3.

TABLE A–3. CONVERSION FACTORS FOR RELATIVE STIFFNESS OF BEAMS UNDER VARIOUS CONDITIONS OF LOADING

Load Condition	Conversion Factor
Beam supported at both ends	
LCM[a] single span	1.0
EDL[b] single span	8/5
Beam fixed or restrained at both ends	
LCM single span	4.0
Beam continuous through 2 equal spans	
LCM on each span	2.3
EDL on each span	3.8
Beam continuous through 3 equal spans	
LCM on each span	1.9
EDL on each span	3.0
Cantilever beam loaded at free end	1/16
Cantilever beam, EDL	1/6

[a] Load concentrated in middle of span. [b] Load evenly distributed.

Applications of Table A-3. If the size and span of the beam and consequently the allowable concentrated load in the middle of the span are known, equivalent allowable loads for other conditions of loading are obtained by multiplying the known allowable load by the conversion factor appropriate to the specific loading condition.

Example: a platform has an internal frame 12′ long in which the top rail, a single piece of 1″ × 4″ white pine, is supported by outside stiles and by two internal stiles creating three equal spans of four feet. To determine the evenly distributed load the rail will carry, find in Graph 4A the allowable load concentrated in the middle of a single span of four feet: 150 lbs. The conversion factor in Table A-3 for equivalent evenly distributed load on a beam continuous over three equal spans is 3.3. There are three spans. Then the allowable evenly distributed load on the top rail is:

$$150 \times 3.3 \times 3 = 1,485 \text{ lbs.}$$

If the load under a specific loading condition is known, the equivalent load concentrated in the middle of a beam supported at both ends is found by dividing the known load by the appropriate conversion factor. The result may be used to enter the curves for loads on beams (Graph 4) to determine the adequate beam sizes.

Example: a cantilevered beam 4′ long must support an evenly distributed load of 500 lbs. To determine what size of white pine beam will be adequate, find in Table A-3 the factor for a cantilever beam, load evenly distributed: 1/6. Hence the equivalent load concentrated in the middle of a span is 6 × 500, or 3,000 lbs. Enter the graph with this and a span of 4′. Find: 1¼ × 10 or 2 × 6 beams adequate.

The conversion factors in Table A-3 are also applicable to pipe and metal beams.

1. To determine the allowable beam span

GIVEN: spacing of beams in feet (i.e., span of flooring), and floor load in lbs/ft². Find the appropriate curve in Graph 4, and at the intersection of this curve and the lumber-size curve, read out at the bottom of the vertical line the allowable beam span (i.e., spacing of posts).

Example: if the desired beam spacing is 3′ and the floor load is 100 lbs/ft²:

Lumber Size	Beam Span	Lumber Size	Beam Span
1″ × 4″	2.2′	1¼″ × 4″	2.5′
1″ × 5″	2.9′	1¼″ × 5″	3.3′
1″ × 6″	3.7′	1¼″ × 6″	4.0′

2. To determine lumber size

GIVEN: floor load, desired beam spacing, and desired post spacing. At the intersection of the floor-load/beam-spacing curve and any beam-span line (vertical), read the size of lumber represented by the line above the point of intersection.

Example 1: if the floor load is 50 lbs/ft², the desired beam spacing 2′, and the desired post spacing 4′, enter any part of Graph 4 on the curve for the first two items, and follow it to the vertical line for 4′. Read out from the graph: 1″ × 5″, 1¼″ × 5″, 1½″ × 4″, 2″ × 4″.

Example 2: if beams are to be rigidly fastened to posts, and the desired post spacing is 5′, floor load 200 lbs/ft², desired beam spacing 3′, determine the size of the beam lumber as follows:

First, divide the floor load by the fixed beam conversion factor (from Table A-3): 200/4 = 50 lbs/ft². In other words, a beam that carries 200 lbs/ft² when fixed at both ends will carry 50 lbs/ft² when supported at both ends, the condition upon which the graphs are based. In each of the graphs find the curve for 50 lbs/ft² and 3′ beam spacing; follow it to the vertical for 5′ post spacing; and read out the possible lumber sizes: 1″ × 8″, 1¼″ × 6″, 1½″ × 6″, 2″ × 6″.

Graph 1. ALLOWABLE LOADS ON DOUGLAS FIR PLYWOOD[a]
(in pounds per square foot)

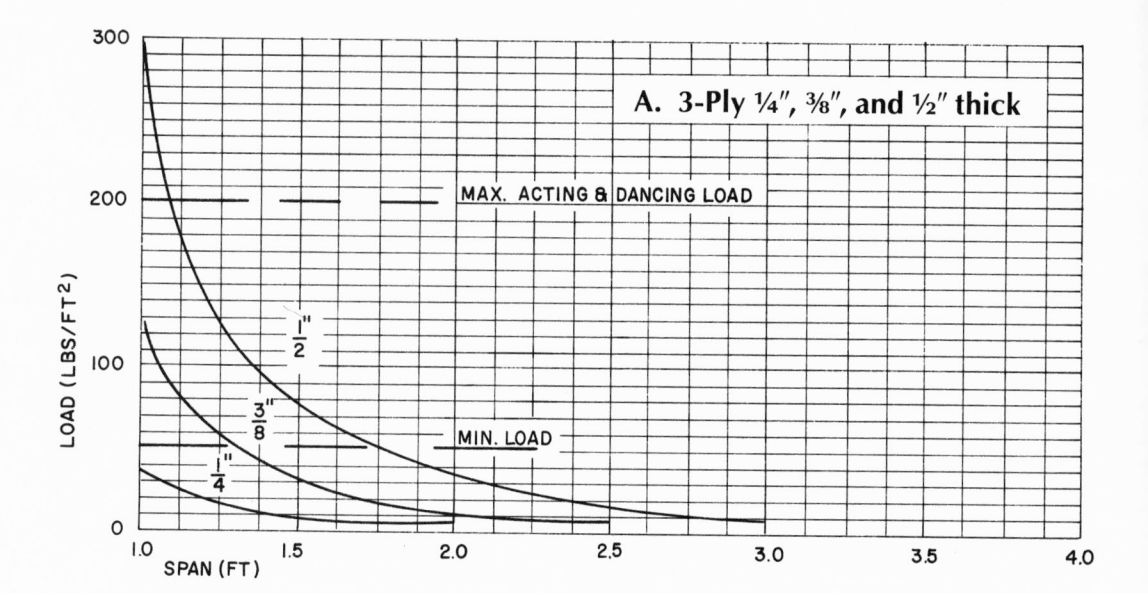

[a]Dominant grain parallel with the span. Deflection: 1/360 span.

Sources: (1) T. Nolan's equation for stiffness of floors, in F. E. Kidder and T. Nolan, eds., *Architects and Builders Handbook* (17th ed.; New York, 1921), p. 730: $T = \sqrt[3]{w(l^3)/19.2e_1}$. Or, expressed in terms of w: $w = T^3 (19.2e_1)/l^3$, in which T is the thickness in inches; w, the load in lbs/ft²; l, the span in feet; and e_1, the coefficient for stiffness. (2) Equations in *The Wood Handbook* (U.S. Department of Agriculture Handbook #72, 1955), p. 284, from which were determined the moduli of elasticity for the several plies and the resulting relative values for the coefficient of stiffness (e_1 in Nolan's equation). The modulus of elasticity for Douglas fir lumber was taken as 1,600,000.

Graph 1. ALLOWABLE LEADS ON DOUGLAS FIR PLYWOOD (*continued*)

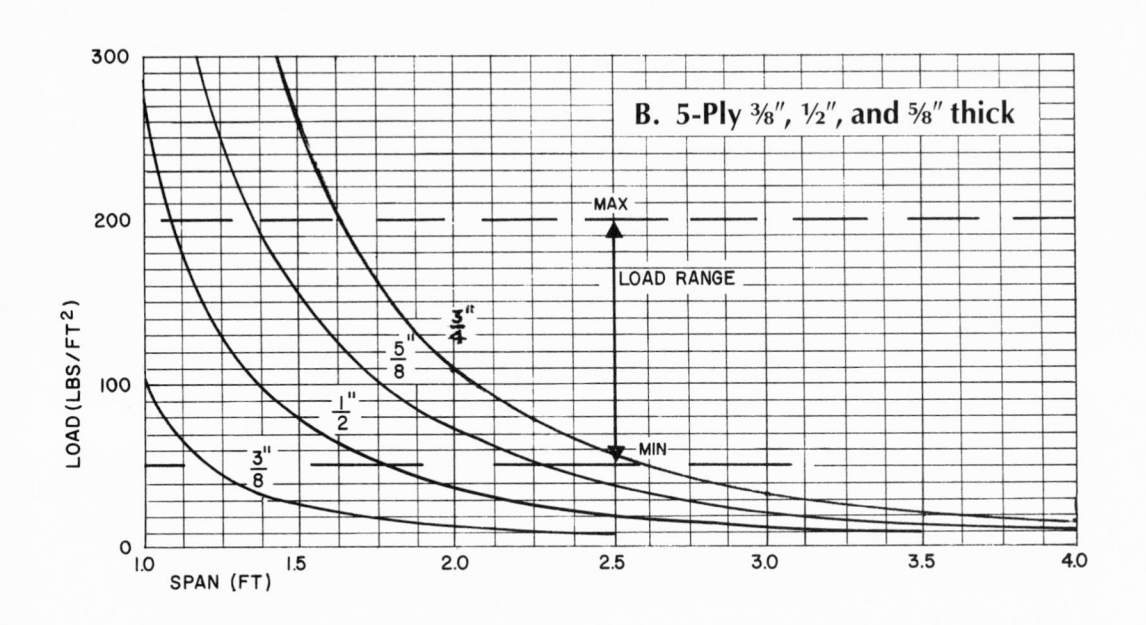

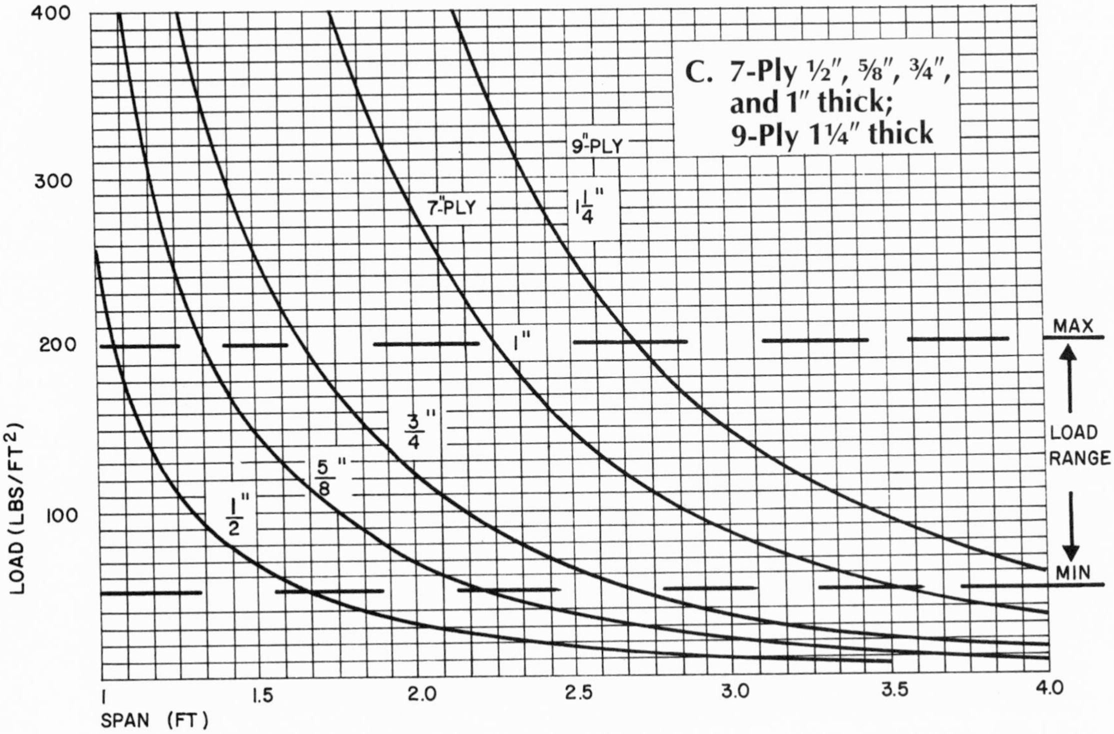

Graph 2. ALLOWABLE LOADS ON WHITE PINE FLOORING[a]
(in pounds per square foot)

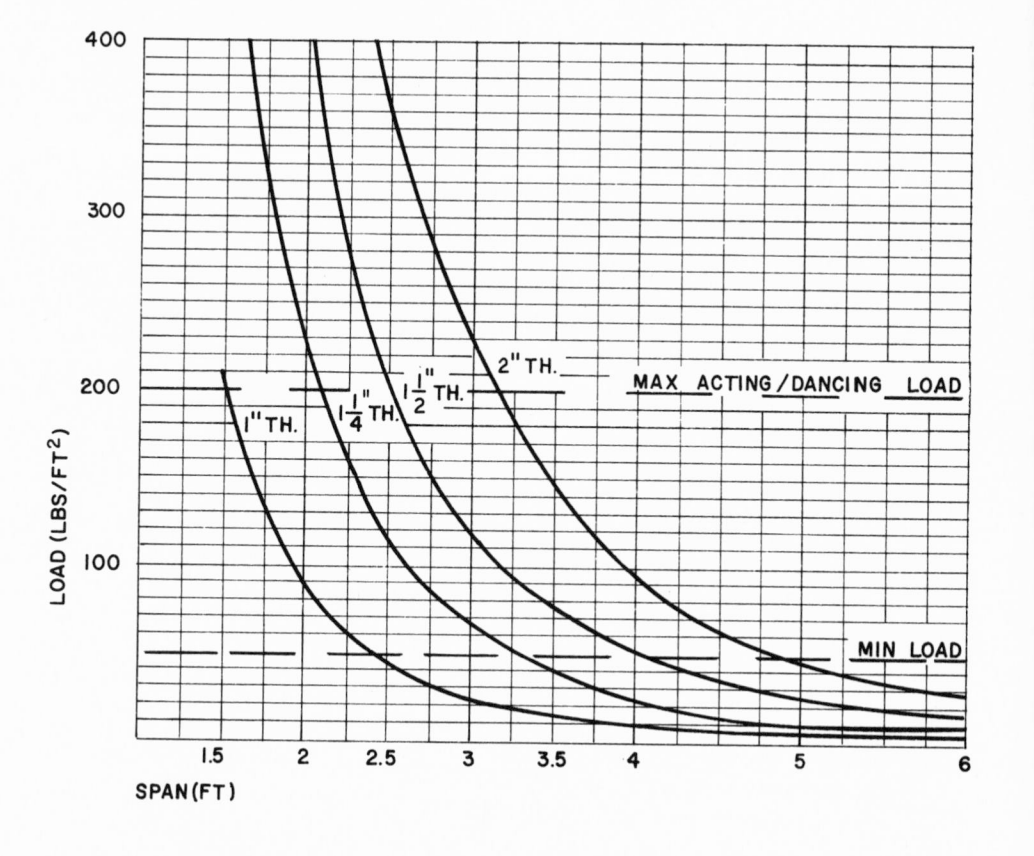

[a]Nominal thicknesses (1′, 1¼″, 1½″, 2″) corrected to minimum standard thicknesses. Deflection: 1/360 span.

Source: Nolan's equation for stiffness of floors (see source note for Graph 1). Coefficient for stiffness: 77 for white pine.

Graph 3. ALLOWABLE LOADS ON WHITE PINE PLANKS[a]
(in pounds; loads concentrated in middle of span)

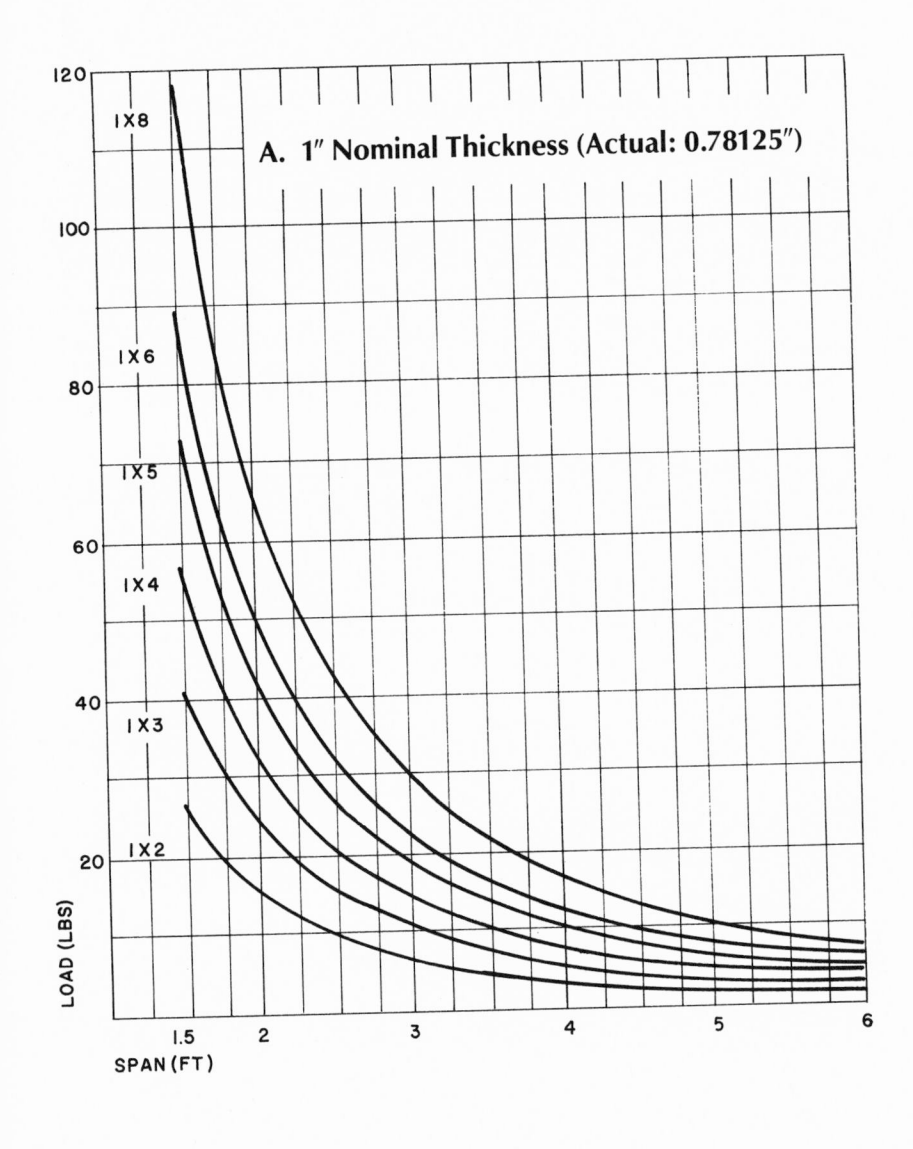

[a]Deflection: 1/360 span.

Source: Warren's equation for stiffness of wooden beams, in F. E. Kidder and T. Nolan, eds., *Architects and Builders Handbook* (17th ed.; New York, 1921), p. 665: $AL = b(d^3)e_1/l^2$, in which AL is the allowable load in pounds, concentrated in the middle of the span; b, the horizontal dimension in inches; d, the vertical dimension (actual thickness) in inches; e_1, the coefficient for stiffness (77 for white pine); and l, the span in feet.

Graph 3. ALLOWABLE LOADS ON WHITE PINE PLANKS (*continued*)

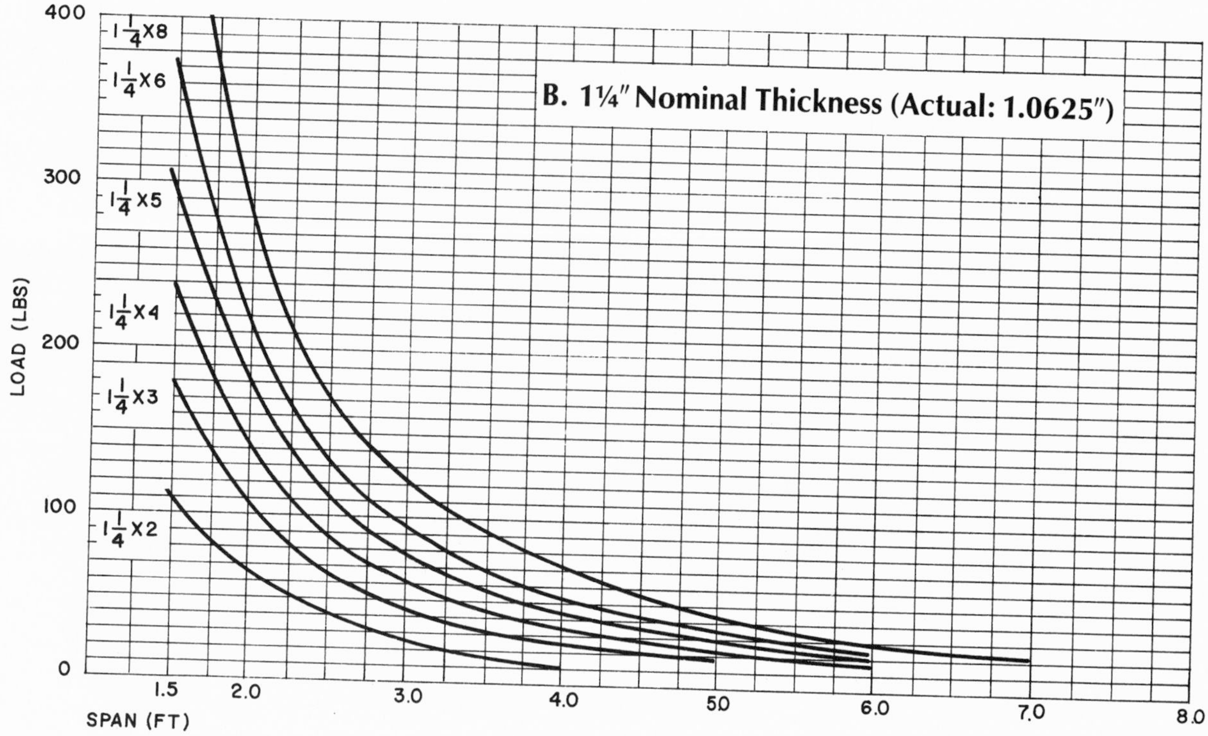

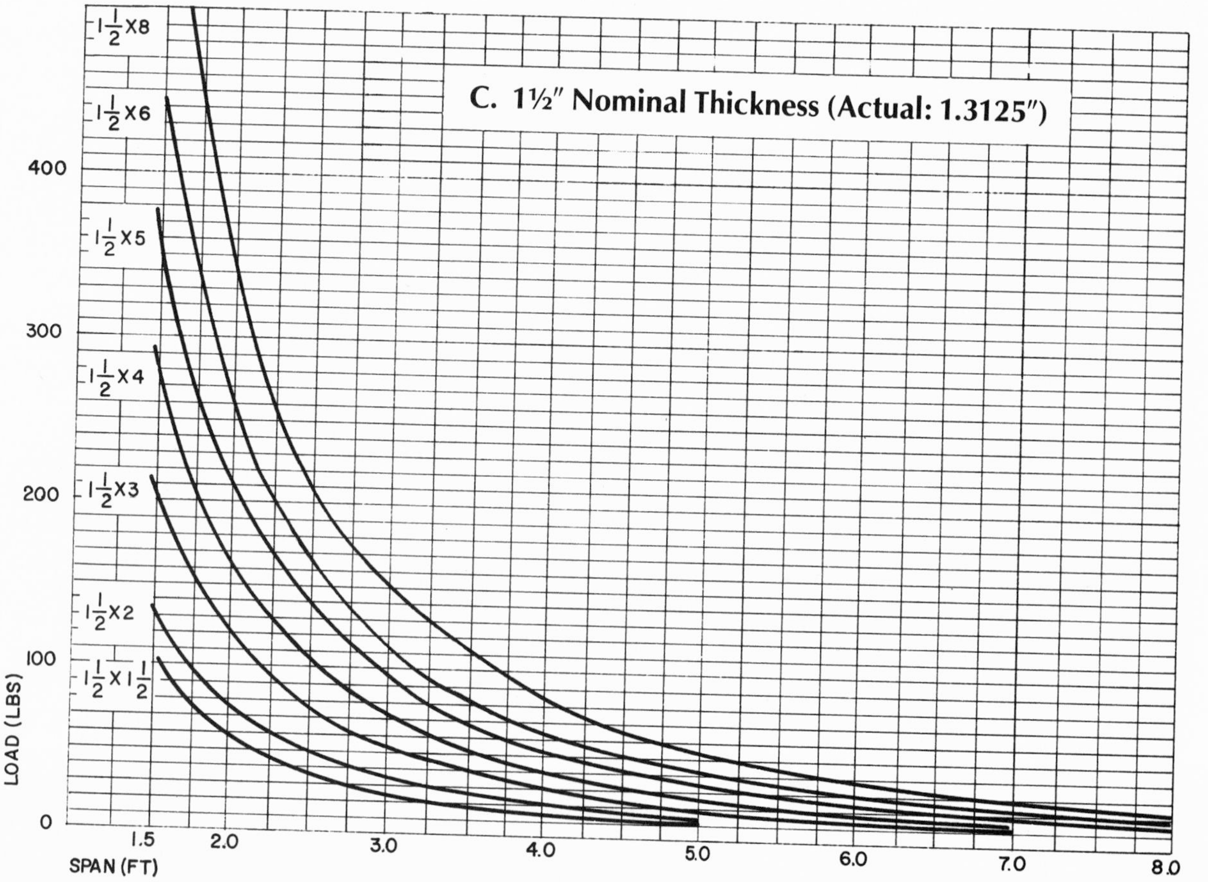

B. 1¼″ Nominal Thickness (Actual: 1.0625″)

C. 1½″ Nominal Thickness (Actual: 1.3125″)

Graph 3. ALLOWABLE LOADS ON WHITE PINE PLANKS (*continued*)

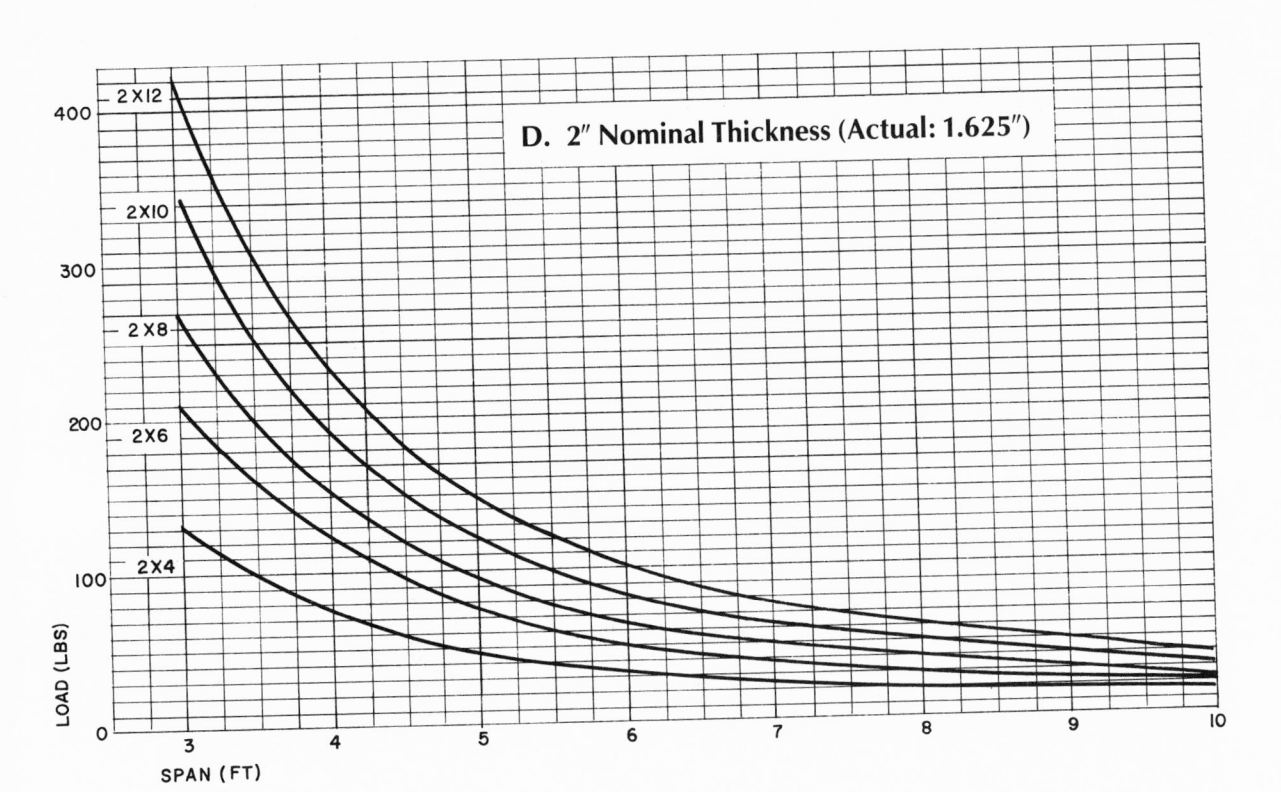

D. 2″ Nominal Thickness (Actual: 1.625″)

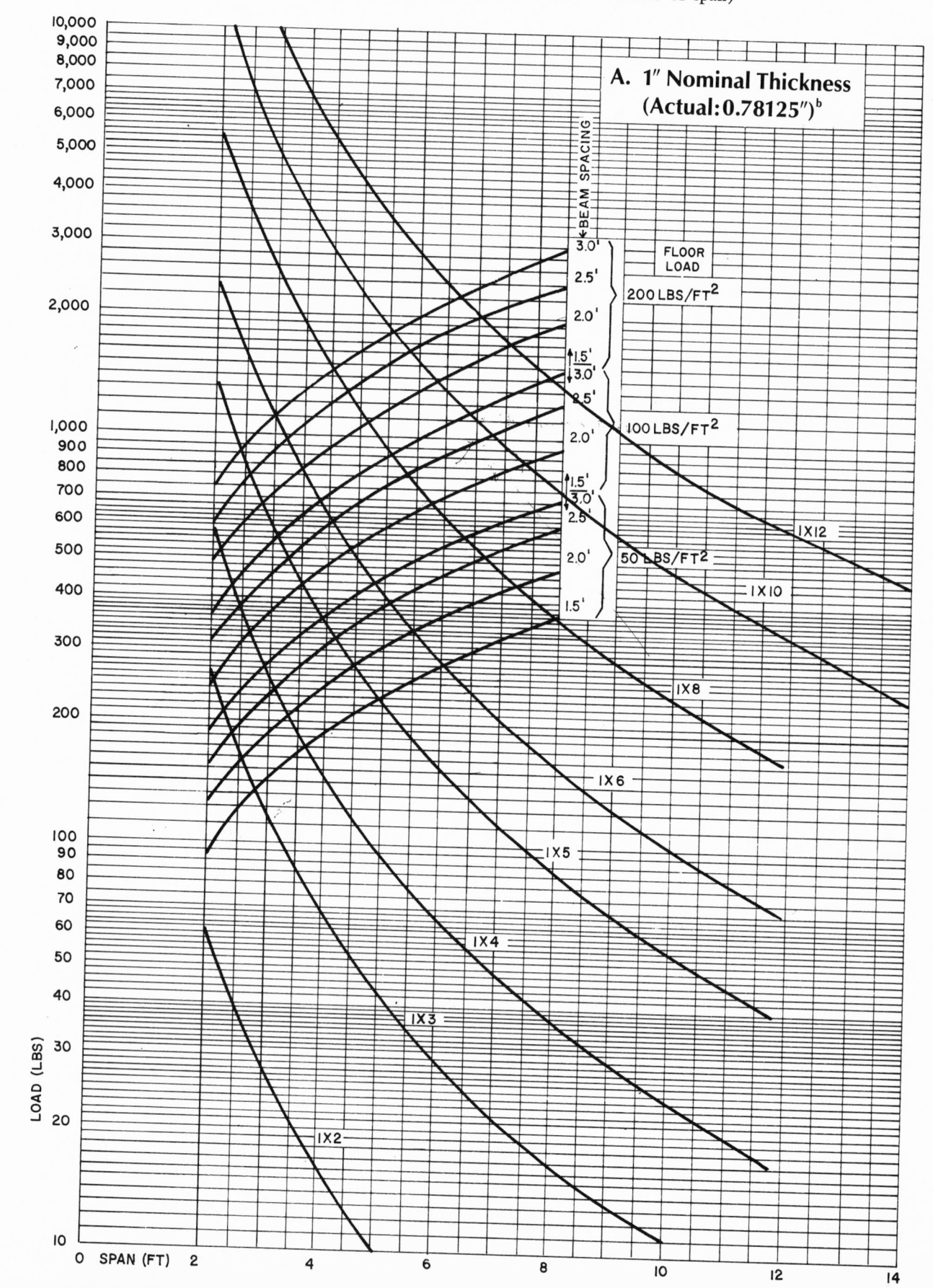

Graph 4. ALLOWABLE LOADS ON WHITE PINE BEAMS[a]
(in pounds; concentrated in middle of span)

**A. 1″ Nominal Thickness
(Actual: 0.78125″)[b]**

BEAM SPACING

FLOOR
LOAD

200 LBS/FT²

100 LBS/FT²

50 LBS/FT²

3.0'
2.5'
2.0'
1.5'
3.0'
2.5'
2.0'
1.5'
3.0'
2.5'
2.0'
1.5'

1X12
1X10
1X8
1X6
1X5
1X4
1X3
1X2

LOAD (LBS)

SPAN (FT)

Graph 4. ALLOWABLE LOADS ON WHITE PINE BEAMS (*continued*)

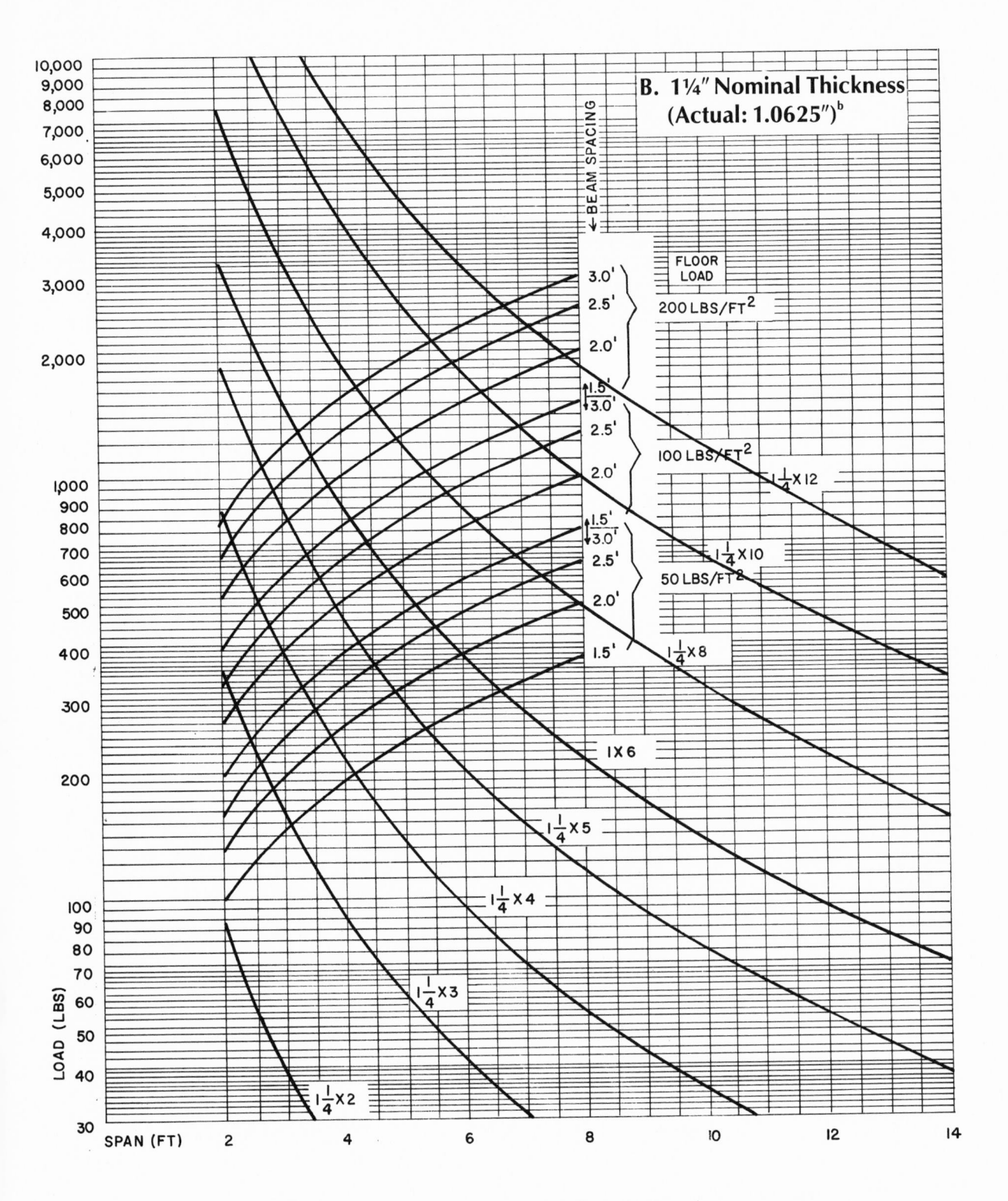

B. 1¼" Nominal Thickness (Actual: 1.0625")[b]

*Deflection: 1/360 span. [b]Actual figure is *b* in the equation (see source note).

Source: equation 6, p. 665, in F. E. Kidder and T. Nolan, eds., *Architects and Builders Handbook* (17th ed., New York, 1921). The values in the curves for floor loads on selected flooring spans were converted from evenly distributed beam loads to loads concentrated in the middle of the beam span, to make them compatible with the beam load values.

Graph 4. ALLOWABLE LOADS ON WHITE PINE BEAMS (*continued*)

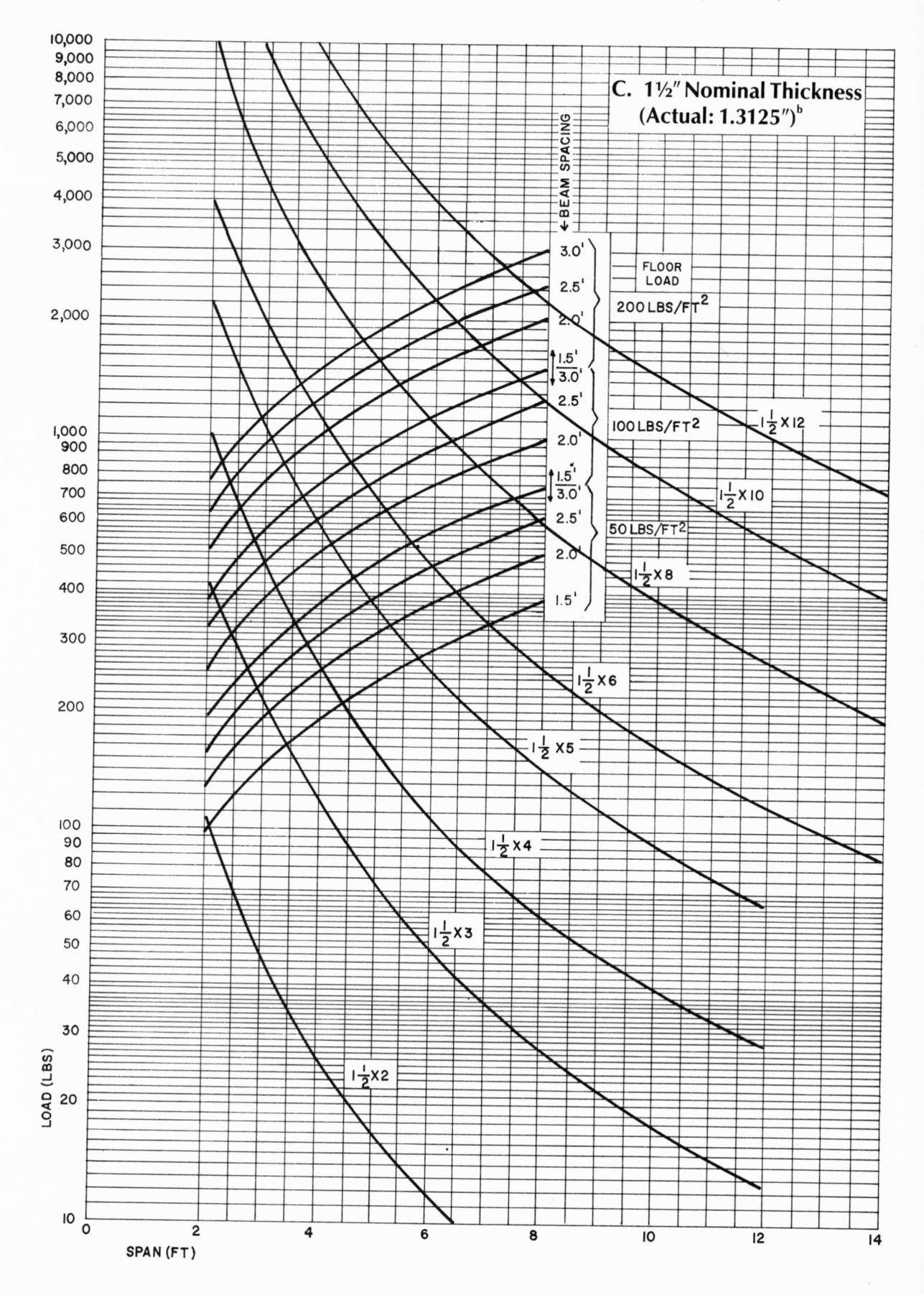

Graph 4. ALLOWABLE LOADS ON WHITE PINE BEAMS (*continued*)

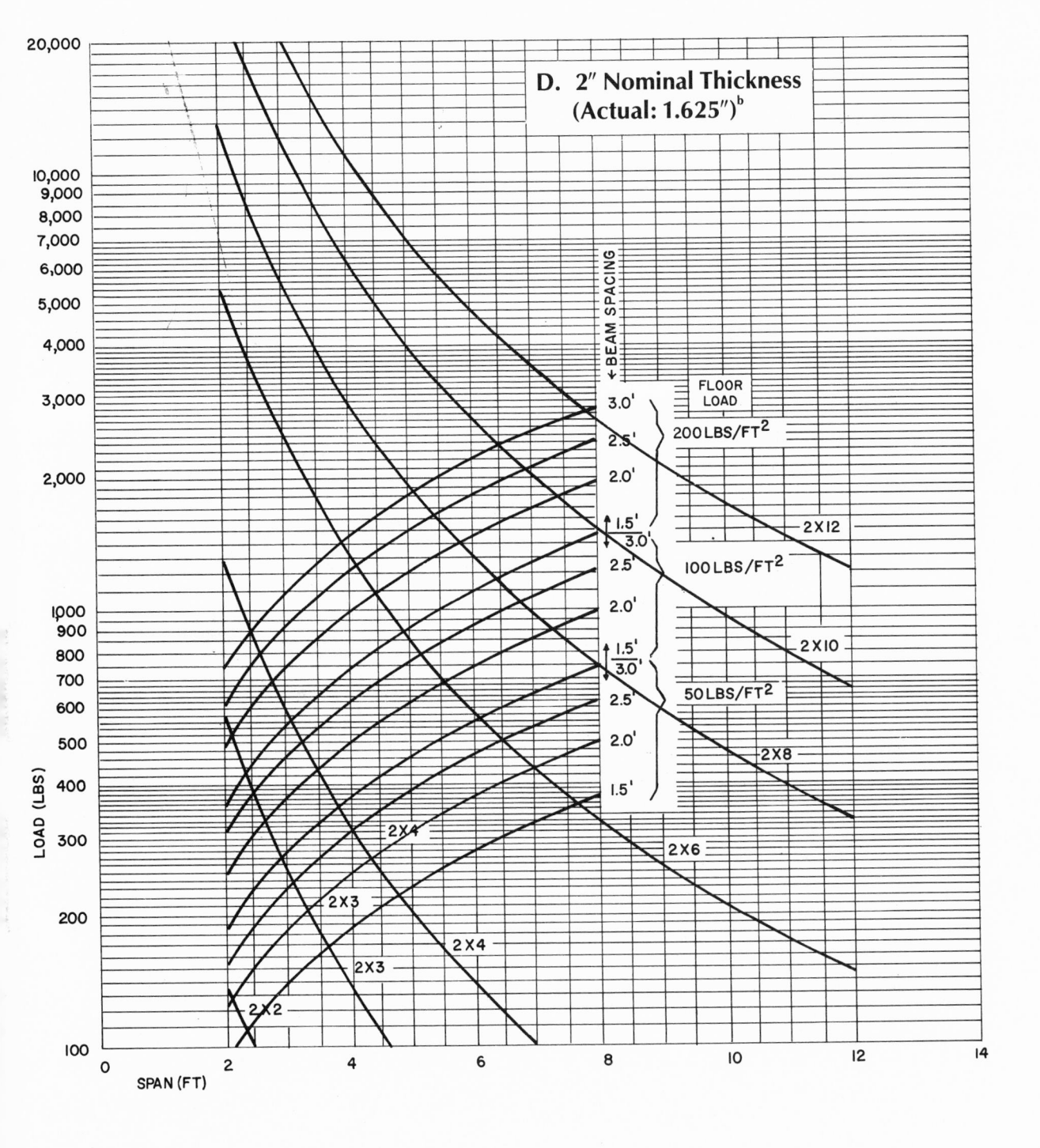

D. 2″ Nominal Thickness (Actual: 1.625″)[b]

Graph 5. ALLOWABLE LOADS ON WHITE PINE COLUMNS[a]

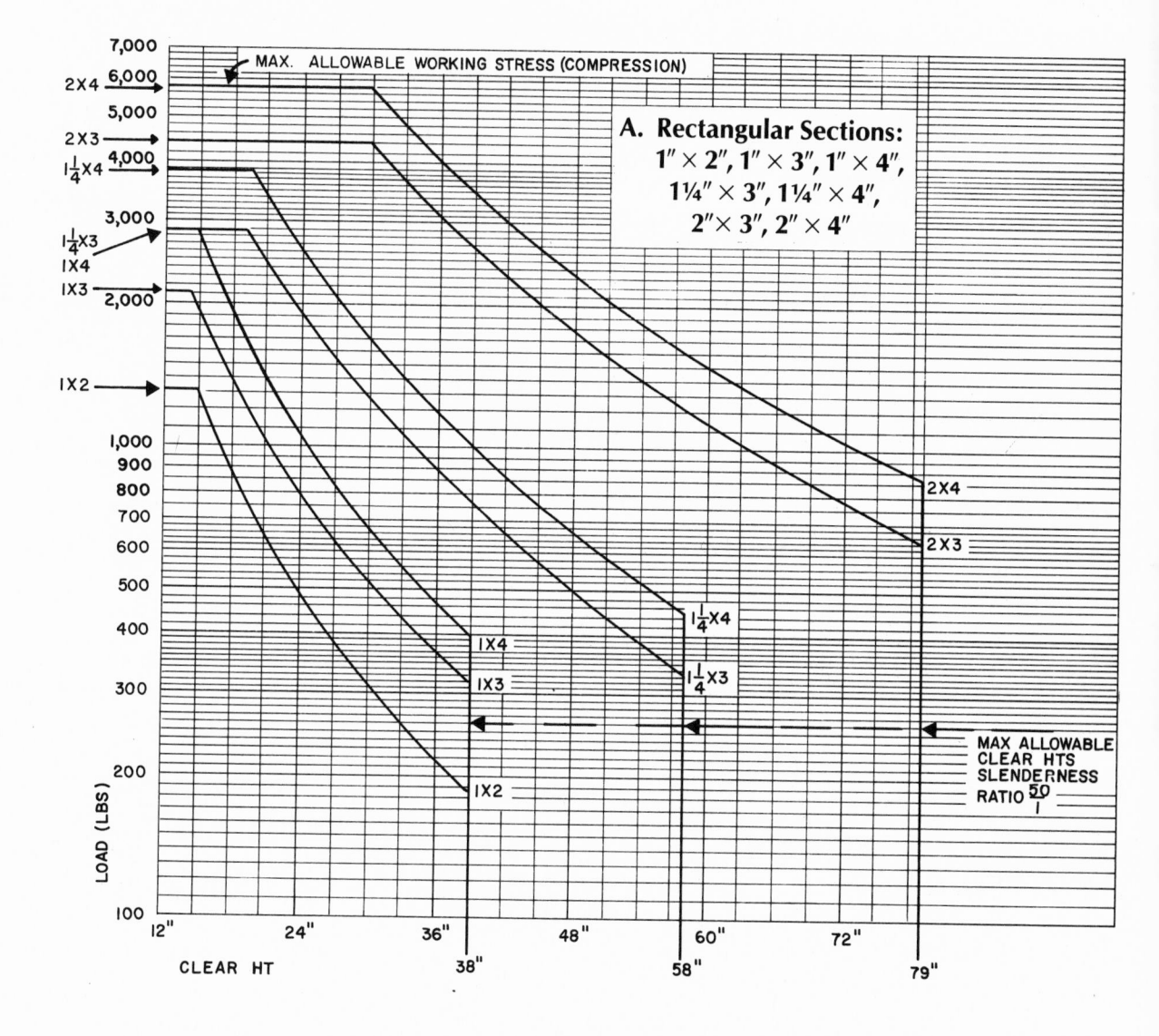

[a]In computing these loads, two limits must be observed: no load on a column must exceed the safe working compression stress parallel with the grain; and no unsupported column (clear height) may have a slenderness ratio (*l* to *d*) exceeding 50 to 1. These limits determine the horizontal and vertical lines at the end of the curves.

Source: equation on p. 238, in H. Parker, *Simplified Engineering for Architects and Builders* (4th ed., New York, 1966): $P/A = 0.30E/(l/d)^2$, in which P is the total load parallel with the grain; A, the cross-section area, in in²; E, the modulus of elasticity (1,200,000 for white pine, according to *The Wood Handbook*); l, the clear height of the column in inches; and d, the least lateral dimension of the column in inches.

Graph 5. ALLOWABLE LOADS ON WHITE PINE COLUMNS (*continued*)

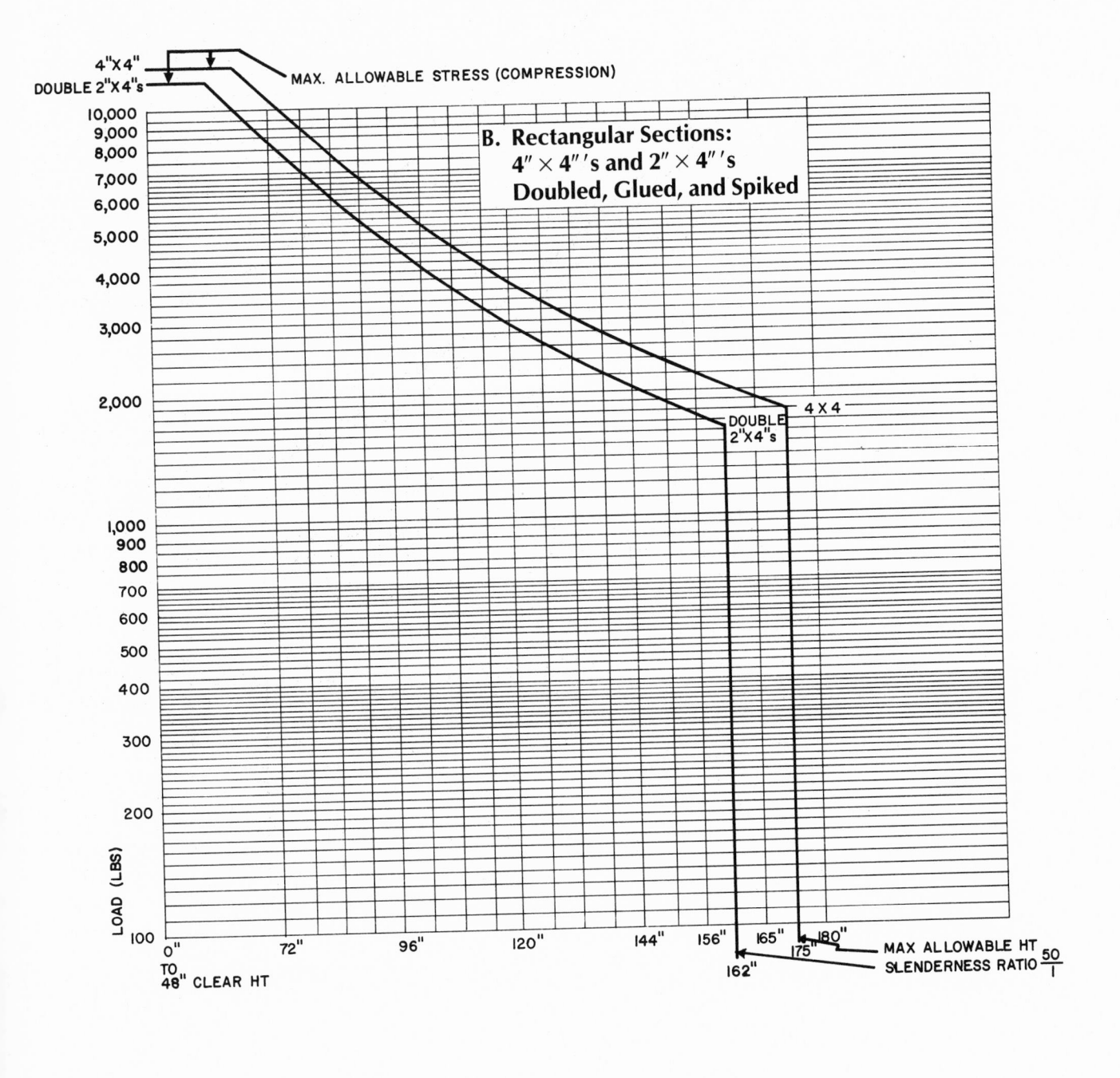

B. Rectangular Sections:
4″ × 4″ 's and 2″ × 4″ 's
Doubled, Glued, and Spiked

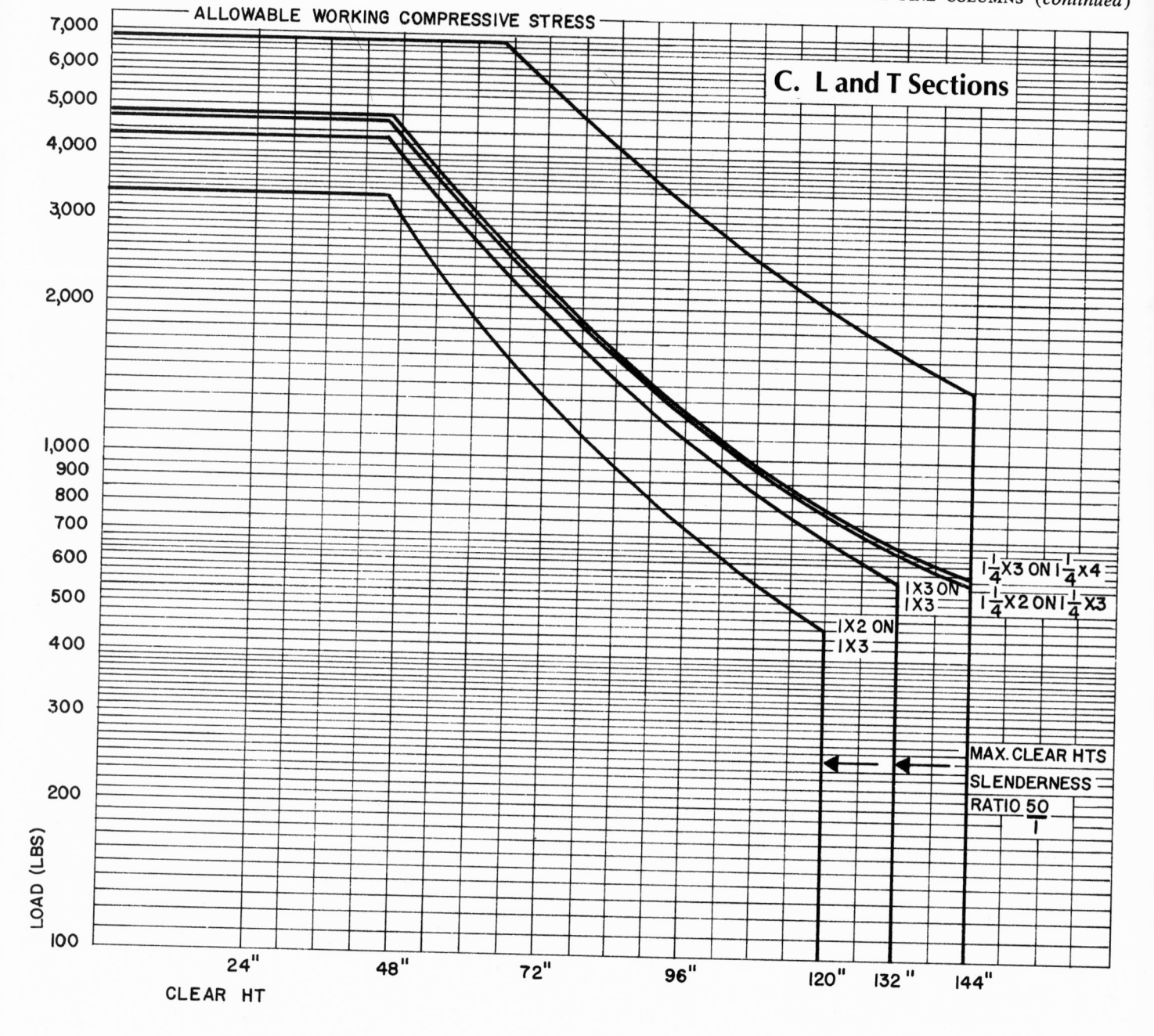

Graph 5. ALLOWABLE LOADS ON WHITE PINE COLUMNS (*continued*)

C. L and T Sections

ALLOWABLE WORKING COMPRESSIVE STRESS

LOAD (LBS)

CLEAR HT

24"   48"   72"   96"   120"   132"   144"

$1\frac{1}{4}$X3 ON $1\frac{1}{4}$X4
1X3 ON
1X3
$1\frac{1}{4}$X2 ON $1\frac{1}{4}$X3
1X2 ON
1X3

MAX. CLEAR HTS
SLENDERNESS
RATIO 50
T

Graph 6. ALLOWABLE LOADS ON STEEL PIPE[a]

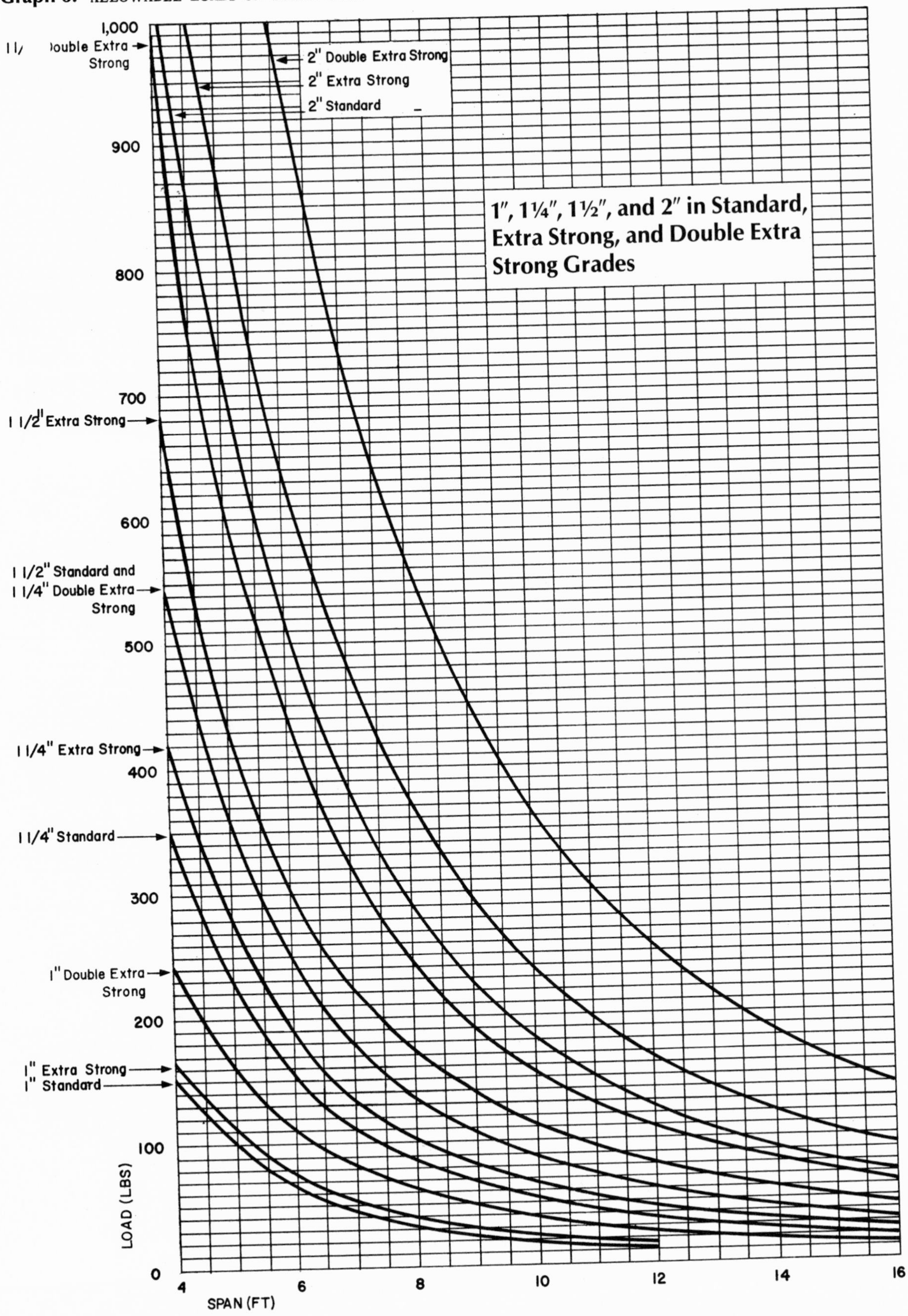

1", 1¼", 1½", and 2" in Standard, Extra Strong, and Double Extra Strong Grades
2" Double Extra Strong
2" Extra Strong
2" Standard
1,000
900
800
700
600
500
400
300
200
100
0
LOAD (LBS)
Double Extra Strong
1 1/2" Extra Strong
1 1/2" Standard and 1 1/4" Double Extra Strong
1 1/4" Extra Strong
1 1/4" Standard
1" Double Extra Strong
1" Extra Strong
1" Standard
4
6
8
10
12
14
16
SPAN (FT)

[a]Deflection: 1/360 span. For deflection 1/200 span, multiply by 1.8. For deflection 1/100 span, multiply by 3.6.

Source: equation on p. 59, in H. Parker, *Simplified Engineering for Architects and Builders* (4th ed., New York, 1966): $D = P(l^3)/48\ EI$ in which D is the deflection (1/360 span); P, the load in pounds concentrated in the middle of the span; l, the span in inches; E, the modulus of elasticity for steel (taken at 30,000,000); and I, the moment of inertia for each size of pipe.

Bibliography

Baumol, William J., and William G. Bowen. *Performing Arts: The Economic Dilemma.* New York: Twentieth Century Fund, 1966.

Bernheim, Alfred L. *The Business of the Theatre.* New York: Actors Equity Association, 1932.

Bowman, Ned. "A Checklist of Publications in Theatre Architecture, 1946–1964," in Maxwell Silverman, ed., *Contemporary Theatre Architecture: An Illustrated Survey.* New York: New York Public Library, 1965.

Burris-Meyer, Harold, and Edward C. Cole. *Theatres and Auditoriums.* 2nd ed. New York: Reinhold, 1964.

Gard, Robert, Marston Balch, and Pauline B. Temkin. *Theatre in America.* Madison, Wis.: Dembar Educational Research Services, 1968.

Kranich, Friedrcih, *Buhnentechnik der Gegenwart.* 2 vols. Munich: Verlag von R. Oldenbourg, 1929.

Mielziner, Jo. *Designing for the Theatre: A Memoir and a Portfolio.* New York: Atheneum, 1965.

————. The Shapes of Our Theatre. New York: Clarkson N. Potter, 1970.

The New York City Record. *Building Code of the City of New York.* City Record Office, Municipal Building, New York, December 6, 1968.

Nicoll, Allardyce. *The Development of the Theatre.* 5th ed., rev. London: Harrap, 1966.

Oenslager, Donald. *Scenery Then and Now.* New York: Norton, 1936.

Parker, W. Oren, and Harvey K. Smith. *Scene Design and Stage Lighting.* New York: Holt, Rinehart and Winston, 1968.

Rockefeller Brothers Fund Panel. *The Performing Arts :Problems and Prospects.* New York: McGraw-Hill, 1965.

Ramsey, Charles George, and Harold Reeve Sleeper. *Architectural Graphic Standards.* 5th ed. New York: Wiley, 1956.

Rubin, Joel E. *Basic Technical Theatre Bibliography.* New York: ANTA National Theatre Service. Copies may be obtained from ANTA, 245 West 52nd Street, New York, N.Y.

Santaniello, A. E. *Theatre Books in Print.* 2nd ed. New York: Drama Book Shop, 1966.

Silverman, Maxwell. *Contemporary Theatre Architecture: An Illustrated Survey.* New York: New York Public Library, 1965.

Simon, Bernard. *Simon's Directory of Theatrical Materials, Services and Information.* New York: Package Publicity Service, 1966.

Simonson, Lee. *The Stage Is Set.* New York: Theatre Arts Books, 1963.

general
books

periodicals

Bühnentechnische Rundschau. Berlin, 1907 —.

ITI (World Theatre). Paris, 1965 —. Vols. I & II published only in French; others in both French and English. Distributed by Theatre Arts Books, New York, N.Y.

TABS. London, 1937 —.

Theatre Crafts. Emmaus, Pa., 1967 —.

Theatre Design and Technology. New York, 1965 —. Journal of the U.S. Institute for Theatre Technology.

catalogs

Sweet's Architectural Catalogs. 4 vols. New York: F. W. Dodge Corporation. Frequent revisions.

organization and production planning

Farber, D. C. *From Option to Opening.* New York: DBS Publications, 1968.

Gruver, Bert. *The Stage Manager's Handbook.* New York: DBS Publications, 1961.

planning the scenery

French, Thomas E., and C. J. Vierck. *Fundamentals of Engineering Drawing.* 2nd ed. New York: McGraw-Hill, 1966.

————. *Graphic Science: Engineering Drawing, Descriptive Geometry, Graphic Solutions.* 2nd ed. New York: McGraw-Hill, 1963.

Giesecke, Frederick E., Alva Mitchell, and Henry Cecil Spencer. *Technical Drawing.* 4th ed., revised by Henry Cecil Spencer. New York: Macmillan, 1958.

Gillette, A. S. *An Introduction to Scene Design.* New York: Harper, 1958.

Jones, Leslie Allen. *Scenic Design and Model Building.* Boston: Walter H. Baker, 1939.

Parker, W. Oren. *Sceno-graphic Techniques.* Pittsburgh: Carnegie-Mellon University, 1964.

U.S. Bureau of Naval Personnel. *Blueprint Reading and Sketching.* NAVPERS 10077-B. Washington, D.C.: U.S. Government Printing Office, 1963.

shop and equipment catalogs

Black & Decker Mfg. Co., Towson, Md. Portable drills and hole saws, screw-drives, impact wrenches, polishers, sanders, grinders, shears and nibblers, trimmers, router-planes, jig saws, disc saws.

Blackhawk Industrial Products Co., Butler, Wis. Enerpac hydraulic power systems.

Bosch-Lesto, Robert Bosch Corp., 2800 S. Twentieth St., Broadview, Ill. 60853. Portable drills, impact drills, grinders, jig saws, screwdrivers, impact wrenches, nibblers, pneumatic handsaw (jig), pneumatic shear, pneumatic nibbler.

Chicago Pneumatic Tool Corp., Chicago, Ill.

Cut-Awl Corporation, Bethel, Conn. 06801. Cut-Awl.

Delta Power Tool Division, Rockwell Mfg. Co., Pittsburgh, Pa. Lathes (metal).

De Walt, Inc., Lancaster, Pa. Division of Black & Decker Mfg. Co., Towson, Md. Radial arm saws.

Greenbee Tool Co., 2136 Twelfth St., Rockford, Ill. 61101. Benders, hand tools.

Hossfeld Manufacturing Co., Winona, Minn. Universal iron bender.

Linde Co., Division of Union Carbide Corp., 270 Park Ave., New York, N.Y. 10017. Welding products.

Milwaukee Electric Tool Corp., Milwaukee, Wis. Drills and hole saws, "Sawzalls" (hack, saber, jig), (reciprocating) shear, lock hammer (sheet metal), sanders, grinders.

Porter-Cable Machine Co., Division of Rockwell Manufacturing Co., 400 N. Lexington Ave., Pittsburgh, Pa. Portable disc, bayonet (jig, saber), band, scroll saws. Portable sanders, portable drills, portable routers, portable planes, portable grinders.

Rockwell Manufacturing Co., 400 N. Lexington Ave., Pittsburgh, Pa. Saws: disc, bayonet, all-purpose, band. Sanders, drills, screwdrivers, hammer drills, breakers, routers, planes, grinders, nailers.

Sears Roebuck and Co., U.S.A. Simpson-Sears Ltd., Canada. Hand and power tools.

Skil Corp., 5033 Elston Ave., Chicago, Ill. Portable disc saws and groovers. Jig saws (bayonet and saber), roto-hammers (drills), sanders, planes, routers, drills, screwdrivers, polishers, grinders.

Stanley Works, New Britain, Conn. Drills, grinders, hammers, screwdrivers, routers, shears, disc saws, groovers, saber saws, hand tools.

Whitney Metal Tool Co., Rockford, Ill. Punches, shears, presses, brakes, hand tools.

W. A. Whitney Mfg. Co., Rockford, Ill. Punches, shears, presses, hand tools, hydraulically powered tools.

Wilton Tool Manufacturing Co., Inc., Schiller Park, Ill. 60176. Vises, clamps, hydraulic and air-hydraulic power systems.

materials

chemicals

Bennett, Harry. *Chemical Formulary.* Vols. 1–13. Brooklyn: Chemical Publishing Co.

————. *Cumulative Index of the Chemical Formulary.* Vols. 1–10. Brooklyn: Chemical Publishing Co. (With names and addresses of companies handling the materials.)

theatrical supplies

Paramount Theatrical Supplies, Alcone Co., Inc., 32A W. 20th St., New York, N.Y. 10011. Catalog.

Theatre Production Service, 53 W. 46th St., New York, N.Y. 10036. Catalog.

fabrics

The Astrup Co., 30 Walker St., New York, N.Y. Flameproofed fabrics. Samples. Catalog.

Dazian's, Inc., 40 E. 29th St., New York, N.Y. 10016. Also Boston, Chicago, Dallas, Los Angeles. Catalog and fabric sample books.

Maharam's, Inc., 130 W. 46th St., New York, N.Y. 10036. Also Chicago and Los Angeles. Fabric samples. Catalog.

wood

U.S. Department of Agriculture, Forest Service, Forest Products Laboratory. *The Wood Handbook.* Agriculture Handbook No. 72. Washington, D.C.: U.S. Government Printing Office, 1955.

metal

American Institute of Steel Construction, Inc. *Manual of Steel Construction.* 6th ed. New York, 1963.

Armco Steel Corp., Metal Products Division, Middletown, Ohio. ARMCO open web joists. Catalog.

Bethlehem Steel Co., General Office, Bethlehem, Pa. Open web steel joists. Catalog.

Inland-Ryerson Construction Products Co., Milwaukee, Wis. Milcor steel studs. Catalog.

Republic Steel Corp., Cleveland, Ohio. Electronite structural steel tubing. Catalog.

Taylor, Douglas C. "Metal Working for the Technician." Unpublished M.F.A. thesis, Yale University, 1966.

The Unistrut Corp., Wayne, Mich. Unistrut and Telespar. Catalog.

plastics

Bryson, Nicholas L. "Thermoplastic Scenery for Theatre." Unpublished M.S. thesis, University of Wisconsin, 1968.

Cadillac Plastic and Chemical Co., 15111 Second Ave., Detroit, Mich. 48203. Catalog.

Milar Coating Products Co., Englewood, N.J. Metallic vinyl laminates. Samples. Catalog.

Sweet, Harvey. "Styrofoam for the Stage." Unpublished M.S. thesis, University of Wisconsin, 1967.

Tobins Lake Studios, 2650 Seven Mile Rd., South Lyon, Mich. 48178. Vacuum-formed plastic ornaments. Catalog.

adhesives

Guttman, Werner H. *Concise Guide to Structural Adhesives.* New York: Reinhold, 1961.

paint

Gothic Color Co., Inc., 90 Ninth Ave., New York, N.Y. Catalog, booklet.

Playhouse Colors, 771 Ninth Ave., New York, N.Y. Catalog.

rope, chain, cable	American Chain & Cable Co., Inc., Bridgeport, Conn. Catalog No. 36.
	American Steel & Wire Co., New York. *Wire Rope.* Catalog.
	Plymouth Cordage Co., North Plymouth, Mass. *Rope for the Boatman* and other publications.
	John A. Roebling's Sons Co., New York, N.Y. *Wire Rope.* Catalog.
construction	DeCristoforo, R. J. *How to Build Your Own Furniture.* New York: Popular Science, 1964. Order from Harper.
	Gillette, Arnold S. *Stage Scenery: Its Construction and Rigging.* New York: Harper, 1960.
painting	Ashworth, Bradford. *Notes on Scene Painting.* Donald Oenslager, ed. New Haven: Whitlock, 1952.
	Munsell Color Company, Inc. *Munsell Book of Color.* Baltimore: Munsell Color Co., 1929.
	Pope, Arthur Upham. *An Introduction to the Language of Drawing and Painting.* 2 vols. Cambridge: Harvard University Press, 1929.
stage equipment and rigging	Automatic Devices Co., Allentown, Pa.
	J. H. Channon Corp., 1455 W. Hubbard St., Chicago, Ill.
catalogs	J. R. Clancy, Inc., West Belden Ave., Syracuse, N.Y.
	Knoxville Scenic Studios, Knoxville, Tenn.
	Mutual Hardware Corp., 5–45 49th Ave., Long Island City, N.Y.
	Olesen Co., 1535 Ivar Ave., Hollywood, Calif.
portable stages	Wenger Corp., 118 W. Rose St., Owatonna, Minn. 55060. Catalog.
knots and splices	Ashley, Clifford W. *The Ashley Book of Knots.* Garden City, N.Y.: Doubleday, 1944.
	Day, Cyrus Lawrence. *The Art of Knotting and Splicing.* Annapolis: Book Department, U.S. Naval Institute, 1955.
	Shaw, George Russell. *Knots, Useful and Ornamental.* New York: Houghton Mifflin, 1924.
stage lighting	Fuchs, Theodore. *Stage Lighting.* New York: Ben Blom, 1963.
	McCandless, S. R. *A Method of Lighting the Stage.* New York: Theatre Arts Books, 1954.
	———. *A Syllabus of Stage Lighting.* New York: DBS Publications, 1964.
	National Board of Fire Underwriters. *National Electrical Code.* New York, 1962.
	Rubin, Joel, and Leland H. Watson. *Theatre Lighting Practice.* New York: Theatre Arts Books, 1954.
catalogs	Century Lighting, Inc., 3 Entin Rd., Clifton, N.J. *Lighting by Century* and *Century Theatre Lighting.*
	Kliegl Brothers, 32-32 48th Ave., Long Island City, N.Y. Catalogs.
projection	Kook, Edward F. *Images in Light for the Living Theatre.* New York: privately printed, 1963.
	Nagy, Elemer. *Multiscreen Scenery Projection System.* West Hartford, Conn.: privately printed, n.d.
	National Theatre Supply, 356 W. 44th St., New York, N.Y. (and other cities). *Planning the Projection Room.* New York: n.d.
	Wilfred, Thomas. *Projected Scenery: A Technical Manual.* New York: Drama Book Shop, 1965.
sound	Burris-Meyer, Harold, and Vincent Mallory. *Sound in the Theatre.* New York: Theatre Arts Books, 1959.
	Napier, Frank. *Noises Off.* 3rd ed. London: J. G. Miller, 1948.

R. A. Moog Co., Trumansburg, N. Y. Electronic music composition-performance
equipment.
Theatre Sound, Inc., 149 Ramsdell St., New Haven, Conn. Sound equipment.

Kidder, Frank E., and Thomas Nolan, eds. *Architects and Builders Handbook.*
17th ed. New York: Wiley, 1921.
Kidder, Frank E., and Harry Parker, eds. *Architects and Builders Handbook,*
18th ed. New York: Wiley, 1931.
Marks, Lionel S. *Mechanical Engineer's Handbook.* 6th ed., revised by Baumies-
ter. New York: McGraw-Hill, 1958. (7th ed. in preparation.)
Parker, Harry S. *Simplified Engineering for Architects and Builders.* 4th ed. New
York: Wiley, 1966.

**mechanical and
structural engineering**

Illustration Credits and Acknowledgments

The photographer's name is given if it could be ascertained; otherwise the institution or organization that commissioned or owned the photograph is named. Photographs not credited were made either by the authors or by persons under contract to the authors or by staff photographers of the Yale School of Drama.

photographs

The authors wish to acknowledge with gratitude the help given them by many persons, institutions, firms, and agencies in obtaining illustrative materials for the book. Where no help is acknowledged, the materials were prepared either by the authors or by persons under contract to the authors or by contributors named in the Preface.

other illustrative materials

PHOTOGRAPHS. *8:* W. H. Spradley. *10-12:* staff of the Loeb Drama Center, Harvard University. *13:* Dartmouth College Photographic Services. *14:* Morris Shapiro.

ILLUSTRATIVE MATERIALS. *1-6:* Archivio di Stato, Parma, Italy (Mario de Grazio, director); and the Yale-Rockefeller Theatrical Collection (Alois Nagler, curator). *7:* Howard Bay, designer. *8:* National Park Service, U.S. Department of the Interior. *9:* Joseph Amisano, architect. *10-12:* Loeb Drama Center, Harvard University (George Hamlin, associate director, and Don Soule, technical director). *13:* George Schoenhut. *14:* Yale School of Drama.

chapter 1

ILLUSTRATIVE MATERIALS. *3-5:* Ann Farris; the Yale Drama Library.

chapter 2

PHOTOGRAPH. *5:* White Studio.

chapter 3

ILLUSTRATIVE MATERIALS. *1-5:* Donald M. Oenslager and Isaac Benesch. *9:* Ann Farris. *10-12:* H. Burris-Meyer and V. Mallory, *Sound in the Theatre* (New York: Theatre Arts Books, 1959).

ILLUSTRATIVE MATERIALS. *12:* Donald M. Oenslager and Isaac Benesch.

chapter 4

PHOTOGRAPHS. *4, 14-16, 28, 36-40, 46, 47, 52, 55-60:* Munro Gabler. *5, 27, 30, 41:*

chapter 5

Clark Mendum. *6, 65, 66, 69:* Morris Shapiro. *17:* George Schoenhut. *19:* The Dadmun Company. *20, 25, 29:* LeRoy V. Stransky. *42, 44, 45:* Roger Sherman. *43, 49:* Arthur Ross. *50, 80-83:* Ward D. Haarbauer. *61:* Ned A. Bowman. *63, 67:* A. Burton Street. *71:* Elemer Nagy. *70, 72:* Allan Hurst, A.R.P.S., and Patrick Robertson. *73-76:* Douglas C. Taylor. *77:* Michael Billingsley. *84:* Elmer Tangerman. *85:* University of Wisconsin Photographic Laboratory. *86:* Daniel Hirsch.

ILLUSTRATIVE MATERIALS. *4, 14-16, 28, 36-40, 46, 47, 52, 55-60:* Nolan Scenery Studios. *5, 6, 20, 25, 27, 29, 41-45, 49, 63-67, 69, 73-76:* Yale School of Drama. *17:* Hopkins Center, Dartmouth College. *24, 25:* Peggy Clark. *50, 80-83:* Gene A. Wilson. *64, 67:* H. Burris-Meyer and E. C. Cole, *Theatres and Auditoriums* (New York: Reinhold, 1964); copyright 1964 by Reinhold Publishing Corporation. *68:* Garson Kanin and David Pardoll. *70, 72:* F. P. Bentham, editor of *Tabs*. *73-76:* Douglas C. Taylor. *77:* University of Delaware Theatre. *78:* Unistrut Corporation; and N. A. Bowman and P. R. Eck, "Modular Platform Systems for the Stage," *Theatre Design and Technology* (December, 1965). *85, 86:* Harvey Sweet.

chapter 6   **NO CREDITS**

chapter 7   PHOTOGRAPHS. *4* (page 172): George Schoenhut. *4* (page 173): Dartmouth College Photographic Services. *6:* Walter Barnes Studio.

ILLUSTRATIVE MATERIALS. *4:* Hopkins Center, Dartmouth College. *5, 6:* Loren Winship, Department of Drama, University of Texas. *7:* University of California at Los Angeles, Jack Morrison, *Education Theatre News,* and Burris-Meyer and Cole, *Theatres and Auditoriums* (see above).

chapter 8   PHOTOGRAPHS. *1, 2:* George Schoenhut. *5-10:* Roger Sherman. *11, 12, 15:* Ralph Sandler. *13, 14:* Curtis J. Senie. *16, 17:* Daniel Hirsch. *18, 19:* Nicholas L. Bryson.

ILLUSTRATIVE MATERIALS. *1, 2:* Hopkins Center, Dartmouth College. *4:* Studio Alliance. *11, 12, 15:* Harvey Sweet. *13, 14:* George C. Izenour. *16-19:* Nicholas L. Bryson.

chapter 9   PHOTOGRAPHS. *4-7:* Munro Gabler. *8, 9 (middle):* Jerry Lewis. *9 (left and right):* Ralph Sandler.

ILLUSTRATIVE MATERIALS. *4-7:* Nolan Scenery Studios. *8, 9:* Harvey Sweet.

chapter 10   PHOTOGRAPH. *30:* Louis Mélançon.

ILLUSTRATIVE MATERIALS. *1:* Robert Bergman. *2-29:* James F. Göhl. *30:* Herman Kravitz, Metropolitan Opera Association. *A-1:* James F. Göhl and Thomas Ford.

chapter 11   PHOTOGRAPHS. *1, 3, 5:* White Studio. *7, 8, 12:* Martin's. *9:* Tribble Studio. *10:* Commercial Illustrators, Ltd. *14, 15:* Peter Clark, Inc. *19, 20:* Manning. *21, 31, 34, 36:* Munro Gabler. *24, 25:* Hartwick. *26:* Morris Shapiro. *27:* Zamsky Studio. *28:* Ned A. Bowman. *29:* Mears. *30:* Arthur Ross. *32:* Vandamm Studio. *33:* Stage Photo Co.

ILLUSTRATIVE MATERIALS. *1-6:* Max Gordon, Eddie Sobol, and Jo Mielziner. *7-10, 12, 19, 20, 24, 25:* Stage Decoration and Supplies, Inc. *13, 15, 22:* Peter Clark, Inc. *16:* Hopkins Center, Dartmouth College. *17:* George C. Izenour. *18:* Hydra Float Systems, Inc., Ralph Alswang, William Cruse. *21, 31, 34, 36:* Nolan Scenery Studios. *26, 30:* Yale School of Drama. *27:* Yale University Dramatic Association. *28:* Ned A. Bowman. *29:* Loren Winship, Department of Drama, University of Texas. *32:* Aline Bernstein, Herman Shumlin. *33:* Max Hasait, Gilbert Miller. *35:* Warren, Knight and Davis, architects; Arnold Powell.

chapter 12   PHOTOGRAPHS. *11, 33:* Ward D. Haarbauer. *15:* George Schoenhut. *16-19, 43-47:* Munro Gabler. *20, 21, 56:* Douglas C. Taylor.

ILLUSTRATIVE MATERIALS. *1-6, 23, 24, 27-32, 34, 81:* Yale School of Drama. *11, 33:* Gene A. Wilson. *15:* Hopkins Center, Dartmouth College. *16-19, 43-47:* Nolan Scenery Studios. *20, 21, 56:* Yale Drama Library. *61:* T. B. McDonald Construction Co.

chapter 13

PHOTOGRAPHS. *2, 18, 19:* LeRoy V. Stransky. *3, 7:* Ward D. Haarbauer. *6, 10, 15-17, 20:* Munro Gabler. *11, 13:* Ralph Sandler. *21:* Arthur Ross. *23, 24:* Douglas C. Taylor. *27-34:* Austin O. Huhn. *36, 37:* De Felice Photography.

ILLUSTRATIVE MATERIALS. *1, 2, 4, 5, 8, 9, 12, 14, 18, 19, 21-26, 35:* Yale School of Drama. *3, 7:* Gene A. Wilson. *6, 10, 15-17, 20:* Nolan Scenery Studios. *11, 13:* Harvey Sweet. *23, 24:* Yale Drama Library. *27-34* NBC-TV Special Effects Department. *36, 37:* Erwin Steward of Theatre Sound, Inc.

chapter 14

ILLUSTRATIVE MATERIALS. *2, 4:* Ann Farris; the Yale Drama Library. *5-11:* Lo Hardin, American Shakespeare Festival Theatre and Academy.

chapter 15

PHOTOGRAPHS. *23, 30:* Roger Sherman. *31-34, 40:* Douglas C. Taylor. *41:* Carolyn Ross. *42, 43, 46-52:* Ward D. Haarbauer. *44, 45:* Gene A. Wilson. *53, 55-57, 60-66:* Ralph Sandler. *54, 59:* Jerry Lewis. *67, 69, 70, 74-77, 80, 81:* Daniel Hirsch. *68, 71, 72:* Daniel Boylen. *73, 78, 79:* Nicholas L. Bryson. *82:* Munro Gabler.

ILLUSTRATIVE MATERIALS. *23, 30:* Yale School of Drama. *31-41:* Douglas C. Taylor; the Yale Drama Library. *35, 36, 39, 40:* Linde Air Products Co., Division of Union Carbide Corp., *The Oxyacetylene Handbook,* 10th ed. (1954); copyright 1943 by Union Carbide Corp. *37: The Oxyacetylene Welder's Hand-Book,* 6th ed. (Morton Grove, Ill.: Welding Engineer Publications, Inc., 1960). *42-52:* Gene A. Wilson. *53-66:* Harvey Sweet. *67-81:* Nicholas L. Bryson. *82:* Nolan Scenery Studios.

Index